Readings in Urban Theory

Readings in Urban Theory

Second Edition

Edited by

Susan S. Fainstein and Scott Campbell

Blackwell
Publishing

© 1996, 2002 by Blackwell Publishing Ltd
except for editorial material and organization © 1996, 2002 by Susan S. Fainstein and
Scott Campbell

BLACKWELL PUBLISHING
350 Main Street, Malden, MA 02148-5020, USA
9600 Garsington Road, Oxford OX4 2DQ, UK
550 Swanston Street, Carlton, Victoria 3053, Australia

First edition published 1996
Second edition published 2002

5   2005

Library of Congress Cataloging-in-Publication Data

Readings in urban theory / edited by Susan S. Fainstein and Scott Campbell. — 2nd ed.
    p.   cm.
    Includes bibliographical references and index.
    ISBN 0–631–22344–4 (hbk : acid-free paper) — ISBN 0–631–22345–2 (pbk : acid-free
paper)
    1. Cities and towns. 2. Urban economics. I. Fainstein, Susan S. II. Campbell, Scott,
1958–
HT151.R35   2002
307.76—dc21

                                                                        2001025968

ISBN-13: 978-0-631-22344-3 (hbk : acid-free paper) — ISBN-13: 978-0-631-22345-0 (pbk :
acid-free paper)

A catalogue record for this title is available from the British Library.

Set in 10 on 12 pt Sabon
by Kolam Information Services Pvt. Ltd, Pondicherry, India
Printed and bound in the United Kingdom
by TJ International, Padstow, Cornwall

For further information on Blackwell Publishing, visit our website:
www.blackwellpublishing.com

Contents

Figures

Tables

Acknowledgments

We wish to thank our editors at Blackwell, Sarah Falkus and Joanna Pyke, for their contributions, and our research assistant at Rutgers, Gregory Godfrey, for his help.

Titles of articles reprinted here are the same as in all the originals. For book excerpts, we have generally used the original book title, the chapter title, or a combination thereof. The texts are, wherever possible, reprinted in full. We have deleted short sections of the original text only when a book chapter refers to another chapter of the book not included in this reader.

We are grateful to the following for their permission to reprint copyright material:

Burns, Carol, Robert Campbell, Andres Duany, Jarold Kayden and Alex Krieger (1997) "Urban or Suburban?" (Roundtable discussion), *Harvard Design Magazine* 1, Winter/Spring, pp. 47–61. Copyright © 1997 by the President and Fellows of Harvard College.

Fainstein, Norman (1993) "Race, Class and Segregation: Discourses about African Americans" *International Journal of Urban and Regional Research* 17, Fall, 384–403. Reprinted by permission of Blackwell Publishers.

Fainstein, Susan S. (1990) "The Changing World Economy and Urban Restructuring" from Dennis Judd and Michael Parkinson (eds.) *Leadership and Urban Regeneration*, Sage Publications Inc., Thousand Oaks, pp. 31–47.

Fishman, Robert (1987) "Bourgeois Utopias: Visions of Suburbia" from *Bourgeois Utopias: The Rise and Fall of Suburbia*, Basic Books, New York, pp. 3–17.

Goldsmith, William W. (2000) "From the Metropolis to Globalization: The Dialectics of Race and Urban Form" from Peter Marcuse and Ronald van Kempen (eds.) *Globalizing Cities: A New Spatial Order*, Blackwell Publishers, Oxford, pp. 37–55.

Gray, Mia, Elyse Golob, Ann Markusen, and Sam Oak Park (1998) "New Industrial Cities? The Four Faces of Silicon Valley" from *Review of Radical Political Economics* 30(4), 1–28. Copyright © the Union of Radical Political Economists.

Hannigan, John (1998) "Fantasy City: Pleasure and Profit" in *The Postmodern Metropolis* Routledge, New York, pp. 81–100. Reprinted by permission of Taylor & Francis, Inc.

Harvey, David (1993) "Social Justice, Postmodernism and the City" *International Journal of Urban and Regional Research* 16, 588–601. Reprinted by permission of Blackwell Publishers.

Judd, Dennis R. (1995) "Promoting Tourism in US Cities" *Tourism Management* 16(3), 178–87.

Kelbaugh, Douglas S. (1997) "The New Urbanism" from *Common Place*, University of Washington Press, pp. 111–21. Reprinted by permission of the University of Washington Press.

Lawson, Roger and William Julius Wilson "Poverty, Social Rights, and the Quality of Citizenship", in McFate, Katherine, Roger Lawson and William Julius Wilson (eds.) (1995) *Poverty Inequality and the Future of Social Policy*, Russell Sage Foundation, 693–714. © 1995 Russell Sage Foundation, New York. Used with permission of the Russell Sage Foundation.

Logan, John R. and Harvey L. Molotch (1987) "The City as a Growth Machine" from *Urban Fortunes: The Political Economy of Place*, The University of California Press, Berkeley, pp. 50–98. Copyright © 1987 The Regents of the University of California, The University of California Press, Berkeley.

Painter, Joe (1995) "Regulation Theory, Post-Fordism and Urban Politics" from David Judge, Gerry Stoker and Harold Wolman (eds.) *Theories of Urban Politics*, Sage Publications, pp. 276–95. Reprinted by permission of Sage Publications Ltd. Copyright © Sage Publications Ltd.

Sachs, Aaron W. (1999) "Virtual Ecology: A Brief Environmental History of Silicon Valley" from *Worldwatch* Jan/Feb, 12–21. Reprinted by permission of Worldwatch Institute, http//www.worldwatch.org.

Sassen, Saskia (2000) "Cities in a World Economy" from *Cities in a World Economy*, 2nd edn, Pine Forge Press, pp 1–31. Copyright © 2000 by Pine Forge Press. Reprinted by permission of Pine Forge Press, Sage Publications Inc.

Smith, Neil (1986) "Gentrification, the Frontier and the Restructuring of Urban Space" from Neil Smith and Peter Williams (eds.), *Gentrification of the City*, Allen and Unwin, Boston, pp. 15–34.

Sorkin, Michael (1992) "See You in Disneyland" from Michael Sorkin (ed.) *Variations on a Theme Park: The New American City and the End of Public Space*, Hill and Wang, New York, pp. 205–32.

Squires, Gregory D. (1991) "Partnership and the Pursuit of the Private City" from Mark Goettdiener and Chris Pickvance (eds.) *Urban Life in Transition*, Sage Publications, Newbury Park, pp. 123–40.

Zukin, Sharon (1995) "Whose Culture? Whose City?" from *The Culture of Cities*, Blackwell Publishers, Oxford, pp. 1–45.

Introduction: Theories of Urban Development and their Implications for Policy and Planning

Susan S. Fainstein and Scott Campbell

This book presents a set of readings that analyze the economic, cultural, and political context of urban and regional policy within the USA and the UK. It is a companion volume to a book of readings on planning theory (Campbell and Fainstein, 2002) but is intended for any reader whose concern is urban and regional development. Thus, it addresses two audiences: first, policy makers, who must understand the context in which they work in order to behave intelligently; and second, people who wish to achieve general insights into urban and regional processes.[1] As discussed in greater detail at the end of this chapter, the readings were selected to address a set of questions concerning the interaction of economy, culture, politics, policy, and space. This introduction discusses the major themes of the readings and presents our viewpoint concerning the determinants and effects of urban form.

Urban Policy and the Urban Condition

At the beginning of the twenty-first century, urban areas are vastly different from the metropolises of a hundred years earlier. The old central cities that still lend their names to metropolitan areas contain a shrinking proportion of regional wealth and population. Although some cities are the command centers of the global economy or nests of technological innovation, others have lost economic function even while they still encompass large populations. Environmental pollution, traffic congestion, racial and ethnic discrimination, and financial crises afflict many urban cores. At the same time, gentrified neighborhoods adjacent to low-income areas display the emblems of affluence, and suburban enclaves of privilege, increasingly set off by walls and gates, sharpen the distinctions between the haves and have-nots. More and more people live in metropolitan areas, but even the most economically successful of these regions manifest sharply uneven development.

The economic, social, and environmental circumstances of urban areas have stimulated calls for reform ever since the Industrial Revolution brought large masses of people to live within cities. The circumstances in which efforts at change are made are not fixed, and reformers can pursue strategies that push the edges of the possible, thereby remaking the circumstances in which they operate. But the situation in which they find themselves at any historical moment limits their range of feasible actions. Existing economic, political, and spatial relations create a web in which those seeking to improve the urban condition must function. Therefore, in addition to requiring a set of techniques, mastery of pertinent information, and entrepreneurship, good policy making demands a deep understanding of what can be done. Numerous blueprints for change have been offered, ranging from the utopian solutions presented by advocates of the garden city to the computer simulations of more recent analysts to the redistributive schemes of equity planners. These efforts, however, have run up against forces that resist the implementation of the reformers' visions. To understand the potential for consciously designed urban change, it is necessary to analyze the elements of the urban context and to calculate their malleability.

Context circumscribes policy in three ways. First, it defines priorities. The historical situation in which policy makers find themselves causes certain issues to become salient to the public and therefore to be at the top of the agenda. For example, rural depopulation and rapid economic growth in the nineteenth century combined with labor exploitation to generate overcrowding and disease within the industrial city. These conditions, in turn, stimulated demands for sanitary regulation, housing codes, and parks development and made these the object of governmental action. After World War II, the release of pent-up consumer demand combined in the USA with political support for home ownership to produce rapid suburbanization and hence the need to develop transportation, education, sanitation, and other services for new suburban residents. Most recently, restructuring of the world economy, industrial flight, heightened competition among places, and the impact of information technology have transformed metropolitan areas in the USA and the UK once again, leading local policy makers to place economic development at the top of their agenda. While policy makers can affect the massive social processes that call for policy responses – and indeed the character of these processes consists partly of policy components – policy is largely reactive rather than formative.

Second, broad cultural and ideological currents constrain the alternatives that policy makers can consider. The expansion of public programs takes place when general public opinion calls for governmental solutions to social problems and opposition of the propertied class to such intervention has declined. Thus, the greatest expansion of planning and the welfare state in the USA occurred during the Great Depression. At that time, social movements of the unemployed, a widespread sense of emergency, and a loss in legitimacy by those whom President Roosevelt called "malefactors of great wealth" changed attitudes toward governmental activism. Working within this permissive framework, the government became the employer of last resort, hiring millions of workers to carry out public works schemes.

Similarly, in the UK, in the immediate aftermath of World War II, the great majority sensed that the country had to be rebuilt for everyone; at the same time, the war had broken down class barriers and weakened conservative opposition to an activist state. Within the context of these broader feelings of responsibility for all members of the national community, Parliament established the National Health Service, and local councils engaged in massive social housing construction programs. In both the USA and the UK, the threat posed by the Soviet Union, and the fear that socialism would spread if government did not improve the general standard of living, further bolstered support for governmental social welfare activities during the postwar period.

Within both these countries, the end of the Cold War, tax revolts, conservative electoral triumphs, and the waning of any effective left-wing threat have delegitimized active government. Privatization and restrictions on governmental intervention have been the order of the day, even under Democratic and Labour national administrations. Although policy analysts often advocate other, more generous ways of dealing with social problems caused by industrial displacement and growing income inequality, the tenor of the times makes adoption of these measures extremely difficult.

Third, short of fundamental restructuring of the whole economic and social system, only certain policy choices are capable of implementation within any territory. It is not the imagination of policy makers that primarily constrains the range of available solutions to urban and regional problems but rather the social facts that they must confront. Thus, in the nineteenth century, utopians proposed ideal cities that gained much popular support but could never achieve successful, stable operation. These idealistic constructs all demanded a level of social equality at odds with the profit-driven market economies in which they had to function. Even the more practical philanthropists who advocated the construction of decent housing for working-class people failed in their aims. They built model tenements to demonstrate the advantages of space, light, and air for the preservation of public health, but their activities did not affect the bulk of the working class. Essentially, the economic system in which they operated precluded the raising of large sums of money to invest in housing for those who could not pay an adequate rent. Only once legislative bodies accepted the legitimacy of using tax money for redistributive purposes did subsidies allow the development of affordable housing.

Later periods reveal similar examples. Within the USA, postwar metropolitan transportation problems could not be addressed through the expansion of rail systems because the sprawling form of metropolitan development meant that population densities were insufficient to provide enough ridership. In both the USA and the UK, contemporary economic development planners are unable to stimulate the growth of jobs appropriate for the skills of displaced industrial workers because jobs at this level have been replaced either by machines or by competition from abroad. Even within the same country, urban policy makers face sharply different circumstances depending on whether they are in growing or declining areas. In regions enjoying rapid expansion, planners can seek to extract public benefits from developers desiring to build while, in declining areas, they desperately offer concessions to investors. In sum, there are objective preconditions to the adoption of a particular policy approach that simply may not be present.

The Determinants of Urban and Regional Form

Economic, cultural, and political factors have interacted to create contemporary spatial forms. Thus, even though the USA and the UK have proceeded through roughly similar stages of economic change, producing many similarities of spatial development, analyses of their metropolitan areas reveal important differences as well (Buck and Fainstein, 1992). The broad forces that, in the century after 1870, created similar outcomes were rooted in a manufacturing economy and a rapidly growing urban population. During the early part of the period, manufacturing developed within industrial districts and required dense agglomerations of workers living nearby to operate the machines; at the same time, commerical and retail activities clustered in central business districts (CBDs). Later, both countries witnessed the rise of suburbanization. The desire of residents to escape urban dangers fueled the outward exodus, as discussed by Fishman (ch. 1, this volume). Changes in transportation technology gradually made it possible for workers to live farther from their places of employment and industries, and to spread out to cheaper, more extensive sites.

The decentralization of jobs and population has produced giant conurbations in both the USA and the UK. At the same time, the two nations continue to display important differences in urban form and housing configuration. British settlements mostly have sharp boundaries demarcated by greenbelts; the endless strip development characterizing the outskirts of American cities is absent. Housing within the UK is mainly attached, even in suburban areas, and lot size is much smaller. There is less rigid income segregation in housing in the UK than in the USA.

Some of the spatial differences between the UK and the USA derive from their differing population densities and racial/ethnic compositions. Others, however, stem from the historically different patterns of settlement in the two countries as well as to the attitudes generated by this history. Whereas British cities trace their roots to close-knit medieval towns and villages, American metropolises mostly began in an epoch of commercial capitalism and speculative land development. These differing starting points, in part, account for differing perceptions of appropriate social and land-development policy. The British public places a higher premium on collectively enjoyed open space than does its American counterpart. British values include the communality resulting from denser settlement, whereas Americans opt strongly for privatism and retain the model of the frontier homestead. The much greater availability and dispersion of publicly subsidized housing in Britain result partly from the absence of the racial and ethnic conflicts that reinforce class division in the USA. Until recently at least, the British electorate supported a larger role for government in providing basic security for individuals. The consequence of the social and cultural dissimilarities between the two countries is stronger land-use regulation and a historically more beneficent welfare state in the UK, which, in turn, amplify the differences in urban form. Thus there are broadly similar socio-spatial patterns produced by past economic and technological forces, and variations within them caused by culture, politics, and policy.

Contemporary Economic Restructuring

Economic restructuring of the last three decades has transformed the shape of cities and regions once again. Production and population have been decentralizing, while economic control has become increasingly concentrated in multinational firms and financial institutions. The new logic of production, employment, and distribution has engendered changes in land use and social occupation; it has caused a reordering of the urban hierarchy and of the economic and political links between places (Sassen, ch. 2, this volume). Common trends within Europe and the USA include the displacement of a manufacturing-based by an information-based economy with corresponding declines in industrial and increases in service employment (Castells, 1996). These have been accompanied by the rapid growth of financial and producer services[2] sectors within cities at the top of the urban hierarchy, and the flight of industry and population from others. Whereas the growth of manufacturing and suburbanization stimulated different policy responses in the UK and the USA, contemporary economic restructuring has evoked similar strategies of deregulation and the promotion of property development through public–private partnerships (Squires, ch. 11, this volume).

Theorists have attempted to understand this transformation through a variety of lenses. Mainstream economic theory emphasizes market competition as the driving force of economic change. Analysts in this tradition point to the lower costs of labor in less developed countries, the entrepreneurship and weaker regulations of the newly industrializing countries (NICs), and the lowering of transportation costs as the key elements pressing on the manufacturers of the wealthy nations; see, for example, Porter (1990). To grapple with competition that can produce at lower cost, these manufacturers must cut their own costs of production. They can do so by moving their factories to locations with cheap labor, by replacing labor with capital, or by shrinking their wage and benefit bill. Within the framework of this analysis, industrialists have no choice but to compete by getting more from their labor forces.

Theorists on the left have emphasized the power of capitalists in bringing about changes that have increased the profitability of investment while weakening the influence of labor. The dominant explanation (although by no means universally held) among these thinkers concerns a switch in "regimes of accumulation" (Amin, 1995). According to this theory, the major capitalist nations previously were dominated by "Fordist" regimes based on mass production, mass consumption, and the welfare state. During the 1970s, however, these regimes resulted in a crisis for capital as profits fell. In response, the leaders of multi-national corporations imposed a new, "post-Fordist" regime that involved very high mobility of capital from sector to sector and place to place ("flexible accumulation"). It was accompanied by flexible production techniques allowing customized manufacturing, just-in-time inventories, and short production runs. A new "mode of regulation" made possible the imposition of this regime. This mode of regulation diminished the welfare state, reduced the power of labor unions, and supported social institutions that would enhance competitiveness.

The two interpretations of capital restructuring are not mutually exclusive. Both outlooks recognize the existence of greater competitiveness within industries and

among places. The progressive/left analysis, however, goes beyond simply identifying the global forces that prompted capital to restructure and attempts to root them
in a theory of capitalist class conflict. The issue between the two portrayals thus
concerns the causes and consequences of a similarly perceived set of processes.
According to mainstream theory, recent changes have resulted inevitably from the
laws of the marketplace. This theory assumes that the benefits of enhanced competitiveness flow to all workers in expanding industries and to all residents of places that
achieve economic growth. In contrast, left analysis attributes global restructuring to
the exercise of class power by a world capitalist class threatened by working-class
absorption of an increasing share of production during the Fordist period. In the
post-Fordist era, capitalists have regained the upper hand, and it is primarily owners,
upper management, and possessors of high informational skills who reap the benefits of economic expansion. Growth and decline occur simultaneously, and the social
distribution of the benefits of growth is highly uneven.

Within the reshaped economic geography of the USA and the UK, a number of
different types of cities and regions with characteristic spatial configurations can be
detected. Those which are discussed in the readings include declining industrial
centers, global cities, expanding and contracting regions, and cities that are centers
of cultural consumption. We look briefly here at each of these types.

Declining industrial centers   The departure of industry has resulted in declining
manufacturing centers afflicted with high levels of unemployment. Although some
of these cities have maintained active CBDs, they all manifest vast empty tracts of
abandoned industrial space.[3] The causes of their plight are manifold (Bluestone and
Harrison, 1982). Competition from other industrial countries, especially within East
Asia, has displaced many of the mature industries of the USA and the UK, particularly in the electronics and automobile sectors. Manufacturing has departed to
suburban areas and peripheral regions both at home and abroad, so as to take
advantage of cheaper land and labor, less burdensome regulation, weaker or non-
existent unions, and government incentives. Whereas until recently less developed
countries specialized in the provision of raw materials, under the "new international
division of labor" many perform the role of "platform economies" that import
capital goods and export finished products at prices lower than manufacturers in
the developed world can meet. As markets for goods grow more rapidly outside the
old core countries than within them, producers increasingly open factories close to
the sources of the new demand. When industry has remained in place but modern-
ized, it has substituted capital for labor, allowing it to simultaneously increase
production and reduce its workforce.

The industrial cities of Europe and the US have all felt the impact of these changes.
Especially striking is the suddenness with which they were affected; many cities lost
as many as a hundred thousand or more manufacturing jobs during the decade
1974–84. They have sought to compensate through nurturing growth in the service
sector, promoting both high-end financial and business-service jobs like law and
accounting and also much less remunerative entertainment and tourism-related
employment. Their primary mechanism for encouraging such growth has been
through inducements to the real-estate industry, either through subsidies or deregulation, but they have also sponsored various employment and training programs.

Global cities The term "global city" refers to those cities in which control of the world financial system rests, where cultural production influences the whole world, and where the business service sector sells its products to the globe (Sassen, ch. 2, this volume). Global cities are cosmopolitan, boasting numerous foreign visitors and a panoply of opportunities to consume. New York, London, and Tokyo are the premier global cities; Los Angeles, Paris, and Hong Kong also have some claim to the title. Global cities have attracted scholarly attention because their financial and business service sectors have seemingly resisted the forces of decentralization that have affected most other industries.

Global pre-eminence, however, does not protect a city from unemployment and neighborhood deterioration. Many commentators have remarked on the sharp discrepancies so visible in these cities, where the world's most affluent people live in close proximity to the impoverished homeless, where extraordinarily prosperous districts abut abjectly poor ones (Mollenkopf and Castells, 1991; Fainstein et al., 1992). Global cities are, however, much more complex than the simple notion of a dual city implies. As well as containing rich and poor, they encompass groups of upwardly mobile immigrants and aspiring artists, masses of unionized government employees, large student populations, and vast numbers of middle-level white collar workers. They have had increasing numbers of both single-parent and multiple-earner households. Because individuals with the same income may have strikingly different family situations and future prospects, simple descriptions of class stratification are inadequate (Mingione, 1991).

Expanding and contracting regions Because the dynamics of restructuring produce uneven development – i.e., simultaneous growth and decline within a nation, a region, and a metropolitan area – it is to be expected that, within the same country, some regions are experiencing expansion while others are suffering from disinvestment. Expanding regions are ones that, because of "good business climates" and governmental investment, are benefiting from the shifts of industry described above. Contracting regions suffer from obsolete industrial structures and socio-political systems that businesses regard as inhospitable to their profit-maximizing goals. Throughout the 1980s, the fortunes of the American southwest and the British southeast improved relative to the rest of the nation. Recent developments, however, indicate that, in the volatile competition among places, no region can easily sustain its advantage. Within the US currently, greater relative growth can be seen in some "rustbelt" areas, while parts of the previously prosperous sunbelt have suffered large employment losses. In the UK, the tilt to the Southeast continues. Moreover, it becomes increasingly clear that the rate of development varies substantially within regions and metropolitan areas. Aggregate figures disguise this unevenness, and terms like "sunbelt" and "frostbelt" are too gross to capture the changes that are occurring.

Implications

From one point of view, the continual ebb and flow of investment from place to place indicate the potential for laggards to catch up and the equalizing characteristics of a

market-based economy. If areas have high labor costs, then business will go elsewhere, the price of labor will drop, and business will come back. Such an assessment, however, does not include the social costs of insecurity, the price that people
pay when communities are broken up because they lose their main sources of
livelihood, the perhaps irredeemable loss of a critical mass of skilled workers and
of relations among producers and consumers (Fainstein and Markusen, 1993). Nor
does it address the growing social inequality that has resulted from a system in which
business has been able to drive down wages by threatening to move away. Despite
the extraordinary growth in aggregate income within both the USA and the UK
during the 1990s, income inequality worsened. In part, this trend was both caused
by and reflected in growing spatial disparities. The changing spatial forms of the era
of restructuring have important consequences that can be summed up by analyzing
the social creation and meanings of urban space.

Social Space

Urban space gains its meanings as a consequence of the activities carried on within
it, the characteristics of the people who occupy it, the form given to it by its physical
structures, and the perceptions with which people regard it. Consequently, such
space does not simply exist; it is, instead, a social creation. Yet, although the product
of creative activity, spatial relations once formed take on a seeming fixity, a life of
their own. For example, ethnic and racial ghettos come into being and perpetuate
themselves through the interaction of majority exclusionary practices and minority
preferences. Once in existence, they become a defined territory, comprising a dependable voting bloc for politicians, a perceived area of danger or source of exotica
for outsiders, a specialized niche in the real-estate market, and a source of particular
types of labor. Central business districts (CBDs) result from a concentration of
investment in office buildings and retail establishments. After they become established, CBDs welcome certain kinds of activities and exclude others, enhance the
potential profitability of buildings within their boundaries, and become symbolic of
the economic health of the cities in which they are located.

The character of the built environment both determines the profits and losses that
derive from investments made within a given territory and reinforces the nature of
social relations between races and classes. Thus, governmental responses to economic restructuring that have depended on a strategy of urban redevelopment have
provoked intense political conflict, and the investment decisions of private property
developers have stimulated both choruses of support and furious antagonisms. The
process of economic restructuring described above has reorganized spatial relations.
Its consequences are visible in revived CBDs, rapidly growing "edge cities," and
increased spatial segregation of class and racial groups. It has produced a fragmented landscape wherein the identities that people formed with place over the
generations have been undercut, often to be replaced by synthetic versions of the
main streets, villages, and marketplaces of old (Sorkin, ch. 16, this volume).

The changes stimulated by economic restructuring have been mediated by the
political process and its policy output. In virtually all cities, policy makers have
perceived their economic base as endangered by competition from other places and

have striven to devise programs that would attract expanding businesses. Usually, they have identified office-based and touristic sectors as offering the most promise for future development. Consequently, they have provided various kinds of financial assistance and regulatory relief to developers and occupiers of new office, retail, and entertainment-oriented space. At the same time, "marginal businesses" have suffered from governmental neglect. Workers in declining sectors have therefore found themselves doubly disadvantaged – by the disappearance of employment opportunities, and by the biases of the public sector in favor of jobs with entry requirements that they cannot meet.

Role of Politics and Polity: The Case of Urban Redevelopment

In both the USA and the UK, there is a typical, though by no means uniform, history of urban redevelopment.[4] Within the USA, business groups, usually in concert with political leaders, promoted their vision of the revitalized city, often forming organizations that provided governments with plans and technical advice (Logan and Molotch, ch. 10, this volume; Squires, ch. 11, this volume).[5] Urban movements, driven by equity, preservationist, and environmental concerns, frequently opposed subsidized downtown redevelopment and unregulated profit-driven expansion. They also, although less frequently, promoted alternative plans for neighborhood redevelopment. The outcomes of these contests have varied. Regardless, however, of whether the result has been growth or decline, greater or less equity, deal making on a project-by-project basis rather than comprehensive planning has been the main vehicle for determining the uses of space.

Overall, business interests have dominated the negotiations among government, community, and the private sector on the content of redevelopment (Stone, 1993). They have been supported by elite and middle-class consumers seeking a more exciting downtown and attractive, centrally located housing. Neighborhood and lower-income groups have received some gains in some places from redevelopment. Generally, however, the urban poor, ethnic communities, and small businesses have suffered increased economic and locational marginalization as a consequence. The emphasis on office-based employment within most large redevelopment schemes has reinforced the decline of manufacturing jobs and contributed to the employment difficulties of unskilled workers. While businesses have received direct subsidies, taxpayers at large have borne the costs and received benefits only as they have trickled down. Neil Smith's (ch. 12, this volume) comments on the discourse surrounding displacement, in which the vanquishing of working class people is justified through frontier imagery. Within this terminology, expulsion of long-time residents becomes the triumph of heroic adventurers.

In many cities, redevelopment strategies have been successful in creating a revitalized core (Frieden and Sagalyn, 1989; Hannigan, ch. 14, this volume). The numbers of people working in city centers has increased, and tourists and suburbanites have patronized the hotels, stores, and restaurants in the renovated shopping districts. The short, sharp recession of the early 1990s called some of these strategies into question, as office vacancies shot up, reflecting the particularly steep loss of employment in financial and related sectors. The overhang of vacant space caused many policy makers to switch their emphasis from the volatile financial services sector to greater promotion of entertainment and tourism. So far, these have proved to be steadily growing sectors, although their contributions to personal income are substantially lower than in other industries (Gladstone and Fainstein, 2001).

In some cities, political leaders have followed a more redistributive strategy. Chicago's late mayor, Harold Washington, while not forgoing CBD-development, gave strong support to non-profit neighborhood organizations for housing construction and fostered community economic development schemes (Mier, 1993). Sheffield's Labour-led city council first embarked on a radical program for industrial revival and social housing construction. When that approach failed, due to conflicts with the central government and an inability to attract capital, the city shifted to a more moderate but nevertheless still progressive method of drawing in investment. While depending on a partnership with the private sector and seeking to stimulate tourism, it also focused on improving educational and training opportunities and expanding the supply of affordable housing for both renters and owners (Lawless, 1990).

A different reform movement, known as "the new urbanism" has sprung up in the USA. Comparable to neo-traditionalism in the UK and the compact city effort on the European continent, the new urbanism addresses some of the consequences of urban deconcentration (Kelbaugh, ch. 17, this volume). Focused primarily on reconstituting American suburbia to make it both more diverse and more communal, the movement calls for the physical redesign of municipalities so as to protect the environment, house a greater diversity of people, and bring households into closer proximity. It is, however, controversial, as is evidenced by the debate contained herein.

US/UK Redevelopment Experiences Compared

British and American experiences differed before the 1980s. Redevelopment in the UK was less dependent on private-sector participation. The intimate relationship between local elected officials and real-estate interests that is a hallmark of American local government, wherein developers are the largest contributors to municipal political campaigns, did not (and still does not) exist in the UK. British local authorities restricted private development and built millions of units of low-rent, publicly or non-profit-owned housing. In contrast, "slum clearance" was a major component of the American urban renewal program, resulting in the demolition but not the replacement of hundreds of thousands of units of poor people's housing. In addition, land taking for highway building produced an even greater loss of units.

In the UK, social housing (i.e. publicly owned or subsidized housing at below-market rents) was placed throughout metropolitan areas, minimizing gross ethnic and income segregation. American public housing, while much more limited in scope, was available to only the poorest residents and was usually located in low-income areas. Urban renewal efforts, often derisively labelled "Negro removal" programs by their opponents, targeted ghetto areas that were near to business centers or to more affluent residential districts. Their intent was either to extend the more prosperous area or to cordon it off from the threat of lower-class invasion. Their effect was to displace nonwhite residents into more isolated, homogeneously minority territories.

As in the USA, British local authorities raised revenues through a tax on business and residential property (known as "rates").[6] Unlike their American equivalents, however, if British local governments were unable to meet the service demands on them through internal sources, they received a compensating central government grant. They therefore did not need to attract business and high-income residents to maintain themselves and could afford to be more attuned to the negative environmental and social impacts of growth.

During the 1980s, development policies in the UK and the USA converged.[7] In general, the dominant objective in both countries was to use public powers to assist the private sector with a minimum of regulatory intervention. Earlier emphases in redevelopment programs on the provision of housing, public amenities, and targeted benefits to low-income people were downplayed, as aggregate economic growth – measured by the amount of private investment "leveraged" – became the criterion of program success.

During the 1990s, British policy once again became more sensitive to the effects of redevelopment on disadvantaged populations. Nevertheless, even after the election of a Labour government, the main thrust of 1980s market-led policies remained in place. Within the USA, despite some increases in housing programs during the Clinton administration, ruthless competition among cities continued unabated.

The sponsors of the regeneration programs of the last part of the twentieth century claimed that they had achieved a remarkable reversal in the trajectory of inner-city decline. Numerous studies, however, have characterized this growth as highly uneven in its impacts, primarily benefiting highly skilled professionals and managers, and offering very little for workers displaced from manufacturing industries except low-paid service-sector jobs. Moreover, as economic restructuring and contraction of social benefits produced a broadening income gap, growing social inequality expressed itself spatially in the increasing residential segregation of rich and poor, black and white (Goldsmith, ch. 7, this volume; N. Fainstein, ch. 9, this volume). Rapid development also produced undesirable environmental effects. While the gleaming new projects upgraded the seedy appearance of many old core areas and brought middle-class consumers back to previously abandoned centers, their bulk and density often overwhelmed their surroundings, stifled diversity, and, in the crowded cores of London and New York, overloaded transportation and pedestrian facilities.[8]

Cultural Manifestations of Urban and Regional Development

The reconstructed urban cores now constitute nodes within a multi-centered system of metropolitan urban regions. These regions have changed significantly from the era when the CBD defined their hearts. Although the old CBD may retain its dominance over certain industries like financial services and tourism, other parts of the region have assumed numerous functions including wholesaling, manufacturing, research, retailing, and commercial services. These activities may be concentrated in technology parks, office complexes, and shopping malls, or they may be strung along highway corridors in single-purpose units. Stylish and expensive residential areas may be close to the old CBD, as in New York's upper east side or London's Mayfair, or far on the periphery but nonetheless in convenient commuting distance of the new suburban work complexes. Residential developments, whether within or outside the boundaries of the central city, are set off by barriers or fully enclosed by walls, separating the homogeneous community within from the more diverse population without.

Some interpreters consider that spatial form breeds culture, and that these new spatial forms have created a more divided society, although the extent to which spatial proximity and distance alone influence perceptions and behavior remains a subject of hot debate. Louis Wirth (1938), in his famous essay "Urbanism as a Way of Life," set forth the case for the relation between spatial configuration and culture, arguing that the urban characteristics of size, density, and heterogeneity produced a culture of impersonality and alienation. Later, critics of suburbia argued that its neatly arranged housing on large lots encouraged conformity and competitive consumerism. Most recently, social commentators like Sharon Zukin and Michael Sorkin, whose essays appear in this volume, have contended that gated communities and "theme-park" developments produce an intolerant public, hostile to diversity and opposed to public programs that would benefit the poor. Their arguments are the obverse side of William Julius Wilson's (1987), who argues that the spatial isolation of low-income African-Americans in inner-city ghettos produces detachment from the labor market, low expectations, and deviant behavior.

Whether or not a less artificial, more diverse environment would, as writers like Richard Sennett (1990) contend, produce a better society is a question not easily answered. Proximity of differing groups can breed enmity as well as tolerance. The indifference encouraged by distance, even while it may produce fear and lack of empathy, can also create a buffer that prevents open warfare. Without settling this debate, however, we can agree with the cultural critics of spatial forms that it is possible to "read" the divisions and values of a society in the lineaments of its spatial configurations; and, that the ways in which people perceive their cities and regions, in turn, shapes their development.

The Readings

The readings selected for this volume all investigate issues concerning the interaction of economy, culture, politics, policy, and space. The criterion of selection was their germaneness to addressing the themes briefly sketched out in this introduction: the changing urban and regional system, its social impacts, the effect of publicly sponsored redevelopment programs, and the cultural meanings of spatial relations. These are, we believe, the fundamental underpinnings of urban and regional theory. Although there are important differences among the authors represented, they mostly share a common paradigm of political-economic analysis.

This volume is a revised edition of a book of readings originally published in 1996. About two thirds of the selections are new. We decided to replace a selection when the same author had written a more recent piece addressing the same subject or when we felt that the original reading was simply too dated. We also somewhat shifted the emphasis of the volume, so that it includes more chapters dealing with culture and with the city as a space of consumption. Finally, we have included two pieces dealing with the New Urbanism, a topic that has recently become much more prominent in American discussions of spatial development.

The volume is intended to address a set of questions rather than to provide a survey of the field. We rejected the approach of being encyclopedic and trying to present at least two viewpoints on every issue. There is considerable merit in such a strategy, but we were unable to find readings that matched up well in this way. Moreover, we were committed to bringing contemporary works to the attention of our readers, and much of the most interesting contemporary writing on urban and regional theory falls within the political-economy paradigm. We also failed to include classic pieces on urban and regional development, although we had originally wished to do so. This omission resulted primarily from space limitations

In sum, then, we have assembled a collection of readings that examines the following questions:

- What is the spatial, economic, social, and political character of the urban and regional system in the USA and the UK, and how has it changed?
- What are the causal factors underlying this change?
- What is the impact of spatial segregation on the economic and social situation of minority groups?
- What have been the economic and social effects of governmental programs for urban redevelopment?
- What has been the cultural significance of changes in the urban and regional system?
- How has the New Urbanism attempted to reverse the tendency toward urban sprawl, and what are its likely effects?

The outlook on theory incorporated here envisions it as a convincing general explanation of events and processes. Theory in social science may assist in predicting the future, may allow the generation of testable hypotheses, and may define the foundations of a discipline. In our view, however, these functions alone do not define the role of theory and are not necessarily all present in works of theoretical significance. For us, theory's transcendent purpose is to make sense of the world and to show how particular phenomena form part of a broader scheme.

We therefore have chosen readings that make coherent arguments buttressed with various kinds of evidence but which do not usually rigorously present their findings as falsifiable hypotheses. Rather, their authors make a number of arguments concerning underlying causes, many of which are open to dispute. We believe that they have incisively depicted the new urban and regional environment, and have developed important approaches to explaining its causes, meaning, and consequences. Our intention, however, is that readers of this book will use these arguments as starting points for the development of their own theories.

NOTES

1 This introduction discusses the major themes of the volume and refers to the readings as they bear on these themes. Summaries of the various contributions introduce each of the sections.

2 The term "producer services" refers to businesses like law, accounting, management consulting, and advertising that sell their products to other businesses.

3 Changes in trade patterns and the containerization of bulk cargo for water-borne shipping has had a similar impact on many port-dependent cities, resulting in desolate waterfront areas that formerly were centers of bustling activity and extreme congestion (Campbell, 1993).

4 This discussion is drawn from Fainstein (2001, ch. 1).

5 The prototype organization was the Allegheny Conference. Organized in 1943 under the leadership of Richard King Mellon, head of Pittsburgh's leading bank, it drew up the plans for the transformation of Pittsburgh from a manufacturing to a service city. The public sector's role was primarily the reactive one of implementing the Allegheny Conference's strategies. The partnership between private and public sectors was institutionalized within the city's Urban Redevelopment Authority (Sbragia, 1990).

6 British businesses no longer pay taxes to local municipal authorities. Instead, all business taxes are collected by the central government and redistributed to localities. Consequently, no local authority achieves any revenue advantage through attracting business development.

7 A number of studies are explicitly comparative and reach something of a consensus concerning the similarities in the impact of global economic restructuring on British and American cities and on the direction of urban policy in the two countries; see, for example, Barnekov et al. (1989), and Sassen (1991).

8 Among the many studies that reach the conclusions summarized in this paragraph, see especially Fainstein et al. (1986), Parkinson et al. (1988), Squires (1989), Judd and Parkinson (1990), Logan and Swanstrom (1990); Brindley et al. (1996) and Imbroscio (1997).

REFERENCES

Amin, Ash, (ed.). 1995. *Post-Fordism*. Oxford: Blackwell.

Barnekov, Timothy, Robin Boyle, and Daniel Rich. 1989. *Privatism and Urban Policy in Britain and the United States*. Oxford: Oxford University Press.

Bluestone, Barry, and Bennett Harrison. 1982. *The Deindustrialization of America*. New York: Basic.

Brindley, Tim, Yvonne Rydin, and Gerry Stoker. 1996. *Remaking Planning: The Politics of Urban Change*. 2nd edn. London: Routledge.

Buck, Nick, and Norman Fainstein. 1992. A comparative history. In Fainstein et al. (1992, pp. 29–67).

Campbell, Scott. 1993. Increasing trade, declining port cities: Port containerization and the regional diffusion of economic benefits. In Helzi Naponen, Julie Graham, and Ann Markusen (eds.). *Trading Industries, Trading Regions*. New York: Guilford Press, pp. 212–55.

Campbell, Scott, and Susan S. Fainstein. 2002. *Readings in Planning Theory*. 2nd edn. Cambridge, MA: Blackwell.

Castells, Manuel. 1996. The informational mode of development and the restructuring of capitalism. In Susan Fainstein and Scott Campbell (eds.). *Readings in Urban Theory*. 1st edn. Oxford: Blackwell.

Fainstein, Susan S. 2001. *The City Builders*. Revised edn. Lawrence, KS: University Press of Kansas.

Fainstein, Susan S., and Ann Markusen. 1993. The urban policy challenge: Integrating across social and economic development policy. *North Carolina Law Review*, 71 (June), pp. 1463–86.

Fainstein, Susan S., Norman Fainstein, Richard Child Hill, Dennis Judd, and Michael Peter Smith. 1986. *Restructuring the City*. Revised edn. New York: Longman.

Fainstein, Susan S., Ian Gordon, and Michael Harloe. 1992. *Divided Cities*. Oxford: Blackwell.

Frieden, Bernard J., and Lynne B. Sagalyn. 1989. *Downtown, Inc*. Cambridge: MIT press.

Gladstone, David, and Susan S. Fainstein. 2001. Tourism in US global cities. *Journal of Urban Affairs*, 23 (1).

Hannigan, John. 1998. *Fantasy City*. London: Routledge.

Imbroscio, David L. 1997: *Reconstructing City Politics*. Thousand Oaks: Sage.

Judd, Dennis and Michael Parkinson (eds.). 1990. *Leadership and Urban Regeneration*. Newbury Park: Sage.

Lawless, Paul. 1990. Regeneration in Sheffield: From Radical Intervention to Partnership. In Dennis Judd and Michael Parkinson (eds.). *Leadership and Urban Regeneration*. Newbury Park: Sage, pp. 133–51.

Logan, John R., and Todd Swanstrom (eds.). 1990. *Beyond the City Limits*. Philadelphia: Temple University Press.

Mier, Robert. 1993. *Social Justice and Local Development Policy*. Newbury Park: Sage.

Mingione, Enzo. 1991. *Fragmented Societies*. Oxford: Blackwell.

Mollenkopf, John, and Manuel Castells. 1991. *Dual City*. New York: Russell Sage.

Parkinson, Michael, Bernard Foley, and Dennis Judd (eds.). 1988. *Regenerating the Cities: The UK Crisis and the US Experience*. Manchester, UK: Manchester University Press.

Porter, Michael. 1990. *The Competitive Advantage of Nations*. New York: Free Press.

Sassen, Saskia. 1991. *The Global City*. Princeton: Princeton University Press.

Sbragia, Alberta. 1990. Pittsburgh's "third way": The nonprofit sector as a key to urban regeneration. In Dennis Judd and Michael Parkinson (eds.). *Leadership and Urban Regeneration*. Newbury Park: Sage, pp. 51–68.

Sennett, Richard. 1990. *The Conscience of the Eye*. New York: Knopf.

Squires, Gregory (ed.). 1989. *Unequal Partnerships*. New Brunswick, NJ: Rutgers University Press.

Stone, Clarence. 1993. Urban regimes and the capacity to govern: A political economy approach. *Journal of Urban Affairs*, 15 (1), pp. 1–28.

Wilson, William Julius. 1987. *The Truly Disadvantaged*. Chicago: University of Chicago Press.

Wirth, Lewis. 1938. Urbanism as a way of life. *American Journal of Sociology*, 44 (July), pp. 9–18.

Part I

The Changing Urban and Regional System

Introduction

The readings in this part examine the changes in spatial relations that have produced the contemporary urban and regional systems of the USA and Great Britain. The elements of this system are: multi-nodal metropolitan areas; a network of cities connected by a web of telecommunications but differentiated by their economic roles and the thickness of their linkages to other places; and regions distinguished by their economic bases and social structures. Some of the factors creating this system trace back to the last century; others have only recently come into prominence.

Robert Fishman (chapter 1) examines the history of the residential suburb, which he regards as the archetypal expression of contemporary Anglo-American civilization. He traces the demand for suburban residence not to changes in transportation modes but to a new form of family life. The demand generated by this family-centered mode of living presented a profitable opportunity for developers. Thus, suburban development spread rapidly as investors bought up inexpensive agricultural land and converted it into far more remunerative buildable lots.

Whereas Fishman recounts the history of peripheral metropolitan growth, Sassen (chapter 2) analyzes the renewed importance of certain central cities and, in particular, of "global cities." It is in these cities that the decisions are made which govern the flows of capital in the world. Their current heightened influence arises from a seemingly paradoxical cause: the simultaneous decentralization of industry and concentration of control in multi-national firms. Both of these factors in turn – the disaggregation of production and the enormous capital needs of huge industrial conglomerates – intensify the role of financial institutions and providers of business services in coordinating economic activity. The financial and producers' services sectors cluster in relatively few locations.[1] Consequently their increased prominence reinforces the position of the cities where they exist in large numbers. Thus, globalization, rather than making place meaningless, has increased the importance of certain locations.

Two essays on Silicon Valley detail the transformation of a recently agricultural setting into the world's most famous high-tech success story. Chapter 3, by Mia Gray et al., examines the relationships among firms in the Valley, disputes the view that attributes its success entirely to local entrepreneurship, and indicates the social costs of its industrial development. Gray et al. note that, despite the credit given to private entrepreneurs in providing the Valley's industrial leadership, the US Department of Defense was a key promoter of its growth; and they doubt that Silicon Valley provides a useful model for other regions in their economic development endeavors.

Aaron Sachs (in chapter 4) is similarly critical of the impact of high-tech development Silicon Valley's poor. In addition, he chronicles the environmental costs associated with economic prosperity. Even though high-tech tends to be considered "clean" industry, the particular form that development has taken in the Valley contributes heavily to air and water pollution, and the decentralized land use pattern, as well as stimulating intense highway usage, has eaten up open space.

In his discussion of regional theory and urban politics (chapter 5), Joe Painter summarizes the arguments that have caused many commentators to argue that we are in a new stage of the development of capitalism. The previous period, labeled "Fordist," was characterized by mass production for mass consumption and an interventionist state maintaining employment and welfare. The present, "post-Fordist" era is defined by flexible, specialized production methods and a political situation wherein the state promotes competitiveness rather than welfare. Painter notes that regulation theory is helpful for the study of urban politics, because it avoids determinism in predicting the causes and outcomes of urban policy making. At the same time, he is critical of mechanistic applications of the terms Fordist and post-Fordist, arguing that the methodological approach of regulation theory does not require a facile division of history by periods. Rather, it calls for an analysis of the complicated relationships between economic forces, consciousness, and urban politics.

Susan Fainstein takes up the debate (in chapter 6) over whether urban change results from deliberate actions or impersonal forces. She contends that both interpretations of urban development are correct and that the usefulness of each depends on what one wishes to explain. She offers a number of suggestions for progressive local policies but concludes that, without a supportive national movement, major local initiatives will be stymied.

NOTE

1   Producers' services firms have other businesses as their customers. Unlike consumer services, which employ many low-wage workers and few highly paid ones, producers' services involve numerous highly trained, well-remunerated employees. Consumer services include shoe repair shops and fast-food operations; producers' services encompass management consulting and public relations firms.

I

Bourgeois Utopias: Visions of Suburbia*

Robert Fishman

Our suburban architecture...reveals the spirit and character of modern civilization, just as the temples of Egypt and Greece, the baths and amphitheaters of Rome, and the cathedrals and castles of the Middle Ages help us to comprehend and penetrate the spirit of previous civilizations.   César Daly, 1864[1]

Every civilization gets the monuments it deserves. The triumph of bourgeois capitalism seems most apparent in the massive constructions of iron and steel that celebrate the union of technology and profit: the railroad terminals, exposition halls, suspension bridges, and skyscrapers. One does not look to suburbia for the modern equivalents of the Baths of Caracalla or Chartres cathedral.

But, if like Daly quoted above, we are seeking the architecture that best reveals "the spirit and character of modern civilization," then suburbia might tell us more about the culture that built the factories and skyscrapers than these edifices themselves can. For suburbia too was an archetypal middle-class invention, perhaps the most radical rethinking of the relation between residence and the city in the history of domestic architecture. It was founded on that primacy of the family and domestic life which was the equivalent of the bourgeois society of the intense civic life celebrated by the public architecture of the ancient city. However modest each suburban house might be, suburbia represents a collective assertion of class wealth and privilege as impressive as any medieval castle. Most importantly, suburbia embodies a new ideal of family life, an ideal so emotionally charged that it made the home more sacred to the bourgeoisie than any place of worship. The hundred years of massive suburban development that have passed since Daly wrote can only confirm his judgment that the true center of any bourgeois society is the middle-class house. If you seek the monuments of the bourgeoisie, go to the suburbs and look around.

* Fishman, Robert (1987) "Bourgeois Utopias: Visions of Suburbia" from *Bourgeois Utopias: The Rise and Fall of Suburbia*, Basic Books, New York, pp. 3–17.

Suburbia is more than a collection of residential buildings; it expresses values so deeply embedded in bourgeois culture that it might also be called the bourgeois utopia. Yet this "utopia" was always at most a partial paradise, a refuge not only from threatening elements in the city but also from discordant elements in bourgeois society itself. From its origins, the suburban world of leisure, family life, and union with nature was based on the principle of exclusion. Work was excluded from the family residence; middle-class villas were segregated from working-class housing; the greenery of suburbia stood in contrast to a gray, polluted urban environment. Middle-class women were especially affected by the new suburban dichotomy of work and family life. The new environment supposedly exalted their role in the family, but it also segregated them from the world of power and productivity. This self-segregation soon enveloped all aspects of bourgeois culture. Suburbia, therefore, represents more than the bourgeois utopia, the triumphant assertion of middle-class values. It also reflects the alienation of the middle classes from the urban-industrial world they themselves were creating.

I wish to understand the significance of suburbia both for modern culture and for the modern city first by tracing this urban form back to its origins in the late eighteenth century and then by showing the evolution of the suburban tradition of design to the present. I adopt this historical method in part because, like so many great inventions, suburbia has always seemed contemporary. In the United States, people are often surprised to learn that suburbs existed before 1945. Even César Daly was unaware that the mid-Victorian English suburbs he observed were the product of an urban evolution that was already a century old at the time he wrote.

Only by examining the eighteenth-century origins of suburbia can one grasp its radical departure from all previous traditions of urban structure as well as its crucial role in reshaping the modern city. In order to clarify this "suburban revolution" in metropolitan structure I must first define the precise meaning of the "suburb." The word means literally "beyond the city," and thus can refer to any kind of settlement at the periphery of a large city. A former mill town in the process of being swallowed up by an expanding metropolis, or a newly built industrial area on the urban fringes – these, strictly speaking, are as much "suburbs" as the most affluent bedroom community.

I am concerned [here] only with the middle-class suburb of privilege, and I shall use the words "suburb" and "suburbia" to refer only to a residential community beyond the core of a large city. Though physically separated from the urban core, the suburb nevertheless depends on it economically for the jobs that support its residents. It is also culturally dependent on the core for the major institutions of urban life: professional offices, department stores and other specialized shops, hospitals, theaters, and the like. The true suburb, moreover, is more than a collection of dense city streets that have reached the edge of the built-up area. The suburb must be large enough and homogeneous enough to form a distinctive low density environment defined by the primacy of the single family house set in the greenery of an open, parklike setting.

I should emphasize that the suburb, in my definition, is not necessarily a separate political unit. In selecting a site for a nineteenth-century suburb, developers carefully considered such questions as topography or access to the central city, but virtually ignored whether an attractive location was within or outside the political jurisdiction of the central city. Only in the twentieth century did a separate political identity become important in maintaining a separate social or design identity. Even today almost all large cities have suburbs as I define them within their borders.

Suburbia can thus be defined first by what it includes – middle-class residences – and second (perhaps more importantly) by what it excludes: all industry, most commerce except for enterprises that specifically serve a residential area, and all lower-class residents (except for servants). These social and economic characteristics are all expressed in design through a suburban tradition of both residential and landscape architecture. Derived from the English concept of the picturesque, this tradition distinguishes the suburb both from the city and from the countryside and creates that aesthetic "marriage of town and country" which is the mark of the true suburb.

One need only contrast this definition with the realities of the eighteenth-century city to see how radically suburbia contradicted the basic assumptions that organized the premodern city. Such cities were built up on the principle that the core was the only appropriate and honorific setting for the elite, and that the urban peripheries outside the walls were disreputable zones, shantytowns to which the poorest inhabitants and the most noisome manufacturers were relegated.

In London – a typical premodern city in this respect and one with a special relevance to this study – income and social standing declined markedly as one moved from the center to the outskirts. These social distinctions were enshrined in the language itself. From its earliest usage in the fourteenth century until the mid-eighteenth century, a "suburbe" – that is, a settlement on the urban fringe – meant (in the definition of the *Oxford English Dictionary*) a "place of inferior, debased, and especially licentious habits of life." The canon's yeoman in Chaucer's *Canterbury Tales* says of himself and his master, a crooked alchemist, that they live "in the suburbes of town. We lurk in corners and blind alleys where robbers and thieves instinctively huddle secretly and fearfully together...."[2]

In Shakespeare's London so many houses of prostitution had moved to these disreputable outskirts that a whore was called "a suburb sinner," and to call a man a "suburbanite" was a serious insult.[3] One nineteenth-century writer has described the inhabitants of the suburb of Cripplegate in the seventeenth century as

> a population of tanners and skinners, catgut makers, tallow melters, dealers in old clothes, receivers of stolen goods, charcoal sellers, makers of sham jewelry, coiners, clippers of coin and silver refiners, who kept their melting-pots ready day and night for any silver plate that might come to hand, toilers in noisome trades and dishonest dealers... Forgers of seals, of bills, of writs, professional pick-purses, sharpers and other thieves, conjurors, wizards and fortune tellers, beggars and harlots found a refuge here.[4]

If the modern suburb can be defined as a peripheral zone in which people of means choose to live, then such a district was literally unthinkable in the premodern city, a contradiction in the basic terms that defined urban structure.

Indeed, even the concept of a residential district from which commerce and industry had been excluded was inconceivable for the premodern city. The basic principle of a city like London before 1750 was that work and residence were naturally combined within each house. Almost all middle-class enterprises were extensions of the family, so that it was not only the Spitalfields weaver who lived with his loom or the grocer who lived above his shop. The banker conducted business in his parlor, the merchant stored his goods in his cellar, and both housed and fed their apprentices along with their families.

This intimate connection of work and residence explained the universal attraction of the wealthy bourgeoisie to the urban core. When workplace and residence are combined, the best location for transacting one's business determined the location of one's house. In a mercantile city this location was almost invariably the most crowded district of the urban core.

I should emphasize here that even the relatively wealthy core areas were never upper-class neighborhoods in the modern sense. Just as the idea of a district devoted to a single function – a residential district or a business district – was foreign to the premodern city, so too was a single-class district. John Strype describes the privileged parish of St Giles in the Fields as possessing "a mixture of rich inhabitants, to wit, of the Nobility, Gentry, and Commonality, but, withal, filled with abundance of poor."[5]

The wealthy might, at best, occupy large townhouses that fronted on the principal streets. But the poor inevitably crowded into the narrow alleyways and courtyards that existed literally in the backyards of the rich. This "medley of neighborhood," as Strype put it, was accepted without question. The poor were often servants in nearby houses, or workers in the multitude of small workshops found throughout the city. As one eighteenth-century writer observed,

> Here lives a personage of high distinction; next door a butcher with his stinking shambles! A Tallow-chandler shall be seen from my Lord's nice Venetian window; and two or three brawny naked Curriers in their Pits shall face a fine Lady in her back Closet, and disturb her spiritual Thoughts.[6]

Here indeed we find the "mixed uses" frequently romanticized by twentieth-century "postsuburban" planners. These mixed uses often had a functional basis, as when workshops clustered around the homes of merchants who dealt in their products. Sometimes they seem bizarre, as when a notorious "crime district" called Alsatia could be found adjoining the Temple, the center of English law.[7] In any case, the basic principles of the modern suburb had no precedents in the premodern city.

The suburb as we know it, therefore, did not evolve smoothly or inevitably from the premodern city; still less did it evolve from those disreputable outlying districts which originally bore the name of "suburbes." The emergence of suburbia required a total transformation of urban values: not only a reversal in the meanings of core and periphery, but a separation of work and family life and the creation of new forms of urban space that would be both class-segregated and wholly residential.

Who then invented suburbia and why? To ask the question is to formulate a major thesis, which is that suburbia was indeed a cultural creation, a conscious choice based on the economic structure and cultural values of the Anglo-American bourgeoisie. Suburbanization was not the automatic fate of the middle class in the "mature industrial city" or an inevitable response to the Industrial Revolution or the so-called transportation revolution.

Yet, if suburbia was an original creation, it was not the product of an architect of genius who conceived the modern suburb in a single vision, which then gradually inspired the design profession and eventually the middle class. Indeed, in this history of suburban design, professional architects and city planners play a remarkably limited role.

Suburbia, I believe, was the collective creation of the bourgeois elite in late eighteenth-century London. It evolved gradually and anonymously by trial-and-error methods. Wealthy London bankers and merchants experimented with a variety of the traditional housing forms available to them to create an original synthesis that reflected their values. Suburbia was improvised, not designed. Its method of evolution paralleled that of the contemporaneous Industrial Revolution, then taking place in the north of England, which also proceeded by trial-and-error adaptation. In both cases one senses the power of a class with the resources and the self-confidence to reorder the material world to suit its needs.

The motives that inspired the creation of suburbia were complex. Here I would emphasize only one, which seems to me the most crucial. The London bourgeoisie who invented suburbia were also experiencing a new form of family, which Lawrence Stone has called "the closed domesticated nuclear family." Inner-directed, united by strong and exclusive personal ties, characterized in Stone's phrase by "an emphasis on the boundary surrounding the nuclear unit," such families sought to separate themselves from the intrusions of the workplace and the city. This new family type created the emotional force that split middle-class work and residence.[8]

The bourgeois residence was now freed from traditional patterns to be redesigned as a wholly domestic environment – the home of a family that acted primarily as an emotional rather than an economic unit. This home, moreover, need not be restricted to the crowded districts of the urban core, as the logic of business location had formerly dictated. It was free to seek a more appropriate setting beyond the city in the picturesque villages that surrounded London. There, within easy commuting distance to the city by private carriage, these merchants and bankers could construct their "bourgeois utopia" of leisure, neighborliness, prosperity, and family life.

To this strong cultural impetus to suburbanization was soon added an equally strong economic motive. The suburban idea raised the possibility that land far beyond the previous range of metropolitan expansion could be transformed immediately from relatively cheap agricultural land to highly profitable building plots. This possibility provided the great engine that drove suburban expansion forward. Builders in both England and the United State adapted more easily to the needs of suburban development than they did to the more difficult challenge of creating middle-class districts within the city. Suburbia proved to be a good investment as well as a good home.

Middle-class suburbanization thus entered into the structural logic of the expanding Anglo-American city. It formed an integral part of what Frederick Law Olmsted perceived to be "the most prominent characteristic of the present period of civilization...the strong tendency of people to flock together in great towns."[9] Suburbia might appear to be a flight from the city but, seen in a larger, regional context, suburbanization was clearly the outer edge in a wider process of metropolitan growth and consolidation that was draining the rural areas and small towns of their population and concentrating people and production within what H. G. Wells called "the whirlpool cities."[10]

In 1800 only 17 percent of the English people lived in settlements larger than 20,000 people.[11] Cities were then places for highly specialized forms of consumption, manufacture, and trade. The real work of the world took place in the villages and in the countryside. By 1890, however, 72 percent of the English population lived in districts classified as "urbanized."[12] In the United States in 1800 less than 4 percent of the population lived in cities of 10,000 or more; by 1890 that figure had reached 28 percent.[13] Behind these statistics lies a fundamental shift in the role of the modern city. Where premodern cities had been parasitic on the larger societies, the new industrial metropolis emerged as the most efficient and productive site for the most characteristic modern industries.[14]

As such "whirlpool cities" as London, Manchester, and New York came to dominate the world economy, their attraction grew ever more powerful. In these centers of exchange and information, crowding seemed to work; in other words, intense congestion led not to chaos and decline but to further expansion. In the nineteenth century the expression "urban crisis" referred to the explosive growth of the great cities, and to horrified critics it seemed that almost the whole population of modern nations would soon be sucked into the already crowded urban centers.[15]

Inevitably, these whirlpool cities had to expand physically, to break the barriers of size that had always constrained urban growth. The only question was if they would grow in the traditional manner, with the wealthy massed at the core and the poor pushed ever farther into the periphery; or if the middle class would use their wealth and resources to seize the unspoiled land at the urban fringe for their suburban "bourgeois utopia," forcing the working class into an intermediate "factory zone" sandwiched between the central business district and the suburbs.

Broadly speaking, continental and Latin American cities opted for the traditional structure, while British and North American cities followed the path of middle-class suburbanization. This distinction, still fundamental in so many of the world's great cities, had nothing to do with the supposed backwardness of continental cities as compared to their Anglo-American counterparts. Paris in the nineteenth century became far more intensively industrialized than London, and the French capital developed a network of omnibuses, streetcars, and railroads that matched the transportation facilities in any English or American city. Yet the Parisian middle class remained loyal to the central city; the transportation system in Paris was used to move Parisian industry and its workers to the suburbs, and every further advance in transportation and industry has meant moving factories and the working class even farther from the city while the Parisian middle class has solidified its hold on the urban core.

However "objective" the "industrial city" might appear in diagrams from the Chicago School of sociology, its form rests ultimately on the values and choices of the powerful groups within the city. The decision of the bourgeoisie in Manchester and the other early industrial cities in the 1840s to suburbanize created the basic structure of the Anglo-American industrial city, while the decision of the comparable group in Paris of the 1850s and 1860s (aided by considerable governmental aid and intervention) to live in apartment houses in the center created the modern continental-style city.

In both cases the key actor was that elite of the middle class, the bourgeoisie. By "bourgeoisie" I mean that part of the middle class which through its capital or its professional standing has attained an income level equal to the landed gentry, but whose daily work in urban offices ties it to middle-class style of life. Their personal resources permit them to create new patterns of living, while the values they share with the rest of the middle class make them the model for eventual emulation by the less prosperous. The history of suburbia must therefore be a cultural and social history of the Anglo-American bourgeoisie. They are the pioneers whose collective style and choices define the nature of suburbia for their era.

For these English and American bourgeois pioneers, the "frontier" was inevitably the urban periphery, with its relatively cheap, undeveloped land. In continental cities massive governmental intervention – the nineteenth-century versions of urban renewal – opened the possibility of reshaping the urban core for bourgeois uses. In England and the United States, laissez-faire urban economics turned the core into a tangle of competing uses. Only the periphery was sufficiently undefined to permit innovation. Indeed, the fate of the periphery was ultimately decisive in defining the whole structure of the Anglo-American city. In this Darwinian struggle for urban space, the bourgeoisie sought not only land for their commercial and industrial enterprises but also land for their dreams: their visions of the ideal middle-class home. These dreams are now deep in the structure of the twentieth-century city.

The history of suburbia is thus a history of a vision the bourgeois utopia – which has left its mark on thousands of individual suburbs, each with its own distinctive history. But I believe that all these communities can be linked to a single suburban tradition of architectural and social history. In attempting to outline the principal stages in the evolution of this tradition, I have been forced to depart from the usual method of suburban history, which is to examine one community over time. No single suburb adequately represents all the stages of suburban evolution, so I have selected a series of communities that seem best to embody the suburban idea at each crucial point of innovation.

These suburbs are not typical of their time but rather exemplary. Built rapidly in periods of unusual growth and prosperity, they incorporate in their design a creative response to contemporary changes in the structure and economy of modern cities. Unconstrained by previous building, responding to new social and cultural forces, these communities are truly "of their time." Through a series of often uncoordinated decisions by developers, builders, and individuals, a new style arises, which is then copied in hundreds of other suburbs. These exemplary suburbs create the image that, at any particular time, defines the suburban tradition. This image then becomes an active force in urban history, shaping subsequent decisions by speculators and home buyers that transform the urban landscape.

The first models for this process – and consequently the inevitable starting point for this book – were those earliest of modern suburbs which took shape on the outskirts of London in the second half of the eighteenth century. They not only defined the essential suburban image for all subsequent development but, in their strict segregation of class and function, they also implied a new structure for the modern city.

These implications were first worked out in practice not in London itself but in the early nineteenth-century industrial cities of northern England. The suburbs of Manchester, which form the second group of exemplary suburbs, were the necessary catalyst in reshaping the whole structure of the modern industrial city. For the first time one sees a middle class that is wholly suburbanized; and, as necessary correlates, a central business district devoid of residents and a crowded, smoky factory zone between the central business district and suburbia. Frenzied land speculation, bitter class conflict, and the alluring image of the bourgeois utopia combined to restructure the basic components of the city.

By the 1840s Manchester had established a model for middle-class suburbanization that was to endure fundamentally unchanged for a century. In the 1850s and 1860s this suburban model established itself outside the rapidly growing cities of the United States but was decisively rejected in France. There, as we have seen, the bourgeoisie maintained their hold on the urban core. This dichotomy creates an important problem for any history of suburbia: why did this bourgeois utopia take hold only among the "Anglo-Saxon" bourgeoisie, when the equally bourgeois French followed a very different vision?

The answer hinges both on long-term differences between French and Anglo-American images of the city and on the specifics of Eugène-Georges Haussmann's massive rebuilding of Paris. In any case, the great apartment houses along the new boulevards of Paris – as well as their counterparts in Vienna's Ringstrasse – created a powerful counterimage that shaped the continental city into a structure diametrically opposed to that of the English city. At the same time, and for equally strong cultural and economic reasons, the American middle class adopted the English model of bourgeois suburbanization so decisively that ever since Americans have been convinced that it was they who invented suburbia.

Indeed, after 1870 the site of the "exemplary" suburb shifted decisively to the United States. It happened not because of any loss of enthusiasm for the suburban ideal in England. The slowing of the British economy, first apparent in the late nineteenth century, combined with the explosive growth of the American industrial city, meant that English suburbs were more constrained by the past, while the United States was forced to innovate.

The suburbs that arose outside the American industrial cities at the end of the nineteenth century were the classic embodiments of the whole history of suburbia. They not only summed up the design tradition now more than a century old, but they provided the model that all subsequent suburbs have attempted to imitate. Structurally, these suburbs were at once separate from the industrial city and yet, through the streetcar and the steam railroad, easily accessible to it. Socially, they housed a powerful and self-conscious bourgeoisie that combined the old business and professional elite with the "new middle class" anxious to establish its separateness from the immigrant cities. In design, the substantial houses set in open, tree-shaded lots summed up that blend of property, union with nature, and family life which defines the suburban tradition. I have chosen the suburbs of Philadelphia to exemplify this era – though the suburbs of Boston, New York, Baltimore, St Louis, and especially Chicago would have served just as well.

If there is a single theme that differentiates the history of twentieth-century suburbia from its nineteenth-century antecedents, it is the attempt to secure for the whole middle class (and even for the working class as well) the benefits of suburbia, which in the classic nineteenth-century suburb has been restricted to the bourgeois elite alone. Inevitably, this attempt was to change the basic nature both of suburbia and of the larger city. For how can a form based on the principle of exclusion include everyone?

This paradox is exemplified in the history of Los Angeles, the suburban metropolis of the twentieth century. From its first building boom in the late nineteenth century, Los Angeles has been shaped by the promise of a suburban home for all. The automobile and the highway when they came were no more than new tools to achieve a suburban vision that had its origins in the streetcar era. But as population spread along the streetcar lines and the highways, the "suburbs" of Los Angeles began to lose contact with the central city, which so diminished in importance that even the new highways bypassed it. In the 1920s, a new urban form evolved in which the industries, specialized shopping, and offices once concentrated in the urban core spread over the whole region. By the 1930s Los Angeles had become a sprawling metropolitan region, the basic unit of which was the decentralized suburb.

This creation of a suburban metropolis signaled a fundamental shift in the relationship of the urban core and its periphery, with implications extending far beyond Los Angeles. As we have seen, the suburb emerged during the era of urban concentration, when the limitations of communications and transportation combined to draw people and production into the crowded core. By the 1920s an interrelated technology of decentralization – of which the automobile was only one element – had begun to operate, which inexorably loosened the ties that once bound the urban functions of society to tightly defined cores. As the most important urban institutions spread out over the landscape, the suburb became part of a complex "outer city," which now included jobs as well as residences.

Increasingly independent of the urban core, the suburb since 1945 has lost its traditional meaning and function as a satellite of the central city. Where peripheral communities had once excluded industry and large-scale commerce, the suburb now becomes the heartland of the most rapidly expanding elements of the late twentieth-century economy. The basic concept of the suburb as a privileged zone between city and country no longer fits the realities of a posturban era in which high-tech research centers sit in the midst of farmland and grass grows on abandoned factory sites in the core. As both core and periphery are swallowed up in seemingly endless multi-centered regions, where can one find suburbia?

This problem forms the heart of my concluding chapter in the book from which this essay is drawn, "Beyond Suburbia: The rise of the Technoburb." Kenneth Jackson in his definitive history of American suburbanization, *Crabgrass Frontier*, interprets post-World War II peripheral development as "the suburbanization of the United States," the culmination of the nineteenth-century and early twentieth-century suburban tradition.[16] I see this development as something very different, the end of suburbia in its traditional sense and the creation of a new kind of decentralized city.

Without anyone planning or foreseeing it, the simultaneous movement of housing, industry, and commercial development to the outskirts has created perimeter cities that are functionally independent of the urban core. In complete contrast to the residential or industrial suburbs of the past, these new cities contain along their superhighways all the specialized functions of a great metropolis – industry, shopping malls, hospitals, universities, cultural centers, and parks. With its highways and advanced communications technology, the new perimeter city can generate urban diversity without urban concentration.

To distinguish the new perimeter city from the traditional suburban bedroom community, I propose to identify it by the neologism "technoburb." For the real basis of the new city is the invisible web of advanced technology and telecommunications that has been substituted for the face-to-face contact and physical movement of older cities. Inevitably, the technoburb has become the favored location for those technologically advanced industries which have made the new city possible. If, as Fernand Braudel has said, the city is a transformer, intensifying the pace of change, then the American transformer has moved from the urban core to the perimeter.[17]

If the technoburb has lost its dependence on the older urban cores, it now exists in a multicentered region defined by superhighways, the growth corridors of which could extend more than a hundred miles. These regions, which (if the reader will pardon another neologism) I call techno-cities, mean the end of the whirlpool effect that had drawn people to great cities and their suburbs. Instead, urban functions disperse across a decentralized landscape that is neither urban nor rural nor suburban in the traditional sense. With the rise of the technoburb, the history of suburbia comes to an end.

NOTES

1   César Daly. *L'Architecture privée au XIXe siècle sous Napoléon III*, 2 vols in 3 (Paris: Morel, 1864), 1:20; my translation.

2   Geoffrey Chaucer. *Canterbury Tales*, Canon's Yeoman's Tale, lines 557–60:
> In the suburbes of town…
> Lurkynge in hernes and in lanes blynde,
> Whereas thise robbours and thise theves by kynde
> Holden hirpryvee fereful residence…

3   *Oxford English Dictionary*, s.v. "suburb."

4   Quoted in Pat Rogers. *Grub Street: Studies in a Subculture* (London: Methuen, 1972), 26.

5   John Strype in John Stow. *A Survey of the Cities of London and Westminster and the Borough of Southwark* [orig. ed. 1598], "corrected, improved, and very much enlarged in the year 1720" by John Strype, 6th edn, 2 vols (London: Innys & Richardson, 1754–55), ii, 76.

6   Anonymous article in *Old England* (London), 2 July 1748.

7   *Encyclopaedia Britannica*, 11th edn, s.v. "London."

8   Lawrence J. Stone. *The Family, Sex and Marriage in England, 1500–1800* (New York: Harper & Row, 1977), part 4.

9   Frederick Law Olmsted. Preliminary Report upon the Proposed Suburban Village at Riverside, near Chicago (New York, 1868); reprinted in S. B. Sutton (ed.). *Civilizing American Cities: A Selection of Frederick Law Olmsted's Writings on City Landscapes* (Cambridge, MA: MIT Press, 1971), 293.

10   H. G. Wells. The Probable Diffusion of Great Cities (1900). In *Anticipations and Other Papers*, vol. 4 of *The Works of H. G. Wells* (New York: Scribner's, 1924), 39. Wells himself attributes the phrase to George Gissing.

11   Adna F. Weber. *The Growth of Cities in the Nineteenth Century*, rev. edn (Ithaca, N. Y.: Cornell University Press, 1963; orig. edn. 1899), 47.

12   Ibid.

13 Ibid., 39.

14 For the best scholarly analysis of the city's changing role over time, see Paul M. Hohen-berg and Lynn H. Lees. *The Making of Urban Europe, 1000–1950* (Cambridge, MA: Harvard University Press, 1985).

15 Andrew Lees. *Cities Perceived: Urban Society in European and American Thought, 1820–1940* (New York: Columbia University Press, 1985), 136–88. As Lees emphasizes, these negative views were balanced by more positive evaluations of the impact of urbanization.

16 Kenneth T. Jackson. *Crabgrass Frontier: The Suburbanization of the United States* (New York: Oxford University Press, 1985).

17 Fernand Braudel. *Capitalism and Material Life, 1400–1800*, trans. Miriam Kochan (New York: Harper & Row, 1975), 373, for the concept of the city as "transformer."

2

Cities in a World Economy

Saskia Sassen

Place and Production in the Global Economy*

At the end of the 20th century, massive developments in telecommunications and the ascendance of information industries led analysts and politicians to proclaim the end of cities. Cities, they told us, would become obsolete as economic entities. With large-scale relocations of offices and factories to less congested and lower-cost areas than central cities, computerized workplaces can be located anywhere: in a clerical "factory" in the Bahamas or in a home in the suburbs. The growth of information industries means that more and more outputs can be transmitted around the globe instantaneously. And the globalization of economic activity suggests that place – particularly the type of place represented by cities – no longer matters.

But this is a partial account. These trends are indeed all taking place, yet they represent only half of what is happening. Alongside the well-documented spatial dispersal of economic activities, we are seeing the growth of new forms of territorial centralization in top-level management and control operations. National and global markets, as well as globally integrated operations, require central places where the work of running global systems gets done. Furthermore, information industries require a vast physical infrastructure containing strategic nodes with a hyperconcentration of facilities. Finally, even the most advanced information industries have a production process that is partly place-bound.

Once these processes are brought into the analysis, funny things happen; secretaries become part of it, and so do the cleaners of the buildings where professionals work. An economic configuration very different from that suggested by the concept

* Sassen, Saskia (2000) "Cities in a World Economy" from *Cities in a World Economy*, 2nd edn, Pine Forge Press, pp 1–31. Copyright © 2000 by Pine Forge Press. Reprinted by permission of Pine Forge Press, Sage Publications Inc.

of information economy emerges. We recover the material conditions, production sites, and place-boundedness that are also part of globalization and the information economy. A detailed examination of the activities, firms, markets, and physical infrastructure involved in globalization, and concentrated in cities, allows us to see the actual role played by cities in a global economy. Thus, when telecommunications were introduced on a large scale in all advanced industries in the 1980s, we saw the central business districts of the leading cities and international business centers of the world – New York, Los Angeles, London, Tokyo, Paris, Frankfurt, São Paulo, Hong Kong, and Sydney, among others – reach their highest density of firms ever. This explosion in the numbers of firms located in the downtown areas of major cities in the 1980s and 1990s goes against what should have been expected according to models emphasizing territorial dispersal; this is especially true when one considers the high cost of locating in a major downtown area.

If telecommunications have not made cities obsolete, have they at least altered the economic function of cities in a global economy? And if this is so, what does it tell us about the importance of place and locale in an era dominated by the imagery and language of economic globalization and information flows? Is there a new and strategic role for major cities, a role linked to the formation of a truly global economic system, a role not sufficiently recognized by analysts and policymakers? And could it be that the reason this new and strategic role has not been sufficiently recognized is that economic globalization – what it actually takes to implement global markets and processes – is misunderstood?

The notion of a global economy has become deeply entrenched in political and media circles all around the world. Yet its dominant images – the instantaneous transmission of money around the globe, the information economy, the neutralization of distance through telematics – are partial, and hence profoundly inadequate, representations of what globalization and the rise of information economies actually entail for the concrete life of cities. Missing from this abstract model are the actual material processes, activities, and infrastructures crucial to the implementation of globalization. Overlooking the spatial dimension of economic globalization and overemphasizing the information dimensions both have served to distort the role played by major cities in the current phase of economic globalization.

The last 20 years have seen pronounced changes in the geography, composition, and institutional framework of economic globalization. Although a world economy has been in existence for several centuries, it has been repeatedly reconstituted over time. A key starting point for this book is the fact that in each historical period, the world economy has consisted of a distinct configuration of geographic areas, industries, and institutional arrangements. One of the most important changes over the last 20 years has been the increase in mobility of capital at both the national and especially the transnational levels. This transnational mobility of capital has brought about specific forms of articulation among different geographic areas and transformations in the role played by these areas in the world economy. This trend in turn has produced several types of locations for international transactions, the most familiar of which are export processing zones and offshore banking centers. One question for us, then, is the extent to which major cities are yet another type of *location* for international transactions in our world economy, although clearly one at a very high level of complexity.

Increased capital mobility not only brings about changes in the geographic organization of manufacturing production and in the network of financial markets, but it also generates a demand for types of production needed to ensure the management, control, and servicing of this new organization of manufacturing and finance. These new types of production range from the development of telecommunications to specialized services that are key inputs for the management of a global network of factories, offices, and financial markets. The mobility of capital also includes the production of a broad array of innovations in these sectors. These types of production have their own locational patterns; they tend toward high levels of agglomeration. We will want to ask whether a focus on the *production* of these service inputs illuminates the question of place in processes of economic globalization, particularly the kind of place represented by cities.

Specialized services for firms and financial transactions, as well as the complex markets connected to these regions of the economy, are a layer of activity that has been central to the organization of major global processes beginning in the 1980s. To what extent is it useful to think in terms of the broader category of cities as key locations for such activities – in addition to the more narrowly defined locations represented by headquarters of transnational corporations or offshore banking centers – to further our understanding of major aspects of the world economy's organization and management?

Much of the scholarly literature on cities has focused on internal aspects of the urban social, economic, and political systems, and it has considered cities to be part of national urban systems. International aspects typically have been considered the preserve of nation-states, not of cities. The literature on international economic activities, moreover, has traditionally focused on the activities of multinational corporations and banks and has seen the key to globalization in the *power* of multinational firms. Again, this conceptualization has had the effect of leaving no room for a possible role for cities.

Including cities in the analysis adds three important dimensions to the study of economic internationalization. First, it breaks down the nation-state into a variety of components that may be significant in understanding international economic activity. Second, it displaces our focus from the power of large corporations over governments and economies to the range of activities and organizational arrangements necessary for the implementation and maintenance of a global network of factories, service operations, and markets; these are all processes only partly encompassed by the activities of transnational corporations and banks. Third, it contributes to a focus on place and on the urban social and political order associated with these activities of the global network. Processes of economic globalization are thereby reconstituted as concrete production complexes situated in specific places containing a multiplicity of activities and interests, many unconnected to global processes. Focusing on cities allows us to specify a geography of strategic places on a global scale, as well as the microgeographies and politics unfolding within these places.

A central thesis...is that the last two decades have seen transformations in the composition of the world economy, accompanied by the shift to services and finance, that have renewed the importance of major cities as sites for certain types of activities and functions. In the current phase of the world economy, it is precisely the combination of the global dispersal of economic activities *and* global integration – under conditions of continued concentration of economic ownership and contro – that has contributed to a strategic role for certain major cities. These I call global cities (Sassen, 1991). Some have been centers for world trade and banking for centuries. Yet beyond these long-standing functions, today's global cities are

1 command points in the organization of the world economy;
2 key locations and marketplaces for the leading industries of the current period – finance and specialized services for firms; and
3 major sites of production for these industries, including the production of innovations in these industries.

Several cities also fulfill equivalent functions on the smaller geographic scales of both trans- and subnational regions. Furthermore, whether at the global or at the regional level, these cities must inevitably engage each other in fulfilling their functions, as the new forms of growth seen in these cities are a result of these networks of cities. There is no such entity as a single global city.

Alongside these new global and regional hierarchies of cities is a vast territory that has become increasingly peripheral, increasingly excluded from the major processes that fuel economic growth in the new global economy. Many formerly important manufacturing centers and port cities have lost functions and are in decline, not only in the less developed countries but also in the most advanced economies. This is yet another meaning of economic globalization. We can think of these developments as constituting new geographies of centrality that cut across the old divide of poor/rich countries, and of new geographies of marginality that also cut across the poor/rich country divide.

The most powerful of these new geographies of centrality binds together the major international financial and business centers: New York, London, Tokyo, Paris, Frankfurt, Zurich, Amsterdam, Sydney, and Hong Kong, among others. But this geography now also includes cities such as São Paulo, Mexico City, Bombay, Buenos Aires, and Seoul. The intensity of transactions among these cities, particularly through financial markets, flows of services, and investment has increased sharply, and so have the orders of magnitude involved. At the same time, there has been a sharpening inequality in the concentration of strategic resources and activities between each of these cities and others in their respective countries. For instance, Paris now concentrates a larger share of leading economic sectors and wealth in France than it did 20 years ago, whereas Marseilles, once a major economic center, has lost its own share and is suffering severe decline. Some national capitals, for example, have lost central economic functions and power to the new global cities, which have taken over some of the coordination functions, markets, and production processes once concentrated in national capitals or in major regional centers. A case in point, São Paulo has gained immense strength as a business and financial center in Brazil over Rio de Janeiro – once the capital and most important city in the country – and over the once powerful axis represented by Rio and Brasilia, the current capital. This is one of the meanings, or consequences, of the formation of a globally integrated economic system.

What is the impact of this type of economic growth on the broader social and economic order of these cities? A vast literature on the impact of a dynamic, high-growth manufacturing sector in highly developed countries shows that it raises wages, reduces economic inequality, and contributes to the formation of a middle class. There is much less literature about the impact on the service economy, especially the rapidly growing specialized services.

Specialized services, which have become a key component of all developed economies, are not usually analyzed in terms of a production or work process. Such services are usually seen as a type of output – that is, high-level technical expertise. Thus, insufficient attention has been paid to the actual array of jobs, from high paying to low paying, involved in the production of these services. A focus on production displaces the emphasis from expertise to work. Services need to be produced, and the buildings that hold the workers need to be built and cleaned. The rapid growth of the financial industry and of highly specialized services generates not only high-level technical and administrative jobs but also low-wage unskilled jobs. Together with the new interurban inequalities mentioned above, we are also seeing new economic inequalities within cities, especially within global cities and their regional counterparts.

The new urban economy is in many ways highly problematic. This is perhaps particularly evident in global cities and their regional counterparts. The new growth sectors of specialized services and finance contain capabilities for profit making vastly superior to those of more traditional economic sectors. The latter are essential to the operation of the urban economy and the daily needs of residents, but their survival is threatened in a situation in which finance and specialized services can earn superprofits. This sharp polarization in the profit-making capabilities of different sectors of the economy has always existed. But what we see happening today takes place on a higher order of magnitude, and it is engendering massive distortions in the operations of various markets, from housing to labor. We can see this effect, for example, in the unusually sharp increase in the beginning salaries of MBAs and lawyers in the corporate sector and in the fall, or stagnation, in the wages of low-skilled manual workers and clerical workers. We can see the same effect in the retreat of many real estate developers from the low- and medium-income housing market who are attracted to the rapidly expanding housing demand by the new highly paid professionals and the possibility for vast overpricing of this housing supply.

The rapid development of an international property market has made this disparity even worse. It means that real estate prices at the center of New York City are more connected to prices in London or Frankfurt than to the overall real estate market in the city. In the 1980s, powerful institutional investors from Japan, for instance, found it profitable to buy and sell property in Manhattan or central London. In the 1990s, this story has multiplied many times. German, Dutch, French, and US investors are buying properties in central London and in major cities around the world. They force prices up because of the competition and raise them even further to sell at a profit. How can a small commercial operation in these cities compete with such investors and the prices they can command?

The high profit-making capability of the new growth sectors rests partly on speculative activity. The extent of this dependence on speculation can be seen in the crisis of the early 1990s that followed the unusually high profits in finance and real estate in the 1980s. That real estate and financial crisis, however, seems to have left the basic dynamic of the sector untouched, and we saw prices and stock market values reach new highs by the mid-1990s – only to have yet another crisis in 1997–98 and, once again, enormous increases as the decade closes. These crises can thus be seen as a temporary adjustment to more reasonable (i.e., less speculative) profit levels. The overall dynamic of polarization in profit levels in the urban economy remains in place, as do the distortions in many markets.

The typical informed view of the global economy, cities, and the new growth sectors does not incorporate these multiple dimensions. Elsewhere, I have argued that we could think of the dominant narrative or mainstream account of economic globalization as a narrative of eviction (Sassen, 1996). In the dominant account, the key concepts of globalization, information economy, and telematics all suggest that place no longer matters and that the only type of worker that matters is the highly educated professional. This account favors

1   the capability for global transmission over the concentrations of material infra-structure that make transmission possible;
2   information outputs over the workers producing those outputs, from specialists to secretaries; and
3   the new transnational corporate culture over the multiplicity of cultural environments, including reterritorialized "immigrant" cultures within which many of the "other" jobs of the global information economy take place.

In brief, the dominant narrative concerns itself with the upper circuits of capital, not the lower ones.

This narrow focus has the effect of excluding from the account the *place*-bound-edness of significant components of the global information economy; it thereby also excludes a whole array of activities and types of workers from the story of global-ization that are in their own way as vital to it as international finance and global telecommunications are. Failing to include these activities and workers ignores the variety of cultural contexts within which they exist, a diversity as present in pro-cesses of globalization as is the new international corporate culture. When we focus on place and production, we can see that globalization is a process involving not only the corporate economy and the new transnational corporate culture but also, for example, the immigrant economies and work cultures evident in our large cities.

The new empirical trends and the new theoretical developments are making cities prominent once again for a still small but growing number of social scientists and cultural theorists. Cities have re-emerged not only as objects of study but also as strategic sites for the theorization of a broad array of social, economic, and political processes central to the current era:

1   economic globalization and international migration
2   the emergence of specialized services and finance as the leading growth sector in advanced economies
3   new types of inequality
4   the new politics of identity and culture

5   the dynamics of radicalization, and
6   the politics of space.

In this context, it is worth noting that we are also seeing the beginning of a repositioning of cities in policy arenas. Two instances in particular stand out. One is the recent programmatic effort at the World Bank to produce analyses that show how important urban economic productivity is to macroeconomic performance. The other is the explicit competition among major cities to gain direct access, bypassing national states, to increasingly global markets for resources and activities ranging from foreign investment, headquarters, and international institutions to tourism and conventions. The mayors of a growing number of cities worldwide have set up offices for foreign economic affairs and appear increasingly interested in dealing directly with mayors of other countries.

The subject of the city in a world economy is extremely broad. The literature on cities is inevitably vast, but it focuses mostly on single cities. It is also a literature that is mostly domestic in orientation. International studies of cities tend to be comparative. What is lacking is a transnational perspective on the subject: that is to say, one that takes as its starting point a dynamic system or set of transactions that by its nature entails multiple locations involving more than one country. This contrasts with a comparative international approach, which focuses on two or more cities that may have no connections between each other.

Given the vastness of the subject and of the literature on cities and given what is lacking in much of that literature, this [chapter] focuses particularly on recent empirical and conceptual developments because they are an expression of major changes in urban and national economies and in modes of inquiry about cities. Such a choice is inevitably limited and certainly cannot account for the cases of many cities that may *not* have experienced any of these developments. Our focus on the urban impact of economic globalization, the new inequalities among and within cities, and the new urban economy is justified by the major characteristics of the current historical period and the need for social scientists to address these changes.

The Urban Impact of Economic Globalization

Profound changes in the composition, geography, and institutional framework of the global economy have had major implications for cities. In the 1800s, when the world economy consisted largely of trade, the crucial sites were harbors, plantations, factories, and mines. Cities were already servicing centers at that time: The major cities of the time typically developed alongside harbors, and trading companies depended on multiple industrial, banking, and other commercial services located in cities. Cities, however, were not the key production sites for the leading industries in the 1800s; the production of wealth was centered elsewhere. Today, international trade continues to be an important fact in the global economy, but it has been overshadowed both in value and in power by international financial flows, whether loans and equities or foreign currency transactions. In the 1980s, finance and specialized services emerged as the major components of international transactions. The crucial sites for these transactions are financial markets, advanced corporate service firms, banks, and the headquarters of transnational corporations (TNCs). These sites lie at the heart of the process for the creation of wealth, and they are located in cities.

Thus, one of the factors influencing the role of cities in the new global economy is the change in the composition of international transactions, a factor often not recognized in standard analyses of the world economy. The current composition of international transactions shows this transformation very clearly. For instance, foreign direct investment (FDI) grew three times faster in the 1980s than the growth of the export trade. Furthermore, by the mid-1980s, investment in services had become the main component in FDI flows, whereas before it had been in manufacturing or raw materials extraction. These trends became even sharper in the 1990s. By 1999, the monetary value of international financial flows was vastly larger than the value of international trade and FDI. The sharp growth of international financial flows has raised the level of complexity of transactions. This new circumstance demands a highly advanced infrastructure of specialized services and top-level concentrations of telecommunications facilities. Cities are central locations for both.

The first half of this chapter will present a somewhat detailed account of the geography, composition, and institutional framework of the global economy today. The second half will focus on two types of strategic places for international financial and service transactions: global cities and offshore banking centers. Finally, we will consider the impact of the collapse of the Pax Americana on the world economy and the subsequent shift in the geographical axis of international transactions.

The global economy today

Here we emphasize new investment patterns and dominant features of the current period. The purpose is not to present an exhaustive account of all that constitutes the world economy today. It is rather to discuss what distinguishes the current period from the immediate past.

Geography   A key feature of the global economy today is the geography of the new types of international transactions. When international flows consist of raw materials, agricultural products, or mining goods, the geography of transactions is in part determined by the location of natural resources. Historically, this has meant that a large number of countries in Africa, Latin America, and the Caribbean were key sites in this geography. When finance and specialized services became the dominant component of international transactions in the early 1980s, the role of cities was strengthened. At the same time, the sharp concentration in these industries means that now only a limited number of cities play a strategic role.

The fact of a new geography of international transactions becomes evident in FDI flows – that is, investors acquiring a firm, wholly or in part, or building and setting up new firms in a foreign country (UNCTAD, 1993). FDI flows are highly differentiated in their destination and can be constituted through many different processes. During the last two decades, the growth in FDI has been embedded in the internationalization of production of goods and services. The internationalization of production in manufacturing is particularly important in establishing FDI flows into developing countries.

Compared with the 1950s, the 1980s saw a narrowing of the geography of the global economy and a far stronger East–West axis. This is evident in the sharp growth of investment and trade within what is often referred to as the *triad*: the United States, Western Europe, and Japan. FDI flows to developed countries grew at an average annual rate of 24% from 1986 to 1990, reaching a value of US$129.6 billion in 1991, out of a total worldwide FDI inflow of US$159.3 billion (see Table 2.1). By the mid-1980s, 75% of all FDI stock and 84% of FDI stock in services was in developed countries. There was a sharp concentration even among developed countries in these patterns: The top four recipient countries (United States, United Kingdom, France, and Germany) accounted for half of world inflows in the 1980s; the five major exporters of capital (United States, United Kingdom, Japan, France, and Germany) accounted for 70% of total outflows. In the early 1990s, there were declines in most of these figures due to the financial crisis but, by the late 1990s, levels of investment had grown sharply, reaching US$233.1 billion in developed countries and US$148.9 in developing countries. Overall, worldwide FDI inflows went from US$175.8 billion in 1992 to US$400.5 billion in 1997 (Table 2.1). Financial concentration is evident in a ranking of the top banks in the world, with only eight countries represented (Table 2.2).

Although investment flows in developing countries in the 1990s were lower than in developed countries, they were high in historic terms – a fact that reflects the growing internationalization of economic activity (Table 2.1). International investment in developing countries lost share in the 1980s, although it increased in absolute value and regained share by the early 1990s. Since 1985, FDI has been growing at an annual rate of 22%, compared with 3% from 1980 to 1984, and 13% from 1975 to 1979. Yet the share of worldwide flows going to developing countries as a whole fell from 26% to 17% between the early 1980s and the late 1980s, pointing to the strength of flows within the triad (United States, Western Europe, and Japan); it grew in the 1990s, reaching 37.2% by 1997 before the financial crisis of the late 1990s. Most of the flow to developing countries has gone into East, South, and Southeast Asia, where the annual rate of growth rose on the average by over 37% a year in the 1980s and 1990s.

There was a time when Latin America was the single largest recipient region of FDI. Between 1985 and 1989, Latin America's share of total flows to developing countries fell from 49% to 38%, and Southeast Asia's share rose from 37% to 48%. However, the absolute increase in FDI has been so sharp that, notwithstanding a falling share, Latin America has actually experienced increases in the amount of FDI, especially toward the end of the 1980s and in the 1990s (although these increases are mostly concentrated in a few countries). These figures point to the emergence of Southeast Asia as a crucial transnational space for production. The Asian region has surpassed Latin America and the Caribbean for the first time ever as the largest host region for FDI in developing countries.

The other two major components of the global economy are trade and financial flows other than FDI. By its very nature, the geography of trade is less concentrated than that of direct foreign investment. Wherever there are buyers, sellers are likely to go. Finance, on the other hand, is enormously concentrated...

Table 2.1 Inflows and outflows of foreign direct investment (FDI), 1986 to 1997 (in US$ billions and percentages)

Year	Developed countries		Developing countries		Central and Eastern Europe		All countries	
	Inflows	Outflows	Inflows	Outflows	Inflows	Outflows	Inflows	Outflows
Value (US$ billions)								
1986–1991	129.6	169.2	29.1	11.3	0.7	0.0	159.3	180.5
1992	120.3	180.0	51.1	20.7	4.4	1.0	175.8	200.8
1993	138.9	205.8	72.5	34.9	6.1	0.2	217.6	240.9
1994	141.5	241.5	95.6	42.5	5.9	0.3	243.0	284.3
1995	211.5	306.5	105.5	45.6	14.2	0.4	331.2	352.5
1996	195.4	283.5	129.8	49.2	12.3	0.9	337.6	333.6
1997	233.1	359.2	148.9	61.1	18.4	3.3	400.5	423.7
Share in total (percentage)								
1986–1991	81.3	93.7	12.3	0.1	0.0*	0.00*	100.0	100.0
1992	68.4	89.6	29.1	10.3	2.5	0.0	100.0	100.0
1993	63.8	85.4	33.3	14.5	2.8	0.0	100.0	100.0
1994	58.2	85.0	39.3	15.0	2.4	0.0	100.0	100.0
1995	63.9	86.9	31.9	12.9	4.3	0.0	100.0	100.0
1996	57.9	85.0	38.5	14.7	3.7	0.0	100.0	100.0
1997	58.2	84.4	37.2	14.4	4.6	0.1	100.0	100.0
Growth rate (percentage)								
1992	−7	6	76	83	575	308	10	11
1993	15	14	42	69	38	58	24	20
1994	2	17	32	22	−4	66	12	18
1995	49	27	10	7	140	52	36	24
1996	−8	−8	23	8	−13	143	2	−5
1997	19	27	15	24	49	232	19	27

Note: Asterisk (*) denotes that the share in total FDI inflows and outflows was below 0.01 and 0.001, respectively.
Source: Based on UNCTAD *World Investment Report* (1998: 361–71).

Table 2.2 Top banks in the world ranked by assets, 1998 (US$ millions)

Asset rank	Name	City	Assets	Net income
1	Bank of Tokyo (22) – Mitsubishi (6)	Tokyo	752,318	352
2	Deutsche Bank (11)	Frankfurt	575,693	1,441
3	Sumitomo Bank (2)	Osaka	513,781	294
4	Dai-Ichi Kangyo Bank (1)	Tokyo	476,696	−1,531
5	Fuji Bank (4)	Tokyo	474,371	942
6	Sanwa Bank (5)	Tokyo	470,336	223
7	ABN Amro Holdings (16)	Amsterdam	444,410	1,790
8	Sakura Bank (3)	Tokyo	470,336	153
9	Industrial & Commercial Bank	Beijing	435,723	622
10	HSBC Holdings	London	405,037	5,330
11	Norinchukin Bank (9)	Tokyo	400,031	267
12	Industrial Bank of Japan (10)	Tokyo	399,509	110
13	Dresdner Bank (24)	Frankfurt	389,626	999
14	Banque Nationale de Paris (12)	Paris	358,187	743
15	Société Générale (20)	Paris	342,760	876
16	Chase Manhattan	New York	336,099	2,461
17	Union Bank of Switzerland (26)	Zurich	325,082	−261
18	Commerzbank	Frankfurt	320,419	773
19	Barclays Bank (13)	London	318,551	2,807
20	National Westminster Bank (18)	London	317,411	752
21	Crédit Lyonnais (9)	Paris	312,926	39
22	Mitsubishi Trust & Banking (15)	Tokyo	312,223	97
23	Westdeutsche Landesbank	Duesseldorf	305,879	441
24	Tokal Bank (14)	Nagoya	296,895	145
25	Cle. Financiè de Paribas	Paris	293,437	838
26	Bank of China	Beijing	292,554	1,067
27	Citicorp (29)	New York	277,653	3,788
28	Swiss Bank	Geneva	268,161	−1,461
29	Sumitomo Trust & Banking (17)	Osaka	266,035	63
30	Bayerische Vereinsbank	Munich	256,371	527

Note: Numbers in parentheses denote standing in 1991. Five banks have dropped out of the top 50 from 1991: Mitsui Trust and Banking Co. Ltd. (19), Kyowa Saltama Bank Ltd. (23), Daiwa Bank (25), Yasuda Trust and Banking Co. Ltd. (27), Instituto Bancario San Paulo di Torino (28). Three banks are still in the top 50 but not reported in the table above: Long-Term Credit Bank (previous rank, 21/35), Crédit Agricole (8/35), and Toyo Trust and Banking (30/48).
Source: Based on *Hoover's Handbook of World Business* (1998).

Composition   In the 1950s, the major international flow was world trade, concentrated in raw materials, other primary products, and resource-based manufacturing. In the 1980s, the gap between the growth rate of exports and that of financial flows widened sharply. Although there are severe problems with measurement, the increase in financial and service transactions, especially the former, is so sharp as to leave little doubt (Table 2.3). For instance, worldwide outflows of FDI nearly

Table 2.3 Sectoral distribution of FDI stock for the largest developed home countries and the largest developed and developing host countries, selected years, 1970 to 1990 (US$ billion and percentages)

Group of countries and sectors	Billions of dollars					Average annual growth rate in percentages					Share in percentages				
	1970	1975	1980	1985	1990	1971–1975	1976–1980	1981–1985	1986–1990	1981–1990	1970	1975	1980	1985	1990
A. Outward stock															
Developed countries[a]															
Primary	29	58	88	115	160	14	8.7	5.5	6.8	6.2	22.7	25.3	18.5	18.5	11.2
Secondary	58	103	208	240	556	11.7	15.1	2.9	18.3	10.3	45.2	45	43.8	38.7	38.7
Tertiary	41	68	179	265	720	10.4	21.4	8.2	22.1	14.9	31.4	27.7	37.7	42.8	50.1
Total	129	229	475	620	1436	11.7	15.7	5.5	18.3	11.7	100	100	100	100	100
B. Inward stock															
Developed countries[b]															
Primary	12	17	18	39	94	4.7	5.9	16.7	19.2	18	16.2	12.1	6.7	9.2	9.1
Secondary	44	79	148	195	439	10.7	13.4	5.7	17.6	11.5	60.2	56.5	55.2	46.2	42.5
Tertiary	17	44	102	188	499	16.5	18.3	13	21.6	17.2	23.7	31.4	38.1	44.5	48.4
Total	73	140	268	422	1032	11.3	13.9	9.5	19.6	14.4	100	100	100	100	100
Developing countries/economies[c]															
Primary	–	7	17	31	46	–	19.4	12.8	8.2	10.5	–	20.6	22.7	24	21.9
Secondary	–	19	41	64	102	–	16.6	9.3	9.8	9.5	–	55.9	54.6	49.6	48.6
Tertiary	–	8	17	34	62	–	16.3	14.9	12.8	13.8	–	23.5	22.7	26.4	29.5
Total	–	34	75	129	210	–	17.1	11.4	10.2	10.8	–	100	100	100	100

[a] Australia, Canada, France, Federal Republic of Germany, Italy, Japan, Netherlands, United Kingdom, and United States; together, these countries accounted for almost 90% of outward FDI stock in 1990. 1970 and 1971 to 1975 growth data exclude Australia and France.

[b] Australia, Canada, France, Federal Republic of Germany, Italy, Japan, Netherlands, United Kingdom, Spain, and United States; together, these countries accounted for approximately 72% of total inward FDI stock in 1990. 1970 and 1971 to 1975 growth data exclude Australia, France, and Spain.

[c] Argentina, Brazil, Chile, China, Colombia, Hong Kong, Indonesia, Malaysia, Mexico, Nigeria, Philippines, Republic of Korea, Singapore, Taiwan Province of China, Thailand, and Venezuela; together, these countries accounted for 68% of total inward FDI in developing countries.

Source: UNCTAD, Programme on Transnational Corporations, *World Investment Report* (1993:62).

tripled between 1984 and 1987, grew another 20% in 1988, and grew yet another 20% in 1989. By 1990, total worldwide stock of FDI stood at US$1.5 trillion and at US$2 trillion by 1992. After the 1981–82 slump and up to 1990, global FDI grew at an average of 29% a year, a historic high. Furthermore, the shares of the tertiary sector grew consistently over the 1980s and 1990s while that of the primary sector fell. Between 1992 and 1997, worldwide FDI inflows grew by 56%. FDI worldwide outward stock stood at US$3.5 trillion in 1997.

Many factors have fed the growth of FDI:

1 Several developed countries became major capital exporters, most notably Japan.
2 The number of cross-border mergers and acquisitions grew sharply.
3 The flow of services and transnational service corporations have emerged as major components in the world economy.

Services, which accounted for about 24% of worldwide stock in FDI in the early 1970s, had grown to 50% of stock and 60% of annual flows by the end of the 1980s. The single largest recipient of FDI in services in the 1980s – the decade of high growth of these flows – was the European Community, yet another indication of a very distinct geography in world transactions. But it should be noted that these flows have also increased in absolute terms in the case of less developed countries.

Another major transformation has been the sharp growth in the numbers and economic weight of TNCs – firms that operate in more than one country through affiliates, subsidiaries, or other arrangements. The central role played by TNCs can be seen in the fact that US and foreign TNCs accounted for 80% of international trade in the United States in the late 1980s (UNCTAD, 1991, ch. 3). By 1997, global sales generated by foreign affiliates of TNCs were valued at US$9.5 trillion, while worldwide exports of goods and services were at US$7.4 trillion, of which one-third was intra firm trade (UNCTAD, 1998). More than 143 countries have adopted special FDI regimes to attract FDI, up from 20 in 1982 (UNCTAD, 1998, ch. 3).

Institutional framework   How does the "world economy" cohere as a system? We cannot take the world economy for granted and assume that it exists simply because international transactions do. One question raised by the developments described above is whether the global economic activities occurring today represent a mere quantitative change or actually entail a change in the international regime governing the world economy. Elsewhere, I have argued that the ascendance of international finance and services produces a new regime with distinct consequences for other industries, especially manufacturing, and for regional development, insofar as regions tend to be dominated by particular industries (Sassen, 1991). One consequence of this new regime is that TNCs have become even more central to the organization of the world economy, and the new, or vastly expanded older, global markets are now an important element in the institutional framework.

In addition to financing huge government deficits, the financial credit markets that exploded into growth in the 1980s served the needs of TNCs to a disproportionate extent. TNCs also emerged as a source for financial flows to developing countries, both through direct inflows of FDI and indirectly, insofar as FDI stimulates other forms of financial flows. In some respects, TNCs replaced banks.[1] The bank crisis of 1982 sharply cut bank loans to developing countries to the point that the aggregate net flow of financial resources to developing countries was negative during much of the 1980s. For better or for worse, the TNC is now a strategic organizer of what we call the world economy.

Global financial markets have emerged as yet another crucial institution organizing the world economy. The central role of markets in international finance, a key component of the world economy today, was in part brought about by the so-called Third World bank crisis formally declared in 1982. This was a crisis for the major transnational banks in the United States, which had made massive loans to Third World countries and firms incapable of repayment. The crisis created a space into which small, highly competitive financial firms moved, launching a whole new era in the 1980s in speculation, innovation, and levels of profitability. The result was a highly unstable period but one with almost inconceivably high levels of profits that fed a massive expansion in the volume of international financial transactions. Deregulation was another key mechanism facilitating this type of growth, centered in internationalization and in speculation. Markets provided an institutional framework that organized these massive financial flows. Notwithstanding two financial crises, one in 1990–91 and the second in 1997–98, the end of the 1990s saw a sharp growth in the value of financial transactions.

The formation of transnational trading blocs is yet another development that contributes to the new institutional framework. The two major blocs are the North American Free Trade Agreement (NAFTA) and the European Economic Community (EEC). According to the World Trade Organization (WTO), there were over 70 regional trade agreements by the late 1990s. The specifics of each of the two major trading blocs currently being implemented vary considerably, but both strongly feature the enhanced capability for capital to move across borders. Crucial to the design of these blocs is the free movement of financial services. Trade, although it has received far more attention, is less significant; there already is a lot of trade among the countries in each bloc, and tariffs are already low for many goods. The NAFTA and EEC blocs represent a further formalization of capital as a transnational category, one that operates on another level from that represented by TNCs and global financial markets. Finally, in 1993, the WTO was set up to oversee cross-border trade. It has the power to adjudicate in cross-border disputes between countries and represents potentially a key institutional framework for the governance of the global economy.

Considerable effort and resources have gone into the development of a framework for governing global finance. This includes the development of new institutional accounting and financial reporting standards, minimum capital requirements for banks, and efforts to institute greater transparency in corporate governance.

These realignments have had pronounced consequences. One consequence of the extremely high level of profitability in the financial industry, for example, was the devaluing of manufacturing as a sector – although not necessarily in all subbranches. Much of the policy around deregulation had the effect of making finance so profitable that it took investment away from manufacturing. Finance also contains the possibility for superprofits by maximizing the circulation of and speculation in money – that is, buying and selling – in a way that manufacturing does not (e.g., securitization, multiple transactions over a short period of time, selling debts). Securitization, which played a crucial role, refers to the transformation of various types of financial assets and debts into marketable instruments. The 1980s saw the invention of numerous ways to securitize debts, a trend that has continued in the 1990s with the invention of ever more complex and speculative instruments. A simple illustration is the bundling of a large number of mortgages that can be sold many times, even though the number of houses involved stays the same. This option is basically not available in manufacturing. The good is made and sold; once it enters the realm of circulation, it enters another set of industries, or sector of the economy, and the profits from subsequent sales accrue to these sectors.

These changes in the geography and in the composition of international transactions, and the framework through which these transactions are implemented, have contributed to the formation of new strategic sites in the world economy. This is the subject of the next section.

Strategic places

Four types of places above all others symbolize the new forms of economic globalization: export processing zones, offshore banking centers, high-tech districts, and global cities. There are also many other locations where international transactions materialize. Certainly, harbors continue to be strategic in a world of growing international trade and in the formation of regional blocs for trade and investment. And massive industrial districts in major manufacturing export countries, such as the United States, Japan, and Germany, are in many ways strategic sites for international activity and specifically for production for export. None of these locations, however, captures the prototypical image of today's global economy the way the first four do. Some geographers now speak of global city regions to capture this development.

Because much has been published about export processing zones and high-tech districts, and because they entail types of activity less likely to be located in cities than finance and services, we will not examine them in detail. As they are less known, let me define the first as zones in low-wage countries where firms from developed countries can locate factories to process and/or assemble components brought in from and re-exported to the developed countries. Special legislation was passed in several developed countries to make this possible. The central rationale for these zones is access to cheap labor for the labor-intensive stages of a firm's production process. Tax breaks and lenient workplace standards in the zones are additional incentives. These zones are a key mechanism in the internationalization of production.

Here we will focus briefly on global cities and offshore banking centers.

Global cities   Global cities are strategic sites for the management of the global economy and the production of the most advanced services and financial operations. They are key sites for the advanced services and telecommunications facilities necessary for the implementation and management of global economic operations. They also tend to concentrate the headquarters of firms, especially firms that operate globally. The growth of international investment and trade and the need to finance and service such activities have fed the growth of these functions in major cities. The erosion of the role of the government in the world economy, which was much larger when trade was the dominant form of international transaction, has displaced some of the organizing and servicing work from governments and major headquarters to specialized service firms and global markets in services and finance. Here we briefly examine these developments, first by presenting the concept of the global city and then by empirically describing the concentration of major international markets and firms in various cities.

The specific forms assumed by globalization over the last decade have created particular organizational requirements. The emergence of global markets for finance and specialized services, along with the growth of investment as a major type of international transaction, has contributed to the expansion in command functions and in the demand for specialized services for firms. Much of this activity is not encompassed by the organizational form of the TNC or bank, even though these types of firms account for a disproportionate share of international flows. Nor is much of this activity encompassed by the power of transnationals, a power often invoked to explain the fact of economic globalization. It involves work and workers. Here some of the hypotheses developed in our recent work are of interest, especially those that examine the spatial and organizational forms of economic globalization and the actual work of running transnational economic operations (Sassen, 1991). This way of framing the inquiry has the effect of recovering the centrality of place and work in processes of economic globalization.

A central proposition in the global city model (Sassen, 1991) is that the *combination* of geographic dispersal of economic activities and system integration that lies at the heart of the current economic era has contributed to a strategic role for major cities. Rather than becoming obsolete because of the dispersal made possible by information technologies, cities instead concentrate command functions. In a somewhat different vocabulary, Friedmann and Wolff (1982) posited this long before it exploded into the research literature it is now; see also Friedmann (1986) and Sassen-Koob (1982).[2] To this role, I have added two additional functions:

1   Cities are postindustrial production sites for the leading industries of this period – finance and specialized services.
2   Cities are transnational marketplaces where firms and governments from all over the world can buy financial instruments and specialized services.

The territorial dispersal of economic activity at the national and world scale implied by globalization has created new forms of concentration. This territorial dispersal and ongoing concentration in ownership can be inferred from some of the figures on the growth of transnational enterprises and their affiliates. Table 2.4 shows how vast the numbers of affiliates of TNCs are. This raises the complexity of management functions, accounting, and legal services, and hence the growth of these activities in global cities.

In the case of the financial industry, we see a similar dynamic of global integration: a growth in the number of cities integrated in the global financial network and a simultaneous increase of concentration of value managed at the top of the hierarchy of centers. We can identify two distinct phases. Up to the end of the 1982

Table 2.4 Number of parent transnational corporations and foreign affiliates, by region and country, selected years (1990–97)

	Year	Parent corporations based in country	Foreign affiliates located in country
All developed countries	1990	33,500	81,800
	1996	43,442	96,620
Select countries			
Australia	1992	1,306	695
	1997	485	2,371
Canada	1991	1,308	5,874
	1996	1,695	4,541
Federal Republic of Germany	1990	6,984	11,821
	1996	7,569	11,445
France	1990	2,056	6,870
	1996	2,078	9,351
Japan	1992	3,529	3,150
	1996	4,231	3,014
Sweden	1991	3,529	2,400
	1997	4,148	5,551
Switzerland	1985	3,000	2,900
	1995	4,506	5,774
United Kingdom	1991	1,500	2,900
	1996	1,059	2,609
United States	1990	3,000	14,900
	1995	3,379	18,901
All developing countries	1990	2,700	71,300
	1996	9,323	230,696
Select countries			
Brazil	1992	566	7,110
	1995	797	6,322
China	1989	379	15,966
	1997	379	145,000
Colombia	1987	–	1,041
	1995	302	2,220
Hong Kong, China	1991	500	2,828
	1997	500	5,067
Indonesia	1988	–	1,064
	1995	313	3,472
Philippines	1987	–	1,952
	1995	–	14,802
Republic of Korea	1991	1,049	3,671
	1996	4,806	3,878
Singapore	1986	–	10,709
	1995	–	18,154
Central and Eastern Europe	1990	400	21,800
	1996	842	121,601
World total	1990	36,600	174,900
	1996	53,607	448,917

Source: Based on UNCTAD, *World Investment Report* (1998:3, 4).

Third World debt crisis, the large transnational banks dominated the financial markets in terms of both the volume and the nature of financial transactions. After 1982, this dominance was increasingly challenged by other financial institutions and the major innovations they produced. These challenges led to a transformation in the leading components of the financial industry, a proliferation of financial institutions, and the rapid internationalization of financial markets. The marketplace and the advantages of agglomeration – and hence, cities – assumed new significance beginning in the mid-1980s. These developments led simultaneously to

1   the incorporation of a multiplicity of markets all over the world into a global system that fed the growth of the industry after the 1982 debt crisis, and
2   new forms of concentration, specifically the centralization of the industry in a few leading financial centers.

Hence, in the case of the financial industry, to focus only on the large transnational banks would exclude precisely those sectors of the industry where much of the new growth and production of innovations has occurred. Also, it would again leave out an examination of the wide range of activities, firms, and markets that compose the financial industry beginning in the 1980s.

The geographic dispersal of plants, offices, and service outlets and the integration of a growing number of stock markets around the world could have been accompanied by a corresponding decentralization in control and central functions. But this has not happened.

If we organize some of the evidence on financial flows according to the places where the markets and firms are located, we can see distinct patterns of concentration. The evidence on the locational patterns of banks and securities houses points to sharp concentration. For example, the worldwide distribution of the 100 largest banks and 25 largest securities houses in 1991 shows that Japan, the United States, and the UK accounted for 39 and 23 of each, respectively (see top half of Tables 2.5 and 2.6). This pattern persists in the late 1990s, notwithstanding multiple financial crises in the world and in Japan particularly (see bottom half of Tables 2.5 and 2.6).

The stock market illustrates this pattern well. From Bangkok to Buenos Aires, governments deregulated their stock markets to allow their participation in a global market system. And they have seen an enormous increase in the value of transactions. Yet there is immense concentration in leading stock markets in terms of worldwide capitalization – that is, the value of publicly listed firms. The market value of equities in domestic firms confirms the leading position of a few cities. In September 1987, before the stock market crisis, this value stood at US$2.8 trillion in the United States and at US$2.89 trillion in Japan. Third ranked was the UK, with US$728 billion. The extent to which these values represent extremely high levels is indicated by the fact that the next largest value was for West Germany, a major economy where capitalization stood at US$255 billion, a long distance from the top three. What these levels of stock market capitalization represent in the top countries is indicated by a comparison with gross national product (GNP) figures: in Japan, stock market capitalization was the equivalent of 64%; in the United States, the equivalent of 119%; in the UK, the equivalent of 118% of GNP; and in Germany, 23% of GNP. The full impact of deregulation and the growth of financial markets

Table 2.5   United States, Japan, and United Kingdom: Share of world's 50 largest banks, 1991 and 1997 (US$ millions and percentage)

	No. of firms	Assets	% of top 50	Capital	% of top 50
1991					
Japan	27	6,572,416	40.7	975,192	40.6
United States	7	913,009	5.7	104,726	4.4
United Kingdom	5	791,652	4.9	56,750	2.4
Subtotal	39	8,277,077	51.3	1,136,668	47.4
Total for Top 50	50	16,143,353	100.0	2,400,439	100.0
1997					
Japan	12	6,116,307	36.4	1,033,421	45.8
United States	6	1,794,821	10.7	242,000	10.7
United Kingdom	5	1,505,686	9.0	130,587	5.8
Subtotal	23	9,416,814	56.0	1,406,008	62.3
Total for Top 50	50	16,817,690	100.0	2,257,946	100.0

Note: Ranked by assets as determined by Dow Jones Global Indexes in association with WorldScope; figures are based on each listed company's 1997 fiscal year results, except data on Japanese banks, which are based on fiscal 1998 results.
Source: Based on "World Business," *Wall Street Journal*, September 24, 1992, R27; "World Business," *Wall Street Journal*, September 28, 1998, R25–27.

Table 2.6   United States, Japan, and United Kingdom: Share of world's 25 largest security firms, 1991 and 1997 (US$ millions and percentage)

	No. of firms	Assets	% of top 25	Capital	% of top 25
1991					
Japan	10	171,913	30.5	61,871	50.5
United States	11	340,558	60.4	52,430	42.8
United Kingdom	2	44,574	7.9	3,039	2.5
Subtotal	23	557,045	98.8	117,340	95.7
Total for Top 25	25	563,623	100.0	122,561	100.0
1997					
Japan	6	236,712	11.9	36,827	14.1
United States	15	1,660,386	83.2	207,181	79.3
United Kingdom	2	41,396	2.1	9,501	3.6
Subtotal	23	1,938,494	97.1	253,509	97.1
Total for Top 25	25	1,995,782	100.0	261,180	100.0

Note: Ranked by capital as determined by Dow Jones Global Indexes; figures based on 1997 fiscal year results.
Source: Based on "World Business," *Wall Street Journal*, September 24, 1992, R27; "World Business," *Wall Street Journal*, September 28, 1998, R25–27.

can be seen in the increases in value and in number of firms listed in all the major stock markets in the world by 1997. The market value of listings rose between 1990 and 1997 from US$2.8 trillion to US$9.4 trillion in New York City and from US$1 trillion to US$2 trillion in London. Similar patterns, although at lower orders of magnitude, are evident in the other stock markets listed in Figure 2.1 [2.7].

The concentration in the operational side of the financial industry is made evident in the fact that most of the stock market transactions in the leading countries are

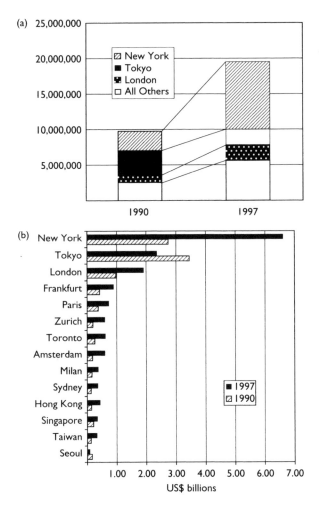

Figure 2.1 (a) New York, Tokyo, and London: Share of world stock market value, 1990 and 1997 (US$ millions and number)*; (b) Top cities ranked by stock market value, 1990 and 1997 (US$ billions)†

Source: Based on Meridian Securities Markets, *World Stock Exchange Fact Book* (1998).

Note: * All others includes Frankfurt, Paris, Zurich, Toronto, Amsterdam, Milan, Sydney, Hong Kong, Singapore, Taiwan, and Seoul stock exchanges.

† For Australia 1997, the number of listed companies is form 1996; when only domestic is listed, it represents the total market value.

concentrated in a few stock markets. The Tokyo exchange accounts for 90% of equities trading in Japan. New York accounts for about two-thirds of equities trading in the United States; and London accounts for most trading in the UK. There is, then, a disproportionate concentration of worldwide capitalization in a few cities.

Certain aspects of the territorial dispersal of economic activity may have led to some dispersal of profits and ownership. Large firms, for example, have increased their subcontracting to smaller firms worldwide, and many national firms in the newly industrializing countries have grown rapidly, thanks to investment by foreign firms and access to world markets, often through arrangements with transnational firms. Yet this form of growth is ultimately part of a chain in which a limited number of corporations continue to control the end product and reap most of the profits associated with selling on the world market. Even industrial homeworkers in remote rural areas are now part of that chain (Sassen, 1988, ch. 4).

Under these conditions, the territorial dispersal of economic activity creates a need for expanded central control and management if this dispersal is to occur along with continued economic concentration. This in turn has contributed to the strategic role played by major cities in the world economy today.

Offshore banking centers   Offshore financial centers are another important spatial point in the worldwide circuits of financial flows. Such centers are above all else tax shelters, a response by private sector actors to government regulation. They began to be implemented in the 1970s, although international tax shelters have existed in various incipient forms for a long time. The 1970s marked a juncture between growing economic internationalization and continuing government control over the economy in developed countries, partly a legacy of the major postwar reconstruction efforts in Europe and Japan. Offshore banking centers are, to a large extent, paper operations. The Cayman Islands, for example, illustrate some of these issues (Roberts, 1994). By 1997, they were ranked as the seventh largest international banking operation in the world and the fifth largest financial center after London, Tokyo, New York, and Hong Kong, according to International Monetary Fund (IMF) data (IMF, 1999). They also were still the world's second largest insurance location with gross capital of US$8 billion in 1997. The value of deposits held in banks in the Cayman Islands grew from US$250 billion in 1990 to US$640 billion in 1997. Its 593 banks in 1997 included 47 of the world's top 50 banks. But even though that tiny country supposedly has well over 500 banks from all around the world, only 69 banks have offices there, and only 6 are "real" banks for cashing and depositing money and other transactions. Many of the others exist only as folders in a cabinet (Walter, 1989; Roberts, 1994).

These offshore centers are located in many parts of the world. The majority of Asian offshore centers are located in Singapore and Hong Kong; Manila and Taipei are also significant centers. In the Middle East, Bahrain took over from Beirut in 1975 as the main offshore banking center, with Dubai following as a close second. In 1999, Abu Dhabi made a bid to create its own offshore financial center on Saadiyat Island. In the South Pacific, we find major centers in Australia and New Zealand and smaller offshore clusters in Vanuatu, the Cook Islands, and Nauru; Tonga and Western Samoa are seeking to become such centers. In the Indian Ocean, centers cluster in the Seychelles and in Mauritius. In Europe, Switzerland tops the list, and

Luxembourg is a major center; others are Cyprus, Madeira, Malta, the Isle of Man, and the Channel Islands. Several small places are struggling to compete with established centers: Gibraltar, Monaco, Liechtenstein, Andorra, and Campione. The Caribbean has Bermuda, the Cayman Islands, Bahamas, Turks and Caicos, and the British Virgin Islands.

Why do offshore banking centers exist? This question is especially pertinent given the massive deregulation of major financial markets in the 1980s and the establishment of "free international financial zones" in several major cities in highly developed countries. The best example of such free international zones for financial activity is the Euromarket, beginning in the 1960s and much expanded today, with London at the center of the Euromarket system. Other examples, as of 1981, were international banking facilities in the United States, mostly in New York City, that allowed US banks to establish special adjunct facilities to accept deposits from foreign entities free of reserve requirements and interest rate limitations. Tokyo, finally, saw the development of a facility in 1986 that allowed transactions in the Asian dollar market to be carried out in that city; this meant that Tokyo got some of the capital being transacted in Hong Kong, Singapore, and Bahrain, all Asian dollar centers.

Compared with the major international centers, offshore banking centers offer certain types of additional flexibility: secrecy, openness to "hot" money and to certain "legitimate" options not quite allowed in the deregulated markets of major financial centers, and tax minimization strategies for international corporations. Thus, offshore centers are used not only for Euromarket transactions but also for various accounting operations aimed at tax avoidance or minimization.

In principle, the Euromarkets of London are part of the offshore markets. They were set up to avoid the system for regulating exchange rates and balance-of-payments imbalances contained in the Bretton Woods agreement of 1945. The Bretton Woods agreement set up a legal framework for the regulation of international transactions, such as foreign currency operations, for countries or banks wanting to operate internationally. Euromarkets were initially a Eurodollar market, where banks from the United States and other countries could do dollar transactions and avoid US regulations. Over the last decade, other currencies have joined.

In finance, *offshore* does not always mean overseas or foreign; basically the term means that less regulation takes place than "onshore" – the latter describing firms and markets not covered by this special legislation (Roberts, 1994). The onshore and offshore markets compete with each other. Deregulation in the 1980s brought a lot of offshore capital back into onshore markets, especially in New York and London – a not insignificant factor in convincing governments in these countries to proceed with deregulation of the financial markets in the 1980s. London's much-noted "Big Bang" and the less-noted "petit bang" in Paris are instances of such a process of deregulation of financial markets.

The Euromarkets are significant in international finance. According to the Bank for International Settlements, the Eurocurrency markets grew from US$9 billion in 1964 to US$57 billion in 1970 and US$661 billion in 1981. The oil crisis was important in feeding this growth. In the 1980s, it was Eurobonds and Eurosecurities – that is, bonds and securities traded "offshore," outside the standard regulatory framework. Securitization was crucial in the 1980s, to launch the new financial era by making liquid what had been illiquid forms of debt. With the launch of the euro in January 1999, Euromarkets are experiencing a period of profound change and growth, with the current value of outstanding international debt in both euro and legacy currencies at US$1,629 billion in 1998 (IMF 1999: Part 2).

Offshore banking centers basically grew out of tax havens in the 1970s, and this is one of the ways in which they differ from the Euromarkets. Some offshore centers today are mere tax havens, whereas some old tax havens have become full-fledged offshore banking centers; many offshore centers specialize in certain branches of banking, insurance, and other financial transactions. There is a clustering of small offshore banking centers within the time zone of each of the three major financial centers (New York City, London, Tokyo); these marginal offshore centers do some servicing of business being transacted in the major centers and within that time zone. But not all offshore activity is related to major centers, nor is location offshore totally determined by time zones.

In brief, offshore banking centers represent a highly specialized location for certain types of international financial transactions. They are also a buffer zone in case the governments of the leading financial centers in the world should decide to reregulate the financial markets. On the broader scale of operations, however, they represent a fraction of the financial capital markets now concentrated in global cities.

Conclusion: After the Pax American

The world economy has never been a planetary event; it has always had more or less clearly defined boundaries. Moreover, although most major industries were involved throughout, the cluster of industries that dominated any given period changed over time, contributing to distinct structurings of the world economy. Finally, the institutional framework through which the world economy coheres has also varied sharply, from the earlier empires through the quasi-empire of the Pax Americana – the period of US political, economic, and military dominance – and its collapse in the 1970s.

It is in this collapse of the Pax Americana, when the rebuilt economies of Western Europe and Japan reentered the international markets, that we see emerging a new phase of the world economy. There is considerable agreement among specialists that in the mid-1970s new patterns in the world economy became evident. First, the geographical axis of international transactions changed from North–South to East–West. In this process, significant parts of Africa and Latin America became unhinged from their hitherto strong ties with world markets in commodities and raw materials. Second was a sharp increase in the weight of FDI in services and in the role played by international financial markets. Third was the break down of the Bretton Woods agreement, which had established the institutional framework under which the world economy had operated since the end of World War II. This breakdown was clearly linked to the decline of the United States as the single dominant economic power in the world. Japanese and European multinationals and banks became major competitors with US firms. The financial crises in Asia in the 1990s have once again strengthened the role of the North-Atlantic system in the global economy.

These realignments are the background for understanding the position of different types of cities in the current organization of the world economy. A limited but growing number of major cities are the sites for the major financial markets and leading specialized services firms. And a large number of other major cities have lost their role as leading export centers for manufacturing, precisely because of the decentralization of production.

NOTES

1 FDI by transnationals may be financed through transnational banks or through the international credit markets. The mid-1980s saw a sharp increase in the share of the latter and a sharp decline in the former (Sassen, 1991, ch. 4).
2 I have traced this emerging scholarly lineage in Sassen (2000). Some of the texts are Castells (1989); Fainstein (1993); Knox and Taylor (1995); Allen, Massey, and Pryke (1999); Short and Kim (1999); and Eade (1997).

REFERENCES

Allen, J. Massey, D and Pryke M. (eds.). 1999: *Unsettling Cities*. London: Routledge.

Castells, M. 1989: *The Informational City*. London: Blackwell.

Eade, J. 1997: *Living the Global City: Globalization as a Local Process*. New York: Routledge.

Fainstein, S. 1993: *The City Builders*. Oxford, UK: Blackwell.

Friedmann, J. 1986: "The World City Hypothesis." *Development and Change*. 17: 69–84.

Friedmann, J. and Wolff, G. 1982: "World City Formation: An Agenda for Research and Action." *International Journal of Urban and Regional Research*. 15 (1): 269–83.

Hoover's Handbook of World Business. 1998: Austin, TX: Reference Press.

IMF (International Money Fund). 1999: *International Capital Markets Report*. Washington, DC: IMF.

Knox, P. and Taylor, P. (eds.). 1995: *World Cities in a World System*. New York: Cambridge University Press.

Meridian Securities Markets. 1998: *World Stock Exchange Fact Book*. Morris Plains, NJ: Electronic Commerce.

Roberts, S. 1994: "Fictitious Capital, Fictitious Spaces: The Geography of Off-shore Financial Flows." In S. Corbridge, R. Martin, and N. Thrift (eds.) *Money, Power, and Space*. Oxford, UK: Blackwell.

Sassen, S. (ed.). 1988: *The Mobility of Labor and Capital: A Study in International Investment and Labor Flow*. New York: Cambridge University Press.

Sassen, S. (ed.). 1991: *The Global City: New York, London, Tokyo*. Princeton, NJ: Princeton University Press.

Sassen, S. (ed.). 1996: *Losing Control? Sovereignty in an Age of Globalization*. The 1995 Columbia University Leonard Hasting Schoff Memorial Lectures. New York: Columbia University Press.

Sassen, S. (ed.). 2000: *Cities and Their Crossborder Networks*. Tokyo: United Nations.

Sassen-Koob, S. 1982: "Recomposition and Peripheralization at the Core." pp. 88–100 *Immigration and Change in the International Division of Labor.* San Francisco: Synthesis. (Reprinted in Contemporary Marxism, Vol. 4).

Short, J. R. and Kim, Y. H. 1999: *Globalization and the City.* New York: Longman.

United Nations Center on Transnational Corporations (UNCTC). 1991: *World Investment Report: The Triad in Foreign Direct Investment.* New York: United Nations.

UNCTAD (United Nations Conference on Trade and Development) 1993: *World Investment Report 1993: Transnational Corporations and Integrated International Production.* New York: United Nations.

UNCTAD, Programme on Transnational Corporations. 1998: *World Investment Report 1998: Trends and Determinants.* New York: United Nations.

Walter, I. 1989: *Secret Money.* London: Unwin Hyman

3

New Industrial Cities? The Four Faces of Silicon Valley*

Mia Gray, Elyse Golob, Ann Markusen, Sam Ock Park

In the search for an American archetypal new industrial district, no place has been more intensely scrutinized than Silicon Valley. The valley has been admired and much emulated, based on its heavily networked, small-firm, innovative electronics sector which is argued to give the region a uniquely cooperative, flexible, and dynamic structure (Borrus, 1988; Gordon and Kimball, 1987; Miller and Cote, 1987; Rogers and Larsen, 1984; Saxenian, 1991b, 1994). If any one place has been anointed as an American version of the "Third Italy," it is Silicon Valley. It has been championed by its admirers as the prototypical city of the future.[1]

In her book, *Regional Advantage*, Saxenian (1994) focuses on the valley's small and medium-sized firms in the electronics industry, and shows how intricately linked they are with each other, how boundaries between firms are often "fuzzy," and how cooperative relationships permit them to reposition themselves rapidly as product and process innovations alter industry circumstances. Saxenian places special emphasis on the evolved entrepreneurial culture of the region, distinguishing it sharply from the Route 128 electronics complex around Boston. The latter, she argues, is encumbered with an industrial structure composed of large, relatively walled-off firms who are unwilling to share and slow to respond to market changes. Silicon Valley's culture, she suggests, in addition to being responsible for the region's superior performance, also makes it a more attractive work environment. In Saxenian's account, which has been contested by others (Florida and Kenney, 1990; Harrison, 1994), Silicon Valley firms engage in reciprocal and mutually advantageous relationships free from the hierarchy, power imbalances, and cultural conservatism of the New England large firm-dominated environment.

* Gray, Mia, Elyse Golob, Ann Markusen, and Sam Oak Park (1998) "New Industrial Cities? The Four Faces of Silicon Valley" from *Review of Radical Political Economics* 30(4), 1–28. Copyright © the Union of Radical Political Economists.

But Silicon Valley is much more than an Italianate agglomeration of small, flexible, cooperating firms. In this paper, we demonstrate that there are three additional "faces" to Silicon Valley, each of which contributes to the region's expertise, its resilience, and its potential. One face is the military industrial portion of the economy which is centered on large public and private institutions (Lockheed, FMC, Ford Aerospace, Stanford, Ames Aeronautical Laboratory). This element of the economy is a large chunk of the region's "export" income, and has been a major source of technological innovation, underwritten by US taxpayers. A second face is the contingent of large civilian high-tech firms like Hewlett-Packard and IBM, who for decades have been conducting research and interacting with smaller valley firms. A third is the more recent increment of branch plants of foreign firms, both Asian and European, doing detective work on the region's innovators and transferring know-how out of the region.

These three components all have arms that reach far afield from the region, calling into question the claim of largely endogenously driven growth celebrated in the industrial districts literature. In this [chapter] each additional face is scrutinized with research findings based on fieldwork in the valley. Through intensive interviewing, which is described in detail in the following section, and secondary research, we find considerable power imbalances among firms; strains in the networking fabric; and processes at work which may undermine the valley's singularity. Relationships among members of different sectors are generally characterized by competitive, arm's length relationships. Larger firms and foreign branch plants are more apt to cooperate with organizations external to the district. Relatively low levels of inter-organizational mobility of personnel predominate. All of these features undermine the cooperative, innovative, and governance conditions celebrated by the new industrial districts scholars. Furthermore, their *modus operandi* tends to raise the regional cost of doing business and exacerbates centrifugal tendencies in corporate location.

On broader economic welfare criteria, Silicon Valley receives only mixed marks, especially when compared with other fastgrowing and widely admired regions like the Third Italy (Piore and Sabel, 1984), Research Triangle Park (Luger and Goldstein, 1990), and Seattle (Gray et al., 1996). Its income distribution is more highly skewed and its labor force less apt to have a voice via collective bargaining relationships. As a model for aspiring regions elsewhere, then, our research suggests that the Silicon Valley recipe is more complex than has been acknowledged in the literature, less likely to be easily replicated, and less attractive from a social welfare point of view.

The Growth and Industrial Structure of Silicon Valley

As one of the fastest growing manufacturing regions in the United States over the past twenty years, Silicon Valley's economy has expanded rapidly since the 1970s while maintaining a relatively stable industrial mix (Table 3.1).[2] From 1970 to 1990, regional employment increased by 128 percent to 1015,000 (US Census, 1992). During this period, manufacturing employment increased by 119 percent and service jobs by 199 percent. Five industries account for much of the growth: computer and office equipment; guided missiles, space vehicles, and parts; electronic components

Table 3.1 Selected US metropolitan employment growth rates, 1970–90

	Employment		Manufacturing		Service	
	1990 (000)	Change (%) 1970–90	Employment 1990 (000)	Change (%) 1970–90	Employment 1990 (000)	Change (%) 1970–90
Colorado Springs, CO	228	104	24	261	60	214
Austin, TX	471	178	50	249	131	253
Reno, NV	145	155	9	202	70	184
Tucson, AZ	316	123	28	199	101	219
Huntsville, AL	163	76	34	177	42	82
Orlando, FL	569	246	56	162	236	465
Albuquerque, NM	305	125	22	131	98	184
Melbourne–Titusville, FL	202	112	31	122	66	119
San Jose, CA	1,015	128	273	119	301	199
San Diego, CA	1,397	120	141	109	390	254
Anaheim–Santa Ana, CA	1,552	192	261	111	464	352
Raleigh–Durham, NC	513	123	66	94	145	175
Seattle, WA	1,339	114	227	73	362	206
Madison, WI	262	73	26	53	62	147
Elkhart–Goshan, IN	116	64	52	50	20	123
Los Angeles–Long Beach, CA	5,200	56	893	9	1,707	129
Boston–Lawrence–Salem, MA	1,672	30	340	–12	894	108
Chicago, IL	3,673	23	569	–33	1,128	101
New York, NY	4,765	2	428	–51	1,704	50
United States	110,321	56	19,742	0	37,573	126

Source: Bureau of Economic Analysis (1970, 1990) as compiled by Andy Isserman, Regional Research Institute, University of West Virginia, and Ann Markusen and Mia Gray, PRIE, Rutgers University.

and accessories; communications equipment; and measuring and controlling devices. Each posted high levels of overall employment and had location quotients significantly higher than one, suggesting strong specialization and comparative advantage (Table 3.2).[3]

These key industrial sectors represent a diverse group of manufacturers, some of which include a high number of small, innovative, locally headquartered firms, as theorized by the regional scholars. Most, however, are also characterized by significant levels of defense production and state-funded R&D, long-standing big firm innovation and leadership, and increasing international interpenetration. In the following sections, we explore each of these three additional dimensions.

Our interpretation is based on evidence from secondary data analysis and interviews with public and private sector managers of larger institutions, as well as the work of others. Our interviews targeted large, prominent firms (both headquarters and branch operations), economic development officials, and industry watchers (venture capitalists, realtors, academics, and business associations) in the valley, and were conducted in the summer of 1993. The set of firms and institutions, 49 interviews in all, was chosen to complement rather than replicate Saxenian's careful study of smaller, innovative firms.[4] We used a standard protocol with many open-ended questions and included some industry specific variations. Relatively few firms or organizations declined to participate, although a few venture capitalists and realtors refused. We could not identify any discernible pattern or bias resulting from the refusals.

We selected firms on the basis of size, significance in previous research, domestic or foreign ownership, and sector. We often interviewed two or three contacts in each firm to validate our responses for institutional consistency. We interviewed executive or senior vice presidents and often interviewed directors in operations, quality, or planning afterward to explore intra-organizational variations or inconsistencies.[5] For the institutions in our set, the president of the organization was the usual interviewee. We asked managers of these larger firms and organizations a series of questions about their relationships with other organizations within the valley and elsewhere, as well as their perspective on the advantages and disadvantages of operating from a valley site.

The Heart of the Valley: The Military Industrial Complex

Although Los Angeles is generally perceived to be California's premium military industrial complex, Silicon Valley gives Los Angeles a stiff run for its money. Silicon Valley is a national leader in the high-tech segment of the defense industry, including guided missiles, electronic components, and measuring and controlling devices (Table 3.2).[6] Although it has expanded its customer base beyond the military over the years, more so than its neighbor to the south, Silicon Valley ranks as the most defense-dependent community in the nation (Table 3.3). In 1988, the San José metropolitan area received $4,590 in prime contracts per employed worker, more than four times the national average. The Los Angeles–Long Beach region, in comparison, received $2,234 prime contracts per worker, less than half the amount of Silicon Valley (US Congress OTA, 1992).

Table 3.2 Location quotients and estimated jobs, Santa Clara County, 1975 and 1989

SIC	Industry	1975		1989		% Defense dependency of sector in 1987
		Jobs	LQ	Jobs	LQ	
3570	Computers and office equipment	21,771	16.03	50,155	19.80	13%
3760	Guided missiles, space vehicles, and parts	15,109	18.63	31,113	18.06	79%
3670	Electronic components and accessories	30,408	17.13	63,938	14.46	20%
3660	Communications equipment	10,043	3.96	15,943	7.73	63%
3820	Measuring and controlling devices	10,120	11.03	15,838	6.88	NA

Sources: US Census, County Business Patterns (1989); estimates by Andrew Isserman, Regional Research Institute, University of West Virginia; sector dependency from David Henry, "Defense Spending: A Growth Market for Industry," US Industrial Outlook (1983): XXXIX–XLVII. These are estimates of direct and indirect output orientation at the national level. Figures are for SIC 3573, 3761, 3676–9, and 3662.

Table 3.3 Defense dependent communities, 1989

Metro area	National rank	Prime contracts per worker employed	Ratio to US average
San Jose	1	$4,590	4.33
Washington, D.C.	2	$3,863	3.64
St Louis	3	$3,850	3.63
Boston	4	$2,863	2.70
Cincinnati	5	$2,778	2.62
Dallas-Fort Worth	6	$2,776	2.62
Nassau-Suffolk	7	$2,691	2.54
Hartford, et al.	8	$2,666	2.52
Los Angeles-Long Beach	9	$2,234	2.11
Anaheim	10	$2,164	2.04
Seattle-Everett	11	$2,127	2.01
San Diego	12	$1,950	1.84
Denver-Boulder	13	$1,949	1.84
Baltimore	14	$1,701	1.60
Minneapolis-St. Paul	15	$1,441	1.36
US Average	n/a	$1,060	1.00

Source: US Congress, Office of Technology Assessment, After the Cold War.

The role of the defense industry in shaping Silicon Valley, both in the past and present, is often downplayed or omitted entirely in "industrial districts" accounts. While some analysts acknowledge the military's leadership role in promoting the early evolution of the valley's high-tech industries, they consider it important only in the early stages of the valley's development and belittle its ongoing significance (Saxenian, 1994; Borrus, 1988). Our field research finds that the defense industry not only played an important role in the valley's initial development, but continues to exert major influence on the region today.

The history of Silicon Valley is inextricably intertwined with the needs of the military. At the turn of the century, Santa Clara county, a large and prosperous agricultural area with fertile grounds and vast fruit orchards, was known as "The Valley of the Heart's Delight." During the first half of the century, two military-related institutions, the Naval Air Station at Moffett Field and Ames Aeronautical Laboratory,[7] complemented the role of Stanford University in establishing a skilled labor force, local business services, and a shared infrastructure. These three institutions served as anchor tenants in a district that came to specialize in aerospace, electronics, and computer industries. The military launched the valley's technological trajectory by funding electronics and aeronautical R&D, setting strict product specifications, and later functioning as a steady and lucrative market for the fledging aerospace, computer, and microelectronics firms (Borrus, 1988; Saxenian, 1985).

The central role of Stanford University in Silicon Valley's development is well documented (Saxenian, 1985; Malone, 1985; Rogers and Larsen, 1984). Frederick Terman, the early dean of Stanford's engineering department and prime mover in its rise to national prominence, aggressively pursued Department of Defense (DoD) patronage. Terman anticipated the magnitude of high-tech requirements in the Cold War economy, and revamped the institution's research and teaching programs to meet military demand. In 1946, Stanford's total government contracts amounted to $127,999; a decade later, due largely to Terman's efforts, total DoD contracts came to $4.5 million (Leslie, 1993). Terman also presided over launching numerous fledgling electronics firms – the founders of Hewlett-Packard, Litton, and Varian were trained and funded under his tutelage – and pioneered Stanford Industrial Park, which opened in 1951.[8]

After the war, Santa Clara County consolidated its position as a center for research in aviation technology and defense electronics. In 1956, Lockheed Missile and Space Co. hived off its operations from Lockheed Aircraft in Los Angeles and moved to Sunnyvale (Schoenberger, 1993). It quickly became the valley's largest employer with a peak of 25,000 workers in the mid-1960s. In the same era, other defense-oriented companies including Syntex, Sylvania, IBM, ESL, Loral, Philco, and Raytheon, located in the region, serving as subcontractors for Lockheed's Polaris missile contracts and space technology projects. By the mid-1970s, 82 percent of all federal R&D funds in the United States were directed to the aerospace and electronics sectors, and Silicon Valley's leading position in these industries ensured its role as primary recipient (Malecki, 1981).

This second wave of high-tech firms reinforced the region's competitive advantage by collectively assembling a pool of talented scientists and engineers, many of them recruited from top-notch engineering schools of the East and Middle West. Defense contracts underwrote expansive recruitment and resettlement – when a firm hired engineers from other parts of the nation, moving expenses were charged to the government on existing contracts. As a result, several generations of scientists and engineers were drawn to Silicon Valley and other defense dependent regions at taxpayer expense, one of the largest and largely unnoticed selective population resettlements in US history (Markusen et al., 1991; Ellis et al., 1993).

Silicon Valley benefited both from crucial federal government purchases in early stages of industrial evolution and from ongoing public investments in research. Steady military and space agency demand served as a lucrative market for the semiconductor, computer, and aerospace industries. The DoD and NASA provided a protected market by acting as the single largest buyer in crucial early commercialization stages, their commitment reinforced by their "buy American" policy (Markusen, 1986). In 1962, the military purchased literally all of the integrated circuits produced in the valley, paying premium prices. Although its market share rapidly declined to 10 percent by 1978, the early patronage was critical to the electronics industry's success. Military sales moved firms swiftly along the technological learning curve which allowed unit costs to fall low enough to permit them to penetrate industrial and commercial markets (Borrus, 1988).

The culture of innovation and rapid technological diffusion, championed in Saxenian's interpretation, owes much to Pentagon-provided incentives for technological innovation and funds for major investments on favorable terms. For prime contractors, military R&D funding set the direction for early product design by stressing miniaturization, high performance, reliability, and continual innovation – attributes fundamental to the subsequent commercialization of microelectronics. Military procurement also promoted technology diffusion by employing patent pooling agreements among defense contractors.[9] When DoD funding produced patentable products such as the transistor and integrated circuit, the DoD and contracting firms obtained the license free of charge (Borrus, 1988).

Low levels of defense-to-civilian sales ratios are often cited by Silicon Valley boosters as evidence that the contemporary valley has weaned itself from defense dependency. However, many firms interviewed still view the military as a "bread and butter" customer, and the more than $4 billion in prime contracts that has been flowing into the valley annually is a major stimulant to the local economy. As seen in Table 3.4, in addition to the large dedicated defense contractors such as Lockheed and Loral, micro-electronic firms such as Sun Microsystems and Stanford Telecommunications serve as major defense contractors. Many of the commercial semiconductor suppliers interviewed in this study sell 15–20 percent of their product to prime defense contractors, while the defense-oriented firms continue to sell 60–90 percent of their product to the Pentagon.

Other Silicon Valley firms are not even trying to wean themselves off of defense. While many defense-oriented firms have coped with a shrinking defense budget by increasing their civilian markets, others are attempting to increase their market share of the defense market or to "gain a larger piece of a smaller pie." One large defense contractor commented:

> Our major customers are the DoD, the intelligence agencies, and some of the arsenals. We tried to find new customers, but it's hard. We've had to refocus on our traditional customers' needs in the DoD and try to fit into their new missions.

But more significantly, numerous valley high-tech companies rely heavily on defense-related R&D for their innovative edge. In both computing and electronics, military contracts remain the major source of funding – over 60 percent of path-breaking research in computing, for instance, is underwritten by national security funds (Yudken and Simons, 1989). This is true for Stanford University, which has consistently ranked among the nation's top recipients of federal R&D funding, as well as the private sector (Table 3.5). The University's progeny, Stanford Research Institute (SRI), created in 1969 in response to student protests over the University–Defense Department link, has a higher percentage of defense and space R&D funding than Stanford itself. In 1991, DoD and NASA together provided over half of SRI's and more than a third of Stanford's federal research funds.

The military industrial presence in the valley today is robust, albeit under intense pressures from defense downsizing. Current military planning and industrial base configuration stress continued high-tech weapons development, favoring electronics and communications over platforms. Silicon Valley's expertise lies heavily in the former areas, where procurement contracts have not been cut as deeply as in existing weapons systems. As a result, the valley has not been hit as severely during the current round of defense cuts as compared to the mass-production aerospace firms in Los Angeles. It is, however, subject to the same centrifugal tendencies undermining Los Angeles, as high costs and a newfound Pentagon frugality drive firms to consider production and even research in lower cost areas of the South and Intermountain West.

Table 3.4 15 Largest defense contractors, Santa Clara County, FY 1991

Company	Contracts (millions)	FT emp		Military product specialization
		In county	In firm	
Lockheed Missile and Space Co.	$1,082	16,359	23,387	Satellites, missile systems, command, and control
FMC Corp.	$0,805	3,200	23,000	Ground combat vehicles
Loral Western Dvlpmt. Labs	$0,280	2,000	26,000	Aerospace, training and simulation, test ranges, spacecraft
Westinghouse Electric Co.	$0,214	1,700	110,000	Missile launching systems
Sun Microsystems	$150+	8,900	12,800	Unix-based workstations and servers
Watkins-Johnson Co.	$0,145	1,200	2,680	Surveillance and reconnaissance, components and subsystems
Kaiser Electronics	$0,136	810	2,000	Aircraft cockpit displays
ESL Inco.	$0,121	2,100	na	Imagery, reconnaissance, communication systems
Varian Associates	~$72	2,600	8,400	Electron devices, including microwave and power-grid tubes
Litton Applied Technology	$0,061	1,046	2,236	Threat warning systems and database storage retrieval
Stanford Telecommunications	$0,052	450	900	Digital satellite communication
Trimble Navigation	$0,043	na	975	Satellite-based navigation systems
Teledyne Microwave	$0,040	450	35,000	Radio frequency & microwave components and systems
Space Applications	$0,032	50	275	Systems software engineering services
Tiburon Systems	$0,025	160	180	Automated software testing

Source: *San Jose Business Journal*, 31 August 1992.

Table 3.5 Federal R&D funds to Stanford and SRI, 1970–91

	Stanford			SRI		
Year	Natl funding rank	Federal R&D $(Thousands)	% R&D from DoD+NASA[a]	Natl funding rank	Federal R&D $ (Thousands)	% R&D from DoD+NASA[a]
1970	2	50,920	30	n/a	34,632	85
1975	6	70,171	16	2	45,565	n/a
1981	4	125,645	23	2	56,229	62
1986	3	201,452	18	3	72,986	75
1991	3	237,842	35	10	54,390	55

Note: [a] DoD and NASA funding as percent of total federal R&D funds.
Source: National Science Foundation (NSF) (1991, 1986, 1981, 1975, 1970). "Selected Data on Support to Universities, Colleges, and Non-profit Institutions."

While some of the unique features of the Silicon Valley complex – its product mix, its familiarity with innovation, and rapid technological diffusion – have their origins in military patronage, others do not. Although military requirements have promoted long-term contracts between primary contractors and their subcontractors, many of our interviewees report that the DoD's strict product specifications discourage the informal trust-based relationships found in the valley's civilian sectors. This issue was raised in numerous interviews. As one manager of a defense-systems firm explained it, "We try to build long-term relationships with our suppliers, because that helps our manufacturing process, but it's pretty hard to do with all the government (procurement) regulations and the sensitive nature of our work." While the constant teaming between competitors serving as prime or subcontractors may superficially resemble a flexible production network, the formality of the defense-oriented procurement system imposes a high degree of rigidity on interfirm relationships.[10] The firms involved in these "teams" are constantly negotiating around the internal contradictions this structure engenders. Subcontractors interviewed report a fairly high degree of power imbalance in relationships with primes. Interviewees emphasized that research and production in this segment of the valley is far from endogenous, with constant communication between area firms and the Pentagon and Congress in Washington, the military users, and major subcontractors elsewhere in the country.

At the Head of the Valley: Big Firm Leadership

The role of small-firm networks in Silicon Valley's success has been extensively documented in Saxenian's work. She depicts a valley economy comprised of flexible networks of small specialized producers who loosely coordinate a decentralized production system through their close and collaborative relationship (Saxenian, 1990a, 1990b). While the flexible production model of small-firm networking captures a unique phenomenon, it only describes one aspect of Silicon Valley's industrial organization, and is most applicable to the semiconductor industry. Our field research suggests that large firms play a more prominent role in the valley's economic success than this model allows for. Furthermore, the additional resources available to large corporations often allows them to dominate existing industrial networks. This unbalanced structure may result in less than optimal results for both entrepreneurs and workers in the region.

Saxenian is right that small firms have played an important role in the valley's success. In the five high-growth industries we studied, small firms represented between 50–69 percent of the total number of establishments (Table 3.6). These figures, however, overstate the significance of small firms to Silicon Valley's economy. While these companies are a vital component of the region's innovation and resilience, large multinational firms still control the lion's share of the market and are the major generators of jobs (Harrison, 1994). Significant barriers to entry and economies of scale continue to ensure big firm dominance in certain sectors. For example, total employment in the valley's guided missiles and space vehicles sector in 1989 was 31,113. Although 50 percent of the firms in this sector are small, Lockheed Missile & Space alone employed more than 20,000 of these workers.

Table 3.6 Firm size by industry, Santa Clara County, 1975 and 1989

SIC	Industry	Total emp. 1989	Distribution by size,[a] 1989		
			Small	Medium	Large
3760	Guided missiles, space vehicles, and parts	31,113	50%	0%	50%
3670	Electronic components and accessories	63,938	64%	24%	11%
3570	Computers and office equipment	50,155	62%	24%	14%
3820	Measuring and controlling devices	15,838	69%	22%	9%
3660	Communication equipment	15,943	61%	28%	11%

Note: [a] Firm size definition: small 1–49, medium 50–249, large 250+.
Source: U.S. Census, County Business Patterns (1989, 1975).

Not only are large firms major employers, but they tend to offer higher pay and better benefits than small firms, especially if they are defense oriented.

Furthermore, an overemphasis on the numerical superiority of small firms ignores subindustry structure and market segmentation. Many of the large Silicon Valley firms are market leaders and dominate their subfield or entire sector. For example, pointing to small-firm totals in the semiconductor industry ignores the sector's internal segmentation. There are three main types of firms in the semiconductor industry: product designers and manufacturers for internal use; product designers and manufacturers for external markets; and product designers renting manufacturing facilities. Small firms tend to dominate the third category, the smallest market segment, while large firms including Hewlett-Packard, Apple, IBM, Lockheed, and Litton dominate the first and second. Intel, a leading Silicon Valley firm, recently surpassed Motorola to become the nation's largest semiconductor supplier.

In addition, firm cooperation and trust, whether between small firms or small and large firms, is an insufficient explanation of the industrial structure within the district. Power relationships between firms also play an important role. While interfirm collaboration is an important feature of industrial organization, it may serve to reinforce the dominance of multinational corporations (Amin and Thrift, 1993). Lopsided collaboration allows large firms to expand market share and reduce the costs and risks of R&D without actually owning the required facilities. The greater organizational, technical, and financial resources of multinational corporations may allow them to shape these relationships to their advantage (Anderson, 1995). Small firms with expertise but little capital must operate in the shadow of large corporations and may be captive to their spatial and product requirements while bearing a disproportionate share of the risk. The result may be a highly structured and formalized, rather than fluid network, in which large firms coordinate the productive capacity of those of smaller size.

Our interviews confirm this power imbalance, as do the relatively high failure rates of smaller firms in the valley (Florida and Kenney, 1990). Although some individuals interviewed spoke of cooperation and collaboration, others alluded to the hierarchy and inequality between firms in the district. A product development executive at a large computer firm summarized the situation as follows: "We use our leverage (over other, smaller firms) whenever we can. It can give us an advantage ... We cooperate when we don't have that power." Furthermore, while some large firms praised the rich local supplier base, others indicated their ability to use their market power to their advantage when negotiating with smaller firms. As the vice president of one large computer firm put it: "You can negotiate (with suppliers) on price and then do some whip-sawing."

Furthermore, large firms are as likely to engage in *global* collaborative relationships as local ones. The recent boom in strategic alliances underscores the importance of national and international links for Silicon Valley firms. Although these partnerships vary tremendously, they tend to be formal agreements between firms to share research and development costs, marketing and distribution networks, and/or production. Our interviews suggest that capability, not proximity, is the key factor for participating firms. As a result, there may be substantial flows of capital from the region. Our research indicates that many Silicon Valley firms are deeply embedded

in these relationships which are quite different from the informal and highly localized linkages stressed in the industrial districts literature.

In addition, the trend towards lean manufacturing systems and corporate downsizing is transforming the valley's industrial network. Production is often hived off
beyond regional and national boundaries. Even R&D, once thought by many as
exclusively the reserve of the valley, is becoming a candidate for relocation. For
example, Intel employed 28,000 people and showed revenues of $5.9 billion in
1993. While its corporate headquarters remain in Santa Clara, production facilities
have been relocated to New Mexico, Ireland, and Israel, and its R&D is performed
in Phoenix and Oregon.

Hewlett-Packard, founded in 1939, has several major product lines including
computers, testing and diagnostic equipment, and medical equipment. Its organization, which includes over 20,000 employees in the Bay area, has always taken a
decentralized approach. In its early years, the company had strong local concentrations of R&D, financing, manufacturing, suppliers, and marketing; now many of
these functions except for R&D are gone. Although corporate headquarters remain
in Palo Alto, the firm currently employs 60,000 workers in other locations. As one
executive commented. "Hewlett-Packard will continue to have Silicon Valley as its
brain and its heart, but its body is a diffuse one."

These observations offer a corrective to the relatively egalitarian and reciprocal
relations governing firm interaction stressed in the Saxenian account. The flexible
specialization model allied with the industrial districts position posits that all firms
have an interest in maintaining a relatively trusting and egalitarian relationship so
that the system as a whole can function. Our research suggests that while the valley
may operate in this manner in some quarters, it also contains a substantial degree of
fierce competition in which relationships are adversarial and less than candid, and
where relationships between oligopolists or oligopsonists and their smaller customers or suppliers are far from egalitarian. Flexibility and openness without equality
leads to a situation where the costs and uncertainties of flexibility are pushed onto
the smaller firms. An example of this comes from the manager of a large electronics
firm who described their relationship with their suppliers this way:

> There's a rich base of suppliers here and that's very helpful for us. We try to be partners
> with them, help them, and to work with them...but, we're also extremely aware of
> costs and when push comes to shove, we can play hard ball, negotiate on price, and play
> them off each other.

Furthermore, many of the valley's large and small firms are deeply embedded in
close collaborative relationships with parties outside the region, calling into question
the depiction of a robust, locally embedded, and endogenously propelled growth
trajectory.

Eyes and Ears in the Valley: The Role of Foreign Investment

The presence of a significant contingent of foreign branch operations in Silicon
Valley is another underemphasized factor in industrial districts' accounts. Over the

past two decades, foreign direct investment (FDI) has provided the valley with additional employment, firm creation, and an important external source of capital. As such, its role is similar to that of the military in the 1940s through 1960s and venture capital in the 1960s to 1980s (Saxenian, 1994). From 1976 to 1987, foreign investment transactions in California grew from 31 to 244 with a value of over $3 billion (Teece, 1992). This presence requires further modification of the district's profile. Even more than operations of large domestic firms in the valley, these facilities have clear loyalties to overseas parents and are only very loosely engaged in local firm networking of the more intensive, cooperative form. In fact, their success in digesting and transferring overseas technological information reveals the vulnerability of the valley to its own openness and interfirm labor mobility.

Although corporations from many countries are found in the valley, our interviews concentrated on Japanese and Korean firms.[11] Since 1986, Japanese firms have collectively constituted California's leading foreign investor, strategically directing the majority of funds towards product development and applied R&D facilities in Silicon Valley. The number of Japanese corporate labs, most of which are owned by electronics firms, increased from 35 in 1985 to 135 in 1993 (Florida and Kenney, 1994).

The United States, especially California, has been a prime target for Korean foreign investment as well. The number of Korean-owned facilities in the United States increased tenfold from 1982 to 1992, with annual total investment rising 316 percent to $4.1 billion, mostly in manufacturing and trade. By 1993, 41 percent of Korean establishments in the United States were located in California and the value of these investments was slightly under $6 million (Bank of Korea, 1993). Our interviews suggest that Korean firms in Silicon Valley specialize in microelectronics, computer components, semiconductors, scientific equipment, and R&D.

Overseas firms engage in foreign direct investment (FDI) in the valley for several reasons. First, companies seeking to enter high-tech sectors often prefer to buy rather than develop expertise. Direct acquisition of an existing firm is the most popular form of FDI, providing an easy way to acquire technology and leapfrog the learning curve (Glickman and Woodward, 1989). Added to this is the desire to monitor competitors and changes in the sector. Almost uniformly, interviewees from high-tech, foreign-owned firms claimed that their Silicon Valley location is strategic – the branch serves as the company's "eyes and ears" on the industry. For example, Daeyoung Electronics, a Korean firm, opened a liaison office in Silicon Valley in 1988 to monitor information and coordinate new product development in computer peripherals. The director of Samsung Information Systems, a Korean-owned R&D lab, offered a similar explanation for his company's San José location:

> Information rises up to the surface here through "invisible networking" before it appears in the newspaper. We can confirm this information easily. Technical evaluations and prospectives (sic) can be done rapidly, and professionals can be secured immediately. As a result, the learning period is shortened and products can be developed quickly.

Second, firms also use FDI as a means of diversification (Teece 1992). Hyundai, Korea's largest chaebol, or industrial conglomerate, used profits earned from its construction division to buy into the high-tech sector. In 1983, it purchased a Silicon Valley semiconductor firm. Only three years later, when manufacturing costs became too costly, they moved their plants and equipment to Korea while retaining the San José facility for R&D and sales.

Third, many foreign firms seek access to manufacturing facilities and distribution channels in order to compete effectively in the US market. American companies, in turn, find themselves in need of "patient" R&D capital[12] and inexpensive entryways to foreign markets, and so often welcome offers to purchase (Glickman and Woodward 1989).

Fourth, locating in Silicon Valley helps foreign branches attract and keep talent which they might otherwise not be able to recruit. Our interviews reveal that a particular target for the Japanese and Korean firms in our study are large pools of Asian and Asian-American students who have graduated from American engineering schools and work in the valley. When not US citizens, they are banned from working on defense projects, and some degree of discrimination on the part of domestic firms creates some advantages for whites over Asians in the local labor market. Some foreign firms have been able to woo educated and experienced engineers into their organizations by locating in the valley – some go on to join the parent company overseas.

Information and expertise, then, is what draws foreign branch operations to the valley while ample cash makes it affordable and enables partnerships and new hires. The result is most often a facility whose chief decision makers as well as production facilities remain far afield. Oki Semiconductor, a subsidiary of Oki Electric in Japan, was established in Sunnyvale in 1978 as an engineering lab, with administrative, marketing, and sales headquarters. An Oki official explained that Silicon Valley was the ideal location because most of the firm's competitors were situated there, and the region represented 30 percent of its US market. Manufacturing, however, takes place primarily in Japan with a new facility recently established in Oregon, while financing and insurance are provided by its holding company, Oki America.

Time and again, interviewees stressed that foreign-owned facilities have a different relationship with the valley firms than do indigenous companies. Although they may participate in local production networks, benefit from agglomeration economies, and interact with suppliers and customers in Silicon Valley, their most significant relationship is with the parent corporation. Decisions regarding finance, strategy, product technology, and often material purchases come from the home country. This situation minimizes the foreign firms' ties with local suppliers. For example, NTK Ceramics, a Japanese firm located in Santa Clara, purchases one-half of its material inputs from Japan due to quality concerns and its commitment to long-term supplier relationships. Hyundai, a Korean firm, buys most of its parts and components from other Korean firms, although some specialized parts are obtained in Silicon Valley.

Some foreign firms play a more active role in the local economy, yielding more financial control to their valley branches and encouraging stronger relations with local suppliers. Samsung Semiconductor, an R&D establishment, has followed this strategy. Although financial decisions come from its parent company, it is more tied into the local economy than most, and has encouraged numerous local spin-offs. In

1993, the firm decided it no longer needed its fabrication facilities, and rather than shut them down, sold them to its employees. In addition, they provided the new firm with $3 million for development and $1 million for a fabrication foundry. But such cases are the exception rather than the rule.

In summary, foreign firms' operations constitute an important though unstable phenomenon in Silicon Valley. Many foreign firms view FDI as a transitional strategy, and thus enter and leave quickly. Firms locate in Silicon Valley with a specific purpose. They gain technical knowledge or information available on the local market, thus cashing in on Marshall's "secrets of industry" found in the air. Once this mission is accomplished, they often downsize, outsource, or abandon the region. The transitory nature of much of the FDI makes it an unstable source of growth. But more ominously, it may presage stiffer competition from overseas parents, which in the future may undermine the valley's comparative (and absolute) advantage. The unusual degree of interfirm mobility in the valley, documented so powerfully by Saxenian, may facilitate this process without capturing much return. Technology rents (broadly defined to include the valley's organizational structure) may, thus, never fully be captured by the region.

Conclusion and Evaluation

Silicon Valley, then, is the product of an overlay of at least five distinct institutional groupings: an impressive cluster of smaller, innovative electronics firms: Stanford University and its SRI and other non-profit research spin-offs; large domestic computing and instrumentation firms, many of them branch operations; research, marketing, and information-gathering operations of foreign firms; and a military industrial component of both private corporations and government offices. Saxenian and other industrial district analysts have concentrated their research on the first two, implying that they are responsible for the valley's success and unique character. We argue that Silicon Valley has also been powerfully shaped by its ongoing military specialization, big firm leadership, and foreign direct investment, and that growth in these segments of the valley is exogenously, not endogenously, driven. Evidence from our interviews with managers from within the latter three groups contradict the notion that the valley sports a unique business culture. We found that among them, relationships are generally competitive or insular rather than cooperative, boundaries are fixed rather than fuzzy, and employees exhibit relatively low degrees of interorganizational mobility.

The valley will undoubtedly continue to be relatively successful for several reasons, not the least of which is the innovative milieu stressed by Saxenian in the electronics sector. But the valley is spatially circumscribed, preventing further expansive growth. Within its confines, then, considerable turmoil is apt to characterize the future, with successive generations of the five institutional groups competing with each other for space. The valley's success already makes it a pricey place to do business, so that less agglomeration-sensitive operations will continue to be hived off to other locales.[13] The military industrial component is apt to be durable – the newly merged Lockheed Martin will have a superior bargaining position in Washington and even less competition from other contractors, and its expertise in communications and space will continue to be fundable. Though even here, certain operations can be decentralized to lower cost regions. Although foreign investment has been a boon to the valley, the transitory nature of FDI makes it an unstable source of future growth and contains, as we have seen, its own longer-term threat.

The phenomenon Saxenian stresses in *Regional Advantage* is significant because it will continue to anchor some innovative activities in the valley, compensating for the maturation and decentralization of other product lines. But even these functions are not immune to competition from other centers. In the past few years, dozens of smaller software and instrumentation firms have migrated to emerging agglomerations in Seattle, Colorado, Arizona, and New Mexico from Silicon Valley, drawn by the lower cost of doing business, a higher quality of life, and the removal of constraints that once held them captive in the valley. The explosive growth of inexpensive communications and overnight shipping has made it possible to collaborate and do business easily across national and even international space.

Heightened international competition and centrifugal forces have slowed the valley's growth in the 1990s. Between 1991 and 1993, total employment in the region decreased by 25,000 due to defense downsizing, firm restructuring, and productivity gains. In 1994, job loss was halted and employment flat, and this trend is expected to continue. As Saxenian (1991a) points out, the valley has not developed industry- or valley-wide governance structures, such as those in the Third Italy, which ameliorate competitive pressures and corrosive rivalry and shore up the agglomerative pull of the region. Our field research shows that the large number of industry associations in the valley act in a traditional, limited, manner to lobby on behalf of the industry, as opposed to socializing some of the costs and supplying collective inputs that small firms are unable to provide on their own.[14] The divided loyalties of many of the larger firms are a major reason for the absence of a strong local governance structure. Their desire to collaborate with firms elsewhere dampens their enthusiasm for valley-reinforcing agreements and behavior that might cement the region's comparative advantage.

How well is the valley performing on broader economic welfare criteria? The generally high but lopsided nature of income distribution in the valley has long been noted (Saxenian, 1983). The average annual wage in Santa Clara County in 1994 is, at $38,991, much higher than the national average, and is supplemented by entrepreneurial income. Real wages in the valley increased by 7.2 percent between 1990 and 1994 as compared to 3 percent nationally. Wage increases were highest in the semiconductor and software industries, 29 percent and 12 percent respectively (Joint Venture, 1995).

But income distribution is highly uneven. In the electronics industry, a largely female, immigrant work force faces low pay and insecure work as large firms continue to subcontract out their work (Cho, 1986). As manufacturing continues to leave the region, the workplace is increasingly composed of high-paid programmers and researchers and low-paid, unorganized service and manufacturing workers. Relatively high salaries in the defense, industrial, and large corporate sectors amplify this tendency.

A plethora of small firms continually forming and disappearing is not an unalloyed blessing, either. The growth of the small-firm sector is often due to large-firm downsizing, rather than small-firm vitality or innovation (Harrison, 1994). At least within the US context, smaller firms usually offer lower wages and fewer benefits, and are associated with lower unionization rates than are large firms.

A relatively small percentage of the workforce in the valley is covered by union contracts compared with the nation and other high-tech regions like Seattle, Los Angeles, or San Diego (Table 3.7). In fact, the rate in San José SMSA is closer to Atlanta's or Tampa-St. Petersburg's service-based economies.[15] The substantially lower rates reflect the structure of the workforce in the valley, the importance of small firms, and the anti-union stance of many defense-oriented and high-tech firms. Wage levels as a result are lower in assembly operations, and workers in these occupations are less apt to be incorporated in the firm's decision making and planning.

Table 3.7 Percent of workforce covered by union contracts for selected SMSAs and the US, 1983 and 1985

SMSA	1983	1985
Seattle-Everett, WA	29.8	29.3
Los Angeles-Long Beach, CA	25.9	24.9
San Diego, CA	21.9	23.4
Denver, CO	16.4	23.0
San José, CA	19.8	16.0
Atlanta, GA	16.4	14.9
Tampa-St. Petersburg, FL	12.3	11.0
Houston, TX	13.3	10.4
United States	23.3	20.5

Source: Curme et al. (1990) and Hirsch and MacPherson, (1993, table 6). No more recent data at the regional level is available.

Silicon Valley's extraordinary growth continues to be the envy of many regions. Governments around the world have attempted, with mixed results, to recreate the conditions that engendered the high-tech cluster's vitality and innovation. Economies diverse as New York City, Seattle, rural Appalachia, and Michigan in the United States; Denmark, London, and Cyprus in Europe; and Japan and Korea in Asia have set up state and local programs to encourage the formation of local industrial districts.

Our research suggests that these efforts are bound to disappoint, because they are based on a misreading or partial understanding of factors contributing to the valley's success. Key institutions like Stanford and the Lockheed missile and space complex are hard to replicate, especially in this era of fiscal squeeze and retrenchment. Rapid rates of innovation associated with ongoing high rates of government and private research spending in the valley are relatively unique to the region and its electronics industry. There will only be a few such nodes built on emerging technologies around the globe, and some of the newer industries – biotechnology, software, communications equipment – exhibit less of a need to agglomerate than electronics has.

Our findings lead us to question both the replicability of Silicon Valley's developmental trajectory and unabashedly admiring interpretations of Silicon Valley as a model regional economy. We see little cause for celebration in the power imbalance found in many relationships among large and small firms, the embeddedness of many firms in externalized relationships, the ease with which foreign firms are able to transmit valley technologies and talent to their home ports, the region's dependency on military contracts, and the lack of job security and/or a participatory role for labor. Certainly, Silicon Valley, the premier example of a US industrial district, has not fulfilled the industrial district advocates' hope for a softer, gentler, form of business organization.

NOTES

1 The Third Italy, located in the central and northeastern sections of the country, refers to an economic region that has undergone tremendous regional renewal and growth since the 1970s. The economy is based on networks of small, decentralized firms that benefit from agglomeration economies and a large measure of economic cooperation. The networks are supported and reproduced by a strong local institutional framework (Becattini, 1990; Best, 1990; Bellandi, 1989; Sforzi, 1989; Brusco, 1986).

2 The data in Table 1 are broken down by county. Santa Clara, while not containing all of Silicon Valley, is the county that captures most of the valley.

3 A location quotient is a measure of spatial concentration: it is a ratio of ratios. The numerator is the total employment for a particular industry in a particular state (or county) divided by total employment for that state (or county). The denominator is the national (or state) employment for that industry divided by total national (or state) employment. Any location quotient over 1 signifies a concentration above the expected county or state average.

4 Certain firms only agreed to be interviewed if their firms were not directly identified.

5 See Schoenberger (1991), Healey and Rawlinson (1993), and Markusen (1994) for an overview of corporate interviewing techniques and problems.

6 These sectors are all heavily dependent on defense spending. See Markusen et al. (1991).

7 A Lockheed official provided details of the historical military links. In 1929, following an extensive local lobbying effort, the Navy selected Sunnyvale in Santa Clara County as the West Coast site to house its newly built dirigibles. The Naval Air Station at Moffett Field, a state-of-the-art aircraft facility, opened in 1935. Four years later, the National Advisory Committee for Aeronautics (NACA) established Ames Aeronautical Laboratory down the road from Moffett Field. Its mission was to perform aeronautical research and development and provide technological assistance to the nation's nascent military and commercial aircraft industries.

8 It is not unusual to have strong university-industry links in the United States. Similar patterns have been seen in agriculture and biotechnology. However, the scale of DoD funding, the scope of Stanford's involvement, and Stanford's first mover advantage made this particular university–industry link extraordinary.

9 Patent pooling occurs when a patent resulting from DoD-funded research is shared among other DoD contractors.

10 This situation may be changing, however, as defense contractors increasingly turn to commercial markets, encouraged by the Pentagon's new emphasis on dual use (emphasizing the development of technologies with civilian as well as military uses), and participate in local production networks in face of military cutbacks. As the current president of a "black box" military contractor remarked: "Defense contractors changed from stealth mode to being much more comfortable in the spotlight. Now there is a lot more networking going on and we're talking more to commercial firms."

11   Countries with a corporate presence in Silicon Valley include Japan, Germany, Israel, and South Korea.

12   Patient capital refers to investments made with a long-term time horizon. This is in contrast to traditional, short-term, "impatient" capital from Wall Street that requires immediate and constant returns.

13   Its success also makes Silicon Valley an extremely expensive place to live. San José, the major city in the valley, is distinguished by having the highest median rental prices in the nation and the third highest median housing prices (US Census, 1992). Many firms mentioned the problem this caused in recruiting employees from other parts of the country. Low-income residents are often pushed out of the region altogether.

14   Examples of socialized costs and collective inputs might include joint international marketing projects, shared equipment schemes, internal "hiring halls," or joint training programs.

15   This difference is especially striking since in 1989 the City of San José had 31.3 percent of its civilian workforce in manufacturing, one of the highest rates in the nation (US Census, 1992).

REFERENCES

Amin, Ash and Nigel Thrift. 1993. Neo-Marshallian Nodes in Global Networks. *International Journal of Urban and Regional Research* 16(4): 571–87.

Anderson, Malcolm. 1995. The Role of Collaborative Integration in Industrial Organization: Observations from the Canadian Aerospace Industry. *Economic Geography* 71(1), January.

Bank of Korea. 1993. *Overseas Direct Investment*. Seoul: Bank of Korea. Nov. 31.

Becattini, Giacomo. 1990. The Marshallian Industrial District as a Socio-Economic Notion. In *Industrial Districts and Inter-Firm Cooperation in Italy*. F. Pyke, G. Becattini, and W. Sengenberger (eds.). Geneva: International Institute for Labour Studies.

Bellandi, Marco. 1989. The Industrial District in Marshall. In *Small Firms and Industrial Districts in Italy*. E. Goodman and J. Bamford (eds.). pp. 136–52. London: Routledge.

Best, Michael. 1990. *The New Competition: Institutions of Industrial Restructuring*. Cambridge: Harvard University Press.

Borrus, Michael. 1988. *Competing for Control: America's Stake in Microelectronics*. Cambridge, Mass.: Ballinger Publishing Company.

Brusco, Sabastiano. 1986. Small Firms and Industrial Districts: The Experience of Italy. *Economia Internazionale* 39(2): 98–103.

Bureau of Economic Analysis (BEA). 1970, 1990. *U.S. Census*. Washington DC: US Government Printing Office.

Cho, Soon Kyoung. 1986. Export-Led Development: A Comparison of the Electronics Industry in Silicon Valley and Seoul, Korea. Unpublished Ph.D. dissertation. University of California, Berkeley.

Curme, Michael, Barry Hirsch, and David MacPherson. 1990. Union Membership and Contract Average in U.S., 1983–1988. *Industrial and Labor Relations Review* 44(1), October, 5–33.

Ellis, Mark, Richard Barff, and Ann Markusen. 1993. Defense Spending and Interregional Labor Migration. *Economic Geography* 69(2): 1–22.

Florida, Richard and Martin Kenney. 1990. Silicon Valley and Route 128 Won't Save Us. *California Management Review* 33: 68–88.

Florida, Richard and Martin Kenney. 1994. The Globalization of Japanese R&D: The Economic Geography of Japanese R&D Investment in the United States. *Economic Geography* 70(4), October.

Glickman, Norman and Douglas Woodward. 1989. *The New Competitors: How Foreign Investors are Changing the U.S. Economy.* New York: Basic Books.

Gordon, Richard and Linda Kimball. 1987. The Impact of Industrial Structures on High Technology Location. In *The Spatial Impact of Technological Change.* J. Brotchie, P. Hall, and P. Newton (eds.). Beckenham, Kent: Croom Helm.

Gray, Mia, Elyse Golob, and Ann Markusen. 1996. Big Firms, Long Arms: A Portrait of a "Hub and Spoke" Industrial District in the Seattle Region. *Regional Studies* 30(7): 651–66.

Harrison, Bennett. 1994. *Lean and Mean: The Changing Landscape of Corporate Power in the Age of Flexibility.* New York: Basic Books.

Healey, Michael and Michael Rawlinson. 1993. Interviewing Business Owners and Managers: A Review of Methods and Techniques. *Geoforum* 24: 339–55.

Hirsch, Barry and David MacPherson. 1993. Union Membership and Coverage Files from the Current Population Surveys: Note. *Industrial and Labor Relations Review* 46(3), April

Joint Ventures. 1995. *Index of Silicon Valley.* San Jose, Calif.: Silicon Valley Network, Inc.

Leslie, Stuart. 1993. *The Cold War and American Science: The Military – Industrial – Academic Complex at MIT and Stanford.* New York: Columbia University Press.

Luger, Michael and Harvey Goldstein. 1990. *Technology in the Garden.* Chapel Hill, N.C.: University of North Carolina.

Malecki, Edward. 1981. Government-Funded R&D: Some Regional Economic Implications. *Professional Geographer* 31(1): 72–82.

Malone, Michael. 1985. *The Big Score: The Billion Dollar Story of Silicon Valley.* New York: Doubleday.

Markusen, Ann. 1986. The Militarized Economy. *World Policy Journal* 9: 495–516.

Markusen, Ann. 1994. Studying Regions by Studying Firms. *The Professional Geographer* 46(4): 477–90.

Markusen, Ann, Peter Hall, Scott Campbell, and Sabina Deitrick. 1991. *The Rise of the Gunbelt: The Military Remapping of Industrial America.* New York: Oxford University Press.

Miller, Roger and Marcel Cote. 1987. *Growing the Next Silicon Valley.* Lexington, Mass.: Lexington Books.

National Science Foundation (NSF). 1970, 1975, 1981, 1986, and 1991. *Selected Data on Federal Support to Universities, Colleges, and Nonprofit Institutions.* Washington DC: NSF.

Piore, Michael and Charles Sable. 1984. *The Second Industrial Divide.* New York: Basic Books.

Rogers, Everett and Judith Larsen. 1984. *Silicon Fever: Growth of High-Technology Culture.* New York: Basic Books.

San Jose Business Journal. August 31, 1992.

Saxenian, Annalee. 1983. The Urban Contradictions of Silicon Valley. *International Journal of Urban and Regional Research* 17(2): 236–57.

Saxenian, Annalee. 1985. The Genesis of Silicon Valley. In *Silicon Landscapes.* Peter Hall and Ann Markusen (eds.). Boston: Allen and Unwin.

Saxenian, Annalee. 1990a. Regional Networks and the Resurgence of Silicon Valley. *California Management Review,* Fall: 89–112.

Saxenian, Annalee. 1990b. Response to Richard Florida and Martin Kenney "Silicon Valley and Route 128 Won't Save Us." *California Management Review* 33(3): 136–142.

Saxenian, Annalee. 1991a. Contrasting Patterns of Business Organization in Silicon Valley. Working paper No 535, Institute of Urban and Regional Development, University of California at Berkeley.

Saxenian, Annalee. 1991b. The Origins and Dynamics of Production Networks in Silicon Valley. *Research Policy* 20: 423–37.

Saxenian, Annalee. 1994. *Regional Advantage*: *Culture and Competition in Silicon Valley and Route 128*. Cambridge, Mass.: Harvard University Press.

Schoenberger, Erica. 1991. The Corporate Interview as a Research Method in Economic Geography. *Professional Geographer* 44: 180–89.

Schoenberger, Erica. 1993. Corporate Transformation and Regional Change: The Case of Lockheed. Working paper, Johns Hopkins University.

Sforzi, Fabio. 1989. The Geography of Industrial Districts in Italy. In *Small Firms and Industrial Districts in Italy*. E. Goodman and J. Bamford (eds.). London: Routledge.

Teece, David. 1992. Foreign Investment and Technological Development in Silicon Valley. *California Management Review* 34(2): 88–106.

US Census. 1992. *City and County Data Book*. Washington DC: Bureau of the Census.

US Congress. Office of Technology Assessment (OTA). 1992. *After The Cold War: Living with Lower Defense Spending*. OTA-ITE-524. US Congress. Washington DC: US Government Printing Office.

US Department of Commerce. Bureau of the Census. 1975 and 1989. *County Business Patterns*. Washington DC: Bureau of the Census.

US Industrial Outlook. 1983. Washington, D.C.: U.S. Department of Commerce, Bureau of Industrial Economics.

Yudken, Joel and Barbara Simons. 1989. Federal Funding in Computer Science: A Preliminary Report. *Directions and Implications of Advanced Computing*. (DIAC-87). Volume 1. Jonathon P. Jacky and Douglas Schuler (eds.). Norwood, N.J.: Ablex Publishing, pp. 51–64.

4

Virtual Ecology: A Brief Environmental History of Silicon Valley*

Aaron W. Sachs

"Dutch" Hamann, City Manager of San José, California, from 1950 to 1970, liked to say that he put Silicon Valley on the map. Despite Hamann's success at spurring economic growth, though, the oil-executive-turned-civic-planner drew much criticism for his expansionist boosterism, for having allowed industrial parks and housing tracts to sprawl perhaps too far, blotting out Santa Clara County's former beauty. His retirement, which came just as the county's high-tech nickname started to enter the national lexicon, was celebrated not only by environmentalists but by economists as well. In September, 1970, *Business Week* ran an article about the challenge of "Correcting San José's Boomtime Mistake." But Hamann himself never doubted his legacy, insisting until his death in 1977 that the benefits of intense development would far outweigh any costs. "They say San José is going to become another Los Angeles," he noted in a 1965 interview, seeming to acknowledge his critics. "Believe me, I'm going to do everything in my power to make that come true."

Twenty years after Hamann's death, his vision has been realized. San José is booming again and Silicon Valley is often lauded as the engine of America's economy: high tech now has just as high a profile as Hollywood. In 1997, Silicon Valley firms created some 53,000 jobs, and profits among the region's top 150 high-tech companies grew by 15 percent to $15.4 billion. City officials from around the world have been visiting the area, desperate for the secret of San José's success. And, in fact, intense cooperation between municipal governments and high-tech firms has resulted in several attempts to copy the Silicon Valley model, from Silicon Desert in Phoenix, Arizona, to Silicon Glen in Livingston, Scotland, to Silicon Plateau in Bangalore, India.

* Sachs, Aaron W. (1999) "Virtual Ecology: A Brief Environmental History of Silicon Valley" from *Worldwatch* Jan/Feb, 12–21. Reprinted by permission of Worldwatch Institute, http//www.worldwatch. org.

Of course, critics and skeptics have argued that the valley's economic upsurge can't last forever, that bust always follows boom. Even the newly minted millionaires of Silicon Valley (there are two more every week) are beginning to acknowledge that they, too, may be held hostage by the cycles of history. An eventual economic downturn, however, is perhaps the least of this region's problems. Evidence is mounting that the boom–bust cycle may be quite dangerous even in good years, that economic growth as we know it may create about as many problems as it solves. While money is certainly flowing freely in Silicon Valley (the average salary of $46,000 is more than 50 percent higher than the national average), most of it is going to a relatively small social and economic elite. As a result, much of the region is becoming unaffordable for the local working-class people, many of whom are immigrants or ethnic minorities. Latinos, for example, make up 24 percent of Santa Clara County's population, but 50 percent of the county's working poor. In addition, housing is in short supply (jobs are being created about 15 times faster than housing units), and the region suffers from stultifying traffic snarls (freeway delays more than doubled between 1994 and 1996). And beneath all this burgeoning development, the soil and water are so battered by the chemicals used in high-tech manufacturing that the region now has 29 Superfund sites, giving it the densest concentration of highly hazardous waste dumps in the country.

San José is similar to Los Angeles, then, not only in terms of its internationally significant industries and economic success, but also in terms of its deep class and ethnic tensions, and the many other frustrations that accompany rapid growth – which tend to be exacerbated by the region's seemingly endless sprawl of strip malls, highways, cookie-cutter housing developments, and office parks. This troubling physical reality is one of the best-kept secrets in America: everyone has heard of Silicon Valley, but few people know what it looks like. Many East Coasters don't even know where in California it's located, as I discovered in 1996 when I told my friends and colleagues in Washington, DC, that I was moving to San José (which is right at the southern tip of the San Francisco Bay). Moreover, the images we have of high-tech companies in Silicon Valley – those offices full of bright, young engineers – rarely reflect the fact that high tech is just as much an industry as a profession, that the valley is actually packed with manufacturing plants. But, then, transcending physical realities is an important theme in the high-tech world, especially for people promoting the Internet, which represents the industry's best bet for future economic growth. When your web browser asks you where you want to go today, the implication is that the space you actually inhabit is irrelevant.

Nowhere is that philosophy more obvious than in Silicon Valley, especially given what Santa Clara County used to look like. Perhaps the most significant difference between Los Angeles and San José is that L.A. used to be a desert, whereas San José used to be home to some of the most fertile soil in the world, which just five decades ago produced close to 50 percent of the world's prunes, apricots, and cherries. People used to come to this area, known in the first half of this century as the Valley of Heart's Delight, not to see Research and Development facilities but to visit the orchards and go on "blossom tours." The recent history of San José represents an almost unparalleled ecological transformation, which begs a fundamental question confronting society at the end of the twentieth century: how long can we sustain economic growth without considering the relevance of our physical surroundings?

The high-tech version of the American Dream is a compelling one: young software engineers flock to Silicon Valley in the same way that young actors and actresses flock to Hollywood, and here the "failures" still make six figures. But in Santa Clara County this new model for success came at the expense of an older version of the American Dream. The Valley of Heart's Delight had fostered a community of thriving agriculturists – one that lasted well into the 1950s. The climate and soil were perfect, and land was so widely available that many cash-poor independent farmers were able to start successful orchards, whether on a subsistence level or as profit-making enterprises.

At the peak of agricultural activity, in the early 1940s, there were about 6000 farms in the Valley. Almost all of them were small, family-run operations covering less than 50 acres each, which together made up 80 percent of the county. About half of the planted area comprised the largest near-continuous orchard the world had ever seen: some 8 million flowering trees spread over 132,000 acres. As paintings, photographs, and old-timers attest, it was an amazing sight. "For 60 miles the beautiful Santa Clara Valley unrolls south, verdant with orchards, vineyards, and groves," wrote N. D. Ford, author of *America's 50 Best Cities*, in 1956. And the fruits of the farmers' labor were like nothing you can get today at your local supermarket. "That asphalt there is covering some of the best land in the world," says Charlie Olson of Olson's Cherries, one of the last remaining fruit stands in the valley. "What hurts me is that people don't even know how good it used to taste. They don't even know what they're missing." When I recently showed some vintage footage of the valley's orchards to an environmental studies class I was teaching at a community college in San José, my students expressed disbelief. Most of them had never seen an orchard.

You can build an electronics plant almost anywhere, but there are truly few places on earth that could match the fertility of Santa Clara Valley in the early twentieth century. The US Department of Agriculture evaluated all the land in the county and designated 32 percent of it – 400 square kilometers – as Class I, the top ranking for the cultivation of fruits and vegetables. Stream systems flowing down to the San Francisco Bay from the Diablo Range and the Santa Cruz Mountains had laid down two alluvial fans in the Valley. In places, the topsoil of fine loam was 40 feet deep. Below that were water-bearing layers of gravel and clay and a huge freshwater aquifer. Nineteenth-century farmers satisfied all their irrigation needs by means of artesian wells, which gushed water straight out of the ground. Not until the early 1970s, at the peak of local computer chip manufacturing, a highly water-intensive industry, did the county have to start importing water.

Until World War II, despite a few rocky periods, the valley was both booming and abloom. Now, all that's left of that era is a few fruit trees scattered along the freeways, a chain of Orchard Supply Hardware stores, and a strip mall called The Pruneyard, where farmers used to lay out their plums to dry in the sun. Wallace Stegner, a long-time resident of Santa Clara County, saw all of these changes first hand, and he captured this region's history succinctly in a 1984 essay. "Silicon Valley is probably a good, in many ways," he wrote. "The Valley of Heart's Delight was a glory. We should have found ways of keeping the one from destroying the other."

The story of Dutch Hamann's proud disregard of the ecological and aesthetic consequences of overdevelopment makes for an important cautionary tale.

Certainly, Santa Clara County provides a particularly dramatic case study, because of the sheer inappropriateness of the industrial growth that occurred here, given the quality of the land. The speed with which that growth occurred, too, is remarkable. By 1970, when Santa Clara County was dubbed Silicon Valley, five of the seven largest semiconductor firms in the country had their headquarters here, and critics were marveling at the near-total disappearance of the orchards that had so dominated the local landscape just two decades before.

What is most significant about the way the valley developed, though, has to do with the central role played by the electronics industry itself. Long before the invention of the Internet, the engineers of Stanford University, Hewlett-Packard, and IBM were playing tricks with physical reality, claiming that they were reinventing industry, that high tech would beautify rather than destroy the local landscape. To an even greater extent than Hamann, it was those engineers who finally determined how this region would develop.

Once the Cold War was launched in the late 1940s, there was a steady stream of research funds flowing from the US Department of Defense to almost anyone interested in electrical engineering and solid state physics. The technicians at Stanford, located in Palo Alto, at the northern tip of the Santa Clara Valley, were among the first to take advantage of the government's largess. Dean of Electrical Engineering Frederick Terman, who had been recruited to lead Harvard's Radio Research Lab during the war, moved back to Palo Alto in 1945, and a year later established the Stanford Research Institute (SRI), which he funded mainly with military contracts.

In 1951, Terman convinced the university to create the Stanford Industrial Park on land that had been earmarked for housing, arguing that the symbiosis of scholarship and industry would give the local area a worldwide reputation for technical expertise. He was right. Especially after the success of fledgling companies like Hewlett-Packard, which set up shop at Stanford Industrial Park in 1952, and Shockley Transistor, the first semiconductor company, Terman was able to lure the giants of the field to Santa Clara County: Lockheed, Sylvania, General Electric, IBM, and Westinghouse all came to the valley in the 1940s and 1950s to take advantage of the free-flowing ideas and money. Today, virtually all of the key players in the high-tech world – except for arch-enemy Microsoft – reside within the valley's borders.

In just a few years, then, Santa Clara County had gone from supplying America's fruit bowls to supplying America's arsenals. Until Intel's invention of the microprocessor in 1971, high tech was essentially a tool of the Space Race and the military industrial complex. As of 1965, the Pentagon purchased 70 percent of all the integrated circuits manufactured in the United States. In 1967, 60 percent of Silicon Valley's electronics employees were working on defense contracts, designing eversmaller, more highly automated guidance and delivery systems for missiles. Terman and his colleagues felt no qualms about applying their research to weapons of mass destruction. From the beginning, though, they were determined to transcend the standard realities of industrial development.

The very phrase "industrial park," oxymoronic as it is, reveals Terman's desire to transform the valley into an employment center that could rival San Francisco and Oakland – without the soot and rowdy laborers. In 1956, Stanford's business manager, Alf E. Brandin, went on record explaining that Stanford Industrial Park was designed to "attract a better class of workers." Terman himself had seen the major industrial cities on the East Coast, and he wanted nothing to do with them: high tech was to be a clean, white-collar industry, fed by the nation's finest engineering departments – which, at the time, consisted almost entirely of well-to-do white males. By the time Silicon Valley got its name, Standford Industrial Park had become Stanford Research Park, and its companies had to follow strict building codes, which included "complete concealment" of things like smokestacks, generators, transformers, ducts, storage tanks, and air conditioning equipment. Even now, many new offices and factories in the valley are laid out on a "campus," so as to evoke the pastoral feel of places like Stanford.

Sprawling office parks and industrial campuses, however, not only take up massive amounts of space in their attempts to appear suburban – they also distract workers and residents from the real consequences of industrial activities. Stanford Research Park conceals not only its ductwork but its actual manufacturing plants, which form the heart of high tech. No industry, after all, can survive on research alone. In fact, while manufacturing was shrinking around the country in the postwar era, as America gradually shifted over to a service-dominated economy, it was growing fast in Santa Clara County. Here, the percentage of employees working in manufacturing increased from 15 percent in 1940 to 35 percent in 1980 (nationwide, the figure had dipped to 21 percent). And while the industry continued catering to its technical professionals, its behind-the-scenes production workers were the ones paying the price for high tech's dependence on toxic chemicals.

In 1970, 70 percent of the production workers in the electronics industry were women, about half of whom were minorities, mostly Mexican-Americans and Filipino-Americans who had migrated to San José as Southern California agriculture became more mechanized. As high levels of employee illness – from headaches to miscarriages to cancer – soon revealed, the hydrocarbon solvents used to clean semiconductors were no safer than the pesticides soaking the fields of vegetables down south. On average, according to Graydon Larrabee of Texas Instruments, making one 15-centimeter silicon wafer – the building-block for a few dozen chips – requires 9 kilograms of liquid chemicals and 6 cubic meters of gases, as well as 8610 liters of water. In so-called "clean rooms," where elaborate circuitry is etched onto the wafers, production workers never breathe in any dust, but they are regularly exposed to known carcinogens like dichloroethylene.

In any case, a few palm trees and heavily watered lawns interspersed among huge, homogeneous office buildings and manufacturing plants do not exactly comprise a park. Terman and his associates may have avoided recreating the heavy industrial landscapes of towns like Pittsburgh and Detroit, but high-tech industries ended up using so much space in the valley that there was little room left over either for housing or for true green spaces. Starting with Palo Alto and moving progressively southward, each town in Santa Clara County devoted more and more land to industry, and Stanford Industrial Park essentially replicated itself several times over – each time spurring the construction of new expressways and strip malls in neighboring areas. The municipal governments of Mountain View, Sunnyvale, Cupertino, Santa Clara, and San José all courted high-tech firms relentlessly, in order to increase their tax base: profit-making companies are worth much more to a city than houses or apartment buildings.

In many cases, just as Stanford had done, these cities offered firms newly rezoned land that had originally been intended for housing, often bending rules in order to make the offers more attractive. In 1966, for example, 65 percent of the approved applications for rezoning in San José did not conform to the city's regulations, according to a study by the Stanford Environmental Law Society. Between 1965 and 1975, the number of housing units accommodated by the zoning plans of the county's major cities actually decreased from 978,000 to 561,000 – while the number of jobs in the country increased by about 150 percent. Meanwhile, by 1970, San José had only 3.2 hectares of open space per 1,000 residents, half of which consisted of school playgrounds – compared to 14.2 hectares per 1000 people in San Francisco and 28.7 per 1000 in Washington, DC. And in Palo Alto, which had a daily influx of some 60,000 electronics workers in the mid-1970s, the municipal governments felt so threatened that it restricted access to the town's beautiful Foothills Park: to this day only Palo Alto residents are allowed inside.

It is no coincidence that the effacement of the Valley of Heart's Delight occurred during Dutch Hamann's tenure as City Manager of San José. Between 1950 and 1970, he annexed 1377 parcels of land, and San José's urbanized area increased from 17 square miles to a sprawling 135 square miles, while the city's population increased from 95,000 to 460,000. Hamann's land-use policies and a rubber-stamp city council were the driving forces behind the elimination of green space in the valley's largest city; contractors, developers, and businesses grew richer during his term in office, but at the expense of residents, since city services – sewers and schools as well as parks – could not keep pace with growth.

Frederick Terman, though, had just as much influence as Hamann, and he was more of a visionary. While Hamann was expanding madly and trumpeting his city's "appointment with destiny," Terman was quietly establishing his "community of technical scholars," bequeathing real power to his heirs in the form of unprecedented economic opportunity. The 20 electronics firms clustered around Stanford Industrial Park in 1951 had become 800 by 1974, and they determined the everyday realities of the region – economically, socially, and ecologically. Terman's seeds had scattered and multiplied, forming the industrial equivalent of a monoculture plantation. As Annalee Saxenian, author of *Regional Advantage: Culture and Competition in Silicon Valley and Route 128*, has argued, it is rare to find a place where the character of development is "so clearly attributable to a particular sector," but that is the case in Santa Clara Country – for better and for worse.

The cover story of *Newsweek* on November 9, 1998 was devoted to "the explosion of Silicon Valley wanna-bes, both domestic and overseas, that have already begun transforming cities, regions and, in some cases, entire countries." Titled "The Hot New Tech Cities," the article confirmed the extent to which the Silicon Valley model has captured the world's imagination. But it offered few hints of the model's troubling track record. An unanswered question still hovers in the smog over Silicon Valley: has high tech's influence over this region's development truly improved the local people's long-term quality of life? And on a broader scale, does this industry's impact on society at large warrnat the kind of uncritical embrace it has received from investors and developers? Here in the valley, as the negative aspects of unbridled growth become more apparent, the debate will continue to rage. It would seem that no one could dispute the benefits of living in a place where the unemployment rate is consistently below 3 percent. Yet the cost of living is so high here that even the gainfully employed have reason to complain. In 1997, according to the estimate of the local Emergency Housing Consortium, 20,000 employed, taxpaying citizens of Santa Clara Country were forced to leave their homes and solicit beds at homeless shelters because of excessive rent hikes.

The jobs–housing imbalance in Silicon Valley is perhaps the most obvious symptom that economic growth here has reached cancerous levels. Local high-tech companies are getting so big that they are threatening to kill off their municipal hosts. In the past three years, Santa Clara County firms added 126,005 employees, a 15.2 percent increase. Meanwhile, housing increased by a mere 1.3 percent, as the county added just 7154 new units. Those who try renting bump up against a 1.4 percent vacancy rate (anything under 15 percent is considered tight). And, of course, scarcity has driven residential costs through the roof – assuming you are lucky enough to have one over your head. Santa Clara Country now has the highest median sale price for new houses in all of America: at $316,250, it's 155 percent higher than the national average, and unaffordable for about 70 percent of the county's population. Meanwhile, rents have doubled since 1990.

This region's international reputation for affluence is justified, in other words, but the wealth isn't trickling down. And, as in Los Angeles, conspicuous consumption on the part of elites is spurring resentment among the valley's working classes. Since 1990, wage rates for the poorest 25 percent of the valley's workers have actually decreased by 14 percent. Meanwhile, between 1987 and 1997, though the average household income rose from $85,741 to $101,010, the median household income stayed constant: it was only the top half of income earners who got richer. In other words, those new, expensive homes are going to wealthy engineers, mostly white males, who move to this area to take high-paying jobs.

Some poorer people, meanwhile, are either being squeezed out or packed into ghettos. And impoverished production workers, besides being exposed to chemical vapors in clean rooms, generally have few benefits and little job security. High-tech firms in Silicon Valley use temporary employees at a rate that is three times the national average, and several companies run seminars for managers on how to prevent unionizing efforts in their plants. There are currently no active unions at local electronics firms. Even if the valley is blessed with continued material success, it seems likely that either the region's social and economic diversity will gradually disappear, or tensions will begin to erupt. In the spring of 1997, at the end of San José's Cinco de Mayo celebration, there was an outbreak of violence and looting that for many Californians evoked the class and race wars of Los Angeles.

Poor workers who opt to keep their jobs in Silicon Valley but who cannot afford to live here end up paying the additional cost of commuting every day, sometimes more than 80 miles each way. And they are joined in the traffic jams by all the software engineers and electronics executives who could have afforded the valley but simply couldn't find space. Even within Santa Clara County, commutes have been bad for a long time. San José was the one city with room to expand during the region's period of heaviest industrial development, so that's where most of the housing is: with 894,000 people, it now has an even larger population

Table 4.1   Population growth in San Jose and Santa Clara County, 1940–98

	San Jose	Santa Clara County
1940	68,000	175,000
1950	95,000	291,000
1960	204,000	642,000
1970	460,000	1,065,000
1980	629,000	1,295,000
1990	782,000	1,498,000
1998	894,000	1,680,000

(by 13 percent) than San Francisco (Table 4.1). But most of the jobs remain clustered around Stanford, in the northern part of the county. These days, traveling the 20 miles from south San José to Palo Alto can take up to two hours in the morning, since San Joseans are competing not only with each other but with commuters who have been forced to live even further south, in Gilroy or even San Benito County.

Next to the housing shortage, traffic is the biggest concern of Silicon Valley employees. The average speed on the freeways during rush hour has already dipped below the figure for Los Angeles County, and while the number of miles driven in L.A. has increased only 2 percent annually since 1994, here the yearly increase has been 11 percent. In 1996, the last year for which data are available, local drivers experienced an average of 20,500 hours of delays per day – without taking construction or accidents into consideration. And no amount of money can fix the problem. "Look at L. A.," says Mike Evanhoe, Director of Santa Clara County's Congestion Management Program, urging politicians to heed the lessons of history and demography. "We just cannot build enough lanes fast enough to accommodate our growth." Even businesses have begun complaining about traffic. According to the Metropolitan Transportation Commission, local freeway delays are costing valley companies $3.4 billion a year.

In addition, heavy commutes create smog – as do the high-tech facilities to which employees are commuting, even if façades hide the smokestacks. Federal Clean-Air regulations and state-wide improvements in car standards have eased this problem considerably in the past 15 years, but there are still many days when you can't see through the haze to the nearby hills. Moreover, as a report by the Santa Clara County Strategic Visions Steering Committee explains, emissions reductions are quickly being "outweighed by the growing number of commuters."

A similar trend is at work with regard to the region's water pollution problems. Chip manufacturers are coming up with innovative techniques that reduce the amount of toxic waste emitted per unit produced; but production is still increasing in the valley (even though some manufacturing and most assembly plants have relocated to developing countries), so overall pollution levels are still rising as well. Indeed, one of the most important lessons other communities can learn from the history of Silicon Valley is that high tech is not a clean industry.

Ever since the infamous 1982 leak at San José's Fairchild Semiconductor plant, as Lenny Siegel and John Markoff have shown in their book, *The High Cost of High Tech*, Silicon Valley companies have struggled to maintain their pristine image.

Countless poisoned wells, leaking chemical tanks, and illegal sludge dumps have been discovered in the past 15 years. The underground plume of pollution from one IBM facility extends for three miles and has shut down 17 public wells. In some cases, even the most sophisticated cleanup methods have had only partial success; when trichlorethylene (TCE), for instance, has time to settle into an aquifer, there is no known method by which it can be completely removed. At the Fairchild factory, toxic solvents used in chip production (including trichloroethane and dichloroethylene) gradually seeped into drinking water supplies from an underground storage tank, and within a few years there were obvious cancer clusters in the neighborhood, and residents were experiencing three times the normal rate of miscarriages and birth defects. Another set of solvents, called glycol ethers, are not even detectable using normal water-testing protocols, and studies by IBM and the Semiconductor Industry Association have linked their use in clean rooms to disruptions of workers' reproductive health.

Meanwhile, high-tech sewage emissions laced with heavy metals such as cadmium, nickel, and lead have had a disastrous impact on the southern reaches of the San Francisco Bay. At the turn of the century, fishers living in shoreline communities harvested about 15 million pounds of oysters annually from the Bay, but since 1970 the entire oyster population has been too contaminated to eat.

The environmental history of this valley, then, is not just about the loss of orchards and farms, and the replacement of an agricultural society with an industrial society. It is not simply a pastoral tragedy. It is about the impact of an almost-exclusive reliance on the high-tech industry and its capacity for economic growth. And for all those would-be Silicon Valleys around the world, it is important to note that, in terms of the residents' overall quality of life, high tech has been a mixed blessing here. Even the most successful executives are beginning to feel the need to escape, finding that even their vast fortunes cannot insulate them from urban sprawl and pollution. Lately, a back-to-the-land movement has arisen among the elites of Silicon Valley. Steve Jobs, one of the founders of Apple Computer, cleared the lot next to his Palo Alto home and planted a small orchard. Many other executives have left the area altogether, heading up to Napa and Sonoma to grow grapes.

Over the last three decades, high tech has matured and come of age. Starting with Intel's microprocessor, developed for a Japanese calculator company, electronics applications have become more and more mainstream and user-friendly, ranging from those first hand-held calculators to laser surgery and the World Wide Web. Computers are helping us to collect, store, organize, and process more information than ever before, facilitating scientific inquiry, global communication, political participation, and even environmental activism. I recently got an e-mail, for instance, from the Silicon Valley Toxics Coalition, one of this country's foremost eco-justice organizations, explaining that thanks to the high-tech industries' own tools and technology, citizens can now map the 178 sites in Santa Clara Country where high-tech firms have polluted the local groundwater. By using a Geographic Information Systems (GIS) project accessible via the Coalition's web site, activists can even overlay contamination maps with demographic data, tracing the links between toxicity levels, race, and economic status.

Countless similar examples reveal the truly paradoxical nature of high tech, in both its global and its local implications. At the local level, the major issue is not necessarily the usefulness of the products but rather the tradeoffs inherent in catering to high tech's development agenda. Cash-poor communities desperate to attract the next Intel microprocessor plant would do well to understand the transformative power of the industry.

Once the problems associated with high tech are recognized, though, improvements and solutions become apparent. There are some positive examples emerging from Silicon Valley itself. The Greenbelt Alliance and the Mid-Peninsula Open Space District, for instance, are both working not only to preserve strips of open land in the valley, but also to stop all further expansion and force cities to pursue "in-fill" development instead of building more mansions in the foothills. The private sector has also joined the battle to preserve land: early in 1998, the foundation established by Silicon Valley pioneer David Packard (one of Frederick Terman's students and the cofounder of Hewlett-Packard) announced that it will spend $175 million over the next five years to protect farms, open space, and wildlife habitat here in California. Several valley chip-making firms have even pioneered the use of natural soaps and citrus solutions in an attempt to clean up their manufacturing processes. And San José, besides adding carpool lanes to local freeways, recently made considerable improvements to its public transit system, with the result that ridership on the city's light-rail line has increased 31 percent in the past five years.

All these initiatives suggest the urgent necessity of pursuing development from a regional perspective. The Silicon Valley model, as elaborated by Frederick Terman, is based on economic regionalism, a conscious effort to build a broad community of business partners and academics all engaged in interrelated pursuits. To be truly successful, though, high-tech development requires regional planning that addresses social and ecological issues as well. Even county-wide plans are not broad enough: Silicon Valley itself has significant influence on traffic patterns in at least five separate counties. Only from a broad bioregional perspective can planners consider the complex interconnections between jobs and profits and housing and farmland and water quality and parks and ethnic diversity and class tensions and freeway back-ups. "Our task," wrote Lewis Mumford, in an essay entitled "The Regional Framework of Civilization," "is to replace the primeval balance that exists in a region ... in a state of nature, by a richer environment, a more subtle and many-weighted balance, of human groups and communities in a state of high culture." For instance, if the developers of Silicon Valley had proceeded a little more cautiously, they might have been able to build just as many chip manufacturing plants without paving over all of the region's Class I agricultural land.

Moreover, just as local communities would profit from examining and planning for the more problematic aspects of high-tech development, society at large would be well-served by a more critical approach to the dark side of the industry as a whole. One of the main reasons Silicon Valley grew the way it did, after all, was that no one thought to question technological "progress." And now many of us are buying "smart" appliances, and computers, and modems, simply assuming that they are going to improve our lives. We are participating in a massive transformation, which is accepted virtually without debate – just like the transformation of the Santa Clara Valley. "No one is stepping forth to suggest that there might be something at stake," writes cultural critic Sven Birkerts, "that the headlong race to wire ourselves might, in accordance with the gain–loss formulae that apply in every sphere of human endeavor like the laws of physics, threaten or diminish us in some way."

It seems clear, though, that high tech writ large, just like unrestrained economic growth, is a mixed bag, as Edward Tenner has documented extensively in his book *Why Things Bite Back: Technology and the Revenge of Unintended Consequences*. Technological devices do often save time, and yet beepers, e-mail, and cellular phones have all extended the work day, especially for Silicon Valley employees, who are among the busiest in the nation. And though the computer keyboard is easier to use than a typewriter, it nevertheless causes more health problems (repetitive strain injury in particular). Meanwhile, the Internet links us all together in the so-called electronic hive, but it may allow actual social skills to atrophy, as people interact less often on what is referred to as an F2F (or face-to-face) basis. Recent studies have even suggested a link between high levels of Internet use and clinical depression.

Nevertheless, the techno-evangelists, like magicians or movie directors, continue to preach, urging us to embrace every aspect of the high-tech revolution, whatever the consequences. High tech is clean, they say, it's democratic, it's profitable, and it makes life easier and more fun. In other words, the industry is fundamentally misleading and ahistorical in its approach. And perhaps most dangerous is the seemingly concerted attempt of high-tech boosters to inspire scorn for the actual, physical world. In celebrating the Virtual, futurists like Gregory Stock also celebrate "comfortable indoor environments" and consider it perfectly appropriate that "the emotional links between humans and the 'natural' environment are weakening," since the best of human experience is now occurring "in an entirely different realm." Confronted with arguments about the need to uphold biodiversity, Stock simply shrugs, and opines that there are only a few animals in the world that really matter, anyway. "There is an immense roster of species," he notes, "that neither affect nor interest the vast majority of humankind."

One major selling point of the high-tech revolution, then, is its power to gloss over physical reality. San José is the Hollywood of the North; people come here to escape Real Life in the Real World. And if we remake other communities in Silicon Valley's image, Virtual Life in a Virtual World will indeed begin to seem like the only logical option. Just spend a few hours exploring some high-tech suburbs, urges Mark Slouka, author of *War of the Worlds: Cyberspace and the High-Tech Assault on Reality*. Slouka's experiences in California led him to conclude that "no life outside the home is possible [in some of these communities]. There is no playground, no park, no field or meadow...So what do people who live in these communities do? What else can they do? They live inside: watching television, listening to their home entertainment systems, playing computer games." This move inside, this preference for Virtual Reality over Real Life, is perhaps the key environmental issue confronting the industrialized world. There can be no ecological protection without a sense of place.

Our saving grace may be that, like the Silicon Valley executives who are now planting vineyards, most of us eventually tend to feel the need to connect with nature, to feel rooted in the soil, to blend in with one particular landscape: that's the way human beings have lived for thousands of years. Until recently, high-tech devotees from around the world were willing to pull up their roots and plant new ones in Silicon Valley: all it took was a call from Hewlett-Packard or Intel or National Semiconductor. These days, though, more and more engineers are declining prestigious jobs in the valley because of quality-of-life issues. Sometimes visiting a virtual park on the World Wide Web just isn't enough.

5

Regulation Theory, Post-Fordism and Urban Politics*

Joe Painter

In seeking to interpret some of the broad shifts in urban politics during the 1980s, a number of urban theorists, urban and political geographers and political scientists began to turn to the writings of a small group of French economists working in the tradition of Marxist economics and known as the 'regulation theorists'. At first sight, this seems a strange move, because the regulation theorists' main concern was with explaining economic changes, and their ideas, at least at first, did not include much consideration of the state, government and politics.

The appeal of regulation theory for urban political theorists, however, stems from three main sources. First, it presents an account of the changing character of capitalist economies and of the role of cities within them. It thus provides a context against which to discuss urban political change. Second, it examines the connections and interrelations between social, political, economic and cultural change. This potentially avoids some of the problems encountered by those theories which focus on one aspect of the political whole (such as elections, leadership or bureaucracy). Third, it tries to avoid a rather different set of difficulties associated with some versions of orthodox Marxism, which accord only a secondary role to political processes. For regulation theory, economic change depends upon, and is partly the product of, changes in politics, culture and social life.

Not all of these advantages have yet been realized in full by urban political theorists, as this chapter will make clear. However, in comparison with many other theoretical traditions, regulation theory is still very young and there is much scope for further development. In this chapter I will discuss the progress that has been made so far in applying the ideas of regulation theory in the sphere of urban politics. After outlining the key concepts of the approach I will consider three

* Painter, Joe (1995) 'Regulation Theory, Post-Fordism and Urban Politics' from David Judge, Gerry Stoker and Harold Wolman (eds.) *Theories of Urban Politics*, Sage Publications, pp. 276–95. Reprinted by permission of Sage Publications Ltd. Copyright © Sage Publications Ltd.

of them in relation to urban politics: the labour process, the 'Fordist mode of regulation', and the 'post-Fordist mode of regulation'. I will then look at some of the criticisms that have been made of these ideas, before concluding with an evaluation of the current position.

Regulation Theory: An Exposition

The concept of regulation

Regulation theory originated in France in the 1970s and early 1980s in the work of a number of Marxist economists including Michel Aglietta, Robert Boyer and Alain Lipietz. It has subsequently been developed by economists, geographers, political theorists and others working in a variety of countries. As a result it has become a rich, but highly diverse, school of thought. There is no one unified 'regulation theory' and many writers now prefer to talk about a 'regulation approach'.[1]

Central to all regulation theory is the concept of regulation itself. There is a certain amount of confusion about the nature of regulation theory, which has arisen partly because of a misinterpretation of this central idea. In English, the term 'regulation' usually refers to 'conscious and active intervention by the *state* or other collective organizations' (Boyer, 1990, p. 20). However, in French, this sense is conveyed by the word '*réglementation*', and not by '*régulation*' (the word used by the regulation theorists). A further problem arises as the term 'regulation' is often used in the context of general systems theory and biology to mean *self*-regulation. (The kind of regulation provided by the regulator on a steam engine.)

By contrast with both the deliberate rule-making of *réglementation* and the auto-regulation of a negative feedback system, regulation theory looks at the kinds of regulation of economic life which are neither wholly deliberate nor automatic. According to the regulationists 'successful' regulation of the crises and contradictions of capitalism does not occur automatically and inevitably but neither does it occur purely by conscious and deliberate design. Instead, when it does occur, it is the often *unintended* consequence of the interaction of activities and processes which may have been undertaken deliberately, but perhaps for quite other reasons. This general principle is given substance by two further core concepts, the *regime of accumulation* (which specifies the nature of the economic relationship between investment, production and consumption) and *mode of regulation* (which specifies the political and sociocultural institutions and practices which secure that relationship).

These two key ideas mean that temporal and spatial variations in the character of capitalism play an important part in regulation theory. Capitalism has been marked by a series of different regimes of accumulation and modes of regulation. The *regime of accumulation* refers to a set of macroeconomic relations which allow expanded capital accumulation without the system being immediately and catastrophically undermined by its instabilities. Within a regime of accumulation, the imbalances in the cycle of reproduction, production, circulation and consumption are postponed or displaced. Acute crises and sharp irregularities are replaced for a time by chronic crisis tendencies and muted economic cycles. A regime of accumulation may be identified when rough balances between production, consumption and investment, and between the demand and supply of labour and capital allow economic growth to be maintained with reasonable stability over a relatively long period.

However, this stability cannot arise simply as the result of the operation of the defining core processes of capitalism. When stabilization does occur (and it is not inevitable that it will) it is the contingent outcome of social and political activities. A sustained compatibility between production and consumption, for example, is not an automatic feature of capitalism. Rather it is generated in and through social and political institutions of various sorts, cultural norms and even moral codes. Such norms and codes are not set up *for the purpose* of sustaining a regime of accumulation, but they can sometimes interact to produce that effect. When this happens, they constitute a *mode of regulation* also referred to as the 'mode of social regulation' or MSR. (Bob Jessop now uses a still more precise term, the 'social mode of economic regulation' in order to stress that it is economic activities which are being regulated, and that they are regulated socially.[2])

'Fordism', 'neo-Fordism' and 'post-Fordism'

The term 'Fordism' was first used in the 1930s by the Italian Marxist, Gramsci (1971). It is most often used today to refer to the 'long-boom' in Western development which lasted from 1945 to 1974. By extension, 'neo-Fordism' refers to an intensification of Fordist arrangements, whereas 'post-Fordism' implies a transition to a qualitatively new set of relationships.

Regulation theory is often mistakenly assumed to be synonymous with theories of Fordism and post-Fordism. Both Jessop and Boyer stress the broadly *methodological* character of regulation theory, seeing it as a set of organizing principles and as an approach to analysis, rather than a series of substantive accounts. Concepts such as Fordism and post-Fordism come lower down the hierarchy of abstraction – they are examples of ideas which some regulationists have developed to make more substantive claims about specific societies.

In relation to Fordism, Jessop (1992) distinguishes four different such categories: the labour process, the regime of accumulation, the mode of regulation, and the mode of societalization. The Fordist *labour process* involves the production of long runs of standardized commodities. Archetypally this involves a moving assembly line staffed by workers executing a limited range of production tasks and separated from the design of both the product and the production process. As a *regime of accumulation*, 'Fordism involves a virtuous circle of growth based on mass production and mass consumption' (Jessop, 1992, p. 47). Mass production provides economies of scale and productivity growth, which in turn allow wage increases, providing a market which can sustain mass consumption.

The *mode of regulation* is the set of social, cultural and political supports which promote the compatibility between production and consumption in the regime of accumulation. These supports operate through particular norms, networks and institutions which are the outcomes of social and political conflicts. In the Fordist mode of regulation they include: the form of the wage relation; the character of social organization within and between firms; a system of money supply based on national central banks and private credit; mass media and mass advertising, marketing and retailing to promote the connection between mass production and mass consumption; and the Keynesian welfare state which manages aggregate demand through fiscal policy and generalizes the norm of mass consumption through collective provision of certain services and transfer payments to the un- (or inadequately) waged. Finally Fordism may be understood as a '*mode of societalization*' which specifies the overall social impact of the characteristics discussed above on wider aspects of society such as cultural life, spatial organization and the political system. Jessop also outlines a series of problems associated with each of these readings of Fordism (1992, p. 53–8), and argues that Fordism is best defined as a mode of regulation.

A mode of regulation can never *permanently* resolve the contradictions of capitalism, but only translate acute crises into crisis tendencies. Eventually, the contradictions *do* build up and prevent the established mode of regulation from operating to promote economic growth. Fordism developed to a greater and more complete extent in some countries than others, and the timing and consequences of its failure also varied considerably. In general, however, the 1970s was the decade when the limits to Fordism began to become apparent, and the 1980s was when a series of (often conflicting) political strategies began to be adopted in attempts to resolve the problems. In due course, if certain of these strategies, or a combination of them, succeed in securing a new phase of economic growth, it may be possible to identify a new 'post-Fordist' phase.

However, the concept of post-Fordism[3] is yet more problematic than the concept of Fordism. As Jessop notes, there is considerable asymmetry between the concepts of Fordism and post-Fordism. Most analysts are agreed that no fully-fledged post-Fordist social relations have yet emerged (while some doubt that they ever will). Therefore, only in the case of Fordism is it possible to discuss the substance within the four categories. Nonetheless, one can consider some of the potential characteristics of post-Fordism under the same four headings.

As Jessop points out, for it to make sense to speak of post-Fordism (rather than non-Fordism, for example) the new developments would have to have the potential to resolve the specific problems of Fordism. The area in which there is most evidence of post-Fordist developments in this sense is the labour process. The emphasis in the post-Fordist labour process is on the use of microelectronic technology to provide significantly increased flexibility and automation in the production process. Jessop argues that new communication and information technologies 'allow new or enhanced flexible specialization by small firms or producer networks even in small-batch production and, indeed, outside manufacturing, could promote flexibility in the production of many types of services in the private, public, and so-called "third" sectors' (1992, p. 61). These developments have the potential to resolve some of the contradictions of the Fordist labour process, and thus justify the label 'post-Fordist'.

In the other three categories of analysis it is more difficult to identify clear lines of development which might serve to resolve for a time Fordist contradictions in each case. However, since the concept of Fordism appeared to have most purchase when defined as a mode of regulation, it is important to consider what might be meant by a post-Fordist mode of regulation. One of the problems with this, as Jessop points out, is that the objects of regulation and the processes which regulate them emerge together. A mode of regulation can therefore only be identified with hindsight. However, some possible trends are apparent in relation to the advanced industrialized economies. It seems likely that the wage relation in a post-Fordist mode of regulation would involve increased flexibility within labour markets and increased polarization between a multiskilled (or at least multitasked) core workforce and an unskilled 'peripheral' workforce recruited from politically marginalized social groups. Corporate organization would probably shift from relatively hierarchical bureaucratic forms, to leaner, flatter structures, with a smaller central organization and a series of subcontracting relations with external bodies. Money may be supplied at least in part through new types of financial instruments and become increasingly internationalized. The link between production and consumption would increasingly become a matter of segmented rather than mass markets promoted by niche forms of advertising and retailing.

Finally, the state would have a particular role to play in a post-Fordist mode of regulation. With the internationalization of financial and productive capital, Jessop argues, the state would play a stronger role in promoting competitiveness of both specific firms and of the overall socio-economic system. Jessop argues that these changes will involve the decline of the postwar 'Keynesian Welfare States' and the emergence of 'Schumpeterian Workfare States' (1993). The state will become more involved in supply side interventions of various kinds, including in the labour market. At the same time, the state may become 'hollowed out'. Some of its powers will be passed upwards to supranational bodies, such as the European Union, which arguably have greater capacity to act in a globalized economic system. Other powers may be devolved downwards to local or regional tiers of the state (Jessop, 1992, pp. 63–5; 1993).

Applications in Urban Politics

Having outlined some of the main arguments of the regulation approach I am now in a position to consider how they relate to the field of urban politics. As I have shown, regulation theory was developed as a theory of economic, not political, change. At first sight, therefore, it seems perverse to adopt it as a framework for analysing urban politics. However, political processes do play a crucial role in regulationist explanations of economic changes.[4] Furthermore, the breakdown of Fordism and the debates over its putative successor have generated considerable discussion among analysts about the implications for urban politics of the supposed transition, and about the implications for any transition of the changing character of urban politics. The emphasis in regulation theory on change and periodization holds out the promise of a theoretical account of urban politics which is historically embedded, and which can deal with qualitative shifts in the character of political processes and institutions. This is in contrast to some other theories which assume that the urban political system is essentially unchanging. Moreover, the contingent character of the emergence of regulation avoids the pitfalls of economic reductionism, while still allowing the crucial relationship between the state and economic processes to remain in the frame.

In the following discussion, I will interpret 'urban politics' as including:

1   Urban *policy* (state policies established to deal with perceived urban problems).
2   The institutions and processes of urban government and governance (involving not only the local tier of state administration, but *all* organizations exercising political authority at the local level – whether public, private or voluntary – and the relationships between these.
3   Political movements and processes operating at the urban scale, but outside institutions of governance (such as local community campaigns).

The elements of regulation theory on which I particularly want to focus are post-Fordist developments of the labour process, Fordism as a mode of regulation and the role of the 'Schumpeterian Workfare State' within a potential future post-Fordist mode of regulation.

Urban politics and the labour process

Aglietta argued that new production techniques and developments in the labour process had the capacity significantly to transform the provision of the means of collective consumption and thereby to reduce their cost (1979, p. 167). Picking up this idea, Hoggett (1987) was among the first to introduce the notions of Fordism and neo-Fordism to an analysis of urban politics. In his consideration of decentralization initiatives by socialist city councils in Britain, he drew an analogy between the organization of production along Fordist lines in manufacturing firms and the 'people-processing' character of the local welfare state. At the same time, the power of local government professionals added a complicating element which had something in common with pre-Fordist craft production in the manufacturing sector. Moreover, the hierarchical and bureaucratic organization of the local government institutions also resonated with corporate organization in the private sector. In Hoggett's view, decentralization might represent part of a shift from a Fordist to a neo-Fordist labour process. The decentralization of local services involved, according to Hoggett, a critique of the 'Fordist' character of welfare state production: its remoteness, inflexibility and unresponsiveness. Decentralization supposedly involved a series of key changes which were characteristic of the neo-Fordist changes in the manufacturing labour process. These included: an emphasis on customer care; leaner, flatter, managerial hierarchies; budgetary devolution; multiskilling and flexibility of the workforce; a key role for information and information technology; and the adoption of new managerial ideologies, notably those associated with Peters (Peters and Waterman, 1982).

Stoker (1989) goes somewhat further than Hoggett in discussing the restructuring of British local government 'for a post-Fordist society'. However, like Hoggett, Stoker regards the labour process within local government as of central significance. Within this he includes the contracting out of service provision to private sector companies. Like Hoggett, he refers to the potential of information technology:

> the availability of information technology in all its forms – data processing, communications and control, computer-aided design, office automation – offers the possibility of recasting traditionally labour-intensive service activities. And one major use of such

technology is to reduce the aggregate cost of a particular service and the employment within it (1989, p. 160).

Geddes also discusses the labour process within the provision of public services in urban areas, through his consideration of the local state (Geddes, 1988). He comes to the same conclusion, that information technology offers opportunities to reorganize state production processes, to cut the costs of collective provision and to provide a more individualized 'product'. There is a wide range of urban public services to which information technology and other forms of technological change is being applied. While these developments are still rather patchy, some interesting examples are discussed in detail in the OECD publication *Cities and New Technology* (OECD, 1992).

Urban politics and the Fordist mode of regulation

A somewhat larger group of writers have concentrated their attention on the part played by urban politics within specific modes of regulation. As I noted above, the Fordist mode of regulation included a key role for the Keynesian welfare state, and in many ways it is in analysing the link between the welfare state and the urban arena that regulation theory has most to offer the study of urban politics.

Urban policy   Florida and Jonas (1991) discuss the link between regulation theory and postwar urban policy in the United States. They argue that the Fordist mode of regulation in the United States was intimately related to federal urban policy (broadly defined). To begin with, the specific character of US Fordism was constituted in part by the ending of the social democratic experiment of the New Deal. This saw, among other things, the Cold War circumscribing the legitimate role for the state, a limited 'class accord', the growth of the military-industrial complex and the emergence of new areas of economic growth in the west and east of the country. In comparison with the situation in Europe, US Fordism was to a significant extent privatized, and depended on a spatial organization at the urban scale in which suburbanization was central: 'suburbanization was propelled by a growing demand for housing, automobiles, consumer durables and public services (eg: education and infrastructure)' (1991, p. 362).

The argument here is that Federal urban policies such as the expansion of education and the 1956 Highway Act promoted the shift to the suburbs, which in turn then helped to generate the demand for goods and services to sustain the virtuous circle of growth of Fordism. Suburbanization thus significantly reduced the 'need' for the state intervention characteristic of Western European modes of regulation. It was accompanied by decentralization of private production and the spatial fragmentation of labour markets. As a result, the Fordist mode of regulation in the United States was more socially divided than in Europe. In inner-urban areas lived a population of poor and disproportionately black 'peripheral' workers, while a suburbanized, affluent and disproportionately white group provided the core, skilled labour force. When linked to the territorial fragmentation characteristic of US urban government, the result was increasing fiscal stress, making it more and more difficult to provide public services in inner-urban areas. This meant that the crisis of the Fordist mode of regulation was developed relatively early, and Florida and Jonas argue that the black civil rights movements in the 1960s were an expression of this crisis. As a result, the Federal government acted to mitigate some of the worst problems of US Fordism with a series of urban renewal programmes and the enhancement of the 'social wage' directed at poorer groups. By contrast, explicitly spatial policies had long been a defining part of the Fordist modes of regulation in Western Europe.

Urban government Surprisingly few regulationist writers have focused on the functions fulfilled by urban government and the local-level institutions of the state under the Fordist mode of regulation. This may reflect the genesis of regulation theory during the crisis of Fordism, and the urgency of interpreting current changes, rather than worrying about the past. Whatever the reason, while there are now several attempts to consider the links between local government, the crisis of Fordism and a supposedly emergent post-Fordist mode of regulation, most of the authors take the character of the Fordist system more or less for granted and no comprehensive account of the local state in the 30 years after the Second World War has so far used regulationist ideas in any detail.

Given that the concept of the Fordist mode of regulation represents one of the richer products of regulation theory, it is disappointing that regulationist writers on urban politics have generated so few developed accounts of the character of local government within Fordism. The following ideas are thus derived from general regulationist principles and the brief accounts which have been provided elsewhere (Stoker, 1989, pp. 149–52; Painter, 1991a, pp. 58–79; 1991b, pp. 23–33).

In most countries in which the Fordist mode of regulation developed, governmental and state institutions operating at the urban scale played a key role in the operation of the Keynesian welfare state. First, they were often instrumental in providing a part of the 'social wage': goods and services provided collectively to all or to those unable to afford them privately. Public housing is a pre-eminent example of this. The social wage was central to the Fordist mode of regulation, because it placed a 'floor' under popular consumption, ensuring that during times of economic difficulty, recession did not turn into slump. This 'subsidy' to the costs of reproducing labour power was one of the ways in which the Fordist mode of regulation ironed out large fluctuations in the process of capital accumulation by helping to match demand to supply.

Second, the Fordist mode of regulation involved an increased degree of government planning of economic and social life. In many cases, urban government was one of the primary agencies through which this planning took place. In the United Kingdom, for example, the local government system was the principal forum for land use and urban infrastructural planning. Related to this, and third, the Fordist mode of regulation involved state intervention to provide vital human and physical infrastructure, such as transportation, environmental improvement, education and health care. Under Fordism, these were vital to the private sector but were often unprofitable for individual firms to provide, at least on a universal basis.

Finally, there is an area which links the mode of regulation with the much more narrow concerns with the labour process discussed above. The organization of state institutions at the local level under Fordism involved the application of bureaucratic principles. Governmental institutions tended to be hierarchical and centralized, with the performance criteria based on procedure, rather than results. As Hoggett noted (see above), they tended to be good at providing a relatively narrow range of services in a fairly inflexible and standard way to a large population, which was implicitly assumed to be fairly homogeneous. Some critics have argued that this reflected the dominance of producer interests within the public services sector over the interests of service users. However, while there are clear links here with the mass consumption norm of the Fordist regime of accumulation, it is not immediately clear whether these features of urban government were an *essential* part of the Fordist mode of regulation. Arguably they do reflect some of the organizational principles of the archetypal Fordist firm. However, as I have already suggested, within Fordism, the public sector in fact often played the role of 'filling-in' gaps left by private provision. In other words, it was distinctively different from the private sector, not a straight-forward mimic of it, and thus where organizational form is concerned, the causal link remains obscure.

Urban political processes   Political processes at the urban scale took a particular form and played a particular role in the Fordist mode of regulation. In particular, the role of local elections played a key role, especially in those countries where Fordism was secured through a form of social democratic political settlement. This representative function conferred a degree of political legitimacy on Fordist arrangements.

According to regulation theory, the 'grand compromise' of Fordism (Lipietz, 1987) accorded a degree of political power to certain (organized) sections of the working class in exchange for a broad toleration of capitalist relations of production. This had two political consequences at the urban scale. First, the organizations of the working class struggled for, and began to be involved in, political decision making. This took place through, for example, certain forms of local corporatism involving trade unions or the development of mass working class-based political parties. The government of many major urban areas, particularly in Western Europe, was, as a result, frequently dominated by social democratic, socialist or communist politicians.

Second, the limits of the compromise circumscribed the boundaries of legitimate political struggle. It was acceptable (though sometimes only just) to fight for labour *within* the limits of the Fordist deal. However, where urban political unrest began to challenge the rules of the game itself, the state was often swift in its retribution. As the mode of regulation of Fordism began to develop its own crises, these challenges, and the retribution, became more intense. Examples include the civil rights movements in the United States, the events of May 1968 in Paris and the public sector strikes in the 1970s in Britain.

Urban politics and potential post-Fordist modes of regulation

Despite, or perhaps because of, the considerably more problematic character of the concept of post-Fordism, much more attention has been focused by regulation theorists on trying to interpret a supposed shift from Fordism to post-Fordism, than on clarifying the nature of Fordism. Moreover, Mark Goodwin and I have recently argued that not only are there empirical reasons for doubting whether a new mode of regulation is emerging, but there are also significant conceptual reasons why it may be unlikely to do so (Goodwin and Painter, 1993).

Nonetheless, the notion of post-Fordism has attracted considerable attention, and in this section I will first briefly outline the 'crisis of Fordism' and then draw on both regulationist principles and existing accounts of change to discuss the relationships between urban politics and post-Fordist modes of regulation.

The crisis of Fordism is a key reference point for any development of the notion of post-Fordism. As I have suggested, the Fordist mode of regulation was itself a contradictory phenomenon and the subject of political struggles and conflicts. Ultimately these aspects compromised its ability to postpone economic difficulties. Most of the standard accounts of regulation theory contain a discussion of the overall character of the crisis, so I will limit myself to the role of urban politics.

The crisis involved a pincer movement in which the 'virtuous circle' of Fordism switched into a downward spiral. The productivity increases on which the regime of accumulation depended could not be sustained indefinitely given the existing technical and organizational approaches. This led to a fall in profits and the growth of structural unemployment in the industrialized countries as multinational corporations in particular shifted production overseas in search of cheaper labour. This simultaneously decreased the pool of finance from which the state drew its resources and increased the demand for public services as workers and their families increasingly faced economic distress. In addition, many of the social groups which had been marginalized in the Fordist mode of regulation began to organize and assert demands on the welfare state (Bakshi et al., 1994; Painter, 1995). In many countries, this placed strains on the urban political system as local government struggled to meet increased demand for welfare services, sometimes in the face of fiscal stringency. In addition, urban policy and the urban political process increasingly became dominated by the need to deal with economic restructuring (frequently involving deindustrialization and only limited growth of new sectors) and the social effects of these changes, such as increases in crime and poverty and shifts of population. In the face of such changes, new political strategies have been adopted by many central and local government organizations. The debate is over whether these have the capacity to secure a new mode of regulation which will resolve or sidestep the contradictions of Fordism and usher in a new phase of enhanced capitalist development.

According to Jessop the broadly neo-liberal strategies adopted by most western governments mean that it is likely that in any new post-Fordist mode of regulation, the state would be a Schumpeterian Workfare State (SWS). In contrast to the Keynesian Welfare State of Fordism, the SWS would: 'promote product, process, organizational, and market innovation and enhance the structural competitiveness of open economies mainly through supply-side intervention; and to subordinate social policy to the demands of labor market flexibility and structural competitiveness' (Jessop, 1993, p. 19). This would imply that urban policy would shift away from an explicit concern with social and spatial equity, full employment and welfare programmes and towards initiatives aimed at promoting workforce flexibility and the economic competitiveness of the private sector. In addition the social polarization implicit in the neo-liberal version of post-Fordism would be likely to require increasingly authoritarian measures of policing and social control (Edwards and Hallsworth, 1992).

Esser and Hirsch (1989) outline the impact of these changes in a study of the then Federal Republic of Germany. Urban policy in Germany, they argue, is increasingly a matter of managing the division in urban areas between the affluent middle-classes who are to take advantages of the growth industries and the marginalized poor and dispossessed. This intra-urban heterogeneity is, they suggest, a stronger feature of contemporary Germany than inter-regional differences. (However, with the incorporation of the former German Democratic Republic, this last point no longer holds as regards the relationship between East and West.)

In Britain, urban policy has changed distinctively towards a system of centrally imposed and non-elected agencies, such as the Urban Development Corporations (UDCs), with wide-ranging powers over specific, and usually fairly small, areas of inner-urban land. The UDCs were explicitly charged with undertaking the regeneration of their areas in ways which prioritized the needs of private investors. Considerable sums of public funding were channelled into transport infrastructure, land reclamation, office and housing developments, and environmental 'improvements'. In some cases the people originally living in the local area have gained relatively little from the changes, with many of the housing and leisure developments aimed deliberately at up-market consumers and incomers with aspirations to an affluent lifestyle (Goodwin, 1991, 1993).

Debates around the agencies of urban government and governance have focused on two connections with post-Fordism. First, some authors have considered the links between public sector organization and new forms of corporate organization in the private sector. Stoker and Mossberger (1995), for example, identify many of the new organizational attributes of urban government and governance in Britain as post-Fordist in part because they reflect management strategies adopted in the private sector in response to the economic impact of the crisis of Fordism. These include in particular: an emphasis on the consumer (often called 'customer care' in the British public sector); a stress on flexible forms of organization; a more diverse range of relationships with external private and public sector bodies.[5] I have elsewhere emphasized the role of increased contracting out in the structures of urban government in Britain (Painter, 1991a, 1991c, 1991d). Although there has not been wholesale privatization of services provided by local councils in the UK, many public utilities outside the control of elected local government have been transferred to the private sector. Privatization of public service provision would have a key role in a new mode of regulation, as it simultaneously reduces the costs of providing labour intensive services as workers are removed from the protection of collective agreements and provides new sources of capital accumulation for the private sector.

The main potential contribution of these kinds of changes to a new mode of regulation would be to help to resolve the fiscal crisis of the local state, and, arguably, its legitimation problems by making the services more responsive to user needs. The second connection is slightly different, however, and involves the *direct* functions of urban governmental organizations within the Schumpeterian Workfare State (SWS). In Britain, the 1990s saw the establishment by the central government of a large number of quangos at the urban level. Foremost among these are the Training and Enterprise Councils (TECs) in England and Wales and the Local

Enterprise Companies in Scotland. These agencies are outside the system of elected local government and are dominated by appointed, private sector interests. They have the responsibility of delivering government training schemes and promoting local economic development and private sector enterprise. This would seem to place them at the centre of any move towards the SWS. Peck and Jones (1994) have studied the work of the TECs from precisely this point of view. They concluded that TECs do look and sound very much like the local level equivalent of the SWS, but they have one fatal flaw. According to Peck and Jones, they are quite efficient at 'disciplining' the unemployed workforce to accept the primacy of employer require-ments in the labour market, but they are not able to provide the entrepreneurial, supply-side innovation which Jessop argues is a necessary feature of the SWS. In other words they are 'workfarist' but not particularly 'Schumpeterian', largely because the funding which the central government provides is mostly targeted at training schemes, with only very limited resources set aside for generating local entrepreneurial activities.

Mayer has usefully summarized a range of the changes underway in urban governance across the western capitalist world relating them to the possible emer-gence of post-Fordism as a new mode of regulation (Mayer, 1994); see also Mayer (1991). Her account emphasizes new forms of economic intervention organized around innovation and new institutional relations in which hierarchical local state structures are supposedly being replaced by more pluralistic ones. She argues that both of these developments could be part of the political strategies of the left as well as the right, with rather different social outcomes.

Goodwin et al. (1993) discuss the changing character of urban politics in three English urban areas: Sheffield, Bracknell and Camden in London. Their account is especially useful in highlighting geographical variations in urban political processes within Fordism, its crisis and its potential successor. In many ways, Goodwin et al. argue, the three locations were archetypes of Fordist urban politics, within which 'a highly skilled labour force reaped the benefits of high wages and increasing levels of service provision in return for increasing productivity' and where 'structures of local politics were in place which were conducive to continued economic growth, social stability, and increasing standards of collective consumption' (1993, p. 76). With the crisis of Fordism, the local political coalitions which allowed this to continue in each place have now been undermined.

In Sheffield, the catastrophic decline of the steel industry initially prompted the city council to develop regeneration strategies based on the public sector promotion of employment. The imposition of central government control of the regeneration process meant that the explicitly socialist inflection and class basis of this strategy gave way to one subordinated to private capital and based on leisure, consumption and place marketing. In Bracknell, a New Town in the South East of England, Fordist growth had been governed by the social democratic and corporatist New Town Development Corporation, which used public sector finance to develop the local infrastructure. Today, some of the characteristics of a post-Fordist mode of regulation are evident:

> owner occupation has replaced council housing as the dominant form of housing tenure in the area, which lies at the centre of the affluent M4 corridor. Per capita expenditure

by the local state on public services is little more than a third of that in Camden, and around two thirds of that in Sheffield. The shift from the postwar version of a one-nation mass-consumption system, as exemplified by Bracknell's successful New Town, has now been completed here to a two-nation model based on private provision for the affluent worker, with only a minimal 'social security state' for those excluded from this. . . . The basis and institutions of collectivist local politics have been systematically challenged by social and economic recomposition, and in their place the local state now facilitates private accumulation and consumption.   (Goodwin et al., 1993: 81)

In Camden, the decline of Fordism was accompanied by the rise of the 'new urban left' with its emphasis on supporting social groups marginalized by Fordism, such as women and black people. These kinds of political movements and particularly the socialist experiment at the Greater London Council in the early 1980s briefly held out the hope of an alternative transition from Fordism; one not based so whole-heartedly on the dominance of the private sector and central government. However, the defeat of many of the groups and movements both locally (Goodwin et al., 1993, p. 82) and nationally, culminating in the abolition of the GLC in 1986, effectively dashed that hope. Nonetheless, the evidence from Goodwin et al.'s research does not support the existence of a smooth transition to a private sector post-Fordist future. If that transition does occur, it will have been highly uneven, partial and, in some places, bitterly contested.

Critiques and Responses

Almost all the authors I have cited so far are, to a greater or lesser extent, proponents of regulation theory or the concept of post-Fordism, or both. However, the regula-tionist approach and (particularly) the idea of post-Fordism, have also been heavily criticized. While there are some who are critical of regulation theory as a whole, the picture is complicated because many of those who accept the principles of regulation theory are themselves critical of the idea of post-Fordism or of its use by certain writers. Furthermore, there are also writers who accept the tenets of regulation theory (and in some cases, also, post-Fordism) but regard its ability to account for changes in urban politics rather limited.

Some of the most trenchant critics of regulation theory as a whole have been other Marxist economists and political theorists; see, for example, Bonefeld (1987, 1993), Clarke (1988, 1990), Bonefeld and Holloway (1991), and Brenner and Glick (1991). Since this account is concerned specifically with urban politics, I will not discuss their criticisms in detail, but they hinge around four main issues.

First, it is argued that regulation theory is *teleological*. That is, it sees history as the unfolding of an inevitable logic of development, from one regime of accumula-tion to the next. This, it is suggested, reduces the scope for political intervention and political conflict, and means that contemporary political events are evaluated purely in terms of their success in advancing society towards a presupposed future (post-Fordism). Second, according to some writers, regulation theory is *functionalist*. In other words it explains the development of a new mode of regulation in terms of its effects in securing capital accumulation: post-Fordism has arisen because the process of capital accumulation needed it. This, it is argued, is problematic, since the effects of a phenomenon cannot serve as an explanation of its origins. Third, regulation theory is sometimes accused of *technological determinism*. That is, the concern with the labour process and product and process innovation leads regulation theorists to assume that social development is essentially driven by new technology. Fourth, critics of regulation theory argue that it overstates the *coherence* of the mode of regulation and assumes that the class compromise around which it is supposedly built is hegemonic and widely accepted. This then leads to an underemphasis on social struggle during modes of regulation, with conflict and new developments only being significant *between* modes of regulation. Once a mode of regulation has been established, the working class, and especially other oppressed groups, simply have to sit it out and wait for its inherent logical contradictions to build up to crisis point.

Regulation theorists have responded vigorously to all these criticisms. Lipietz, in particular, has been especially concerned to develop a version of regulation theory which avoids functionalism and teleology (Lipietz, 1987). Technological determinism is arguably a feature of some regulationist writing, but it can only really apply in the sphere of the labour process, which as we have seen is but one aspect of regulation. Some accounts of modes of regulation have indeed tended to stress their coherence and unity, rather than their contradictions and diversity. Given that regulationism is a developing theory, what is required here are more detailed and nuanced accounts of particular modes of regulation operating at particular times in particular countries. In discussing concrete cases, it may well make sense to talk about 'regulatory processes' or 'tendencies towards regulation', rather than coherent 'modes of regulation'. Furthermore, all those who would abandon regulation theory are still left with the conundrum posed at the beginning of this chapter, namely, how, given the inherently contradictory nature of capital accumulation, has capitalism not only survived, but from time to time generated relatively stable economic growth?

In addition to these criticisms of regulation theory as a whole, a number of specialists in urban politics have criticized its application there. Cochrane (1993, pp. 81–93) has recently neatly summarized many of these sceptical reactions, and also considers the problems of the concept of post-Fordism. He begins by discussing the debates around post-Fordism as a technological paradigm, which I have referred to here as the labour process.

Focusing on the work of Hoggett and Geddes, he argues that the notion of post-Fordism in this narrow technical and organizational sense implies a determinism, which makes it difficult for local government to resist or affect the changes:

> However qualified the argument, political processes still tend to be relegated to second-ary status. This makes it difficult to explain why particular technological opportunities are taken up at one time rather than another, and also makes it easy to under-estimate the extent to which the direction of change remains contested.   (Cochrane, 1993: 84)

In addition Cochrane suggests that the analogy between private sector organizational forms and the local welfare state may be overstated. There may be parallels, though he suggests that these are sometimes more apparent than real, but parallels and analogies cannot explain why the public sector adopted certain methods at certain times.

Moreover, as I have argued elsewhere, Hoggett's argument that the production of public services approximated to Fordist production in the manufacturing sector is actually sharply at odds with Aglietta who 'insists that it is precisely those goods and services whose production cannot be organized on Fordist lines which then have to be produced by the state, given a politically-determined consumption norm' (Painter, 1991b, p. 33).

Unlike some critics of the regulation approach, Cochrane is careful and correct to distinguish debates around post-Fordism as labour process and organizational form from debates around shifts in the mode of regulation. In assessing the latter he outlines and discusses Stoker's (1989) description of local government under Fordism and post-Fordism. First, in Cochrane's view, the case presented by Stoker is an oversimplification of the complexities of the British local state and urban politics. He regards Stoker's account of Fordism as applying at best only to the formal structures of elected local government, but failing to allow for the informal processes of negotiation and political conflict in any real political system. On the other hand, Stoker also points out that 'the Fordist character of local government organization and management...should not be overstated' (1989, p. 151). Second, contracting out is often regarded as a key element of post-Fordist local government, and yet as Cochrane points out, such arrangements can actually reduce the flexibility which is supposed to be one of its other defining features. However, 'flexibility' can apply in a number of different spheres. Contracting out does seem to be associated with a deregulation of the labour market, for example, and there is no reason in principle why a contract could not specify that the contractor should provide a service which responds ('flexibly') to public demand. Third, according to Cochrane, in some countries, including the United States, local government during the so-called Fordist period actually has a lot in common with Stoker's model of post-Fordist local government in Britain (Cochrane, 1993, p. 89). Finally, in the case of Britain, Cochrane agrees with the regulation theorists that local government did indeed play a key role in the welfare state. However, he argues that regulation theory underemphasizes the degree of contestation and conflict around that role.

Evaluation

The concepts of regulation theory and the idea of post-Fordism have only been applied in the field of urban politics for some six or seven years, and then somewhat sporadically. Stoker and Mossberger point out that in comparison with other available theories, 'the post-Fordist literature has a reasonable claim to have most effectively captured the broad complexity of the changes that are occurring in the system of local governance' (1995). In practice, however, the application of regulation theory to these issues has been very patchy.

First, more work is required to specify the complex and uneven relationship between urban politics and Fordism. At least some of the difficulties with the notion of post-Fordism stem, in my view, from a too glib assumption about the link between politics, the urban arena and the Fordist mode of regulation.

Second, the so far extremely limited geographical reach of most of the accounts I have discussed needs to be addressed. For example, how far is the so-called post-

Fordist local government system a peculiarity of the British case where an unusually right-wing government has been in power for an unusually long time. How were different modes of regulation articulated differently with urban politics in different societies? (According to Kevin Cox (personal communication), the debate over Fordism and post-Fordism has 'little resonance' with research into urban politics in the United States.) More research will be required to address these questions.

Third, modes of regulation can only firmly be identified retrospectively. Regulation theory is much better at describing the character (and contradictions) of an established mode of regulation than it is at explaining the emergence of new forms. These, it insists, are the product of social struggles and political conflicts. What is therefore required, and what regulation theory currently lacks, is a complementary set of theoretical tools that can account for the development of potential new regulatory practices and processes, without falling into the traps of teleology and functionalism.

Fourth, the prevalence of post-Fordist forms of local governance and urban politics remains unclear and extensive empirical research is required to assess it. In Britain, at the time of writing, such research is underway as part of the Local Governance Research Programme established by the Economic and Social Research Council.

This preliminary assessment suggests, first, that changes in contemporary urban politics in all its senses can be viewed in terms of competing political strategies in response to the decline of Fordist arrangements, whether social, economic or political. A major strength of regulation theory lies in its attempt to disclose and explain the *links between* the economic, political and sociocultural spheres. However, second, there is as yet relatively little evidence that urban politics is playing any clear role in the emergence of a new, coherent, post-Fordist mode of regulation. Certain developments are certainly not incompatible with such a future. On the other hand, since, as Jessop points out, the objects and processes of regulation are mutually constituting, it is likely that a definite assessment will only be possible retrospectively. At its present stage of development, regulation theory is perhaps best seen as a specialized, rather than a general theory. It may be of only limited application in specifying the detail of political shifts, but is particularly helpful in making sense of the social and economic context within which those shifts are taking place.

NOTES

1 I have space here only to outline the main concepts. Fuller accounts are provided in Robert Boyer's excellent survey of regulation theory (1990) and by Peck and Tickell (1992).
2 Jessop further distinguishes the pattern of market relations as constituting an additional '*economic* mode of economic regulation'.
3 Some writers (including the founder of regulation theory, Michel Aglietta) prefer the concept of neo-Fordism, implying that the new arrangements are a development of Fordist systems, rather than a wholesale transformation of them. While the concept of neo-Fordism is arguably more precise and less open to some of the criticisms discussed in this chapter, it has not been widely adopted.

4 Jessop (1990, p. 200) argues that it should be possible to use regulationist methods to develop an account of the state, rather than the economy. This would involve identifying the state as an *object* of regulation (a contradictory and unstable phenomenon which itself is regulated, or needs regulation) rather than (or as well as) something which participates in the regulation of the economy. While Goodwin et al. (1993) begin to take up this point in their discussion of urban politics, it remains the case that most regulationist writers are concerned with the regulation of the economy, rather than the state.

5 Stoker and Mossberger also consider the role of the local state in managing the changed economic and social circumstances of local areas.

REFERENCES

Aglietta, M. (1979) *A Theory of Capitalist Regulation: The US Experience*. London: Verso.

Bakshi, P. K., Goodwin, M., Painter, J. and Southern, A. (1994) 'Monitoring the transition from Fordism in British local government', paper presented at the Institute of British Geographers' Annual Conference, Nottingham.

Bonefeld, W. (1987) 'Reformulation of state theory', *Capital and Class*, 33: 96–127.

Bonefeld, W. (1993) 'Crisis of theory: Bob Jessop's theory of capitalist reproduction', *Capital and Class*, 50: 25–47.

Bonefeld, W. and Holloway, J. (eds) (1991) *Post-Fordism and Social Form*. London: Macmillan.

Boyer, R. (1990) *The Regulation School: A Critical Introduction*. New York: Columbia University Press.

Brenner, R. and Glick, M. (1991) 'The regulation approach: Theory and history', *New Left Review*, 188: 45–119.

Clarke, S. (1988) 'Overaccumulation, class struggle and the regulation approach', *Capital and Class*, 36: 59–92.

Clarke, S. (1990) 'New utopias for old: Fordist dreams and post-Fordist fantasies', *Capital and Class*, 42: 131–55.

Cochrane, A. (1993) *Whatever Happened to Local Government?* Buckingham: Open University Press.

Edwards, A. and Hallsworth, S. (1992) 'Regulation theory and crime control: A future for Marxist criminology?', paper presented at the Political Studies Association Marxism Specialist Group Annual Conference, Leicester.

Esser, J. and Hirsch, J. (1989) 'The crisis of Fordism and the dimensions of a "post-Fordist" regional and urban structure', *International Journal of Urban and Regional Research*, 13 (3): 417–37.

Florida, R. and Jonas, A. (1991) 'U.S. urban policy: The postwar state and capitalist regulation', *Antipode: A Journal of Radical Geography*, 23 (4): 349–84.

Geddes, M. (1988) 'The capitalist state and the local economy: "Restructuring for labour" and beyond', *Capital and Class*, 35: 85–120.

Goodwin, M. (1991) 'Replacing a surplus population: The policies of the London Docklands Development Corporation', in J. Allen and C. Hamnett (eds), *Housing and Labour Markets: Building the Connections*. London: Allen and Unwin.

Goodwin, M. (1993) 'The city as commodity: The contested spaces of urban development', in G. Kearns and C. Philo (eds), *Selling Places: The City as Cultural Capital, Past and Present*. Oxford: Pergamon.

Goodwin, M. and Painter, J. (1993) 'Local governance, the crisis of Fordism and uneven development', paper presented at the Ninth Urban Change and Conflict Conference, Sheffield.

Goodwin, M., Duncan, S. and Halford, S. (1993) 'Regulation theory, the local state, and the transition of urban politics', *Environment and Planning D: Society and Space*, 11 (1): 67–88.

Gramsci, A. (1971) 'Americanism and Fordism', in Q. Hoare and G. Nowell Smith (eds), *Selections from the Prison Notebooks of Antonio Gramsci*. London: Lawrence and Wishart.

Hoggett, P. (1987) 'A farewell to mass production? Decentralisation as an emergent private and public sector paradigm', in P. Hoggett and R. Hambleton (eds), *Decentralisation and Democracy: Localising Public Services*. Bristol: School for Advanced Urban Studies.

Jessop, B. (1990) 'Regulation theories in retrospect and prospect', *Economy and Society*, 19 (2): 153–216.

Jessop, B. (1992) 'Fordism and post-Fordism: A critical reformulation', in M. Storper and A. J. Scott (eds), *Pathways to Industrialization and Regional Development*. London: Routledge.

Jessop, B. (1993) 'Towards a Schumpeterian Workfare State? Preliminary remarks on post-Fordist political economy', *Studies in Political Economy*, 40 (Spring): 7–40.

Lipietz, A. (1987) *Mirages and Miracles: The Crises of Global Fordism*. London: Verso.

Mayer, M. (1991) 'Politics in the post-Fordist city', *Socialist Review*, 21 (1): 105–24.

Mayer, M. (1994) 'Post-Fordist city politics', in A. Amin (ed.), *Post-Fordism: A Reader*. Oxford: Blackwell.

OECD (ed.) (1992) *Cities and New Technology*. Paris: OECD.

Painter, J. (1991a) 'Responding to restructuring: The geography of trade union responses to the restructuring of local government services in Britain, 1979–89', Ph.D. dissertation, Open University, Milton Keynes.

Painter, J. (1991b) 'Regulation theory and local government', *Local Government Studies*, 17 (6): 23–44.

Painter, J. (1991c) 'The geography of trade union response to local government privatization', *Transactions of the Institute of British Geographers*, 16: 214–26.

Painter, J. (1991d) 'Compulsory competitive tendering in local government: The first round', *Public Administration*, 69 (2): 191–210.

Painter, J. (1995) 'The regulatory state', in R. J. Johnston, P. J. Taylor and M. Watts (eds), *World Problems: Geographical Perspectives*. Oxford: Blackwell.

Peck, J. and Jones, M. (1994) 'Training and Enterprise Councils: Schumpeterian workfare state, or what?', paper presented at Institute of British Geographers' Annual Conference, Nottingham.

Peck, J. and Tickell, A. (1992) 'Accumulation, regulation and the geographies of post-Fordism', *Progress in Human Geography*, 16 (2): 190–218.

Peters, T. and Waterman, R. (1982) *In Search of Excellence*. New York: Harper and Row.

Stoker, G. (1989) 'Creating a local government for a post-Fordist society: The Thatcherite project?' in J. Stewart and G. Stoker (eds), *The Future of Local Government*. London: Macmillan.

Stoker, G. and Mossberger, K. (1995) 'The post-Fordist local state: The dynamics of its development', in J. Stewart and G. Stoker (eds) *Local Government in the 1990s*. London: Macmillan.

6

The Changing World Economy and Urban Restructuring*

Susan S. Fainstein

Restructuring and Locality

There are two ways of analyzing cities, neither incorrect. The first, or global, approach scrutinizes the international system of cities (and its national and regional subsystems). While noting particularities, this mode of explanation attributes them to the niche or specific node that a city occupies within the overall network. Scholars using this perspective predict uneven development and consequent territorial difference; from their vantage point, which particular places win or lose matters less than that there inevitably will be winners and losers.[1] In contrast, the second approach, which works from the inside out, examines the forces creating the particularities of a specific place – its economic base, its social divisions, its constellation of political interests, and the actions of participants. Within the first framework, differences among cities are manifestations of the varying components that comprise the whole. The second traces urban diversity to internal forces and the tactics used by local actors.

The same city can thus be regarded both as part of a totality and as a unique outcome of its particular history. To offer an example that illustrates the point: it is possible to tell the story of Houston using either analytic framework. Using a world system approach, we see Houston as building its prosperity on its unique function as the center of the US oil industry and the headquarters of firms dominating world petroleum exploration and marketing. The economic decline that it suffered during the 1980s resulted from global economic factors including plummeting oil prices and overvaluation of the dollar, which heavily damaged the ability of Texas manufacturing firms to export. Moreover, its role as a regional financial center weakened

* Fainstein, Susan S. (1990) "The Changing World Economy and Urban Restructuring" from Dennis Judd and Michael Parkinson (eds.) *Leadership and Urban Regeneration*, Sage Publications Inc., Thousand Oaks, pp. 31–47.

as a consequence of bank failures caused by over-extension during the preceding boom period, particularly lavish financing of real estate development, which itself was premised on ever-increasing affluence. From this perspective Houston's rise and decline can be traced to its place in controlling, financing, and marketing one of the most important commodities in international trade, and one that has been particularly affected by world political and economic currents.[2]

Most important, this approach provides insight into the general relationship between macroeconomic forces and urban outcomes. This argument is as follows: changing modes of corporate finance and control, causing and produced by the geographic decentralization of production, globalization of financial and product markets, and internationalization of the giant corporations, increase the vulnerability of places to disruptions in the markets of commodities on which they are dependent for their economic well-being. Moreover, the instability of foreign exchange levels increases their exposure to uncontrollable outside forces, regardless of their efficiency of production, since it causes the world-market price of their output to vary independently of their production costs.

The inside-out approach to explaining urban restructuring, on the other hand, allows us to identify the dynamic factors driving Houston's adaptation to changing circumstances. Applying this analytic mode, we explain the city's past status by relating its development as the capital of the petroleum industry to its entrepreneurial culture and favorable business climate. We identify the industry leaders who founded enterprises in Houston and trace the city's expansion to federal subsidies attracted by well-connected politicians (Feagin, 1988, ch. 6). One reason for the sharpness of Houston's recent decline and the extremity of its effects on its poorest residents is the past reluctance of the public sector to intervene in the economy and to provide social welfare. At least part of the explanation for Houston's present turnaround lies in an increased willingness to plan and manage growth.

We can similarly assess the decline of many other old commercial and industrial cities and the regeneration of some. Probably no city in the advanced capitalist world has been unaffected by the reorganization of the global economy of the past two decades. For those places especially dependent on dying manufacturing and port industries, local leadership has been one element that could improve their competitive position, although always within the serious constraints posed by historic economic base, regional location, and national policy.

To understand the process by which improvement has occurred, we must identify the changes in economic functions resulting from shifts in the world and national economy and examine the activities of groups and leaders within particular cities that affected their new roles. Thus, Pittsburgh and Sheffield similarly suffered from the world's increase in steel capacity, reduced demand for metals products, and heightened international competition. Both have had local leadership that sought to restructure their economies so as to develop new economic functions and indeed have seen economic revivals. A similar transformation has occurred in the old port cities of Baltimore and Hamburg: after long periods of decline, enterprising municipal administrations identified new opportunities and managed to attract outside investment to their locales. In the case of Baltimore these were primarily tourist oriented, while Hamburg followed the high-tech route.

This chapter briefly recapitulates the now extremely familiar story of economic restructuring and urban transformation. It then examines the varying interpretations of urban trajectories and potential according to the two vantage points sketched above. It will summarize the right and left ideological responses to economic restructuring; and finally it will set forth the types of policies available to progressive local regimes and oppositional movements, concluding with a discussion of the relationship between the politics of locality, economic forces, and national governments.

Economic Change and Urban Restructuring

We remember now only with difficulty the immediate post-World War II period, when industrialization seemingly offered the key to economic prosperity. Cities with large, diverse manufacturing bases promised secure growth and stable employment; the Soviet Union set its goal as outpacing the West through the development of heavy industry; and the task in front of war-ravaged Europe was the reconstruction of its manufacturing capacity. Now, in a world awash in commodities, peripheral locations have become the most advantageous sites for manufacturing. The future of older cities appears to depend on capturing the financial, informational, and managerial functions that determine the world's capital flows, although some areas can alternatively rely on tourism, scientific or medical services, and high-technology manufacturing to maintain a competitive edge. Overall, in the advanced capitalist world, massive employment losses in manufacturing sectors have been balanced or mitigated by gains in services and wholesale and retail trade; many places, however, have never fully recovered from the rapid loss of manufacturing jobs and are still characterized by high unemployment rates and continued outflow of population.

One of the main lessons of the past two decades is that the economic composition of places seems to have become less and less permanent (Harvey, 1989). While restructuring of manufacturing industry may have passed its peak, a similar rationalization of tertiary industries has possibly just begun. During the 1980s many cities have shown signs of regeneration, evidenced in new office towers, gentrified inner-city neighborhoods, and job creation. However, the internationalization of economic competition, which was one of the principal causes of manufacturing decline, also threatens this new vitality. While globalization has enhanced the importance of financing, informational, and control functions, it has also enlarged the number of competitors in the tertiary sector. Within Europe, each nation has hopes of housing the control center of the European Community after 1992 and is competing fiercely to attract headquarters and financing operations; the glut of office space that currently characterizes United States metropolitan areas may soon spread to Europe, where numerous large office projects are under construction in anticipation of European Union. In the United States, financial interests look warily at the expanding Japanese presence in the banking and investment industries, which threatens to make Tokyo the world's financial capital.

Within each country, even domestically owned financial and service firms have become increasingly footloose as they emulate industrial corporations by separating their routine processing functions from more complex operations and decentralizing them to low-cost areas. Furthermore, prosperity based on the advanced-service and financial sectors remains hostage to the health of financial markets. The shock of October 1987 continues to reverberate through diminished employment in financial sector firms and reduced consumption in cities dependent on that industry.

Even successful regeneration, therefore, demonstrates signs of instability and social fragmentation. While financial centers benefit from merger and acquisition activities, other cities find that consolidation of the new conglomerates results in the closing down of formerly profitable establishments now redundant or too encumbered with debt to remain viable. Efforts to spur central business district development and the "realistic" dismissal of manufacturing as the future basis for growth have displaced residents and small firms and left blue-collar workers stranded.

Along with deindustrialization has come the decline of a homogeneous, relatively well-paid working class and the growth in size of income strata at both extremes of the spectrum (Harrison and Bluestone, 1988, ch. 5). The outmigration or closing of factories and obsolete shipping facilities has produced desolate landscapes of unused structures in once central locations. Changes in social groupings have resulted in homelessness and the decay of formerly stable working-class residential districts, on the one hand; on the other, they have heightened the demand for converted, well-located structures and luxury new construction. Combined with demographic changes due to dropping birth rates, growing numbers of single-member and female-headed households as well as high-income, two-earner couples, and large-scale immigration, these factors have heightened the fragmentation of urban space (Mingione, 1991). Moreover, cities with low unemployment rates and new investment still face fiscal problems that severely restrict governmental efforts on behalf of low-income residents and limit necessary investment in the physical infrastructure required for future growth.

Social scientists generally agree that the trickle-down effects of new development in "successfully" restructured cities have excluded a large proportion of the population and may even have worsened their situation (Parkinson and Judd, 1988; Squires, 1989). For the many locales that remain trapped in the trajectory of industrial decline and high unemployment, circumstances are obviously worse. To formulate a political stance that effectively addresses the economic distress of old cities requires identifying points of indeterminacy as global forces operate on particular places. Only after such an analysis do local policies stand a chance of stimulating growth; it, however, offers no guarantee and in some cases may prove extremely discouraging to local action.

The Global Perspective

Localities are forever in the position of adjusting to forces beyond their control. The oil crises of the 1970s, the rise of manufacturing economies of the Far East, the management failures of Western oligopolistic industries, the rationalization of firms through decentralization of their various components into least-cost locations, global sourcing, and modern telecommunications have all had profound effects on urban economic structures. While technology is not the cause of increased capital mobility, the loosening of natural and technical constraints on location has allowed firms to further exploit socially created locational advantages (Fainstein and Fainstein, 1988). Most important of these advantages is the group of attributes often called the business climate. Also significant is proximity to markets, which matters far more to most businesses than closeness to raw materials or natural features like rivers.[3] Proximity to markets, however, may only require location close to an airport rather than placement within an actual agglomeration.

For many medium-size cities the weakening in importance of their natural advantages has meant the termination of their *raison d'être*. For example, although port facilities continue to be important generators of economic growth, their existence depends less on the quality of the available water berths than on the pricing of dock labor and the presence of modern container-handing operations. The enhanced capacity of a few ports to handle greatly increased amounts of tonnage along with the ease of transferring containerized loads to trucks and trains reduces the need for numerous ports dotting a single shoreline (Hoyle, 1988). While for London and New York the decline of the port was within the context of diverse other economic functions, for Liverpool or Baltimore port-related activities defined their specialized niche in the system of cities. Consequently, they were particularly vulnerable to technological transformation, and they lacked economic leaders capable of developing other functions since they had few sectors independent of the port. A similar problem exists for the steel-fabricating areas of northern France or the American Midwest.

Such cities then are systemically disadvantaged. The lack of vital private business outside the declining sectors leaves only the public sector to offer a potential engine for stimulating new growth. For the public sector to do so means finding a new niche that the locality can occupy.[4] It is in this possibility of identifying a new niche that indeterminacy exists within the global framework of analysis, and it is here that the two approaches to urban analysis complement each other (Riley and Shurmer-Smith, 1988).

Urban growth coalitions, however, find themselves in a prisoner's dilemma in that their success in finding a new area of specialization depends on leadership groups elsewhere not initiating the same strategy. Festive retailing may work for the first cities that revitalize their waterfronts using this formula, but impulse-buying tourists can support only so many stores selling brass ships' furnishings and Irish shawls. Research parks have spurred development in Cambridge, England, and Charlotte, North Carolina, but they are predestined to languish in most places. Just as in the market economy as a whole, latecomers to an industrial sector will not see the profits of the innovators, so cities that are imitators are unlikely to flourish. Hence, while a city's economic leadership has leeway in choosing new niches, it does so within the framework of a system of competing cities, putting the public's investment at risk.

The Local Autonomy Perspective

Viewing from the inside, we can see each city as having a potential for regeneration that is dependent on the actions of its constituent groups. There are three major dimensions on which cities vary according to the character of state intervention aimed at economic regeneration:

1   Extent of governmental entrepreneurship
2   Amount of planning
3   Level of priority to those in greatest need

Which growth strategy is followed within a city and the city's commitment to targeting low-income groups are consequences of political struggle and are largely independent of external forces (Smith, 1988) – although, as indicated above, whether the growth strategy works is less open.[5]

Entrepreneurship

Whereas city governments once restricted their activities to building infrastructure and providing services, virtually all now take an active role in promoting economic growth. Eisinger (1988) contends that, within the US, city and state governments have moved from an initial, naive "supply-side" strategy for stimulating private investment to "demand-side" policies:

> What guides the entrepreneurial state is attention to the demand side of the economic growth equation. Underlying the actions of the entrepreneurial state is the assumption that growth comes from exploiting new or expanding markets. The state role is to identify, evaluate, anticipate, and even help to develop and create these markets for private producers to exploit, aided if necessary by government as subsidizer or coinvestor. The policies of the entrepreneurial state are geared to these functions. They include the generation of venture capital for selected new and growing businesses, the encouragement of high-technology research and product development to respond to emerging markets, and the promotion of export goods produced by local businesses to capitalize upon new sources of demand.   (Eisinger, 1988, p. 9)

This terminology is confusing since the term "demand side" usually refers to a policy that subsidizes consumers rather than investors. By *demand side* Eisinger simply means a more entrepreneurial or active policy that identifies market opportunities rather than indiscriminately subsidizing all investors. His general point, however, is that subnational governments in the United States increasingly seek to encourage specialized development where their economic policymakers have identified a strategic advantage. He considers that this entrepreneurship represents a new and important role for the subnational state, although he considers the resultant programs of "modest dimensions and uncertain impact" (Eisinger, 1988, p. 34).[6]

Planning

Cities also vary according to the amount of planning they do, both within countries and from country to country. The United States and Great Britain differ considerably from Canada and continental Europe in the extent to which growth is channeled through the planning process. The construction of La Défense in Paris as a corporate center, for example, and the current development of that city's southeast sector as a financial district result from a very strong governmental role in guiding development (Savitch, 1988, ch. 5). In contrast, almost all US cities allow office developers broad limits within which to choose their sites. British restrictions on office locations have been greatly relaxed, allowing simultaneous competing projects. According to the head of the London Regional Planning Office, "boroughs that had formerly tried to stop office development will do so no longer." Or, in the words of the chief planner of one of London's boroughs, "even developers would like more planning."[7]

Growth regulation for environmental protection, the preservation of low-income housing, or the maintenance of manufacturing sites is frequently criticized. Critics assert that such planning is, depending on whether it is in growing or declining areas, either exclusionary or a luxury that deteriorating communities cannot afford (Sternlieb, 1986). Without planning, however, urban landscapes become the product of impersonal market forces, dominated by the interests of capital (Foglesong, 1986). Not only does the absence of planning prevent the general public from being able to affect urban outcomes, but it also denies real-estate interests a regulatory body to insure against overdevelopment. Consequently we see the oversupply of office space that now threatens the future stability of regenerating cities.

Economic growth at the bottom

Within the capitalist countries that have undergone restructuring, urban regeneration has largely taken place under elite leadership, although some exceptions like the "Third Italy" exist. As might be expected from a top-down phenomenon, participating economic elites have been the primary direct beneficiaries of the growth of new industries and the rehabilitation of housing in old industrial settings. Relatively few city governments have devoted themselves consistently to using municipal instruments to direct the dividends of growth toward improving the economic situation of low-income people.

During the period when public housing construction flourished in Europe, municipalities led in providing the social wage. Recent policies of privatization and fiscal conservatism, however, indicate a major withdrawal by local governments from social welfare provision, although a few progressive governments in the United States (Clavel, 1986), some of the "red" municipalities of Italy and France, and local administrations in the north European welfare states continue to offer housing and services to low-income residents (Pickvance and Preteceille, 1990). In the United Kingdom, withdrawal of the local state from its former redistributional role has been sharpest; Margaret Thatcher's "enterprise state" remains committed to encouraging private-sector activity without the imposition of either planning or linkage policies (Martin, 1986).

While municipalities have become more active and autonomous in their pursuit of growth policies, in the United States and United Kingdom national economic and political forces have restricted their freedom of action when they have tried to improve conditions at the bottom of the social hierarchy. US firms, reacting to the high costs of doing business in cities with substantial welfare and social service budgets, fled to more hospitable locales, effectively punishing those municipalities substituting public benefits for private wages. Simultaneously, the federal government sharply reduced its subsidies for urban social programs. In Britain, central government terminated the metropolitan governments, which it regarded as under-cutting its policies, and severely limited the financing powers of local government, effectively preventing it from taxing its constituents to pay for higher levels of service. Thus, increases in municipal capacity in one arena have been balanced off by restrictions in another.

Ideological Interpretations

Neither the systemic nor the localistic perspective on urban restructuring is neces-sarily connected with a particular ideological interpretation. Rather, ideology is associated with identification of the heroes and villains of the piece. The right attributes economic decline to overpaid and unproductive workers, governmental welfarism, insufficient incentives to entrepreneurship, and political intrusion into the market. While, according to this view, much of the fault lay outside municipal boundaries in national unionism and the welfare state, it also had specifically local roots:

> Current legislation to reduce local government autonomy is only the latest episode [for the Thatcherites] in a recurrent problem [with local political consciousness]. Those political processes leading to "municipal Marxism" in Sheffield or Lambeth can be replaced by "neutral" equations and civil service procedures in Marsham Street [where the Department of the Environment is located]; the Docklands Action Group can be shunted aside and "sensible" development, free of the inefficiencies of local politics, can be undertaken by the Docklands Development Corporation.
>
> (Duncan and Goodwin, 1982, p. 94)

The right's prescription for regeneration therefore requires shifting the role of government from inhibitor of growth to provider of incentives. Its ideological triumphs have been enhanced by the recent introduction of market processes to the eastern socialist economies and the explicit admissions of economic failure by the Eastern Bloc leadership. Whatever the weaknesses of the logic of free markets as the basis for renewal, the right can point to the failures of communism and, in the United States and Great Britain, the economic stagnation that occurred under Democratic and Labour governments. The strength of mixed economies in northern Europe is usually underestimated or ignored in these arguments.

For leftists, urban restructuring has been produced by the greed of corporate capitalists rather than as a necessary response to the heavy hand of the state. Its outcome has been increased wealth for investors, particularly financial and real-estate speculators, and impoverishment of a growing proportion of the population. The stimulus for the process was an initial crisis of profitability caused by inter-national competitive pressure resulting from unmanaged international trade and overproduction. Capital responded by heightening the rate of exploitation of labor. A combination of tactics was used to achieve this end, including union busting, automation, relocation of production sites, and reduction of social welfare programs that competed with the private wage (Harrison and Bluestone, 1988). At the local level, capitalists worked through urban growth coalitions to establish environments favorable to cost-cutting through reduced expenditures on labor, taxes, and physical plant. Nationally and internationally they sought the locales promising the greatest return on investment, whipsawing one against the other.

According to this analysis, the effort to alleviate the situation in which most people are seeing increased insecurity and declining living conditions requires far more than a strategy for growth. Rather, it necessitates finding a formula that will limit capitalist hegemony within both the workplace and the community. No benign assumption can be sustained that, once economic growth is reestablished in a city, wage increases and a growing public fisc will follow. For instance, the recent Boeing Aircraft strike in Seattle, Washington, illustrates the way in which business seeks to exclude labor from the gains of growth. Boeing, which is the largest US exporter and which currently has a huge backlog of orders, was offering a pay raise of only 10 percent over three years, based on the grounds of needing to compete internationally. Its union contended that when the firm was having hard times, it had accepted give-backs; now that the company was enormously profitable, the question was entirely one of the division between wages and profits, not of the need to sacrifice in order to promote competitiveness (Uchitelle, 1989c).

The fiscal effects of economic growth are similarly contested. For example, New York City business leaders, after a decade of economic growth, were pressing for across-the-board tax reductions despite dramatically growing service needs. And, in the face of serious budgetary shortfall, New York State was embarking on the third phase of a multiyear tax-reduction program, which had originally been enacted on the basis of mistaken estimates of revenue expansion. Again, the justification is competitiveness. A report sponsored by the top executives of New York City's leading firms declared:

> The increase in competitive pressures in the financial services industry has made firms more cost conscious than ever before. While cost control has always been important in choosing locations for back offices and data centers, front offices are also increasingly concerned about operating costs... New York City and State impose the highest tax burden in the nation. Reducing this burden is the most important step that the city and state can take to reduce the cost of doing business in New York City, and thereby retain and promote financial services job growth in New York City.
>
> (New York City Partnership, 1989, p. 23)

The triumph of progressive regimes is as important as a successful growth strategy to the well-being of citizens of declining cities. Indeed, economic stagnation may well be preferable to development if the latter is based on ruthless tax and cost reductions. The policies of progressive regimes involve public and/or worker participation in economic decision making, emphasis on indigenous business development, linkage policies, housing subsidies, and a stress on neighborhood over downtown development. For cities to escape from total determination by outside forces, local entrepreneurship, planning, and distributive policies are a necessary condition. The character of the local regime determines whether, and how, these functions are carried out. But, in the old Marxist phrase, "not under conditions of their own making."

Growth and Equity

The flaw of the leftist analysis, with which this chapter is otherwise generally sympathetic, is that it does not offer a formula for growth. So far, the left has not discovered an effective method for stimulating substantial investment in declining areas that differs significantly from the business subsidy approach of the right.

There are four conceivable sources of risk capital for economic regeneration: the private, for-profit sector; the state; employee savings and benefit funds; and the nonprofit sector. To attract private capital to territories not regarded as inherently profitable by capitalist managers, state officials feel compelled to offer incentives with all the likely negative consequences outlined above. State participation in quasi-governmental corporations has saved failing industries and is more amenable to public control of the outcomes than is state subsidy of purely private entities. (AMTRAK, the US passenger railroad corporation which connects a number of old US central cities and whose revival has spun off an important employment and retailing multiplier, is a good example of revitalization through the use of this kind of instrument.) Such corporations, though, when they are profitable and capitalized on a large scale, tend to behave little differently from private firms (Rueschemeyer and Evans, 1985, pp. 57–9) and, when not restricted locationally, will also seek least-cost locations. In contrast, firms run directly by the state will be less profit-oriented and, theoretically at least, susceptible to democratic control. They tend, however, to avoid risks, invest insufficiently, and avoid cost reduction measures.

Employee-owned firms offer the greatest potential for maintaining efficient operations without abandoning geographic locations that have been the site of private disinvestment. Employee takeovers, however, obviously can occur only when a firm is already in existence and must usually confront heavy debt encumbrance. Economic development corporations and economic cooperatives of various sorts have opened new enterprises and prospered in different places ranging from Chicago to Mondragon to Emilio-Romagna (Piore and Sabel, 1984). Except in Italy, however, their total contribution to economic development is tiny, and few locales possess established traditions of this sort of enterprise.

A workable, large-scale strategy based on local economic development corporations or cooperatives needs the formation of new kinds of credit institutions. Eisinger (1988, ch. 10) lists a number of innovative development banking institutions that now exist in the United States to provide loans to small businesses. Although the amount of capital so far expended is very small, Eisinger anticipates long-term cumulative benefits. As presently constituted, however, these loan funds simply do what private banking institutions do at a higher level of risk. Such funds, if constituted on more progressive principles, would issue loans containing assurances that successful firms could not be bought out, then moved or folded up. Alternatively, they could include recapture provisions such that profits from a buy-out would revert to the community.

The left needs to devise its own version of the public–private partnership. This means a reorientation away from manufacturing toward the service sector, recognition of the importance of management and entrepreneurship, and a coming-to-terms with the multinational corporation. The reality that giant multinational corporations dominate economic transactions means that the left must find ways of tapping into their economic power rather than dismissing them on moral grounds. Public–private partnerships under these conditions are inevitable; what needs to be done is ensure that the public component is more controlling and shares more in the proceeds.[8]

Romanticization of the Italian machine shop cooperatively run by worthy artisans will not suffice as a model for development of old inner cities. Public sponsorship of consulting, computer, high-tech, restaurant franchise, nursing home, home health care, and similar enterprises could generate a stable, small business sector to occupy inner-city sites. If such businesses are to thrive, they will involve internal hierarchies with sufficient returns to managers as to induce competent, experienced individuals to assume these roles. They will also have to allow managers discretion in rewarding worker performance. Social equalization, if it is to occur, would come through redistribution within the tax and welfare system rather than the firm. In other words, the left will have to accept serious inequalities in the rewards to labor if it is to stimulate growth.

The task for progressive movements within declining cities is to formulate a strategy that is as creative and less destructive than the *modus operandi* of typical urban growth coalitions. Social democrats need to do what is necessary to foster incentives and reward entrepreneurship. Without a program for growth, except in cities like Santa Monica or Toronto that have to fend off private capital, the left has little chance of achieving political power. Criticisms of the depredations caused by unregulated capital or prescriptions for cooperative industry are insufficient. Most people will accept growing inequality in preference to stagnation or absolute decline in the standard of living.

To speak, however, of the tasks for progressive local forces without noting their national context is to dodge a central issue. Cities are limited in their autonomy not only by general economic forces but also by the national political system of which they form a part. Ideological, institutional, and fiscal factors constrain their ability to operate in political isolation from the rest of the nation. Within the United States and the UK, where conservative forces dominate nationally, local regimes with a different agenda must swim against the ideological current. The trickle-down model dominates the definition of economic improvement in these countries, causing other methods to be automatically suspect. Progressive local forces have difficulty maintaining a broad base of support when the national propaganda attack pictures them as loony or unrealistic. In the continental European states, where planning and social welfare maintain much greater national legitimacy, national regimes are less inclined to glorify the unshackled free market and, therefore, they give localities greater capabilities for managing development.

The extent of local entrepreneurship also depends on the amount of institutional decentralization existing within a nation's urban system. In the United States the federal system and the widespread acceptance of "home rule" have both heightened interurban competition and given cities considerable leeway to determine their own policies (Fainstein and Fainstein, 1989). In contrast, Britain's increasingly centralized system has blocked radical local councils from pursuing their own development and expenditure policies (Lawless, 1987). France, previously the most centralized of

European nations, has gone through a period of decentralization that has made possible more active local efforts to foster growth.

Finally, the availability of funds to local governments and the terms under which they can use them significantly affects their capabilities. Subnational governments in the United States can tap into national financial resources through issuing tax-free industrial revenue bonds, but they have no similar source of funds for job-training and placement programs. There have been sharp reductions in direct federal support of local development and welfare programs, but localities may use their own tax revenues as they please. In contrast, in the UK, local councils, which have also seen major cutbacks in national subventions, are largely prevented from making up for the shortfall locally.

In conclusion, then, we have seen an upsurge in public-sector entrepreneurship and considerable variation in the extent to which local governments have sought to spread the benefits of growth to the whole population. We can propose programs that will increase the public benefits of growth even while encouraging private sector participation in regeneration activities. Without a broad national movement to support such programs, however, we must expect that local initiatives will be blocked by higher levels of government and by footloose capital that will play one locality against another. Entrepreneurship by urban progressive coalitions thus requires that they aim not only at stimulating local investment but also at building a national movement for growth with equity.

NOTES

1 There are two variants of the systemic perspective. The first, exemplified by Noyelle and Stanback's (1983) study of the changing American urban hierarchy, emphasizes impersonal economic forces (increasing size of markets; changes in transport and technology; increased importance of public and nonprofit sector activities; corporate concentration) that produce economic growth and decline in particular locations. The second, most strongly presented in the work of David Harvey (1985), stresses the role of the capital-controlling class in maximizing profits through use of the "spatial fix." For Harvey, uneven development is not an unintended consequence of investment processes; rather capitalists create and use it so as to lower production costs, protect themselves from regulation, increase profitability, and produce speculative gains.

2 This kind of analysis is susceptible to the criticism that it assumes any phenomenon fulfills a necessary function and that any existing institution or activity had to be. One need not, however, engage in a totally deterministic argument to accept that certain social practices do serve the ends of dominant groups and that these practices can be institutionalized so that concerted, conscious activity is not required to perpetuate them. Because some system requirements are fulfilled does not mean that all are, and when they are, the outcome is not an automatic response to need, but can ultimately be traced back to human agency. Moreover, practices may also exist that are dysfunctional for achieving the aims of dominant social interests, and systems produce contradictions as well as functionalities.

3 A pair of articles in *The New York Times* (Uchitelle, 1989a, 1989b) chronicled the globalization of the Stanley Tool Company, an old New England manufacturer of screwdrivers, tape measures, and other common tools. Even though it made a seemingly low-tech, standard product, Stanley needed to be close to its foreign markets:

The ... [tape measure's] popularity at home raises the possibility that Stanley could increase production in New Britain [Connecticut], which turns out 200,000 tape rulers a day for the American market, and simply export the rest from here. But this approach violates principles held by Mr. Ayers [the chief executive officer] and other advocates of global manufacturing.

One is that factories should be close to the customers they serve – to get inside tariff barriers, to give the impression that they are local companies, to reduce delivery time, and to "capture" manufacturing techniques not readily available back home.

Another is that big factories are inefficient. The maximum for Mr. Ayers, and for many others intent on globalizing, is 500 employees, the number at the tape factory here [in France].

Finally, Mr. Ayers does not like to have, as he puts it, all his eggs in one basket. "With one plant, if there is a strike or shutdown you're out of business," he said. "With several, you can switch production to another country or back and forth among countries."

(Uchitelle, 1989a, p. 10)

4 The problem is more acute in America than European cities, because the jurisdictional fragmentation of US metropolitan areas means that even if new functions arise in an area (e.g., Greater Cleveland or Greater Saint Louis), they may be located outside the boundary of the central city and spin off few benefits for its residents.

5 Peterson (1981) argues that growth and redistribution are necessarily antagonistic at the urban level and that the general consensus in favor of growth therefore precludes local redistributional activity, or at any rate should do so. The literature disputing his argument is by now vast, particularly concerning whether growth strategies really are supported by a consensus on values (Fainstein and Fainstein, 1988; Sanders and Stone, 1987).

6 The active agency in promoting growth within metropolitan areas in both the United States and Europe is often an intermediate level of government (states or regional authorities).

7 Quotations are from interviews carried out by the author in 1989.

8 Robert Beauregard (1989) discusses the importance of the state playing a role in requiring preferential hiring agreements for residents when it participates in development. His analysis is restricted to construction hiring, but the principle can be extended to operating firms. Another example of the public capture of benefits from major private investment is the Battery Park City project in New York. Since a public authority maintains ownership of the land, it receives an escalating rental based on profits from the structures constructed. More than $1 billion of this revenue is currently designated for low-income housing construction. This is far greater than the amounts typically allocated under linkage programs.

REFERENCES

Beauregard, R. A. (1989). Local politics and the employment relation: Construction jobs in Philadelphia. In R. A. Beauregard (ed.). *Economic Restructuring and Political Response* (pp. 149–80). Newbury Park, CA: Sage.

Clavel, P. (1986). *The Progressive City*. New Brunswick, NJ: Rutgers University Press.

Duncan, S. S., and Goodwin, M. (1982, January). The local state: Functionalism, autonomy and class relations in Cockburn and Saunders. *Political Geography Quarterly*, 1, 77–96.

Eisinger, P. K. (1988). *The Rise of the Entrepreneurial State*. Madison: University of Wisconsin Press.

Fainstein, S. S., and Fainstein, N. (1988). Technology, the new international division of labor, and location: Continuities and disjunctures. In R. A. Beauregard (ed.). *Economic Restructuring and Political Response* (pp. 17–40). Newbury Park, CA: Sage.

Fainstein, S. S., and Fainstein, N. (1989, September). The ambivalent state: Economic development policy in the U.S. federal system under the Reagan administration. *Urban Affairs Quarterly*, *20*, 41–62.

Feagin, J. R. (1988). *Free Enterprise City*. New Brunswick, NJ: Rutgers University Press.

Foglesong, R. E. (1986). *Planning the Capitalist City*. Princeton: Princeton University Press.

Harrison, B., and Bluestone, B. (1988). *The Great U-turn*. New York: Basic Books.

Harvey, D. (1985). *The Urbanization of Capital*. Baltimore: Johns Hopkins University Press.

Harvey, D. (1989). *The Condition of Postmodernism*. Oxford: Basil Blackwell.

Hoyle, B. (1988). Development dynamics at the port-city interface. In B. S. Hoyle, D. A. Pinder, and M. S. Husain. *Revitalising the Waterfront* (pp. 3–19). London: Belhaven Press.

Lawless, P. (1987). Urban development. In M. Parkinson (ed.). *Reshaping Local Government* (pp. 122–37). New Brunswick, NJ: Transaction Books.

Martin, R. (1986). Thatcherism and Britain's industrial landscape. In R. Martin and B. Rowthorn. *The Geography of De-industrialisation* (pp. 238–90). London: Macmillan.

Mingione, E. (1991). *Fragmented Societies*. Oxford: Basil Blackwell.

New York City Partnership, Financial Services Task Force. (1989). *Meeting the Challenge: Maintaining and Enhancing New York City as the World Financial Capital*. New York: New York City Partnership.

Noyelle, T. J. and Stanback, T. M., Jr. (1983). *The Economic Transformation of American Cities*. Totowa, NJ: Rowman and Allanheld.

Parkinson, M., and Judd, D. (1988). Urban revitalisation in America and the U.K. – the politics of uneven development. In M. Parkinson, B. Foley, and D. Judd. *Regenerating the Cities* (pp. 1–8). Manchester, UK: Manchester University Press.

Peterson, P. (1981). *City limits*. Chicago: University of Chicago Press.

Pickvance, C., and Preteceille, E. (1990). *State and Locality: A Comparative perspective on State Restructuring*. London: Frances Pinter.

Piore, M. J., and Sabel, C. F. (1984). *The Second Industrial Divide*. New York: Basic Books.

Riley, R., and Shurmer-Smith, L. (1988). Global imperatives, local forces and waterfront redevelopment. In B. S. Hoyle, D. A. Pinder, and M. S. Husain. *Revitalising the Waterfront* (pp. 38–51). London: Belhaven Press.

Rueschemeyer, D., and Evans, P. B. (1985). The state and economic transformation: Toward an analysis of the conditions underlying effective intervention. In P. B. Evans, D. Rueschemeyer, and T. Skocpol. *Bringing the State Back in* (pp. 44–77). Cambridge: Cambridge University Press.

Sanders, H. T., and Stone, C. N. (1987, June). Developmental politics reconsidered. *Urban Affairs Quarterley*, *22*, 521–39.

Savitch, H. V. (1988). *Post-industrial Cities*. Princeton: Princeton University Press.

Smith, M. P. (1988). *City, State, and Market*. Oxford: Basil Blackwell.

Squires, G. D. (ed.). (1989). *Unequal Partnerships*. New Brunswick, NJ: Rutgers University Press.

Sternlieb, G. (1986). *Patterns of Development*. New Brunswick, NJ: Rutgers University Center for Urban Policy Research.

Uchitelle, L. (1989a, July 23). The Stanley Works goes global. *The New York Times*, sec. 3.

Uchitelle, L. (1989b, July 24). Only the bosses are American. *The New York Times*, p. D1.

Uchitelle, L. (1989c, October 12). Boeing's fight over bonuses. *The New York Times*.

Part II

Race and Inequality

Introduction

American cities differ from European ones in their relation to their suburban periphery. Whereas European urban centers have remained desirable places to live, many of their American counterparts have suffered from depopulation and impoverishment. Individual preferences for a suburban lifestyle constitute one factor causing the discrepancy between the center and its outskirts in the US; another is the economic advantage that accrues to ownership of a single-family house. In almost every American metropolitan area, however, race has been an additional, powerful causal element in determining spatial patterns. "White flight" and, more recently, an outmigration of middle-class African-Americans has resulted in the ghettoization, relative poverty, and neighborhood homogeneity of the central city. The readings in this part examine aspects of the relationship between the changing global economy, ghettoization processes, and the life chances of people residing within racially homogeneous areas.

According to William Goldsmith (chapter 7), American politicians and the public more broadly have accepted the pattern of uneven development and spatial segregation as an inevitable product of market forces. He further argues that this pattern of uneven development is not only self-perpetuating within the US but is being exported abroad, where it is influencing the development of European metropolises formerly characterized by much greater diversity. In Europe, where economic globalization has fostered increased flows of immigration, growing communities of relatively poor foreigners are becoming excluded from the benefits of the European welfare state. Thus, spatial segregation reinforces initial disadvantage in cities that once were models of integration.

The relationship between spatial isolation and disadvantage formed the basis of William Julius Wilson's extremely influential book, *The Truly Disadvantaged* (1987). Wilson's argument is that conditions of discrimination in the first half of the century had resulted in highly segregated neighborhoods. The relaxation of measures that had forced upwardly mobile elements of the black community to stay within undesirable neighborhoods led to their rapid outmigration. The consequence is neighborhoods of extreme deprivation, singularly lacking in role models and employment opportunities. In the absence of supportive family structures and employment skills, the occupants of ghetto neighborhoods constitute an underclass isolated from the labor market.

In the selection by Lawson and Wilson included as chapter 8, the authors retain the argument concerning spatial isolation but place it in a broader political context. They examine the relationship between poverty and racial and ethnic difference in the US and in the welfare states of Europe. They conclude that, although the situation of the poor in the USA is worse than in Europe, considerable convergence is occurring between the two areas in terms of worsening income inequality and spatial segregation. Finally they argue that, to the extent that levels of deprivation in Europe are lower than in the US, these differences are the consequence of public policy.

Norman Fainstein (chapter 9) contends that Wilson's original thesis resulted in a focus on the characteristics of the underclass that distracted researchers from examining the situation of working- and middle-class blacks. He documents the continuing economic disadvantage of employed African-Americans and relates it to the overall socio-economic structure. In examining the question of the relative importance of class versus race in shaping the situation of African-Americans, he argues that racial discrimination continues to exact a toll even among those who have seemingly escaped its worst ravages.

REFERENCE

Wilson, William Julius. 1987. *The Truly Disadvantaged*. Chicago: University of Chicago Press.

7

From the Metropolis to Globalization: The Dialectics of Race and Urban Form*

William W. Goldsmith

The European city is threatened by change. The danger results in part from a peculiarity of the US city and its spatial form. This chapter is about that spatial form, how it spreads a pernicious influence through social and economic connections, and how those connections work internationally. The chapter focuses on the United States, but it ultimately traces a (global) connection to Europe.[1]

European cities are the envy of the world. They enjoy prosperity and harmony, especially in contrast to cities elsewhere, cities that are so often stressed either by poverty or by ethnic conflict.[2] This urban well-being is in good part a consequence of the ebb and flow of the global economy. Europe for decades has stood in a privileged position, influential throughout the world in economics and politics, and its city centers have profited from the wealth of hinterlands near and far.[3] The shape of these cities is distinctive and congenial and their governance is reasonably competent and compassionate.[4] They have exercised abilities to incorporate new residents and accommodate change, providing transportation, housing, and safety, even for many who elsewhere would be pushed to the margins.[5]

Today, however, the urban prosperity and harmony of Europe are threatened. They are threatened by shifts in the global economy...[6] But the character of European cities is also now threatened by a particular influence originating in a very strange way, as a consequence of the peculiar geographic pattern of the US city.

Usually...we expect global economic forces to impress their influence on the city, not the other way around. That is, we expect the push and pull of market competition and corporate power, ever more sensitive to overseas causes, to bring about industrial change, generate the economics of land use, arrange and rearrange residential neighborhoods, and finally, affect the way people are housed, transported,

* Goldsmith, William W. (2000) "From the Metropolis to Globalization: The Dialectics of Race and Urban Form" from Peter Marcuse and Ronald van Kempen (eds.) *Globalizing Cities: A New Spatial Order*, Blackwell Publishers, Oxford, pp. 37–55.

and served. Indeed, in an earlier study Edward Blakely and I found the global economy to constitute one of the roots of the US urban dilemma, producing in US cities a pair of *Separate Societies* (1992), as our book on the subject is titled.[7]

In contrast, the reasoning below turns the usual argument on its head. We will see that the pattern of urban form itself brings about social and economic change. More particularly, the peculiar physical patterning of the US city partially causes many of the problems the European city is just beginning to experience. Because this is an unusual argument, I offer an outline in this introduction, elaborating and providing evidence in the sections to follow.

In the post-war period until quite recently, it is especially notable that the European city has avoided the racial-caste character of US cities.[8] It has also avoided their poverty and squalor. But now, as we near the end of the twentieth century, the vibrant centers, good transit, adequate housing, and decent social services of Europe's cities are threatened not only by cutbacks, but in some cities also by a new urban geography. As governments and employers cut benefits and protections, workers turn against darker skinned immigrants. Class struggle tends to take on the persona of "race" struggle, allowing governments to ignore further the demands of workers and residents.[9] I contend that these threats to Europe result in good part from a very particular set of American influences – not as direct copies, but through hidden influences. To understand these influences, we must focus attention on the US city and US politics and economics, the main subjects of this chapter. There are six parts to the argument.

First, racial segregation is an essential feature and a leading cause of the bizarre spatial form the US metropolis has taken in this century, especially since World War II. Second, the social separation resulting from this spatial pattern has powerfully and detrimentally affected US politics not just at the municipal level, but also nationally. Third and partly because of these political effects, US leaders and the public have accepted deep social inequalities as though they were God-given, and they have embraced an exaggerated belief in the efficacy and fairness of the market. Fourth, because of the dominant position of the United States in international economics and politics, this market model has been exported worldwide. Fifth, the broad force of this market model itself has combined with the ideology of advertising and the media, and practical influence from American corporations, to put US-like pressure on cities elsewhere. Finally, with the sixth part, we turn fully around the vicious circle: For various reasons connected with the enlargement of the world economy and increased international migration, we find that neighborhood conflict and class struggle in big cities throughout Europe take on more and more the features of "race" and ethnic struggle, including segregation, as has long been the case in the United States.

This chain of reasoning is intrinsically interesting. Its logic suggests fascinating topics for research, challenging ideas, and peculiar historical twists, as well as troublesome questions for theory. Equally important, these issues have practical consequences.

The United States has occupied the dominant position in the world economy over the past 50 years. Racial inequality and discrimination have exerted unique and powerful effects on US politics and economics.[10] One expects *a priori* to find some linkage between the politics that come from racial segregation and global economics. Urban residential segregation lies at the core of racial politics in the United States, so segregation, also, is part of the story. This is where the argument begins.

Background

Students of urban affairs frequently remind us that international trade, exchange rates, flows of funds, and patterns of innovation affect spatial form. In particular, they explain how the dramatic changes in international economic and industrial structure that have transformed commerce and politics in so much of the world in recent decades have also transformed the physical pattern of cities. Although many questions arise about the extent, the form, and especially the time lag for these transformations, it is indisputable that there are such effects. What this chapter argues, however, is that there are also important effects in the other direction. That is, peculiarities of urban spatial form can influence the contours of the global economy. In particular, *patterns of residential racial segregation in US cities have had pernicious effects on cities outside the United States*. These post-war urban geographies in the United States have not simply reflected but have actually contributed to the troublesome "globalization" of the 1980s and 1990s.

Now, some might agree immediately but reluctantly by saying, "well, of course, in social reality all causes and effects are mutual, and influences run in both (or all) directions." "By such bi-directional or multi-directional logic," they might add, "we would expect that the social and economic worlds (of globalization) and the physical worlds (of city geography) would be mutually influential." Nevertheless, they would warn that the effects in the second direction, from city spatial-form to international economy, would necessarily be minimal, even trivial, like a butterfly's flight affecting the wind. Surely, these are good reasons for caution. After all, most urban theorists and researchers are nervous in general about assigning much weight to the social or economic power of the physical form, and properly so. Not so long ago hard-thinking planners and urban scholars found it necessary to reject the popular but simple-minded social physics that suggested we could eradicate urban poverty by tearing down old buildings or destroying old neighborhoods.[11] Nevertheless, however true it may be that slum neighborhoods do not cause poverty, it does not necessarily follow that pervasive distortions in residential patterns have no important social, economic, and political consequences.

Indeed, the argument of this chapter may be open to even broader challenge because it is potentially more inclusive than the old error-laden theory from social physics. An even more extensive view of physical form looks not simply at the social, economic, and political effects of a particular building or project or neighborhood, but also at the effects of the overall pattern of spatial segregation in cities and metropolitan areas. The argument also has a much longer reach, for it claims not just local, or even national, but also international effects. These are indeed very strong claims. Still, although it is difficult to subject these claims to strong statistical testing, the chapter will show that they are well rooted in the historical facts.

Apartheid in America

Racial exclusion and residential segregation are essential, perhaps *the* essential qualities of the US metropolis in the last half of the 20th century. The standard, one almost must say approved, condition for African Americans in US cities is to live in neighborhoods that are racially homogeneous. Numerous surveys have demonstrated that black people do not wish to be segregated any more than do people belonging to any other group; statistics show that income differences explain very little of black segregation. In fact, African Americans are kept to restricted ghettos simply because white people, via numerous mechanisms of prejudice and privilege, do not allow blacks to live or live comfortably in white neighborhoods. It may be difficult for many liberal white Americans to swallow this pill, but the bad taste must be admitted – all evidence points to the primacy of overwhelming and effective racial discrimination in the development of cities and suburbs in the United States.[12]

The first important thing to remember here, because it is so often forgotten when related subjects are brought forth, is that – with the exception of a very small proportion of the black population who live in integrated neighborhoods – to live in highly segregated conditions is simply a fact of life. Nothing else is expected. For many Americans, nothing else can be imagined. The second thing to keep in mind is this – *no other group in US history has been similarly segregated* except American Indians, who have been segregated formally, by law, on reservations. Various white ethnic and immigrant groups have bunched together in neighborhoods, sometimes unwillingly and under oppressive circumstances, but their degrees of separation from others were relatively minor. Even Asians and Hispanic populations, among whom recent immigrants today *are* vigorously segregated, are by all measures segregated much less than African Americans.[13] Waters (1990) deconstructs the popular but undocumented argument that ethnic-Americans had it as bad as African Americans. She shows how such claims are based on false histories invented by ethnics as racist defenses against affirmative action.

Segregation, Politics, and the State

The racially segregated nature of the city in the United States has poisoned American politics. Extensive and intense isolation of one group from another can distort, damage and ultimately poison any chance for coalition and cooperation. As Lubiano (1997) says in her introduction to *The House that Race Built*:

> The idea of race and the operation of racism are ... the means by which a state and a political economy largely inimical to most of the US citizenry achieve the consent of the governed. They act as a distorting prism that allows that citizenry to imagine itself functioning as a moral and just people while ignoring the widespread devastation directed at black Americans particularly, but at a much larger number of people generally.

More specifically, as Susan J. Smith (1993) writes of Britain, "the process of residential differentiation and, crucially, the imagery of 'racial segregation,' have played key roles in the social reproduction of 'race' categories and in sustaining material inequalities between 'black' and 'white'" (p. 128).

In *The Uses of Disorder: Personal Identity and City Life* (1970), Richard Sennett argues from the perspective of social psychology to show that isolation of people in separated neighborhoods and suburbs can lead not just to lack of sympathy, but to misinformation and misunderstanding. When groups learn about one another only by means of distant, indirect, vicarious experience – through what they read or hear, or much worse, through what they see on television – they have shallow understanding, based only on superficialities. Living in separate neighborhoods, they are unable to learn to develop, to be tolerant, to work things through, to compromise. As Manuel Castells (1994, p. 22) says, "the exclusion of the other is not separable from the suppression of civil liberties and a mobilization against alien cultures."

Current racial segregation causes white suburban residents to be not just ignorant of but actually afraid of the city. They see it quite literally as a case of the "other," the alien, the hostile and the dangerous. In the social climate of the 1990s and amidst the growing number of gated communities, it is worth recalling that suburbanites' antipathy toward city people and their neighborhoods long predates the drug violence that today suffocates so many people with fear, inner-city residents included.[14]

Today, influential politicians and business leaders are almost exclusively drawn from among the suburban population.[15] Sennett (1970) refers to what he calls a permanent state of adolescence among these white suburbanites. He can be taken to mean that the leaders of the United States have never quite grown up – that their discomfort and inability to experience diversity, work through conflict, and arrange for compromise doom them, and their adversaries, to a permanent, psychological underdevelopment. Without much stretch in logic, we can see that these shortcomings might doom the rest of us to unrepresentative government. This may not be a bad explanation for the current state of national affairs, for such "conservative" absurdities as large and growing budgets for prisons but parsimony for public schools.[16]

Research on municipal and metropolitan governmental affairs demonstrates in detail how segregation has poisoned politics, and numerous studies document the rarity in US cities of cooperation across racial lines. Coalitions between blacks and whites are not simply rare, but they depend, argues Sonenshein (1993), on convergent political ideologies and willing leadership (particularly among whites) rather than simply on shared material interests. "Racial attitudes structure political choices. A racial conservative is highly unlikely to join a biracial coalition, especially if one of the coalition's explicit goals is African American political incorporation. Shifting interests are unlikely to shake that basic view of the world" (p. 56).

Most white Americans are highly conservative when it comes to racial matters. They have grown up in isolation, separated from others, and have developed their attitudes and behaviors toward African Americans in the absence of rich and productive interaction. They are nurtured on simplified myths of difference, danger and hostility.[17]

Damaging prejudices exist as well inside (Western) European countries, and they cross European borders. One does not expect instant sympathy among the English regarding some problem afflicting Germans or French or Italians, or vice versa, for the groups live in separate territories, grow up with separate cultures, and learn myths about the strange habits of foreigners. They develop knee-jerk animosities that are little based on fact and greatly influenced by prejudice. These are conservative prejudices, not easily amenable to change, not leaning toward tolerance. The difference in Europe is that most of these prejudices, damaging as they may be, have historically operated across borders, bounded by lines of national sovereignty, so they have had small immediate effect on the progress of national social legislation.[18]

To explain the special and unusual cases in which American cross-race politics *has* worked even to a limited extent, we must turn to situations in which blacks and whites *live nearby* one another. In Los Angeles in the 1960s, African Americans with relatively high incomes and extensive schooling lived in the predominantly white Tenth District, from which Tom Bradley, later to become the city's (first black) mayor, was elected to the City Council. In the Tenth, white political reformers and black entrants to the middle class formed a biracial alliance. The district was "a bridge between two worlds." "Black and white liberal activists worked together day by day, developing an understanding of each other's abilities and personalities." A key white activist remembers that blacks and whites who lived and worked together avoided "misunderstandings and serious disagreements and collisions... [thus avoiding] errors that other political campaigns may make just because they don't... have the people who know the differences among people" (Sonenshein, 1993, pp. 55–6).

After the South Central rebellion of 1992, and the election of a white, conservative mayor, presumably no one would argue that Los Angeles reflects deep racial harmony and cooperation. And no one can claim that Los Angeles is *not* highly segregated, given the powerful statistical evidence of racial segregation and the dismaying histories of white conspiracies to erect and maintain barriers against integration in Los Angeles.[19] The point is that political collaboration, the little there was, resulted only as a result of the daily interaction of black and white residents, who shared their lives in a *relatively* unsegregated district.

Moving from the municipal and metropolitan to the national level, it would be difficult to dispute the central influence that "race" has always had on American politics. As Michael Goldfield (1990) argues, white supremacy was essential to the development of American capitalism. Southern planters used slavery, crop liens and debt bondage in share cropping. Northern industrialists kept wages down with cheap cotton, racial strike breaking, and ethnic hierarchies. With minor exceptions – in the early Populist movement, organizing by the Knights of Labor in the 1880s and 1890s, the IWW in the first two decades of the present century, and the Communist Party in the 1930s – labor unions and labor-based political parties in the United States generally excluded blacks and ethnics. Although one expects to find the most liberal attitudes among prominent reformers, in fact there is considerable evidence that even the New Deal welfare state was racially biased. Lest these words be regarded as notes on ancient history, recall that not until 1967 did the Supreme Court rule against the numerous state laws then still prohibiting interracial marriages.[20]

To sum up: The general failures at building cross-racial coalitions in cities played and still play a major role in reinforcing the racism that exists at the deep core of US national politics. Big-city racial hostilities were developed and then sustained more and more by residential segregation as the nation urbanized throughout the 20th century. These hostilities have affected the formation of social movements, the selection of candidates, the conduct of elections, and the design and implementation of policies of all kinds.[21]

All Roads Lead to the Market

This racial tilt of US politics has led to many difficulties. It has long led to reinforcement of the traditional American reliance on "free" markets, rather than on cooperation, planning and the regulation of markets.[22] Most recently this tilt has predisposed American leaders to develop a preposterously exaggerated enthusiasm for market deregulation.[23] In the absence of strict regulation, markets (as opposed to planning, public intervention, legislation, and redistribution) generate high degrees of inequality of income. (This tendency of markets to reward some players handsomely but others barely is recognized by economists of all political colors.) Each person's or family's well-being is based almost entirely on the ability-to-pay, derived mainly from market-earned incomes, from either paid employment or, in a few fortunate cases, inheritance.[24] In the United States, these inequalities are tolerated more than elsewhere in good part because they conform so closely to racial hierarchies.[25] The truncated nature of political discussion finds people of color kept at bay and their interests denied, thus limiting serious consideration of the various alternatives to markets and preventing their adoption. Without intervention from outside the market, this alignment of poverty and political weakness is self-reinforcing in a grim, downward spiral. Not only do people of color suffer the consequences, but so do all others who slip into market failure.

Over the past century and a half, the experience outside the United States is quite different. Most industrialized countries have responded to pressures from workers and their families by establishing rather broad guarantees of economic equality. The wealthy nations of Western Europe and Canada administer national health care programs and guarantee vacations typically four to six weeks per year in addition to eight or ten national holidays and generous sick leave. They also provide housing subsidies (or "social" housing) to large proportions of their residents and support comprehensive systems of public transit inside cities and among them.[26] American capitalists alone have successfully resisted pressures for broad social guarantees, so that poor Americans must cope with the inadequacies of the bottom of the market in private health care and housing and most Americans must suffer from short vacations and poor public transportation. Why?

Some explanations for US exceptionalism are well known. Most commonly it is argued that the frontier was an escape for oppressed workers, providing them an alternative to the need for working class organizations. Furthermore, the frontier served as an alternative to the city, giving workers a means of sustaining high private wages, thus negating the need for social supports.[27] However true these arguments may be, and there is ample room for dispute, the racial factor is central to any theory of difference for America: White workers have organized less successfully for social benefits. Instead, they have been able to shift much of the burden of inequality and poverty to people of color. The politics of whites have been truncated as well because they have *believed* they could shift the burden to blacks and also because whites derive status and pleasure directly from the experience of racial dominance itself.[28] This psychological and practical ability to shift the burden has been generated, reinforced, and protected by the ignorance bred of isolation and segregation.

If whites and blacks had lived together in the same neighborhoods, segmented mainly and less drastically by income as is true of whites, then history might have been different, and that would negate the entire argument. Then whites might have observed more directly individuals' differential successes and failures with the economy, and they or their acquaintances would personally have suffered more of the consequences. Instead, in real history, whites observed failure at a safe distance, which made it easy to excuse the society and blame the victims.

The Washington Consensus

The anti-social character of US politics has begun to spread to other countries. Indeed, many have remarked on the worldwide marketing of the US model of individualism, deregulation, free trade, and privatization that threatens to cut into the guarantees of social democracy nearly everywhere. This has come to be called the Washington Consensus.[29] The most obvious routes for this free-market influence run directly and legally from Wall Street to the US Treasury, then to the World Bank and the International Monetary Fund (IMF), then to the rest of the world. These Washington-based and US-dominated "multilateral institutions" operate prodigious and technically proficient propaganda campaigns to assure the ascendancy of the market approach to economic management and political life.[30]

The World Bank and IMF derive most of their power as bankers who can withhold funds, their own and those of other lenders. They influence domestic policies through their insistence on "structural adjustment" and similar austerity programs not only in the Third World but in many rich industrial countries.[31] The World Bank and the IMF insist as a condition for life-sustaining loans that countries "get the prices right" by allowing supply and demand to operate unchallenged by government intervention. This often plays into the hands of monopoly or other unfair foreign competition and regularly promotes the worsening of income distributions. The World Bank and the IMF push countries to reduce public services and to charge more for them. And they push relentlessly for countries to privatize everywhere that it is possible.[32]

It would be a mistake to attribute the worldwide diffusion of pro-market hysteria to an organized conspiracy. Rather, the sweeping service cutbacks and planetary market enthusiasm find a welcoming climate because of the prior and general spread of US-based corporate attitudes, preferences, management styles, and activities, and because of the need to successfully compete against firms not regulated elsewhere.[33] These patterns of universal corporate behavior exist in good part as a result of expectations developed domestically, on the unregulated US scene. Because of their experience in the United States, corporations insist that their "markets" everywhere be "unregulated" and that the rules that protect their competitive domination be assured, not just at home but abroad. In fact, accompanying the Washington Consensus on economic management, we find another US ideological export, rhetoric on the value of democracy, putatively running 180 degrees in the opposite direction, but in fact often reinforcing the pro-market rules to the detriment of real democracy.[34]

The Global Escape to the Suburbs

My chain of reasoning began with American apartheid, which has led to truncated politics in the United States. Those damaged politics led to worship of the market, which has led to market-based political systems worldwide. The final link can now be forged: The dynamism of worldwide market deregulation leads to new pressures on the European metropolis. If Western Europe is, in the words of Manuel Castells (1994, p. 22), a "fragile island of prosperity, peace, democracy, culture, science, welfare and civil rights," then its cities are now threatened with social stratification, with exaggerated segregation by incomes, and especially by ethnic and racial segregation. Increased social stratification, in turn, fuels costly new suburban sprawl. There are, of course, many variants of pressures tending in the same direction. The syndrome begins to display some of the internal dynamics of the US metropolitan model, with national variations, as in the impoverished immigrant peripheries of Paris, Lyon and Marseilles.[35] But how do pressures descend from world markets to the European city?

To take the most obvious instance first, there is the celebrated influence of Hollywood and of US television programming, including much of the news. Either because they show better entertainment, or more likely because they are better funded, the American movie and television industries are dominant worldwide, issuing direct messages, indirect messages, and advertising. They spread not only the false, pastoral, romantic image of the suburb, but lately also the equally false, demonic, barbarian image of the city. Aside from the divisive and distorted racial imagery in these false pictures, there is also the transfer of preferences for high material consumption. How much social and psychological damage this misleading information causes is difficult to say with precision. But the overall effect is very likely to be negative in its nurturing of hostile racial stereotypes, its denigration of the inner city, and its celebration of the suburb.[36]

How do these damages connect with market deregulation? They connect directly, as we can observe when other governments object to the spread of these images. For example, when political bodies decide they want to interfere with markets – as when the French government tries to keep out Hollywood movies – they are beaten back by a panoply of structures erected to protect unrestricted competition. These structures include free-trade agreements, such as the North American Free Trade Agreement (NAFTA), the General Agreement on Tariffs and Trade (GATT), the new World Trade Organization, and compensatory award clauses in commerical treaties, etc.[37] Such damages connect indirectly, as deregulation stimulates international economic transfers. These transfers in turn stimulate sales of movies and TV shows and lead (through normal market operations) to dominance by the stronger and more developed (US) competitors.

There are less noticed influences from the internationalizing of affairs through the expansion of market-based rules. As markets expand to encompass more of social life, nonmarket welfare guarantees such as national health care or broad housing subsidies are reduced. These reductions began in Western Europe in the 1980s largely as a result of the pressures felt as a result of diminished restrictions against overseas competitors.[38] After nonmarket guarantees and subsidies are reduced, then social inequalities increase. Take the case of urban transportation. Under circumstances in which the public sector is shortchanged, funds for public mass transit decline precisely as the need grows. At the same time, incomes rise in those households who can afford to commute in individual automobiles. Pressures to build roads and manage automobile traffic thus explode, just as the capacity to provide mass transit declines, and the vicious cycle so well known in US cities takes hold. Traffic chokes city streets and arterial connectors, suburbs grow, and complaints pile up.[39] Suburbanites strengthen their hand in public affairs, and the pattern of expenditures, subsidies, taxes, and individual preferences for auto mobility smother the collective benefits of transit in cities. These trends are abetted by the actively pursued self-interest of industries that manufacture and maintain autos, construct roads, and refine oil.[40]

As neighborhoods inside the city become identified with particular ethnic groups of (poorer) people, these suburbanizing tendencies reinforce themselves with the pernicious weight of national, ethnic and racial bias. Services decline, public authorities permit lax standards of housing and welfare, commercial interests transfer their loyalties, real estate markets shift, and the relative advantages of suburban relief are compounded. Small businesses decline in poor neighborhoods but expand in areas of wealth; major employers move their offices to follow the skilled population. By the same logic applied in the United States, this segregated spatial form in Western European cities can be expected to degrade politics, further reducing protections for citizens and workers, so that the deleterious cycle will be reinforced.

In the largest European cities, resistance to this model may be pronounced, and in many smaller ones the pressures may be barely felt, the tendencies hardly evident. National budgets for central-city vitality can fight the trend. The French government, for example, throws huge quantities of public funding at Paris, which strengthens a historic pattern that has subsidized the upper middle class in the city and put workers' residences at the periphery, the worst of them by now occupied by immigrants.[41] But as the pressures expand to cut public expenditures, there are likely to be reversions even here – witness the 1995 French decision to scale back drastically its plans for expansion of the Metro system.

Race and Class in the Global City

Just as "globalized" workers in European cities have lost benefits and protections, more of them have become darker skinned, since many are immigrants enabled or forced to move as markets expand.[42] Class struggle has begun to intertwine with racial conflict. These historical developments allow governments to ignore further the demands of (increasingly minority) workers and residents.

Here, of course, it becomes difficult to distinguish any longer between two phenomena – the effects of city form on economic organization, on the one hand, and the effects of the overall economy (and its worldwide extensions) on city form, on the other hand. One can thus see US exceptionalism in a very broad light. The US colonial situation was internal: the southern slave-holding states were like the overseas colonies of Western Europe. As slavery, reconstruction, and Jim Crow were attacked and partially defeated in the Southern colonies, the subject population fled, seeking freedoms, livelihoods, and new opportunities in the North. From that basic structural divide comes the story we have just reviewed, of the pervasive effects of racism and racial politics on the development, including the urban development, of the United States, with all its circular and destructive logic. A parallel phenomenon now involves Europe with its ex-colonial people of color, as physical boundaries of nations fall to the axes of cheap transportation and instant communication, and as both people and goods tend to move with fewer restraints. Globalization and the market economy are indeed colorizing European cities, just as local control over resources and politics shifts in favor of elites and corporations, causing the attendant conflict, resistance, hostility, and violence.

Combined with the techno-economic pressures put on cities by suburbanization and national budgetary shortfalls, there are also the spread of the drug wars, the widespread availability of murderous weaponry, and a more generalized level of violence. To the extent that newly "dangerous classes" are segregated into ghettos either in city centers or on the outskirts, the US city form tends to be reproduced elsewhere.

NOTES

1 An earlier version of this chapter appeared in the *American Behavioral Scientist* of November 1997 (Goldsmith, 1997). Karen Westmont provided excellent and extensive research assistance for the revisions.
2 Castells (1994) correctly points out that all (Western) Europe, not only its cities, is a site of great privileges in today's troubled world.
3 In fact, the European city has profited over a much longer period. Beginning with the early emergence of the city from the Dark Ages, Western European ruling classes took profits from overseas trade and exploited domestic workforces to establish splendid private residences, churches, municipal buildings, and urban (later to become thoroughly public) spaces. See Bairoch (1991, 1988) and Braudel (1985).
4 These cities themselves – as physical structures *and* as social spaces – have long served and remain still today as enormously attractive magnets for tourism by the "middle classes" from all other parts of the world. It is a peculiar contradiction that Americans, who so neglect their city centers and so heavily subsidize the outskirts of the metropolis, take so much pleasure in visiting dense European city centers.
5 To take the example of Rome: even in the worst peripheral neighborhoods – the miserably designed Corviale high-rise project is one – residents find frequent and reliable access to city bus lines, some local shopping, schools, and programs for the elderly. The people who live in these places do not suffer the deep sense of isolation and despair that afflict so many of those who live in the worst parts of US cities. For further discussion of the US case, see, e.g. Wilson (1996).
6 These kinds of pressures sprang vividly into view when television newscasts showed refugees from Kosovo in small Italian cities, with public debate balancing local capacity for housing, schooling, and other public services against the emergency needs of the

suffering immigrants. Similar pressures in Sweden force progressive, anti-racist politicians to cope with the tensions involved in the segregation of darker-skinned immigrants
and their unassimilated children. See incidents described in newspaper articles by Allen-
Mills (11/1/1998) and Williams (10/31/1998).

7   *Separate Societies* argues that rapid expansion of the international economy has led to a
rearrangement of industry, resulting in a pattern that has left many city people stranded
without jobs and city governments unable to collect sufficient taxes. New funds are
required to provide the public services needed by the additional unemployed or increasingly poorly paid workforce. These municipal fiscal shortcomings in turn make the city
still less attractive for reinvestors, thus aggravating the cycle. This circular causation of
decline is further reinforced by, and especially reinforces, racial discrimination and
segregation.

8   For an excellent comparison of US and French cities see Wacquant (1993). For (up-to-
date statistical) studies of segregation in cities in Britain, the Netherlands, Belgium,
Sweden, Germany, and Austria, see Van Kempen and Özüekren (1998), *passim.*

9   Some papers in the special issue of *Urban Studies* (1998) on ethnic segregation, edited by
Van Kempen and Özüekren, show that European cities provide much better conditions,
compared to US cities, for minority residents (by "race," ethnicity, or foreign origin)
relative to conditions for native citizens. Still, these papers also suggest considerable
uncertainty about future social policy and urban results. It is difficult to summarize
across very different situations, and (as Van Kempen and Van Weesep point out) statistical indices of segregation are highly sensitive to scale and other factors. Still, a reading
of the entire special issue leads one to a sense of a growing concern with racial bias and
danger to the proper functioning of the city.

10 Only in South Africa and, in some ways, Brazil do conditions parallel the stark ones
produced by the US colorline, but since those two countries are also subject to the
widespread poverty of Third World status, the US case stands alone. See Seidman
(1994), Degler (1971) and Goldsmith (1994).

11 The same environmental determinism was sometimes employed in reverse, as in the case
of the newly planned city of Brasília. There, as throughout the early modern movement,
the planners and designers believed the city's physical form would help usher in more
modern, egalitarian, and democratic social practices, not only in the city itself, but in the
whole country. See Goldsmith (1998), pp. 1207–8) and Holston (1989), *passim.*

12 An enormous literature documents the depth of this segregation and discrimination. The
standard source is now Massey and Denton (1993), which compiles exhaustive evidence
of racial segregation and examines the social forces behind it. Also see Goldsmith (1974),
Farley (1996), Wacquant (1997), and Hanchett (1998). On the notion of "white privilege," see the seminal papers by McIntosh (1988, 1990). For discrimination arising more
from institutional – rather than personal – causes, see Jackson (1985), Federal (1989),
Munnell et al. (1992), Carr and Megbolugbe (1993), Yinger (1995), Baar (1981), and the
South Burlington case (1975, 1983).

13 In addition to the works cited in the previous footnote, see Philpott's *The Slum and The
Ghetto* (1978). Due to the complex social definitions of the "race" of Hispanic people,
US Census categories rarely enable researchers to distinguish between light-skinned and
dark-skinned Hispanics. Special, detailed demographic studies, however, suggest that
light-skinned Hispanics suffer little segregation, after accounting for income, while dark-
skinned Hispanics are victimized much like non-Hispanic blacks. See Massey and Denton (1993, pp. 113–14) Massey and Bitterman (1985), Denton and Massey (1989) and
Massey (1978).

14 Blakely and Snyder (1995) refer to "fortification," Marcuse (1997a, 1997b) refers to
"citadels," and Christopherson (1994) refers to "fortress city," as they document how

thoroughly the better-off people in US cities have isolated and insulated themselves in the 1980s and 1990s.

15   Formal representation of cities in the Congress has declined more quickly than has central city population as a proportion of the national population. While central city population fell only moderately, from 31 percent in the 1970s to 28 percent in the 1990s, the number of representatives in the House from districts with central-city-majority populations fell more, from 103 to only 84. The main change, however, has been decline in rural membership and growth of the suburbs. In spite of advantages from disproportionate seniority, such city membership on the (key) House Banking, Housing, and Urban Affairs Committee fell from 37 percent in 1983–84 to only 24 percent in 1993–94, while suburban membership rose from 21 percent to 54 percent (Wolman and Marckini, 1998). In the US Senate, rural power remains intact. As Stephens (1996) explains, "Because small states are generally less urban, the Senate heavily underrepresents central cities and ethnic minorities and massively overrepresents suburban and rural/small-town residents..." Stephens concludes that the "institutional lock" in the Senate held by 26 states comprising less than 18 percent of the national population appears to cause bias in the distribution of federal grants.

16   Prison budgets have exploded along with prison populations in the United States since 1980. The number of prisoners rose from 320,000 to 992,000 from 1980 to 1994, according to the Justice Policy Institute's 1997 report using data from the US Justice Department as cited in *Jet Magazine* (1997). As noted by Davis (1995), since California's penal system has become the third-largest in the world after China and the United States, its prison–industrial complex threatens to become the dominate political force in the state. According to Skolnick (1995), "most Americans have come to assume that lengthy imprisonment, determinate sentencing, mandatory minimum sentencing, and severe habitual offender laws offer safety along with retribution. Recent statistics from California... demonstrate the shortcomings of this assumption. Despite the 600 percent increase in the state's prison population and the 400 percent rise in its prison budget over the past decade, California's violent crime rate has increased by 40 percent." For the arguments of this paper, note that these huge increases in "crime," prisoners and budgets accompany the disproportionate criminalizing of the African American population, almost entirely for victimless use of drugs or for commerce in drugs. As researchers of various political or ideological stripes find, this terrible domestic consequence of the wrong-headed US-sponsored War on Drugs finds its match in the equally terrible consequences for supplier countries, especially in Central America and South America. See Kohl (1996, pp. 3–4), Farthing (1997) and Sanabria (1997).

17   Note two indirect but telling indications of continuing political pressures to promote privileges of whites. Trent Lott, the majority leader in the 105th and 106th US Senates, seeks and finds support from the openly racist Council of Conservative Citizens (Herbert, 1999). US Supreme Court Chief Justice William Rehnquist, in an incautious document written when he was a law clerk, revealed his support for the open discrimination embodied in the separate-but-equal doctrine of 1896 in *Plessy v. Ferguson* (Rosen, 1999).

18   The domestic case in (Western) Europe is like a double-edged sword. In some cases minority groups are too small and weak to have affected either politics or budgets. In others, working class parties have maintained class solidarity above racial conflict. Unfortunately, in other cases nativist movements offer an ugly challenge. Where inequality as well as prejudice crosses national boundaries, even in the absence of the "race" factor, social damages can be profound.

19   On the astonishing history of deliberate racial discrimination by Los Angeles' early academic and civic leaders, see Davis (1990). Robert Millikan, a founder of both the California Institute of Technology and of the California military-industrial complex,

sought a white-dominated pattern of growth. Millikan was happy that the Los Angeles population was "twice as Anglo-Saxon as that existing in New York, Chicago or any of the great cities of this country" (p. 56).

20 Numerous instruments of public policy prohibited or inhibited non-white residents from moving into white areas. See Goldsmith (1974) and Jackson (1985). Today, although such formal rules against racial integration would be illegal, many barriers still operate against minorities or prevent the mixing of households with different incomes. For example, the universal form of the Federal National Mortgage Association (FNMA) allows appraisers to adjust loan amounts by rating neighborhood for internal "compatibility" and by deciding whether the house is "compatible to [the] neighborhood." See FNMA Form RE-414W (12/89). Federal Reserve Bank statisticians found significant racial discrimination in mortgage lending. Their study [see Munnell et al. (1992), and also Carr and Megbolugbe (1993)] found white families denied mortgages only 11 percent of the time while comparable minority families (including Hispanic) were denied 17 percent of the time. Further raising the barrier to ownership, homes in low-income areas are assessed at higher rates than others (Baar, 1981), thereby raising taxes and offering the inescapable presumption of assessors' biases against non-white neighborhoods. By using "audits" to prove differential treatment of black and Hispanic auditors who were seeking to buy or rent housing, Yinger (1995) found extensive discrimination by brokers and agents in real estate offices. Compared to whites shown houses, minority households were told that nothing is available 5–10 percent of the time, and they were shown fewer units 19–23 percent of the time.

21 I have purposefully cited interpretations and evidence provided by white scholars and writers in this century. African American scholars, from W. E. B. Du Bois (1903) to John Henrik Clarke (1976), to mention only two of the most prominent and well-respected, provide abundant evidence of the pervasive and malicious violence of racism in all aspects of life. Also see Marable (1991).

22 For a thorough discussion of how politicians in the United States use "race" to obscure issues of income or class inequalities, see Silver (1993) especially page 345.

23 Knowing that markets generate inequality and acknowledging the fact are sometimes two very different things. For a discussion of the World Bank's refusal to acknowledge how markets create inequality, see Goldsmith (1977). Recent arguments emphasize the benefits of planning – rather than free markets – even in celebrated instances of "market-led" development. See e.g. Amsden (1997); Singh (1994) and Amsden (1993) on Asia; and Amsden et al. (1994) on Eastern Europe.

24 To some extent, the evidence from Europe post-1980, where deregulation has proceeded apace, especially in Thatcherite Britain, must be counted as the effect of the American experience, not as a parallel development.

25 As Goldsmith and Blakely (1992, p. 54) put it, "African Americans are increasingly isolated from mainstream American jobs, education, culture, and economic life, as are Puerto Ricans, Chicanos, Central Americans, women who manage families alone, and slum dwellers. These groups form the base for the evolution of new patterns of urban poverty."

26 For international comparisons of income distributions, see Atkinson et al. 1995). On European–US differences in public transportation, see Pucher and Lefèvre (1996). On social services, see Anderson (1996). Even compensation of top executives is hugely more skewed in US than in European firms. In 1998, e.g., while top US firms paid an average of $1.1 million, German firms (with higher costs of living) paid $398,000 (*New York Times*, January 17, 1999, Business Section, p. 1).

27 For application of American exceptionalism to current biases in the distribution of services, see Quadagno (1998), Lipset (1996), and Halpern and Morris (1997).

28   Peggy McIntosh (1988, 1990) wrote of "white privilege" to describe the many ways in which whites, compared to blacks, unconsciously enjoy advantages in everyday life as do men versus women, but my argument here goes further to assert that some whites consciously enjoy the advantage itself. Similarly, Massey and Denton (1993, p. 213) argue that whites want an absence of discrimination in principle but not in practice.

29   The term "*Washington Consensus*" suggests for some an overbearing and arrogant imposition of US power (originating more on Wall Street than in Washington, but carried there via the Treasury Department). The term seems to be used without self-consciousness by its self-described promoters. Williamson (1994, pp. 22, 26–8), e.g., who supplies a set of rules for the consensus, writes that the "Chicago boys" economics team that refashioned the Chilean economy under the Pinochet dictatorship, "implemented the Washington Consensus long before the concept was conceived..." (p. 22). Oddly, Washington sometimes accompanies its pressure to expand markets with parallel pressure to expand democracy. See for example, Kohl (1999).

30   The most sustained effort in recent years was the World Bank's to promote the idea that the best, for them the only, route to development for poor countries would employ markets functioning entirely on their own, without public intervention. See, e.g., World Bank (1993) and critiques cited above by Singh, Amsden, and others. Celarier (1998) writes in *Euromoney* magazine of 18 years of a "mantra of free markets." According to the *Institutional Investor*, "Despite their failures (...) this coterie of insiders [Treasury Secretary Robert Rubin, IMF managing director Michael Camdessus, World Bank president James Wolfensohn and Federal Reserve Chairman Alan Greenspan] still believes it is the world's best hope to devise an answer to the mess" (Muehring, 1998, p. 74).

31   Structural Adjustment Programs (SAPs) are the latest versions of international economic strictures dictating austerity in public budgets. In the many countries where the World Bank, the IMF, and local banking/conservative/public authorities have imposed SAPs, the short-run results for the – mostly poor – population has been a tragic shortfall in incomes, social services, and supply of basic goods. For examples, see Stein and Nafzier (1990), Ruderman (1990), Bello et al. (1994), and Beneria and Mendoza (1995). Even the international institutions themselves have acknowledged this problem, subsequently trying to impose SAPs "with a human face." See, e.g., the UNICEF study, Cornia et al. (1987) and more recent World Bank admissions of difficulties with SAPs. Also see Fitch (1977).

32   This sort of austerity program is familiar to students of urban politics and budgets, especially in the United States and Britain. In the 1970s and 1980s, authorities often responded to municipal "fiscal crises" with draconian austerity programs, such as those spawned by the Big MAC (Municipal Assistance Corporation) in New York City. See Shefter (1985, 1992). Of New York City's budget cuts, Jack Newfield (1976) said, "Every day I get a phone call, or a press release or meet someone who tells a small, personal horror story of the budget cuts."

33   A *New York Times* journalist, R. Cohen (1997) refers to the "velvet hegemony" of the US corporate style. For an articulate summary of the effects of free-market economies, see Larudee's (1993) discussion of NAFTA's approximation of a non-regulated economy and its resulting shift of earnings from labor to capital. The gap between European and US corporate compensation to top executives is now shrinking, partly through the effects of mergers, as US corporate style dominates and as individual European-employed executives take the opportunity to escape their national restraints on greed (*New York Times*, January 17, 1999, Business Section, p. 1 ff).

34   Notably, the academic world of the 1990s is having a run on the idea of "democracy," or "democratic theory," involving at its best a politics with transparency, accountability, and participation (see, e.g., Putnam, 1995, and Putnam et al., 1993, and critical

responses by Lemann (1996) and Tarrow (1996)). Too often authorities use superficial coatings of democratic forms to disguise power grabs by powerful economic groups. In an unusually blunt exercise, Crozier et al. (1975) forthrightly argued the counter-case to the Trilateral Commission, that an excess of democracy would threaten market capitalism.

35 See the insightful analysis by Wacquant (1993).

36 See Goldsen's (1978) analysis of the "working over" that American television programming does to its viewers. Recently, Pasquier (1993) has documented that the industrial nature of the Hollywood "salt mine" torpor of doing business is overwhelming the public service ethic of French TV. See related work mentioned below by Dorfman and Mattelart (1975). More generally, Cohen (1997) writes that although the French compete with the United States to offer the world their "universal model" of "Liberty, Equality, Fraternity," still the French ethos in not praising wealth and personal enrichment is a "feeble dike to the global tide." Although there are many excellent works on the biases in the media, Jones (1996) captures perhaps best the ideas of both the racism and the ghettoization of the central city.

37 For an interesting discussion in the context of GATT of cultural protectionism by European governments from the US point of view, see Van Elteren (1996). On the invasion of images and corporate culture, Cohen (1997) writes about the negative reaction of French business to an American-styled high-technology firm in their midst. The effectiveness of the US commercial culture has been documented by – among others – Dorfman and Mattelart (1975).

38 On the damage of free markets, Larudee (1993) explains how NAFTA imitates free-market mechanisms to shift earnings from labor to capital.

39 For a full treatment of the inherently contradictory nature of auto-based urban growth, see Vietorisz et al. (1998). Also see Vasconcellos (1997).

40 For comparisons of US and European transportation and public transport, see Pucher (1995a, 1995b) and Pucher and Lefèvre (1996).

41 The national government pays 40 percent of Paris' budget, thereby allowing lower taxes in Paris itself relative to the ratios of services/tax in surrounding localities. See Greenhouse (1992). In contrast to most US cities, the poor live in the periphery of Paris. See Wacquant (1993).

42 At the end of the 1980s, Sutcliffe (1994) finds that non-natives make up an average of 2.5 percent of Western European populations, with France having more than 6 percent and Spain, Portugal, Ireland and Greece each having less than 1 percent. Sutcliffe comments that governments in Europe – and the US – react with anti-immigration policies, thereby encouraging the expression of racist attitudes.

REFERENCES

Allen-Mills, T. 1998: Disco Survivors accuse Neo-Nazis. *Sunday Times*, 1 November 1998.

Amsden, A. H. 1993: Asia's Industrial Revolution: "Late Industrialization" on the Rim. *Dissent*, 40, 324–32.

Amsden, A. H. 1997: Editorial: Bringing Production Back. *World Development*, 25 (4), 469–80.

Amsden, A. H., Kochanowicz, J. and Taylor, L. 1994: *The Market Meets its Match: Restructuring the Economies of Eastern Europe*. Cambridge (MA): Harvard University Press.

Anderson, F. A. 1996: National Differences in Social Welfare Policies. Paper presented at the Conference of the Status of Women, Copenhagen.

Atkinson, A. B. et al. 1995: *Income Distribution in OECD Countries: Evidence from the Luxembourg Income Study.* Paris: OECD.

Baar, K. K. 1981: Property Tax Assessment Discrimination against Low-income Neighborhoods. *The Urban Lawyer,* 13 (3), 333 ff.

Bairock, P. 1988: *Cities and Economic Development: From the Dawn of History to the Present.* Chicago: University of Chicago Press.

Bairock, P. 1991: The City and Technological Innovation. In P. Higonnet, D. S. Landes and H. Rosovsky (eds.). *Favorites of Fortune: Technology, Growth, and Economic Development since the Industrial Revolution.* Cambridge (MA): Harvard University Press.

Bello, W., Cunningham, S. and Rau, B. 1994: *Dark Victory: The United States, Structural Adjustment, and Global Poverty.* London: Pluto; Oakland, CA: Institute for Food and Development; Amsterdam: Transnational Institute.

Beneria, L. and Mendoza, B. 1995: Structural Adjustment and Social Investment Funds: The Cases of Honduras, Mexico and Nicaragua. *European Journal of Development Research,* June, 53–7.

Blakely, E. J. and Snyder, M. G. 1995: *Fortress America: Gated and Walled Communities in the United States.* Cambridge, MA/ Washington DC: Lincoln Institute of Land Policy/ Brookings Institution Press.

Braudel, F. 1985: *Civilization and Capitalism, 15th–18th Century: Volume 2, The Wheels of Commerce.* New York: Harper and Row.

Carr, J. H. and Megbolugbe, I. F. 1993: *The Federal Reserve Bank of Boston Study on Mortgage Lending Revisited.* Washington, DC: FNMA.

Castells, M. 1994: European Cities, the Informational Society, and the Global Economy. *New Left Review,* 204, 18–34.

Celarier, M. 1998: Too Many Risks, Too Few Rewards. *Euromoney,* 353 ff.

Christopherson, S. M. 1994: Fortress City, Privatized Spaces, Consumer Citizenship. In A. Amin (ed.). *Post-Fordism: A Reader.* Oxford: Blackwell, pp. 409–27.

Clarke, J. H. 1976: *Black–White Alliances: A Historical Perspective.* Chicago: Institute of Positive Education.

Cohen, R. 1997: Liberty, Equality, Anxiety: A Special Report. For France, Sagging Self-Image and Esprit. *The New Yorker,* 2 November 1997.

Cornia, G. A., Jolly, R. and Stewart, F. (eds.). 1987: *Adjustment with a Human Face.* Oxford: Clarendon Press.

Crozier, M., Huntington, S. P. and Watanuki, J. 1975: *The Crisis of Democracy: Report of the Governability of Democracies to the Trilaterial Commission.* New York: New York University Press.

Davis, M. 1990: *City of Quartz: Excavating the Future of Los Angeles.* London/ New York: Verso.

Davis, M. 1995: Hell Factories in the Field. *In the Nation,* 260 (7), 229 ff.

Degler, C. N. 1971: *Neither Black nor White: Slavery and Race Relations in Brazil and the United States.* New York: MacMillan.

Denton, N. A. and Massey, D. S. 1989: Racial Identity among Caribbean Hispanics: The Effect of Double Minority Status on Minority Segregation. *American Sociological Review,* 54, 790–808.

Dorfman, A. and Mattelart, A. 1975: *How to Read Donald Duck: Imperialist Ideology in the Disney Comic.* New York: International General.

Du Bois, W. E. B. 1903/ 1965: *The Souls of Black Folk in Three Negro Classics: Up From Slavery; The Souls of Black Folk; The Autobiography of an Ex-Colored Man.* New York: Avon Books.

Farley, R. 1996: Black–White Residential Segregation: The Views of Myrdal in the 1940s and Trends of the 1980s. In O. Clayton Jr. (ed.). *America Dilemma Revisited: Race Relations in a Changing World*. New York: Russell Sage Foundation, pp. 45–75.

Farthing, L. 1997: Social Impacts Associated with Anti-Drug Law 1008. In M. B. Leons and H. Sanabria (eds.). *Coca/Cocaine, and the Bolivian Reality*. Albany: State University of New York Press, 253–69.

Fitch, R. 1977: Planning New York. In R. E. Alcaly, E. Roger and D. Mermelstein (eds.). *The Fiscal Crisis of American Cities*. New York: Vintage Books.

Goldfield, M. 1990: Class, Race and Politics in the United States. *Research in Political Economy*, 12, 83–117.

Goldsen, R. K. 1978: *The Show and Tell Machine: How Television Works and Works You Over*. New York: Dell Publishing Company.

Goldsmith, W. W. 1974: The Ghetto as a Resource for Black America. *Journal of the American Institute of Planners*, 40, 17–30. Reprinted in Jay Stein (ed.). (1995) *Classic Readings in Planning*. New York: McGraw Hill.

Goldsmith, W. W. 1977: The War on Development. *Monthly Review*, (March), 50–7.

Goldsmith, W. W. 1994: Introduction to the U.S. Edition, São Paulo as a World City: Industry, Misery, and Resistance. In L. Kowarick (ed.). *Social Struggles and the City: The Case of São Paulo*. New York: Monthly Review Press, pp. 13–29.

Goldsmith, W. W. 1997: The Metropolis and Globalization: The Dialectics of Racial Discrimination, Deregulation, and Urban Form. *American Behavioral Scientist*, 41 (3), 299–310.

Goldsmith, W. W. 1998: Fishing Bodies out of the River: Can University Help Troubled Neighborhoods? *Connecticut Law Review*, 30 (4), 1205–46.

Goldsmith, W. W. and Blakely, E. J. 1992: *Separate Societies: Poverty and Inequality in U.S. Cities*. Philadelphia: Temple University Press.

Greenhouse, S. 1992: Why Paris Works. *The New York Times Magazine*, 19 July 1992.

Halpern, R. and Morris, J. (eds.). 1997: *American Exceptionalism? U.S. Working-Class Formation in an International Context*. New York: St. Martin's Press.

Hanchett, T. W. 1998: *Sorting Out the New South City: Race, Class, and Urban Development in Charlotte, 1875–1975*. Chapel Hill: University of North Carolina Press.

Herbert, B. 1999: Mr. Lott's "Big Mistake." *New York Times*, New York, NY, A-31.

Holston, J. 1989: *The Modernist City: An Anthropological Critique of Brasilia*. Chicago: University of Chicago Press.

Jackson, K. T. 1985: *Crabgrass Frontier: The Suburbanization of the United States*. New York: Oxford University Press.

Jet Magazine. (1997), 91 (17) 23. Chicago, IL: Johnson Publications.

Jones, J. 1996: The New Ghetto Aesthetic. In V. T. Berry and C. L. Manning-Miller (eds.). *Mediated Messages and African-American Culture: Contemporary Issues*. Thousands Oaks: Sage, pp. 40–51.

Kohl, B. 1996: Coca/ Cocaine Control Policy in Bolivia. *Colloqui*, 11, 1–7.

Kohl, B. 1999: Market and Government Reform in Bolivia: Global Trends and Local Responses. Ithaca, NY, Cornell University (doctoral thesis).

Larudee, M. 1993: Trade Policy: Who Wins? Who Loses? In G. Epstein, J. Graham and J. Nembhard (eds.). *Creating a New World Economy: Forces of Change & Plans for Action*. Philadelphia: Temple University Press, pp. 47–63.

Lemann, N. 1996: Kicking in Groups (Alleged Decline of America's Communal Culture). *The Atlantic Monthly*, 277 (4), 22 ff.

Lipset, S. M. 1996: *American Exceptionalism: A Double Edged Sword*. New York: W. W. Norton.

Lubiano, W. (ed.). 1997: *The House That Race Built: Black Americans, United States Terrain*. New York: Pantheon.

McIntosh, P. 1988: *White Privilege and Male Privilege: A Personal Account of Coming to See Correspondences Through Work in Women's Studies.* Wellesley: Wellesley College, Center for Research on Women.

McIntosh, P. 1990: White Privilege: Unpacking the Invisible Knapsack. *Independent School,* (Winter), 31–6.

Marable, M. 1991: *The Crisis of Color and Democracy: Essays on Race, Class, and Power.* Monroe, ME: Common Courage Press.

Marcuse, P. 1997a: The Enclave, The Citadel, and The Ghetto: What Has Changed in the Post-Fordist U.S. City. *Urban Affairs Review,* 33 (2); 228–64.

Marcuse, P. 1997b: The Ghetto of Exclusion and the Fortified Enclave; New Patterns in the United States. *American Behavioral Scientist,* 41 (3); 311–26.

Massey, D. S. 1978: Residential Segregation of Spanish Americans in the United States Urbanized Areas. Princeton: University of Princeton (thesis).

Massey, D. S. and Bitterman, B. 1985: Explaining the Paradox of Puerto Rican Segregation. *Social Forces,* 64 (2); 306–31.

Massey, D. S. and Denton N. A. 1993: *American Apartheid: Segregation and the Making of the Underclass.* Cambridge, MA: Harvard University Press.

Muehring, K. 1998: The Fire Next Time. *Institutional Investor,* 32 (9), 74 ff.

Munnell, A. H., Browne, L. E., McEnearney, J. and Tootell, G. M. B. 1992: Mortgage Lending in Boston: Interpreting the HMDA Data. Boston: Federal Reserve Bank of Boston (working paper # 92–7)

New York Times, 17 January 1999. Business Section, P. 1.

Newfield, J. 1976: How the Power Brokers Profit. In R. E. Alcaly and D. Mermelstein (eds.). *The Fiscal Crisis of American Cities.* New York: Random House, pp. 296–314.

Pasquier, D. 1993: The Salt Mines: Television Authors and Scriptwriters. *Sociologue du Travail,* 35 (4); 409–30.

Philpott, T. L. 1978: *The Slum and the Ghetto: Neighborhood Deterioration and Middle Class Reform, Chicago, 1880–1930.* New York: Oxford University Press.

Pucher, J. 1995a: Urban Passenger Transport in the United States and Europe: A Comparative Analysis of Public Policies, Part 1: Travel Behaviour, Urban Development and Automobile Use. *Transport Reviews,* 15 (2); 99–177.

Pucher, J. 1995b: Urban Passenger Transport in the United States and Europe: A Comparative Analysis of Public Policies, Part 2: Public Transport, Overall Comparisons and Recommendations. *Transport Reviews,* 15 (3), 211–27.

Pucher, J. and Lefèvre, C. 1996: *The Urban Transport Crisis in Europe and North America.* London: MacMillan Press.

Putnam, R. D. 1995: Bowling Alone: America's Declining Social Capital. *Journal of Democracy,* 6 (1); 65–78.

Putnam, R. D. et al. 1993: *Making Democracy Work. Civic Traditions in Modern Italy.* Princeton: Princeton University Press.

Quadagno, J. 1998: Social Security Policy and the Entitlement Debate: The New American Exceptionalism. In Y. H. Lo, and M. Schwartz (eds.). *Social Policy and the Conservative Agenda.* Malden: Blackwell.

Rosen, J. 1999: Rehnquist's Choice, Annals of Laws. *The New Yorker,* 11 January 1999.

Ruderman, A. P. 1990: Economic Adjustment and the Future of Health Services in the Third World. *Journal of Public Health Policy,* 11 (4); 481–9.

Sanabria, H. 1997: The Discourse and Practice of Repression and Resistance in the Chapare. In M. B. Leons and H. Sanabria (eds.). *Coca/Cocaine, and the Bolivian Reality.* Albany: State University of New York Press, 169–93.

Seidman, G. W. 1994: *Manufacturing Militance: Worker's Movements in Brazil and South Africa, 1970–1985.* Berkeley: University of California Press.

Sennett, R. 1970: *The Uses of Disorder: Personal Identity and City Life*. New York: Vintage.

Shefter, M. 1985: *Political Crisis, Fiscal Crisis: The Collapse and Revival of New York City*. New York: Basic Books.

Shefter, M. 1992: *Political Crisis, Fiscal Crisis: The Collapse and Revival of New York City*. New York: Columbia University Press.

Silver, H. 1993: National Conceptions of the New Urban Poverty: Social Structural Change in Britain, France and the United States. *International Journal of Urban and Regional Research*, 17 (3); 336–54.

Singh, A. 1994: Openness and the Market Friendly Approach to Development: Learning the Right Lessons from Development Experience. *World Development*, 22 (12); 1811–23.

Skolnick, J. H. 1995: What Not To Do About Crime; The American Society of Criminology's 1994 Presidential Address. *Criminology*, 33 (1), 1–15.

Smith, S. J. 1993: Residential Segregation and the Politics of Racialization. In M. Cross, and M. Keith (eds.). *Racism, The City and the State*. New York: Routledge and Kegan Paul, pp. 128–43.

Sonenshein, R. J. 1993: *Politics in Black and White*. Princeton (NJ): Princeton University Press.

South Burlington County NAACP v Mt. Laurel, 336 A.2d. 713 (1975) and 450 A.2d. 390 (1983).

Stein, H. and Nafzier, E. W. 1990: Structural Adjustment, Human Needs, and the World Bank Agenda. *Journal of Modern African Studies*, 29 (1), 173–89.

Stephens, G. R. 1996: Urban Underrepresentation in the U.S. Senate. *Urban Affairs Review*, 31 (3), 404–18.

Sutcliffe, B. 1994: Migration, Rights, and Illogic. *Index on Censorship*, 23 (3), 27–37.

Tarrow, S. 1996: Making Social Science Work Across Space and Time: A Critical Reflection on Robert Putman's Making Democracy Work. *American Political Science Review*, 90 (2), 389–97.

Van Elteren, M. 1996: GATT and Beyond: World Trade, The Arts and American Popular Culture in Western Europe. *Journal of American Culture*, 19 (3), 59–73.

Van Kempen, R. and Özüekren, A. S. 1998: Ethnic Segregation in Cities: New Forms and Explanations in a Dynamic World. *Urban Studies*, 35 (10), 1631–56.

Vasconcellos, E. 1997: The Making of the Middle-Class City: Transportation Policy in São Paulo. *Environment and Planning A*, 29, 293–310.

Vietorisz, T., Goldsmith, W. W. and Grengs, J. 1998: *Air Quality Urban Form, and Coordinated Urban Policies*. Ithaca: Cornell University, Department of City and Regional Planning (working papers in Planning).

Wacquant, L.J.D. 1993: Urban Outcasts: Stigma and Division in the Black American Ghetto and the French Urban Periphery. *International Journal of Urban and Regional Research*, 17 (3), 366–83.

Wacquant, L. J. D. 1997: Three Pernicious Premises in the Study of the American Ghetto. *International Journal of Urban and Regional Research*, 22 (2), 341–53.

Waters, M. C. 1990: *Ethnic Options: Choosing Identities in America*. Berkeley: University of California Press.

Williams, C. J. 1998: Arson, Racist Attack Feared in Deadly Sweden Disco Fire. *The Buffalo News*, 31 October 1998.

Williamson, J. (ed.). 1994: *The Political Economy of Policy Reform*. Washington DC: Institute for International Economics.

Wilson, W. J. 1996: *When Work Disappears; The New World of Urban Poor*. New York: Alfred Knopf.

Wolman, H. and Marckini, L. 1998: Changes in Central-City Representation and Influence in Congress since the 1960s. *Urban Affairs Review*, 34 (2), 291–312.

World Bank 1993: *The East Asian Miracle: Economic Growth and Public Policy.* New York: Oxford University Press.

Yinger, J. M. 1995: *Closed Doors, Lost Opportunities: The Continuing Costs of Housing Discrimination.* New York: Russell Sage Foundation.

8

Poverty, Social Rights, and the Quality of Citizenship*

Roger Lawson and William Julius Wilson

"New Poverty" in Europe and North America

The period since the late 1970s marks a watershed in poverty, inequality, and social policy on both sides of the Atlantic. With the erosion of the protective systems of social and economic cooperation erected in the earlier postwar era, a growing section of the workforce is now more likely to be exposed to the vagaries of the labor market. Economic insecurity has been accompanied by family breakdown and inferior and uncertain forms of public assistance. For an increasingly vulnerable minority population, the prospects are a life more or less detached from the broader economic and social experiences of mainstream society.

On both continents, a variety of economic, social, and political forces have been producing powerful new configurations of inequality. Described as "the new poverty," these recent forms of inequality reflect changes in the size and composition of economically marginal groups, the crystallization of racial cleavages among them, a downward turn in their life chances, and an increase in their social and political isolation.

In contrast to the period between the 1940s and 1970s, poverty rates have not only been rising in most Western societies, they have grown disproportionately among the younger sections of society and the prime-age workforce. The most significant rises have occurred, as the data from the Luxembourg Income Study (LIS) reveal, among the more vulnerable younger families and their children, particularly among the increasing numbers of lone-parent families.

* Lawson, Roger and William Julius Wilson "Poverty, Social Rights, and the Quality of Citizenship", in McFate, Katherine, Roger Lawson and William Julius Wilson (eds.) (1995) *Poverty Inequality and the Future of Social Policy*, Russell Sage Foundation, 693–714. © 1995 Russell Sage Foundation, New York. Used with permission of the Russell Sage Foundation.

The period since the late 1970s has also seen a hardening of racial cleavages, especially among the more disadvantaged segments of the population. In the United States, deindustrialization, the growing plethora of low-wage and part-time jobs, rising unemployment, and the rolling back of greatly needed social and urban programs have affected all economically marginal groups. But the urban black poor have been particularly devastated, mainly because their plight has been compounded by their spatial concentration in deteriorating inner-city ghettos (Wilson, 1987, 1991). In Western Europe, links between race or minority status and social exclusion and deprivation have also become increasingly evident over the past decade, and they have been compounded by the upsurge of xenophobia and racism since the late 1980s.

What most characterizes the "new poverty" is that it affects the life chances of the poor more acutely than in the recent past. It has involved qualitative changes in the status, social relations, and expectations of the poor and does not just represent new forms of material inequality and deprivation. Terms like *feminization* and *racialization* of poverty and various explanations of poverty, which now center around labor market processes and work relationships, are used to convey or demonstrate these changes. In Europe, especially, efforts to treat poverty in the 1960s focused mainly on providing adequate services and benefits. Today, the new poor are exposed to more grudging, bureaucratic forms of welfare that many would regard as denying them the dignity and status essential to their social citizenship (Vincent, 1991).

In the tougher environment on both sides of the Atlantic, the "moral worth" of the poor (i.e., their willingness to work, sexual arrangements, and honesty) is subjected to more detailed scrutiny in means-tested programs. Recent research in the United Kingdom (Dean and Taylor-Gooby, 1993) has shown how changes in the official orientation to welfare tend to strengthen claimants' inclinations to view the state as adversary and to reduce the likelihood of their cooperation with the authorities. Rather than the creation of a "dependency culture," in the sense propounded by conservative theorists, the research pointed to an emerging "'captivity culture': claimants may be trapped unwillingly into dependency, and policies intended to promote 'independence' may serve in practice to sustain state dependency as a 'manageable' phenomenon." It should come as no surprise that the reactions of many poor people to such trends have been a willingness to "fiddle" the system to some degree and, among some, to turn to an alternative social economy based on illicit or semi-legal activities and earnings.

Furthermore, the social and political isolation of the poor has become more marked in the 1980s and 1990s. In the United States, poverty has become more urban, more concentrated, and more firmly implanted in inner-city neighborhoods in large metropolises, particularly in older industrial cities with immense and highly segregated numbers of black and Hispanic residents. Even the most pessimistic observers of urban life in America during the ghetto riots of the 1960s hardly anticipated the massive breakdown of social institutions in these neighborhoods and the severity of the problems of joblessness, family disruption, teenage pregnancy, failing schools, and crime and drugs that now involve many of those who live in the inner city. These social dislocations derive in part from macro-structural changes in the broader society, most notably from the declining labor market opportunities for the poor (Wilson, 1987).

An important aspect of the urban poor's predicament is the way the dwindling presence of nonpoor families has deprived ghetto neighborhoods of key resources, including structural resources, such as a social buffer to minimize the effects of growing joblessness, and cultural resources, such as conventional role models for neighborhood children. The absence of these resources increases social isolation (as reflected, e.g., in the rapidly decreasing access to job information network systems), which further reinforces already weak labor force attachment. Moreover, a social context that also includes poor schools, a lack of legitimate employment opportunities, and a depletion of other social resources increases the probability of illegal or deviant activities. This weakens attachment to the legitimate labor market even further (Wilson, 1987, 1991).

Europe and the United States provide a sharp contrast on the issue of urban inequality. No European city has experienced the level of concentrated poverty and racial and ethnic segregation typical of American metropolises. Nor does any European city include areas that are as physically isolated, deteriorated, and violence prone as the inner-city ghettos of urban America. As Loïc Wacquant's comparison of La Corneuve in Paris and Woodlawn in Chicago [McFate et al., 1995; See Lawson and Wilson in Acknowledgements on p. xi] suggests, there is, as yet, no real European equivalent of the plight of the American ghetto. Nevertheless, the omens are not always as favorable as they appear in La Corneuve. In France and in other parts of Europe, many inner-city communities and outer-city public housing estates have been cut off from mainstream labor market institutions and informal job networks, creating the vicious cycle of "weak labor force attachment," growing social exclusion, and rising tensions. As in the United States, evidence is now accumulating that once this process gets under way, it has serious consequences for the socialization of the next generation (Ashton and Maguire, 1991).

Although these European communities are more mixed than in the United States, their population is invariably drawn disproportionately from various ethnic minorities. Trends in a number of European countries suggest the beginnings of a social polarization in the cities that has been characteristic of American metropolises, featuring a growing gap in the concentration of social problems between some areas and others.

Moreover, European research has been documenting how poverty, as it becomes more concentrated, multiplies forms of deprivation, and leads to a qualitative and not just material deterioration of conditions. A study of *Poverty and Labour in London*, conducted in the 1980s, notes the growing inequalities between boroughs in social and health conditions, particularly in the "geography of death." It also found

> a lot more evidence of hostile and fearful relationships within local communities than did a corresponding team 17 years ago. The volume of concern about safety on the streets, burglaries and muggings has gained a major grip and affects ordinary people deeply in an increasing number of communities.... This makes poverty worse because it isolates people and stultifies community support and the readiness of others to offer... services to mitigate or compensate for the privations which old people and unemployed people experience.   (Townsend et al., 1987:52)

Given these developments, it should not be surprising that in several quarters and with increasing frequency, European observers have been warning that if present trends continue, in a few years cities in Europe will feature ghettos that resemble those in the United States. However, when such comparisons are made, differences in the social and political organization of American and European cities are rarely taken into account.[1] In American cities, groups can be more easily separated by income, race, and ethnicity because of differences in land use policy, housing policy, the organization of social policy, and federal urban policy. Municipalities in the United States have much greater autonomy than do those in Europe. They have much greater control over population movements and urban developments. Through zoning and other measures ostensibly designed to ensure a community's health, they have the power "to determine what kinds of people can live and what kinds of business activities can be conducted within their borders" (Weir, 1993, p. 18).

A major factor in the movement to create separate political jurisdictions has been the organization of social policy that reflects the greater autonomy of localities in the United States. This is particularly true with respect to education. Given the middle class's long-established norm of enrolling its children in public schools, a strong impetus for groups to separate themselves by income, and/or by race, has been the traditional use of local property taxes to finance education.

Also, federal government policies have contributed to the growth of local fragmentation. On the one hand, the building of numerous federally financed freeways and the creation of federal government programs to subsidize private homeownership in order to meet the postwar housing demands contributed substantially to the growth of suburban communities, including many new political jurisdictions. On the other hand, the federal government "bowed to local opposition to subsidize housing that might promote integration" (Weir, 1993, p. 19). Indeed, opposition from organized community groups to the building of public housing in their neighborhoods and *de facto* federal policy to tolerate extensive segregation against blacks in urban housing markets have led to massive, segregated housing projects that have become ghettos for the minorities and disadvantaged (Sampson and Wilson, 1994). Accordingly, because local acceptance dictated federal housing policies, public housing was overwhelmingly concentrated in the overcrowded and deteriorating inner-city ghettos – the poorest and least socially organized sections of the city and the metropolitan area. In America, public housing represents a federally funded, physically permanent institution for the isolation of families by race and class and, therefore, has contributed to the isolation of many minority residents in inner-city ghettos in recent years.

Finally, since 1980, a fundamental shift in the federal government's support for basic urban programs has contributed to the worsening conditions of the urban ghettos in the United States. Spending on direct aid to cities, including general revenue sharing, urban mass transit, public service jobs and job training, compensatory education, social service block grants, local public works, economic development assistance, and urban development action grants, was sharply cut during the Reagan and Bush administrations. The federal contribution to city budgets declined from 18 percent in 1980 to 6.4 percent in 1990. In addition, the latest economic recession, which began in the Northeast in 1989, sharply reduced urban revenues that the cities themselves generated, thereby creating budget deficits that resulted in further cutbacks in basic services and programs, and increases in local taxes.

Unlike during the Ford and Carter presidencies, in which countercyclical programs, such as emergency public service jobs, emergency public works and countercyclical cash payments were used to fight recessions, there was no antirecession legislation in 1990 and 1991 to combat economic dislocations in urban areas. As Demetrios Caraley (1992) has pointed out, if the antirecession package voted by Congress in 1976 and 1977 had been introduced during the early 1990s, it would have amounted to $17 billion dollars in 1990 dollars.

Caraley (1992) also noted that the combination of the New Federalism, which resulted in sharp cuts in federal aid to local and state governments, and the recession created for many cities, especially the older cities of the East and Midwest, the worst fiscal and service crisis since the Depression. Cities have become increasingly underserviced, and many are on the brink of bankruptcy. Therefore, they have not been in a position to combat effectively three unhealthy social conditions that have emerged or become prominent since 1980:

1   The outbreaks of crack-cocaine addiction and the murders and other violent crimes that have accompanied them
2   The AIDS epidemic and its escalating public health costs
3   The sharp rise in the homeless population not only for individuals but for whole families as well

Although these unhealthy social conditions are present in many neighborhoods throughout the city, the high jobless and socially unstable inner-city ghetto areas are natural breeding grounds for violent crime, drug addiction, AIDS, and homelessness. Life in inner-city ghetto neighborhoods, already imperiled by unprecedented levels of joblessness and social disorganization, has become even more difficult in the face of these new epidemics. Fiscally strapped cities have had to watch in helpless frustration as these problems – the new urban poverty, the decline of social organization of inner-city neighborhoods, the rise of unhealthy social conditions, the reduction of social services – escalated during the 1980s and made the larger city itself seem like a less attractive place in which to live. Accordingly, many urban residents with the economic means have followed the worn-out path from the central city to the suburbs and other areas, thereby shrinking the tax base and further reducing city revenue.

As Margaret Weir (1993) has pointed out, in 1960 the nation's population was evenly divided among cities, suburbs, and rural areas. By 1990, both urban and rural populations had declined, leaving suburbs with nearly half of the nation's population. The urban population dipped to 31 percent by 1990. And as cities lost population, they became poorer and more minority in their racial and ethnic composition, so much so that in the eyes of many in the dominant white population, the minorities symbolize the ugly urban scene left behind. Today, the divide between the suburbs and the city is, in many respects, a racial divide. For example, whereas 68 percent of all the residents in the city of Chicago were minority in 1990, 83 percent of all suburban residents in the Chicago metropolitan area were white. Across the nation, whereas 74 percent of the dominant white population lived in suburban and rural areas, a majority of blacks and Hispanics resided in urban areas in 1990.

These demographic changes are associated with the declining influence of American cities. The shift of the population to suburban areas made it possible to win national elections without a substantial urban vote. Suburbs cast 36 percent of the vote for president in 1968, 48 percent in 1988, and a majority in the 1992 election. The sharp drop in federal support for basic urban programs since 1980 is associated with the declining political influence of cities and the rising influence of electoral coalitions in the suburbs.

These aspects of the American political system (land use policy, housing policy, the organization of social policy, and federal urban policy) contribute to greater racial differences and "make the problems of racially-identified concentrated poverty more extreme and intractable." (Weir, 1993, p. 2). Consider, by comparison, Britain and France, two countries that also have a significant number of citizens who are members of racial minorities and who tend to be concentrated in deteriorated areas.

In Britain, the strong central government has exerted a good deal of control over population movements and urban development. Local authorities have little autonomy in the highly centralized British political system. Until recently the only local source of revenue to which they had access was the property tax levied on businesses and property owners. Thus, unlike in the United States, the quality of local public schools is far less determined by the resources of local governments and, therefore, the association between schooling and residence is not as strong. Because of lack of autonomy and of discretion in financing, competition between local jurisdictions is far less apparent than in the United States.

Furthermore, unlike in the United States, where the federal government subsidized suburban home ownership to satisfy postwar housing demands, the rebuilding of housing stock in Britain occurred mainly through the construction of public housing. "By the end of the 1970s, a third of British households lived in 'council housing.' The very size of the British sector made some level of income mixing inevitable" (Weir, 1993, p. 21). Moreover, council housing in Britain was less concentrated in certain locations. The government's aim to decentralize the urban population resulted in the construction of council housing outside the central city. By the late 1980s, although 43 percent of council housing was located in poorer inner London, 29 percent was located in central London and 23 percent in outer London.

Although the postwar population sorting in Britain did affect racial mixing, the sharp racial concentration so characteristic of cities in the United States did not occur because public housing was not deliberately segregated. With the absence of preexisting ghettos, many public housing units were built in working-class neighborhoods that were not defined racially. Moreover, opportunities for the working class to move to suburban owner-occupied housing were restricted because of limited financing and less favorable tax treatment of mortgages (Weir, 1993).

A somewhat different pattern prevails in France. French cities tend to be more desirable as places to reside, with the more disadvantaged segments of the population concentrated in the suburbs. Overseen by the central planning agency, the public housing program, traditionally populated mainly by the lower middle classes and working classes, has recently opened up to immigrant minorities, and their representation in public housing has gradually increased since 1970.

Fourteen percent of the French population now resides in public housing, and the proportion of immigrants in public housing has reached 30 percent in some estates (Weir, 1993).

Although poor ethnic and racial minorities are often concentrated in suburban high-rise public housing, which leads to problems of physical isolation, French land use and housing policies controlled population movements more and permitted more mixing of people by income, ethnicity, and race than in either Britain or the United States (Weir, 1993).

However, recent population movements and government action in Britain and France that have increased concentrated poverty and racial/ethnic segregation suggest a growing convergence between these countries and the United States. Just as the promotion of home ownership by the United States government in the 1950s increased sharply the suburbanization of the middle class, so, too, has the central government's promotion of home ownership more than a decade later in both France and Britain contributed to the suburbanization of the middle classes there. Moreover, as the barriers to their entry have been removed, the minority poor have become more concentrated in public housing in both countries (Weir, 1993).

These two developments have separated populations along racial and ethnic lines in a manner that resembles historic racial sorting in the United States. And the problems associated with the construction of high-rise public housing have contributed to the growing segregation of the British and French minority populations. "Difficult to maintain, many of the housing blocks quickly became dilapidated, undesirable places to live, propelling those who were able to find housing elsewhere" (Weir, 1993, pp. 24–5).

Nonetheless, for the reasons discussed earlier, it is unlikely that Britain and France will eventually experience the degree of income and racial segregation that characterizes metropolitan areas in the United States. The central government's control over the formation of new political jurisdictions in Britain and France reduces the opportunities and incentives for the spatial separation by race and income. Structural arrangements, such as local control over education and taxation, and political arrangements that enable localities to incorporate and to resist federal government efforts to site public housing are far fewer in the two European countries. Accordingly, the "tipping" phenomena so characteristic of the ghettoization process in American cities is far less likely to develop in France and Britain. When the "tipping" mechanism is triggered, it is much more likely to be restricted to, say, a particular public housing project and can be more easily reversed by government interventions. As Weir, (1993, p. 26) has observed, "In neither country have residents had the same incentives or opportunities to act on their racial antipathies as in the United States."

Finally, in neither Britain nor France has suburbanization been associated with the abandonment of cities as residential areas. In France especially, governments have "continued to treat cities as a national resource to be protected and nurtured" (Weir, 1993, p. 25). These arguments are presented not to suggest that the new poverty in Europe does not represent some fundamental and major change in the system of inequality but rather to indicate that different structural and political arrangements in European countries reduce the likelihood that American-style ghettos will emerge in the near future.

Policy Lessons from the United States

So far we have drawn attention to the emergence of the new poverty on both continents, the various economic, social, and political forces associated with it, and the special problems and challenges it presents. However, the chapters in this volume also raise important questions about variations between countries in the extent to which problems of poverty and inequality are addressed. Foremost among these are questions about the dismal record of the United States. Although poverty and inequality have increased in Europe and in Canada, the most severe consequences of the social and economic dislocations of the past two decades have occurred in the United States. This was already readily apparent in the late 1970s but became more pronounced during the 1980s, when the Reagan administration pursued policies aimed at improving the living standards of the broad middle class and relied on economic growth to trickle down and take care of the problems of the poor.

The comparisons based on the LIS data illustrate the effects of these policies. By the second half of the 1980s, the American poverty rate among the nonelderly population rose to more than double that of most European countries and to almost three times the level in West Germany. Even when the elderly are included, the United States had the highest national poverty rate of all 13 countries represented in the LIS data base (Rainwater, 1991). Even more significant were the changing depth or severity of poverty in the United States and the sharply divergent patterns of poverty concentration between racial minorities and whites.

In recent years, the United States Census Bureau established what might be called "the poorest of the poor" category, that is, those individuals whose annual income falls at least 50 percent below the officially designated poverty line. In 1975, 30 percent of all the poor had incomes below 50 percent of the poverty level; in 1988, 40 percent did so. Among blacks, the increase was much sharper, from 32 percent in 1975 to nearly half (48%) in 1988 (U.S. Bureau of the Census, 1988).

As the comparisons with Europe suggest, these trends can be seen as the outcome of a distinctive response to poverty that has long prevailed in the United States. As Rainwater (1991) has noted, "America's various wars on poverty, unlike those of some continental European countries, have been particularly preoccupied with the situation of the very worst off in society, with the situation of the lower class rather than that of the working class more broadly." This difference has been reflected in the way antipoverty and social policy agendas have been structured. In most European welfare states, the prevailing view for much of the postwar period has been similar to that described by a French official. "A policy for the poor," he suggested, "is a poor policy...the general principle underlying steps to help the most disadvantaged is to ensure that they get the maximum benefit from programs which apply to the population as a whole. Rather than specific measures, the idea is to pay specific attention to groups in difficulty within the context of general measures" (Lion, 1984).

By contrast, most American "welfare" and antipoverty programs, including the Great Society's War on Poverty programs in the 1960s, have emphasized targeting and means testing rather than universalistic social policy. As such, they have been relatively autonomous arrangements for the "poor" that have developed largely in isolation from broader national concerns with employment or indeed from macro-economic interventions more generally. Politically and institutionally they have been sharply differentiated from mainstream social policies, especially social security, health, and housing, for the "stable" working class and middle class. Moreover, the American response to poverty has been typically characterized by a predilection for "programs" rather than "policy" and especially for decentralized and fragmented programs and experiments.

A number of excellent historical studies have shown that the American approach to poverty is part of the peculiar policy legacy of the New Deal (Weir et al., 1988; Katz, 1986, 1989; Patterson, 1981). These studies demonstrate how the development of nationwide social security programs under the New Deal marked an important extension of social citizenship to the "deserving" working class (i.e., workers with good job prospects and the ability to pay regular contributions). These programs were not only backed by a strong federal bureaucracy, they also had a broad base of public support, including support from the middle classes who gained from the improvements in social security entitlements.

However, the New Deal did much less to address the problems facing people with low skills and status, including many blacks migrating out of the rural South, who were prone to bouts of joblessness, low and fluctuating incomes, and poor health. Policy initiatives that would have rebounded to their benefit, such as attempts to establish a firm national commitment to full employment or to a nationwide health care program, were notably unsuccessful in the 1930s and 1940s. As Paul Osterman's chapter notes [McFate et al., 1995; see Lawson and Wilson in Acknowledgments on p. xi], the United States also lacked the combination of laws, union power, and customs used in Europe after 1945 to raise the bottom of the labor market. Instead, under the New Deal system, efforts to combat the real threat of poverty among the weakest sections of society were confined to a number of disjointed, second-tier programs grouped under the rubric of "welfare." With much weaker administrative capacities than social security, the fate of these programs was largely dependent on the altruism of the nonpoor.

The historical analysis shows how the development of second-tier "welfare" programs from the New Deal not only restricted the scope of antipoverty initiatives but also reinforced traditional concerns with the "undeserving poor" and, more importantly, images of the poor and of many black Americans as a class apart in American society. In many important respects, the Great Society programs of the 1960s helped sustain these images.

Although the War on Poverty appeared to herald a new and less divisive era in social policy, its impact on social rights contrasted sharply with the extension of political and civil rights to blacks in the 1960s. The poor gained some notable improvements in welfare benefits, but from policies that did little in practice to integrate the recipients into the economic and social life of mainstream society. On the contrary, issues like unemployment and the growth of female-headed households among the newly urbanized black poor were still treated as distinctive welfare issues to be addressed through "special interest" programs. As one study puts it, "despite a greater willingness to expend resources on the poor...the labor economists and sociologists who became architects of the poverty programs in the 1960s saw efforts to change the behavior of the poor as the most promising route to ending poverty – for poverty was, by definition, not a national economic problem" (Weir et al., 1988, p. 206). Even the more radical measures of the War on Poverty, such as the efforts in the Community Action Programs to secure poor and minority group control of social policy institutions, effectively maintained the separation of poverty policy from broader issues of social solidarity and wider economic and workplace concerns (Klass, 1983).

The events of the past two decades have exposed the real weaknesses of the targeted welfare programs. As Skocpol (1988, p. 309) has argued, "When the political going gets rough for public social policies, as it has in the United States since the 1970s, policies that lack clear political and cultural legitimation as expressions of social compassion and collective solidarity are difficult to either defend or extend against individualist, market-oriented, and anti-statist attacks." Put another way, the most significant welfare state backlash in this period has occurred, not where social spending is highest, but in countries like the United States, where there has been a more marked "us/them" divide in social policy between programs for the broad middle mass in society and programs for the poor. As Korpi (1980) explains, this dualism "in effect splits the working class and tends to generate coalitions between the better off workers and the middle class thus creating a larger constituency for welfare-backlash. In fact, the 'welfare backlash' becomes rational political activity for the majority of citizens."

But the welfare backlash is also activity that has been fueled by the way America's antipoverty efforts have, in the long run, fostered group misunderstanding and isolation and distrust of the poor. A weakening of community support for the poor – or what Alan Ryan (1992) has called "the retreat from caring" – is another of the broader themes associated with the new configurations of poverty. Ryan used the phrase in a commentary on the new "tough love" policies advocated by both Democrats and Republicans in the 1992 US presidential campaign and particularly on the way even Democrats appeared to despair of the poor. The 1992 Democratic party platform took a line that 10 years earlier would have been denounced as "blaming the victim." Why this exasperated mood seemed so widespread was, to Ryan, a puzzle, given the low costs of the social programs that evoked so much hostility. However, he attributed it partly to despair at the apparent intractability of black poverty and, more specifically, to the decline of basic formal and informal institutions in ghetto neighborhoods. This placed severe constraints on welfare services in locating their clients but, more importantly, made it "harder to recruit community organizers who provide grassroots support to go with government assistance."

The problem of who now speaks for the poor is raised in Guy Standing's discussion [McFate et al., 1995; see Lawson and Wilson in Acknowledgements on p.xi] of the dramatic erosion of trade union rights and influence on both sides of the Atlantic. As he argues, unions have sometimes been castigated for representing mainly relatively secure male employees. But, in reality, union membership has often in the past made a substantial difference for the most vulnerable groups in the labor market. His figures for the United States in the late 1980s are worth repeating: "whereas white men gained a wage premium of about 50 cents an hour from union membership, black men gained about $1.61, Hispanic men about $2.18, white women about $0.83, black women $1.23 and Hispanic women $1.53."

The retreat from caring in the United States reflects a more widespread sense of pessimism about the intractability of poverty and the failure of welfare programs than has been evident in Europe. The European comparisons indicate that much of the problem in the United States stems from the limited range of tools available for combating poverty. Without the support of more universal social services or labor market interventions, welfare programs have attempted to do too much, not too little. However, the prevalent mood in America by the 1970s and 1980s offered a very different interpretation. To many middle Americans, the nation's poorest citizens had come to be virtually synonymous with a "welfare class" posing a growing threat to the public peace and to dominant American norms. To be more specific, as a study of social standing in America in the 1970s showed, lower America was seen to be separated into two status subdivisions. At the bottom of the ladder was the welfare class, people who were described in terms of their behavioral and cultural deficiencies by the great majority of those interviewed in the study, and who were seen as being caught up in a "welfare way of life" that undermined initiative and encouraged apathy, alienation, and normlessless. Above them were people who were "lower class but not the lowest": Significantly, they were "accorded their superior standing 'because they are never on welfare' or 'only occasionally' (and 'if on, they're trying to get off')" (Coleman and Rainwater, 1979).

The heavy emphasis on the individual traits of the welfare poor and on the duties or social obligations of welfare recipients is not unique to the general public. This "common wisdom" has been uncritically incorporated into the work of many poverty researchers. Throughout the 1960s and 1970s, the expanding network of poverty researchers in the United States paid considerable attention to the question of individuals' work attitudes and the association between income maintenance programs and the work ethic of the poor. They consistently ignored the effects of basic economic transformations and cyclical processes on the work experiences and prospects of the poor.

However, despite this narrow focus, these very American researchers have consistently uncovered empirical findings that undermine, rather than support, assumptions about the negative effects of welfare receipt on individual initiative and motivation. Yet these assumptions persist among policy makers, and "the paradox of continuing high poverty during a period of general prosperity has contributed to the recently emerging consensus that welfare must be reformed" (Melville and Doble, 1988). Although it is reasonable to argue that policy makers are not aware of a good deal of the empirical research on the effects of welfare, the General Accounting Office (GAO), an investigative arm of Congress, released a study in early 1987 that reported that there was no conclusive evidence for the prevailing beliefs that welfare discourages individuals from working, breaks up two-parent families, or affects the child-bearing rates of unmarried women, even young unmarried women.

The GAO report reached these conclusions after reviewing the results of more than 100 empirical studies on the effects of welfare completed since 1975; analyzing the case files of more than 1,200 families receiving public assistance in four states, and interviewing officials from federal, state, and local government agencies. Nonetheless, despite the report's findings, the growth of social dislocations among the inner-city poor and the continued high rates of poverty have led an increasing number of policy makers to conclude that something should be done about the current welfare system to halt what they perceive to be the breakdown of the norms of citizenship. Indeed, a liberal–conservative consensus on welfare reform has recently emerged that features two themes:

1   The receipt of welfare should be predicated on reciprocal responsibilities whereby society is obligated to provide assistance to welfare applicants who, in turn, are obligated to behave in socially approved ways.
2   Able-bodied adult welfare recipients should be required to prepare themselves for work, to search for employment, and to accept jobs when they are offered. These points of agreement were reflected in the discussions of the welfare reform legislation passed in the United States Congress in 1988.

These two themes are based on the implicit assumption that a sort of mysterious "welfare ethos" exists that encourages public assistance recipients to avoid their obligations as citizens to be educated, to work, to support their families, and to obey the law. In other words, and in keeping with the dominant American belief system, *it is the moral fabric of individuals, not the social and economic structure of society, that is taken to be the root of the problem* (Wacquant and Wilson, 1989).

The poverty tradition in the United States, including the lack of comprehensive programs to promote the social rights of American citizens, is especially problematic for poor inner-city blacks who are also handicapped by problems that originated from the denial of civil, political, and social rights to the previous generations. And their degree of current economic deprivation and social isolation is in part due to the limited nature of institutionalized social rights in the United States (Schmitter-Heisler, 1991). Indeed, the effects of joblessness on all the poor in the United States are far more severe than those experienced by disadvantaged groups in other advanced industrial Western societies. While economic restructuring and its adverse effects on lower-income groups has been common to all these societies in recent years, the most severe consequences of social and economic dislocations have been in the United States because of the underdeveloped welfare state and the weak institutional structure of social citizenship rights. Although all economically marginal groups have been affected, the inner-city black poor have been particularly devastated because their plight has been compounded by their spatial concentration in deteriorating ghetto neighborhoods, neighborhoods that reinforce weak labor force attachment.

In short, the socioeconomic position of the inner-city black poor in American society is extremely precarious. The cumulative effects of historic racial exclusion have made them vulnerable to the economic restructuring of the advanced industrial economy. Moreover, the problems of joblessness, deepening poverty, and other woes that have accompanied these economic changes cannot be relieved by the meager welfare programs targeted to the poor. Furthermore, these problems tend to be viewed by members of the larger society as a reflection of personal deficiencies, not structural inequities.

Accordingly, if any group has a stake in the enhancement of social rights in the United States, it is the inner-city black poor. Unfortunately, given the strength of the American belief system on poverty and welfare, any program that would improve the life chances of this group would have to be based on concerns beyond those that focus on life and experiences in inner-city ghettos. The poor and the working classes struggle to make ends meet, and even the middle class has experienced a decline in its living standard. Indeed, Americans across racial and class boundaries continue to worry about unemployment and job security, declining real wages, escalating medical and housing costs, childcare programs, the sharp decline in the quality of public education, and crime and drug trafficking in their neighborhoods.

These concerns are reflected in public opinion surveys. For the last several years national opinion polls consistently reveal strong public backing for government labor market strategies, including training efforts, to enhance employment. A 1988 Harris poll indicated that almost three-quarters of the respondents would support a tax increase to pay for childcare. A 1989 Harris poll reports that almost 9 out of 10 Americans would like to see fundamental change in the United States' health care system. And recent surveys conducted by the National Opinion Research Center at the University of Chicago reveal that a substantial majority of Americans want more money spent on improving the nation's educational system and on halting rising crime and drug addiction.

These poll results suggest the possibility of new alignments in support of the enhancement of social rights. If a serious attempt is made to forge such an alignment, perhaps it ought to begin with a new public rhetoric that does two things: focuses on problems that afflict not only the poor, but the working and middle classes as well; and emphasizes integrative programs that promote the social and economic improvement of all groups in society, not just the truly disadvantaged segments of the population.

European Responses to Poverty

While the experience of the United States suggests the need for a fundamental shift in policy away from the emphasis on targeted, fragmented, and "isolationist" anti-poverty programs, the various economic crises facing European welfare states over the past two decades provide a sobering reminder of the difficulties now involved in sustaining more universal and integrative social citizenship rights. Europe's postwar commitment to universal programs and social inclusion was premised, as Guy Standing [McFate et al., 1995; see Lawson and Wilson in Acknowledgments on p. xi] emphasizes, on assumptions of steady growth and full employment and, although this occurred in varying degrees in different countries, on improvements in a range of closely interrelated employment and labor market securities. It was also closely – and, many would now argue, too inflexibly – identified with notions of collective solidarity associated with organized "wage labor" and class-based labor movements, and revolving primarily around the risks facing the male "breadwinner." Fundamental to the postwar version of social inclusion were conceptions of citizenship that assumed a fair degree of cultural homogeneity, or at least played down the significance of historic cleavages between Catholics and Protestants or between various ethnic groups.

In the 1990s, by contrast, issues of race, ethnicity, and cultural diversity loom large in all discussions of citizenship in western Europe. The future of the European welfare states depends crucially on the ability of European countries to widen their definitions of citizenship to embrace their new minority and immigrant communities, and prevent the emergence of a racialized underclass, marginalized by the welfare state as well as the economy. However, this itself depends on the capacity and willingness of governments to revitalize "social citizenship" by combating broader marginalizing tendencies in the welfare state that have accompanied the return of mass unemployment and the growing fragmentation of European labor markets.

Since the late 1970s, increasing numbers of indigenous workers as well as immigrants in western Europe have found themselves in the "secondary labor market," with a high risk of unemployment, low skills, poor working conditions, and weak trade union protection. Many are on temporary or part-time contracts, or in the gray areas of employment where employers can evade social or labor rights. At the same time, the growth of long-term unemployment – in 1993 it constituted about half of all Western European unemployment, compared with 10–20 percent in the rest of the industrialized world – has created a substantial group more or less detached from the labor force. It includes many young people unable to enter the employed labor force, as well as those "pushed into long-term unemployment or economic activity through discouragement, illness, alcoholism, disability, drugs or crime, much of which could be linked to experience of unemployment in one way or another" (Standing, 1986, p. 20).

An important, interdisciplinary study of poverty and marginalization in West Germany (Leibfried and Tennstedt, 1985) reveals the effects of growing economic dislocations on social rights. The study shows how during the 1970s and 1980s, those that formed the "productive core" of German society and who could continue to rely on regular, stable employment consolidated their hold on the established social insurance system, the traditional nucleus of the German welfare state. Despite cuts in social insurance provisions, most of the beneficiaries of the system still enjoyed comparatively high standards of social security, health, and welfare and on the whole succeeded in preserving their relative position in the income hierarchy. By contrast, a growing German *lumpenproletariat* – those in more precarious employment or increasingly detached from the labor force – was effectively excluded from many of these provisions and forced to depend for its livelihood on an "alternative welfare state in reserve," mainly localized public welfare and assistance, or on family support, or on illegal forms of "self-help."

The study showed, for example, how prior to the onset of the recession in the 1970s, the idea of applying for local means-tested public assistance was anathema to most German workers, and less than 1 percent of those receiving such assistance were registered as unemployed. By the mid-1980s the proportion had grown to more than 25 percent, with surveys suggesting that more than half of all the unemployed eligible for these benefits were still not applying, mainly because of feelings of shame and the stigma attached to public assistance (Balsen et al., 1984).

This bifurcation of the welfare state remains evident in newly unified Germany in the 1990s. Indeed, it has acquired new dimensions, as growing numbers of East Germans have been forced to depend on public assistance and – a more disturbing trend, if it persists – as Germany's large foreign population appears to have become more ghettoized and more dependent on means-tested welfare in the aftermath of unification. Until the end of the 1970s, foreign workers and their families were much less likely than native Germans to rank among the "official poor" receiving public assistance. Since then, but particularly in the 1990s, the situation has changed markedly. During 1991, almost 15 percent of all foreigners at some stage drew upon public assistance, compared with less than 5 percent of the German population (Statistisches Bundesamt, 1993). Foreigners are also disproportionately affected by the cuts in social benefits in the much heralded "Solidarity Pact" of 1993 aimed at diverting resources to the former GDR. This involves major savings in benefits paid to asylum seekers and refugees and, more generally, in means-tested poverty programs, in which foreign workers and their families tend to be overrepresented (Schneider, 1993).

Similar developments have been evident throughout western Europe, though the form they have taken and their effects have varied from country to country. In the United Kingdom, for example, the Thatcher governments of the 1980s consciously accentuated the "splitting apart" of the welfare state by encouraging the growth of tax-supported private and company-based welfare among the middle classes and more affluent workers. At the same time, major cost-cutting reforms in social security and housing led not only to an increased association of residual care for the poorer sections of society with social security and housing, but also to a toughening of entitlement requirements and reducing of minimum standards for the poor. By the second half of the 1980s, around 8 million people or one in seven of the total British population were living in households dependent on a national means-tested and last-resort income support program. This compared with 4 million people in 1973 and 1.2 million in 1950 (Lawson, 1987). A shift toward more targeted welfare has been a feature of recent French and Dutch policies, although with less pronounced effects than in Britain. In the Dutch case, a period of "self-discipline" in the 1980s involved austerity measures significantly reducing the proportion of national income allocated to social security, more emphasis on individually earned social insurance, and a strategy focusing benefits more on the *echta minima* (the truly needy).

While trends like these point to a growing convergence between western Europe and the United States, it is important not to overstate the case. Despite clear tendencies in social policy in the 1980s that appear to promote group separation rather than social integration, a commitment to universal social services remains firmly institutionalized in most European welfare states. ... much of the difference between Europe and America in the incidence of family and child poverty, particularly among lone-parent families, can be attributed to family policy packages that still receive wide popular support in Europe. In addition to income transfers to all or almost all families with children, family policy packages include a range of measures providing mothers at work, as Sheila Kamerman [McFate et al., 1995; see Lawson and Wilson in Acknowledgments on p. xi] emphasizes, with a "social infrastructure ... far ahead of the United States." Europe's commitment to publicly provided health care is another area where efforts to contain costs and trim programs have had to contend with a deeply entrenched popular preference for universal services, as well as strong support for universalism from health professionals. Although not a direct focus of our inquiries in this volume, differences in health care provision would seem to have a major bearing on the quality of life among the poor.

For the United States, important lessons can be learned from recent European efforts to coordinate economic and social policies, and to adjust social policies and public expectations of welfare to the new economic situation. The new policies emerging in Sweden following the much publicized defeat of the Social Democrats in 1991 are one example that will be interesting to follow. The liberal–conservative coalition that took office has introduced a wide-ranging reform package aimed at stimulating industrial restructuring and more competitiveness and "enterprise" in Swedish society through tax and public expenditure cuts and curbs on the state monopoly in social policy.

However, the Swedish reform package involves a commitment not to dismantling the welfare state but rather to revitalizing it by giving priority to those components seen to be more consistent with the obligations and rights of "active citizenship." Foremost among these components are the labor market programs pioneered in Sweden in the 1950s, programs that subsequently played a key role in one of the most effective strategies in facilitating social participation and eliminating poverty found in Europe. The programs, which have deliberately sought to avoid passive reliance on welfare among the working-age population by using alternative labor market measures, include retraining measures and publicly supported job creation in areas of high unemployment, subsidized travel for job search, paid costs for movement to a new residence, and an active labor market exchange system.

Germany is another country with a tradition of active labor market measures and close links between industries and educational institutions in its "dual" apprenticeship system. Germany sought to foster a "community of skills" and a successful partnership between economic and social policies. This partnership suffered, however, between the mid-1970s and mid-1980s, when cuts and retrenchment in public expenditures were the overriding concern of governments. Between 1982 and 1984, in the early years of Chancellor Kohl's coalition, almost half the cuts in the federal budget were in labor market and unemployment measures, creating what was dubbed "a new labor market policy without the unemployed."

As Bernard Case [McFate et al., 1995; see Lawson and Wilson in Acknowledgments on p.xi] shows, it also became clear in these years that Germany's much admired dual system was failing to integrate many young people into permanent, core employment. Inspired by the problems of restructuring and reskilling the former East German economy, a more determined effort has been made to revamp the provisions of the dual system since 1989. But, as Casey indicates, the situation was already improving prior to unification, partly as a result of a well-directed trade union campaign, but mainly because of successful pressure on government from two national institutes, the Federal Labour Institute and the Federal Training Institute, comprised of employers, union representatives, and government. As in Sweden, powerful, semi-independent bodies overseeing labor market and training programs and setting goals for employers have played a key role in Germany.

Paul Osterman [McFate et al., 1995; see Lawson and Wilson in Acknowledgments on p.xi] shows how other European countries have witnessed an explosion of interest in altering the relationship between schools and the workplace, inspired partly by the German system. In countries like France, the United Kingdom, and the Netherlands, there has been a noticeable reaction against more passive, compensatory social rights for the working-age population, with their connotations of welfare dependence, and a movement to reorient social protection toward forward-looking interventions aimed at improving skills and job opportunities. This reaction includes more acknowledgment than has been given in the past to the potential of workfare and to the obligations, responsibilities, and rights of "social citizenship." But it also reflects a new interest in developing mixed packages of work and welfare in line with what the Organization for Economic Cooperation and Development (OECD) has described as the central role of public social policy in the 1990s: "to design interventions so as to maximize both the numbers of people who have opportunities for active social roles, and the duration of their lives over which they can experience such activity" (OECD, 1988, p. 18).

While these are promising trends, their prospects of revitalizing social rights are by no means secure. So far, as McFate [McFate et al., 1995] emphasizes, many of the new employment and training innovations have been ill-planned and poorly co-ordinated, partly because they have been developed in a period that has emphasized decentralized program delivery. It has become abundantly evident in the deepening recession of the early 1990s that efforts to combat the problems of economic dislocation through employment and training strategies can only be effective as part of broader national programs of economic recovery and adjustment to struc-tural change. With European unemployment rates climbing again in 1993 to around 10 percent of the workforce, many of the new training initiatives now look more like remedial actions serving to delay the onset of unemployment.

While the recession of the 1990s has set back the prospects for more "active" social rights, it has also created situations ripe for the demagogic mobilization of racism and anti-immigrant feelings. As economic conditions in Europe have worsened, generating a widespread urban housing crisis and insecurities in the labor market, many in the majority white population have come to view the growth of minorities and immigrants as a source of the problem. The new inflow of refugees and asylum seekers from eastern and southeastern Europe has further exacerbated this feeling. Although extremist violence in Germany and France has attracted the greatest attention, heightened racial and ethnic antagonisms have been evident in most countries. In the United Kingdom, for example, 7,780 racially motivated attacks were officially reported in 1991; the total had climbed by around 1,000 a year over the previous 3 years (*Economist*, 1992).

The recession has also underlined the particular vulnerability of immigrant and minority communities to economic stagnation, industrial restructuring, and the decline of traditional manufacturing. Immigrant unemployment rates are commonly more than double those of the indigenous workforce, reaching levels ranging from 25 to 50 percent in cities that have experienced unprecedented high levels of unemployment overall. At a time of growing strains on the welfare state, the minority population, thus, has become more dependent on public assistance for survival. Studies of poverty and welfare benefits show that the onus is often put on minorities and immigrants to prove their entitlement in ways that are not required of the majority, while among more recent immigrants rights are even less often secured (Smith, 1989, p. 176; Townsend et al. 1987, p. 56). As the German example discussed earlier indicates, immigrants are often ready and easy targets for government cut-backs, particularly when they lack citizenship and effective political voice. Moreover, many of those most acutely affected by the recession have been the second and third generation of minority youths who "often suffer from educational deficiencies, are unable to find meaningful employment and are culturally and institutionally removed from the societies of their parents. Their isolation, dislocation, and alienation have been increasing" (Schmitter-Heisler, 1991).

However, as Loïc Wacquant [McFate et al., 1995; see Lawson and Wilson in Acknowledgments p.xi] stresses in his comparisons of urban deprivation in Paris and Chicago, we ought not to exaggerate the salience of race in European countries. The new social tensions in Europe may be manifested in xenophobia and racial enmity, but they stem primarily from the deteriorting economic and social conditions and declining organizational resources in poorer working-class neighborhoods that afflict the native populations and immigrants alike and that create situations that enhance racial antagonisms. Accordingly, if Europe is to avoid the levels of poisonous racial flareups and antagonisms that have plagued America, it will be important to generate public recognition and appreciation of the impact of these changes on the lives of the poor, including the minority poor, and on intergroup relations.

Conclusion

In this chapter we have argued that a new poverty has emerged on both sides of the Atlantic represented by changes in the size and composition of disadvantaged groups, the hardening of racial cleavages among them, an increase in their social and political isolation, and a worsening of their life chances. Although aspects of the new poverty are more severe in America than in Europe, recent trends in a number of European countries suggest a growing convergence of income and racial segregation between the two continents. However, as we have attempted to show, different structural and political arrangements in European countries reduce the likelihood of the emergence of American-style ghettos in the near future.

Moreover, there are still notable differences between the United States and Europe in the extent to which problems of poverty and inequality are addressed. In contrast to many European nations, the United States has not created comprehensive programs to promote the social rights of American citizens. Antipoverty programs have been largely targeted and fragmented. Instead of helping to integrate the poor into the broader economic and social life of mainstream society, they tend to stigmatize and separate them (Schmitter-Heisler, 1991).

However, recent economic crises in Europe have made it difficult to sustain programs that embody universal and integrative social citizenship rights. With the growth of mass unemployment and the growing fragmentation of European labor markets, pressures to cut back on welfare state benefits have mounted. Moreover, the increase of racial and ethnic diversity has led some to reexamine the postwar commitment to universal programs and social inclusion, a commitment originally based on conceptions of citizenship that assumed a fair degree of cultural homogeneity. Recent challenges to this commitment often reflect racial bias. As economic conditions have worsened, many in the majority white population view the growth of minorities as part of the problem. Stagnant economies and slack labor markets have placed strains on the welfare state at the very time when the immigrant population, facing mounting problems of joblessness, has become more dependent on public assistance for survival.

Nonetheless, although the conditions for the expressions of racial antagonisms have increased, as pointed out earlier, because of differences in political organization, Europeans do not have the same opportunities as Americans to act on their racial antipathies. Moreover, official and scholarly explanations of the new poverty in Europe tend to focus much more on the changes and inequities in the broader society than on individual deficiencies and behavior and, therefore, lend much greater support to the ideology of social citizenship rights. Furthermore, welfare programs that benefit wide segments of the population, including the poor and minorities, such as childcare, child allowances, housing subsidies, education, and medical care, have been firmly institutionalized in many Western European democracies. Efforts to cut back on these programs in the face of growing joblessness have met firm resistance.

However, changes in Europe are occurring very rapidly. The extent to which the multiracial and multiethnic countries there will approach the United States in the levels of racial and income segregation, belief systems on poverty and welfare, and commitment to social rights is a question that cross-cultural researchers will pursue with considerable interest.

NOTE

1   In the following discussion in this section, we are indebted to the stimulating work of Margaret Weir (1993) and Demetrios Caraley (1992). Parts of this discussion are also based on Wilson (1995).

REFERENCES

Ashton, D., and Maguire, M. 1991. "Patterns and Experiences of Unemployment." In *Poor Work: Disadvantage and the Division of Labour*, edited by P. Brown and R. Scase, 40–55. Milton Keynes and Philadelphia: Open University Press.

Balsen, W. et al. 1984. *Die Neue Armut*, Cologne: Bund Verlag.

Caraley, D. 1992. "Washington Abandons the Cities." *Political Science Quarterly* 107: 1–27.

Coleman, R., and Rainwater, L. 1979. *Social Standing in America*. London: Routledge & Kegan Paul.

Dean, H., and Taylor-Gooby, P. 1993. *Dependency Culture: The Explosion of a Myth*. New York and London: Harvester Wheatsheaf.

Economist. 1992. "All Quiet on the Racial Front?" 325 (7788), 5–11 December, London.

Katz, M. 1986. *In the Shadow of the Poorhouse: A Social History of Welfare in the United States*. New York: Basic Books.

Katz, M. 1989. *The Undeserving Poor: From the War on Poverty to the War on Welfare*. New York: Pantheon.

Klass, G. 1983. "Explaining America and the Welfare State: An Alternative Theory." *British Journal of Political Science* 15: 427–50.

Korpi, W. 1980. "Social Policy and Distributional Conflict in the Capitalist Democracies." *West European Politics* 3(1).

Lawson, R. 1987. "Social Security and the Division of Welfare." In *Inside British Society: Continuity, Challenge and Change*, edited by G. Causer, 77–97. New York: St. Martin's Press.

Leibfried, S., and Tennstedt, F. (eds.). 1985. *Politik der Armut und die Spaltung des Sozialstaats*. Frankfurt am Main: Suhrkamp.

Lion, A. 1984. "An Anti-Poverty Policy or a Social Development Policy? A French Point of View." In *Anti-Poverty Policy in the European Community*, edited by J. Brown, 100–12. London: Policy Studies Institute.

Melville, K., and Doble, J. 1988. "The Public's Perspective on Social Welfare Reform." The Public Agenda Foundation, January.

OECD. 1988. *The Future of Social Protection: The General Debate*. Paris: Organisation for Economic Co-operation and Development.

Patterson, J. 1981. *America's Struggle Against Poverty*. Cambridge, MA: Harvard University Press.

Rainwater, L. 1991. "Poverty in American Eyes." Luxembourg Income Study, CEPS/INSTEAD, mimeo.

Ryan, A. 1992. "The Retreat from Caring." *The Times*, London, August 12.

Sampson, R., and Wilson, W. J. 1994. "Toward a Theory of Race, Crime, and Urban Inequality." In J. Hagan and R. Peterson, *Crime and Inequality*. Stanford: Stanford University Press.

Schmitter-Heisler, B. 1991. "A Comparative Perspective on the Underclass." *Theory and Society* 20: 455–83.

Schneider, U. 1993. *Solidarpakt gegen die Schwachen: Der Rückzug des Staates aus der Sozial politik*. München: Knaur.

Skocpol, T. 1988. "The Limits of the New Deal System and the Roots of Contemporary Welfare Dilemmas." In *The Politics of Social Policy in the United States*, edited by M. Weir, S. Orloff, and T. Skocpol, 293–312. Princeton, NJ: Princeton University Press.

Smith, S. 1989. *The Politics of "Race" and Residence*. London: Polity Press.

Standing, G. 1986. *Unemployment and Labour Market Flexibility: The United Kingdom*. Geneva: International Labour Office.

Statistisches Bundesamt. 1993. *Sozialhilfe*. Wiesbaden: Statistisches Bundesamt.

Townsend, P., et al. 1987. *Poverty and Labour in London*. London: Low Pay Unit.

US Bureau of the Census 1988. "Money Income and Poverty Status in the U.S." In *Current Population Reports*, Series P-60. Washington, DC: Government Printing Office.

Vincent, D. 1991. *Poor Citizens*. London and New York: Longman.

Wacquant, L., and Wilson, W. J. 1989. "Poverty, Joblessness and the Social Transformation of the Inner City." In *Reforming Welfare Policy*, edited by D. Ellwood and P. Cottingham, 70–102. Cambridge, MA: Harvard University Press.

Weir, M. 1993. "Race and Urban Poverty: Comparing Europe and America." Center for American Political Studies, Harvard University, occasional paper 93–9, March.

Weir, M., Orloff, A., and Skocpol, T. 1988. "The Future of Social Policy in the United States: Political Constraints and Possibilities." In *The Politics of Social Policy in the United States*, edited by M. Weir, S. Orloff and T. Skocpol, 421–46. Princeton, NJ: Princeton University Press.

Wilson, W. J. 1987. *The Truly Disadvantaged: The Inner City, The Underclass, and Public Policy*. Chicago: University of Chicago Press.

Wilson, W. J. 1991. "Studying Inner-City Social Dislocations: The Challenge of Public Agenda Research." *American Sociological Review* 56: 1–14.

Wilson, W. J. 1995. *Jobless Ghettoes: The Disappearance of Work and Its Effect on Urban Life*. New York: Knopf.

9

Race, Class, and Segregation: Discourses about African Americans*

Norman Fainstein

It is common in the social sciences for research topics, evidence, interpretations and intellectual conflict to be organized within a dominant discourse. Examples that come readily to mind include modernization, community power structure and pluralism. Like great hippopotamuses, these linguistic animals take up much space and eat up resources within academic disciplines, the media and government. Of course, there are usually other intellectual animals lurking around these giants, not merely raising dissenting voices, but even trying to speak other languages. Dominant discourses become dominant in the first place, however, because they reflect and reinforce an array of interests – cultural, political, economic – generally, though not solely, those of the rich and powerful. So it is not easy for other voices to be heard, much less to redefine the reigning way of talking about things. Yet ways of speaking do change when the moment is right. Perhaps we are at that point now with regard to the discourse about class and race in America, where the *underclass* has been the reigning hippopotamus. This paper constitutes a modest effort to sum up some of the dissident voices and dissonant evidence with regard to the topic of the social–economic situation of African Americans,[1] and perhaps thereby to break free of our obsessive use of underclass discourse to frame our discussions.

The Underclass Narrative

In sociological research on African Americans, the present dominant discourse was established in the latter part of the 1970s. At that time, two strands of thought were woven together. One may be attributed to William Julius Wilson, who displaced

* Fainstein, Norman (1993) "Race, Class and Segregation: Discourses about African Americans" *International Journal of Urban and Regional Research* 17, Fall, 384–403. Reprinted by permission of Blackwell Publishers.

Charles Hamilton and his black power paradigm and emerged as arguably the leading African American social scientist with the publication of *The Declining Significance of Race* (Wilson, 1978). In that influential book, Wilson looked back over the first three-quarters of the century and saw a sharp decline in racism in the United States, with blacks being treated more and more like whites, that is, stratified and differentiated by class. Black society was, he argued, increasingly bifurcated, with the 'black poor falling further and further behind middle- and upper-income blacks'. These 'talented and educated blacks' were experiencing rapid upward mobility, 'opportunities that [were] at least comparable to whites with equivalent qualifications' (Wilson, 1978, pp. 151–2).

The second strand of thought predated Wilson, though it was developed by him in a series of publications culminating in *The Truly Disadvantaged* (1987). Low-income, typically black, inner city neighbourhoods were being described in the media as increasingly wild, inhabited by a socially deviant, dependent and lawless population – 'The American underclass', as it was called on the cover of *Time magazine* (1977). Ten years later, nothing had changed for the better:

> Today's ghetto neighborhoods are populated almost exclusively by the most disadvantaged segments of the black urban community, that heterogeneous grouping of families and individuals who are out of the mainstream of the American occupational system. Included in this group are individuals who lack training and skills and either experience long-term unemployment or are not members of the labor force, individuals who are engaged in street crime and other forms of aberrant behavior, and families that experience long-term spells of poverty and/or welfare dependency. These are the populations to which I refer when I speak of the underclass. *I use this term to depict a reality not captured in the more standard designation lower class.*   (Wilson, 1987, pp. 7–8)

In combination, the ideas of the declining significance of race and the growing pathology and danger posed by people who were, it seemed, under or outside of the 'normal' class structure established the dominant discourse of the underclass, the study of which has become a veritable industry, nearly monopolizing foundation and government resources committed to research on poverty, constituting the subject of numerous conferences and, of course, generating a considerable literature.[2] A real sign that the underclass discourse is indeed dominant may be found in the fact that it subsumes debate over class, race and poverty. The underclass hippopotamus takes up nearly the whole political spectrum in the social sciences, as radical, liberal and conservative analysts each impart their particular spin to its interpretation, differing in their emphases on economic versus cultural factors, in their attachment of culpability to members of the underclass, and especially in whether they blame prior liberal government policies or extant conservative ones for the growth and bad behaviour of the underclass.

Whatever their political and theoretical perspective, participants in the discourse of the underclass share a deep narrative. Like other deep narratives[3] – the collapse of socialism is a ubiquitous story these days – that of the underclass is both explicit and implicit, saying much in its omissions. Its logic is relatively transparent, constructed along four lines. *First, underclass terminology offers a way of speaking about race in a language of class that implicitly rejects the importance of race.* While the term in theory should be deployed universally against all those who fit its behavioural conditions – like its ancient relative 'the undeserving poor', and its modern cognate 'the culture of poverty' – in practice it is reserved for African Americans. That is why Wilson (1991), responding to criticism, could ask in his 1990 presidential address to the American Sociological Association that 'ghetto poor' replace 'underclass' in the language of the social sciences. 'Ghetto' we all understand here to be a contraction of 'black ghetto', or simply a euphemism for black. Yet race itself is not theorized in any kind of direct manner, possibly because of the obvious implication that the black poor may share certain structural, political or cultural attributes that differentiate them from others with low income – in other words, that race continues to matter.

Second, research on the underclass tends to study the attributes or behaviours of a category of the population that is nominally separated from other groups and from processes that affect larger populations. This, instead of beginning with labour and housing markets which establish the life chances for all black persons, underclass research quickly focuses on blacks who are poor, unemployed and concentrated in 'ghetto' neighbourhoods.[4] Such a theoretical or methodological approach allows the researcher to avoid highly politicized questions about wage structure, the condition of the millions of poor blacks and others who are fully employed at poverty wages, or about the ways in which public finance and services affect the life chances of low-income populations. To understand the high incidence of out-of-wedlock births among poor black women, for example, it makes more intellectual sense to study marriage and the family across the class and ethnic spectrum than to focus on the cluster of attributes that define the behaviour of the ghetto poor. The latter approach does however, garner much better funding, since it addresses 'one of the most important domestic problems of the last quarter of the twentieth century' (Wilson, 1991, p. 1).

The explanation of the situation of the underclass encompasses a variety of elements, the precise mix depending to some extent on the politics of the researcher.[5] But common to all approaches is *the third component of the underclass narrative: recognition of the increasing concentration and isolation of the ghetto poor, which, according to the plot, has resulted in significant part, and ironically, from the success of working-and middle-class blacks in escaping the ghetto.* These non-underclass African Americans used to live in the ghetto, in a (vaguely specified) past when all blacks faced racial discrimination. At that time, the narrative asserts, working- and middle-class blacks provided the poor with role models, connections to the labour market, and economically heterogeneous institutions like the church; they generally policed and stabilized the potentially unruly who finally came to comprise an underclass.

> In the 1940s, 1950s, and as late as the 1960s such [black] communities featured a vertical integration of different segments of the urban black population. Lower-class, working-class, and middle-class black families all lived more or less in the same communities (albeit in different neighborhoods), sent their children to the same schools, availed themselves of the same recreational facilities, and shopped in the same stores … Accompanying the black middle-class exodus has been a growing movement of stable working-class blacks from ghetto neighborhoods to higher income neighbor-

hoods in other parts of the city and to the suburbs. In the early years, the black middle and working classes were confined by restrictive covenants to communities also inhabited by the lower class; their very presence provided stability to inner city neighborhoods and reinforced and perpetuated mainstream patterns of norms and behavior.   (Wilson, 1987, p. 7)[6]

By an unstated logic, therefore, the underclass not only results from the increasing bifurcation of black society, but reaffirms by its existence the reality of black success. It would not be too much to say, in fact, that the narrative of the underclass tells whites that working- and middle-class blacks, including, of course, black professionals, are *not* the underclass, that the appropriate lens with which to examine the economic situation of African Americans is class, not race.[7]

Thus, we arrive at *the final element of the underclass narrative, namely, that it does not need to tell the story of African Americans who are in the 'stable' working and middle class.* These blacks, perhaps two-thirds or more of the black population, are assumed to have benefited from increasing educational attainment and better employment, using these advantages to move out of the ghetto (the term no longer being used, we must remember, for all segregated black districts, but limited to impoverished black neighbourhoods inhabited by the underclass). Where they have moved to is not an object of discussion, but is assumed to be nice city neighbourhoods or the suburbs. Justifying this lacunae in the research agenda is an even deeper premise that racial residential segregation must have decreased substantially or that, at worst, better-off blacks live in all-black neighbourhoods far away from impoverished blacks, receiving advantages of spatial economic segregation similar to their white counterparts. Rarely are these assertions tested with evidence by the active voices of the underclass discourse.

An Other-narrative: The Story of Working- and Middle-class Blacks

Three recent books (Jencks, 1992; Orfield and Ashkinaze, 1991; and Hacker, 1992), written by prominent and definitely mainstream social scientists, have challenged in different ways the dominant narrative of the underclass.[8] Christopher Jencks (1992) directs most of his attention to the intersection of race and poverty. He undermines assumptions that the 'underclass' is a single social type by showing that its various dimensions are but weakly correlated, and that the underclass has not on the whole expanded during the last two decades.

Gary Orfield and Carole Ashkinaze[9] (1991) take on a broader subject by examining the situation of black households in Atlanta and its suburbs. That city has often been held aloft as a model of economic growth, enlightened government and black progress – social, economic and political. Orfield and Ashkinaze show instead that a black mayor and regional economic development have been unable to overcome local racism and conservative national policies: black progress in Atlanta has been greatly exaggerated. In particular, they find that non-poor African Americans were kept segregated during the 1980s in city neighbourhoods and suburbs sharply inferior in housing quality, government services and schools to those of whites of similar social class. The other-narrative of Atlanta leads Orfield and Ashkinaze (1991, p. 15) to take on underclass mythology:

> [William Julius] Wilson's work strongly deemphasizes the racial problems faced by middle-class blacks and sees isolation primarily as a problem of the inner-city 'underclass' population. This study finds the vast majority of blacks in metropolitan Atlanta in segregated neighbourhoods and schools, reflecting, in part, a very large pattern of segregated suburbanization. It reports evidence of continuing racial discrimination in housing and in mortage lending. In a society where the maintenance of middle class status is strongly dependent upon the provision of college education for the next generation, it shows sharp declines in college access. We estimate that racial barriers directly affect and harm a much larger portion of the black population than is suggested in Wilson's work.

In a widely reviewed work, Andrew Hacker (1992) examines an extensive body of evidence from every sphere of life to show that the United States remains *Two Nations* – the title of his book drawn from Disraeli and the subtitle, 'Black and white, separate, hostile, and unequal', from the 1968 Report of the National Advisory Commission on Civil Disorders, which warned of this possible negative trajectory for America. Hacker has importantly added the word 'hostile' to the Commission's prediction, for he discovers that not only have material differences remained large between the races across the class spectrum, but political–cultural cleavages appear to have widened as well.

Together these books might finally shove the underclass hippopotamus sufficiently aside to make room for a fresh discussion of class and race, especially one that incorporates the considerable scholarship of the last five or so years, which emphasizes the continuing significance of race and may even suggest the declining significance of class in explaining the situation of African Americans.[10] An other-narrative of race can be pieced together from this literature and reinforced by recent census data. In outlining its elements, I will not dwell on its critique of the underclass narrative, since it seems most important to discuss that part of African-American society about which the underclass narrative has been silent or rather misleading.

Growing economic inequality

The other-narrative of race begins by telling the story of our economy over the last 20 years, a history of slow growth and increasing inequality, with the richest Americans reaping nearly all of the wealth created in the Reagan fantasy.[11] Median household income, controlled for inflation, was $29, 108 in 1973 – the peak year of the postwar American boom – and $29,943 in 1990, virtually unchanged.[12] But this income was redistributed upward, as the percentage of households receiving more than $50,000 increased, with the sharpest gain among those in the $100,000 and above category – from 2.3 to 4.3 per cent of all households. Conversely, middle-income households with annual incomes of $25–50,000 declined from 37.1 per cent of all households to 33.3 per cent.

Many other measures show the same pattern of a declining middle and expanding top of the income distribution, especially the very top. For example, the richest 5 per cent of American families received 25.7 per cent of total *after-tax* income in 1992, compared with 18.5 per cent in 1977 (and the richest 1 per cent, 13.4 per cent of after-tax income in 1992 as against 7.3 per cent in 1977); however, the share of the middle quintile declined from 16.3 per cent to 14.9 per cent in these same years.[13] Wage patterns followed a similar course (Harrison and Gorham, 1992). Such an aggregate social economy creates a pattern of zero-sum games among racial groups – improvement can only be at someone else's expense. Everyone tries to protect his or her own position.

In this kind of a situation, African Americans, who were disadvantaged at the start, could not be expected to make much economic progress along the way (Swinton, 1991). So it is unremarkable that black median household income increased by less than $1000 dollars between 1973 and 1990, with the typical black household remaining at only 59–60 per cent of the income of a typical white household (table 9.1). The black middle class (incomes of $25–50,000) *contracted* slightly during the period.[14] And while upper-middle-class and elite black households grew in these 17 years, they still comprised but 12 per cent of all black households compared with 26 per cent of white households. By contrast, the percentage of blacks in poverty has *not* increased since 1973; in fact, it contracted by more than 1.5 per cent, though of course it remains very high, at more than two-fifths of all black households. These data explain why our counter to the underclass story should begin by describing the economic situation of all African Americans. That situation reflects the continued racial disadvantage experienced across the entire black class structure, rather than just the impoverishment of lower-class blacks.

Table 9.1 Race and income structure, 1973–90: distribution of households among income classes (1990 $, CPI-U-X1)

	Poverty ≤ 14,999	Marginal 15–24,999	Middle 25–49,999	Upper mid. 50–99,999	Elite ≥100,000	Median
Black distribution						
1973	43.8	21.8	27.3	6.8	0.4	$17,957
1985	44.0	20.3	25.5	9.5	0.8	$18,000
1990	42.4	19.1	26.6	10.8	1.1	$18,676
White distribution						
1973	23.3	17.6	38.3	18.4	2.5	$30,507
1985	23.6	18.1	34.5	20.3	3.6	$30,255
1990	22.0	17.7	34.1	21.5	4.7	$31,231

Note: The ratio of black to white median incomes was .59 in 1973 and 1985, and .60 in 1990. The median income of all US households was $29,108 in 1973, $28,688 in 1985 and $29,943 in 1990.
Source: US Bureau of the Census (1991), table B-10.

Conservative public policy

The other-narrative continues by examining the impact of government policies –
again, not as they are directed particularly at the black poor, much less the so-
called underclass, but as they affect blacks at every economic level. The relative
lack of economic progress of the great majority of non-poor African Americans
is what must be explained. Put most briefly, governments throughout the federal
system have been influenced by the conservative tide since the late 1970s, with
the national government directing the redeployment of public policies in ways
that have badly harmed African Americans. Federal aid to individuals above
the poverty line contracted sharply, both in direct transfers like grants for
college attendance, and in indirect transfers which passed through subnational governments, for instance for public schools and job training. Washington
virtually eliminated long-extant housing programmes for low- and moderate-
income groups, from which blacks benefited disproportionately. And the withdrawal of federal aid to cities helped precipitate the tax revolts which compounded the decline in services to African Americans. Working- and middle-
class blacks who had gained much in the 1960s and early 1970s saw their
mobility routes blocked, as government employment grew only slowly or contracted in the older cities where they are concentrated. John Jacob (1991, p. 1),
president of the politically centrist National Urban League, summed up what had
happened:

> A strategic goal of the Reagan administration was to limit government's ability to
> undertake social and economic programs by choking off available resources through
> tax cuts and higher military spending. The success of that strategy was seen in the
> virtual abandonment of important job training, health, and housing programs and
> crippling cuts in other domestic programs. But it was most obvious in the recurring
> refrain that responded to virtually all proposals for government programs that
> would...create opportunities in the 1980s – 'we can't afford to do it.'

Moreover, the conservative regimes in Washington reversed the policies of the
Civil Rights Commission, the Department of Justice and the Equal Employment
Opportunity Commission, packed the Supreme Court, and in numerous other
ways effectively ended federal actions to reduce racial discrimination in employment, education, housing and public services. Playing their part in the story, actors
in all sectors of our society – whether realtors, school superintendents,
employers, firefighters' unions or suburban government officials – took their
cues from Washington and reduced their commitment to racial integration,
however low had been its previous level. Blacks for their part, too, stopped
pushing for integration, with a small but vocal minority preaching black
separatism, a message that many whites took to heart. Separatism between
the races expanded in political – cultural space, even as it failed to contract geographically.[15]

Persistent residential segregation

The geographical separation of the races continues through processes that involve the segmentation of housing markets, active racial discrimination by realtors and banks (Galster, 1987) and the use of governmental boundaries as racial barricades.[16] Far from the pleasant but undocumented picture of working- and middle-class dispersal from the ghetto assumed in the underclass narrative, the students of residential segregation describe a very different scene as of 1980, the latest year for which national data are available, and more recent evidence gives little reason to believe there has been much improvement since then.[17] In fact, except for metropolitan areas with very small black populations, racial segregation remained virtually constant in the 1970s (Massey and Gross, 1991). The small increase in the suburbanization of African Americans was largely in jurisdictions contiguous to urban black neighbourhoods, and signified neither a substantial increase in the deconcentration of blacks[18] (relative to white decentralization) nor much improvement in the likelihood that even middle-class blacks would be living in racially integrated neighbourhoods (Massey and Denton, 1988; Galster, 1991). Douglas Massey (1990, p. 354), perhaps America's leading contemporary expert on racial segregation, reminds us that

> two decades after the passage of the Fair Housing Act, levels of black segregation remain exceedingly high in large urban areas...This high level of segregation cannot be explained by blacks' objective socioeconomic characteristics, their housing preferences, or their limited knowledge of white housing markets. Rather, it is linked empirically to the persistence of discrimination in housing markets and to continuing antiblack prejudice.[19]

The underclass narrative emphasizes the departure of higher-income black households from impoverished 'ghettos'.[20] We know that most of these households will none the less continue to live in all-black neighbourhoods, whether in the central cities or in suburbs. The question by our other-narrative is one of degree: how much income segregation is there among blacks compared with other social groups, and how much has it changed? In the only study of its kind, Massey and Eggers (1990, table 2) examined 60 metropolitan areas in 1980. Using the index of dissimilarity (see note to Table 9.7), they compared levels of *economic* segregation among whites, blacks, hispanics and Asians. They found that blacks showed moderate levels of segregation (0.342), higher than whites (0.254), but lower than hispanics (0.479) and Asians (0.565). *Segregation by income among blacks is, in fact, less than half the level of segregation by race among persons with similar incomes* (table 9.7).[21] While economic segregation among blacks increased in the 1970s, the changes were quite small (0.029) and may largely reflect increasing inequality within the black income distribution. 'Because of persisting segregation, middle- and upper-class blacks are less able to separate themselves from the poor than the privileged of other groups, and recent increases in black interclass segregation probably represent a movement toward parity with other groups' (Massey and Eggers, 1990, p. 1186).[22]

Before wrapping up all the strands of our other-narrative, I would like to examine some recent evidence about the economic situation of middle-class blacks and, more generally, about the extent to which racial differences are narrowed by keeping social class constant. If race really has declined in significance, we should be seeing a great deal of progress among middle-class blacks relative to middle-class whites.

Class Differences and Life Chances

The data in Table 9.2 allow us to compare black and white earnings among college graduates (those with passports into the middle class), high school graduates and the entire population for three age cohorts in 1990. Let us first consider the case of males. We see that among the youngest workers, higher education improves the earnings ratio between black and white men (from 74.5 per cent among all men to 83.3 per cent among college grads). For older male workers, however, education has little effect. In fact, the wage ratio of black to white male high school graduates among 45–54-year-olds is actually better than among college graduates of the same age. One possible explanation for these cohort differences is that racial

Table 9.2 Income of cohorts with similar education, YRFT workers: Median annual earnings and percentage of white male earnings, 1990

	25–34 yrs		35–44 yrs		45–54 yrs	
Males						
College grads						
Black	26,787	(83.3)	35,931	(80.9)	38,560	(76.6)
White	32,130		44,125		50,325	
HS grads						
Black	17,197	(74.8)	21,778	(79.3)	26,426	(84.5)
White	22,985		27,472		31,255	
All						
Black	19,200	(74.5)	26,023	(79.5)	25,965	(73.4)
White	25,767		32,750		35,364	
Females						
College grads						
Black	25,714	(80.0)	28,978	(65.2)	33,378	(66.3)
White	26,787	(83.4)	30,939	(69.6)	31,209	(62.0)
HS grads						
Black	14,132	(61.5)	18,033	(65.6)	18,954	(60.6)
White	16,481	(71.7)	18,733	(68.1)	18,460	(59.1)
All						
Black	17,121	(66.4)	20,875	(63.7)	19,699	(55.7)
White	19,974	(77.5)	21,833	(66.6)	21,113	(59.7)

Note: 'YRFT' (year-round full-time) are persons employed every week in the specified year on a full-time basis; 'HS grads' are persons who graduated high school but have never attended college; 'College grads' are persons who have completed at least four years of college.
Source: US Bureau of the Census (1991, Table 29), and author's calculations.

discrimination is declining for highly educated young blacks, compared to older blacks. But if we look at the actual dollar amounts in the table, another conclusion is much more likely. Young workers enter jobs with a relatively small wage spread. As male workers age and move up the job hierarchy, the variance in salaries increases substantially. White male college graduates move farther up the income scale with age than do black college graduates. For example, the median income of prime age white college graduates (45–54-years-old) exceeds that of young white workers by more than $18,000, while the comparable difference among blacks is less than $12,000. There is little reason from this evidence to think that college education is closing the racial gap in earnings.

For women, the picture is quite different. Table 9.2 presents women's income as a percentage of white male earnings. We find that racial differences in earnings among women are quite small, whether we look at all women, or at college and high school grads separately. While college education increases earnings, the wage spread of all women is relatively narrow, and the median wages of women in every category but the youngest college graduates remains in the range of 60–65 per cent of comparable white males. This happens because there is almost no wage hierarchy for women. For example, the spread between young and prime age white women college graduates is less than $5,000, compared with more than $18,000 among men. In sum, then, black women do quite as well as white women of similar education, sometimes even better, and education increases the earnings of all women, but women as a gender receive significantly lower wages than men. Because black households are much more dependent on women's earnings than are white households, the depressed level of women's earnings, even among prime age college graduates, contributes to the economic disadvantage of blacks across the class structure.

Did racial differences in earnings within the middle class decline during the last decade? Tables 9.3 and 9.4 provide several indicators that address the question respectively for male and female college graduates. The results are mixed, leaning toward the negative. The median earnings of black male college graduates improved versus that of whites, as did that of full-time year-round workers (Table 9.3), but among women there was either no improvement or actual decline (Table 9.4). The percentage of both black men and black women who occupied high-wage jobs decreased substantially – though the absence of comparable white figures means that we do not know if the racial gap widened or narrowed (Table 9.3).

Finally, blacks in the cohort of young, college-educated workers slipped further behind whites during the decade. The real salaries of all young male college graduates declined in the 1980s (Table 9.3), but those of black males declined more than those of white males; young college-educated black men, who had mean earnings of 80.6 per cent of those of similar whites in 1980, dropped to 73.6 per cent in 1990.[23] Given the pattern we saw in Table 9.2 of increasing racial differences as workers age, these data portend quite negatively for black male college graduates, and suggest that intraclass racial differences may grow larger in coming years.

An even wider gap developed among young female college graduates during the 1980s (Table 9.4). Whereas black female mean earnings were 122.2 per cent of the white figure in 1980, they were only 91.2 per cent of the white level in 1990 – another sign of growing racial differences within the middle class. Overall, then, the

Table 9.3   Incomes of male college graduates in the 1980s (expressed in constant (1990) dollars)

	Black	White	B/W (%)
Median earnings[a] persons 25 yrs and older			
1982	25,904	36,916	70.2
1990	30,282	37,996	79.7
Median earnings YRFT[b] workers 25 yrs and older			
1982	29,482	41,813	70.5
1990	32,145	41,661	77.2
Persons earning $40,000 or more on an annualized[c] basis (%)			
1979	23.4	NA	
1987	19.5	NA	
Mean[d] annual earnings persons aged 25–34			
1980	27,744	34,408	80.6
1990	25,241	34,272	73.6

Notes: [a] All dollar amounts are converted using the CPI-U-XI cost of living index.
[b] Year-round, full-time workers.
[c] Annualized wages are calculated by extrapolating actual earnings to a YRFT equivalent. Since not all workers were employed YRFT, this figure overestimates the percentage with high earnings. The deflator used here is the poverty line, with high earnings defined as 3 or more times the annual income for a family of 4 at the prevailing poverty line.
[d] The use of mean earnings slightly increases the dollar amounts compared with medians. The 1980 figures are drawn from the decennial census, which uses a methodology different from the 1990 Current Population Surveys, and are not strictly comparable to CPS estimates. The census methodology relies on self-reporting and tends to underestimate income by a few percentage points compared to the CPS, which uses trained interviewers following a detailed protocol.
Source: US Bureau of the Census (1983, Table 47), 1990, 1991, Table 29); Harrison and Gorham (1992, p. 66); Farley and Allen (1987, Table 11.4). US Bureau of the Census (1991, Table B-1).

evidence in Tables 9.2, 9.3 and 9.4 hardly supports the notion that race is declining in significance as a determinant of the economic situation of blacks, even among the best educated.

At a time when the penalty for not graduating from college is increasing for all workers, blacks are falling further behind whites. Table 9.5 presents college enrol-ment and graduation rates normalized for cohort size. The performance on both indicators of young blacks has deteriorated steadily since 1976 compared with that of whites. For example, the ratio of the black male college graduation rate to the white male rate declined from 41 per cent to 35 per cent. Much attention has been devoted to the high proportion of black college graduates who are female (about 57 per cent of the cohort in 1989), yet the fact remains that black females found themselves well below white females in both college attendance and graduation rates in 1976, and the gap has steadily and substantially widened. Whereas the female black/white graduation ratio stood at 58.1 percent in 1976, it had declined to 44.2 per cent by 1989. The import of the data in Table 9.5 for both genders is, then,

Table 9.4 Incomes of female college graduates in the 1980s (expressed in constant (1990) dollars)

	Black	White	B/W (%)
Median earnings persons 25 yrs and older			
1982	21,012	18,169	115.6
1990	25,874	23,598	109.6
Median earnings YRFT workers 25 yrs and older			
1982	23,619	26,833	88.0
1990	25,874	29,109	88.9
Persons earning $40,000 or more on an annualized basis (%)			
1979	12.4	NA	
1987	7.6	NA	
Mean annual earnings persons aged 25–34			
1980	21,436	17,480	122.6
1990	21,850	23,962	91.2

Notes: [a] All dollar amounts are converted using the CPI-U-XI cost of living index.
[b] Year-round, full-time workers.
[c] Annualized wages are calculated by extrapolating actual earnings to a YRFT equivalent. Since not all workers were employed YRFT, this figure overestimates the percentage with high earnings. The deflator used here is the poverty line, with high earnings defined as 3 or more times the annual income for a family of 4 at the prevailing poverty line.
[d] The use of mean earnings slightly increases the dollar amounts compared with medians. The 1980 figures are drawn from the decennial census, which uses a methodology different from the 1990 Current Population Surveys, and are not strictly comparable to CPS estimates. The census methodology relies on self-reporting and tends to underestimate income by a few percentage points compared to the CPS, which uses trained interviewers following a detailed protocol.
Source: US Bureau of the Census (1983, Table 47), 1990, 1991, Table 29); Harrison and Gorham (1992, p. 66); Farley and Allen (1987, Table 11.4); US Bureau of the Census (1991, Table B-1).

that the black middle class is likely to contract in coming years, at least to the extent that the human capital stock of the next generation remains on its current downward trajectory.

Nor can blacks depend much on actual capital to improve their economic situation or to at least guarantee intergenerational reproduction of prior gains. The median wealth of African American households was less than 10 per cent of that of white households in 1988 (Table 9.6). While the gulf narrowed with increasing income, among middle-income blacks, household net worth was only about one-quarter that of whites with similar incomes, and even among households with the greatest monthly income (the top 8.1 per cent of black households), the wealth ratio between the races was only 39.6 per cent.[24] From this we conclude that even black households with relatively high incomes are asset-poor. Measured by wealth, in fact, the black middle class is minute and the working class would be classified as poor, were it white.

A significant reason for this racial capital disadvantage undoubtedly stems from the depressed value of black housing at every income level, since throughout most of

Table 9.5   College completion rates for persons 18–24 years

	Enrolled in college (%)			Graduated college (%)		
	Black	White	B/W	Black	White	B/W
Men						
1976	22.0	28.8	76.4	1.6	3.9	41.0
1981	18.8	27.7	67.9	1.4	3.4	41.0
1985	20.1	29.3	68.6	1.3	3.6	36.1
1989	19.6	31.5	62.2	1.4	4.0	35.0
Women						
1976	23.0	25.6	89.8	1.8	3.1	58.1
1981	20.7	25.8	80.2	1.8	3.2	56.3
1985	19.5	28.2	69.1	1.7	3.7	45.9
1989	23.5	32.2	73.0	1.9	4.3	44.2

Note: 'College graduation rate' is calculated by dividing the number of bachelor's degrees conferred by the number of 18–24-year-olds in that year. This measure therefore controls approximately for cohort size. The ratio B/W (expressed as a percentage) indicates the relative probability of a black person in the black cohort receiving a bachelor's degree versus a white person in the white cohort. Thus, in 1976 the chances of the average black male aged 18–24 graduating college was 41.0 per cent of that of the average white male; by 1989, it was 35.0 percent.
Source: American Council on Education (1992, Tables 2, 10), and author's calculations.

Table 9.6   Wealth versus income for African Americans and whites: Median net worth by average household monthly income, 1988

	Black		White		B$/W$(%)
	Median $	(% hhds)	Median $	(% hhds)	
Income quintile ($ range)					
Lowest (0–939)	0	(37.4)	8,839	(17.7)	0.0
Second (940–1699)	2,408	(22.5)	26,299	(19.7)	9.2
Third (1700–2568)	8,461	(17.9)	32,802	(20.4)	25.8
Fourth (2569–3883)	20,215	(14.1)	50,372	(20.8)	40.1
Highest (3884 +)	47,160	(8.1)	119,057	(21.4)	39.6
All	4,169	(100.0)	43,279	(100.0)	9.6

Note: Net worth includes houses, furnishings, automobiles, real property, stocks, bonds, savings accounts, accounts and all other forms (current) of wealth except vested interest in pension funds less all mortgages, debts and liabilities.
Source: US Bureau of the Census (1990).

the USA income distribution equity in home ownership is the principal source of household wealth. The devalorization of houses owned by blacks itself results from the racism and segmentation in housing markets, and the persistence of interracial segregation at every class level. In Table 9.7 we look at evidence of black–white segregation using both income and education as indicators of social class. The first column shows the degree of segregation of blacks at specified income or education

Table 9.7 Segregation of African Americans from whites: Index of racial residential segregation (D) in Standard Metropolitan Areas (SMAs) with largest black populations, 1980

	Index of segregation from white persons	
	Regardless of income or education of white persons	White persons with same income or education
Black persons		
Family income		
Under $ 10,000	0.79	0.76
$15–19,999	0.76	0.75
$25–34,999	0.77	0.79
$50,000 or more	0.79	0.79
Education		
9–11 years	0.83	0.77
High school graduate	0.78	0.76
Some college	0.75	0.71
College graduate	0.72	0.71

Note: Both columns exhibit values of the index of dissimilarity (D), a measure of residential segregation. It measures the number of black households that would have to change census tracts within a metropolitan area in order to be distributed in the same manner as the comparative white population. D ranges between zero and 1.000. (In this table, D is rounded off to 100ths and ranges between zero and 1.00.) For the distribution of D, 0–0.300 is considered low, 0.300–0.600 moderate, and 0.600–1.000 high. Thus, all values of D in this table are in the high range.

The columns are drawn from two somewhat different but overlapping samples. The first comprises the 10 metropolitan areas with the largest black populations in 1980. Here D shows how many black persons with a particular characteristic of family income or personal education would have to be redistributed to match the distribution of all whites among census tracts in each SMA. The final number is a weighted average of D for all 10 SMAs. The second column uses the same methodology for the 16 SMAs with the largest black populations. But here D measures the redistribution of black persons required to match the distribution of white persons with the *same* characteristic. For example, the number 0.71 in the lower right-hand corner of the table means that 71 percent of college-educated black persons would need to change census tract in order to match the distribution of college-educated white persons.

Sources: (First column) Denton and Massey (1988, Table 1); (second column) Farley and Allen (1987, Table 5.10).

levels from whites in any income or education. For example, the index number is 0.79 for blacks with income of $50,000 or more in 1980. This means the 79 per cent of these black persons would have had to move from their census tracts in order to match the distribution of whites as a whole within their metropolitan area. It is apparent from the data that blacks at every class are equally isolated from white society. In the second column, we look at segregation with class controlled for both blacks and whites, in other words, at the level of interracial segregation of blacks and whites with the same incomes or educations. Again, race overwhelms class. Middle-class blacks, working-class blacks and poor blacks are equally segregated from their white class counterparts. Clearly, better class standing does little to buy African Americans a racially integrated environment.[25]

Table 9.8 African-American and white class capacity for spatial isolation: Probability of residential contact (P*) between high-status persons and low-status persons by race, city of Philadelphia, 1980

| | Low-status persons, all races | | |
	High-school dropout	Family on welfare	Female-headed family
High-status persons			
White collar			
Black	0.406	0.227	0.214
White	0.336	0.081	0.074
Ratio: B/W	1.2	2.8	2.9
Some college or more			
Black	0.393	0.221	0.210
White	0.289	0.080	0.080
Ratio: B/W	1.4	2.8	2.6
Middle-class income			
Black	0.398	0.216	0.206
White	0.336	0.076	0.068
Ratio: B/W	1.2	2.8	3.0

Note: The cells indicate the probability (P*) of a random person in the high-status group having residential contact with a person in the low-status category. Residential contact is defined as living in the same census tract. In effect, then, P* is the percentage of persons in the low-status category living in the census tract of an average person in the high-status group. For example, the first cell value of 0.406 means that the average black person with a white-collar occupation lives in a census tract where 0.406 persons of any race are high-school dropouts. The ratio B/W measures the relative likelihood of a black person versus a white person within the high-status group encountering a person of any race with a specific low-status attribute. For example, white-collar black persons are 1.2 times more likely than white-collar white persons to have residential contact with a high-school dropout of any race.
Source: Massey et al. (1987, Table 6).

Nor does it allow black households to distance themselves from lower-class cultural influences to the same extent as whites. Table 9.8 persents evidence from a study of Philadelphia, a city with black neighbourhoods at every class level. Using three different indicators of social class, the table shows that middle-class whites are much less likely than middle-class blacks to encounter people with so-called underclass attributes in their neighbourhoods. Equally important, the study examines in great detail other measures of the quality of life in neighbourhoods occupied by working- and middle-class blacks versus those occupied by whites of similar class. It finds that class simply does not buy blacks the environment that it buys whites in a society where class stratification is expressed spatially:

> High status blacks, like whites, seek to convert past socioeconomic attainments into improved residential circumstances. However, very few blacks are successful in achieving these location outcomes. The vast majority live in segregated neighborhoods where blacks have long been, or are rapidly becoming, the majority, areas characterized by high crime, poor schools, economic dependency, unstable families, dilapidated housing,

and poor health. All evidence indicates that blacks are no different than whites in trying to escape such an environment, when they are able. They are just less able.

(Massey et al., 1987, p. 52)

The authors suggest the consequences of the relative social heterogeneity of middle-income black neighbourhoods for reducing the ability of the black middle class to reproduce itself through cultural capital transmission:

> Because of residential segregation, middle class blacks must send their children to public schools with children far below their own class standing, children with more limited cognitive, linguistic, and social skills. Given the strong effect of peer influences and environment on aspirations, motivation, and achievement, it is hardly surprising that so many young black people, even those from middle class families, fail to achieve high test scores or educational distinction.[26]   (Massey et al., 1987: 54)

There is much evidence that class background simply does not translate into educational performance for blacks to the same extent as it does for whites.[27] Table 9.9 illustrates these findings. The upper panel arrays SAT scores by family income. Even if critics of the Scholastic Aptitude Tests are right when they claim that these tests are culturally biased and largely reflect middle-class white language and knowledge, the SAT can at least be interpreted as a measure of cultural capital among students who aspire to college educations and good incomes. The results are only slightly encouraging. On the positive side, black SAT scores improved between 1984 and 1990, reducing the interracial gap from 217 to 196 points. And in both years, black–white differences were reduced with increasing family income. Nonetheless, these differences remain so large that in 1984 and in 1990, black students from families with upper-middle-class incomes of better than $70,000 did worse on the SAT than white students from families in or near poverty, with incomes between $10,000 and $20,000. Clearly, some combination of lower cultural capital among the parents of black children, inferior schooling and perhaps reduced motivation, must be at work to explain such large and persistent differences in an important national measure of cultural and linguistic convergence (or divergence).

The lower panel presents evidence of the power of family background in predicting children's educational attainment. This is another indicator of the transmission of class advantage among blacks compared to whites. Table 9.9 shows that the regression coefficient for whites has remained relatively constant since the Second World War. For blacks, however, the coefficient has declined steadily, beginning at a level higher than that for whites and reaching a point more than one-third below the white coefficient for children who were 15 years old between 1970 and 1982. For whatever reasons – possibly including differences in family composition – the educational attainment of black parents has been less and less a predictor of the educational attainment of black children. This is another sign of a declining significance of class as a differentiating factor within the black population.[28]

A last piece of evidence along the same lines may be found in out-of-wedlock childbirth (Table 9.10). Among the least educated whites, more than 65 per cent were married when their child was born in 1986. That figure rises to well over 90 per cent in the white middle class (those with some college or college graduates). Among

Table 9.9   Effect of family background on educational performance

	SAT[a]Score 1984			SAT Score 1990		
	Black	White	Diff.	Black	White	Diff.
Family income (1990 dollars)						
10–20,000	646	863	217	704	879	175
30–40,000	724	908	174	751	908	157
50–60,000	773	948	175	790	947	157
70,000 +	832	981	149	854	998	144
Median	715	932	217	737	933	196

	Decade when child was 15 years of age			
	1940–49	1950–59	1960–69	1970–82

Effect of parental[b] education on children's educational attainment: Regression of child's schooling on father's (mother's) schooling

	1940–49	1950–59	1960–69	1970–82
Blacks	0.331	0.260	0.214	0.199
Whites	0.326	0.315	0.324	0.315

Note: [a] SAT (Scholastic Aptitude Test) scores are the sum of the verbal and mathematical scores. The sum ranges between 400 and 1600. In each case, this table employs median scores. The table combines two data sources with different presentations of income ranges, so there might be minor variations from actual scores. None the less, the basic picture would remain unchanged.
[b] Father's education is used as the independent variable unless only mother was present when child was 15. The regression coefficients predict additional years of school of child for an increase of one year in parental education. For example, one year more parental education on average resulted in 0.331 years of greater education among black children who were 15 in 1940–49. The overall data set encompasses respondents over the age of 25 interviewed between 1972 and 1989.
Source: *Chronicle of Higher Education*, 16 January 1985; Hacker (1992, p. 143); Jencks (1992, Table 5.8).

Table 9.10   Percentage of mothers unmarried when baby was born

	Education of mother			
	Less than high school	HS graduate	Some college	College graduate
1969				
Black	41.9	28.0	21.5	6.6
White	7.9	4.1	4.1	1.2
B/W	5.3	6.8	5.2	5.5
1986				
Black	79.4	61.9	45.5	20.8
White	34.8	13.9	7.2	2.2
B/W	2.3	4.5	6.3	9.5

Source: Jencks (1992, Table 5.15).

whites, the class background of the mother is thus a very strong predictor of normative behaviour. The same is much less true of black mothers. The illegitimacy rate was 45.5 per cent in 1986 among black mothers who attended college and 20.8 percent among college graduates. Whereas in 1969 the black/white illegitimacy ratio remained constant across class categories, by 1986 it increased steadily with ascending class. Thus, while among the least educated mothers of both races the ratio was 2.3:1, among college graduates it was 9.5:1. Here we have a final, and telling, example of the declining significance of class in controlling, much less eliminating, racial differences.

Boyz'n the Hood

The well-publicized story of the decade may be the presence in many of our cities of a disorderly, impoverished black population, but alongside that story must be placed the narrative of the working-poor and of the better-off African American population, who have neither moved up economically nor become more integrated into white society. Indeed, in this other-narrative, the two subplots must be related. On the one hand, the continuing isolation of non-poor blacks from white America is undoubtedly encouraging their greater alienation, a growing disillusion with the possibility of escaping race and racism, and the continued delegitimization of American social and political institutions – a consciousness widely shared within the black community. On the other hand, the presence of impoverished black households, the drug culture, criminal behaviour, all those elements of the 'underclass', may well be exacerbating the difficulties of working- and middle-class blacks in maintaining their economic gains and seeing their children move up socially, or at least not sink into poverty and/or criminality.

Many of us have seen the film *Boyz 'n the Hood*.[29] It presents this same other-narrative, albeit in a more graphic and much more entertaining manner. The plot is well known. Hard-working black people, some with professional careers, occupy a reasonably attractive LA black neighbourhood. Within that same neighbourhood live lower-income blacks. The streets and schools where adolescents spend their lives are a constant source of exposure to temptations and dangers, which lead to economic failure at best, and death at worst. Some of the sons and daughters of working- and middle-class black families escape this environment unharmed (though none are benefited by it); many others succumb. This is not the underclass narrative. It is the other-narrative of a racially segregated and segmented society where class means one thing for whites and another for blacks, where for African Americans, class (in the white sense) is not nearly as important as race, and may actually be declining in significance.

NOTES

1   I will use the terms 'African Americans' and 'blacks' interchangeably.

2 For example, conferences devoted to the subject culminated in a special issue of the *Annals* (Wilson, 1989) on 'The ghetto underclass' and in *The Urban Underclass* (Jencks and Peterson, 1991). Since the mid-1980s the influential Social Science Research Council has sponsored a research committee on the underclass. Many foundations have provided Wilson and others with very substantial funding.

An incisive review of the literature may be found in Marks (1991).

3 The term 'myth', in the sense made famous by Roland Barthes, could equally well be utilized.

4 Wacquant and Wilson (1989) further add to the linguistic confusion by defining ghettos as places inhabited largely by the underclass, while one of the characteristics of poor people that places them in the underclass is their concentration in ghettos – a line of reasoning that is uncomfortably tautological. Wilson and other underclass researchers have by this linguistic sleight of hand deprived themselves of any commonly understood term which might describe the places into which non-underclass blacks are segregated. If these are no longer ghettos, just what are they?

I should note that despite his co-authorship with Wilson of the aforementioned article, Wacquant (1992) rejects the concept of 'underclass'. Instead, he recognizes the term to be an ideological construct that functions to demonize the poor and mystify the role of state policy in determining the condition of inner-city neighbourhoods. None the less, he is quite adamant about reserving the term 'ghetto' just for the areas with extreme levels of misery, crime and social disorganization (undergoing what he calls de-civilization).

'A ghetto,' according to Wacquant, 'is not simply a segregated neighbourhood but a specific set of spatially-articulated mechanisms of racial closure. To put it differently: all segregated (even racially segregated) areas are not [*ipso facto*] ghettos. What to call the segregated neighborhoods founded by the new black (petty) [*sic*] bourgeoisie outside the historic Black Belt is difficult but it's certainly not a ghetto in the sociological, communal sense' (personal correspondence, 6 October 1992).

In my view, Wacquant is mistaken. A ghetto *is* 'simply' a segregated neighbourhood, to the extent that segregation is societally imposed and based on race, ethnicity or religion. In fact, black ghettos in the USA most certainly are produced by exactly the 'spatially articulated mechanisms of racial closure' that Wacquant specifies. Like the Jewish ghettos of Venice and eastern Europe, black ghettos encompass a range of class groupings, housing quality and lifestyles. That is just the point – everyone who is black is compelled to live within a racially defined district, regardless of their other attributes. Of course, all blacks do not live under the same conditions in the ghetto; rather, they occupy different quarters with varying economic characteristics. Why not identify these places, for example, as 'poor', 'working-class', 'middle-class' and 'mixed-income' *neighbourhoods* in the ghetto under discussion? (See n.6 for discussion of the term 'communal' in Wacquant's definition.)

5 Conservatives like Lawrence Mead (1989) placed much of the blame on social welfare programmes which undermine the work ethic among low-income blacks. Social democrats like Wilson usually rely on the work of John Kasarda (1985; 1989), who has popularized the notion that there is a mismatch between the skills of central city residents and the demands of employers in 'knowledge-intensive' service industries. Elsewhere (Fainstein, 1986) I have provided a lengthy critique of mismatch theory as an adequate economic analysis of the labour-market situation of African Americans.

6 The literature is replete with such assertions, always presented in global terms, and rarely supported by evidence. For example, in a well-known study of Philadelphia in the 1980s, Elijah Anderson (1990, pp. 58–9) refers frequently to the time 'in the past [when] blacks of various social classes lived side by side', when 'successful people' were 'effective, meaningful role models, lending the community a certain moral integrity'. He cites as support

Drake and Cayton (1945), who never set foot in Philadelphia and, as noted previously, took a much less sanguine view of the Chicago ghetto. He also cites, again without specifics, Kenneth Clark's *Dark Ghetto* (1964: 81). Yet Clark said of Harlem in the 1950s and early 1960s: 'The dark ghetto is institutionalized pathology.' Much of his book was, in fact, devoted to excoriating Harlem's leaders and institutions.

The extent of 'community' in a ghetto as a whole, or in its neighbourhoods, must be determined empirically. In general, however, one should be careful about supposing that there was ever a period when the ghetto was internally integrated, when its institutions effected social control over all, when social anomie did not accompany extreme poverty. Thus, Drake and Cayton (1945, ch. 18) in their study of the Chicago black ghetto during its supposedly most 'communal' days – the 1930s – find a world divided by class, religious commitment and varying degrees of criminality. Their description of the worst, lower-class neighbourhoods sounds remarkably contemporary (see ch. 21).

7   The narrative here reinforces its first element through an entirely circular process of reasoning. The correct lens is one of class, but class as applied to the underclass somehow elides into being a racial category, since it is really only the *black* underclass that gets discussed.

8   A radical attack against the prevailing discourse may be found in Raymond Franklin's (1991) recent book, which will probably be viewed as falling beyond the boundaries of 'responsible' social science. Although I do not discuss it here, Michael Katz's *The Underserving Poor* (1989) should be reread along with the new books by Jencks, Orfield and Ashkinaze, and Hacker.

9   Gary Orfield's co-author, Carole Ashkinaze, is a journalist who has won a Pulitzer Prize for investigative reporting.

10   Aside from the work on residential segregation which I will discuss below, see, for example, Landry (1987), Collins (1989), Fainstein and Fainstein (1989), Jaynes and Williams (1989), Feagin (1991), Swinton (1991), Waldinger and Bailey (1991) and Galster and Hill (1992).

11   Other interrelated changes were also involved, of course, including economic restructuring, decentralization of production, shifts in the occupational structure, and growth in female employment. There is a vast literature on these subjects which I cannot address here.

12   These data are in constant (1990) dollars and are drawn from US Bureau of the Census (1991, Table B-10).

13   These data are based on a Congressional Budget Office simulation model using actual data through 1989 and projecting to 1992. Comparisons that reflect actual data, e.g. 1977 versus 1988, are virtually identical (US House of Representatives, Committee on Ways and Means, 1991, Appendix J, Table 23).

14   Table 9.1 also shows that the proportion of white households in the middle-income category declined by more than 4 per cent. Thus, the contraction of the middle class was not particularly a black phenomenon.

15   For an excellent review of policies, politics and political culture, see Edsall and Edsall (1991). Hacker (1992) also documents the differing and increasingly disparate mentalities of blacks and whites. Judd (1991) discusses the historical and continuing role of the national government in promoting racial segregation.

16   On the role of governmental units in metropolitan areas, see Weiher (1991) and Stearns and Logan (1986).

17   See Orfield and Ashkinaze (1991) and the first analysis of 1990 census data from New York City, discussed below.

18   Galster (1991, p. 624) examines three indicators of suburbanization of blacks in 40 metropolitan areas, comparing 1970 and 1980. Using simply the percentage of blacks

living in suburbs, he finds an increase of 4.2 per cent in black suburbanization, from 20.2 to 24.4. When he controls for the change in the percentage of whites living in suburbs by employing the ratio between the races, the improvement in black suburbanization is only 2.3 per cent, from 33.8 to 36.1 (in other words, in both years blacks were about one-third as likely as whites to be suburbanized). Galster then constructs a measure of decentralization which ignores nominal jurisdictional boundaries, reflecting only distance from the metropolitan core. This measure actually shows a minute increase in racial segregation during the 1970s: compared to the decentralization of the white population in the 1970s, the black population did not improve its position, remaining just as concentrated in the central rings of metropolitan areas.

19 Massey (1990) here includes numerous references which I have omitted, but see, for example, Denton and Massey (1988), Farley and Allen (1987), Massey and Denton (1988).

20 An interesting case in point is provided by Wacquant and Wilson (1989), who contrast the differences between life in extremely poor black neighbourhoods ('ghettos') and merely low-income ones in Chicago in 1980. The authors criticize conservatives who fail to recognize the 'unprecedented concentration of the most socially excluded and economically marginal members of the dominated economic and racial group', i.e. African Americans. To that end, they demonstrate that social pathology is concentrated in the poorest black neighbourhoods (with a poverty rate of 40 per cent or more) and that black neighbourhoods with somewhat lower poverty rates (20–30 per cent) are not nearly so bad, being much more economically heterogeneous. In these ('non-ghetto') neighbourhoods, working-class (55 per cent) and even middle-class blacks (11 per cent) live in proximity to the welfare poor, the long-term unemployed, in short, to households that have been characterized as belonging to the underclass. Instead of asking what this means for 'stable' black households and for the dynamics of race and class, Wilson and Wacquant use their evidence to demonstrate that many blacks who live in low-income neighbourhoods do not have the attributes of the underclass. What they are doing there, and what happens to their children (do they disproportionately fall into the underclass?) is not the subject of analysis. (In other respects, the article deviates from the usual underclass interpretation. Perhaps its ambiguous approach reflects an effort to reconcile the quite divergent approaches of its two authors.)

21 Initial evidence from a study of 5700 block groups (units smaller than census tracts) in New York City indicates that the pattern has persisted in the 1980s (Roberts, 1992). Andrew Beveridge, analysing the 1990 census, finds that segregation by race is much greater than by income within and between racial groups, and that the level of racial segregation (even when income is controlled) remained at the same level in 1990 as in 1980 (with an index of dissimilarity above 0.80) (Roberts, 1992).

22 The main thrust of this article was not to study the situation of higher-income blacks, but to test Wilson's thesis that increasing spatial separation between the poor and higher-income blacks contributed to the growth of the underclass. Based on a regression of poverty concentration against various measures of segregation, Massey and Eggers (1990, p. 1183) reject the underclass narrative:

> In short, the class-based arguments put forth by Wilson and others to explain levels and trends in the concentration of poverty are seriously incomplete without reference to patterns and levels of racial and ethnic segregation. Our results suggest that unusually high and rising concentrations of poverty among blacks outside the West and Hispanics in the Northeast cannot be attributed to the flight of middle-class minorities from ghetto or barrio neighborhoods. Rather, they reflect the bifurcation of black and Hispanic income distribution during a period of unusual economic stress and the consequent rise of poverty within a highly segregated residential environment.

23 Note that Tables 9.3 and 9.4 present *mean* earnings, while Table 9.2 uses *median* earnings, which are, of course, much less affected by high-end earners.

24 Upper-income blacks (i.e. those with incomes that would place them within the top 20 per cent of the national household income distribution) actually saw their relative position slip from four years earlier, when it had stood at 45 per cent of white net worth for households in the same income category.

25 As noted earlier, preliminary evidence from the 1990 census (Roberts, 1992) shows that racial segregation remained unchanged during the decade of the 1980s, whether or not social class is controlled.

26 I should note that in spite of the common sense of this idea, and the fact that everyone in America tries to isolate themselves from economic or racially undesirable neighbours, social scientists have had a difficult time demonstrating that neighbourhood effects actually 'matter'. As I read it, the recent lengthy review of the literature by Jencks and Mayer (1990) proves to be largely inconclusive. None the less, I continue to throw in my lot with logic and actual behaviour, noting that few social scientists are personally willing to take the chance of raising their children in even a working-class neighbourhood, not to mention an impoverished one.

27 Hacker (1992) and Jencks (1992) both offer lengthy reviews and thoughtful discussions.

28 Further evidence reinforces the point. In 1985, the Educational Testing Service examined a sample of American young adults (aged 21–25) to determine their level of functional literacy (Jaynes and Williams, 1989, pp. 353–4). The tests measured reading comprehension, ability to use documents like grocery store coupons and street maps, and practical quantitative reasoning. The results showed strong racial differences. For example, about 90 per cent of whites could find a location on a street map compared with 56 per cent of blacks. Sixty-five per cent of whites could use a map and follow directions to a particular location, compared with 20 per cent of blacks. Practical tests associated with everyday life produced similar results on the other measures.

   Moreover, controlling for income had relatively little effect on reducing these racial differences. Thus, without any controls, black–white differences averaged between 51 and 60 points on the various measures (the standard deviation was about 50 points). When class background and education attainment were factored out, racial differences were reduced only by about ten points, to between 41 and 50 points. In other words, among young adults of similar social class, black performance in functional literacy remained nearly a standard deviation below that of whites.

29 In standard English: 'Boys in the neighbourhood'.

REFERENCES

American Council on Education (1992). *Minorities in Higher Education 1991, tenth annual status report*. American Council on Education, Washington DC.

Anderson, E. (1990). *Streetwise*. University of Chicago Press, Chicago.

Clark, K. (1964). *Dark Ghetto*. Harper and Row, New York.

Collins, S. M. (1989). The marginalization of black executives. *Social Problems* 36, 4, 317–31.

Denton, N. A. and D. S. Massey (1988). Residential segregation of blacks, hispanics, and Asians by socioeconomic status and generation. *Social Science Quarterly* 69, 797–817.

Drake, St C. and H. R. Cayton (1945). *Black Metropolis*. Harcourt, Brace, New York.

Edsall, T. B. and M. D. Edsall (1991). *Chain Reactions*. W. W. Norton, New York.

Fainstein, N. (1986). The underclass/mismatch hypothesis as an explanation for black economic deprivation. *Politics and Society* 15, 403–51.

Fainstein, S. and N. Fainstein (1989). The racial dimension in urban political economy. *Urban Affairs Quarterly* 25.2, 187–99.

Farley, R. and W. Allen (1987). *The Color Line and the Quality of Life in America*. Russell Sage Foundation, New York.

Feagin, J. R. (1991). The continuing significance of race. *American Sociological Review* 56, 101–16.

Franklin, R. (1991). *Shadows of Race and Class*. University of Minnesota Press, Minneapolis.

Galster, G. (1987). The ecology of racial discrimination in housing. *Urban Affairs Quarterly* 23.1, 84–107.

Galster, G. (1991). Black suburbanization: Has it changed the relative location of races? *Urban Affairs Quarterly* 26.4, 621–8.

Galster, G. and E. Hill (eds.). (1992). *The Metropolis in Black and White: Place, power and polarization*. Rutgers University Center for Urban Policy Research, New Brunswick, NJ.

Hacker, A. (1992). *Two Nations: Black and white, separate, hostile, unequal*. Scribners, New York.

Harrison, B. and L. Gorham (1992). What happened to African American wages in the 1980s? In Galster and Hill (1992).

Jacob, J. (1991). Black America 1990: an overview. In National Urban League, *The State of Black America*. National Urban League, New York.

Jaynes, G. D. and R. M. Williams Jr (eds.). (1989). *A Common Destiny: Blacks and American Society*. National Academy Press, New York.

Jencks, C. (1992). *Rethinking Social Policy: Race, poverty, and the underclass*. Harvard University Press, Cambridge, MA.

Jencks, C. and S. E. Mayer (1990). The social consequences of growing up in a poor neighborhood. In National Research Council, *Inner-city Poverty in the United States*. National Research Council, Washington DC.

Jencks, C. and P. E. Peterson (eds.). (1991). *The Urban Underclass*. Brookings Institution, Washington DC.

Judd, D. R. (1991). Segregation forever? *The Nation*, 9 December, 740–4.

Kasarda, J. (1985). Urban change and minority opportunities. In P. Peterson (ed.). *The New Urban Reality*. Brookings Institution, Washington DC.

Kasarda, J. (1989). Urban industrial transformation and the underclass. In Wilson (1989).

Katz, M. B. (1989). *The Undeserving Poor*. Pantheon, New York.

Landry, B. (1987). *The New Black Middle Class*. University of California Press, Berkeley.

Marks, C. (1991). The urban underclass. *Annual Review of Sociology* 17, 445–66.

Massey, D. S. (1990). American apartheid: Segregation and the making of the underclass. *American Journal of Sociology* 96.2, 329–57.

Massey, D. S. and N. A. Denton (1988). Suburbanization and segregation in US metropolitan areas. *American Journal of Sociology* 94.1, 592–626.

Massey, D. S. and M. L. Eggers (1990). The ecology of inequality: Minorities and the concentration of poverty, 1970–1980. *American Journal of Sociology* 95.5, 1153–88.

Massey, D. S. and A. B. Gross (1991). Explaining trends in racial segregation, 1970–1980. *Urban Affairs Quarterly* 27.1, 13–35.

Massey, D. S., G. A. Condran and N. A. Denton (1987). The effect of residential segregation on black social and economic well-being. *Social Forces* 66.1, 29–56.

Mead, L. (1989). The logic of workfare: The underclass and work policy. In Wilson (1989).

Orfield, G. and C. Ashkinaze (1991). *The Closing Door: Conservative policy and black opportunity*. University of Chicago, Chicago.

Roberts, S. (1992). Shifts in 80's failed to ease segregation. *New York Times*, 15 July, B1.

Stearns, L. B. and J. R. Logan (1986). The racial structuring of the housing market and segregation in suburban areas. *Social Forces* 65.1, 28–42.

Swinton, D. H. (1991). The economic status of African Americans: Permanent poverty and inequality. In National Urban League, *The State of Black America, 1991*. National Urban League, New York.

Time Magazine (1977). The American underclass: Destitute and desperate in the land of plenty. 29 August, 14–27.

US Bureau of the Census (1983). *Current Population Reports*. Series P-60, no. 142.

US Bureau of the Census (1990). *Household Wealth and Asset Ownership: 1988. Current Population Reports*. Series P-70, no. 22.

US Bureau of Census (1991). *Current Population Reports*. Series P-60, no. 174.

US House of Representatives, Committee on Ways and Means (1991). *Overview of Entitlement Programs, 1991 Green Book*. US Government Printing Office, Washington DC.

Wacquant, L. (1992). Décivilisation et diabolisation: La mutation du ghetto noir américain. In T. Bishop and C. Faure (eds.). *L'Amérique des français*. Editions François Bourin, Paris.

Wacquant, L. and W. J. Wilson (1989). The cost of racial and class exclusion in the inner city. In Wilson (1989).

Waldinger, R. and T. Bailey (1991). The continuing significance of race. *Politics and Society* 19.3, 291–323.

Weiher, G. (1991). *The Fractured Metropolis: Political fragmentation and metropolitan segregation*. SUNY Press, Albany, NY.

Wilson, W. J. (1978). *The Declining Significance of Race*. University of Chicago Press, Chicago.

Wilson, W. J. (1987). *The Truly Disadvantaged*. University of Chicago Press, Chicago.

Wilson, W. J. (1989). The ghetto underclass: Social science perspectives. Edited volume, *Annals*, 501, (January).

Wilson, W. J. (1991). Studying inner-city social dislocations: the challenge of public agenda research. *American Sociological Review* 56, 1–14.

Part III

Redevelopment and Urban Transformation

Introduction

The dominant development trend in both the USA and the UK has been towards decentralization of employment and population. Nevertheless, considerable investment has gone into central business districts (CBDs), and there has been a detectable migration of well-to-do people into formerly working-class inner-city residential districts. These movements have resulted from the interaction of governmental policy and the private market. Even while these trends have been celebrated as an urban renaissance, they have also been widely criticized for channeling their benefits narrowly to developers, downtown businesses, and upper middle-class gentrifiers at the expense of the working class and the poor.

Logan and Molotch (chapter 10) scrutinize the economic interests that constitute the "growth machine." They show its deep historical roots and the role played by political rather than purely impersonal market forces in affecting urban growth. Finally, they reveal the factors that make the political objectives of this coalition so potent and subject these objectives to a broad critique.

Squires (chapter 11) focuses on the principal vehicle for inner-city redevelopment – the public-private partnership. In his discussion of this supposedly new phenomenon of government–business cooperation, Squires contends that it has existed throughout American history. He roots it in an ideology of privatism, which he criticizes for insulating policy makers from accountability and for inflicting serious costs on vulnerable groups. He concludes by proposing alternative paths for central-city redevelopment.

In chapter 12, Neil Smith's examination of gentrification – the displacement of lower- by upper-income people in urban neighborhoods – likewise points to ideological elements in shaping developmental patterns. He shows how the ideology of the frontier connects with the profitability of developing previously devalued urban land. Like many of the authors in this volume, he links the flows of investment into and out of the city to the larger processes of global economic restructuring.

In his discussion of the 'tourist bubble' (chapter 13), Dennis Judd, like many of the authors in this book, links the themes of global competition, urban regeneration, and exclusion. He concerns himself with the increasingly important strategy of tourism development, which city officials have relied on more and more as a basis for urban revival. He contends that, in American cities, the presentation of a favorable image to outsiders requires both intense marketing and the encasing of the tourist milieu in a bubble that buffers visitors from the more unpleasant aspects of urban life. The result is a sanitized, standardized space, which may provide amenities for urban residents but which also creates islands of affluence segregated from the rest of the city.

10

The City as a Growth Machine*

John R. Logan and Harvey L. Molotch

Traditional urban research has had little relevance to the day-to-day activities of the place-based elites whose priorities affect patterns of land use, public budgets, and urban social life. It has not even been apparent from much of the scholarship of urban social science that place is a market commodity that can produce wealth and power for its owners, and that this might explain why certain people take a keen interest in the ordering of urban life.

Research on local elites has been preoccupied with the question "Who governs?" (or "Who rules?"). Are the politically active citizens of a city split into diverse and competing interest groups, or are they members of a coordinated oligarchy? Empirical evidence of visible cleavage, such as disputes on a public issue, has been accepted as evidence of pluralistic competition (Banfield, 1961; Dahl, 1961). Signs of cohesion, such as common membership in voluntary and policy groups, have been used to support the alternative view (Domhoff, 1970).

We believe that the question of who governs or rules has to be asked in conjunction with the equally central question "For what?" With rare exceptions (Smith and Keller, 1983), one issue consistently generates consensus among local elite groups and separates them from people who use the city principally as a place to live and work: the issue of growth. For those who count, the city is a growth machine, one that can increase aggregate rents and trap related wealth for those in the right position to benefit. The desire for growth creates consensus among a wide range of elite groups, no matter how split they might be on other issues. Thus the disagreement on some or even most public issues does not necessarily indicate any fundamental disunity, nor do changes in the number or variety of actors on the scene – what Clark (1968) calls "decentralization" – affect the basic matter. It does not even

* Logan, John R. and Harvey L. Molotch (1987) "The City as a Growth Machine" from *Urban Fortunes: The Political Economy of Place*, The University of California Press, Berkeley, pp. 50–98. Copyright © 1987 The Regents of the University of California, The University of California Press, Berkeley.

matter that elites often fail to achieve their growth goal; with virtually all places in the same game, some elites will inevitably lose no matter how great their effort (Lyon et al., 1981; Krannich and Humphrey, 1983).

Although they may differ on which particular strategy will best succeed, elites use their growth consensus to eliminate any alternative vision of the purpose of local government or the meaning of community. The issues that reach public agendas (and are therefore available for pluralists' investigations) do so precisely because they are matters on which elites have, in effect, agreed to disagree (Molotch and Lester, 1974, 1975; Schattschneider, 1960). Only under rather extraordinary circumstances is this consensus endangered.

For all the pluralism Banfield (1961) uncovered in Chicago, he found no disagreement with the idea that growth was good. Indeed, much of the dissension he did find, for example, on where to put the new convention center, was part of a dispute over how growth should be internally distributed. In his studies of cities on both sides of the southern US border, D'Antonio found that when community "knowledgeables" were "asked to name the most pressing problems facing their respective cities," they cited finding sufficient water for both farming and urban growth (Form and D'Antonio, 1970, p. 439). Whitt (1982) found that in formulating positions on California transportation policies, elites carefully coordinated not only the positions they would take but also the amount of money each would give toward winning relevant initiative campaigns. Thus on growth infrastructure, the elites were united.

Similarly, it was on the primacy of such growth and development issues that Hunter found Atlanta's elites to be most unified, both at the time of his first classic study and during its replication twenty years later (Hunter, 1953, 1980). Hunter (1953, p. 214) reports, "They could speak of nothing else" (cited in Domhoff, 1983, p. 169). In his historical profiles of Dallas and Fort Worth, Melosi (1983, p. 175) concludes that "political power in Dallas and Fort Worth has typically been concentrated in the hands of those people most willing and able to sustain growth and expansion." Finally, even the ecologically oriented scholars with a different perspective, Berry and Kasarda (1977, p. 371), have remarked, "If in the past urbanization has been governed by any conscious public objectives at all, these have been, on the one hand, to encourage growth, apparently for its own sake, and on the other hand, to provide public works and public welfare programs to support piecemeal, spontaneous development impelled primarily by private initiative." And even Hawley (1950, p. 429) briefly departs from his tight ecological schema to remark that "competition is observable . . . in the struggle for transportation and communication advantages and superior services of all kinds; it also appears in efforts to accelerate rates of population growth."

All of this competition, in addition to its critical influence on what goes on *within* cities, also influences the distribution of populations throughout cities and regions, determining which ones grow and which do not. The incessant lobbying, manipulating, and cajoling can deliver the critical resources from which great cities are made. Although virtually all places are subject to the pervasive rule of growth boosters, places with more active and creative elites may have an edge over other areas. In a comparative study of forty-eight communities, Lyon et al. (1981) indeed found that cities with reputedly more powerful elites tended to have stronger growth rates. This may mean that active elites stimulate growth, or it may mean that strong growth emboldens elites to actively maintain their advantage. Although we suspect that both perspectives are valid, we stress that the activism of entrepreneurs is, and always has been, a critical force in shaping the urban system, including the rise and fall of given places.

Growth Machines in US History

The role of the growth machine as a driving force in US urban development has long been a factor in US history, and is nowhere more clearly documented than in the histories of eighteenth- and nineteenth-century American cities. Indeed, although historians have chronicled many types of mass opposition to capitalist organization (for example, labor unions and the Wobblie movement), there is precious little evidence of resistance to the dynamics of value-free city building characteristic of the American past. In looking back we thus have not only the benefit of hindsight but also the advantage of dealing with a time in which "the interfusing of public and private prosperity" (Boorstin, 1965, p. 116) was proudly proclaimed by town boosters and their contemporary chroniclers. The creators of towns and the builders of cities strained to use all the resources at their disposal, including crude political clout, to make great fortunes out of place. The "lively competitive spirit" of the western regions was, in Boorstin's view (1965, p. 123), more "a competition among communities" than among individuals. Sometimes, the "communities" were merely subdivided parcels with town names on them, what Wade (1959) has called "paper villages," on whose behalf governmental actions could nonetheless be taken.[1] The competition among them was primarily among growth elites.

These communities competed to attract federal land offices, colleges and academies, or installations such as arsenals and prisons as a means of stimulating development. These projects were, for many places, "the only factor that permitted them to outdistance less favored rivals with equivalent natural or geographic endowments" (Scheiber, 1973, p. 136). The other important arena of competition was also dependent on government decision making and funding: the development of a transportation infrastructure that would give a locality better access to raw materials and markets. First came the myriad efforts to attract state and federal funds to link towns to waterways through canals. Then came efforts to subsidize and direct the paths of railroads (Glaab, 1962). Town leaders used their governmental authority to determine routes and subsidies, motivated by their private interest in rents.

The people who engaged in this city building have often been celebrated for their inspired vision and "absolute faith." One historian characterizes then as "ambitious, flamboyant, and imaginative" (Fuller, 1976, p. 41). But more important than their personalities, these urban founders were in the business of manipulating place for its exchange values. Their occupations most often were real estate or banking (Belcher, 1947). Even those who initially practiced law, medicine, or pharmacy were rentiers in the making. These professional roles became sidelines: "Physicians became merchants, clergymen became bankers, lawyers became manufacturers" (Boorstin, 1965, p. 123). Especially when fortunes could be made from growth, the elite division of labor was overwhelmed and "specialized skills...had a new unimportance" (Boorstin, 1965, p. 123). Speaking of the early settlers' acquisition of speculative lands through the preemption regulations of the 1862 Homestead Act, Leslie Decker remarks that "the early comers to any town – from lawyers to doctors to merchants, to just plain town developers – usually diversified in this fashion" (quoted in Wolf, 1981, p. 52); see also Swierenga (1966).

The city-building activities of these growth entrepreneurs in frontier towns became the springboard for the much celebrated taming of the American wilderness. As Wade (1959) has argued, the upstart western cities functioned as market, finance, and administrative outposts that made rural pioneering possible. This conquering of the West, accomplished through the machinations of "the urban frontier," was critically bound up with a coordinated effort to gain rents. For town leaders to achieve their goals, there was "ingenious employment of the instruments of political and economic leverage at [their] disposal" to build the cities and regions in which they had made investments (Scheiber, 1973, p. 136).

Perhaps the most spectacular case of urban ingenuity was the Chicago of William Ogden. When Ogden came to Chicago in 1835, its population was under four thousand. He succeeded in becoming its mayor, its great railway developer, and the owner of much of its best real estate. As the organizer and first president of the Union Pacific (among other railroads) and in combination with his other business and civic roles, he was able to make Chicago (as a "public duty") the crossroads of America, and hence the dominant metropolis of the Midwest. Chicago became a crossroads not only because it was "central" (other places were also in the "middle") but because a small group of people (led by Ogden) had the power to literally have the roads cross in the spot they chose. Ogden candidly reminisced about one of the real estate deals this made possible: "I purchased for $8,000, what 8 years thereafter, sold for 3 millions of dollars" (Boorstin, 1965, p. 117). The Ogden story, Boorstin says (p. 118), "was re-enacted a thousand times all over America."

This tendency to use land and government activity to make money was not invented in nineteenth-century America, nor did it end then. The development of the American Midwest was only one particularly noticed (and celebrated) moment in the total process. One of the more fascinating instances, farther to the West and later in history, was the rapid development of Los Angeles, an anomaly to many because it had none of the "natural" features that are thought to support urban growth: no centrality, no harbor, no transportation crossroads, not even a water supply. Indeed, the rise of Los Angeles as the preeminent city of the West, eclipsing its rivals San Diego and San Francisco, can only be explained as a remarkable victory of human cunning over the so-called limits of nature. Much of the development of western cities hinged on access to a railroad; the termination of the first continental railroad at San Francisco, therefore, secured that city's early lead over other western towns. The railroad was thus crucial to the fortunes of the barons with extensive real estate and commercial interests in San Francisco – Stanford, Crocker, Huntington, and Hopkins. These men feared the coming of a second cross-country railroad (the southern route), for its urban terminus might threaten the San Francisco investments. San Diego, with its natural port, could become a rival to San Francisco, but Los Angeles, which had no comparable advantage, would remain forever in its shadow. Hence, the San Francisco elites used their economic and political power to keep San Diego from becoming the terminus of the southern route. As Fogelson (1967, pp. 51, 55) remarks, "San Diego's supreme asset, the bay, was actually its fatal liability," whereas the disadvantage of Los Angeles – "its inadequate and unprotected port – was its saving grace." Of course, Los Angeles won in the end, but here again the wiles of boosters were crucial: the Los Angeles interests managed to secure millions in federal funds to construct a port – today the world's largest artificial harbor – as well as federal backing to gain water (Clark, 1983, pp. 273, 274).

The same dynamic accounts for the other great harbor in the Southwest. Houston beat out Galveston as the major port of Texas (ranked third in the country in 1979) only when Congressman Tom Ball of Houston successfully won, at the beginning of this century, a million-dollar federal appropriation to construct a canal linking landlocked Houston to the Gulf of Mexico (Kaplan, 1983, p. 196). That was the crucial event that, capitalizing on Galveston's susceptibility to hurricanes, put Houston permanently in the lead.

In more recent times, the mammoth federal interstate highway system, hammered out by "a horde of special interests representing towns and cities" (Judd, 1983, p. 173), has similarly made and unmade urban fortunes. To use one clear case, Colorado's leaders made Denver a highway crossroads by convincing President Eisenhower in 1956 to add three hundred miles to the system to link Denver to Salt Lake City by an expensive mountain route. A presidential stroke of the pen removed the prospects of Cheyenne, Wyoming, of replacing Denver as a major western transportation center (Judd, 1983, p. 173). In a case reminiscent of the nineteenth-century canal era, the Tennessee–Tombigbee Waterway, opened in 1985, dramatically altered the shipping distances to the Gulf of Mexico for many inland cities. The largest project ever built by the US Corps of Engineers, the $2 billion project was questioned as a boondoggle in Baltimore, which will lose port business because of it (Maguire, 1985), but praised in Decatur, Alabama, and Knoxville, Tennessee, which expect to profit from it. The opening of the canal cut by four-fifths the distance from Chattanooga, Tennessee, to the Gulf, but did almost nothing for places like Minneapolis and Pittsburgh, which were previously about the same nautical distance from the Gulf as Chattanooga.

Despite the general hometown hoopla of boosters who have won infrastructural victories, not everyone gains when the structural speculators of a city defeat their competition. It is too easy, and misleading, to say that "the public benefits... because it got the railroads" (Grodinsky, as cited in Klein, 1970, p. 294).[2] Given the stakes, the rentier elites would obviously become engulfed by the "booster spirit." But despite the long-held supposition of an American "antiurban bias" (White and White, 1962), researchers have made little effort to question the linkage between public betterment and growth, even when they could see that specific social groups were being hurt. Zunz reports that in industrializing Detroit, city authorities extended utility service into uninhabited areas to help development, rather than into existing residential zones whose working-class residents went without service even as they bore the costs (through taxes) of the new installations. There was a "bias in favor of speculators and against the working class" (Zunz, 1982, p. 116). Even the great urban reformers, such as Detroit's Mayor Hazen Pingree, while working to change this "standard practice" for financing growth (p. 118), were doing so in order to increase the overall efficiencies of urban services and hence "engineer growth better" (p. 111). "Real estate specialists and builders were more involved in the city-building process," Zunz (p. 162) says, "than anybody else."

Reviewing urbanization from 1850 to 1930, Lewis Mumford observed: "That a city had any other purpose than to attract trade, to increase land values, and to grow is something, if it uneasily entered the mind of an occasional Whitman, never exercised any hold on the minds of our countrymen" (quoted in Mollenkopf, 1983, p. 14).

This is the consensus that must be examined, particularly in light of recent urban development. Let us turn now to a description of the ingenious modern incarnations of the growth machines and to an analysis of how they function, a task made more difficult for modern times because the crucial participants seldom speak so openly as did Mr Ogden.

The Modern-day Good Business Climate

The jockeying for canals, railroads, and arsenals of the nineteenth century has given way since to more complex and subtle efforts to manipulate space and redistribute rents. The fusing of public duty and private gain has become much less acceptable (both in public opinion and in the criminal courts); the replacing of frontiers by complex cities has given important roles to mass media, urban professionals, and skilled political entrepreneurs. The growth machine is less personalized, with fewer local heroes, and has become instead a multifaceted matrix of important social institutions pressing along complementary lines.

With a transportation and communication grid already in place, modern cities typically seek growth in basic economic functions, particularly job intensive ones. Economic growth sets in motion the migration of labor and a demand for ancillary production services, housing, retailing, and wholesaling ("multiplier effects"). Con-temporary places differ in the type of economic base they strive to build (for example, manufacturing, research and development, information processing, or tourism). But any one of the rainbows leads to the same pot of gold: more intense land use and thus higher rent collections, with associated professional fees and locally based profits.

Cities are in a position to affect the "factors of production" that are widely believed to channel the capital investments that drive local growth (Hawley, 1950; Summers et al., 1976). They can, for example, lower access costs of raw materials and markets through the creation of shipping ports and airfields (either by using local subsidies or by facilitating state and federal support). Localities can decrease corporate overhead costs through sympathetic policies on pollution abatement, employee health standards, and taxes, Labor costs can be indirectly lowered by pushing welfare recipients into low-paying jobs and through the use of police to constrain union organizing. Moral laws can be changed; for example, drinking alcohol can be legalized (as in Ann Arbor, Mich., and Evanston, Ill.) or gambling can be promoted (as in Atlantic City, N.J.) to build tourism and convention business. Increased utility costs caused by new development can be borne, as they usually are (see, for an example, Ann Arbor, Michigan, Planning Department, 1972), by the public at large rather than by those responsible for the "excess" demand they generate. Federally financed programs can be harnessed to provide cheap water supplies; state agencies can be manipulated to subsidize insurance rates; local polit-ical units can forgive business property taxes. Government installations of various sorts (universities, military bases) can be used to leverage additional development by guaranteeing the presence of skilled labor, retailing customers, or proximate markets for subcontractors. For some analytical purposes, it does not even matter that a number of these factors have little bearing on corporate locational decisions (some certainly do; others are debated); just the *possibility* that they might matter invigorates local growth activism (Swanstrom, 1985) and dominates policy agendas.

Following the lead of St. Petersburg, Florida, the first city to hire a press agent (in 1918) to boost growth (Mormino, 1983: 150), virtually all major urban areas now use experts to attract outside investment. One city, Dixon, Illinois, has gone so far as to systematically contact former residents who might be in a position to help (as many as twenty thousand people) and offer them a finder's fee of up to $10,000, for directing corporate investment toward their old home town (*San Francisco Chronicle*, May 10, 1984). More pervasively, each city tries to create a "good business climate." The ingredients are well known in city-building circles and have even been codified and turned into "official" lists for each regional area. The much-used Fantus rankings of business climates are based on factors like taxation, labor legislation, unemployment compensation, scale of government, and public indebtedness (Fantus ranks Texas as number one and New York as number forty-eight). In 1975, the Industrial Development Research Council, made up of corporate executives responsible for site selection decisions, conducted a survey of its members. In that survey, states were rated more simply as "cooperative," "indifferent," or "antigrowth"; the results closely paralleled the Fantus rankings of the same year (Weinstein and Firestine, 1978, pp. 134–44).

Any issue of a major business magazine is replete with advertisements from localities of all types (including whole countries) striving to portray themselves in a manner attractive to business. Consider these claims culled from one issue of *Business Week* (February 12, 1979):

> New York City is open for business. No other city in America offers more financial incentives to expand or relocate . . .

The state of Louisiana advertises

> Nature made it perfect. We made it profitable.

On another page we find the claim that "Northern Ireland works" and has a workforce with "positive attitudes toward company loyalty, productivity and labor relations." Georgia asserts, "Government should strive to improve business conditions, not hinder them." Atlanta headlines that as "A City Without Limits" it "has ways of getting people like you out of town" and then details its transportation advantages to business. Some places describe attributes that would enhance the lifestyle of executives and professional employees (not a dimension of Fantus rankings); thus a number of cities push an image of artistic refinement. No advertisements in this issue (or in any other, we suspect) show city workers living in nice homes or influencing their working conditions.

While a good opera or ballet company may subtly enhance the growth potential of some cities, other cultural ingredients are crucial for a good business climate. There should be no violent class or ethnic conflict (Agger, Goldrich, and Swanson, 1964, p. 649; Johnson, 1983, pp. 250–1). Rubin (1972, p. 123) reports that racial confrontation over school busing was sometimes seen as a threat to urban economic development. Racial violence in South Africa is finally leading to the disinvestment that reformers could not bring about through moral suasion. In the good business climate, the workforce should be sufficiently quiescent and healthy to be productive; this was the rationale originally behind many programs in workplace relations and public health. Labor must, in other words, be "reproduced," but only under conditions that least interfere with local growth trajectories.

Perhaps most important of all, local publics should favor growth and support the ideology of value-free development. This public attitude reassures investors that the concrete enticements of a locality will be upheld by future politicians. The challenge is to connect civic pride to the growth goal, tying the presumed economic and social benefits of growth in general (Wolfe, 1981) to growth in the local area. Probably only partly aware of this, elites generate and sustain the place patriotism of the masses. According to Boorstin, the competition among cities "helped create the booster spirit" as much as the booster spirit helped create the cities (1965, p. 123). In the nineteenth-century cities, the great rivalries over canal and railway installations were the political spectacles of the day, with attention devoted to their public, not private, benefits. With the drama of the new railway technology, ordinary people were swept into the competition among places, rooting for their own town to become the new "crossroads" or at least a way station. "The debates over transportation," writes Scheiber (1973, p. 143), "heightened urban community consciousness and sharpened local pride in many western towns."

The celebration of local growth continues to be a theme in the culture of localities. Schoolchildren are taught to view local history as a series of breakthroughs in the expansion of the economic base of their city and region, celebrating its numerical leadership in one sort of production or another; more generally, increases in population tend to be equated with local progress. Civic organizations sponsor essay contests on the topic of local greatness. They encourage public celebrations and spectacles in which the locality name can be proudly advanced for the benefit of both locals and outsiders. They subsidize soapbox derbies, parade floats, and beauty contests to "spread around" the locality's name in the media and at distant competitive sites.

One case can illustrate the link between growth goals and cultural institutions. In the Los Angeles area, St Patrick's Day parades are held at four different locales, because the city's Irish leaders can't agree on the venue for a joint celebration. The source of the difficulty (and much acrimony) is that these parades march down the main business streets in each locale, thereby making them a symbol of the life of the city. Business groups associated with each of the strips want to claim the parade as exclusively their own, leading to charges by still a fifth parade organization that the other groups are only out to "make money" (McGarry, 1985, II, p.1). The countercharge, vehemently denied, was that the leader of the challenging business street was not even Irish. Thus even an ethnic celebration can receive its special form from the machinations of growth interests and the competitions among them.

The growth machine avidly supports whatever cultural institutions can play a role in building locality. Always ready to oppose cultural and political developments contrary to their interests (for example, black nationalism and communal cults), rentiers and their associates encourage activities that will connect feelings of community ("we feelings" [McKenzie, 1922]) to the goal of local growth. The overall ideological thrust is to deemphasize the connection between growth and exchange values and to reinforce the link between growth and better lives for the majority. We do not mean to suggest that the only source of civic pride is the desire to collect rents; certainly the cultural pride of tribal groups predates growth machines. Nevertheless, the growth machine coalition mobilizes these cultural motivations, legitimizes them, and channels them into activities that are consistent with growth goals.

The Organization of the Growth Coalition

The people who use their time and money to participate in local affairs are the ones who – in vast disproportion to their representation in the population – have the most to gain or lose in land-use decisions. Local business people are the major participants in urban politics (Walton, 1970), particularly business people in property investing, development, and real estate financing (Spaulding, 1951; Mumford, 1961). Peterson (1981, p. 132), who applauds growth boosterism, acknowledges that "such policies are often promulgated through a highly centralized decision-making process involving prestigious businessmen and professionals. Conflict within the city tends to be minimal, decision-making processes tend to be closed." Elected officials, says Stone (1984, p. 292), find themselves confronted by "a business community that is well-organized, amply supplied with a number of deployable resources, and inclined to act on behalf of tangible and ambitious plans that are mutually beneficial to its own members."

Business people's continuous interaction with public officials (including supporting them through substantial campaign contributions) gives them *systemic* power (Alford and Friedland, 1975; Stone, 1981, 1982). Once organized, they stay organized. They are "mobilized interests" (Fainstein et al., 1983, p. 214). Rentiers need local government in their daily money-making routines, especially when structural speculations are involved. They are assisted by lawyers, syndicators, and property brokers (Bouma, 1962), who prosper as long as they can win decisions favoring their clients. Finally, there are monopolistic business enterprises (such as the local newspaper) whose futures are tied to the growth of the metropolis as a whole, although they are not directly involved in land use. When the local market is saturated with their product, they have few ways to increase profits, beyond expansion of their surrounding area. As in the proverbial Springdale, site of the classic Vidich and Bensman (1960, p. 216) ethnography of a generation ago, there is a strong tendency in most cities for "the professionals (doctors, teachers, dentists, etc.), the industrial workers, the shack people and the lower middle-class groups [to be] for all intents and purposes disenfranchised except in terms of temporary issues."

Because so much of the growth mobilization effort involves government, local growth elites play a major role in electing local politicians, "watchdogging" their activities, and scrutinizing administrative detail. Whether in generating infrastructural resources, keeping peace on the home front, or using the city mayor as an "ambassador to industry" (Wyner, 1967), local government is primarily concerned with increasing growth. Again, it is not the only function of local government, but it is the key one.

In contrast to our position, urban social scientists have often ignored the politics of growth in their work, even when debates over growth infrastructures were the topic of their analyses (Banfield, 1961; Dahl, 1961). Williams and Adrian (1963) at least treat growth as an important part of the local political process, but give it no priority over other government issues. There are a number of reasons why growth politics is consistently undervalued. The clue can be found in Edelman's (1964) distinction between two kinds of politics.

The first is the "symbolic" politics of public morality and most of the other "big issues" featured in the headlines and editorials of the daily press: school prayer, wars on crime, standing up to communism, and child pornography, for example. News coverage of these issues may have little to do with any underlying reality, much less a reality in which significant local actors have major stakes. Fishman (1978) shows, for example, that reports of a major crime wave against the elderly in New York City appeared just at a time when most crimes against the elderly were actually on the decline. The public "crime wave" was created by police officials who, in responding to reporters' interest in the topic, provided "juicy" instances that would make good copy. The "crime wave" was sustained by politicians eager to denouce the perpetrators, and these politicians' pronouncements became the basis for still more coverage and expressions of authoritative police concern. Once this symbiotic "dance" (Molotch, 1980) is in motion, the story takes on a life of its own, and fills the pages and airwaves of news media. Such symbolic crusades provide the "easy news" (Gordon, Heath, and leBailly, 1979) needed by reporters pressed for time, just as these crusades satisfy the "news needs" (Molotch and Lester, 1974) of politicians happy to stay away from issues that might offend growth machine interests. The resulting hubbubs often mislead the general public as well as the academic investigator about what the real stuff of community cleavage and political process might be. To the degree that rentier elites keep growth issues on a symbolic level (for example, urban "greatness"), they prevail as the "second face of power" (Bachrach and Baratz, 1962), the face that determines the public agenda (McCombs and Shaw, 1972).

Edelman's second kind of politics, which does not provide easy news, involves the government actions that affect the distribution of important goods and services. Much less visible to publics, often relegated to back rooms or negotiations within insulated authorities and agencies (Caro, 1974: Friedland, Piven, and Alford, 1978), this is the politics that determines who, in material terms, gets what, where, and how (Lasswell, 1936). The media tend to cover it as the dull round of meetings of water and sewer districts, bridge authorities, and industrial development bonding agencies. The media attitude serves to keep interesting issues away from the public and blunt widespread interest in local politics generally. As Vidich and Bensman (1960, p. 217) remark about Springdale, "business control rests upon a dull but unanimous political facade," at least on certain key issues.

Although there are certainly elite organizational mechanisms to inhibit them (Domhoff, 1971, 1983; Whitt, 1982), cleavages within the growth machine can nevertheless develop, and internal disagreements sometimes break into the open. But even then, because of the hegemony of the growth machine, *its* disagreements are allowable and do not challenge the belief in growth itself. Unacceptable are public attacks on the pursuit of exchange values over citizens' search for use value. An internal quarrel over where a convention center is to be built, Banfield (1961) shows us, becomes the public issue for Chicago; but Banfield didn't notice that there was no question about whether there should be a convention center at all.

When elites come to see, for example, that inadequate public services are repelling capital investment, they can put the issue of raising taxes on the public agenda. Trillin (1976:154) reports on Rockford, Illinois, a city whose school system was bankrupted by an antitax ideology. Initially, local elites opposed taxes as part of their efforts to lure industry through a low tax rate. As a result, taxes, and therefore tax money for schools, declined. Eventually, the growth coalition saw the educational decline, not the tax rate, as the greatest danger to the "economic vitality of the community." But ironically, elites are not able to change overnight the ideologies they have put in place over decades, even when it is in their best interests to do so.[3] Unfortunately, neither can the potential *opponents* of growth. As the example of Rockford shows, even such issues as public school spending can become subject to the growth maximization needs of locality. The appropriate level of a social service often depends, not on an abstract model of efficiency or on "public demand" (Tiebout, 1956), but on whether the cost of that service fits the local growth strategy (past and present).

By now it should be clear how political structures are mobilized to intensify land uses for private gain of many sorts. Let us look more closely, therefore, at the various local actors, besides those directly involved in generating rents, who participate in the growth machine.

Politicians

The growth machine will sustain only certain persons as politicians. The campaign contributions and public celebrations that build political careers do not ordinarily come about because of a person's desire to save or destroy the environment, to repress or liberate the blacks or other disadvantaged groups, to eliminate civil liberties or enhance them. Given their legislative power, politicians may end up doing any of these things. But the underlying politics that gives rise to such opportunities is a person's participation in the growth consensus. That is why we so often see politicians springing into action to attract new capital and to sustain old investments. Even the pluralist scholar Robert Dahl observed in his New Haven study that if an employer seriously threatened to leave the community, "political leaders are likely to make frantic attempts to make the local situation more attractive" (quoted in Swanstrom, 1981, p. 50).

Certainly, politicians differ in a number of ways. Like Mayor Ogden of Chicago, some are trying to create vast fortunes for themselves as they go about their civic duties on behalf of the growth machine. Robert Folson, the mayor of Dallas, has direct interests in over fifty local businesses, many of which have stakes in local growth outcomes. When the annexation of an adjacent town came up for a vote, he had to abstain because he owned 20 percent of it (Fullinwider, 1980). Another Texan, former governor John Connally, has among his holdings more than $50 million in Austin-area real estate, property slated to become its county's largest residential and commercial development ("Austin Boom," *Santa Barbara News Press*, June 24, 1984, p. B-8). According to Robert Caro (1974), Commissioner Robert Moses was able to overcome opposition to his vast highway and bridge building in the New York City area in part because the region's politicians were themselves buying up land adjacent to parkway exits, setting themselves up for huge rent gains. Most of Hawaii's major Democrat politicians, after winning election on a reform platform in 1954, directly profited as developers, lawyers, contractors, and investors through the zoning and related land-use decisions they and their colleagues were to make over the next thirty years of intensive growth and speculation (Daws and Cooper, 1984). Machine politics never insulated candidates from the development process; builders, railroaders, and other growth activists have long played crucial roles in boss politics, both in immigrant wards (Bell, 1961) and in WASP suburbs (Fogelson, 1967, p. 207). All this is, as George Washington Plunkitt said in 1905, "honest graft" as opposed to "dishonest graft" (quoted in Swanstrom, 1985, p. 25).[4]

Although a little grease always helps a wheel to turn, a system can run well with no graft at all unless using campaign contributions to influence elections is considered graft. Virtually all politicians are dependent on private campaign financing (Alexander, 1972, 1980, 1983; Boyarsky and Gillam, 1982; Smith, 1984), and it is the real estate entrepreneurs – particularly the large-scale structural speculators – who are particularly active in supporting candidates. The result is that candidates of both parties, of whatever ideological stripe, have to garner the favor of such persons, and this puts them squarely into the hands of growth machine coalitions. Thus many officeholders use their authority, not to enrich themselves, but to benefit the "whole community" – that is, to increase aggregate rents. Again, this does not preclude politicians' direct participation in property dealing on occasion and it certainly does not preclude giving a special hand to particular place entrepreneurs with whom a politician has a special relationship.

Elected officials also vary in their perception of how their authority can best be used to maximize growth. After his thorough study of the Cleveland growth machine, Swanstrom (1985) concluded that there are two types of growth strategists: the "conservative" and the "liberal." The former, paramount during the city's age of steel, favors unbridled exploitation of the city and its labor force, generally following the "free economy" political model. Programs of overt government intervention, for purposes of planning, public education, or employee welfare, are all highly suspect. The liberal growth machine strategy, in contrast, acknowledges that longer-term growth can be facilitated by overt government planning and by programs that pacify, co-opt, and placate oppositions. This is a more modern form of growth ideology. Some politicians, depending on place and time, tend to favor the hard-line "unfettered capitalism" (Wolfe, 1981); others prefer the liberal version, analogous to what is called, in a broader context, "pragmatic state capitalism" (Wolfe, 1981); see also Weinstein (1968). These positions became more obvious in many regions when urban renewal and other federal programs began penetrating cities in the postwar period. Especially in conservative areas such as Texas (Melosi, 1983, p. 185), elites long debated among themselves whether or not the newfangled growth schemes would do more harm than good.

On the symbolic issues, politicians may also differ, on both the content of their positions and the degree to which they actually care about the issues. Some are no doubt sincere in pushing their "causes"; others may cynically manipulate them to obscure the distributional consequences of their own actions in other matters. Sometimes the results are positive, for example, when Oklahoma City and Dallas leaders made deliberate efforts to prevent racist elements from scaring off development with "another Little Rock." Liberal growth machine goals may thus help reform reactionary social patterns (Bernard, 1983, p. 225; Melosi, 1983, p. 188). But despite these variations, there appears to be a "tilt" to the whole system, regardless of time and place. Growth coalition activists and campaign contributors are not a culturally, racially, or economically diverse cross-section of the urban population. They tend to give a reactionary texture to local government, in which the cultural crusades, like the material ones, are chosen for their acceptability to the rentier groups. Politicians adept in both spheres (material and symbolic) are the most valued, and most likely to have successful careers. A skilled politician delivers growth while giving a good circus.

The symbolic political skills are particularly crucial when unforeseen circumstances create use value crises, which can potentially stymie a locality's basic growth strategy. The 1978 Love Canal toxic waste emergency at Niagara Falls, New York, reveals how local officials use their positions to reassure the citizens and mold local agendas to handle disruptive "emotional" issues. In her detailed enthnographic account, Levine (1982, p. 59) reports that "the city's chief executives, led by the mayor, minimized the Love Canal problem in all public statements for two years no matter how much personal sympathy they felt for the affected people whose health was threatened by the poisons leaking into their homes"; see also Fowlkes and Miller (1985). Lester (1971) reports a similar stance taken by the Utah civic leadership in response to the escape of nerve gas from the US military's Dugway Proving Grounds in 1969; see also Hirsch (1969). The conduct of politicians in the face of accidents like the leakage of poison into schoolyards and homes in Niagara Falls or the sheep deaths in Utah reveal this "backup" function of local leaders (Molotch and Lester, 1974, 1975).

Still another critical use of local politicians is their ability to influence higher-level political actors in their growth distribution decisions. Although capital has direct links to national politicians (particularly in the executive office and Senate, see Domhoff (1967, 1970, 1983)), rentier groups are most parochial in their ties, although they may have contact with congressional representatives. Hence, rentiers need local politicians to lobby national officials. The national politicians, in turn, are responsive because they depend on local political operators (including party figures) for their own power base. The local politicians symbiotically need their national counterparts to generate the goods that keep them viable at home.

The goods that benefit the local leaders and growth interests are not trivial. The development of the Midwest was, as the historical anecdotes make clear, dependent on national decisions affecting canal and railroad lines. The Southwest and most of California could be developed only with federal subsidies and capital investments in water projects. The profound significance of government capital spending can be grasped by considering one statistic: direct government outlays (at all levels) in 1983 accounted for nearly 27 percent of all construction in the United States (Mollenkopf,

1983, p. 43). The figure was even higher, of course, during World War II, when federal construction expenditures laid the basis for much of the infrastructural and defense spending that was to follow.

Local media

One local business takes a broad responsibility for general growth machine goals – the metropolitan newspaper. Most newspapers (small, suburban papers are occasionally an exception) profit primarily from increasing their circulation and therefore have a direct interest in growth.[5] As the metropolis expands, the newspaper can sell a larger number of ad lines (at higher per line cost), on the basis of a rising circulation base; TV and radio stations are in a similar situation. In explaining why his newspaper had supported the urbanization of orchards that used to cover what is now the city of San José, the publisher of the *San Jose Mercury News* said, "Trees do not read newspapers" (Downie, 1974, p. 112, as cited in Domhoff, 1983, p. 168). Just as newspaper boosterism was important in building the frontier towns (Dagenais, 1967), so today "the hallmark of media content has been peerless boosterism: congratulate growth rather than calculate consequences; compliment development rather than criticize its impact" (Burd, 1977, p. 129); see also Devereux (1976) and Freidel (1963). The media "must present a favorable image to outsiders" (Cox and Morgan, 1973, p. 136),[6] and only "sparingly use their issue-raising capacities" (Peterson, 1981, p. 124).

American cities tend to be one-newspaper (or one-newspaper company) towns. The newspaper's assets in physical plant, in "good will," and in advertising clients are, for the most part, immobile. The local newspaper thus tends to occupy a unique position: like many other local businesses, it has an interest in growth, but unlike most others, its critical interest is not in the specific spatial pattern of that growth. The paper may occasionally help forge a specific strategy of growth, but ordinarily it makes little difference to a newspaper whether the additional population comes to reside on the north side or the south side, or whether the new business comes through a new convention center or a new olive factory. The newspaper has no ax to grind except the one that holds the community elite together: growth.

This disinterest in the specific form of growth, but avid commitment to development generally, enables the newspaper to achieve a statesmanlike position in the community. It is often deferred to as a neutral party by the special interests. In his pioneering study of the creation of zoning laws in New York City in the 1920s, Makielski (1966, p. 149) remarks, "While the newspapers in the city are large landholders, the role of the press was not quite like that of any of the other nongovernmental actors. The press was in part one of the referees of the rules of the game, especially the informal rules, calling attention to what it considered violations." The publisher or editor is often the arbiter of internal growth machine bickering, restraining the short-term profiteers in the interest of more stable, long-term, and properly planned growth.

The publishing families are often ensconced as the most important city builders within the town or city; this is the appropriate designation for such prominent families as Otis and Chandler of the *Los Angeles Times* (Clark, 1983, p. 271; Halberstam, 1979); Pulliam of the *Arizona Republic* and *Phoenix Sun* (Luckingham, 1983, p. 318); and Gaylord of the *Daily Oklahoman* (Bernard, 1983, p. 216). Sometimes these publishers are directly active in politics, "kingmaking" behind the scenes by screening candidates for political office, lobbying for federal contracts and grants, and striving to build growth infrastructure in their region (Fainstein et al. 1983, p. 217; Judd, 1983, p. 178). In the booming Contra Costa County suburbs of the San Francisco Bay Area, the president of the countrywide organization of builders, real estate investors, and property financiers was the owner of the regional paper. In his home county, as well as in the jurisdictions of his eleven other suburban papers, owner Dean Lesher ("Citizen Lesher") acts as "a cheerleader for development" who simply kills stories damaging to growth interests and reassigns unsympathetic reporters to less controversial beats (Steidtmann, 1985). The local newspaper editor was one of the three "bosses" in Springdale's "invisible government" (Vidich and Bensman, 1960, p. 217). Sometimes, the publisher is among the largest urban landholders and openly fights for benefits tied to growth in land: the owners of the *Los Angeles Times* fought for the water that developed their vast properties for both urban and agricultural uses. The editorial stance is usually reformist, invoking the common good (and technical planning expertise) as the rationale for the land-use decisions the owners favor. This sustains the legitimacy of the paper itself among all literate sectors of society and helps mask the distributive effects of many growth developments.

The media attempt to attain their goals not only through news articles and editorials but also through informal talks between owners and editors and the local leaders. Because newspaper interests are tied to growth, media executives are sympathetic to business leaders' complaints that a particular journalistic investigation or angle may be bad for the local business climate, and should it nevertheless become necessary, direct threats of advertising cancellation can modify journalistic coverage (Bernard, 1983, p. 220). This does not mean that newspapers (or advertisers) control the politics of a city or region, but that the media have a special influence simply because they are committed to growth *per se*, and can play an invaluable role in coordinating strategy and selling growth to the public.

This institutional legitimacy is especially useful in crises. In the controversy surrounding the army's accidental release of nerve gas at the Dugway Proving Grounds, Lester found that the Utah media were far more sympathetic to the military's explanations than were media outside Utah (Lester, 1971). The economic utility of the Dugway Proving Grounds (and related government facilities) was valued by the local establishment. Similarly, insiders report that publicizing toxic waste problems at Love Canal was hindered by an "unwritten law" in the newsroom that "a reporter did not attack or otherwise fluster the Hooker [Chemical Company] executives" (Brown, 1979, cited in Levine, 1982, p. 190).

As these examples indicate, a newspaper's essential role is not to protect a given firm or industry (an issue more likely to arise in a small city than a large one) but to bolster and maintain the predisposition for general growth. Although newspaper editorialists may express concern for "the ecology," this does not prevent them from supporting growth-inducing investments for their regions. The *New York Times* likes office towers and additional industrial installations in the city even more than it loves "the environment." Even when historically significant districts are threatened, the *Times* editorializes in favor of intensification. Thus the *Times* recently admonished opponents to "get out of the way" of the Times Square renewal, which would replace landmark structures (including its own former headquarters at 1 Times Square) with huge office structures (*New York Times*, May 24, 1984, p. 18). Similarly, the *Los Angeles Times* editorializes against narrow-minded profiteering that increases pollution or aesthetic blight – in other cities. The newspaper featured criticism, for example, of the Times Square renewal plan (Kaplan, 1984, p. 1), but had enthusiastically supported development of the environmentally devastating supersonic transport (SST) for the jobs it would presumably lure to Southern california. In an unexpected regional parallel, the *Los Angeles Times* fired celebrated architectural critic John Pastier for his incessant criticisms of Los Angeles's downtown renewal projects (Clark, 1983, p. 298), and the *New York Times* dismissed Pulitzer Prize winner Sydney Schanberg as a columnist apparently because he "opposed civic projects supported by some of New York's most powerful interests, particularly those in the real estate industry" (Rosenstiel, 1985, p. 21).

Although newspapers may openly support "good planning principles" of a certain sort, the acceptable form of "good planning" does not often extend to limiting growth or authentic conservation in a newspaper's home ground. "Good planning principles" can easily represent the opposite goals.

Utilities

Leaders of "independent" public or quasi-public agencies, such as utilities, may play a role similar to that of the newspaper publisher: tied to a single locale, they become growth "statesmen" rather than advocates for a certain type of growth or intralocal distribution of growth.

For example, a water-supplying agency (whether public or private) can expand only by acquiring more users. This causes utilities to penetrate deep into the hinterlands, inefficiently extending lines to areas that are extremely costly to service (Gaffney, 1961; Walker and Williams, 1982). The same growth goals exist within central cities. Brooklyn Gas was an avid supporter of the movement of young professionals into abandoned areas of Brooklyn, New York, in the 1970s, and even went so far as to help finance housing rehabilitation and sponsor a traveling slide show and open houses displaying the pleasant lifestyles in the area. All utilities seem bent on acquiring more customers to pay off past investments, and on proving they have the good growth prospects that lenders use as a criterion for financing additional investments. Overall efficiencies are often sacrificed as a result.

Transportation officials, whether of public or private organizations, have a special interest in growth: they tend to favor growth along their specific transit routes. But transportation does not just serve growth, it creates it. From the beginning, the laying-out of mass transit lines was a method of stimulating development; indeed, the land speculators and the executives of the transportation firms were often the same people. In part, because of the salience of land development, "public service was largely incidental to the operation of the street railways" (Wilcox, quoted in Yago, 1984, p. 44). Henry Huntington's Pacific Electric, the primary commuting system of Los Angeles, "was built not to provide transportation but to sell real estate"

(Clark, 1983, p. 272); see also Binford (1985), Fogelson (1967) and Yago (1984). And because the goal of profitable transportation did not guide the design and routing of the system, it was destined to lose money, leaving Los Angeles without a viable transit system in the end (Fogelson, 1967).

Transit bureaucrats today, although not typically in the land business, function as active development boosters; only in that way can more riders be found to support their systems and help pay off the sometimes enormous debts incurred to construct or expand the systems. On the national level, major airlines develop a strong growth interest in the development of their "hub" city and the network it serves. Eastern Airlines must have growth in Miami, Northwest Airlines needs development in Minneapolis, and American Airlines rises or falls with the fortunes of Dallas-Fort Worth.

Auxiliary Players

Although they may have less of a stake in the growth process than the actors described above, certain institutions play an auxiliary role in promoting and maintaining growth. Key among these auxiliary players are the cultural institutions in an area: museums, theaters, universities, symphonies, and professional sports teams. An increase in the local population may help sustain these institutions by increasing the number of clients and support groups. More important, perhaps, is that such institutions often need the favor of those who are at the heart of local growth machines – the rentiers, media owners, and politicians, who can make or break their institutional goals. And indeed, cultural institutions do have something to offer in return.

Universities

The construction and expansion of university campuses can stimulate development in otherwise rural landscapes; the land for the University of California at Los Angeles (UCLA) was originally donated for a state normal school in 1881 "in order to increase the value of the surrounding real estate" (Clark, 1983, p. 286). Other educational institutions, particularly the University of California campuses at Irvine and Santa Barbara, had similar origins, as did the State University of New York at Stony Brook and the University of Texas at San Antonio (Johnson, 1983). Building a university campus can be the first step in rejuvenating a deteriorated inner-city area; this was the case with the Chicago branch of the University of Illinois (Banfield, 1961), the expansions of Yale University in New Haven (Dahl, 1961; Domhoff, 1978), and the University of Chicago (Rossi and Dentler, 1961). The use of universities and colleges as a stimulus to growth is often made explicit by both the institution involved and the local civic boosters.

The symbiotic relationship between universities and local development intensified in the 1980s. Drawing on the precedent of Silicon Valley (with Stanford University as its intellectual center) and Route 128, the high-tech highway, in the Boston area (with MIT as its intellectual center), many localities have come to view universities as an infrastructure for cutting edge industrial growth. Universities, in turn, have been quick to exploit this opportunity to strengthen their local constituency. A clear illustration is the Microelectronics and Computer Technology Corporation (MCTC), a newly created private firm with the mission of keeping the United States ahead of Japan in the microelectronics field. Jointly funded by twelve of the most important American firms in advanced technology, the new company had to build, at its founding, a $100 million installation. Austin, Texas, won the project, but only after the local and state governments agreed to a list of concessions, including subsidized land, mortgage assistance for employees, and a score of faculty chairs and other positions at the University of Texas for personnel relevant to the company mission (Rivera, 1983).

The Austin victory reverberated especially through California, the location of the runner-up site. A consensus emerged, bolstered by an MCTC official's explicit statement, that faltering support for California higher education had made Texas the preferred choice. The view that a decline in the quality of higher education could drive away business may have been important in the fiscally conservative governor's decision to substantially increase allocations to the University of California in the following year. Budget increases for the less research-oriented state college system were at a much lower level; the community college system received a decrease in real dollar funding. The second and third groups of institutions play a less important role in growth machine strategies. As the president of the University of Texas said after his institution's victory, "The battle for national leadership among states is being fought on the campuses of the great research universities of the nation" (King, 1985, p. 12).

Museums, theaters, expositions

Art and the physical structures that house artworks also play a role in growth strategies. In New York City, the art capital of the country, the arts generate about $1.3 billion in annual economic activity, a sum larger than that contributed by either advertising or computer services (Pittas, 1984). In Los Angeles, another major art center, urban redevelopment funds are paying for the new Museum of Contemporary Art, explicitly conceived as a means of enhancing commercial success for adjacent downtown residential, hotel, and office construction. Major art centers are also being used as development leverage in downtown Miami, Tampa (Mormino, 1983, p. 152), and Dallas. The new Dallas Museum of Art will be the central focus of "the largest downtown development ever undertaken in the United States" (Tomkins, 1983, p. 92). Whatever it may do to advance the cause of artists in Texas, the museum will do much for nearby rents. According to a Dallas newspaper report, "The feeling persists that the arts have been appropriated here primarily to sell massive real estate development" (quoted in Tomkins, 1983, p. 97).

Other sorts of museums can be used for the same purpose. Three Silicon Valley cities are locked in a battle to make themselves the site for a $90 million Technology Museum that "is expected to draw one million visitors a year, boost hotel occupancy and attract new business" (Sahagun and Jalon, 1984, p. 1). Two of the competing cities (Mountain View and San José), in promising millions in subsidies, would use the museum as a focal point for major commercial developments. In a not dissimilar, though perhaps less highbrow effort, the city of Flint, Michigan ("the unemployment capital of America") invested city money in a Six Flags Auto World Theme Park that displayed cars (old and new) and used the auto as a motif for its other attractions. The facility was situated so as to boost the city's crumbling downtown; unhappily, gate receipts were poor and the park was closed, and the $70 million public–private investment was lost (Risen, 1984).

Theaters are also being used as a development tool. Believing that the preservation of the legitimate theater will help maintain the "vitality" of Midtown Manhattan, city officials are considering a plan to allow theater owners to sell the "development rights" of their properties, which the dense zoning in the theater district would otherwise permit. The buyer of these rights would then be allowed bonus, or greater, densities on other nearby sites, thereby protecting the theaters' existence while not blocking the general densification of the area (New York Times, September 19, 1983, p. 1). In many parts of the country, various individuals and groups are encouraging (and often subsidizing) the construction and rehabilitation of theaters and concert halls as growth instruments. Downtown churches are looking to the heavens for financial returns, arranging to sell air rights over their imposing edifices to developers of nearby parcels.

These programs allow cultural institutions, in effect, to collect rents they otherwise could gain only by tearing down their structures. The arrangements heads off any conflict between developers and those oriented to the use values that theaters and historic buildings might provide and helps to maintain these "city treasures" that help sustain the economic base. But aggregate levels of development are not curtailed.

Still another kind of cultural institution involved in the growth apparatus is the blue-ribbon committee that puts together local spectaculars, like annual festivals and parades, or a one-shot World's Fair or Olympics competition. These are among the common efforts by Chambers of Commerce and Visitors Bureaus to lure tourists and stimulate development. There are industrial expositions, music festivals, and all manner of regional annual attractions. Such events are considered ways of meeting short-term goals of generating revenue, as well as ways of meeting long-term goals of attracting outside businesses. They show off the locality to outsiders who could generate additional investments in the future. Los Angeles business leaders, for example, "created the Rose Parade to draw national attention to Southern California's balmy weather by staging an outdoor event with fresh flowers in the middle of winter" (Clark, 1983, p. 271).

The short-term results of big events can mean billions of dollars injected into the local economy, although costs to ordinary citizens (in the form of traffic congestion, higher prices, and drains on public services) are notoriously understated (Clayton, 1984; Shlay and Gilroth, 1984). To help gain the necessary public subsidies for such events, the promoters insist that "the community" will benefit, and they inflate revenue expectations in order to make trickle-down benefits at least seem plausible (Hayes, 1984). The 1983 Knoxville World's Fair, one of the few World's Fairs to actually produce a profit on its own books, nevertheless left its host city with $57 million in debts (Schmidt, 1984), a debt large enough to require an 8 percent increase in property taxes in order to pay it off. The 1984 New Orleans World's Fair showed a $100 million loss (Hill, 1984). Other spectaculars, like the Los

Angeles Olympics, do come out ahead, but even so, certain costs (like neighborhood disruption) are simply not counted.

Clearly, a broad range of cultural institutions, not often thought of in terms of land development, participate closely as auxiliary players in the growth process for many reasons. Some participate because their own organizational goals depend on local growth, others because they find it diplomatic to support the local rentier patrons, others because their own properties become a valuable resource, and still others because their boards of directors are closely tied to local elites. Whatever the reasons, the growth machine cuts a wide institutional swath.

Professional sports

Professional sports teams are a clear asset to localities for the strong image they present and tourist traffic they attract (Eitzen and Sage, 1978: 184). Baseball, the American pastime, had its beginning in amusement parks; many of the team owners were real estate speculators who used the team to attract visitors to the subdivisions they offered for sale. Fans would ride to the park on trolley lines that the team owner also owned (Roderick, 1984). In more recent years, baseball and football stadia and hockey and basketball arenas have been used by local *governments* to provide a focus for urban renewal projects in Pittsburgh, Hartford, Minneapolis, and other cities (Roderick, 1984). New Orleans used the development of the Superdome "to set the stage for a tourist-based growth strategy for the future development of downtown" (Smith and Keller, 1983, p. 134). The facility ended up costing $165 million (instead of the projected $35 million), and has had large annual operating losses – all absorbed by the state government.

St. Petersburg, Florida, seems to be following the example of New Orleans. The Florida city has agreed to invest $59.6 million in a new stadium *in the hope* that it will lure a major league franchise to a city that woefully lacks the demographic profile necessary to support major league sports. So far the project has required displacement of four hundred families (primarily black) and saddled the city with a huge debt. A city official insists it will be worth it because

> When you consider what it would mean in new business for hotels, jobs, pride, tourism
> – then it's a real good deal. We believe for every dollar spent inside a stadium, seven are
> spent outside.
>   (Roderick, 1984, p. 24)

In an even more dubious effort, the city of Albany, New York, gained popular support (and some state funding) for a $40 million multipurpose downtown civic center on the grounds that it *might* attract a hockey team to the city (D'Ambrosio, 1985). Like the New Orleans project, this plan puts sports boosters behind a project that will help local business with its other events (such as conventions), regardless of its success in attracting a professional team.

Local teams are an industry in themselves. Atlanta's professional sports organizations have been estimated to be worth over $60 million annually to the local economy (Rice, 1983, p. 38). But a local team does much more than the direct expenditures imply: it helps a city's visibility, putting it "on the map" as a "big league city," making it more noticeable to all, including those making investment decisions. It is one of "the visible badges of urban maturity" (Rice, 1983, p. 38). Within the city, sports teams have an important ideological use, helping instill civic pride in business through jingoistic logic. Whether the setting is soccer in Brazil (Lever, 1983) or baseball in Baltimore, millions of people are mobilized to pull for the home turf. Sports that lend themselves to boosting a locality are the useful ones. Growth activists are less enthusiastic about sports that honor individual accomplishment and are less easily tied to a locality or team name (for example, tennis, track, or swimming). Only when such sports connect with rent enhancement, for example, when they are part of an Olympic competition held on home ground, do they receive major support.

The mobilization of the audience is accomplished through a number of mechanisms. Money to construct stadia or to attract or retain the home team is raised through public bond issues. About 70 percent of current facilities were built with this tool, often under conditions of large cost overruns (Eitzen and Sage, 1978). Enthusiastic corporate sponsorship of radio and TV broadcasts greatly expands public participation (and by linking products with local heroes this form of sponsorship avoids any danger of involving the corporate image with controversial topics). Finally, the news media provide avid coverage, giving sports a separate section of the newspaper and a substantial block of broadcast time during the period designated for the news (including the mention of the city name on national news). No other single news topic receives such consistent and extensive coverage in the United States.

The coverage is, of course, always supportive of sports itself and the home team in particular. There is no pretense of objectivity. It is all part of the ideological ground for other civic goals, including the successful competition of cities for growth-inducing projects. Professional teams serve many latent social functions (Brower, 1972); sustaining the growth ideology is clearly one of them.

Organized labor

Although they are sometimes in conflict with capitalists on other issues, labor union leaders are enthusiastic partners in growth machines, with little careful consideration of the long-term consequences for the rank and file. Union leadership subscribes to value-free development because it will "bring jobs," particularly to the building trades, whose spokespersons are especially vocal in their support of development. Less likely to be openly discussed is the concern that growth may bring more union members and enhance the power and authority of local union officials.[7]

Union executives are available for ceremonial celebrations of growth (ribbon cuttings, announcements of government contracts, urban redevelopment ground breakings). Entrepreneurs frequently enlist union support when value-free development is under challenge; when growth control was threatened in the city of San Diego in 1975, three thousand labor union members paraded through downtown, protesting land-use regulations they claimed were responsible for local unemployment (Corso, 1983, p. 339). Labor leaders are especially useful when the growth machine needs someone to claim that development opponents are "elitist" or "selfish." Thus, in a characteristic report on a growth control referendum in the city of Riverside, California, Neiman and Loveridge (1981, pp. 764–65) found that the progrowth coalition "repeated, time and again, that most of organized labor in the area opposed Measure B, firms wishing to locate in Riverside were being frightened away...and thousands of voters would lose their jobs if Measure B passed." Although this technique apparently worked in Riverside at the pools and in San Diego in the streets, it is doubtful that the majority of the rank and file share the disposition of their leaders on these issues. Nevertheless, the entrepreneurs' influence over the public statements and ceremonial roles of union leaders, regardless of what their members think, helps the rentiers to achieve their aggressive growth policies.

The co-optation of labor leadership is again evident in its role in national urban policy. Labor essentially is a dependable support of growth – anywhere, anytime. Although its traditional constituency is centered in the declining areas of the country, the unions' national hierarchy supports policies little more specific than those that provide "aid to the cities." The active campaign by the United Auto Workers (UAW) for increased investment in Detroit and other sections of the country's "automotive realm" (Hill, 1984) is an exception. Although unions may be especially concerned with the future of the declining areas, they have not tried to develop an effective strategy for directing investment toward these places, at the expense of other places. Labor cannot serve the needs of its most vulnerable and best organized geographical constituency because it will not inhibit investment at any given place. The inability of labor to influence the distribution of development within the United States (much less across world regions) makes organized labor helpless in influencing the political economy of places. Labor becomes little more than one more instrument to be used by elites in competing growth machines.

Self-employed professionals and small retailers

Retailers and professionals ordinarily have no clear interest in the generation of aggregate rents. The stake of these groups in growth depends on their particular situation, including the possibility that growth may displace a clientele upon which they are dependent. Any potential opposition from these groups is, however, blunted by a number of factors, two of which are especially important. Retailers need customers and this often leads them to equate aggregate growth in a locality with an increase in sales and profits for themselves. They also have social ties with local rentier groups, whose avid growth orientation may have a strong influence.

By contrast, larger but locally based retailing chains with substantial local market shares have a direct interest in local growth. They can grow more cheaply by expanding in their own market area (where media and other overhead costs can be spread among existing stores) than by penetrating distant regions. But a larger population base also draws new competitors, since retailing is more competitive than most other businesses. In particular, on reaching a certain size, markets become more attractive to higher-volume, national retailers, such as McDonald's or chain department stores and the malls that house them. Large operations are especially drawn to fast-growing areas in which an early decision to locate can preempt other national competitors. Department stores and chain restaurants displace an enormous number of smaller entrepreneurs (Friedland and Gardner, 1983). Despite these prospects, small retailers are often supporters of local growth machines, even when it means bringing in directly competitive operations. In this instance, ideology seems to prevail over concrete interests and the given record.

Well-paid professionals such as doctors and lawyers sometimes invest their own high salaries in property syndicates (often unprofitable ones) that are put together for them by brokers and financial advisers. This gives the professionals the direct stake in growth outcomes that we ordinarily associate with place entrepreneurs. As social peers of the rentiers, and as vague supporters of value-free production generally, these professionals are often sympathetic to growth. They seem less supportive than business groups, but more supportive than lower-paid professionals or members of the working class (Albrecht et al. 1986). A critical issue for the affluent professionals is whether their own use of places – to live, shop, and earn money – is compatible with growth. Professionals can avoid the dilemma by investing at a distance from their own homes.... professionals not tied to the growth machine make particularly effective citizen opponents of the growth coalition.

Corporate capitalists

Most capitalists, like others whose primary attachment to place is for use values, have little direct interest in land-use intensification in a specific locality. They are in business to gain profits, not rents. Particularly when local corporate leaders are division heads of multilocational firms, there is little reason for direct involvement (Schulze, 1961). In his report on Houston's historical development, Kaplan quotes a local observer who remarks that the "pro-growth faction" consists of people "whose very good livelihoods depend on a local government that will continue to make the 'right' policy decisions." "Surprisingly," Kaplan comments (1983, p. 204), "the oil and gas industry remains aloof from local Houston politics, preferring to concentrate on the national and international policies crucial to its interests." This disinterest of the large industrials is not a surprise to us.

Nevertheless, corporate actors do have an interest in sustaining the growth machine ideology (as opposed to the actual growth of the area surrounding their plant). This ideology helps make them respected people in their area. Their social worth is often defined in terms of "size of payroll," and their payroll in turn helps them get land-use and budget policies consistent with corporate needs. As long as the rentiers dominate locality, capitalists and their managers need not play a direct role. They may choose to do so anyway, particularly when they are natives of the locale (not branch plant functionaries) with ties to rentier groups (Friedland and Palmer, 1984; Galaskiewicz, 1979a, 1979b). But the absence of corporate officials in local politics (especially branch plant managers), repeatedly observed by various investigators (Banfield and Wilson, 1963; Dahl, 1961; Schulze, 1961), is not a sign of their lack of power. It can instead be evidence that the local agenda is so pervasively shaped by their interests that they have no need to participate. Like good managers generally, they work through others, leaving their relative invisibility as a sign of their effectiveness. Only when there is a special opportunity, as in modern-day company towns, or when ordinary hegemonic mechanisms fail, do we find corporate functionaries again active in urban politics.

The Effects of Growth

By claiming that more intensive development benefits virtually all groups in a locality, growth machine activists need pay no attention to the distinction between use and exchange values that pervades our analysis. They assert that growth strengthens the local tax base, creates jobs, provides resources to solve existing social problems, meets the housing needs caused by natural population growth, and allows the market to serve public tastes in housing, neighborhoods, and commerical development. Similarly, Paul Peterson speaks of development goals as inherently uncontroversial and "consensual" because they are aligned with the "collective good" (1981, p. 147), "with the interests of the community as a whole" (p. 143). Speaking in characteristically sanguine terms even about urban renewal (widely known by then for its detrimental effects on cities), Peterson says in his celebrated book: "Downtown business benefits, but so do laborers desiring higher wages, homeowners hoping house values will rise, the unemployed seeking new jobs, and politicians aiming for reelection" (p. 147).

Some of these claims, for some times and places, are true. The costs and benefits of growth depend on local circumstance. Declining cities experience problems that might be eased by replacement investments. Even in growing cities, the costs of growth can conceivably be limited by appropriate planning and control techniques. Nevertheless, for many places and times, growth is at best a mixed blessing and the growth machine's claims are merely legitimating ideology, not accurate descriptions of reality. Residents of declining cities, as well as people living in more dynamic areas, are often deceived by the extravagant claims that growth solves problems. These claims demand a realistic evaluation.

Fiscal health

Systematic comparative analyses of government costs as a function of city size and growth have found that cost is positively related to both size of place and rate of growth, at least for middle-size cities (Appelbaum et al., 1976; Follett, 1976). Of course, the *conditions* of growth are important. The overall fiscal state of a city depends on the kind of growth involved (industrial versus residential, and the subtypes of each) and the existing capacities of the local infrastructure. In general, most studies (Stuart and Teska, 1971) conclude that housing development represents a net fiscal loss because of the service costs that residents require, although housing for the rich is more lucrative than housing for the poor. Industrial and commercial growth, on the other hand, tends to produce net benefits for the tax base, but only if the costs of servicing additions to the local labor force are omitted from the calculations. If local government provides special tax incentives or other sorts of subsidies to attract new industries, the fiscal costs of development will obviously be higher.

Growth can also at times save a local government money. A primary factor in this possibility is the existence of "unused capacities." If a town has a declining birth rate and thus a school district with empty classrooms, officials may try to attract additional families to increase the efficient use of the physical plant and thereby reduce the per capita costs. If a city is paying off a bonded debt on a sewer plant that could serve double its present demand, officials may seek additional users in order to spread the costs to a larger number and thus decrease the burden for current residents.

Under other conditions, however, even small increases in demand can have enormous fiscal costs if the increases entail major new public expenditures. In many cases infrastructures must be built "all at once"; these are "lumpy" costs. Additional water supplies can sometimes be gained only by constructing a vast aqueduct system that can transport 100,000 acre feet annually as easily as a single acre foot. The costs of such utility investments are usually shared equally by all users; the "new people" do not have to pay more because of the extraordinary costs their presence creates. The developer of a "leapfrog" housing tract (one that jumps beyond existing urban development) does not pay more than previous entrepreneurs to run utilities a greater distance, despite the higher costs entailed by the location. This pricing system, in which each user pays the same amount regardless of when or how the user joined the client group, tends to mask the cost of additional growth (or the irrationalities of its distribution). These costs can be especially high because the cheap sources of water, power, and highway rights of way are the first ones tapped; expansion thus tends to be increasingly expensive.

Costs to existing residents can be particularly high if the anticipated growth does not materialize. In what Worster (1982, p. 514) calls the "infrastructural trap," localities that place bets on future growth by investing in large-scale capacities then must move heaven and earth to make sure they get that growth. Whether through deceitful plot or inadvertent blunder, the results can be a vicious cycle of crisis-oriented growth addiction as various infrastructures collapse from overuse and are replaced by still larger facilities, which then can only be paid for with additional growth that again creates another crisis of overuse.

All of this resembles the infrastructure crises of much earlier efforts at growth inducement in the nineteenth century. Scheiber (1973) reports absurd redundancies in the canal-building spree of the state of Ohio as each politically powerful land group demanded a linkage to the great waterways. The scenario was repeated with turnpikes and railroads, leading to absurd overcapacity and the "intolerable indebtedness" that led to bond defaults by several states (Goodrich, 1950). Costs of construction were considerably increased through corrupt management, and the viability of the completed projects was eroded by duplication and irrational routings. The result was "bitter disillusionment" (Scheiber, 1973, p. 138) when prosperous towns did not materialize where expected (almost everywhere) and the costs of overbuilt infrastructures remained as a continuous drain on public budgets.

It is less likely today that a single project could bring about such a fiscal disaster, although the nuclear power bankruptcy in 1983 of the major utility in the state of Washington is one case in point, just as similar nuclear power problems threaten other ratepayers elsewhere. In most instances, growth spending corrodes subtly, slowly eroding fiscal integrity as the service costs of new developments outweigh the revenues they generate. Some localities have demanded "hard looks" at the precise cumulative costs, and have come up with striking results. A 1970 study for the city of Palo Alto, California, found that it would be cheaper for that city to purchase its privately owned undeveloped foothills at full value, rather than allow the land to be developed and enter the tax rolls (Livingston and Blayney, 1971).

Again, a study of Santa Barbara, California, demonstrated that service expenditures for virtually any population growth would require raising property taxes and utility rates, with no compensatory public service benefits for local residents (Appelbaum et al., 1976). Similar conclusions on the costs of growth have resulted from studies of Boulder, Colorado (cited in Finkler, 1972), and Ann Arbor, Michigan (Ann Arbor, Michigan, Planning Department, 1972). In their review of case studies of the effects of industrial growth in small towns, Summers and Branch (1984) report that increments to the local tax base were in most cases outweighed by added service burdens, except when industrial development was not subsidized by local government and new employees lived in other communities.

The kinds of cities that have undertaken these studies, primarily university towns, are by no means typical US places; in the declining cities of the frostbelt, the results might well be different. And cities can, in reality, manipulate the fiscal consequences of growth to benefit them. Here we want to stress that growth cannot, just because it "adds to the tax base," be assumed beneficial to a city's fiscal well-being. Only a careful analysis of the details can yield accurate conclusions about a specific place at a given time. We suspect that the promised benefits of growth would be found, more often than not, to have been greatly exaggerated by the local growth activists, who, while portraying themselves as the prudent guardians of the public purse, often lead their cities into terrible fiscal troubles.

Employment

A key ideological prop for the growth machine, especially in appealing to the working class, is the assertion that local growth "makes jobs." This claim is aggressively promulgated by developers, bankers, and Chamber of Commerce officials – people whose politics otherwise reveal little concern for problems of the working class. The emphasis on jobs becomes a part of the statesmanlike talk of media editorialists. Needless to say, the benefits in profits and rents are seldom brought up in public.

The reality is that local growth does not make jobs: it only distributes them. In any given year, the United States will see the construction of a certain number of new factories, office units, and highways – regardless of where they are put. Similarly, a given number of automobiles, missiles, and lampshades will be made in this country, regardless of where they are manufactured. The number of jobs in this society, whether in the building trades or in any other economic sector, will therefore be determined by rates of return on investments, national trade policy, federal decisions affecting the money supply, and other factors unrelated to local decision making. Except for introducing draconian measures that would replicate Third World labor conditions in US cities (not as remote a possibility as we might think), a locality can only compete with other localities for its share of newly created US jobs. Aggregate employment is unaffected by the outcome of this competition among localities to "make" jobs. The bulk of studies that search, either through cross-sectional or longitudinal analysis, for relations between size or growth of places and unemployment rates fail to show significant relationships (Appelbaum et al., 1976; Follett, 1976; Garrison, 1971; Greenberg, n.d; Hadden and Borgatta, 1965, p. 108;

Samuelson, 1942; Sierra Club of San Diego, 1973; Summers et al., 1976; Summers and Branch, 1984), but see Eberts (1979).

Despite the pain and difficulty often associated with interurban migrations, there is enough worker mobility, at least within national boundaries, to fill jobs at geographically distant points, including even the wilds of Alaska. When jobs develop in a fast-growing area, workers from other areas are attracted to fill the developing vacancies, thus preserving the same unemployment rate as before the growth surge. Indeed, especially in cases of rapid, "boom town" growth, enthusiastic media coverage can prompt large numbers of workers to migrate, much in excess of immediate job openings. A large surplus of workers results when the boom comes to its inevitable end, often with many of the infrastructural costs still to be paid (Markusen, 1978). The human strain of migration – people forced to leave their relatives and neighborhood behind – may prove to have been for nothing. Unemployment rates in the state of Alaska, a boom region for many years, exceeded the national average from 1972 to 1982 every year except one. In 1978, even before oil prices began their precipitous fall, the national unemployment rate was 6.1 percent and the Alaska rate was 11.2 percent.

Similarly, just as "new jobs" may not change the aggregate *rate* of unemployment (either locally or nationally), they may also have little effect on unemployed *individuals* in a given place. For example, cities that are able to reverse chronic economic decline and stagnation, as Atlantic City has done through its recent gambling boom, often provide new jobs primarily for suburbanites and other "outsiders," rather than for the indigenous working class in whose name the transformation was justified (Sternlieb and Hughes, 1983); see also Greenberg (n.d) and Summers et al. (1976). Summers and Branch (1984) draw the same conclusion in their review of the effects of growth on small towns, reporting that typically less than 10 percent of new industrial jobs are filled by persons who were previously unemployed (of whatever residential origin). Evidently, the new jobs are taken by people who already have jobs, many of whom are migrants.[8] Summers observes that "newcomers intervene between the jobs and the local residents, especially the disadvantaged," because they possess "more education, better skills, or the 'right' racial heritage" (as quoted in Bluestone and Harrison, 1982, p. 90).

It is still possible that certain patterns of growth may stimulate employment without attracting migrants. New jobs that bring underemployed women or youths into the workforce may have this effect. It is also true that certain categories of workers can be especially penalized if local labor markets fail to expand, for example, those immobilized by ill health, family commitments, or other factors that limit mobility. But overall, even though local growth may sometimes have beneficial effects on specific individuals and subgroups, both the weight of empirical evidence and the logic of the process indicate that net benefits do not follow as a matter of course. Indeed, our conclusions reinforce what has been called the "unanimous" agreement among economists that "the only jurisdiction that should be concerned with the effects of its policies on the level of employment is the Federal government. Small jurisdictions do not have the power to effect significant changes in the level of unemployment" (Levy and Arnold, 1972, p. 95).

The real problem is that the United States is a society of constant joblessness, with unemployment rates conservatively estimated by the Department of Commerce at

4–11 percent of the workforce defined as ordinarily active. A game of musical chairs is being played at all times, with workers circulating around the country, hoping to land in an empty position when the music stops. Redistributing the stock of jobs among places may move the chairs around, but it does not alter the number of chairs available to the players.

Job and income mobility

Related to the issue of unemployment is the question of occupational mobility in general. It seems obvious that only in the largest places is it possible to attain the highest incomes in the lucrative occupations; for individuals with such ambitions, large may be the only option. Other than moving (the more efficient mechanism), growth of place is the only answer. In general, studies that have compared wage rates among places have found that urban areas with more people have higher wages rates, although the differences between places are small (Alonso, 1973; Appelbaum, 1978; Fuchs, 1967; Hoch, 1972).

More relevant in the present context than the issue of how size affects wages is the issue of how income is influenced by urban *growth*. In his study of matched "self-contained" cities, Appelbaum (1978) found that there was indeed a positive relation between family income and rate of urban growth, see Eberts (1979) for similar results using Northeast counties. But the size and growth effects together had a small *net* effect: controlling for other variables, size and growth explained about 8 percent of the variance in income among places. More crucially, we do not learn in these studies whether growth tends to merely attract higher-wage workers from other areas (which then "decline" in median income as a result), or growth itself benefits indigenous populations.

Also complicating the interpretation of the growth-related income difference is evidence that larger places (and in particular fast-growing ones) have higher living costs, which offset the higher wages. The degree to which this occurs is a matter of debate (Appelbaum, 1978; Hoch, 1972; Shefer, 1970). Although most evidence suggests that *size* has little effect on living costs, *growth* has a much greater effect. This is especially true for housing costs; the effects of growth on prices are especially strong for both single-family houses and apartments (Appelbaum, 1978, pp. 36–7; Appelbaum and Gilderbloom, 1983). Because so many detrimental effects of growth on costs are not reflected in these studies of household income – for example, the effects of pollution on health care and building maintenance expenses – we must conclude that growth does not benefit a family in terms of net income or quality of life.

An alternative way of investigating the connection between growth and the personal income of local populations is through case studies of how growth has affected the wages of specific social and occupational groups in given places. Greenberg (n.d.) carried out such a study with a special focus on low-wage groups and, in particular, poor blacks in southern counties of three subregions that were experiencing different patterns of development. Although all the areas in her study experienced rates of growth exceeding the national growth rate between 1960 and 1980, the economic basis of that growth was different in each place and had distinct consequences for specific labor groups. There were three different patterns:

1   Growth in service industry in an area of declining low-wage manufacturing
2   Invasion of manufacturing jobs into an agricultural zone
3   Major expansion of government jobs in an area with a mixed economy

   In the first case, found in Durham, North Carolina, the transition from a manufacturing to a service economy meant "that blacks simply exchanged low wage jobs in low growth sectors of the economy for low wage jobs in high growth sectors" (Greenberg, n.d., p. 23). In the second pattern, found in the area outside Durham, in which manufacturing invaded a former agricultural zone, Greenberg found that incoming industrialization did not bring higher living standards: "The transition from agriculture to low wage manufacturing has done little to improve the relative economic position of blacks in most types of nonagricultural employment. Whites also earn substantially less than their counterparts in the adjacent urban counties" (Greenberg, n.d., p. 24). In Greenberg's third growth pattern, there were substantial gains for blacks and, presumably, the poor in general. In Wake Country, the growth in employment was based heavily on expansion by the government. The number of blacks in high-level jobs increased and their wage gains outpaced the national average for blacks during this period. Although Greenberg attributes these gains for blacks to the increased "diversity" of the economy that government employment provided, we might put equal stress on the civil service and affirmative action requirements of government hiring and promotion (Baron and Bielby, 1980).
   Whatever the specific reasons for the differences among places, Greenberg's findings indicate that "growth *per se* is no panacea for urban poverty" (Greenberg, n.d., p. 26). Instead, the issue is the *kind* of growth that is involved, and the degree (ordinarily, limited) to which local residents are given an advantage over migrants in the competition for jobs. Otherwise, local growth may be only a matter of making the local rich even richer, or, alternatively, of moving those already priviledged in their jobs from one part of the country to another part of the country. To stay with our metaphor of musical chairs, the number of *comfortable* chairs and the basis for allocating them does not change; only their *location* is altered. As Summers and Branch conclude on the basis of their own growth studies, "Industrial location has a small or even negative effect on the local public sector and on economically disadvantaged citizens" (1984, p. 153); see also Garrison (1971). This is hardly consistent with the myth of opportunity promoted by supporters of the growth machine.

Eliminating social problems

The idea that an increase in numbers and density leads to severe social pathology has been, at long last, thoroughly discredited (Fischer et al., 1975). We do believe, however, that size and rate of growth have a role in creating and exacerbating urban problems such as segregation and inequality.
   The great population explosions that marked America's industrial cities earlier in the twentieth century cannot be said to have increased levels of either equality or class and racial integration. Instead, greater numbers seem to have increased spatial and social segregation between rich and poor, black and white (Lieberson, 1980; Zunz, 1982). In a more contemporary context, Sternlieb and Hughes (1983)

have studied the social effects of the growth of gambling in Atlantic City, New Jersey – the revitalization of a service sector industry. Sternlieb and Hughes report that the consequences have been extremely negative for existing residents. The growth boom has set up "walled off universes" of casino-generated wealth, with the old people and poor finding their former "dismal comforts being swept away," without the compensation of better jobs.[9] The original residents are not participating in the new economy, except at the bottom (as is consistent with Greenberg's findings, discussed above), and the overall effect of the gambling boom on the community is to exacerbate visible cleavages between the rich and the poor (Markusen, 1978).

More generally, growth may not be the cause of problems, but increases in scale make it more difficult to deal with those that do exist. Racial integration is more difficult when members of a minority are concentrated in large ghettos within a vast, and often politically divided, region. It becomes harder to accomplish school integration without busing pupils over long distances and across jurisdictional lines. Busing generates controversy and high costs to public budgets as well as taking up children's time. In small places, racially and economically diverse social groups can more easily end up in the same schools, as well as the same shopping, recreation, and work settings. Whether through fortuitous movements of people or through managed intervention programs, small places can be more easily integrated, racially and economically. Under current jurisdictional and ecological patterns, growth tends to intensify the separation and disparities among social groups and communities.

Growth is likely to increase inequality within places through its effects on the distribution of rents. Increases in urban scale mean larger numbers of bidders for the same critically located land parcels (for example, the central business district or the site for a freeway intersection), inflating land prices relative to wages and other wealth sources. Although growth expands the center zone (as well as stimulating other pockets in the area) the critical locations remain unique. Hence we see the familiar pattern of an intense use of critical spots (for example, Wall Street or Rodeo Drive) with a sharp drop in rent levels just outside their boundaries. Growth disproportionately increases the value of strategic parcels, generating monopoly effects for their owners. Thus, in terms of rental wealth, urban growth is likely to increase inequality.

There is some empirical evidence showing greater income disparities within larger and faster-growing places, whether from monopoly rent effects or another factor (Haworth et al. 1978); but see Walker (1978). Other studies, however, find little or no impact of size or growth rates on wealth distribution (Alonso, 1973; Appelbaum, 1978; Betz, 1972). Our own conclusion is that growth mainly hurts those in its direct path whose primary tie to place is for its residential use value. When tracing the effect of growth, we must look at how particular groups, at a given time and place, are affected by development.

Environment

Growth has obvious negative consequences for the physical environment; growth affects the quality of air and water, and the ease of getting around in a town or city. Growth obliterates open spaces and damages the aesthetic features of a natural terrain. It decreases ecological variety with a consequent threat to the larger ecosystem.

Though sometimes viewed as trivial concerns of an idle middle class ("rich housewives," according to the stereotype), these blows to the physical environment most heavily affect the less well-to-do. A high-quality physical environment constitutes a free public good for those who have access to it (Harvey, 1973). Those who are unable to buy amenities in the market lose most from the unavailability of such resources. More concretely, since the poor are most likely to live and work in close proximity to pollution sources, the poor are more affected by growth-induced environmental decay than are the rich.

Perhaps nowhere are the effects of environmental decline more dramatically displayed than in those places with the most rapid growth experiences. Feagin (1983), for example, has compiled a list of Houston's problems that have accompanied that city's emergence as "capital of the sunbelt." These include crises in sewage disposal, toxic dumps, water supplies, and transportation. In addition to the visible increases in pollution and congestion, past environmental sins will entail vast cleanup costs – what Worster (1982, p. 514) calls "ecological backlash." By 1983, Houston was second only to New York City in per capita bonding liability. Environmental decline, here as elsewhere, can exacerbate fiscal problems and inequality of life chances among rich and poor.

Accommodating natural increase

Growth activists incessantly raise the problem of providing "homes and jobs for our children." To avoid the forced exile of their youth, towns and cities might reasonably have as a goal the maintenance of economic expansion sufficient to provide jobs and housing for new generations. These expansions would be modest in scale, given the low rates of birth that are characteristic of US urban populations. The difficulty is "reserving" the right openings for the right youths, a goal that is unrealistic given the nature of the hiring queue and the constitutional limitations on restraint of trade. Virtually no local growth policy could effectively guarantee local jobs for local people. Many of the young prefer, of course, to leave their home town anyway, and this in itself probably eliminates the problem of having to create large numbers of jobs to accommodate local youth.

Satisfying public taste

The current pattern of urbanization is not necessarily a response to people's wishes. As Sundquist has remarked,

> The notion commonly expressed that Americans have "voted with their feet" in favor of the great cities is, on the basis of every available sampling, so much nonsense... What is called "freedom of choice" is, in sum, freedom of employer choice or, more precisely, freedom of choice for that segment of the corporate world that operates mobile

enterprises. The real question, then, is whether freedom of corporate choice should be automatically honored by government policy at the expense of freedom of individual choice where those conflict.   (1975, p. 258)

Most evidence suggests that people prefer living in small places or rural areas (Appelbaum et al., 1974, pp. 4.2–4.6; Finkler, 1972, pp. 2, 23; Hoch, 1972, p. 280; Mazie and Rowlings, 1973; Parke and Westoff, 1972). Although only 8 percent of Americans in 1977, for example, lived in small towns and farm areas, 48 percent gave such places as their residential preference (Fischer, 1984, p. 20). The larger the metropolis, the greater the proportion of people (in both the central city and suburbs) who express a desire to move away (Gallup, 1979, p. 85). If people's responses to surveys are any indication, a substantial portion of the migration to the great metropolitan areas of the postwar decades was more in spite of tastes than because of them.

Growth Trade-offs

Although there is clear evidence on some of the effects of growth, urban size is fundamentally a political or value issue in which one person's criteria are lined up against another's (Duncan, 1957). It may, for example, be necessary to sacrifice clean air to build a population base large enough to support a major opera company. If one loves music enough, the price may be worth paying. But in reality, differential material interests influence the trade-offs. If one happens to be on the winning side of the rent intensification process (or in the opera business), the pleasures of cleaner air or lower taxes will be easier to forgo.

Besides the variations between individuals and groups, the actual price to be paid for growth and the willingness to pay it will vary somewhat. Having an opera house is probably more important to the Viennese than to the residents of Carmel, California, and in the same way the preferred trade-offs in population size will vary. On more prosaic grounds, certain places may need additional population to absorb the costs of existing road and sewer systems, however misguided the initial commitment to build them. People in some small towns may want a population increase in order to make rudimentary specialization possible in their public school system. In other instances, a past history of outmigration may have left behind a surplus of unused capacities, which would easily accommodate additional growth and provide public benefits of various sorts.

These variations notwithstanding, the evidence on fiscal health and economic or social problems indicates clearly that the assumptions of value-free development are false. In many cases, probably in most, additional local growth under current arrangements is a transfer of wealth and life chances from the general public to the rentier groups and their associates. Use values of a majority are sacrificed for the exchange gains of the few. To question the wisdom of growth for any specific locality is to threaten a benefit transfer and the interests of those who gain from it.

NOTES

1   The same phenomenon is found today in Chicago suburbs formed principally to benefit from state fiscal codes.

2   We were struck by the naive wording used by one historian in commenting upon the life of an urban booster-lawyer: "*despite* [our emphasis] his extensive business career, Brice delved deeply into politics as well. His devotion to the State [Ohio] and its economic interests won him wide popularity there" (Klein, 1970, p. 110).

3   Trillin remarks that rejection of high taxes by the citizens of Rockford is "consistent with what the business and industrial leadership of Rockford has traditionally preached. For years, the industrialists were considered to be in complete control of the sort of local government industrialists traditionally favor – a conservative, relatively clean administration committed to the proposition that the highest principle of government is the lowest property tax rate" (Trillin, 1976, p. 150).

4   Local planning officials also sometimes get in on some of the corruption; they may make real estate investments of their own. Los Angeles Planning Director Calvin Hamilton was pressured to resign after twenty years on the job in part because of revelations that he accepted free rent from developers for a side business and had other conflicts of interest (Clifford, 1985).

5   Although many suburban newspapers encourage growth, especially of tax-generating businesses, the papers of exclusive suburban towns may instead try to guard the existing land-use patterns and social base of their circulation area. Rudel (1989, p. 104) describes just this sort of situation in Westport, Connecticut. There are a number of reasons for this occasional deviation from the rule we are proposing. When trying to attract advertising dollars, newspapers prefer a small, rich readership to a larger but poorer one. Maintaining exclusivity is itself occasionally a growth strategy for smaller communities. Opposition to growth in these cases is consistent with the desires of local elites.

6   Cox and Morgan's study of British local newspapers indicates that the booster role of the press is not unique to the United States.

7   Unions oppose growth projects that bring nonunion shops; the UAW did not welcome Japanese-owned auto plants that would exclude the union.

8   Further, new industrial investment in one city often eliminates jobs at another city, with no net gain.

9   "Atlantic City Hurt by Gambling, Study Finds," *Los Angeles Times*, November 2, 1983, sec. I. p. 11.

REFERENCES

Agger, Robert, Daniel Goldrich, and Bert E. Swanson. 1964. *The Rulers and The Ruled: Political Power and Impotence in American Communities*. New York: Wiley.

Albrecht, Don, Gordon Bultena, and Eric O. Hoiberg. 1986. "Constituency of the Antigrowth Movement: A Comparison of the Growth Orientations of Urban Status Groups." *Urban Affairs Quarterly* 21 (June):607–16.

Alexander, Herbert E. 1972. *Money in Politics*. Washington, DC: Public Affairs Press.

Alexander, Herbert E. 1980. *Financing Politics: Money, Elections and Political Reform*. 2nd edn. Washington, DC: Congressional Quarterly Press.

Alexander, Herbert E. 1983. *Financing the 1980 Election*. Lexington, MA: D. C. Heath.

Alford, Robert, and Roger Friedland. 1975. "Political Participation and Public Policy." *Annual Review of Sociology* 1:429–79.

Alonso, William. 1973. "Urban Zero Population Growth." *Daedalus* 102(4):191–206

Ann Arbor, Michigan, Planning Department. 1972. *The Ann Arbor Growth Study.* Ann Arbor, Mich.: City Planning Department.

Applebaum, Richard P. 1978. *Size, Growth and U.S. Cities.* New York: Praeger

Applebaum, Richard P., and John Gilderbloom. 1983. "Housing Supply and Regulation: A Study of the Rental Housing Market." *Journal of Applied Behavioral Science* 19(1): 1–18.

Applebaum, Richard P., Jennifer Bigelow, Henry Kramer, Harvey Molotch, and Paul Relis. 1974. *Santa Barbara: The Impacts of Growth.* Santa Barbara, CA: Office of the City Clerk.

Applebaum, Richard P., Jennifer Bigelow, Henry Kramer, Harvey Molotch, and Paul Relis. 1976. *The Effects of Urban Growth.* New York: Praeger.

Bachrach, Peter, and Morton Baratz. 1962. "The Two Faces of Power." *American Political Science Review* 56:947–52.

Banfield, Edward C. 1961. *Political Influence.* New York: Macmillan.

Banfield, Edward C., and James Q. Wilson. 1963. *City Politics.* Cambridge, Mass.: Harvard University Press.

Baron, James N., and William T. Bielby. 1980. "The Organization of Work in a Segmented Economy." *American Sociological Review* 49(4):454–73.

Belcher, Wyatt W. 1947. *The Economic Rivalry between St. Louis and Chicago, 1850–1880.* New York: Columbia University Press.

Bell, Daniel. 1961. "Crime as an American Way of Life." In Daniel Bell. *The End of Ideology: On the Exhaustion of Political Ideas in the Fifties.* New York: Collier Books, pp. 127–50.

Bernard, Richard M. 1983. "Oklahoma City: Booming Schooner." In Richard M. Bernard and Bradley R. Rice (eds.). *Sunbelt Cities: Politics and Growth since World War II.* Austin: University of Texas Press, pp. 213–34.

Berry, Brian J. L., and John Kasarda. 1977. *Contemporary Urban Ecology.* New York: Macmillan.

Betz, D. Michael. 1972. "The City as a System Generating Income Inequality." *Social Forces* 51(2):192–8.

Binford, Henry C. 1985. *The First Suburbs: Residential Communities on the Boston Periphery 1815–1860.* Chicago: University of Chicago Press.

Bluestone, Barry, and Bennett Harrison. 1982. *The Deindustrialization of America.* New York: Basic Books.

Boorstin, Daniel. 1965. *The Americans: The National Experience.* New York: Random House.

Bouma, Donald. 1962. "Analysis of the Social Power Position of a Real Estate Board." *Social Problems* 10, (Fall):121–32.

Boyarsky, Bill, and Jerry Gillam. 1982. "Hard Times Don't Stem Flow of Campaign Gifts." *Los Angeles Times,* 4 April, sec. I, pp. 1, 3, 22, 23.

Brower, John. 1972. "The Black Side of Football." Ph.D. dissertation, Department of Sociology, University of California, Santa Barbara.

Burd, Gene. 1977. "The Selling of the Sunbelt: Civic Boosterism in the Media." In David Perry and Alfred Watkins (eds.). *The Rise of the Sunbelt Cities.* Beverly Hills, CA: Sage, pp. 129–50.

Caro, Robert A. 1974. *The Power Broker: Robert Moses and the Fall of New York.* New York: Knopf.

Clark, David L. 1983. "Improbable Los Angeles." In Richard M. Bernard and Bradley R. Rice (eds.). *Sunbelt Cities: Politics and Growth since World War II.* Austin: University of Texas Press, pp. 268–308.

Clark, Terry. 1968. "Community Structure, Decision-Making, Budget Expenditures, and Urban Renewal in Fifty-One American Cities." *American Sociological Review* 33, (August):576–93.

Clayton, Janet. 1984. "South-Central L. A. Fears Olympics to Disrupt Lives." *Los Angeles Times*, 5 February, sec. II, p. 1.

Clifford, Frank. 1985. "Ouster of City Planner Sought." *Los Angeles Times*, 15 July, Sec. I, pp. 1, 13.

Corso, Anthony. 1983. "San Diego: The Anti-City." In Richard M. Bernard and Bradley R. Rice (eds.). *Sunbelt Cities: Politics and Growth since World War II*. Austin: University of Texas Press, pp. 328–44.

Cox, Harvey, and David Morgan. 1973. *City Politics and the Press: Journalists and the Governing of Merseyside*. Cambridge: Cambridge University Press.

Dagenais, Julie. 1967. "Newspaper Language as an Active Agent in the Building of a Frontier Town." *American Speech* 42(2):114–21.

Dahl, Robert Alan. 1961. *Who Governs?* New Haven: Yale University Press.

D'Ambrosio, Mary. 1985. "Coyne Slates Talks on Hockey Franchise." *Albany Times Union*, 14 February, sec. B, p. 1.

Daws, Gavan, and George Cooper. 1984. *Land and Power in Hawaii: The Democratic Years*. Honolulu: Benchmark Press.

Devereux, Sean. 1976. "Boosters in the Newsroom: The Jacksonville Case." *Columbia Journalism Review* 14:38–47.

Domhoff, G. William. 1967. *Who Rules America?* Englewood Cliffs, NJ: Prentice-Hall.

Domhoff, G. William. 1970. *The Higher Circles: The Governing Class in America*. New York: Random House.

Domhoff, G. William. 1971. *The Higher Circles: The Governing Class in America*. New York: Random House.

Domhoff, G. William. 1978. *Who Really Rules: New Haven Community Power Re-Examined*. Santa Monica, CA: Goodyear.

Domhoff, G. William. 1983. *Who Rules America Now? A View for the 80's*. Englewood Cliffs, NJ: Prentice-Hall.

Duncan, Otis Dudley. 1957. "Optimum Size of Cities." In Paul K. Hatt and Albert J. Reiss, Jr. (eds.). *Readings in Urban Sociology*, 2nd edn. Glencoe, Ill.: Free Press, pp. 759–73.

Eberts, Paul R. 1979. "Growth and the Quality of Life: Some Logical and Methodological Issues." In Gene F. Summers and Arne Selvik (eds.). *Nonmetropolitan Industrial Growth and Community Change*. Lexington, MA: Lexington Books, pp. 159–84.

Edelman, Murray. 1964. *The Symbolic Uses of Politics*. Urbana: University of Illinois Press.

Eitzen, D. Stanley, and George H. Sage. 1978. *Sociology of American Sport*. Dubuque, Iowa: William C. Brown.

Fainstein, Susan, Norman Fainstein, and P. Jefferson Armistead. 1983. "San Francisco: Urban Transformation and the Local State." In Susan Fainstein (ed.). *Restructuring the City*. New York: Longman, pp. 202–44.

Feagin, Joe R. 1983. "The Capital of the Sunbelt: Houston's Growth and the Oil Industry." Unpublished manuscript, Department of Sociology, University of Texas, Austin.

Finkler, Earl. 1972. "No-Growth as a Planning Alternative." Planning Advisory Report No. 283. Chicago: American Society of Planning Officials.

Fischer, Claude S. 1984. *The Urban Experience*. San Diego: Harcourt Brace Jovanovich.

Fischer, Claude S., Mark Baldasarre, and R. J. Ofshe. 1975. "Crowding Studies and Urban Life – A Critical Review." *Journal of the American Institute of Planners* 41(6):406–18.

Fishman, Mark. 1978. "Crime Waves as Ideology." *Social Problems* 25(5):532–43.

Fogelson, Robert M. 1967. *The Fragmented Metropolis: Los Angeles, 1850–1930*. Cambridge, MA: Harvard University Press.

Follett, Ross. 1976. "Social Consequences of Urban Size and Growth: An Analysis of U.S. Urban Areas." Ph.D. dissertation, Department of Sociology, University of California, Santa Barbara.

Form, William H., and William V. D'Antonio. 1970. "Integration and Cleavage among Community Influentials in Two Border Cities." In Michael Aiken and Paul E. Mott (eds.). *The Structure of Community Power*. New York: Random House, pp. 431–42.

Fowlkes, Martha R., and Patricia Miller. 1985. "Toward a Sociology of Unnatural Disaster." Paper presented at the 80th annual meeting of the American Sociological Association, Washington, DC, August 31.

Freidel, Frank. 1963. "Boosters, Intellectuals and the American City." In Oscar Handlin and John Burchard (eds.). *The Historian and the City*. Cambridge, MA: MIT Press, pp. 115–20.

Friedland, Roger, and Carole Gardner. 1983. "Department Store Socialism." Testimony before the City of Santa Barbara Redevelopment Agency. Photocopy.

Friedland, Roger, and Donald Palmer. 1984. "Park Place and Main Street: Business and the Urban Power Structure." In Ralph Turner (ed.). *Annual Review of Sociology*, vol. 10. Beverly Hills, CA: Sage, pp. 393–416.

Friedland, Roger, Frances Piven, and Robert Alford. 1978. "Political Conflict, Urban Structure, and the Fiscal Crisis." In Douglas Ashford (ed.). *Comparing Urban Policies*. Beverly Hills, CA: Sage, pp. 175–225.

Fuchs, Victor. 1967. "Differentials in Hourly Earnings by Region and City Size, 1959." Paper 101. New York: National Bureau of Economic Research.

Fuller, Justin. 1976. "Boomtowns and Blast Furnaces: Town Promotion in Alabama, 1885–1893." *Alabama Review* 29, (January):37–48.

Fullinwider, John. 1980. "Dallas: The City with No Limits?" *In These Times* 5(6):12–13.

Gaffney, M. Mason. 1961. "Land and Rent in Welfare Economics." In *Land Economics Research* (papers presented at a symposium on land economics research, Lincoln, Nebraska, June 16–23). Washington, D.C.: Resources for the Future. Distributed by Johns Hopkins University Press, Baltimore, pp. 141–67.

Galaskiewicz, Joseph. 1979a. *Exchange Networks and Community Politics*. Beverly Hills, Calif.: Sage.

Galaskiewicz, Joseph. 1979b. "The Structure of Community Organizational Networks." *Social Forces* 57(4):1346–64.

Gallup, George H. (ed.). 1979. *The Gallup Poll: Public Opinion, 1978*. Wilmington, Del.: Scholarly Resources.

Garrison, Charles B. 1971. "New Industry in Small Towns: The Impact on Local Government." *National Tax Journal* 21(4):493–500.

Glaab, Charles N. 1962. *Kansas City and the Railroads*. Madison: State Historical Society of Wisconsin.

Goodrich, Carter. 1950. "The Revulsion against Internal Improvements." *Journal of Economic History* 10:145–51.

Gordon, Margaret T., Linda Heath, and Robert leBailly. 1979. "Some Costs of Easy News: Crime Reports and Fear." Paper presented at the annual meeting of the American Psychological Association, New York.

Greenberg, Stephanie. n.d. "Rapid Growth in a Southern Area: Consequences for Social Inequality." Unpublished manuscript, Denver Research Institute, University of Denver, Denver, Colorado.

Hadden, Jeffrey K., and Edgar Borgatta. 1965. *American Cities: Their Social Characteristics*. Chicago: Rand McNally.

Halberstam, David. 1979. *The Powers That Be*. New York: Knopf.

Harvey, David. 1973. *Social Justice and the City*. Baltimore: Johns Hopkins University Press.

Hawley, Amos. 1950. *Human Ecology: A Theory of Community Structure.* New York: Ronald Press.

Haworth, Charles T., James E. Long, and David W. Rasmussen. 1978. "Income Distribution, City Size, and Urban Growth." *Urban Studies* 15(1):1–7.

Hayes, Thomas C. 1984. "Shortfall Likely in Olympic Income." *New York Times.* 9 May p. 5.

Hill, Richard Child. 1984. "Economic Crisis and Political Response in the Motor City." In Larry Sawers and William K. Tabb (eds.). *Sunbelt/Snowbelt: Urban Development and Regional Restructuring.* New York: Oxford University Press, pp. 313–38.

Hirsch, Seymour. 1969. "On Uncovering the Great Nerve Gas Coverup." *Ramparts* 3 (July):12–18.

Hoch, Irving. 1972. "Urban Scale and Environmental Quality." In US Commission on Population Growth and the American Future, Ronald G. Ridker (ed.). *Population, Resources, and the Environment,* vol. 3 of Commission Research Reports. Washington, DC: Government Printing Office, pp. 231–86

Hunter, Floyd. 1953. *Community Power Structure: A Study of Decision Makers.* Chapel Hill: University of North Carolina Press.

Hunter, Floyd. 1980. *Community Power Succession.* Chapel Hill: University of North Carolina Press.

Johnson, David R. 1983. "San Antonio: The Vicissitudes of Boosterism." In Richard M. Bernard and Bradley R. Rice (eds.). *Sunbelt Cities: Politics and Growth since World War II.* Austin: University of Texas Press, pp. 235–54.

Judd, Dennis. 1983. "From Cowtown to Sunbelt City." In Susan S. Fainstein (ed.). *Restructuring the City.* New York: Longman, pp. 167–201.

Kaplan, Barry J. 1983. "Houston: The Golden Buckle of the Sunbelt." In Richard M. Bernard and Bradley R. Rice (eds.). *Sunbelt Cities: Politics and Growth since World War II.* Austin: University of Texas Press, pp. 196–212.

Kaplan, Sam Hall. 1984. "Will Times Square Plan Destroy it?" *Los Angeles Times,* 3 October, sec. 1, p. 1.

King, Wayne. 1985. "U. of Texas Facing Cuts in Its Budget." *New York Times,* 17 March, p. 12.

Klein, Maury. 1970. *The Great Richmond Terminal: A Study of Businessmen and Business Strategy.* Charlottesville: University Press of Virginia.

Krannich, Richard S., and Craig R. Humphrey. 1983. "Local Mobilization and Community Growth: Toward an Assessment of the 'Growth Machine' Hypothesis." *Rural Sociology* 48(1):60–81.

Lasswell, Harold. 1936. *Politics: Who Gets What, When, How.* New York: McGraw-Hill.

Lester, Marilyn. 1971. "Toward a Sociology of Public Events." Master's thesis, Department of Sociology, University of California, Santa Barbara.

Lever, Janet. 1983. *Soccer in Brazil: Sports' Contribution to Social Integration.* Chicago: University of Chicago Press.

Levine, Adeline Gordon. 1982. *Love Canal: Science, Politics and People.* Lexington, MA: D. C. Heath.

Levy, Steven, and Robert K. Arnold. 1972. "An Evaluation of Four Growth Alternatives in the City of Milpitas, 1972–1977." Technical memorandum report. Palo Alto, CA: Institute of Regional and Urban Studies.

Lieberson, Stanley. 1980. *A Piece of the Pie: Blacks and White Immigrants since 1800.* Berkeley and Los Angeles: University of California Press.

Livingston, Laurence, and John A. Blayney. 1971. "Foothill Environmental Design Study: Open Space vs. Development." Final report to the City of Palo Alto. San Francisco: Livingston and Blayney.

Luckingham, Bradford. 1983. "Phoenix: The Desert Metropolis." In Richard M. Bernard and Bradley R. Rice (eds.). *Sunbelt Cities: Politics and Growth since World War II*. Austin: University of Texas Press, pp. 309–27.

Lyon, Larry, Lawrence G. Felice, M. Ray Perryman, and E. Stephen Parker. 1981. "Community Power and Population Increase: An Empirical Test of the Growth Machine Model." *American Journal of Sociology* 86(6):1387–400.

McCombs, Maxwell E., and Donald Shaw. 1972. "The Agenda Setting Function of Mass Media." *Public Opinion Quarterly* 36:176–87.

McGarry, T. W. 1985. "Irish Will March to Four Different Drummers." *Los Angeles Times*, 14 March, sec. II, pp. 1, 3.

McKenzie, R. D. 1922. "The Neighborhood: A Study of Local Life in the City of Columbus Ohio – Conclusion." *American Journal of Sociology* 27:780–99.

Maguire, Miles. 1985. "Boondoggle or Marvel: Tenn-Tom Waterway Locks Open." *Baltimore Sun*, 13 January, sec. D, p. 1.

Makielski, Stanislaw J. 1966. *The Politics of Zoning: The New York Experience*. New York: Columbia University Press.

Markusen, Ann. 1978. "Class, Rent and Sectoral Conflict: Uneven Development in Western U.S. Boomtowns." *Review of Radical Political Economics* 10(3):117–29.

Mazie, Sara Mills, and Steve Rowlings. 1973. "Public Attitude toward Population Distribution Issues." In Sara Mills Mazie (ed.) *Population Distribution and Policy*. Washington, DC: Commission on Population Growth and the American Future, pp. 603–15.

Melosi, Martin. 1983. "Dallas-Fort Worth: Marketing the Metroplex." In Richard M. Bernard and Bradley R. Rice (eds.). *Sunbelt Cities: Politics and Growth since World War II*. Austin: University of Texas Press, pp. 162–95.

Mollenkopf, John. 1983. *The Contested City*. Princeton, NJ: Princeton University Press.

Molotch, Harvey. 1980. "Media and Movements." In Mayer Zald and John McCarthy (eds.). *The Dynamics of Social Movements*. Cambridge, MA: Winthrop, pp. 71–93.

Molotch, Harvey, and Marilyn Lester. 1974. "News as Purposive Behavior: On the Strategic Use of Routine Events, Accidents, and Scandals." *American Sociological Review* 39(1): 101–13.

Molotch, Harvey, and Marilyn Lester. 1975. "Accidental News: The Great Oil Spill as Local Occurrence and National Event." *American Journal of Sociology*, 81(2):235–60.

Mormino, Gary R. 1983. "Tampa: From Hell Hole to the Good Life." In Richard M. Bernard and Bradley R. Rice (eds.). *Sunbelt Cities: Politics and Growth since World War II*. Austin: University of Texas Press, pp. 138–61.

Mumford, Lewis. 1961. *The City in History*. New York: Harcourt.

Neiman, Max, and Ronald O. Loveridge. 1981. "Environmentalism and Local Growth Control: A Probe into the Class Bias Thesis." *Environment and Behavior* 13(6): 759–72.

Parke, Robert, Jr., and Charles Westoff (eds.). 1972. *Aspects of Population Growth Policy* (report of the U.S. Commission on Population Growth and the American Future, vol. 6). Washington, DC: Commission on Population Growth and the American Future.

Peterson, Paul E. 1981. *City Limits*. Chicago: University of Chicago Press.

Pittas, Michael. 1984. "The Arts Edge: Revitalizing Economic Life in California's Cities." Speech presented at a conference sponsored by the California Economic Development Commission Local Government Advisory Committee, Santa Barbara, July 15.

Rice, Bradley R. 1983. "If Dixie Were Atlanta." In Richard M. Bernard and Bradley R. Rice (eds.). *Sunbelt Cities: Politics and Growth since World War II*. Austin: University of Texas Press, pp. 31–57.

Risen, James. 1984. "Auto World Theme Park to Close." *Los Angeles Times*, 12 June, sec. IV, p. 1.

Rivera, Nancy. 1983. "High Tech Firm Picks Austin over San Diego." *Los Angeles Times*, 18 May, sec. IV, pp. 1, 2.

Roderick, Kevin. 1984. "Cities Play Hardball to Lure Teams." *Los Angeles Times*, 30 June, sec. I, pp. 1, 24.

Rosenstiel, Thomas B. 1985. "'Killing Fields' Writer Loses N. Y. Times Column, To Be Reassigned." *Los Angeles Times*, 21 August, sec. I, p. 21.

Rossi, Peter, and Robert Dentler. 1961. *The Politics of Urban Renewal*. New York: Free Press.

Rubin, Lillian B. 1972. *Busing and Backlash: White against White in an Urban School District*. Berkeley and Los Angeles: University of California Press.

Rudel, Thomas K. 1989. *Situations and Strategies in American Land-Use Planning*. New York: Cambridge University Press.

Sahagun, Louis, and Allan Jalon. 1984. "Cities Battle to House Technology Museum." *Los Angeles Times*, 29 November, sec. IV, pp. 1, 4.

Samuelson, Paul. 1942. "The Business Cycle and Urban Development." In Guy Greer (ed.). *The Problems of Cities and Towns*. Cambridge, MA: Harvard University Press, pp. 6–17.

San Francisco Chronicle. 1984. "Reagan's Hometown Offers Bounty to Lure More Business to the Area." *San Francisco Chronicle*, 10 May, p. 4.

Schattschneider, Elmer Eric. 1960. *The Semisovereign People*. New York: Holt, Rinehart and Winston.

Scheiber, Harry N. 1973. "Urban Rivalry and Internal Improvements in the Old Northwest, 1820–1860." In Alexander B. Callow, Jr. (ed.). *American Urban History*, 2nd edn. New York: Oxford University Press, pp. 135–46.

Schmidt, William E. 1984. "Suburbs' Growth Pinches Atlanta." *New York Times*, 24 April, sec. A, p. 14.

Schulze, Robert O. 1961. "The Bifurcation of Power in a Satellite City." In Morris Janowitz (ed.). *Community Political Systems*. Glencoe, Ill.: Free Press, pp. 19–80.

Shefer, Daniel. 1970. "Comparable Living Costs and Urban Size: A Statistical Analysis." *Journal of the American Institute of Planners* 36, (November):417–21.

Shlay, Anne B., and Robert P. Gilroth. 1984. "Gambling on World's Fairs: Who Plays and Who Pays." *Neighborhood Works* 7, (August):11–15.

Sierra Club of San Diego. 1973. *Economy, Ecology, and Rapid Population Growth*. San Diego: Sierra Club.

Smith, Michael Peter, and Marlene Keller. 1983. "Managed Growth and the Politics of Uneven Development in New Orleans." In Susan S. Fainstein (ed.). *Restructuring the City*. New York: Longman, pp. 126–66.

Smith, Reginald. 1984. "Willie Brown's Big Income Revealed in State Report." *San Francisco Chronicle*, 7 March, p. 12.

Spaulding, Charles. 1951. "Occupational Affiliations of Councilmen in Small Cities." *Sociology and Social Research*, 35(3):194–200.

Steidtmann, Nancy. 1985. "Citizen Lesher: Newspaper Publisher." *Bay Area Business Magazine* IV, (October 3):14–18.

Sternlieb, George, and James W. Hughes. 1983. *The Atlantic City Gamble*. Piscataway, NJ: Center for Urban Policy Research.

Stone, Clarence N. 1981. "Community Power Structure – A Further Look." *Urban Affairs Quarterly* 16(4):505–15.

Stone, Clarence N. 1982. "Social Stratification, Non-Decision-Making and the Study of Community Power." *American Politics Quarterly* 10(3):275–302.

Stone, Clarence N. 1984. "City Politics and Economic Development: Political Economy Perspectives." *Journal of Politics* 46(1):286–99.

Stuart, Darwin, and Robert Teska. 1971. *Who Pays for What: Cost Revenue Analysis of Suburban Land Use Alternatives*. Washington, DC: Urban Land Institute.

Summers, Gene F., and Kristi Branch. 1984. "Economic Development and Community Social Change." *Annual Review of Sociology*, 10:141–66.

Summers, Gene F., et al. (eds.). 1976. *Industrial Invasion of Nonmetropolitan America: A Quarter Century of Experience*. New York: Praeger.

Sundquist, James, 1975. *Dispersing Population: What America Can Learn from Europe*. Washington, DC: Brookings Institute.

Swanstrom, Todd. 1981. "The Crisis of Growth Politics: Cleveland, Kucinich, and the Challenge of Urban Populism." PhD dissertation, Princeton University.

Swanstrom, Todd. 1985. *The Crisis of Growth Politics: Cleveland, Kucinich, and the Challenge of Urban Populism*. Philadelphia: Temple University Press.

Swierenga, Robert P. 1966. "Land Speculator 'Profits' Reconsidered: Central Iowa as a Test Case." *Journal of Economic History* 26(1):1–28.

Tiebout, Charles M. 1956. "A Pure Theory of Local Expenditures." *Journal of Political Economy* 64, (October):416–24.

Tomkins, Calvin. 1983. "The Art World: Dallas." *New Yorker* 59(17):92–7.

Trillin, Calvin. 1976. "U.S. Journal: Rockford, Illinois – Schools without Money." *New Yorker* 52(38):146–54.

Vidich, Arthur J., and Joseph Bensman. 1960. *Small Town in Mass Society: Class, Power and Religion in a Rural Community*. Garden City, NY: Doubleday.

Wade, Richard C. 1959. *The Urban Frontier: The Rise of Western Cities, 1790–1830*. Cambridge, MA: Harvard University Press.

Walker, Richard A. 1978. "Two Sources of Uneven Development under Advanced Capitalism – Spatial Differentiation and Capital Mobility." *Review of Radical Political Economics* 10(3):28–38.

Walker, Richard A., and Matthew J. Williams. 1982. "Water from Power: Water Supply and Regional Growth in the Santa Clara Valley." *Economic Geography* 58(2):95–119.

Walton, John. 1970. "A Systematic Survey of Community Power Research." In Michael Aiken and Paul Mott (eds.). *The Structure of Community Power*. New York: Random House, pp. 443–64.

Weinstein, Bernard L., and Rober E. Firestine. 1978. *Regional Growth and Decline in the United States*. New York: Praeger.

Weinstein, James. 1968. *The Corporate Ideal in the Liberal State, 1900–1918*. Boston: Beacon Press.

White, Morton, and Lucia White. 1962. *The Intellectual versus the City*. Cambridge, MA: Harvard University Press.

Whitt, J. Allen. 1982. *Urban Elites and Mass Transportation: The Dialectics of Power*. Princeton, NJ: Princeton University Press.

Williams, Oliver, and C. R. Adrian. 1963. *Four Cities: A Study of Comparative Policy Making*. Philadelphia: Temple University Press.

Wolf, Peter. 1981. *Land in America: Its Value, Use and Control*. New York: Pantheon.

Wolfe, Alan. 1981. *America's Impasse: The Rise and Fall of the Politics of Growth*. New York: Pantheon.

Worster, Donald. 1982. "Hydraulic Society in California: An Ecological Interpretation." *Agricultural History* 56, (July):503–15.

Wyner, Allen. 1967. "Governor-Salesman." *National Civic Review* 61, (February):81–6.

Yago, Glenn. 1984. *The Decline of Transit: Urban Transportation in German and U.S. Cities, 1900–1970*. New York: Cambridge University Press.

Zunz, Olivier. 1982. *The Changing Face of Inequality: Urbanization, Industrial Development, and Immigrants in Detroit, 1880–1920*. Chicago: University of Chicago Press.

11

Partnership and the Pursuit of the Private City*

Gregory D. Squires

...Two hundred and sixty-eight years of *laissez-faire* economics had left the city in a hell of a mess.

Joseph S. Clark, Jr.,
Mayor of Philadelphia 1952–1956
(Warner, 1987, p. xi)

Public–private partnerships have become the rallying cry for economic development professionals throughout the United States (Davis, 1986; Porter, 1989). As federal revenues for economic development, social service, and other urban programs diminish such partnerships are increasingly looked to as the key for urban revitalization (G. Peterson and Lewis, 1986). These partnerships take many forms. Formal organizations of executives from leading businesses have been established that work directly with public officials. In some cases public officials as well as representatives from various community organizations are also members. Some partnerships have persisted for decades working on an array of issues while others are ad hoc arrangements that focus on a particular time-limited project. Direct subsidies from public agencies to private firms have been described as public–private partnerships. If economic development has emerged as a major function of local government, public–private partnerships are increasingly viewed as the critical tool.

The concept of partnership is widely perceived to be an innovative approach that is timely in an age of austerity. In fact, "public–private partnership" is little more than a new label for a long-standing relationship between the public and private sectors. Growth has been the constant, central objective of that relationship, though in recent years subsidization of dramatic economic restructuring has become a

* Squires, Gregory D. (1991) "Partnership and the Pursuit of the Private City" from Mark Goettdiener and Chris Pickvance (eds.) *Urban Life in Transition*, Sage Publications, Newbury Park, pp. 123–40.

complementary concern. While that relationship has evolved throughout US history, it has long been shaped by an ideology of privatism that has dominated urban redevelopment from colonial America through the so-called postindustrial era (Barnekov et al. 1989; Krumholz, 1984; Levine, 1989; Warner, 1987). The central tenet of privatism is the belief in the supremacy of the private sector and market forces in nurturing development, with the public sector as a junior partner whose principal obligation is to facilitate private capital accumulation. Individual material acquisitiveness is explicitly avowed, but that selfishness is justified by the public benefits that are assumed to flow from the dynamics of such relations.

One need look no further than the roadways, canals, and railroads of the eighteenth and nineteenth centuries to see early concrete manifestations of large-scale public subsidization of private economic activity and the hierarchical relationship between the public and private sectors (Krumholz, 1984; Langton, 1983). These relationships crystallized in the urban renewal days of the 1950s and 1960s and the widely celebrated partnerships of the 1980s. Structural changes in the political economy of cities, regions, and nations altered the configuration of specific public–private partnerships, but not the fundamental relationship between the public and private sectors. These structural changes have, however, influenced the spatial development of cities and exacerbated the social problems of urban America.

The continuity reflected by public–private partnerships, despite some new formulations in recent years, is revealed by the persistence in the corporate sector's efforts to utilize government to protect private wealth, and primarily on its terms. Demands on the state to subsidize a painful restructuring process have placed added strains on public–private relations. The glue that holds these efforts together, despite these tensions, is the commitment to privatism.

Focusing on the postwar years, this chapter examines the ideology of privatism, its influence on the evolution of public–private partnerships, and their combined effects on the structural, spatial, and social development of cities in the United States, and the lives of people residing in the nation's urban neighborhoods. Perhaps the most striking feature of the evolution of American cities, to be explored in the following pages, is the uneven nature of urban development. To many, such uneven development simply reflects the "creative destruction" that Schumpeter (1942) asserted was essential for further economic progress in a capitalist economy. To others, however, the unevenness generated by unrestrained market-based private capital accumulation constitutes the core of the nation's urban problems. After reviewing the theoretical debates over privatism, various contours of uneven development and the role of partnerships in particular and privatism generally in nurturing such inequalities are examined. Industrial restructuring and uneven spatial development of urban America, along with the many social costs associated with such development, are delineated, with a particular focus on the changing dynamics of racial inequality. Drawing from data pertaining to national trends in urban development as well as developments within specific cities, the mutually reinforcing effects of race and class are explored. This chapter concludes with a discussion of recent challenges to the ideology of privatism. City dwellers, many community organizations, and a significant number of public officials have begun to develop specific policy alternatives, including more inclusive partnerships, in hopes of achieving something better than the "mess of laissez-faire."

Privatism

The American tradition of privatism was firmly established by the time of the Revolution in the 1700s. According to this tradition, individual and community happiness are to be achieved through the search for personal wealth. Individual loyalties are to the family first, and the primary obligation of political authorities is to "keep the peace among individual money-makers" (Warner, 1987, p. 4). Always implicit, and frequently explicit, from colonial days to the present has been the primacy of private action and actors.

Consistent with free market, neoclassical economic theory generally, theory and policy in economic development and urban redevelopment circles have focused on private investors and markets as the appropriate dominating forces. Private economic actors are credited with being the most productive, innovative, and effective. Presumably neutral and impersonal market signals are deemed the most efficient and therefore appropriate measures for determining the allocation of economic resources. Given Adam Smith's invisible hand, the greatest good for the greatest numbers is achieved by nurturing the pursuit of private wealth.

Public policy, from this perspective, should serve private interests. Government has an important role, but one that should focus on the facilitation of private capital accumulation via the free market. (Privatism should not be confused with privatization. The former refers to a broader ideological view of the world generally and relationships between the public and private sectors in particular. The latter constitutes a specific policy of transferring ownership of particular industries or services from government agencies to private entrepreneurs.) While urban policy must acknowledge the well-known problems of big cities, it can do so best by encouraging private economic growth. A critical assumption is that the city constitutes a unitary interest and all citizens benefit from policies that enhance aggregate private economic growth (P. Peterson, 1981). Explicit distributive or allocational choices are to be avoided whenever possible, with the market determining where resources are to be directed. Public policy should augment but not supplant market forces (Barnekov et al., 1989; Levine, 1989).

The ideology of privatism has been tested in recent years by regional shifts in investment and globalization of the economy in general that have devastated entire communities (Bluestone and Harrison, 1982; Eisinger, 1988). Advocates of privatism attribute such developments primarily to technological innovation and growing international competition. They claim the appropriate response is to accommodate changes in the national and international economy. Given that redevelopment is presumed to be principally a technical rather than political process, cities must work more closely with private industry to facilitate such restructuring in order to establish more effectively their comparative advantages and market themselves in an increasingly competitive economic climate. Such partnerships, it is assumed, will bring society's best and brightest resources (which reside in the private sector) to bear on its most severe public problems.

Where such efforts cannot succeed cities must adjust, which in some cases means to downsize, just like their counterparts in the private sector. So-called pro-people rather than pro-place policies are offered to help individuals accommodate such changes. These adjustments may well mean moving from one city and region to another. Policies that might intervene in private investment decision making or challenge market forces for the betterment of existing communities are explicitly rejected (Kasarda, 1988; McKenzie, 1979; President's Commission for a National Agenda for the Eighties, 1980).

Concretely, the policies of privatism consist of financial incentives to private economic actors that are intended to reduce factor costs of production and encourage private capital accumulation, thus stimulating investment, ultimately serving both private and public interests. The search for new manufacturing sites, retooling of obsolete facilities, and restructuring from manufacturing to services have all been facilitated by such subsidization. During the postwar years, cities have been dramatically affected by the focus on downtown development that has generally taken the form of office towers, luxury hotels, convention centers, recreational facilities, and other paeans to the postindustrial society. Real estate investment itself is frequently viewed as part of the antidote to deindustrialization. All of this is justified, however, by the assumption that a revitalized economy generally and a reinvigorated downtown in particular will lead to regeneration throughout the city. As more jobs are created and space is more intensively utilized, more money is earned and spent by local residents, new property and income tax dollars bolster local treasuries, and new wealth trickles down throughout the metropolitan area. Among the specific policy tools are tax abatements, low-interest loans, land cost writedowns, tax increment finance districts (TIFS), enterprise zones, urban development action grants (UDAGs), industrial revenue bonds (IRBs), redevelopment authorities, eminent domain, and other public–private activities through which private investment is publicly subsidized. The object of such incentives, again, is the enhancement of aggregate private economic growth by which it is assumed the public needs of the city can be most effectively and efficiently met.

Privatism has been a powerful ideological force in all areas of American life. That it has dominated urban policy should come as no surprise. But the pursuit of the private city has had its costs. And the advocates of privatism have had their critics.

Responses to Privatism

The most fundamental intellectual and political challenges to privatism are directed to its central assumptions regarding the neutrality and impersonality of the market. Rather than viewing the market as a mechanism through which random decisions made by many individual willing buyers and sellers yields the most efficient production and distribution of resources for cities and society generally, it is argued that the market is an area of conflict. Logan and Molotch (1987) observe that markets themselves are cultural artefacts bound up with human interests. Markets are structured by, and reflect differences in, wealth and power. They reinforce prevailing unequal social relations and dominant values, including a commitment to privatism. Markets are not simply neutral arbiters maximizing efficiency in production and distribution. They are social institutions firmly embedded in the broader culture of American society.

A related critique of privatism is the argument that a city does not constitute a unitary interest that can best be advanced through aggregate private economic growth, but rather a series of unequal and conflictual interests, some of which are advanced through a political process. As Stone (1987) has argued, local economic development policy represents the conscious decisions made by individuals with highly unequal power in a community in efforts by competing groups to further their own interests. Assumptions of a unitary interest or the benevolence of market-based allocation mystifies important decisions made at the local level that clearly favor some interests at the expense of others. Development, therefore, is not a technical problem but rather a political process. As Stone concludes, "urban politics still matters" (1987, p. 4).

While economic development and urban redevelopment are political matters, one consequence of the pursuit of the private city has been a reduction in the public debate over development policy and the accountability of public officials and other actors for the consequences of their activities. Quasi-public redevelopment author-ities have provided selected private investors with responsibilities traditionally vested in the public sector. Hidden incentives have been provided through such off-budget subsidies as industrial revenue bonds and bailouts for large but failing firms. Eminent domain rights have been granted to and exercised for private inter-ests where public interests are most vaguely identified (Barnekov et al., 1989). The beneficaries of these policies include real estate developers, commercial business interests, manufacturers, and others who view the city primarily in terms of the exchange value of its land at the expense of the majority, for whom the city offers important use values as a place to live, work, and play (Logan and Molotch, 1987). But it is not just the immediate beneficiaries who share this view of local governance. As Gottdiener concluded, "The reduction of the urban vision to instrumental capital growth, it seems, gains hegemony everywhere" (Gottdiener, 1986, p. 287).

Declining accountability may be a factor contributing to a more concrete chal-lenge to privatism. Simply put, it has not worked. That is, the array of subsidies and related supply-side incentives have not created the anticipated number of jobs or jobs for the intended recipients, tax revenues have not been stabilized as initially expected, and the urban renaissance remains, at best, a hope for the future (Barne-kov et al., 1989; Center for Community Change, 1989; Levine, 1987). While not always ineffective, such incentives are not primary determinants of private invest-ment decisions. And they often embody unintended costs resulting in minus-sum situations as public subsidies outrun subsequent public benefits (Eisinger, 1988, pp. 200–24). One reason for the disappointing results is that with the proliferation of incentives, the competitive advantage provided by any particular set of subsidies is quickly lost when other communities match them. The number of state location incentive programs alone increased from 840 in 1966 to 1,633 in 1985 (Eisinger, 1988, p. 19). Indeed, many states and municipalities feel obligated to offer add-itional incentives of acknowledged questionable value simply to keep up with their neighbors and provide symbolic assurance that they offer a good business climate. As Detroit Mayor Coleman Young observed:

Those are the rules and I'm going by the goddamn rules. This suicidal outthrust competition among the states has got to stop but until it does, I mean to compete. It's

too bad we have a system where dog eats dog and the devil takes the hindmost. But I'm
tired of taking the hindmost.   (Greider, 1978)

Ironically, one of the costs is the reduced ability of local municipalities to provide
the public services that are far more critical in assuring a favorable climate for the
operation of successful businesses. Tax dollars that are utilized as subsidies for
private development are dollars that are not available for vital public services. In
Detroit, for example, the quality of public education has declined precipitously in
recent years, undercutting the ability of that city's youth to compete for jobs and the
city's ability to attract employers (Thomas, 1989).

Another factor contributing to the disappointing results strikes at the heart of the
ideology of privatism. As Bluestone and Harrison (1982) concluded in discussing
such approaches to reindustrialization, "all share a studied unwillingness to question
the extent to which conventional private ownership of industry and the more-or-less
unbridled pursuit of private profit might be the causes of the problem" (1982,
p. 230).

If privatism has not generated the anticipated positive outcomes, economic restructuring associated with privatism has generated a host of social costs that are
either ignored or accepted by its proponents as an inevitable price to be paid for
progress. Job loss and declining family income resulting from a plant closure are just
the most obvious direct costs. There are also "multiplier effects." Economic stress
within the family often leads to family conflicts, including physical abuse, frequently
culminating in divorce. Increasing physical and medical health problems, including
growing suicide rates, have been clearly connected to sudden job loss. The economic
stability of entire communities and essential public services have been crippled
(Bluestone and Harrison, 1982). Even the winners of the competition have suffered
severe social costs. Sudden growth has generated unmanageable traffic congestion
and skyrocketing housing costs often force families out of their homes and business
to pay higher salaries for competent employees (Dreier, Schwartz and Greiner,
1988). Gentrification moves many poor people around but does little to reduce
poverty. Even in Houston, the "free enterprise city," sudden private economic
growth has generated serious problems in sewage and garbage disposal, flooding,
air and water pollution, congestion, and related problems (Feagin, 1988). Perhaps
the most destructive aspect of this "creative" process is the uneven nature of the
spatial development of cities and the growing inequality associated with race and
class (Bluestone and Harrison, 1988). Privatism and the economic restructuring that
it has nurtured have created costs that are quite real, but not inevitable. As the critics
of privatism note, it reflects political conflicts and political decisions (discussed in
the following section), not natural outcomes of ultimately beneficial market forces.

The pursuit of the private city appears to have produced many ironies. Given the
array of incentives, those firms intending to expand or relocate anyway often shop
around for the best deal they can get. Consequently, local programs designed to
leverage private investment are turned on their head. That is, the private firms
leverage public funds for their own development purposes; and they can punish
local governments that are not forthcoming with generous subsidies. A logical
consequence of these developments is that private economic growth has become
its own justification. As William E. Connolly observed:

at every turn barriers to growth become occasions to tighten social control, to build new hedges around citizen rights, to insulate bureaucracies from popular pressures while opening them to corporate influence, to rationalize work processes, to impose austerity on vulnerable constituencies, to delay programs for environmental safety, to legitimize military adventures abroad. Growth, previously seen as the means to realization of the good life, has become a system imperative to which elements of the good life are sacrificed.   (1983, pp. 23–4)

But perhaps these outcomes are not ironic. In fact, they may well be the intended results. As Barnekov et al. concluded in evaluating privatism in the 1980s, "The overriding purpose of the 'new privatism' was not the regeneration of cities but rather the adaptation of the urban landscape to the spatial requirements of a post-industrial economy" (1989, p. 12). That adaptation has been the central objective of public–private partnerships in the "postindustrial" age of urban America.

The postwar debate over privatism, like debates over redevelopment in general, has taken place within the context of dramatic structural changes in the political economy of American cities. The spatial development of urban America has clearly been influenced by these changes. In turn, the structural and spatial developments of cities have given rise to a host of social problems with which policy makers continue to wrestle. These struggles have included efforts to challenge the ideology and politics of privatism; challenges that have met with some success, including capturing the mayor's office in a few major cities. These efforts are discussed in the concluding section. The following section examines the evolving dynamics of privatism and partnerships for urban America during the postwar years, developments that have prepared the ground for challenges to privatism in recent years.

Structural, Spatial, and Social Development

Urban renewal and the prosperous postwar years

The United States emerged from World War II as a growing and internationally dominant economic power. Given its privileged structural position at that time, the end of ideology was declared and optimism for future growth and prosperity was widespread (Bell, 1960).

Yet blighted conditions within the nation's central cities posed problems for residents trapped in poverty and for local businesses threatened by conditions within and immediately surrounding the downtown business center. Recognizing the "higher uses" (i.e., more profitable for developers and related businesses) for which such land could be utilized, a policy of urban renewal evolved that brought together local business and government entities in working partnerships with the support of the federal government. At the same time, federal housing policy and highway construction stimulated homeownership and opened up the suburbs, while reinforcing the racial exclusively of neighborhoods.

As Mollenkopf (1983) has observed, urban renewal and related federal programs reflected a political coalition of disparate groups. Local entrepreneurial Democratic politicians, along with their counterparts at the federal level, created large-scale downtown construction projects that benefited key local contractors and unions, machine politicians and reformers, and white ethnic groups along with at least some racial minorities. These emerging political alliances were clearly, though not always explicitly, committed to economic growth (particularly downtown) with the private sector as the primary engine for, and beneficiary of, that development (Mollenkopf, 1983).

Although urban renewal was launched and initially justified as an effort to improve the housing conditions of low-income urban residents, it quickly became a massive public subsidy for private business development, particularly downtown commercial real estate interests (Barnekov et al., 1989, pp. 39–48; Hays, 1985, pp. 173–91). Shopping malls, office buildings, and convention centers rather than housing became the focus of urban renewal programs. Following the lead of the Allegheny Conference on Community Development formed in Pittsburgh in 1943, coalitions of local business leaders were organized in most large cities to encourage public subsidization of downtown development. Examples include the Greater Milwaukee Committee, Central Atlanta Progress, Inc., Greater Philadelphia Movement, Cleveland Development Foundation, Detroit Renaissance, the Vault (Boston), the Blyth-Zellerback Committee (San Francisco), Greater Baltimore Committee, and Chicago Central Area Committee. Using their powers of eminent domain, city officials generally would assemble land parcels and provide land cost writedowns for private developers. In the process local business associations frequently operated as private governments as they designed and implemented plans that had dramatic public consequences but did so with little public accountability.

If such developments were justified rhetorically as meeting important public needs, indeed urban renewal took sides. Not all sides were represented in the planning process and the impact of urban renewal reflected such unequal participation (Friedman, 1968). Some people were forcefully relocated so that others could benefit. According to one estimate, by 1967 urban renewal had destroyed 404,000 housing units, most of which had been occupied by low-income tenants, while just 41,580 replacement units for low- and moderate-income families were built (Friedland, 1983, p. 85). As Chester Hartman concluded, "the aggregate benefits are private benefits that accrue to a small, select segment of the city's elite 'public,' while the costs fall on those least able to bear them" (Hartman, 1974, p. 183).

At the same time that the public sector was subsidizing downtown commercial development, it was also subsidizing homeownership and highway construction programs to stimulate suburban development. Through Federal Housing Administration (FHA), Veterans Administration (VA) and related federally subsidized and insured mortgage programs launched around the war years, long-term mortgages requiring relatively low down payments made homeownership possible for many families who previously could not afford to buy. With the federal insurance, lenders were far more willing to make such loans (Hays, 1985; Jackson, 1985). An equally if not more compelling factor leading to the creation of these programs was the financial assistance they provided to real estate agents, contractors, financial institutions, and other housing related industries (Hays, 1985). Since half the FHA and VA loans made during the 1950s and 1960s financed suburban housing, the federal government began, perhaps unwittingly, to subsidize the exodus from central cities to suburban rings that characterized metropolitan development during these decades

(Hays, 1985, p. 215). The Interstate Highway Act of 1956, launching construction of the nation's high-speed roadway system, further subsidized and encouraged that exodus.

A significant feature of these developments was the racial exclusivity that was solidified in part because the federal government encouraged it. Through the 1940s, the FHA's underwriting manuals warned of "inharmonious racial or nationality groups" and maintained that "if a neighborhood is to retain stability, it is necessary that properties shall continue to be occupied by the same social and racial classes" (Jackson, 1985, p. 208). If redlining practices originated within the nation's financial institutions, the federal government sanctioned and reinforced such discriminatory practices at a critical time in the history of suburban development. The official stance of the federal government has changed in subsequent decades, but the patterns established by these policies have proven to be difficult to alter.

During the prosperous postwar years of the 1950s and 1960s urban redevelopment strategies were shaped by public–private partnerships. But the private partner dominated as the public sector's role consisted principally of "preparing the ground for capital." Spatially, the focus was on downtown and the suburbs. Socially, the dominant feature was the creation and reinforcement of racially discriminatory dual housing markets and homogeneous urban and suburban communities. The basic patterns have persisted in subsequent years when the national economy was not so favorable.

Partnerships in an age of decline

The celebrated partnerships of the 1980s reflect an emerging effort to undermine the public sector, particularly the social safety net it has provided, and to reaffirm the "privileged position of business" (Lindblom, 1977) in the face of declining profitability brought on by globalization of the US economy and its declining position in that changing marketplace. Government has a role, but again it is a subordinate one. As Bluestone and Harrison (1988) recently argued:

> Leaders may call these deals "public–private partnerships" and attempt to fold them under the ideological umbrella of laissez-faire. But they must be seen for what they really are: the re-allocation of public resources to fit a new agenda. That agenda is no longer redistribution, or even economic growth as conventionally defined. Rather, that agenda entails nothing less than the restructuring of the relations of production and the balance of power in the American economy. In pursuit of these dubious goals, the public sector continues to play a crucial role. (pp. 107–8)

Global domination by the US economy peaked roughly 25 years following the conclusion of World War II. After more than two decades of substantial economic growth subsequent to the war, international competition, particularly from Japan and West Germany but also from several Third World countries, began to challenge the US position as productivity and profitability at home began to decline (Bluestone and Harrison, 1988; Bowles et al., 1983; Reich, 1983). As both a cause and effect of the general decline beginning in the late 1960s and early 1970s, the US economy experienced significant shifts out of manufacturing and into service industries. Between 1970 and 1987, the US economy lost 1.9 million manufacturing jobs and gained 13.9 million in the service sector (Mishel and Simon, 1988 p. 25). Perhaps even more important than the overall trajectory of decline has been the response to these developments on the part of corporate America and its partners in government. Such economic and political restructuring provided the context that has shaped the spatial development of cities and, in turn, the quality of life in urban America.

Between 1960 and 1980 the US share of the world's economic output declined from 35 percent to 22 percent (Reich, 1987, p. 44). As profitability began to decline, US corporations responded with an array of tactics aimed at generating short-term profits at the expense of long-term productivity (Hayes and Abernathy, 1980).

Rather than directing investment into manufacturing plants and equipment or research and development to improve the productivity of US industry, corporate America pursued what Robert B. Reich labeled "paper entrepreneurialism" (Reich, 1983, pp. 140–72). That is, capital was expended on mergers and acquisitions, speculative real estate ventures, and other investments in which "some money will change hands, and no new wealth will be created" (Reich, 1983, p. 157). Rather than strategic planning for long-term productivity growth, the pursuit of short-term gain has been the objective.

Reducing labor costs has constituted a second component of an overall strategy aimed at short-term profitability. A number of tactics have been utilized to reduce the wage bill including decentralizing and globalizing production, expanding part-time work at the expense of full-time positions, contracting out work from union to non-union shops, aggressively fighting union organization campaigns, implementing two-tiered wage scales, and outright demands for wage concessions. Rather than viewing human capital as a resource in which to invest to secure productivity in the long run, labor has increasingly been viewed as a cost of production to be minimized in the interests of short-term profitability (Bluestone and Harrison, 1988).

If production has been conceded by corporate America, control has not. Administration and a range of professional services have been consolidated and have grown considerably in recent years. If steel, automobile, and electronics production has shifted overseas, legal and accounting – along with other financial and related services – have expanded. Other service industries that have also grown include health care, state and local government, and personal services. Such developments lead some observers to dismiss the significance of a decline in manufacturing and celebrate the emergence of a postindustrial society (Becker, 1986; Bell, 1973). Yet at least half of those jobs in service industries are dependent on manufacturing production, though not necessarily production within the United States. Service and manufacturing are clearly linked; one cannot supplant the other. The health of both manufacturing and services depends on their mutual development. A service economy, without a manufacturing base to service, is proving to be a prescription for overall economic decline within those communities losing their industrial base (Cohen and Zysman, 1987).

True to the spirit of privatism, government has nurtured these developments through various forms of assistance to the private sector. Federal tax laws encourage investment in new facilities, particularly overseas, rather than reinvestment in older but still usable equipment, thus exacerbating the velocity of capital mobility (Bluestone and Harrison, 1982). State and local governments have offered their own inducements to encourage the pirating of employers in all industries ranging from heavy manufacturing to religious organizations (Eisinger, 1988; Goodman, 1979). Further inducements have been offered to the private sector through reductions in various regulatory functions of government. Civil rights, labor law, occupational health and safety rules, and environmental protection were enforced less aggressively in the 1980s than had been the case in the immediately preceding decades (Chambers, 1987; Taylor, 1989). If the expansion of such financial incentives and reductions in regulatory activity were initially justified in terms of the public benefits that would accrue from a revitalized private sector, in recent years unbridled competition and minimal government have become their own justification and not simply means to some other end (Bender, 1983; Connolly, 1983; Smith and Judd, 1984).

The impact of these structural developments is clearly visible on the spatial development of American cities. Accommodating these national and international trends, local partnerships have nurtured downtown development to service the growing service economy. If steel is no longer produced in Pittsburgh, the Golden Triangle has risen as the city's major employers now to include financial, educational, and health care institutions (Sbragia, 1989). If auto workers have lost jobs by the thousands in Detroit, the Renaissance Center, a major medical center, and the Joe Louis Sports Arena have been built downtown (Darden, Hill, Thomas and Thomas, 1987). Most major breweries have left Milwaukee, but the Grand Avenue Shopping Mall, several office buildings for legal, financial, and insurance companies, a new Performing Arts Center, and the Bradley Center housing the professional basketball Milwaukee Bucks are growing up in the central business district (Norman, 1989). With the US economy deindustrializing and corporations consolidating administrative functions, downtown development to accommodate these changes is booming. These initiatives are more ambitious than urban renewal efforts that focused on rescuing downtown real estate, but many of the actors are the same and the fundamental relationships between the public and private entities prevail. In city after city, such developments are initiated by the private side of local partnerships, usually with substantial public economic development assistance in the forms of UDAGs, IRBs, and other subsidies.

As cities increasingly become centers of administration, they experience an influx of relatively high-paid professional workers, the majority of whom are suburban residents (Levine, 1989, p. 26). Despite some pockets of gentrification, most of the increasing demand for housing for such workers has been in the suburbs. Retail and commercial businesses have expanded into the suburbs to service that growing population. To the extent that metropolitan areas have experienced an expansion of existing manufacturing facilities or have attracted new facilities, this growth has also disproportionately gone to the suburbs (Squires et al., 1987; White et al., 1989). Extending a trend that goes back before the war years, suburban communities have continued to grow.

The city of Chicago, often labeled the prototypical American industrial city, is also illustrative of the postindustrial trends. Between 1979 and 1987, downtown investment exceeded $6 billion as parking lots and skid row hotels have been replaced with office towers, up-scale restaurants and shops, and luxury housing (Schmidt, 1987). Yet overall during the postwar decades, manufacturing employment in the city has been cut in half while it tripled in the suburban ring. Total employment in the city of Chicago in the 1970s dropped by 14 percent while it increased by almost 45 percent in the suburbs (Squires et al., 1987). Continuation of downtown and suburban growth, coupled with decline of urban communities in between, led *Chicago Tribune* columnist Clarence Page to describe his city as having a "dumbbell economy" (personal communication, 19 March 1987).

Throughout urban America, the rise of service industry jobs has fueled downtown and suburban development while the loss of manufacturing jobs has devastated blue-collar urban communities. Such uneven development is not simply the logical or natural outcome of impersonal market forces. The "supply-side" revolution at the federal level with the concomitant paper entrepreneurialism in private industry, the array of subsidies offered by state and local governments, and other forms of public intervention into the workings of the economy and the spatial development of cities, reveal the centrality of politics. As Mollenkopf concluded in reference to the post-industrial transformation of the largest central cities in the United States, "while its origins may be found in economic forces, federal urban development programs and the local progrowth coalitions which implemented them have magnified and chan-neled those economic forces" (Mollenkopf, 1983, p. 19). Uneven development therefore reflects conscious decisions made in both the public and private sectors in accordance with the logic of privatism, to further certain interests at the expense of others. Ideology has remained very much alive. Consequently, serious social costs have been paid.

Many of the social costs of both sudden economic decline and dramatic growth have been fully documented. As indicated above they include a range of economic and social strains for families, mental and physical health difficulties for current and former employees, fiscal crises for cities, and a range of environmental and commu-nity development problems. Among the more intangible yet clearly most consequen-tial costs have been a reduction in the income of the average family and increasing inequality among wage earners and their families. Uneven economic and spatial development of cities has yielded unequal access to income and wealth for city residents.

For approximately 30 years after World War II, family income increased and the degree of income inequality remained fairly constant. These trends turned around in the mid-1970s. Between 1977 and 1988, the vast majority of Americans experienced a decline in the buying power of their family incomes. Families in the lower 80 percent of the income distribution (four out of five families) were able to purchase fewer goods with their incomes by the end of the 1980s than they were able to do just 10 years earlier. The most severely affected were those in the bottom 10th who experienced a drop of 14.8 percent. Only those in the top 10th experienced a significant increase that, for them, was 16.5 percent. (Families in the 9th decile experienced a 1.0 percent increase.) Most of this increase went to families in the upper 1 percent who enjoyed a gain of 49.8 percent. While GNP grew during these years and the purchasing power of the average family income increased by 2.2 percent, the top 20 percent received all of the net increase and more, reflecting the increasing inequality. Consequently, when adjusted for inflation, the lower 80 percent experienced a net decrease in the purchasing power of their family incomes (Gottdiener, 1990; Levy, 1987; Mishel and Simon, 1988, p. 6).

This growing inequality in the nation's income distribution reflects two basic trends. First is the shift from relatively high-paid manufacturing positions to lower-paid service jobs. While service sector jobs include some highly paid professional positions, the vast majority of service jobs are low-paid, unskilled jobs. To illustrate, the Bureau of Labor Statistics projects an increase of approximately 250,000 computer systems analysts between 1986 and 2000 but more than 2.5 million jobs for waiters, waitresses, chambermaids and doormen, clerks, and custodians. There have also been income declines within industrial sectors reflecting the second trend, noted above, which includes the increasingly successful efforts by US corporations to reduce the wage bill (Bluestone and Harrison, 1988).

Perhaps more problematic has been the growing racial gap. Racial disparities did decline in the first two decades following the war. Between 1947 and 1971, median black family income rose gradually from 51 percent to 61 percent of the white median. It fluctuated for a few years, reaching 61 percent again in 1975 but dropping consistently to 56 percent in 1987 (US Bureau of the Census, 1976, 1980 [Table H7], 1989). For black men between the ages of 25 and 64 the gap improved between 1960 and 1980 from 49 percent to 64 percent, but dropped to 62 percent by 1987 (Jaynes and Williams, 1989, p. 28). Within cities, and in particular big cities, the racial gaps have grown larger. Between 1968 and 1986, black median family income in metropolitan areas dropped from 63.7 percent to 57.4 percent of the white median. And in metropolitan areas with more than one million people, the ratio within the central city dropped from 69.7 percent to 59.0 percent (Squires, 1991).

Racial disparities in family wealth are even more dramatic. The median wealth of black households is 9 percent of the white household median. At each level of income and educational attainment, blacks control far fewer assets then do whites. Among those with monthly incomes below $900, black net worth is 1 percent that of whites with similar incomes. Education helps but does not close the gap. Among college educated householders 35 years of age or less with incomes of more than $48,000 annually, black net worth is 93 percent that of whites (Jaynes and Williams, 1989, pp. 276, 292).

Not only are blacks and whites separated economically, but racial segregation in the nation's housing markets persists. During the 1970s, the degree of racial isolation in the nation's major cities remained virtually unchanged according to several statistical measures, leading two University of Chicago sociologists to identify 10 cities as "hypersegregated" (Massey and Denton, 1987, 1989). The degree of segregation differs little if at all by income for racial minorities. Among the consequences are unequal access to areas where jobs are being created and inequitable distribution of public services including education for minorities, and heightened racial tensions and conflicts for all city residents (Orfield, 1988).

Not surprisingly, it is predominantly black neighborhoods that have been most adversely affected by the uneven development of US cities. For example, in Chicago between 1963 and 1977, the city experienced a 29 percent job loss, but predominantly black communities lost 45 percent of all jobs. The increasing incidence of crime, drug abuse, teenage pregnancy, school dropout rates, and other indicators of so-called underclass behavior are clearly linked to the deindustrialization and disinvestment of city neighborhoods outside the central business district (Harris and Wilkins, 1988; Wilson, 1987).

Uneven structural and spatial development of cities adversely affects racial minorities. But racial inequalities in US cities are not simply artefacts of those structural and spatial developments. Racism has its own dynamic. Blacks who have earned all the trappings of middle-class life in terms of a professional occupation, four-bedroom house, and designer clothes are still routinely subjected to demeaning behavior that takes such forms as name calling on the streets by anonymous passers-by, discourteous service in restaurants and stores, and harassment on the part of police, all simply because of their race (Feagin, n.d.). Racially motivated violence in Bensenhurst and Howard Beach, Sambo parties and other racially derogatory behavior on several college campuses, and letter bombings of civil rights lawyers and judges confirm the continuity of vicious racism. The dynamics of class and race remain very difficult to disentangle, but the effects of both are all too real in urban America.

Alternatives to the Pursuit of the Private City

Privatism and the policies that flow logically from that ideology have benefited those shaping redevelopment policy, including members of most public–private partnerships. But these policies have not stimulated redevelopment of cities generally. Structural, spatial, and social imbalances remain and are reinforced by the dynamics of privatism. To address the well-known social problems of urban America successfully, policies must be responsive to the structural and spatial forces impinging on cities. At least fragmented challenges to privatism have emerged in local redevelopment struggles in recent years. Alternative conceptions of development, the nature of city life, and human relations in general have been articulated and have had some impact on redevelopment efforts.

In several cities community groups have organized, and in some cases captured the mayor's office, in efforts to pursue more balanced redevelopment policies (Clavel, 1986). Explicitly viewing the city in terms of its use value rather than as a profit center for the local growth machine, initiatives have been launched to democratize the redevelopment process and to assure more equitable outcomes of redevelopment policy. Among the specific ingredients of this somewhat inchoate challenge to privatism are programs to retain and attract diverse industries including manufacturing, targeting of initiatives to those neighborhoods and population groups most in need, human capital development, and other public investments in the infrastructure of cities. A critical dimension of many of these programs is a conscious effort to bring neighborhood groups and residents, long victimized by uneven development, into the planning and implementation process as integral parts of urban partnerships.

When Harold Washington was elected mayor of Chicago in 1983, he launched a redevelopment plan that incorporated several of these components. The planning actually began during the campaign when people from various racial groups, economic classes, and geographic areas were brought together to identify goals and policies to achieve them under a Washington administration. Shortly after the election, Washington released *Chicago Works Together: Chicago Development Plan 1984*, which reflected that involvement. Explicitly advocating a strategic approach to pursuing development with equity, the plan articulated five major goals: increased job opportunities for Chicagoans; balanced growth; neighborhood development via partnerships and coordinated investment; enhanced public participation in decision making; and pursuit of a regional, state, and national legislative agenda (*Chicago Works Together*, 1984, p. 1). As development initiatives proceeded under Washington, strategic plans were implemented that involved industrial and geographic sector-specific approaches to retain manufacturing and regenerate older neighborhoods, affirmative action plans to bring more minorities and women into city government as employees and as city contractors, provision of business incentives that were conditioned on locational choices and other public needs, and a planning process that involved community groups, public officials, and private industry.

Specific tactics included funding the Midwest Center for Labor Research to create an early warning system for the purposes of identifying potential plant closure and where feasible, interventions that would forestall the closure. Linked development programs were negotiated with specific developers to spread the benefits of downtown development. Planned manufacturing district legislation was enacted to control conversion of industrial zones to commercial and residential purposes, thus retaining some manufacturing jobs that would otherwise be lost. As the widely publicized "Council Wars" attested, Washington encountered strong resistance to many of his proposals (Bennett, 1988). The efforts of his administration demonstrated, however, that uneven urban development was not simply the outcome of natural or neutral market forces. Politics, including the decisions of public officials, mattered and those decisions under Washington were responsive to both public need and market signals (Giloth and Betancur, 1988; Mier, 1989; Mier et al., 1986).

In 1983, Boston also held a significant mayoral election. At the height of the Massachusetts miracle, the city's economy was prospering and Raymond L. Flynn was elected with a mandate to "share the prosperity." Several policies have been implemented in order to do so.

Boston's strong real estate market in the early 1980s led to a shortage of low- and middle-income housing. Flynn played a central role in the implementation of a linkage program that took effect one month before he was elected. Under the linkage program, a fee was levied on downtown development projects to assist construction of housing for the city's low- and middle-income residents. Shortly after taking office, the Flynn administration negotiated inclusionary zoning agreements with individual housing developers to provide below-market-rate units in their housing developments or to pay an "in lieu of" free into the linkage fund. To further alleviate the housing shortage, in 1983 the Boston Housing Partnership was formed to assist community development corporations in rehabilitating and managing housing units in their neighborhoods. The partnership's board includes executives from leading banks, utility companies, and insurance firms; city and state housing officials; and directors of local community development corporations.

Boston also established a residents' job policy under which developers and employers are required to target city residents, minorities, and women for construction jobs and for the permanent jobs created by these developments. These commitments hold for publicly subsidized developments and, in an agreement reached by the mayor's office, the Greater Boston Real Estate Board, the Buildings Trade Council, and leaders of the city's minority community, for private developments as well.

The Boston Compact represents another creative partnership in that city. Under this program, the public schools agreed to make commitments to improve the schools' performance in return for the business community's agreement to give hiring preferences to their graduates. Schools have designed programs to encourage students to stay in school, develop their academic abilities, and learn job readiness skills. Several local employers, including members of the Vault, have agreed to provide jobs paying more than the minimum wage and financial assistance for college tuition to students who succeed in the public schools.

As in Chicago, the Flynn administration in Boston has consciously pursued balanced development and efforts to bring previously disenfranchised groups into the development process. The specific focus has been on housing and jobs, but the broader objective has been to share the benefits of development generally throughout the city (Dreier, 1989).

The Community Reinvestment Act (CRA) passed by Congress in 1977 has led to partnerships for urban reinvestment in cities across the nation. The CRA requires federally regulated banks and savings and loans providers to assess and be responsive to the credit needs of their service areas. Failure to do so can result in lenders being denied charters, new branches, or other corporate changes they intend to make. Neighborhood groups can challenge lenders' applications for such business operations with federal regulators, thus providing lenders with incentives to meet their CRA obligations (Potomac Institute, 1980). Subsequently, community groups and lenders have negotiated CRA agreements in more than 125 cities totaling approximately $6 billion in neighborhood reinvestment (Bradford, 1989). Examples include a $100-million loan pool created by 46 California banks to finance low-income housing, a $200-million commitment by Chase Manhatten Bank of New York for a community development fund, and a $245-million agreement negotiated by Chicago housing and neighborhood groups with several Chicago area lenders for various housing and business development projects (Guskind, 1989).

A unique lending partnership was created in Milwaukee in 1989. In response to the 1989 study finding Milwaukee to have the nation's highest racial disparity in mortgage loan rejection rates, the city's Democratic Mayor and Republican Governor created a committee to find ways to increase lending in the city's minority community. The Fair Lending Action Committee (FLAC) (1989) included lenders, lending regulators, real estate agents, community organizers, civil rights leaders, a city alderman, and others. An ambitious set of recommendations was unanimously agreed to in its report *Equal Access to Mortgage Lending: The Milwaukee Plan*. The key recommendation in the report was that area lenders would direct 13 percent of all residential, commercial real estate, and business loans to racial minorities by 1991. (After much debate the 13 percent figure was agreed to because that was the current minority representation in the population of the four-county Milwaukee metropolitan area.) Several low-interest loan programs were proposed to be financed and administered by lenders, city officials, and neighborhood groups. Fair housing training programs were recommended for all segments of the housing industry including lenders, real estate agents, insurers, and appraisers. The lending community was advised to provide $75,000 to support housing counseling centers that assist first-time home buyers. The city, county, and state were called upon to consider a linked deposit program to assure that public funds would go to those lenders responsive to the credit needs of the entire community. Specific recommendations were made to increase minority employment in the housing industry. And a permanent FLAC was called for to monitor progress in implementing the report's recommendations. The report concluded:

> There is a racial gap in mortgage lending in the Milwaukee metropolitan area. Implementation of these recommendations will be a major step in eliminating that gap. The Fair Lending Action Committee constitutes a partnership that is committed to the realization of fair lending and the availability of adequate mortgage loans and finance capital for all segments of the Milwaukee community. Building on the relationships that have been established among lenders, public officials, and community groups, neighborhood revitalization throughout the city and prosperity throughout the entire metropolitan area can and will be achieved.   (Fair Lending Action Committee, 1989, p. 14)

At the press conference releasing the report, Governor Tommy G. Thompson "eloquently" stated, "Neither I nor the Mayor are the kind of guys who commission reports only to see them collect dust." The lenders indicated their own institutions and the local trade associations would support the report and implement its recommendations. Representatives of community groups, whose own reports have gathered much dust on bureaucrats' book cases, nodded approvingly in an expression of most cautious optimism.

Release of the report concluded what had been several months of contentious debates. The unanimous support for the report expressed by committee members at the conclusion did not negate the differences of opinion that prevailed or the fact that compromises were made in the interest of a show of unity. Yet the very existence of this wide-ranging report offers some additional hope for revitalization in Milwaukee. What remains to be seen is the extent of implementation.

These diverse initiatives are illustrative of experiments being launched in small towns and large cities in all regions of the United States. While they constitute an array of programs addressing a variety of problems, there are important underlying commonalities. They are responsive to the structural and spatial underpinnings of critical urban social problems. They are premised on a commitment to growth with equity; the notion that economic productivity and social justice can be mutually reinforcing. And the objective is to make cities more liveable, not just more profitable. A more progressive city is certainly not inevitable, but these efforts are vivid reminders that the major impediments have as much to do with politics as markets.

Beyond *Laissez-Faire*?

The trajectory of future redevelopment activity is blurred. The ideology of privatism is being challenged. Experiments with more progressive policies have occurred. But no linear path in the overall direction of public–private partnerships in particular or urban redevelopment in general has emerged. Harold Washington was soon followed by a Daley in Chicago. Boston's economy in the early 1990s does not look as promising as it did in the early 1980s and the demand for more incentives to the business community is getting louder in the wake of the Massachusetts miracle (personal communication, Peter Dreier of the Boston Redevelopment Authority, 6 January 1990). Milwaukee's mayor frequently expresses concern about the local business climate as civil rights' groups challenge him to respond to the city's racial problems. Redevelopment remains a highly contentious political matter.

The grip of privatism has waned since the height of the Reagan years. HUD abuses, the savings and loan bailout, insider trading scandals, and other manifestations of the excesses of the pursuit of personal wealth serve as reminders of the importance of a public sector role beyond subsidization of private capital accumulation. Experiments in strategic planning to achieve balanced growth in Chicago, to share the prosperity in Boston, and to expand memberships in partnerships in Milwaukee and elsewhere demonstrate the capacity to conceive a different image of the city and the ability to implement programs in hopes of realizing that image. Yet as Warner concluded, "The quality which above all else characterizes our urban inheritance is privatism" (1987, p. 202). For better or for worse, that remains the bedrock on which future plans will be built.

REFERENCES

Barnekov, T., Boyle, R., and Rich, D. (1989). *Privatism and Urban Policy in Britain and the United States*. New York: Oxford University Press.

Becker, G. (1986). The prophets of doom have a dismal record. *Business Week*, 27 January, p. 22.

Bell, D. (1960). *The End of Ideology*. New York: Free Press.

Bell, D. (1973). *The Coming of Post-Industrial Society: A Venture of Social Forecasting*. New York: Basic Books.

Bender, T. (1983). The end of the city? *Democracy*, 3 (Winter), 8–20.

Bennett, L. (1988). Harold Washington's Chicago: Placing a progressive city administration in context. *Social Policy*, 19(2), 22–8.

Bluestone, B., and Harrison, B. (1982). *The Deindustrialization Of America: Plant closings, community abandonment, and the dismantling of basic industry*. New York: Basic Books.

Bluestone, B., and Harrison, B. (1988). *The Great U-turn: Corporate restructring and the polarizing of America*. New York: Basic Books.

Bowles, S., Gordon, D. M., and Weisskopf, T. E. (1983). *Beyond the Waste Land: A democratic alternative to economic decline*. Garden City, NY: Anchor Press/Doubleday.

Bradford, C. (1989). Reinvestment: The quiet revolution. *The Neighborhood Works*, 12(4), 1, 22–6.

Center for Community Change. (1989). *Bright Promises, Questionable Results: An examination of how well three government subsidy programs created jobs*. Washington, DC: Center for Community Change.

Chambers, J. L. (1987). The law and black Americans: Retreat from civil rights. In J. Dewart (ed.). *The State of Black America 1987*. New York: National Urban League, pp. 18–30.

Chicago Works Together: Chicago development plan 1984. (1984). City of Chicago.

Clavel, P. (1986). *The Progressive City: Planning and participation, 1969–1984.* New Brunswick, NJ: Rutgers University Press.

Cohen, S. S., and Zysman, J. (1987). *Manufacturing Matters: The myth of the post-industrial economy.* New York: Basic Books.

Connolly, W. E. (1983). Progress, growth, and pessimism in America. *Democracy*, 3 (Fall): 22–31.

Darden, J., Hill, R. C., Thomas, J., and Thomas, R. (1987). *Detroit: Race and uneven development.* Philadelphia: Temple University Press.

Davis, P. (1986). *Public–Private Partnerships: Improving urban life.* New York: Academy of Political Science.

Dreier, P. (1989). Economic growth and economic justice in Boston: Populist housing and jobs policies. In G. D. Squires (ed.). *Unequal Partnerships: The political economy of urban redevelopment in postwar America.* New Brunswick, NJ: Rutgers University Press, pp. 35–58.

Dreier, P., Schwartz, D. C., and Greiner, A. (1988). What every business can do about housing. *Harvard Business Review*, 66(5), 52–61.

Eisinger, P. K. (1988). *The Rise of the Entrepreneurial State: State and local economic development policy in the United States.* Madison: University of Wisconsin Press.

Fair Lending Action Committee. (1989). Equal Access to Mortgage Lending: The Milwaukee plan. Report to Mayor John Norquist and Governor Tommy G. Thompson (October).

Feagin, J. R. (1988). *Free Enterprise City: Houston in political and economic perspective.* New Brunswick, NJ: Rutgers University Press.

Feagin, J. R. (n.d.). The continuing significance of race: The black middle class in public places. Unpublished manuscript.

Friedland, R. (1983). *Power and Crisis in the City: Corporations, unions and urban policy.* New York: Schocken.

Friedman, L. M. (1968). *Government and Slum Housing: A century of frustration.* Chicago: Rand McNally.

Giloth, R. and Betancur, J. (1988). Where downtown meets neighborhood: Industrial displacement in Chicago, 1978–1987. *Journal of the American Planning Association*, 54(3), 279–90.

Goodman, R. (1979). *The Last Entrepreneurs: America's regional wars for jobs and dollars.* Boston: South End Press.

Gottdiener, M. (1986). Retrospect and prospect in urban crisis theory. In M. Gottdiener (ed.). *Cities in Stress: A new look at the urban crisis.* Beverly Hills, CA: Sage, pp. 277–91.

Gottdiener, M. (1990). Crisis theory and state-financed capital: The new conjuncture in the USA. *International Journal of Urban and Regional Research*, 14(3), 383–404.

Greider, W. (1978). Detroit's streetwise mayor plays key role in city's turnaround. *Cleveland Plain Dealer* (3 July), cited in T. Swanstrom. (1985). *The Crisis of Growth Politics: Cleveland, Kucinich, and the challenge of urban populism.* Philadelphia: Temple University Press.

Guskind, R. (1989). Thin red line. *National Journal*, 21(43), 2639–43.

Harris, F., and Wilkins, R. W. (eds.) (1988). *Quiet Riots: Race and poverty in the United States.* New York: Pantheon.

Hartman, C. (1974). *Yerba Buena: Land grab and community resistance in San Francisco.* San Francisco: Glide.

Hayes, R. H., and Abernathy, W. J. (1980). Managing our way to economic decline. *Harvard Business Review*, 58, July/August 67–77.

Hays, R. A. (1985). *The Federal Government and Urban Housing: Ideology and change in public policy.* Albany: SUNY Press.

Jackson, K. T. (1985). *Crabgrass Frontier: The suburbanization of the United States.* New York: Oxford University Press.

Jaynes, G. D., and Williams, R. M. (eds.). (1989). *A Common Destiny: Blacks and American society.* Washington, DC: National Academy Press.

Kasarda, J. (1988). Economic restructuring and America's urban dilemma. In M. Dogan and J. Kasarda (eds.). *The Metropolis Era: Vol. 1. A world of giant cities.* Newbury Park: Sage, (pp. 56–84).

Krumholz, N. (1984). Recovery of cities: An alternate view. In P. R. Porter and D. Sweet (eds). *Rebuilding America's Cities: Roads to recovery.* New Brunswick, NJ: Center for Urban Policy Research, pp. 173–92.

Langton, S. (1983). Public-private partnerships: Hope or hoax? *National Civic Review,* 72 (May), 256–61.

Levine, M. V. (1987). Downtown redevelopment as an urban growth strategy: A critical appraisal of the Baltimore Renaissance. *Journal of Urban Affairs,* 9(2), 103–23.

Levine, M. V. (1989). The politics of partnership: Urban redevelopment since 1945. In G. D. Squires (ed.). *Unequal Partnerships: The political economy of urban redevelopment in postwar America.* New Brunswick, NJ: Rutgers University Press, pp. 12–34.

Levy, F. (1987). *Dollars and Dreams: The changing American income distribution.* New York: Russell Sage.

Lindblom, C. E. (1977). *Politics and Markets: The world's political–economic systems.* New York: Basic Books.

Logan, J. R., and Molotch, H. L. (1987). *Urban Fortunes: The political economy of place.* Berkeley: University of California Press.

McKenzie, R. (1979). *Restrictions on Business Mobility: A study in political rhetoric and economic reality.* Washington, DC: American Enterprise Institute.

Massey, D. S., and Denton, N. A. (1987). Trends in the residential segregation of blacks, Hispanics, and Asians. *American Sociological Review,* 52(6), 802–25.

Massey, D. S., and Denton, N. A. (1989). Hypersegregation in U.S. metropolitan areas: Black and Hispanic segregation along five dimensions. *Demography,* 26(3), 373–91.

Mier, R. (1989). Neighborhood and region: An experiential basis for understanding. *Economic Development Quarterly,* 3(2), 169–74.

Mier, R., Moe, K. J., and Sherr, I. (1986). Strategic planning and the pursuit of reform, economic development, and equity. *Journal of the American Planning Association,* 52(3), 299–309.

Mishel, L., and Simon, J. (1988). *The State of Working America.* Washington, DC: Economic Policy Institute.

Mollenkopf, J. H. (1983). *The Contested City.* Princeton, NJ: Princeton University Press.

Norman, J. (1989). Congenial Milwaukee: A segregated city. In G. D. Squires (ed.). *Unequal Partnerships: The Political economy of urban redevelopment in postwar America.* New Brunswick, NJ: Rutgers University Press, pp. 178–201.

Orfield, G. (1988). Separate societies: Have the Kerner warnings come true? In F. R. Harris and W. Wilkins (eds.). *Quiet Riots: Race and poverty in the United States.* New York: Pantheon, pp. 100–22.

Peterson, G. and Lewis, C. (eds.). (1986). *Reagan and the Cities.* Washington, DC: The Urban Institute.

Peterson, P. E. (1981). *City Limits.* Chicago: University of Chicago Press.

Porter, D. R. (1989). Balancing the interests in public/private partnerships. *Urban Land,* 48(5), 36–7.

Potomac Institute. (1980). *Lender's Guide to Fair Mortgage Policies.* Washington, DC: Author.

President's Commission for a National Agenda for the Eighties. (1980). *A National Agenda for the Eighties.* Washington, DC: Government Printing Office.

Reich, R. B. (1983). *The Next American Frontier.* New York: Times Books.

Reich, R. B. (1987). *Tales of a New America*. New York: Times Books.

Sbragia, A. (1989). The Pittsburgh model of economic development: Partnership, responsiveness, and indifference. In G.D. Squires (ed.). *Unequal Partnerships: The political economy of urban redevelopment in postwar America*. New Brunswick, NJ: Rutgers University Press, pp. 103–20.

Schmidt, W. (1987). U.S. downtowns: No longer downtrodden. *The New York Times*, 11 October.

Schumpeter, J. (1942). *Capitalism, Socialism and Democracy*. New York: Harper & Row.

Smith, M. P., and Judd, D. R. (1984). American cities: The production of ideology. In M. P. Smith and D. R. Judd (eds.). *Cities in Transformation: Class, capital, and the state*. Beverly Hills, CA: Sage, pp. 177–96.

Squires, G. D. (1991). Deindustrialization, economic democracy, and equal opportunity: The changing context of race relations in urban America. *Comparative Urban and Community Research*, 3, 188–215.

Squires, G. D., Bennett, L., McCourt, K., and Nyden, P. (1987). *Chicago: Race, class, and the response to urban decline*. Philadelphia: Temple University Press.

Stone, C. N. (1987). The study of the politics of urban development. In C. N. Stone and H. T. Sanders (eds.). *The Politics of Urban Development*. Lawrence: University of Kansas Press, pp. 3–22.

Taylor, W. L. (1989). Special report: Supreme Court decisions do grave damage to equal employment opportunity law. *Civil Rights Monitor*, 4(2), 1–28.

Thomas, J. M. (1989). Detroit: The centrifugal city. In G. D. Squires (ed.). *Unequal Partnerships: The political economy of urban redevelopment in postwar America*. New Brunswick, NJ: Rutgers University Press, pp. 142–60.

US Bureau of the Census. (1976). *The Statistical History of the United States: From colonial times to the present*. New York: Basic Books.

US Bureau of the Census. (1980). *Structural Equipment and Household Characteristics of Housing Units*. Washington, DC: Government Printing Office.

US Bureau of the Census. (1989). *Statistical Abstract of the United States: 1989*. Washington, DC: Government Printing Office.

Warner, S. B. Jr (1987). *The Private City: Philadelphia in three periods of its growth*. Philadelphia: University of Pennsylvania Press.

White, S. B., Reynolds, P. D., McMahon, W., and Paetsch, J. (1989). *City and Suburban Impacts of Industrial Change in Milwaukee, 1978–87*. Milwaukee: University of Wisconsin-Milwaukee, The Urban Research Center.

Wilson, W. J. (1987). *The Truly Disadvantaged: The inner city, the underclass, and public policy*. Chicago: University of Chicago Press.

12

Gentrification, the Frontier, and the Restructuring of Urban Space*

Neil Smith

In his seminal essay on "The significance of the frontier in American history," written in 1893, Frederick Jackson Turner (1958 edn) wrote:

> American development has exhibited not merely advance along a single line, but a return to primitive conditions on a continually advancing frontier line, and a new development for that area. American social development has been continually beginning over again on the frontier... In this advance the frontier is the outer edge of the wave – the meeting point between savagery and civilization... The wilderness has been interpenetrated by lines of civilization growing ever more numerous.

For Turner, the expansion of the frontier and the rolling back of wilderness and savagery were an attempt to make livable space out of an unruly and uncooperative nature. This involved not simply a process of spatial expansion and the progressive taming of the physical world. The development of the frontier certainly accomplished these things, but for Turner it was also the central experience which defined the uniqueness of the American national character. With each expansion of the outer edge by robust pioneers, not only were new lands added to the American estate but new blood was added to the veins of the American democratic ideal. Each new wave westward, in the conquest of nature, sent shock waves back east in the democratization of human nature.

During the twentieth century, the imagery of wilderness and frontier has been applied less to the plains, mountains and forests of the West, and more to the cities of the whole country, but especially of the East. As part of the experience of suburbanization, the twentieth-century American city came to be seen by the white middle class as an urban wilderness; it was, and for many still is, the habitat of disease and

* Smith, Neil (1986) "Gentrification, the Frontier and the Restructuring of Urban Space" from Neil Smith and Peter Williams (eds.), *Gentrification of the City*, Allen and Unwin, Boston, pp. 15–34.

crime, danger and disorder (Warner, 1972). Indeed these were the central fears expressed throughout the 1950s and 1960s by urban theorists who focused on urban "blight" and "decline," "social malaise" in the inner city, the "pathology" of urban life; in short, the "unheavenly city" (Banfield, 1968). The city becomes a wilderness, or worse a jungle (Long, 1971; Sternlieb, 1971); see also Castells (1976). More vividly than in the news media or social science theory, this is the recurrent theme in a whole genre of "urban jungle" Hollywood productions, from *West Side Story* and *King Kong* to *The Warriors*.

Anti-urbanism has been a dominant theory in American culture. In a pattern analogous to the original experience of wilderness, the last 20 years have seen a shift from fear to romanticism and a progression of urban imagery from wilderness to frontier. Cotton Mather and the Puritans of seventeenth-century New England feared the forest as an impenetrable evil, a dangerous wilderness, but with the continual taming of the forest and its transformation at the hands of human labor, the softer imagery of Turner's frontier was an obvious successor to Mather's forest of evil. There is an optimism and an expectation of expansion associated with "frontier"; wilderness gives way to frontier when the conquest is well under way. Thus in the twentieth-century American city, the imagery of urban wilderness has been replaced by the imagery of urban frontier. This transformation can be traced to the origins of urban renewal, see especially Abrams (1965), but has become intensified in the last two decades, as the rehabilitation of single-family homes became fashionable in the wake of urban renewal. In the language of gentrification, the appeal to frontier imagery is exact: urban pioneers, urban homesteaders and urban cowboys are the new folk heroes of the urban frontier.

Just as Turner recognized the existence of Native Americans but included them as part of his savage wilderness, contemporary urban-frontier imagery implicitly treats the present inner-city population as a natural element of their physical surroundings. Thus the term "urban pioneer" is as arrogant as the original notion of the "pioneer" in that it conveys the impression of a city that is not yet socially inhabited; like the Native Americans, the contemporary urban working class is seen as less than social, simply a part of the physical environment. Turner was explicit about this when he called the frontier "the meeting point between savagery and civilization," and although today's frontier vocabulary of gentrification is rarely as explicit, it treats the inner-city population in much the same way (Stratton, 1977).

The parallels go further. For Turner, the westward geographical progress of the frontier line is associated with the forging of the national spirit. An equally spiritual hope is expressed in the boosterism which presents gentrification as the leading edge of an American urban renaissance; in the most extreme scenario, the new urban pioneers are expected to do for the national spirit what the old ones did: to lead us into a new world where the problems of the old world are left behind. In the words of one Federal publication, gentrification's appeal to history involves the "psychological need to re-experience successes of the past because of the disappointments of recent years – Vietnam, Watergate, the energy crisis, pollution, inflation, high interest rates, and the like" (Advisory Council on Historic Preservation, 1980, p. 9). No one has yet seriously proposed that we view James Rouse (the American developer responsible for many of the highly visible downtown malls, plazas, markets and tourist arcades) as the John Wayne of gentrification, but the proposal would be quite in keeping with much of the contemporary imagery. In the end, and this is the important conclusion, the imagery of frontier serves to rationalize and legitimate a process of conquest, whether in the eighteenth- and nineteenth-century West or in the twentieth-century inner city. The imagery relies on several myths but also has a partial basis in reality. Some of the mythology has already been hinted at, but before proceeding to examine the realistic basis of the imagery, I want to discuss one aspect of the frontier mythology not yet touched upon: nationalism.

The process of gentrification with which we are concerned here is quintessentially international. It is taking place throughout North American and much of western Europe, as well as Australia and New Zealand, that is, in cities throughout most of the Western advanced capitalist world. Yet nowhere is the process less understood than in the United States, where the American nationalism of the frontier ideology has encouraged a provincial understanding of gentrification. The original pre-twentieth-century frontier experience was not limited to the United States, but rather exported throughout the world; likewise, although it is nowhere as rooted as in the United States, the frontier ideology does emerge elsewhere in connection with gentrification. The international influence of the earlier American frontier experi-ence is repeated with the twentieth-century urban scene; the American imagery of gentrification is simultaneously cosmopolitan and parochial, general and local. It is general in image if often contrary in detail. For these reasons, the critique of the frontier imagery does not condemn us to repeating Turner's nationalism, and should not be seen as a nationalistic basis for a discussion of gentrification. The Australian experience of frontier, for example, was certainly different from the American, but was also responsible (along with American cultural imports) for spawning a strong frontier ideology. And the American frontier itself was as intensely real for potential immigrants in Scandinavia or Ireland as it was for actual French or British immi-grants in Baltimore or Boston.

However, as with every ideology, there is a real, if partial and distorted, basis for the treatment of gentrification as a new urban frontier. In this idea of frontier we see an evocative combination of economic and spatial dimensions of development. The potency of the frontier image depends on the subtlety of exactly this combination of the economic and the spatial. In the nineteenth century, the expansion of the geographic frontier in the US and elsewhere was simultaneously an economic expan-sion of capital. Yet the social individualism pinned onto and incorporated into the idea of frontier is in one important respect a myth; Turner's frontier line was extended westward less by individual pioneers and homesteaders, and more by banks, railways, the state and other speculators, and these in turn passed the land on (at profit) to businesses and families (Swierenga 1968). In this period, economic expansion was accomplished in part through absolute geographical expansion. That is, expansion of the economy involved the expansion of the geographical arena over which the economy operated.

Today the link between economic and geographical development remains, giving the frontier imagery its present currency, but the form of the link is very different. As far as its spatial basis is concerned, economic expansion takes place today not through absolute geographical expansion but through the internal differentiation of geographical space (Smith, 1982). Today's production of space or geographical development is therefore a sharply uneven process. Gentrification, urban renewal, and the larger, more complex, processes of urban restructuring are all part of the differentiation of geographical space at the urban scale; although they had their basis in the period of economic expansion prior to the current world economic crisis, the function of these processes today is to lay one small part of the geographical basis for a future period of expansion (Smith, 1984). And, as with the original frontier, the mythology has it that gentrification is a process led by individual pioneers and homesteaders whose sweat equity, daring, and vision are paving the way for those among us who are more timid. But even if we ignore urban renewal and the commercial, administrative and recreational redevelopment that is taking place, and focus purely on residential rehabilitation, it is apparent that where the "urban pioneers" venture, the banks, real-estate companies, the state or other collective economic actors have generally gone before. In this context it may be more appropriate to view the James Rouse Company not as the John Wayne but as the Wells Fargo of gentrification.

In the public media, gentrification has been presented as the pre-eminent symbol of the larger urban redevelopment that is taking place. Its symbolic importance far outweighs its real importance; it is a relatively small if highly visible part of a much larger process. The actual process of gentrification lends itself to such cultural abuse in the same way as the original frontier. Whatever the real economic, social and political forces that pave the way for gentrification, and no matter which banks and realtors, governments and contractors are behind the process, gentrification appears at first sight, and especially in the USA, to be a marvelous testament to the values of individualism and the family, economic opportunity and the dignity of work (sweat equity). From appearances at least, gentrification can be played so as to strike some of the most resonant chords on our ideological keyboard.

As early as 1961, Jean Gottmann not only caught the reality of changing urban patterns, but also spoke in a language amenable to the emerging ideology, when he said that the "frontier of the American economy is nowadays urban and suburban rather than peripheral to the civilized areas" (Gottmann, 1961, p. 78). With two important provisos, which have become much more obvious in the last two decades, this insight is precise. First, the urban frontier is a frontier in the economic sense, before anything else. The social, political and cultural transformations in the central city are often dramatic and are certainly important as regards our immediate experience of everyday life, but they are associated with the development of an economic frontier. Second, the urban frontier is today only one of several frontiers, given that the internal differentiation of geographical space occurs at different scales. In the context of the present global economic crisis, it is clear that international capital and American capital alike confront a global "frontier" that incorporates the so-called urban frontier. This link between different spatial scales, and the importance of urban development to national and international recovery, was acutely clear in the enthusiastic language used by supporters of the urban Enterprise Zone, an idea pioneered by the Thatcher and Reagan administrations. To quote just one apologist, Stuart Butler (a British economist working for the American right-wing think tank, the Heritage Foundation):[1]

It may be argued that at least part of the problem facing many urban areas today lies in our failure to apply the mechanism explained by Turner (the continual local development and innovation of new ideas)...to the inner city "frontier." Cities are facing fundamental changes, and yet the measures applied to deal with these changes are enacted in the main by distant governments. We have failed to appreciate that there may be opportunities in the cities themselves, and we have scrupulously avoided giving local forces the chance to seize them. Proponents of the Enterprise Zone aim to provide a climate in which the frontier process can be brought to bear within the city itself.

(Butler, 1981, p. 3)

The circumspect observation of Gottmann and others has given way 20 years later to the unabashed adoption of the "urban frontier" as the keystone to a political and economic program of urban restructuring in the interests of capital.

The frontier line today has a quintessentially economic definition – it is the frontier of profitability – but it takes on a very acute geographical expression at different spatial scales. Ultimately, this is what the twentieth-century frontier and the so-called urban frontier of today have in common. In reality, both are associated with the accumulation and expansion of capital. But where the nineteenth-century frontier represented the consummation of *absolute geographical expansion* as the primary spatial expression of capital accumulation, gentrification and urban re-development represent the most advanced example of the *redifferentiation* of geographical space toward precisely the same end. It is just possible that, so as to understand the present, what is needed today is the substitution of a true geography in place of a false history.

The Restructuring of Urban Space

It is important to understand the present extent of gentrification so as to comprehend the real character and importance of the restructuring process. If by gentrification we mean, strictly, the residential rehabilitation of working-class neighborhoods, then, in the United States (where the process is probably most dramatic), it shows up clearly in data at the census tract level but not yet at the scale of the Standard Metropolitan Statistical Area (Chall, 1984; Schaffer and Smith, 1984). For a number of cities, income, rent and other indicators from the 1980 census show clear evidence of gentrification in central tracts. However, the process has not yet become significant enough to reverse or even seriously counter the established trends toward residential suburbanization. Although this is an interesting empirical pattern, alone it hardly amounts to a secular change in patterns of urban development. If, however, we eschew the narrow ideology fostered around gentrification, and see the process in relation to a number of broader if still less "visible" urban developments; if, in other words, we examine the momentum of the process, not a static empirical count, then a coherent pattern emerges of a far more significant restructuring of urban space.

Before examining the precise trends that are leading toward the restructuring process, it is important to note that the question of spatial scale is central to any relevant explanation. We can say that the restructuring of the urban-space economy is a product of the uneven development of capitalism or of the operation of a rent gap, the result of a developing service economy or of changed lifestyle preferences, the suburbanization of capital or the devalorization of capital invested in the urban built environment. It is, of course, a product of all of these forces, in some way, but to say so tells us very little. These processes occur at several different spatial scales, and although previous attempts at explanation have tended to fasten on one or the other trend, they may not in fact be mutually exclusive. Where authors have attempted to incorporate more than one such trend, they have generally been content to list these as factors. Yet this version of "factor analysis" is quite unambitious. The whole question of explanation hinges not upon identifying factors but upon understanding the relative importance of, and relation between, so-called "factors." In part, this is a question of scale.

But there is a second question of scale concerning levels of generality. We accept here that the restructuring of urban space is general but by no means universal. What does this mean? It means, first, that the restructuring of urban space is not, strictly speaking, a new phenomenon. The entire process of urban growth and development is a constant patterning, structuring and restructuring of urban space. What *is* new today is the degree to which this restructuring of space is an immediate and systematic component of a larger economic and social restructuring of advanced capitalist economies. A given built environment expresses specific patterns of production and reproduction, consumption and circulation, and as these patterns change, so does the geographical patterning of the built environment. The walking city, we have been told, is not the automobile city, but of greater importance, perhaps, the city of small craft manufacturing is not the metropolis of multinational capital.

The geographical restructuring of the space economy is always uneven; thus urban restructuring in one region of a national or international economy may not be matched in either quality or quantity, character or extent, by restructuring in another. This is immediately evident in the comparison of developed and underdeveloped parts of the world economy. The basic structure of most Third World cities, and the processes at work, are quite different from those in Europe, Oceania or North America. But equally, within the developed economies, there are strong regional differences. If Baltimore and Los Angeles are both experiencing a rapid transformation of their space economies, there are as many differences between them as similarities. Still other cities, such as Gary, Indiana, may be experiencing a secular decline and little restructuring (as opposed to continued destruction). In short, there is an overlay of regional and international patterns that complicate the extent urban patterns. Although they focus on the general causes and background to the contemporary restructuring of urban space, the explanations offered will be successful only to the extent that they can begin to explain the diversity of urban forms resulting from the process as well as complete exceptions to the apparent rule. This again calls not for a "factor analysis" (a list of factors) but for an integrated explanation; we have to explain not just the location but also the timing of such dramatic urban change. But perhaps the most basic distinction that will emerge is between those trends and tendencies which are predominantly responsible for the *fact* of urban restructuring and those responsible for the *form* the process takes.

The most salient processes responsible for the origins and shaping of urban restructuring can perhaps be summarized under the following headings:

- Suburbanization and the emergence of the rent gap
- The deindustrialization of advanced capitalist economies and the growth of white-collar employment
- The spatial centralization and simultaneous decentralization of capital
- The falling rate of profit and the cyclical movement of capital
- Demographic changes and changes in consumption patterns

In consort, these developments and processes can provide a first approximation toward an integrated explanation of the different facets of gentrification and urban restructuring.

Suburbanization and the emergence of the rent gap

The explanation of suburban development is more complex than is often thought, and a revisionist alternative to traditional, transport-based explanations is beginning to emerge (Walker, 1978, 1981). The point here is not to give a comprehensive account of suburbanization but to summarize some of the most important conclusions.

The suburbanization process represents a simultaneous centralization and decentralization of capital and of human activity in geographical space. On the national scale, suburbanization is the outward expansion of centralized urban places, and this process should be understood in the most general way as a necessary product of the spatial centralization of capital. It is the growth of towns into cities into metropolitan centers.

At the urban scale, however, from the perspective of the urban center, suburbanization is a process of decentralization. It is a product not of a basic impulse toward centralization but of the impulse toward a high rate of profit. Profit rates are location specific, and at the urban scale as such, the economic indicator that differentiates one place from another is ground rent. Many other forces were involved in the suburbanization of capital, but pivotal in the entire process was the availability of cheap land on the periphery (low ground rent). There was no natural necessity for the expansion of economic activity to take the form of suburban development; there was no technical impediment preventing the movement of modern large-scale capital to the rural backwaters, or preventing its fundamental redevelopment of the industrial city it inherited, but instead the expansion of capital led to a process of suburbanization. In part this had to do with the impetus toward centralization (see below), but given the economics of centralization, it is the ground-rent structure that determined the suburban location of economic expansion (Smith, 1984).

The outward movement of capital to develop suburban, industrial, residential, commercial, and recreational activity results in a reciprocal change in suburban and inner-city ground-rent levels. Where the price of suburban land rises with the spread of new construction, the relative price of inner-city land falls. Smaller and smaller quantities of capital are funneled into the maintenance and repair of the inner-city building stock. This results in what we have called a *rent gap* in the inner city between the actual ground rent capitalized from the present (depressed) land use and the potential rent that could be capitalized from the "highest and best" use (or at least a "higher and better" use), given the central location. This suburbanization occurs in consort with structural changes in advanced economies. Some of the other processes we shall examine are more limited in their occurrence; what is remarkable about the rent gap is its near universality. Most cities in the advanced capitalist world have experienced this phenomenon, to a greater or lesser extent. Where it is allowed to run its course at the behest of the free market, it leads to the substantial abandonment of inner-city properties. This devalorization of capital invested in the built environment affects property of all sorts, commercial and industrial as well as residential and retail. Different levels and kinds of state involvement give the process a very different form in different economies, and abandonment (the logical end-point of the process) is most marked in the US, where state involvement has been less consistent and more sporadic.

At the most basic level, it is the movement of capital into the construction of new suburban landscapes and the consequent creation of a rent gap that create the economic *opportunity* for restructuring the central and inner cities. The devaloriza-tion of capital in the center creates the opportunity for the revalorization of this "underdeveloped" section of urban space. The actual realization of the process, and the determination of its specific form, involve the other trends listed earlier.

Deindustrialization and the growth of a white-collar economy

Associated with the devalorization of inner-city capital is the decline of certain economic sectors and land uses more than others. This is a product primarily of broader changes in the economic structure. In particular, the advanced capitalist economies (with the major exception of Japan) have experienced the onset of deindustrialization, whereas there has been a parallel if partial industrialization of certain Third World economies. Beginning in the 1960s, most industrial economies experienced a reduction in the proportion of workers in the industrial sectors (Blackaby, 1978; Harris, 1980, 1983; Bluestone and Harrison, 1982). But many urban areas began to experience the effects of deindustrialization much earlier than the last two decades. Thus the growth in manufacturing, at the national scale, since World War II was very uneven between regions. Whereas some regions, such as the West Midlands and South east of England, or many of the southern and western states of the USA, experienced a rapid growth of modern manufacturing, other regions experienced a relative disinvestment of capital in manufacturing jobs. At the urban scale the process is even more marked; most of the expanding industrial capacity of the postwar boom was not located in the inner cities, the traditional home of industry in the Chicago model of urban structure, but in suburban and peripheral locations. The result was a period of systematic disinvestment in urban industrial production, dating, in the case of some British cities, as far back as before World War I (Lenman, 1977). This was the case despite the overall growth of indus-trial production in the UK economy, taken as a whole, even following World War II.

The corollary to this deindustrialization is increased employment in other sectors of the economy, especially those described loosely as white-collar or service occupa-tions. Within these broad categories, many very different types of employment are

generally included, from clerical, communications and retail operatives to managerial, professional and research careers. Within this larger trend toward a growing
white-collar labor force, therefore, there are very different tendencies and these have
a specific spatial expression, as we shall see in the next section. By themselves, the
processes of deindustrialization and white-collar growth do not at all explain
the restructuring of the urban centers. Rather, these processes help to explain,
first, the kinds of building stock and land use most involved in the development of
the rent gap, and, second, the kinds of new land uses which can be expected where
the opportunity for redevelopment is taken. Thus, although the media emphasis is
on recent gentrification and the rehabilitation of working-class residences, there has
also been a considerable transformation of old industrial areas of the city. This did
not simply begin with the conversion of old warehouses into chic loft apartments;
much more significant was the early urban renewal activity which, although certainly a process of slum clearance, was also the clearance of "obsolete" (meaning
also devalorized) industrial buildings – factories, warehouses, wharves, etc. – where
many of the slum dwellers had once worked.

Although the devalorization of capital and the development of the rent gap
explain the possibility of reinvestment in the urban core around which gentrifying
areas are developing, and the transformation in economic and employment structures suggests the kinds of activity that are likely to predominate in this reinvestment, there remains the question as to why the burgeoning white-collar employment
is, at least in part, being centralized in the urban core. The existence of the rent gap is
only a partial explanation; there is, after all, cheap land available elsewhere,
throughout the rural periphery.

Spatial centralization and decentralization of capital

With the emergence of the capitalist mode of production, that which had hitherto
been accidental disappears, is neglected, or is converted into a necessity. The accumulation of wealth had been accidental in the sense that, however much it was the
goal of individuals, it was nowhere in precapitalist societies a general social rule
upon which the survival of the society depended. With the emergence of capitalism,
the accumulation of capital becomes a social necessity in exactly this way. Marx
(1967, vol. I, ch. 25) demonstrated that both a prerequisite and a product of the
accumulation of capital is a certain social concentration and centralization of that
capital. In short, this means that increasingly large quantities of capital are centralized under the control of a relatively small number of capitalists.

This social centralization is accomplished only through the production of specific
geographical patterns, but the attendant spatial patterns are complex. At its most
basic, the centralization of capital leads to a dialectic of spatial centralization and
decentralization (Smith, 1982). If the expansion of nineteenth-century capital
throughout the world is the most visible manifestation of the latter process (decentralization), the development of the urban metropolis is the most palpable product of
spatial centralization. Centralization occurs at a number of spatial scales, however,
besides the urban. It occurs at the level of plant size and at the level of national
capitals in the world economy, and at each scale there are quite specific mechanisms

that engender the process. At the urban scale, traditional theories have emphasized "agglomeration economies." The expansion of capital involves a continued division of labor, again at different scales, and thus in order to provide necessary commodities and services, a large number of separate operations have to be combined. The less the distance between these different activities, the less is the cost and time of production and transportation. Placed in the context of capital accumulation, this explanation is essentially correct concerning the original centralization of capital into urban "agglomerations."

In an interesting insight, Walker (1981, p. 388) notes that

> as capitalism develops, economies of agglomeration have diminished; they are a historically contingent force. But they are in part replaced by economies of (organizational) scale with the concentration of capital, so that gigantic nodes of activity still structure the urban landscape.

The central insight here is that such forces as agglomeration economies are historically contingent. Viewed from the urban centre, the suburbanization of industry represented a clear weakening of agglomeration economies, and was facilitated (not "caused") by developments in the means of transportation. Yet from the perspective of the national economy, the suburbanization of industry represented a clustering of massive and not so massive industrial facilities around established urban cores, and was thus a reaffirmation (at this scale) of the operation of agglomeration economies, however weakened. What Walker senses, though, is real; agglomeration economies operate in a different manner today, leading to clear spatial consequences. The most obvious of these involves the rapidly changing locational patterns associated with the expansion of white-collar employment.

The problem as regards white-collar employment is that a strong tendency toward centralization is matched by an equally strong if not stronger tendency toward decentralization – the movement of offices and other white-collar jobs to the suburbs. How can such apparently opposite tendencies coexist? How can suburbanization and agglomeration be coexistent? The explanation for this seeming paradox lies with a consideration of two interrelated issues. The first is the relationship between space and time *vis-à-vis* different forms of capital, and the second is the division of labor within the so-called white-collar sectors.

It is a cliché today to suggest that the revolution in communications technology will lead to spatial decentralization of office functions. This annihilation of space by time, as Marx had it, has indeed led to a massive suburbanization of white-collar jobs following on the heels of industrial suburbanization. With the computerization of many office functions, this trend continues. But consistent with the ideology of classlessness which first sponsored the notion of white collar, this trend is generally treated as a suburbanization of any and all types of office work from senior executives to word-processor operatives. Yet the further the trend develops, the clearer it becomes that this is not so. Thus the simultaneous centralization and decentralization of office activities represents the spatial expression of a division of labor within the so-called white-collar economy. For the most part, the office functions that are decentralized are the more routine clerical systems and operations associated with the administration, organization and management of governmental as well as corporate activities. These represent the "back offices," the "paper factories," or, more accurately, the "communication factories" for units of the broader system (Wald, 1984).

Much less usual is the suburbanization of central decision making in the form of corporate or governmental headquarters. The office boom experienced by many cities in the advanced capitalist world during the past 15 years seems to have been of this sort; it has been a continued centralization of the highest decision-making centers, along with the myriad ancillary services required by such activities: legal services, advertising, hotels and conference centers, publishers, architects, banks, financial services, and many other business services. There are exceptions to the rule, and one of the most obvious is Stamford, Connecticut, which has attracted several new corporate headquarters. Yet Stamford is in no way typical. Rather it is unique, precisely in having attracted the decentralization of ancillary administrative and professional functions central to corporate headquarters, thus resulting less in a decentralization process than in a *recentralization* of executive functions in Stamford. Whether or not this strengthens the tendency to a "multi-modal metropolis" (Muller, 1976) remains to be seen.

The question we are left with, then, is why, with the decentralization of industrial and communications factories, there continues to be a centralization of headquarter and executive decision-making centers. Traditional explanations focus on the importance of face-to-face contact. However, although the face-to-face explanation begins to identify the relevant issues, it is too unspecific. It tends to evoke a certain sentimentality for personal contact, but we can be sure that no mere sentimentality is responsible for the overbuilt skyscraper zones of contemporary central business districts. Behind the sentimentality lies a more expedient reason for personal contact, and this involves the very different standards by which time is managed in different sectors of the overall production and circulation of capital. Briefly, in the industrial factory and in the communications factory, the system itself (either the machinery or the administrative schedule) determines the basic daily, weekly and monthly rhythms of the work process. Serious change in this long-term stability comes either from external decisions or from only periodic internal disruptions such as strikes, mechanical faults, or systems' failures. The temporal regularity of these production and administration systems, along with their dependence on readily available skills in the labor force and the ease of transportation and communication with ancillary activities, make suburbanization a rational decision. They have little to gain by a centralized location in the urban core, and with high ground rents they have a lot to lose.

But the temporal rhythm of the executive administration of the economy and of its different corporate units is not stable and regular in this fashion, much to the chagrin of managers and executives. At these higher levels of control, long-term strategic planning coexists with short-term response management. Changes in interest rates or stock prices, the packaging of financial deals, labor negotiations and bailouts, international transactions in the foreign exchange market or the gold market, trade agreements, the unpredictable behavior of competitors and of government bodies – all activities of this sort can demand a rapid response by corporate financial managers, and this, in turn, depends on having close and immediate contact with a battery of professional, administrative and other support systems, as well as with one's competitors. At this level, and in a multitude of ways, the clichéd expression that "time is money" finds its most intense realization. (On time and interest, see Harvey, 1982, p. 258). Less commonly voiced is the corollary that space too is money; spatial proximity reduces decision times when the decision system is sufficiently irregular that it cannot be reduced to a computer routine. The anarchic time regime of financial decision making in a capitalist society necessitates a certain spatial centralization. It is not just that executives *feel* more secure when packed like sardines into a skyscraper can of friends and foes. In reality, they *are* more secure when rapid decisions require direct contact, information flow, and negotiation. The more the economy is prone to crisis, and thus to short-term crisis management, the more one might expect corporate headquarters to seek spatial security. Together with the expansion of this sector *per se* and the cyclical movement of capital into the built environment, this spatial response to temporal and financial irregularity helps to explain the recent office boom in urban centers. "White collar" is clearly a "chaotic concept" (Sayer, 1982) with two distinct components, each with a distinct spatial expression.

If, in the precapitalist city, it was the needs of *market exchange* which led to spatial centralization, and in the industrial capitalist city it was the agglomeration of *production* capital, in the advanced capitalist city it is the *financial* and administrative dictates which perpetuate the tendency toward centralization. This helps to explain why certain so-called white-collar activities are centralized and others are suburbanized, and why the restructuring of the urban core takes on the corporate/professional character that it does.

The falling rate of profit and the cyclical movement of capital

Given, then, the spatial character of the process, how are we to explain the timing of this urban restructuring? This question hinges on the historical timing of the rent gap and the spatial switch of capital back to the urban center. Far from accidental occurrences, these events are integral to the broader rhythm of capital accumulation. At the most abstract level, the rent gap results from the dialectic of spatial and temporal patterns of capital investment; more concretely, it is the spatial product of the complementary processes of valorization and devalorization.

The accumulation of capital does not take place in a linear fashion but is a cyclical process consisting of boom periods and crises. The rent gap develops over a long period of economic expansion, but expansion that takes place elsewhere. Thus the valorization of capital in the construction of postwar suburbs was matched by its devalorization in the central and inner cities. But the accumulation of capital during such a boom leads to a falling rate of profit, beginning in the industrial sectors, and ultimately toward crisis (Marx, 1967, vol. III). As a means of staving off crisis at least temporarily, capital is transferred out of the industrial sphere, and as Harvey (1978, 1982) has shown, there is a tendency for this capital to be switched into the built environment where profit rates remain higher and where it is possible through speculation to appropriate ground rent even though nothing is produced. Two things come together, then; toward the end of a period of expansion when the rent gap has emerged and has provided the opportunity for reinvestment, there is a simultaneous tendency for capital to seek outlets in the built environment.

The slum clearance and urban renewal schemes in many Western cities following World War II were initiated and managed by the state, and though not unconnected to the emergence of the rent gap, cannot adequately be explained simply in these economic terms. However, the function of this urban renewal was to prepare the way for the future restructuring which would emerge in the 1960s and become very visible in the 1970s. In economic terms, the state absorbed the early risks associated with gentrification, as in Philadelphia's Society Hill, which was itself an urban renewal project. It also demonstrated to private capital the possibility of large-scale restructuring of the urban core, paving the way for future capital investment.

The timing of this spatial restructuring, then, is closely related to the economic restructuring that takes place during economic crises such as those the world economy has experienced since the early 1970s. A restructured economy involves a restructured built environment. But there is no gradual transition to a restructured economy; the last economic crisis was resolved only after a massive destruction of capital in World War II, representing a cataclysmic devalorization of capital and a destruction prior to a restructuring of urban space. Today, 50 years later, we are again facing the same threat.

Demographic changes and consumption patterns

The maturation of the baby-boom generation, the increased number of women taking on careers, the proliferation of one- and two-person households and the popularity of the "urban singles" lifestyle are commonly invoked as the real factors behind gentrification. Consistent with the frontier ideology, the process is viewed here as the outcome of individual choices. But in reality too much is claimed. We are seeing a much larger urban restructuring than is encompassed by residential rehabilitation, and it is difficult to see how such explanations could at best be more than partial. Where such explanations might just be conceivable for St. Katherine's Dock in London, they are irrelevant for understanding the London office boom and the redevelopment of the docklands. Yet these are all connected. The changes in demographic patterns and lifestyle preferences are not completely irrelevant, but it is vital that we understand what these developments can and cannot explain.

The importance of demographic and lifestyle issues seems to be chiefly in the determination of the surface *form* taken by much of the restructuring rather than explaining the fact of urban transformation. Given the movement of capital into the urban core, and the emphasis on executive, professional, administrative and managerial functions, as well as other support activities, the demographic and lifestyle changes can help to explain why we have proliferating quiche bars rather than Howard Johnsons, trendy clothes boutiques and gourmet food shops rather than corner stores, American Express signs rather than "cash only, no cheques." As Jager (1986) suggests, the architecture of gentrified housing is also a product of a specific class culture and set of lifestyles. Thus some of the newer, less elite gentrification projects, especially those involving new construction, are beginning to replicate the worst of suburban matchbox housing, leading to a social and aesthetic suburbanization of the city.

Sharon Zukin (1982a, 1982b) offers an excellent illustration of this point in her analysis of the development of loft living in SoHo and the entire Lower Manhattan area. Under the Rockefeller-inspired Lower Manhattan Plan, hatched in the 1960s, the old warehouses, wharves and working-class neighborhoods of the area were to be demolished in favor of the usual centralized, high-finance, "high-rise, high-technology modes of construction." The successful struggle against corporate redevelopment was waged in the name of "historic preservation and the arts," and, in 1971, in an extraordinary ruling, SoHo was zoned an "artists' district." However, as Zukin points out, this did not represent a victory of culture (far less "consumer preference") over capital. In fact, it represented an alternative strategy (involving different factions of capital) for the "recapitalization" of Lower Manhattan:

> revalorization by preservation, rather than by new construction, became an "historic compromise" in the urban core...In Lower Manhattan the struggle to legalize loft living for artists merely anticipated, to some degree, a conjunctural response to crisis in traditional modes of real estate development. In fact, the widening of the loft market after 1973 provided a base for capital accumulation among new, though small-scale, developers.   (Zukin, 1982a, pp. 262, 265)

Since 1973, of course, large-scale developers have become involved in the area. Where once loft co-ops were spontaneously put together among groups of prospective residents, today developers will renovate and fit a building, then put it on the market ready-made as a "co-op." And, of course, fewer and fewer SoHo dwellers today are artists, despite the zoning ordinance which still stands.

The point here is that even SoHo, one of the most vivid symbols of artistic expression in the landscape of gentrification, owes its existence to more basic economic forces (Stevens, 1982). The concentration of artists in SoHo is today more a cover for, and less a cause of, the area's popularity. This is nowhere clearer than in the exploitation of the area's artistic symbolism in aggressive real-estate advertising.

Direction and Limits of Urban Restructuring

If the restructuring that has now begun continues in its current direction, then we can expect to see significant changes in urban structure. However accurate the Chicago model of urban structure may have been, there is general agreement that it is no longer appropriate. Urban development has overtaken the model. The logical conclusion of the current restructuring, which remains today in its infancy, would be an urban center dominated by high-level executive–professional, financial, and administrative functions, middle- and upper-middle-class residences, and the hotel, restaurant, moving, retail, and cultural facilities providing recreational opportunities for this population. In short, we should expect the creation of a bourgeois playground, the social Manhattanization of the urban core to match the architectural Manhattanization that heralded the changing employment structure. The corollary of this is likely to be a substantial displacement of the working class to the older suburbs and the urban periphery.

This should not be taken, as it often is, as a suggestion that suburbanization is coming to an end. On the contrary, the flurry of excitement during the 1970s about so-called "non-metropolitan growth" in the USA represents less a reversal of established urbanization patterns (Berry, 1976; Beale, 1977) than a continuation of metropolitan expansion well beyond the established statistical boundaries (Abu-Lughod, 1982). There is little reason to assume that suburbanization will not be more extensive than ever, should there be another period of strong economic expansion. Nor should this pattern be seen as excluding absolutely the working class from the inner urban core. Just as substantial enclaves of upper-middle-class residences remained in the largely working-class inner cities of the 1960s and 1970s, enclave working-class neighborhoods will also remain. Indeed, these would be functional in so far as the machinery and services of the bourgeois playground require a working population. The comparison – and contrast – with South Africa is instructive in this respect (Western, 1981).

The opposite alternative (that the central and inner cities would continue their absolute decline toward more widespread abandonment) could appear viable only in the United States. And indeed it *is* a possibility for some cities in the USA. In so far as the restructuring of the core depends on a continued concentration and recentralization of economic control functions, it can be expected to happen strongly in national and regional centers. But the situation is less clear with smaller industrial cities, such as Gary, Indiana, where the administrative and financial functions associated with the city's industries are located elsewhere. Detroit provides an even more significant example, because the suburbanization of offices has affected not only the "back offices" but many of the headquarters themselves, and the substantial efforts at recentralization, through the Ford-inspired Renaissance Center, have not yet attracted substantial capital to downtown Detroit.

There is also little reason to doubt that the rapid devalorization of capital invested in the inner-city built environment will continue despite the beginnings of a reinvestment. In the present economic crisis, with interest rates high, it is not just new construction which is adversely affected. The same forces engender a reduction in capital invested in the maintenance and repair of existing buildings, and the consequent devalorization will lead to the outward extension of the "land value valley" of physically decayed buildings; the spatial extent over which the rent gap occurs is thus enlarged. Thus the restructuring of urban space leads to a simultaneous as well as subsequent decline and redevelopment, devalorization and revalorization.

In conclusion, we have emphasized that the restructuring of urban space is part of the larger evolution of the contemporary capitalist economy. Thus in the present context of deepening world economic crisis, our conclusions and speculations must be provisional. It is quite possible that the present economic crisis will result in very different political and economic forces, institutions, and modes of control, and this could well result in very different patterns of urban growth. In particular, I have focused here on the economic background to restructuring rather than attempting to examine the political "growth coalitions" (Mollenkopf, 1978, 1983) which execute specific redevelopment plans. This was in part a choice of scale; no matter how general the process, local experiences differ greatly.

In addition, the emphasis on the logic of accumulation and its role in urban restructuring in no way presupposes a philosophical adherence to a "capital logic" approach rather than one emphasizing class struggle. As a philosophical dichotomy this is a false issue; but as an historical dialectic it is everything. The unfortunate truth is that the comparatively low levels of working-class struggle since the Cold War (with the exception of those during the late 1960s, and in much of Europe during the early 1970s) have meant that capital has had a fairly free hand in the structuring and restructuring of urban space. This does not invalidate the role of class struggle; it means that with few exceptions it was a lopsided struggle during this period, so much so that the capitalist class was generally able to wage the struggle through its economic strategies for capital investment. The investment of capital is the first weapon of struggle in the ruling-class arsenal.

An important exception to the general hegemony of capital concerns the role of European social democratic governments in providing public housing, the struggles over privatization of housing, and the rebellions in several European cities in the early 1980s over housing. These issues are not covered here and that is an important omission. What this experience suggests, however, is a further progression in our understanding of the urban frontier. The urban wilderness produced by the cyclical movement of capital and its devalorization have, from the perspective of capital, become new urban frontiers of profitability. Gentrification is a frontier on which fortunes are made. From the perspective of working-class residents and their neighborhoods, however, the urban frontier is more directly political rather than economic. Threatened with displacement as the frontier of profitability advances, the issue for them is to fight for the establishment of a political frontier behind which working-class residents can take back control of their homes: there are two sides to any frontier. The larger task is organizing to advance the political frontier, and like the frontier itself, Turneresque or urban, there are lulls and spurts in this process.

NOTE

1   For an assessment of the Enterprise Zone experience, see Anderson (1983).

REFERENCES

Abrams, C. 1965. *The City is the Frontier*. New York: Harper & Row.
Abu-Lughod, J. 1982. The Myth of Demetropolitanization. Paper presented at the Symposium on Social Change, University of Cincinnati.
Advisory Council on Historic Preservation 1980. *Report to the President and the Congress of the United States*. Washington, DC: Government Printing Office.
Anderson, J. 1983. Geography as ideology and the politics of crisis: The Enterprise Zones experiment. In *Redundant Spaces in Cities and Regions?*. J. Anderson and R. Hudson (eds.). London: Academic Press, pp. 313–50.
Banfield, E. C. 1968. *The Unheavenly City: The nature and future of our urban crisis*. Boston: Little & Brown.
Beale, C. 1977. The recent shift of the United States population to non-metropolitan areas, 1970–75. *International Regional Science Review* 2(2), 113–22.

Berry, B. J. L. 1976. The counterurbanization process: Urban America since 1970. In *Urbanization and Counterurbanization*, B. Berry (ed.). *Urban Affairs Annual Review*, vol. II. Beverly Hills: Sage Publications, pp. 17–30.

Blackaby, F. (ed.). 1978. *De-industrialization*. London: Heinemann.

Bluestone, B. and B. Harrison 1982. *The Deindustrialization of America: Plant closing, community abandonment, and the dismantling of basic industry*. New York: Basic Books.

Butler, S. 1981. *Enterprise Zones: Greenlining the inner cities*. New York: Universe Books.

Castells, M. 1976. The wild city. *Kapitalistate* 4–5 (Summer), 2–30.

Chall, D. 1984. Neighborhood changes in New York City during the 1970s. *Quarterly Review of the Federal Reserve Bank of New York*, Winter 1983–84, 38–48.

Gottmann, J. 1961. *Megalopolis. The urbanized northeastern seaboard of the United States*. New York: Twentieth Century Fund.

Harris, N. 1980. Deindustrialization. *International Socialism* 7, 72–81.

Harris, N. 1983. *Of Bread and Guns: The world economy in crisis*. Harmondsworth: Penguin.

Harvey, D. 1978. The urban process under capitalism: A framework for analysis. *International Journal of Urban and Regional Research* 2(1), 100–31.

Harvey, D. 1982. *The Limits to Capital*. Oxford: Basil Blackwell.

Jager, M. 1986. Class definition and the esthetics of gentrification: Victoriana in Melbourne. In *Gentrification of the City*. N. Smith and P. Williams (eds.). Boston, London and Sydney: Allen & Unwin, pp. 78–91.

Lenman, B. 1977. *An Economic History of Modern Scotland, 1660–1976*. Hamden, Conn.: Archon Books.

Long, 1971. The city as reservation. *Public Interest* 25, 22–38.

Marx, K. 1967 *Capital* (3 volumes). New York: International Publishers.

Mollenkopf, J. H. 1978. The postwar politics of urban development. In *Marxism and the Metropolis: New perspectives in urban political economy*. W. K. Tabb and L. Sawyers (eds.). New York: Oxford University Press, pp. 117–52.

Mollenkopf, J. H. 1983. *The Politics of Urban Development*. Princeton: Princeton University Press.

Muller, P. 1976. The Outer City. Resource paper 75–2. Association of American Geographers, Washington, DC.

Sayer, A. 1982. Explanation in economic geography: Abstraction versus generalization. *Progress in Human Geography* 6 (March), 68–88.

Schaffer, R. and N. Smith 1984. The gentrification of Harlem. Paper presented at the annual conference of the American Association for the Advancement of Science, May 27.

Smith, N. 1982. Gentrification and uneven development. *Economic Geography* 58(2) (April), 139–55.

Smith, N. 1984. *Uneven Development*. Oxford: Basil Blackwell.

Sternlieb, G. 1971. The city as sandbox. *Public Interest* 25, 14–21.

Stevens, E. 1982. Baltimore renovates, rebuilds and revitalizes. *Art News* 81(8), 94–7.

Stratton, J. 1977. *Pioneering in the Urban Wilderness*. New York: Urizen Books.

Swierenga, R. P. 1968. *Pioneers and Profits: Land speculation on the Iowa frontier*. Ames, Iowa: Iowa State University Press.

Turner, F. J. 1958. *The Frontier in American History*. New York: Holt, Rinehart & Winston.

Wald, M. 1984. Back offices disperse from downtowns. *New York Times*, 13 May.

Walker, R. A. 1978. The transformation of urban structure in the nineteenth century and the beginnings of suburbanization. In *Urbanization and Conflict in Market Societies*. K. R. Cox (ed.). London: Methuen, pp. 165–211.

Walker, R. A. 1981. A theory of suburbanization: capitalism and the construction of urban space in the United States. In *Urbanization and Urban Planning in Capitalist Society*. M. Dear and A. J. Scott (eds.). London: Methuen, pp. 383–429.

Warner, S. B. 1972. *The Urban Wilderness: A history of the American city.* New York: Harper & Row.

Western, J. 1981. *Outcast Cape Town.* London: George Allen & Unwin.

Zukin, S. 1982a. Loft living as "historical compromise" in the urban core: The New York experience. *International Journal of Urban and Regional Research* 6(2), 256–67.

Zukin, S. 1982b. *Loft Living: Culture and capital in urban change.* Baltimore: Johns Hopkins University Press.

13

Promoting Tourism in US Cities*

Dennis R. Judd

Urban tourism is a relatively recent phenomenon but is now being embraced by most US cities, which are using substantial funds to compete for visitors, creating elaborate new infrastructures in the process. This article provides an analytical overview of the steps a variety of US cities are taking – such as developing a new brand image, refurbishing run-down areas, touting for conference business, building shopping malls and creating 'carousal' zones – to promote tourism. The author also examines how far these strategies translate into economic and social success.

Tourism is an important economic sector being promoted by virtually all larger cities in the United States. There are two principal components of local tourism strategies. First, cities attempt to market images attractive to tourists and to the institutions that compose the tourist industry. The construction and projection of images is now managed by a well-organized, professionalized industry that specializes in place marketing. Second, US cities have been investing in an elaborate, costly infrastructure to support tourism. Between 1976 and 1986, 250 convention centers, sports arenas, community centers and performing arts halls were constructed or started, at a cost of more than $10 billion (*US News and World Report* 'Convention centers spark civic wars', February, 1986, 45). Since the early 1980s, the downtowns of American cities have experienced a conversion of land use that approaches, in its scale, the restructuring of downtown economies and land use wrought by the massive urban renewal clearance projects of the 1950s and 1960s (Fainstein et al., 1986). In their attempts to attract tourists, cities have been aggressively reconstructing their physical environments.

In the United States, city-building and entrepreneurialism always have gone hand in hand. In the 19th century, cities became engaged in a 'struggle for primacy and

* Judd, Dennis R. (1995) 'Promoting Tourism in US Cities' *Tourist Management* **16** (3) 175–87.

power' in which, 'Like imperial states, cities carved out extensive dependencies, extended their influence over the economic and political life of the hinterland, and fought with contending places over strategic trade routes' (Wade, 1959, p. 336). In fighting for railroad connections in the 19th century, cities gave away land, purchased railroad bonds and sometimes helped finance construction. Up to 1861, cities supplied $300 million in railroad subsidies, compared with $229 million from the states and $65 million from the federal government (Chalmers, 1976, p. 4). In the years from 1866 to 1873, the legislatures of 29 states granted 800 authorizations for aid by local governments to railroad projects (Goodrich, 1960, pp. 266–7).

Since the early 1980s, cities in the United States have been engaged in a competitive struggle that parallels the railroad wars of more than a century ago. Upon assuming office in 1981, the Reagan Administration moved rapidly to reduce or eliminate all urban policies that tried to help distressed cities. To make up for the loss of federal funds, President Reagan's first *National Urban Policy Report* observed, 'state and local governments will find it is in their best interests to concentrate on increasing their attractiveness to potential investors, residents, and visitors' (US Department of Housing and Urban Development, 1982, p. 14). After only a brief pause to lobby the federal government to reconsider its policy, local officials began doing what their predecessors had so often done before: they threw themselves into the competitive struggle by initiating a major round of local public investment.

Since the early 1980s, cities have been involved in a competition so fierce that Ruth Messinger, a member of the City Council of New York, appropriately compared it to the international arms race of the Cold War. Cities are far more aggressive in the fight for tourists than either the states or the federal government. Cities are subsidizing and building elaborate infrastructures to support local recreation and tourist economies. States, in contrast, do little more than fund tourist stations along interstate highways (sometimes with free coffee), print color brochures, take out ads in newspapers and magazines, and finance promotional junkets for politicians. For these and few other purposes, all 50 states spent $343 million in 1991–92 (Cooke and Azucenas, 1994, p. 165). The federal government does far less. There is a 'US Tourism Week', and under the Carter Administration federal spending to attract overseas visitors to the United States rose to just over $13 million.[1] In 1981, the Reagan Administration slashed tourism spending to $4.1 million. By the time George Bush took office, spending had crept up to about $12 million. Reflecting his habit of substituting symbolic gestures for substantive policy, Bush scheduled a photo opportunity with officials of the tourism industry and became the first president to appear in a video promoting US tourism (Richter, 1994, p. 219).

The tourist industry has become increasingly well organized by organizations and entrepreneurs skilled at promoting their industry. They have learned the art of playing cities off against one another. In a word, the industry has become professionalized. In 1992, the meetings market in the United States was a $61.4 billion industry. Two-thirds of convention and trade shows and a large proportion of other meetings were coordinated by professional meetings planners (*Successful Meetings* 'State of the industry 1993' Bill Communications, New York, July 1993, p. 7). The planners' job is to secure the best deal possible in rental rates for convention centers and other facilities. For cities, too, the competition is no longer left to amateurs

(Guskind, 1987), with visitors' and convention bureaux steadily increasing in number and staff size.

Reflecting the organization and political muscle (and the pretensions) of an increasingly well-organized industry, in 1993 representatives of the World Travel and Tourism Council (WTTC) lobbied US Commerce Secretary Ron Brown, asking him to support a move to create a cabinet-level post for tourism. The immediate objective of the lobbying effort was to oppose a proposal in Clinton's tax bill, which ultimately reduced the deductibility of business meal and entertainment expenses from 80% to 50%. In its trade magazine, the WTTC complained that the industry's voice was insufficiently strong to prevent such measures because 'travelers don't vote as a block' (*Meeting News* 1993 17(12), p. 11). In an opinion piece bristling with outrage, an editor of *Successful Meetings* maintained that Clinton's proposal revealed a lack of appreciation for the penultimate importance of the tourism industry to the US economy: 'The meetings industry represents the most important marketing and educational medium for people in business. It is the primary means of retraining Americans, of rethinking how we do business, and of remaining competitive in the world marketplace' (Conlin, 1993, p. 38).

Cities compete vigorously to host industry meetings; like textbook publishers who know that their books must be marketed first to professors before they can be sold to students, convention and tourism bureaux realize that they must appeal, if at all possible, to the gatekeepers of the tourist industry. In September 1993, the 5000 agents of the American Society of Travel Agents met at the convention center in St Louis, Missouri. Scores of booths representing countries all over the world, plus state and city exhibits, were set to persuade the travel agents that they ought to promote particular destinations. Aside from picking among the mounds of key rings, luggage tags, pens and other paraphernalia, the agents could watch folk dances, eat and drink a variety of ethnic foods, beers and wines, and keep themselves entertained by watching craft demonstrations and promotional films. When interviewed by reporters from the *St Post-Dispatch*, the travel agents talked about being 'pleasantly surprised' by a city they had thought was 'a little bumpkinish'. A travel agent from California said, 'I had a bad impression of St Louis before I came. All I've heard of St Louis is that downtown is a war zone, that it is dirty and horrible'. She said she had always told her clients to 'give it a miss', but after her visit she was converted to the view that the city could be part of 'an overall American vacation' (Tipton, 1993, pp. 1, 7).

Tourism and Image-making

The competition for tourists begins with advertising, the essence of which is the projection of an image. In his path-breaking book, *Images of the American City*, Anselm Strauss (1961, p. 8) noted that 'the city, as a whole, is inaccessible to the imagination unless it can be reduced and simplified...'. Civic boosters utilize images as weapons in the tourism arms race, invariably invoking the '"greatness" of the city' through a 'host of catch phrases, songs, and physical artifacts' which allegedly 'represent the "character" of the place' (Suttles, 1985).

To attract tourists, it is important for local boosters to be able to project a 'place identity' (Pagano and Bowman 2001) that can transform 'ordinary places and times into extraordinary tourist worlds' (Hummon, 1988). For old port and industrial cities, with their slums, high crime rates and the detritus left from the past, this is not easily accomplished. First, cities must try to avoid negative images that are at least as salient and representative of their cultures and histories as are positive ones. No mention must be made of slums, trash heaps, wrecking and junk yards, abandoned factories – exactly the kinds of scenery that normally litter the landscape alongside most rapid transit lines connecting airports to the downtowns of older American cities.

The positive images projected by civic boosters or the advertising firms they hire amount to a 'coaching' process: advertisements and tourist articles (such as those found in tourism trade journal and airline magazines) interpret a city's essence, its history and culture, and tell the tourist what to do, even what to feel (Strauss, 1961, pp. 72–3). The difficulty – and importance – of accomplishing an image make-over for older cities can be appreciated by considering the tourism brochures produced by states. In state tourism brochures, photos and text rarely refer to cities. Almost all photos and text refer to seashores, lakes, clear streams, woods, mountains and wildlife – and this is as true for midwestern states like Missouri and Illinois as for more scenic states like Colorado. When they do mention cities, the brochures 'rarely describe cities as productive sites of work, industry, learning' (Hummon, 1988, p. 192). Instead, cities are mentioned to convince the tourist that there is great diversity within the state, lots to do. The orientation to nature no doubt reflects, in part, the fact that states are angling for vacationers, whereas cities try to attract specific-site tourists, meetings and conferences. Even for cities, however, tourist images invariably invoke a romanticized, nostalgic sense of history and culture. For cities, such impressions are conveyed by photographic or stylized citiscapes composed of architecturally significant or famous mansions, public buildings, museums, symphony halls, and the like, all set (depending on what is available) within a tableaux of scenic vistas, harbors, oceans, rivers, mountains in the distance, promenades and parks. What such images trade on is a sense of nostalgia for what cities allegedly have been or ought to be (Graburn and Moore, 1994, p. 236). The overt and subliminal messages embedded in the tourist images of cities are similar to those conveyed by the urban tableaux often found in malls and similar tourist venues (Boyer, 1992). They are meant to reassure but, equally important, they are designed to make the consumer desire the nostalgic city (or past) more than the actual present.

In recent ads, Tucson, Arizona and Salt Lake City, Utah, abandoned entirely a presentation of citiscapes in favor of full-page photographs of a desert scene (in the case of Tucson) (*Meeting News*, 1993 17(2)) and a mountain meadow (for Salt Lake) (*Meeting Manager*, September, 1993). Cities located in or near scenic natural features like oceans, lakes or mountains possess an inherent tourism advantage, of course, but citiscapes themselves – the physical features that make up the built environment – are crucial to most cities' identity. In his study of the 'imageability' of cities, Kevin Lynch found that residents of Jersey City, New Jersey possessed no clear image of their city; they were unable to draw accurate maps or recognize photographs of its significant features. Residents of Los Angeles had a difficult time describing or recognizing the built environment as well; their images tended to focus not on buildings but on highway systems. In contrast, residents of Boston easily recognized the long vistas and historic areas that define that city (Lynch, 1960).

Cities that find it easy to project a tourist image are characterized by memorable citiscapes. Such citiscapes are, of course, not self-defining; they are necessarily represented through photographs and art as charicture. Thus, New York City enters the mind's eye through stylized images of Times Square, Wall Street and the Empire State Building, San Francisco through the Golden Gate Bridge and the Transamerica Tower, Paris through the Eiffel Tower, and St Louis, Missouri, through its only universally recognized urban monument, the Gateway Arch (meant to signify the city as the gateway to the West). A few symbols have proven to be extraordinarily riveting, so much so that they overwhelm all other images of a city. The Gateway Arch is one such monument; it pervades all tourist advertising, appears on the logo of the University of Missouri's St Louis campus, and businesses identified with the Arch appear on page after page in the city's Yellow Pages. The Arch is hugely successful as a tourist attraction, ranking fourth behind Lenin's Tomb, Disneyland and Disney World. From its opening in 1965 to 1990, 50 million people visited the Gateway Arch (Mehrhoff, 1992, p. 90).

The Eiffel Tower is doubtless the most ubiquitous city symbol in the world. Roland Barthes (1979, p. 3) has said it is impossible to be in or even to think of Paris without confronting images of the Tower:

> The Tower is present to the entire world. First of all as the universal symbol of Paris, it is everywhere on the globe where Paris is stated as an image; from the Midwest to Australia, there is no journey to France which isn't made, somehow, in the Tower's name, no school book, poster, or film about France which fails to propose it as the major sign of a people and of a place...

According to Barthes, the Tower succeeds because it stands as a symbol of so many things, evoking images of 'modernity, of communication, of science or of the nineteenth century, rocket, stem, derrick, phallus, lightning rod or insect'. By provoking such a kaleidoscope of associations, the Tower 'makes the city into a kind of nature; its constitutes the swarming of men into a landscape, it adds to the frequently grim urban myth a romantic dimension, a harmony, a mitigation...' (Barthes, 1979, p. 8).

Cities that lack image cannot easily be promoted to tourists. When the Chamber of Commerce of Columbia, South Carolina undertook a survey to discover what people across the United States knew about their city, the answers unsettled local boosters: responses ranged from 'It's a country in South America' to 'Isn't that the next space shuttle?'. In response, the Chamber launched a somewhat doubtful advertising campaign with the slogan, 'We're Growing Proud' (Pagano and Bowman, 1995, p. 7). It is hard to imagine that this phrase will gain quite the same currency as 'I Love New York' ('Love' in the shape of a heart) or 'I Left My Heart in San Francisco'.

The Tourism Infrastructure

Insofar as European cities are still vibrant in the center, tourism blends into and becomes a permanent, even mundane, feature of daily life. In the United States, some cities – notably San Francisco, New York, even Seattle and Phoenix – absorb tourists in this way. Where urban decay or social problems make parts of a city inhospitable to tourists – as is the case for every city in the United States – specialized areas must be set aside as virtual tourist reservations. These become the 'public' parts of town, making it unnecessary for visitors to see the 'private' spaces where people live and work (Strauss, 1961, p. 76). Tourist venues typically are constructed on a site that was once devoted to primary production, and frequently such places build a theme on a foundation of a nostalgic and idealized version of city life. The 'entertainment cities', such as South Street Seaport in New York, try to create an ambience evoked by 'authentic reproductions' of a working harbor, a Main Street, frontier town or colonial village (Boyer, 1992, pp. 189–90). (Thus The Wharf in San Francisco and the renovated Union Stations in city after city). Recently I took an out-of-town guest to the Rouse mall in St Louis's Union Station. Thus does tourism change a city, so that its projected tourist image not only competes with but begins to overwhelm other, more mundane, features that define its daily life.

In just three decades downtowns have been transformed from centers of wholesale and retail trade to centers of high-level corporate services and recreation. Tourist and entertainment facilities coexist in symbiotic relationship with the corporate towers, and there is some overlap: shopping malls, restaurants and bars cater to daytime professionals who work downtown as well as to visitors. The transformation of downtown economies has been supported by and produced as expensive infrastructure, virtually all of it constructed over the last two to three decades by governments or supported with an array of public subsidies. The mix that comprises the corporate/entertainment complex is remarkably standardized from city to city – so much so that it constitutes a virtual template for economic revitalization, copied by cities all over the United States. Bernard Frieden and Lynn Sagalyn (1990, p. 43) refer to the various components of the new downtowns as every mayor's 'trophy collection', typically made up of an atrium hotel, festival mall, a convention center, a restored historic neighborhood, a domed stadium, an aquarium, new office towers and a redeveloped waterfront.

From Hamburg to Glasgow and Liverpool, and from Boston to San Francisco, virtually every port city in both Europe and North America has tried to redevelop its harbor and riverfront for tourism and recreation (Judd and Parkinson, 1990). In preparation for the activities associated with its designation in 1990 as European City of Culture, Glasgow built an exposition grounds and miles of brick walkway along the abandoned banks of the River Clyde (Boyle, 1990). In the 1980s, with considerable national assistance, Liverpool undertook a comprehensive revitalization of Merseyside, demolishing abandoned docks and warehouses and replacing them with shopping, recreational and apartment facilities, complete with a promenade, reflecting pools, a maritime museum and other accoutrements of tourism. Since the opening of Quincy Market in 1976, Boston has virtually remade its harbor. San Francisco, of course, has long been famous for Ghirardelli Square, The Wharf, and the miles of tourist attractions that line the bay.

Called the 'Cinderella city of the 1980s' (Pierce et al., 1983), Baltimore has transformed its harbor by replacing the abandoned, desolate buildings that once lined its waterfront with open vistas and tourist facilities. The anchor for the Inner Harbor plan is Harbor Place, made up of two block-long, translucent pavilions designed by James Rouse. Opened in 1980, in the first year of its operation it earned

$42 million. A year later the National Aquarium was completed, and over the next decade it attracted 15 million visitors (Corbett, 1992). Between 1980 and 1986 the number of tourists visiting the Inner Harbor and the number of hotels rooms tripled. The city's manpower programs placed 1300 people in jobs in the Inner Harbor development (Berkowitz, 1987, p. 129), 40% of them minorities ('He digs downtown' *Time*, 24 August 1981, p. 47).

St Louis is a relative latecomer to this style of riverfront development. Though the Gateway Arch and its grounds were opened in 1975, the downtown is cut off from the Mississippi River by a freeway and by the Arch grounds, which comprise a large park rather than the kind of development found in Baltimore. North of the Arch, a small renovated 19th-century warehouse district sits virtually on the river's banks, but access to the river is not easy, and there is little to do along the river anyway. Stretching for miles south of the Arch and its grounds, chemical companies line the river.

In March 1994, city officials announced a comprehensive, $250 million riverfront development plan (Prost, 1994a,b). Its features follow the model of development already worked out elsewhere: a promenade and parks along the river, a marina, sports and recreational facilities, an entertainment and retail district. The new element of the plan – indeed, its anchor – was expected to be riverboat casino gambling. In this respect, St Louis is trying to cash in on the latest tourism craze, one that has spread like wildfire across the United States. By 1992, meetings planners ranked gaming fifth on a list of leisure activities in convention cities, right behind tennis and water sports (*Successful Meetings* 'State of the industry 1993' Bill Communications, New York, July 1993).

Cities must, usually, invest in all or most of the components making up a tourist space. One or two pieces are not likely to be sufficient. Agglomeration economies apply to tourist districts not principally because concentration lowers costs or increases the efficiency of business transactions, but because a full panoply of services and businesses is necessary to make the space maximally attractive to consumers of the tourist space (in the economics literature, it is axiomatic that agglomeration economies occur when 'the location of any one economic unit depends upon the location of all the others' (Heilbrun, 1981, p. 18).

There is, to be sure, some variation among cities in how tourist and visitor spaces are constructed. Indianapolis has constructed a critical mass of sports facilities; as a result the city hosts a large number of events and training facilities requiring Olympic-regulation swimming pools, tennis courts, weight rooms and so forth. The annual Indianapolis 500 is immensely important to the city. There is also a unique tourist space in New Orleans; its Mardi Gras and sin industry has not been successfully mimicked in any other city. With few exceptions, however, the tourist strategy has become an extraordinarily standardized phenomenon in the United States. In the remainder of this paper, I explore the character of the various components making up the standard central city tourist venue.

Convention centers

There is keen competition among cities for a share of the nation's meetings and convention business. It is a big business. In 1992, associations spent $32 billion for meetings and corporations spent almost $29 billion on off-premises meetings and conventions (*Successful Meetings* 'State of the industry 1993' Bill Communications, New York, July 1993. pp. 32–3). Although only from 4–5% of these meetings are held in convention centers (*Successful Meetings* 'State of the industry 1993' Bill Communications, New York, July 1993. p. 11), the size of the convention business is large enough to prompt cities to compete vigorously. By the 1980s virtually every major city in the United States had formed a convention and visitors' bureau.

Convention bureaux construct lists of international, national, regional and local associations that regularly sponsor or organize conventions. The bureaux send them promotional literature and frequently attend the meetings of these organizations, where they may stage rather elaborate promotional presentations or exhibits. Cities often invite representatives of the tourist industry and of important business and professional groups for a complimentary visit. In November 1975, for instance, the St Louis Convention and Visitors Bureau hosted representatives of 227 associations for a weekend tour in an effort to promote the city's new convention center, which was then under construction (*St Louis Globe-Democrat, Sunday Magazine*, 9 November 1975, p. 8).

Aside from the nature of the conventional facilities and the availability of hotel space, tourist appeal is a central consideration for meetings planners. Convention centers do not exist in isolation from the cities they are located within. Large cities, with their multitude of entertainment, cultural and commercial attractions, remain the primary drawing cards for national and international conventions. A combination of things is essential: there must be available hotel space, entertainment and sightseeing, restaurants, and so forth (*Successful Meetings*, 1993, pp. 60–1). Smaller cities have one major advantage – lower costs (Teibel, 1994, pp. 32–7). Even these cities, however, are bound to invest, if necessary, in some of the components that make up a tourist space. As observed by a meetings planner, 'If we're going to use a second-tier city and promote it as an attraction, then we have to make it an attraction. We bill it as a tourist destination and give that equal billing with the technical [meeting] program' (Tiebel, 1994, p. 37).

Whatever cities spend for promotion, it pales in comparison with the cost of building convention facilities. *Aud-Arena Stadium Guide* conducted a survey in 1972 showing that 70 cities ranging in size from Pontiac, Michigan, to New York City had recently opened, had under construction, or had planned new or expanded convention centers to enable them to achieve or maintain competitive positions as convention sites. In the 1980s and 1990s, still another round of construction was taking place. Smaller cities were building new convention centers and those cities that already had them were either expanding them or replacing them with new structures. From 1980 to 1987 the number of convention centers increased by 37%, but the square feet of exhibition space rose even faster, by 60% (Tabak, 1993, 1994). Forty cities were constructing or expanding new convention centers in the late 1980s (Fenich, 1992). By the end of the 1980s, 331 convention centers were operating, which constituted a 50% increase in only a decade. It was expected that 434 centers would be on line by 1995 (Fenich, 1992).

The convention business is extraordinarily competitive. Table 13.1 ranks the top 33 convention cities by their shares of the convention market in 1981 (for meetings with exhibits). New York and Chicago easily led the nation as magnets for conventions.

Table 13.1   Convention trade, US cities, 1981

Top 33 cities meetings with exhibits	% of total attendance
1 New York	10.6
2 Chicago	6.7
3 Atlanta	4.4
4 Las Vegas	3.8
5 Dallas	3.8
6 Los Angeles	3.7
7 Anaheim, CA	3.5
8 San Francisco	2.9
9 New Orleans	2.6
10 Boston	2.3
11 Detroit	2.0
12 Kansas City	2.0
13 Philadelphia	1.7
14 Indianapolis	1.7
15 Houston	1.5
16 St Louis	1.4
17 Atlantic City	1.3
18 Columbus	1.2
19 Minneapolis	1.2
20 San Antonio	1.1
21 Louisville	1.1
22 Miami Beach	1.1
23 Seattle	1.1
24 San Diego	1.0
25 Denver	1.0
26 Cleveland	0.8
27 Orlando	0.8
28 Phoenix	0.6
29 Cincinnati	0.6
30 Oklahoma City	0.6
31 Memphis	0.5
32 Pittsburgh	0.5
33 Tulsa	0.3

Source: *Successful Meetings Magazine, Convention and Exhibit Market Profile* (1983).

The convention trade rapidly diminishes as one goes down the list. The top 10 cities accounted for 44% of total attendance, with the other cities listed in the table contending for a 25% share. All the cities outside the top 33 received about 31% of the nation's convention business in 1981.

As the number of cities competing for conventions increases, it becomes difficult for a particular city to change its national share of the convention business very much. Nevertheless, as revealed by Table 13.2, by 1992 New York City had fallen from 1st to 7th place, Anaheim had dropped from 7th to 18th place, but Orlando had shot up from 27th to 2nd place. Even year-by-year rankings change somewhat, though one must be careful not to put too much store by them; Table 13.2 shows Orlando slipping from 2nd in 1990 to 5th in 1991, then rebounding to 2nd in 1992.

Table 13.2 Top US cities[a] booked 1992–90

City	1992 rank	1991 rank	1990 rank
Chicago	1	1	1
Orlando	2	5	2
Dallas	3	2	3
Atlanta	4	3	6
Los Angeles	5	4	5
San Diego	5	7	9
New York	7	8	6
Boston	8	9	8
New Orleans	9	14	14
Phoenix	10	12	13
San Francisco	10	6	4
Houston	12	10	10
Las Vegas	13	13	10
Washington DC	14	11	18
Nashville	15	–	–
Denver	16	16	18
Philadelphia	17	20	15
Anaheim	18	14	31
Miami	18	–	–
St Louis	18	–	–

Note: [a] Duplicate rankings indicates ties.
Source: *Successful Meetings* Magazine 1993 (July) 62.

Evidence of volatility in the convention wars doubtless gives heart to civic boosters who imagine they might experience Orlando's success. There is abundant evidence, however, that larger and more elaborate convention centers may not be the answer. Since 1986 the number of delegates attending conventions has declined, as did overall delegate spending. For convention halls with 25 000 or more square feet, attendance slid 8% from 1986 to 1991 (Tabak, 1994, p. 30).

It may seem illogical that cities have responded by investing in larger and more elaborate convention facilities. From the point of view of local boosters, however, the competition for tourism requires them to be aggressive just to stay even. As Jim Hutchinson, of the Kansas City Convention and Visitors Bureau said, 'It's even more important to be aggressive when competition is up and the economy of the industry down. This industry is just like any other industry. To be competitive, you have to continue to improve the business' (Tabak, 1994, p. 30).

The position that cities find themselves in has not escaped the associations and groups that use convention facilities. The biggest associations already assume that they can persuade cities to give them convention space rent-free, and it can only get worse. In 1993 the Future Farmers of America, a youth organization that has traditionally met in Kansas City, demanded that the city give it cash subsidies, lower hotel rates and other incentives. Since their annual convention brings 28 000 visitors to the city, the city's Convention and Visitors Bureau chair thought it was worth it to spend 'whatever it takes' to keep the group from going elsewhere (Tabak, 1994). Such an approach can only become more common as tourism entrepreneurs and associations become more adept at playing cities off against one another.

Professional sports franchises[2]

Professional sports franchises occupy a pivotal position in urban recreational and tourism economies. In 1992, there were 102 North American franchises in four major sports worth almost $9.5 billion (two new National Football League franchises have been awarded since then). Major league baseball franchises are valued from $75 million dollars for the Montreal Expos to $200 million for the New York Yankees. National Football League teams range in value from $103 million for the New England Patriots to $150 million for the Miami Dolphins and the New York Giants. Some National Basketball Association franchises can be bought for smaller sums; the Indiana Pacers, for examples, would cost only $43 million dollars. However, the Detroit Pistons are valued at $120 million, while the Los Angeles Lakers are the most valuable professional basketball team at $150 million. Professional hockey teams go for less, with values ranging from $30 million for the Winnipeg Jets to $70 million for the Detroit Red Wings.[3]

Cities are willing to go to extraordinary lengths to get and keep a professional sports team. Teams are increasingly mobile, and owners realize that public subsidies are theirs for the asking. It is probably true, as civic boosters argue, that the most important benefits of a major sports franchise are intangible and therefore impossible to measure solely in economic terms. Sports carry huge symbolic power in American culture. Having professional sports teams allegedly is necessary to make a city 'big league', and, indeed, for instant and maximum impact, few events can match a World Series or a Super Bowl champion.

Professional baseball franchises had their origins in amusement parks. Just as streetcar companies tended to lay track to drive up the value of land, team owners were often real estate speculators who used the teams to attract buyers to their subdivisions (Logan and Molotch, 1987). Until the 1950s, franchises rarely moved. The first baseball franchise relocation occurred in 1953, when the Boston Braves relocated to Milwaukee. Between 1950 and 1982 there were 78 franchise relocations in the four major professional sports: 11 in baseball, 40 in basketball, 14 in hockey and 13 in football (Johnson, 1985, p. 232).

Since the early 1980s the relocation game has heated up. The data in Table 13.3 reveal that from 1980 to June 1992 there was an incredible amount of activity involving baseball and football teams. During this $12\frac{1}{2}$-year period, 20 cities sought baseball and 24 cities sought football teams, an interesting statistic considering that there were, at that time, a total of 28 North American major league baseball and football franchises (two new expansion football franchises were added in 1993, with several cities competing for them). Eleven cities built or were building stadiums, and 28 more considered building or had plans to build stadiums. Eleven teams threatened to move in the 1980s and early 1990s, and six actually did.

The baseball franchise relocation game began in earnest in 1957 when Walter O'Malley moved the Brooklyn Dodgers to Los Angeles. The Brooklyn Dodgers were one of the most lucrative franchises in baseball, with fanatically loyal fans who

Table 13.3 Supply and demand of professional, baseball and football franchises, 1980–June 1992

Cities	Teams in residence	Activity
Albuquerque	None	Seeks B
Alexandria, VA	None	In 1992 governor proposes building F stadium
Anaheim	B F	Lured F Rams in 1978; F threatened to leave over stadium development dispute in 1988
Arlington, TX	B	Plans new B stadium
Atlanta	B F	Opened new F stadium in 1992; plans new B stadium in conjunction with 1996 Olympic games
Austin, TX	None	May ally with San Antonio to seek F
Baltimore	B	Opened a B stadium in 1992; seeks F; plans F stadium
Birmingham, AL	None	Seeks B and F; considers building stadium
Boston	B	Considers building F stadium; occasional talk of building new B stadium
Buffalo	F	Seeks B; built new stadiums for B and F
Casa Grande, AZ	None	Sought F; considered stadium
Charlotte	None	Seeks B or F; plans stadium
Chicago	B(2) F	Opened B stadium in 1991; plans F stadium
Cincinnati	B F	No recent developments
Cleveland	B F	Building B stadium; plans new F stadium
Columbus, OH	None	Seeks B or F; considers stadium; attempted to lure F Cardinals in 1987–88
Denver	B F	Awarded expansion B; plans new stadium
Detroit	B	Plans new B stadium; location under dispute
East Rutherford, NJ	F (2)	Lured F Giants and Jets from NY; referendum defeated B stadium proposal
Fort Lauderdale	None	Seeks B and F; plans new stadium
Foxboro, MA	F	F team threatens to move
Green Bay, WI	F	Occasional stadium renovations; team plays some games in Milwaukee
Honolulu	None	Seeks F
Houston	B F	Plans stadium renovations to keep F; occasional threats by B to move, calls for new B stadium
Indianapolis	F	Lured F Colts from Baltimore with new stadium in 1984; seeks B; occasional proposals for new B stadium
Irving, TX	F	Occasional proposals for new F stadium; F lured from Dallas
Jacksonville	None	Seeks F; regular talk of building new stadium
Kansas City	B F	No recent developments
Knoxville	None	Considers alliance with Memphis and Nashville to seek expansion F
Los Angeles	B F	Competes to keep F; plans for $200 million renovation in doubt; talk of new stadium
Louisville	None	Seeks B and F, considers stadium
Memphis	None	Seeks B and F; considers stadium
Miami	B F	Awarded expansion B; new F stadium opened in 1987

Table 13.3 *continued*

Cities	Teams in residence	Activity
Milwaukee	B F	Considers new stadium; shares F with Green Bay
Minneapolis	B F	B and F play in new domed facility
Montreal	B	B occasionally considers moving
Nashville	None	Seeks B and F; considers new stadium or renovation
New Orleans	F	Seeks B; renovates Superdome; F considers move
New York	B(2)	Considers new F stadium
Norfolk	None	Considers stadium
Oakland	B	Lost F to Los Angeles, 1982; seeks F
Oklahoma City	None	Seeks F, considers stadium
Orlando	None	Seeks B and F; considers stadium
Philadelphia	B F	Almost lost F; renovates stadium
Phoenix	F	Seeks B; lured F from St Louis, 1988; building new stadium
Pittsburgh	B F	Almost lost B; mayor proposed new stadium; retracted after opposition
Portland, OR	None	Seeks B or F; considers stadium
Raleigh-Durham	None	Seeks F; considers stadium
Sacramento	None	Seeks B and F; developer proposes new stadium; attempted to entice F Raiders
St Louis	B	Lost F to Phoenix in 1988; new F stadium due to open in 1995; seeks F
St Petersburg	None	Seeks B; opened dome in 1987 without tenet
Salem, OR	None	Sought F; gave up in 1991
San Antonio	None	Seeks F, possibly with Austin; plans stadium
San Diego	B F	No recent developments
San Francisco	B F	B attempted move to St Petersburg, 1992; two B stadium proposals defeated in referendum
San José	None	Proposed B stadium defeated in referendum
Santa Clara Co, CA	None	Proposed B stadium defeated in referendum
Seattle	B F	Almost lost B; new dome opened in 1977
Tampa	F	Seeks B, now in alliance with St Petersburg; considered stadium
Toronto	B	Opened new dome in 1989 to keep B
Tucson	None	Sought F; considers stadium
Vancouver, BC	None	Opened new stadium in 1983, seeks B
Washington DC	F	Seeks B; mayor committed to building new stadium
Worcester	None	Seeks F; considers stadium

Note: (B denotes baseball; F denotes football).
Source: Euchner (1993, pp. 8, 9).

packed the seats at Ebbetts field. At first O'Malley wanted to built a new stadium with public assistance, but he was thwarted by Robert Moses, who controlled the public authorities in the New York region. To lure the Dodgers out of New York, Los Angeles agreed to renovate its minor league stadium at Chavez Ravine, install 22 000 more seats than Ebbetts field, and then give the stadium to O'Malley. As the clincher, they offered him 300 acres of downtown Los Angeles real estate. O'Malley jumped at the chance to add to his personal fortune (Sullivan, 1987).

It did not take long for other owners to follow O'Malley's lead. Threats to move became potent weapons for prying more subsidies out of cities. Between 1980 and 1986 more than half the cities with major league sports franchises were confronted with demands for increased subsidies, with relocation an implied if not always explicit threat hanging over negotiations (Johnson, 1986, p. 411). As teams become more and more footloose, cities found themselves in a poor bargaining position. In an attempt to improve their positions, cities now build stadiums even when they don't have teams. In the 1980s Indianapolis built a football stadium, then persuaded the owner of the Baltimore Colts, Robert Isray, to move. After the Maryland legislature passed an eminent domain law to make it possible for Baltimore to seize the Colts for public use, Isray moved the team in the middle of the night.

St Petersburg, Florida, built a $139 million domed stadium in 1988 in the hopes of attracting a major-league baseball team. Called 'heaven's waiting room', boosters justified the Florida Suncoast Dome as a way of changing the city's image as a conservative retirement community (Smothers, R. 'No hits, no runs, one error: the dome' *The New York Times* 15 June 1991). For years the stadium remained the site of tractor pulls and concerts. In the 1990s, St Petersburg tried to lure several major league baseball teams, including the Seattle Mariners, the San Francisco Giants and a National League expansion team. When Florida won a baseball team in 1991, it was awarded to Miami. In October 1993, an expansion team of the National Football League was awarded to Jacksonville; St Petersburg's stadium was purpose-built for baseball and would not have been suitable for football. St Louis, which also put in a bid for one of the NFL expansion teams, lost out, but it is constructing a domed stadium anyway, which will open in 1995.

Stadiums require generous land, infrastructure and direct public subsidies because almost all of them lose money. Annual operating deficits are generally considerable; the New Orleans Superdome lost about $3 million a year during the 1980s, for example, compared with the annual $1 million loss for the Pontiac, Michigan, Silverdome. In its first year, the Florida Suncoast Dome lost $1.3 million, plus $7.7 million debt payments (Euchner, 1993, p. 67).[4] Modern domed stadiums cost so much to build that they cannot conceivably schedule enough events or charge enough for them to avoid large operating deficits. Toronto ended up paying $400 million for its domed stadium, while Baltimore spent $200 million for its new open stadium. St Louis's domed stadium, which is now under construction, is estimated to cost $250 million. Since estimates on construction costs of stadiums are typically far too low (Euchner, 1993, p. 67), the St Louis stadium may end up costing more than projected.

Do stadiums justify their enormous costs by bringing large sums of money into local economies? A careful review of studies on the economic effects of stadiums concludes that they may have an extremely limited economic impact – and that some may even have a negative effect by replacing some local spending with expenditures that exit the local economy quickly (Euchner, 1993 p. 71). Claims that spending on sports stadiums will have a multiplier effect by introducing a stream of new economic activity into a local economy are, therefore, suspect. The economic impact varies enormously, and it is, in any case, hard to estimate. Two studies of the impact of the NFL Eagles on the Philadelphia economy came to the conclusion either that the team brought in $500 million in 1983 alone or, if one believed the other study, that the team's presence contributed practically nothing (Euchner, 1993, p. 73).

Festival malls

Enclosed malls have become a principal weapon used by cities in the competition for recreational shopping and tourism. Since the early 1980s, at least one downtown mall has become an essential feature of every mayor's trophy collection. Malls are important because they are a means of creating defenced space even in the midst of urban crime and decay. The largest, most dramatic downtown malls have been built by developers James Rouse and John Portman. Rouse and Portman malls and their imitators have become such ubiquitous features of American downtowns that it is hard to keep in mind how recently they have been constructed. Portman's Peachtree complex dates back to the original cylindrical towers of his first atrium hotel, which opened in downtown Atlanta in 1967. It was an instant hit with architectural critics, the media and the public. Rouse opened his first mall on 26 August 1976 in the old Fanueil Hall in Boston, amid much skepticism about its viability (Frieden and Sagalyn, 1990, p. 43; Teaford, 1990). Few people were convinced that a primarily retail mall could make it in the middle of an older city.

Portman's developments are mammoth. Peachtree Center, his other projects – the Renaissance Center in Detroit, the Hyatt at Embarcadero Center in San Francisco, the Bonaventure Hotel in Los Angeles, the Marriott on Times Square – are virtually cities within cities. Shops, hotels and their lobbies, offices, food courts and atriums are connected by a maze of skywalks and arcades. Rouse's so-called festival malls are generally less grand in scale and are focused more narrowly on recreational shopping. In places such as Faneuil Hall in Boston, Union Station in St Louis, Trolley Square in Salt Lake and South Street Seaport in Manhattan, Rouse has attempted to create a carnival-like atmosphere by mixing specialty shops, clothing stores, restaurants and food stands, and by employing musicians, jugglers, acrobats and mimes to entertain shoppers.

Like Peachtree Center, many of the enclosed malls began modestly and then accreted block by block over many years, with tubes and skyways connecting the various components. In Minneapolis a sprawling mall complex has grown by eating away the interiors of the downtown buildings, leaving their historic facades intact. In Kansas City, the Crown Center has inexorably spread from its beginnings as a luxury hotel. In Montreal and Dallas veritable underground cities have been formed through a network of mole-like tunnels. The mall's assault on Atlanta has been much more direct; the huge Peachtree complex has been built on the rubble of the historic downtown.

The malls increasingly engulf and centralize activities that were formerly spread through the urban community at large. The glassed-in skyways that connected the various atriums and lobbies of Peachtree Center isolate the inhabitants of Peachtree from the streets below. There is a pure segregation between the consumers of the private space inside and the public space shared by people using the streets. Such complexes are easily criticized as 'fortified cells of affluence' (Davis, 1992, p. 155), but there can be little doubt that as locations for tourism and recreation, these spaces are incredibly successful. In 1992, Atlanta ranked fourth among cities in the United States for convention business.

Because they are considered an essential component of downtown leisure activities, cities typically have subsidized the construction of downtown malls heavily. To support mall development they devoted Community Development Block Grant and Urban Development Action Grant funds, floated bonds to finance site acquisition and loans to developers, offered property tax abatements, created tax increment districts, built utilities tunnels, constructed sewer lines and water mains, and rerouted and repaved streets. The melding of public subsidies and private dollars took place through new public–private entities established specifically to receive both public subsidies and private investment funds. Such agencies took on a wide variety of projects but, in the case of sports stadiums and malls, private–public authorities were usually created specifically for the purpose. Some cities took profit-sharing positions in development projects. In the case of Quincy Market in Boston, for example, Boston provided $12 million – almost 30% of the total cost of the project – and gave the Rouse Corporation a 99-year lease on the property. In exchange, the city was guaranteed a minimum cash payment plus a portion of income from store rents above the minimum.

Casino gambling

Historically, Nevada has served as the casino gambling mecca for most of the United States, making it possible for the state to keep its property taxes low and to avoid a state income tax altogether. In 1967, New Jersey adopted a lottery and, in 1978, Atlantic City, New Jersey, broke Nevada's monopoly on casino gambling. All through the 1970s and 1980s states adopted lotteries either through legislative action or referenda; by 1993, 35 states ran lotteries, and three more were readying legislation. Following the spread of state lotteries, gambling became legitimized as a source of tax revenues. Several states now allow restricted casino gambling, and year by year more are jumping onto the bandwagon. Gallup polls conducted in 1993 seemed to show that over 60% of Americans approved of riverboat or Indian-land gaming in their states, an increase of 30 percentage points in 20 years (Donaldson et al., 1993, p. 6).

As a means of promoting economic development on Indian reservations, in 1988 Congress passed the Indian Gaming Regulatory Act. The legislation permitted Indian tribes to negotiate with states to run gaming operations and, notably, required the states to negotiate with the tribes. Since then, gaming in some form has been adopted on Indian lands in 24 states, and many more states will no doubt be added to the list over the next five years. Though in many cases the gaming is limited to bingo games or slot machines, the type of gaming operations allowed is certain to be enlarged. In 1992, gaming on Indian lands generated $750 million in revenues (Donaldson et al., 1993, p. 18).

In 1990, Iowa became the first state to approve riverboat gambling. After the opening of the first boat in Iowa in April, 1991, six riverboats generated $12 million in state income taxes within eight months, prompting neighboring states to begin steps to join the competition (Faust, 1994, pp IE–SE). In 1992, riverboats began operating in Illinois, two near St Louis (one in East St Louis, Illinois, directly across from St Louis and the Gateway Arch). Mississippi began operating boats in 1993. Missouri, Louisiana and Indiana have all approved riverboat gambling, with operations beginning in 1994 (Donaldson et al., 1993, pp. 10–12). Alabama, Florida, Massachusetts, Pennsylvania, Rhode Island, Texas, West Virginia and Virginia are likely to follow soon *Monthly Casino Review* (Prudential Securities Incorporated, June 1993).

In the 1990s, it is probable that casino gambling will spread across the country in a manner paralleling the spread of state lotteries. Public officials are desperate for new sources of revenue and, as states and cities adopt gaming, neighboring jurisdictions will be pressured to follow suit. As if to illustrate this, in April 1994, the Missouri legislature amended the gaming statute that had been rejected by voters in a referendum earlier that month to allow games of 'skill' rather than 'chance' on riverboats. On 27 and 28 April, riverboats opened for business in Missouri, but without slot machines and roulette (Linsalata and Ganey, 1994, p. 12). Another referendum aimed at allowing full-scale gaming was held in Missouri in November 1994. This time it passed.

Gambling entrepreneurs and politicians make extraordinary claims about the potential economic benefits of gaming. The 23 applications filed for gaming licenses in Missouri by late March 1994 made it appear that gambling would earn $1.5 billion in gross receipts each year, which would yield $300 million in state and $60 million in local taxes (Mannies and Schlinkmann, 1994). Developers promised officials and voters in Boonville, which is located on the Missouri River in the center of the state, that if a riverboat were approved they would build a riverfront promenade complete with full tourist facilites, plus, they promised, they would renovate two historic buildings. The financing for St Louis's proposed $250 million riverfront project completely depended upon riverboat gambling (Prost, 1994b).

Chicago, Illinois is pushing for five riverboat casinos, in the expectation that these would finance an enormous $800 million entertainment complex (Pacatte, 1994; *Casino Journal's National Gaming Summary* Casino Journal Publishing Group, Las Vegas, NV, 18 April 1994, p. 1). Such extraordinary projections of gambling revenues, if even close to accurate, would constitute the biggest boost to central city economies since the urban renewal programs of the 1950s. Gambling, is, however, vulnerable to competition. Atlantic City is contemplating steps to expand its attractions beyond its casinos, an initiative prompted by the fact that the states of New York, Connecticut, New Jersey and Pennsylvania are all considering gambling legislation. Most of the people who go to Atlantic City are daytrippers who would gamble closer to home if they could. Atlantic City's problem is that its casinos are isolated in a sea of urban decay; casino operators discourage customers from going onto the city streets (Nordheimer, 1994). In a competitive environment, cities must treat casino gambling as one element in an increasingly expensive tourism infrastructure because, with few exceptions, gambling will not work as the main engine for tourism. For almost all cities, casino gambling is sustained by daytrippers, not tourists. City officials expect to reap huge benefits from casino gambling. As more casinos open in more locations, however, it is certain that gambling will often yield less than its promoters promise.

Diversion districts

What we may label as 'carousal zones' have sometimes comprised a component of the tourism space in central cities. Typically, carousal districts are composed of strip clubs, topless bars and stores that sell sex paraphernalia and pornography. Sometimes legitimate bars and restaurants may be sprinkled among the seedier dives. The French Quarter in New Orleans is, no doubt, the most famous example of this kind of zone in the United States and probably the only one to succeed as a long-run tourist magnet. A number of carousal zones have existed in the past, including, among countless others, the Battle Zone in Boston, Rush Street in Chicago, the pre-renovation Atlanta Underground and North Beach in San Francisco.

Carousal zones are inherently unstable, constantly subject to being displaced by luxury hotels, office buildings and other uses that raise land values and rents. Though they undoubtedly generate business volume and tax revenues for a city, they cannot survive successful downtown development. Indeed, they seem to be disappearing from most downtowns. Thus, within the last decade the sex clubs that lined 42nd Street in New York City have been pushed out by office invasion and gentrification. The Battle Zone in Boston was pushed out by a combination of gentrification and an official crackdown on vice. Atlanta Underground has been renovated to look and feel as squeaky clean as any suburban mall. With the notable exception of New Orleans, such zones may threaten the tourism image a city wishes to project, and thus though they may be tolerated from time to time by public officials, they are rarely, if ever, actively encouraged.

A tamer version of the carousal zone may be labelled the 'diversion district', characterized by a concentration of jazz and blues clubs and saloons and bars. Typically these districts are supported by public subsidies in the form of cobble-stoned streets, historic street lamps, waterfront redevelopment, street malls and the like. Unlike carousal zones, diversion districts have become a necessary component and sometimes the anchor for a tourism space. Though these areas succeed best as locations for partying rather than illicit sin, they are likely to fail if they are excessively sterile. For the tourist, they must manage to convey, simultaneously, an ambience of security and fun. Obviously, some cities are more likely to be able to accomplish this balancing act than others.

Urban Tourism in the United States: Image and Economics

In the United States, the competition for tourists has brought about large-scale changes in land use in central cities. Critics often note that sports stadiums, convention centers and other components of the recreation and tourist infrastructure rarely pay for themselves. Public officials and civic boosters do not, on the whole, care much if they do. This apparently cavalier attitude toward taxpayers' money can be explained by noting the general irrelevance – to city officials and civic boosters – of cost–benefit analyses of tourism infrastructure. Public officials' attitudes toward development projects have 'little to do with the...profitability...of a project', and far more to do with the vision or image officials share about the overall direction a city is taking (Pagano and Bowman 2001, ch. 3, p. 3). Such a stance often means that cities become driven by a vision of regeneration that is not entirely of their own invention. Cities exist in a complex political environment shaped by economic changes, national policies, the actions of other cities and, in the case of tourism, a well-organized industry. The manner in which inter-urban competition in the United States is conducted, however, dictates that cities must compete, they must be as generous as their competitors in providing subsidies, and they must adopt every new variation on a theme that comes along. The result is the production of a remarkably standardized tourism space from one city to the next.

Obviously a limitless number of cities cannot attract enough tourists to justify the investment in a completely elaborated tourist zone. As the number of tourist spaces proliferates in central cities, a sorting-out process has to occur. Just as some cities failed to become successful sites of production in the industrial age, in the next few years some will fail to succeed as sites of consumption. In some cases, the indebtedness incurred by cities will become a crushing fiscal burden. It is more likely, however, that success and failure will continue to elude precise measurement. City officials will continue to do what they see other cities doing. The competition imposes a logic of its own that is hard to resist.

For public officials tempted to proceed on blind faith alone, it is useful to keep in mind that abject, total failure is possible. Flint, Michigan tried to make itself into a tourist city, and the unanticipated result was that its often sad and sometimes pathetic efforts were subsequently portrayed in a low-budget but popular movie, *Roger and Me*.[5] After the closing of its General Motors plant had devastated the local economy, public officials in Flint launched an effort at regeneration behind the motto, 'Our New Spark Will Surprise You'. The city committed $13 million in subsidies to the construction of a luxury hotel, the Hyatt Regency. Within a year it closed its doors. Approximately $100 million in public money was used to build AutoWorld, a museum that contained, among other items, the 'world's largest car engine' and a scale model that portrayed downtown Flint in its more prosperous days. AutoWorld closed within six months. Still more public subsidies were committed to the construction of the Water Street Pavilion, a theme park/festival market built by the developer of the South Street Seaport in New York City. Most of its shops closed within the first year. Commenting on Flint's failure to become a magnet for tourism, the former director of AutoWorld said, 'You can't make Palm Beach out of the Bowery. If you want to make Palm Beach, you have to go to Palm Beach'.

It is difficult to know what lesson to draw from Flint's failure to make itself into a Palm Beach. Some cities possess built-in advantages as tourist destinations. In Europe, Rome, Edinburgh and Athens stand as examples of cities that could hardly avoid drawing tourists even if they wanted to, short of destroying their historic monuments. Their histories define them to the world. There is no exact equivalent in the United States, but New Orleans and San Francisco (for instance) also convey powerful images that derive from their unique history and architecture. Though quite a few cities are located near or in scenic spots, very few cities can lay claim to great advantages inherent to the urban landscape itself. Consequently, if they want to claim a share of the fastest-growing sector of the world economy, most cities in the United States are obliged to create the spaces that tourists might inhabit. When they do so, they create tourist reservations that transform part of the historic city into an artificial, segregated space at odds with the city around it; or, from another perspective, they restructure the city to fit contemporary economic realities.

NOTES

1 Undoubtedly a large proportion of Urban Development Action Grants and funds from other federal programs were used by cities to build tourism-related facilities. Cities, however, had discretion in the use of these funds, and the federal government's purpose was not to promote tourism *per se*.
2 I want to express my appreciation to Todd Swanstrom for allowing me to use some material from our coauthored book, *City Politics*, for this paper. Todd researched and drafted the original material on Baltimore's HarborPlace for the book, as well as some of the material on sports politics. Though I have revised and recast those discussions, I want to note that I have continued to rely on some of Todd's research for those sections.
3 Data are from *Financial World Magazine*, as reported in *The New York Times* 17 June 1992.
4 Euchner's book is the most thorough, and readable, treatment of the location politics of professional sports available.
5 A Dog Eat Dog Films Production. Written, produced and directed by Michael Moore (Warner Bros Pictures).

REFERENCES

Barthes, R. (1979) *The Eiffel Tower and Other Mythologies* Hill and Wang, New York.
Berkowitz, B. L. (1987) 'Rejoinder to downtown redevelopment as an urban growth strategy: a critical appraisal of the Baltimore renaissance' *Journal of Urban Affairs* 9 (2).
Boyer, C. (1992) 'Cities for sale: merchandising history at South Street Seaport' in Sorkin, M. (ed) *Variations on a Theme Park: The New American City and the End of Public Space* Hill and Wang, New York.
Boyle, R. (1990) 'Regeneration in Glasgow: stability, collaboration, and inequity' in Judd, D. and Parkinson, M. (eds) *Leadership and Urban Regeneration: Cities in North America and Europe* Sage, Newbury Park, CA.
Chalmers, D. (1976) *Neither Socialism Nor Monopoly* Lippincott, Philadelphia 4.
Conlin, J. (1993) 'Time to rally: we must resist the proposed cut in business meal deductions' *Successful Meetings* April.
Cooke, S. D. and Azucenas, V. (1994) 'Research in state and provincial travel offices' in Ritchie, J. R. and Goeldner, C. R. (eds) *Travel, Tourism, and Hospitality Research: A Handbook for Managers and Researchers* 2nd edn, Wiley, New York.
Corbett, C. (1992) 'What's doing in Baltimore' *The New York Times*, 23 February.
Davis, M. (1992) 'Fortress Los Angeles; the militarization of urban space' in Sorkin, M. (ed) *Variations on a Theme Park: The New American City and the End of Space* Noonday Press, New York 155.
Donaldson, Lufkin, (1993) & Jenrette Securities Corporation *Company Analysis* Donaldson, Lufkin & Jenrette 23 June.
Euchner, C. C. (1993) *Playing the Field: Why Sports Teams Move and Cities Fight to Keep Them* Johns Hopkins University Press, Baltimore.

Fainstein, S. S., Fainstein, N. I., Child Hill, R., Judd, D. and Smith, M. P. (1986) *Restructuring the City* revised edn, Longman, New York.

Faust, F. (1994) 'It wasn't in the cards' *St Louis Post-Dispatch* 10 April.

Fenich, G. G. (1992) 'The dollars and sense of convention centers' doctoral dissertation, The Graduate School of Rutgers University, New Brunswick, New Jersey 34.

Frieden, B. J. and Sagalyn, L. B. (1990) *Downtown, Inc.: How America Builds Cities* MIT Press, Cambridge, MA.

Goodrich, C. (1960) *Government Promotion of American Canals and Railroads, 1800–1890* Columbia University Press, New York.

Graburn, N. H. H. and Moore, R. S. (1994) 'Anthropological research on tourism' in Ritchie, J. R. and Goeldner, C. R. (eds) *Travel, Tourism, and Hospitality Research: A Handbook for Managers and Researchers* 2nd edn, Wiley, New York.

Guskind, R. (1987) 'Bringing Madison Avenue to Main Street' *Planning* 53.

Heilbrun, J. (1981) *Urban Economics and Public Policy* 2nd edn, St Martin's Press, New York.

Hummon, D. (1988) 'Tourist worlds: tourist advertising, ritual, and American culture' *Sociology Quarterly* **29** (Summer) 179–202.

Johnson, A. T. (1985) 'The sports franchise relocation issue and public policy responses' in Johnson, A. T. and Frey J. H. (eds) *Government and Sport: The Public Policy Issues* Rowman & Allanheld, Totowa, NJ.

Johnson, A. T. (1986) 'Economic and policy implications of hosting sports franchises: some lessons from Baltimore' *Urban Affairs Quarterly* **21** (3).

Judd, D. and Parkinson, M. (1990) *Leadership and Urban Regeneration: Cities in North America and Europe* Urban Affairs Annual Reviews 37 Sage, Newsbury Park, CA.

Linsalata, P. and Ganey, T. (1994) 'Casinos prepare to throw the dice' *St Louis Post-Dispatch* 27 April 1, 12.

Logan, J. R. and Molotch, H. L. (1987) *Urban Fortunes: The Political Economy of Place* University of California Press, Berkeley.

Lynch, K. (1960) *The Image of the City* Cambridge Technology Press, Cambridge, MA.

Mannies, Jo and Mark Schlinkmann, (1994) 'Gambling's allure: is it fiscal fuel or fool's gold' *St Louis Post-Dispatch* 20 March 1, 7A.

Mehrhoff, W. A. (1992) *The Gateway Arch: Fact and Symbol* Bowling Green State University Popular Press, Bowling Green, OH.

Nordheimer, J. (1994) 'Atlantic City seeks to lure non-bettors' *The New York Times* 10 April 1490.

Pacatte, M. (1994) 'Chicago ready to gamble' *St Louis Post-Dispatch* 8 April 1, 14.

Pagano, M. A. and Bowman, A. O'M. (1995) *Markets and Images: Development Policy in America's Cities* Johns Hopkins University Press, Baltimore.

Pierce, N. R., Guskind, R. and Gardner, J. (1983) 'Politics is not the only thing that is changing America's big cities' *National Journal* (26 November) 2480.

Prost, C. (1994a) 'City Plans to float its ideas for river' *St Louis Post-Dispatch* 15 March 1, 4.

Prost, C. (1994b) 'Riverfront vision: city plans gamble on park' *St Louis Post-Dispatch* 20 March 4B.

Richter, L. K. (1994) 'The political dimensions of Tourism' in Ritchie, J. R. and Goeldner, C. R. (eds) *Travel, Tourism, and Hospitality Research: A Handbook for Managers and Researchers* 2nd edn, Wiley, New York.

Strauss, A. L. (1961) *Images of the American City* Free Press, Glencoe, IL.

Sullivan, N. J. (1987) *The Dodgers Move West* Oxford University Press, New York.

Suttles, G. D. (1985) 'The cumulative textures of local urban culture' *American Journal of Sociology* **90** (2) 282–304.

Tabak, L. (1993) 'How much do we want their money?' *Ingram's* (February) (Kansas City, MO) 30.

Tabak, L. (1994) 'Wild about convention centers' *The Atlantic* (April) 28–34.

Teaford, J. C. (1990) *The Rough Road to Renaissance: Urban Revitalization in America, 1940–1985* Johns Hopkins University Press, Baltimore.

Teibel, A. (1994) 'The pros and cons of second-tier cities' *Convene* **IX** (1) (Professional Convention Management Association) Birmingham, AL.

Tipton, V. (1993) 'Travel agents: a visit here removes a few bad impressions' *St Louis Post-Dispatch* 22 September 1, 7.

US Department of Housing and Urban Development (1982) *The President's National Urban Policy Report* US Government Printing Office, Washington, DC.

Wade, R. C. (1959) *The Urban Frontier: Pioneer Life in Early Pittsburgh, Cincinnati, Lexington, Louisville, and St Louis* University of Chicago Press.

Part IV

Culture, Design, and Urban Form

Introduction

Recent interpretations of urban development have incorporated many of the insights of cultural studies. The authors represented in this part investigate the symbolic meanings of urban form and interactions, particularly focusing on the language in which space is depicted. They deconstruct the messages transmitted by the shining office buildings and malls, the gated communities, and the seedy barrios and ghettos of contemporary metropolitan areas. Based on criteria of diversity as well as equity, they evaluate the restructured urban realm and criticize it for its inauthenticity and its failure to reflect the values of its less favored populations. The "new urbanism," which has arisen as a response to American suburbanization, represents an attempt to formulate a counter-vision to the prevailing metropolitan form. Its authenticity and equity are, however, open to dispute.

John Hannigan, in chapter 14, continues the argument presented by Dennis Judd in chapter 13. His analysis of the contemporary fantasy city identifies three major trends: the dominance of rational techniques of production; the proliferation of themed environments; and the use of synergies, or tie-ins, as a key business strategy. He sees these trends as resulting in the convergence and overlap of what had formerly been separate consumer activities: shopping, dining, entertainment, and education and culture. Fantasy city thus becomes the almost wholly commercialized or commodified city.

Chapter 15 – a brief excerpt from Sharon Zukin's book, *The Cultures of Cities* – treats the concerns raised by the preceding authors at a more abstract level. She defines the "symbolic economy" and deconstructs the message sent by public spaces which intertwine cultural symbols and entrepreneurial capital. She argues that to understand the symbolic economy of cities, analysis must go beyond political economy to encompass visual and spatial strategies of social differentiation.

It is these visual and spatial strategies that Michael Sorkin (in chapter 16) seeks to uncover in his discussion of the Disney theme parks, which he terms "America's stand-in for Elysium." He traces their antecedents to the World's Fair and calls

London's 1851 Great Exhibition "the first great utopia of global capital." In their physical form, the Disney parks recall Ebenezer Howard's model of the garden city, thereby transmuting their references to exotic locales and urban variety into a safe suburbia. Arguing that Disney has provided a model for office complexes and shopping centers throughout the world, Sorkin compares Disneyland to an airport in which the traveler "submits to an elaborate system of surveillance with the ultimate rationale of self-protection." In its orderliness and artificiality, it is the negation of the city as it really exists: "it produces a kind of aura-stripped hypercity, a city with billions of citizens (all who would consume) but no residents."

The "new urbanism" constitutes a movement within the design professions to create a more physically and socially diverse urban space than the American suburb provides. In chapter 17 Kelbaugh presents strategies for suburban design that conform to the precepts set forth by the Congress for the New Urbanism. He defends these concepts of walkable neighborhoods, dense development, and neotraditional design against accusations of anti-urbanism, elitism, formulaic design, and isolationism. He concludes that, whatever its flaws, the new urbanism is a superior mode of development to the other available models of peripheral growth and that continued suburbanization is inevitable.

The pros and cons of the new urbanism are taken up again in a transcript of a discussion held at Harvard's Graduate School of Design ("Urban or Suburban?"). In chapter 18, Andres Duany, one of the founders of the Congress for the New Urbanism and, with Elizabeth Plater-Zyberg, its best-known advocate, defends the merits of his model. He contends that what this movement is trying to do is to distill from the past what works best and incorporate it into new development. He further argues that design is critical to enabling people to lead better lives and that bad design fails people. He turns the accusation of elitism on his critics and argues that it is they who are refusing to give people what they want.

The concluding essay in this book of readings is an analysis by David Harvey of the issue of social justice and the city that takes into account the cultural insights of post-modernist thought. In chapter 19, Harvey, a Marxist geographer, wrestles with divisions based on gender, ethnicity, race, religion, lifestyle, and taste, as well as class. While recognizing the differences among the groups generated by these varying forces, he nevertheless argues for the possibility of coalition among disparate interests. He offers social justice as a basic ideal that would have sufficiently universalistic appeal to forge such a coalition. He rejects the post-modernist viewpoint that any effort at universalism is illegitimate. In doing so, he contends that "justice and rationality take on different meaning across space and time and persons, yet the existence of everyday meanings . . . gives the terms a political and mobilizing power. . . ." He then lists six dimensions of justice. He concludes by arguing that social policy and planning must apply them both in confronting the issues of daily life and in attacking the underlying structure that he regards as the source of injustice.

14

Fantasy City: Pleasure and profit in the postmodern metropolis*

John Hannigan

While it is possible to find individual elements of Fantasy City in earlier times, notably in the "golden age" at the turn of the twentieth century, it is the convergence of three major trends in the 1990s which has led to the emergence of the contemporary theme park city. These are:

(i)   an increasing dominance of rational techniques of production (i.e. the "McDonaldization" of the market place);
(ii) the proliferation of themed environments;
(iii) and the elevation of "synergies" of form, content and structure as a key business strategy.

The "McDonaldization" of the Market Place

In his book, *The McDonaldization of Society*, sociologist George Ritzer (1993) argues that we have increasingly moved toward a rationalized society which adheres to the principles of the fast food restaurant. Four pillars support the immensely successful McDonald's operational model: efficiency, calculability, predictability and control. That is, McDonald's, and similar establishments, offer service which is rapid, emphasizes products that can be easily calculated, counted and quantified (a "Big Mac," a "Whopper"), holds few suprises, and, by substituting nonhuman for human technology, exerts a maximum degree of organizational control over both customers and employees. Among the type of businesses which follow this formula are theme parks, shopping malls, professional sports venues and tourist resorts.

* Hannigan, John (1998) "Fantasy City: Pleasure and Profit" in *The Postmodern Metropolis* Routledge, New York, pp. 81–100. Reprinted by permission of Taylor & Francis, Inc.

Theme parks such as Disneyland, Disney World and Busch Gardens offer "a world of predictable, almost surreal orderliness" (Ritzer, 1993, p. 92) which depend on a sophisticated infrastructure of efficient people-moving mechanisms. As Alan Bryman (1995, p. 119–20) has observed, one reason for the presence of audio-animatronic figures (i.e. talking robots) everywhere in Disney parks, is that they are consistent and, therefore, predictable, compared to flesh and blood staff. Furthermore, in return for the assurance of safety and certainty, theme park visitors surrender an extraordinary degree of control, both in terms of freedom of movement and freedom of imagination. The Disney parks are not somewhere you go to explore, as individualized itineraries disrupt the standardized visitor flows which are central to their smooth and efficient operation. It could be argued that Walt Disney, rather than Ray Kroc (the founder of McDonald's), first pioneered the rational model described in *The McDonalization of Society*, although Ritzer counters that the fast food model is a more useful template to use because it reaches a wider cross-section of consumers on a daily basis.

Shopping malls as well, exert considerable control over both their customers and their retail tenants. Shopkeepers are subject to innumerable rules and regulations including the approval of their location, design and even name (Ritzer, 1993, p. 111). Shoppers, especially young ones, are tightly regulated in terms of what they may or may not do. Included in the latter is anything which is judged by the management to be "disruptive" behavior, for example, loitering, picketing or protesting. In contrast to traditional commercial streets, the unpredictabilities of the weather are eliminated. Similarly, the illusion of safety from crime is created through the omnipresence of closed-circuit television cameras, private security guards and other such measures.

Standardization is also frequently the case with professional sporting events. In baseball, artificial turf, domed roofs and alike, symmetrical stadium designs are brought together so as to eliminate the possibility of rain-outs, bad hops of the ball, fan interference and other inconsistencies. (Although the newer generation of neo-traditional baseball fields have reinstated some elements which were discarded during the 1970s and 1980s.) Some venues, for instance Toronto's Skydome, have even rationalized food service during games and other events by bringing in such chains as the Hard Rock Cafe and McDonald's. Rather than depend on the spontaneous appearance of some boisterous and charismatic fan to lead the cheer, teams now hire professional mascots and, in case anyone might miss it, the instructions are displayed on a giant electronic scoreboard.

The travel and tourism industry has also followed the organizational model described by Ritzer. One of the more memorable marketing campaigns in recent years was a series of ads for the Holiday Inn hotel chain, which promised customers "no suprises." Similarly, American Express, in a long-running series of ads, made the claim that replacing lost or stolen traveler's checks in a foreign country is fast, easy and efficient with them (and, allegedly, a nightmare with those of their competitors). Mass-marketed tourist resorts such as Club Med offer a large selection of routinized activities in interchangeable exotic settings where a guest can stay without having to venture into the unknown and unpredictable environs of local life on a tropical island (Ritzer, 1993, p. 23).

Yet, contrary to the principles which propel it, the fast food society often turns out to be neither efficient nor inexpensive. Frequently a victim of their own success, theme parks and fast food restaurants generate long queues. "Big Macs" may be good value in America, but the case is different in Geneva, Berlin or Moscow where they are still considered a novelty. Why, then, has the McDonald's model been so successful? Ritzer contends that what is really on offer is the possibility of fun. Fast food restaurants with their explosion of color and garish signs and symbols are entertaining in the same way that, traditionally, amusement parks have been seen to be. Unlike traditional restaurant menus which are presented as individual docu-ments to be handheld, the fast food menu is displayed on a marquee which is reminiscent of the movie options at a local cineplex (Ritzer, 1993, p.127). Some McDonald's outlets even have playgrounds and children's rides. Malls are designed to be fantasy worlds. Not only is the mall itself "a huge stage setting loaded with lots of props" but there are such entertaining extras as restaurants, bars, movie theaters, exercise centers and, on weekends, clowns, balloons, magicians and bands (p. 128). When Ritzer was completing the first edition of his book, the Mall of America near Minneapolis was not yet open, but he cites it as evidence of a future trend toward shopping malls as entertainment palaces.

What can explain the seemingly unstoppable spread of McDonaldization? Ritzer points to three significant factors:

- Economics (lower corporate costs as a result of rationalization equals higher profits), familiarity on the part of consumers (growing up with the Golden Arches), and an attunement to broader societal lifestyle changes (dual-career families who are pressed for time)
- Greater mobility, including greater car use
- Increased affluence and available discretionary income

The first, lower corporate costs, refers to factors internal to the business world, whereas the other two touch the lives of the ordinary consumer. Inexplicably, Ritzer does not include on his shortlist something which he notes earlier on in his book: "our national obsession with amusement" (1993, p. 128), although this would seem to be one key to understanding its desirability. We may be, as Neal Postman (1985) has termed it, "amusing ourselves to death," but nevertheless, this is an important trend in the final years of the millennium.

Ritzer's book has been much praised, but it has also been criticized for underplay-ing the cultural and symbolic aspects of the fast food society. Featherstone (1995, p. 8), for example, insists that McDonaldization not only entails economic efficiency gains but also represents a globalized cultural message which equates the "good life" with American commercial culture. Gottdiener (1997, p. 132) acknowledges that Ritzer's argument is persuasive but claims that he has missed an important point about the human interactive side of the fast food experience. Outlets such as McDonalds are successful, he maintains, not just because they follow rational techniques of production but because they offer easy-to-decipher signs and stand-ardized behaviors, no matter where you go in the world. So too do theme parks, hotels, hospitals, casinos, airports, office buildings and other built spaces in which past experience proves to be a reliable guide.

While writing this section of the book, I encountered several good examples which highlight Gottdiener's point. As a regular patron of a downtown Burger King, I have come to appreciate the concise, almost robotic four-question interrogation by the counter server: "What would you like? To drink? For here? Salt or ketchup?" One day, feeling like a change, I went to a submarine sandwich bar. The specials were numbered, but the choices were more numerous, the direction of the queue was less clear, and you needed to tell the clerk behind the counter a lot of information: type of bread, length of sandwich, choice of toppings, size of beverage cup. This was too much for one patron several places ahead of me, who fled out of the store. An equally confusing incident happened to guests staying with me who, unacquainted with the routines of a popular local hamburger outlet, were left standing in limbo between the order desk and the preparation area where the burgers are dressed and delivered to the customer.

Nevertheless, Ritzer's thesis is useful in helping us to understand the organizational context in which fantasy cities develop. . . . one of the leading principles of UED development is the minimization of risk. To optimize this, leisure merchants must be able to "roll out" new entertainment concepts across the country and the world in a standardized, predictable form very similar to that described by Ritzer for the fast food society. Furthermore, many of the elements of predictability and control which are central to the discussion in his book can be seen in the design and operation of Fantasy City.

The Theming of America

A second noteworthy trend is the proliferation of themed environments as part of the everyday social fabric. In his book, *The Theming of America*, urban sociologist Mark Gottdiener (1997) argues that since the 1960s new modes of thematic representation have come to organize our lives. In contrast to the past, the postmodern 1990s is awash in symbolic motifs created by commercial interests in order to promote mass consumption.

At the turn of the century, city structures tended to be monochromatic with relatively little symbolic embellishment. Space was functional and material culture was relatively straightforward. Gottdiener devotes several pages in his book to contrasting the early modernist city to the ancient cities of Athens and Beijing (formerly Peking), both of which possessed an overarching sacred symbolic structure which imbued the physical layout with meaning. With the arrival of the Industrial Revolution this rich iconography went into decline within secular society, whose leaders were practical men of business. Their consumption patterns were meant to proclaim their financial success and power, emphasizing luxury, ostentation and "conspicuous consumption" (Veblen, 1925). Unlike their counterparts in ancient and medieval societies, ordinary people led lives stripped bare of signification, unless they were active in certain forms of religion, notably Roman-Catholicism.

In marked contrast, Gottdiener characterizes the history of the twentieth century as an escalating development of commodity fantasy themes by capitalist entrepreneurs eager to exploit the rising purchasing power of the swelling middle class. In particular, he points to the emergence of advertising as a crucial activity. Whereas sales people such as the once ubiquitous door-to-door "Fuller Brush man" had sold products on the basis of their utility and performance, marketing people now devised sophisticated psychological techniques with which they identified the insecurities and aspirations of particular socio-demographic population segments and then produced images of desire tailored to appeal to these perceived needs.

Such image clusters were not just restricted to advertisements in magazines and catalogues but also pervaded the built environment. Standardized suburban housing, for example, was differentiated and promoted through endowing subdivisions, streets and house models with names suggesting mountains, nature or tropical scenery. Despite the fact that minimal downpayments and low mortgage rates had made suburbia virtually open to all whites, developers continued to sell an image of an exclusive enclave of upwardly mobile Americans nestled close to the land (Palen, 1995, pp. 95–6). Shopping centers were architecturally themed to suggest a fusion of modernity and Old World familiarity, the latter represented by open courts, fountains, terraces and skylights (Rowe, 1991, pp. 126–7).

While Gottdiener's account is generally convincing, there are a few significant gaps and inconsistencies in his argument. Although he cites the world's fairs and commercial arcades as partial exceptions, Gottdiener labels the large industrial city of the nineteenth and early twentieth centuries as "hyposignificant," meaning that their symbolic content was limited to signifying functionality. Consequently, they "could hardly be called a themed environment" (1997, p. 42). This dichotomy between the functional modernism of the industrial period and the later era of thematization breaks down, however, insomuch as functionalism and modernization can in themselves be considered broad themes (Purcell, 1997). Curiously, he makes no reference to the "golden age" of public amusements. While they tended to look back into history for their imagery, fantasy entertainments such as those presented at Coney Island, Luna Park and the New York Hippodrome were elaborately themed, even by today's standards. So too were the movie palaces of the 1920s and 1930s. It's fair to say that it is no coincidence that contemporary megaplexes have modeled themselves after these exotic picture palaces: with their Hispano-Persian lobbies, Mexican-baroque auditoria and Italian-Renaissance ceilings, most of which "bore no resemblance whatsoever to models closer at hand in the city or in the memories of those who resided there" (Nasaw, 1993, p. 230). It is hard to understand, therefore, why Gottdiener would conclude that urban spaces prior to the 1960s were not particularly based around a theme and were not very entertaining.

At the same time, Gottdiener overemphasizes the extent to which the 1960s and 1970s landscapes were dominated by themed developments. While the advertising for suburban homes was theme led, the product itself was usually more mundane, unleashing a torrent of architectural and literary criticism of suburban vistas as homogeneous, bland and incoherent. Recall, for example, the first generation of multiplex theaters which were little more than "concrete screening rooms" with thin walls, sticky floors and overpowering sound systems.

Finally, Gottdiener's historical and semiotic approach is not very helpful in telling us much about the political economy of Fantasy City. While he does a good job demonstrating how advertising paved the way to widespread popular acceptance of commercial images as a feature of everyday life, his account falters at the approach of the 1990s, frequently reverting back to general bromides about those evil twin processes: commodification and mass media influence. Such broad forces do not explain the reason why projects which could not get off the ground in the 1980s have moved ahead in the 1990s. That is, the fact that the air may be pregnant with "motif milieus," as Gottdiener terms them, does not explain how or why these themes actually find their way to become finished UED projects.

Building Synergies

The third major factor which has sparked the growth of Fantasy City is the increasing emphasis placed by corporate decision makers on "synergistic" opportunities, otherwise known as "tie-ins." Along with "downsizing" and "globalization," exploiting synergies has become one of the dominant business strategies of the 1990s.

Consider, for example, the road to success traveled by three of the most successful individual entrepreneurs operating in the entertainment industry in the 1990s. Relationships guru John Gray supplements his best-selling advice books on gender relations with an "infomercial," audiotapes, weekend seminars, a CD-ROM, themed vacations, a string of "Mars and Venus" counseling centers and even a solo performance show which had its debut at the Gershwin Theater in New York, and, at the time of writing, is scheduled to continue at arenas across the US (Gleick, 1997). Entertaining and home interiors doyenne, Martha Stewart, is no less devoted to building an empire of spin-offs. Her interrelated enterprises, all of which bear her name, include a syndicated television show, a radio spot, a magazine, a mail-order business and a line of designer bedlinen at K-Mart stores.

Perhaps the most accomplished Merlin of brand synergies is the British entrepreneur Richard Branson who has successfully embossed the Virgin brand name on a mind-boggling array of products and services, among them, Virgin Megastores (music, books, videos, computer games), Virgin Cinemas (the largest movie exhibitor in Britain), Virgin Atlantic Airways (the "no frills" successor to Laker Airways), Virgin Communications (publishing, educational computer software, film production), and Virgin Direct (consumer financial services). Like Stewart, Branson is an iconic figure, popping up as the principal in a series of "events," which range from attempting to span the globe in a hotair balloon trip to modeling a wedding dress from Virgin Bride (another of his companies, founded on a suggestion from an enterprising employee). When BBC Radio asked 1,200 people who they thought would be most qualified to rewrite the Ten Commandments, Branson rated fourth behind Mother Teresa, the Pope and the Archbishop of Canterbury (Fabrikant, 1997).

More or less the same strategy is pursued by the entertainment giants who are prime movers in the growth of Fantasy City. Observe, for example, recent events at Sony Corporation, the Japanese consumer electronics conglomerate, which counts recordings, films, and computers among its other entertainment related interests. Compared to some of its competitors, notably Disney, Warner Bros. and Universal, Sony has been slow off the mark to explore the synergistic potential of its varied holdings. But, early in 1996, Sony hired Matt Mazer, former chief of Disney's promotions department, to head up a new unit, the Gateway Group, which was given the task of exploiting the value of the Sony brand wherever it occurred in the consumer market place (Gelsi, 1997, p. 20). Mazer began by assembling a web of tie-ins around his firm's existing contract to outfit cruise ships owned by the London-based Celebrity Cruise Lines Inc., with audio and video equipment. With

Celebrity's approval, he arranged for the gala opening on board one of their ships to screen Hollywood movie *Jerry Maguire*, released by Sony-owned TriStar Pictures. As a lead up to the event, movies released by TriStar and Sony Pictures were placed in the ship's video-on-demand center, the gift shop was equipped with a Sony concept area, Sony PlayStations were installed in children's play areas and computer classes were arranged for passengers who tired of swimming and shuffleboard. The project became a floating demonstration platform for Sony products, witnessed by roughly 200,000 passengers a year and constituting a new outlet for its movie software (Gelsi, 1997).

According to American media and entertainment consultant Michael Wolf, there are three significant ways through which commercial value is created or enhanced by implementing strategies such as that undertaken by Sony (Koselka, 1995). First, incremental revenue streams from repackaging and/or reworking existing properties and distributing them in new formats. As far back as the 1950s, Walt Disney pioneered this stategy by putting together *Davy Crockett* episodes first shown on television into a feature film and instaling a "Crockett" attraction in the Adventure-land sector of Disneyland. Today, the Disney Company continues the same practice, only on a larger scale. Animated movies such as *Beauty and the Beast* are turned into theatrical stage productions. Another Disney feature, *Hercules*, was launched at the newly renovated New Amsterdam Theater supported by a stage show and publicized through an "Electrical Parade" down Fifth Avenue in New York. Other entertainment companies have converted popular video games into movies (*Mortal Kombat, Street Fighter*) and films have become the basis for popular theme park rides (*Back to the Future*).

A second way of creating value is to forge cross-business opportunities. Much to the consternation of traditionalist hockey fans, Disney named its Anaheim professional hockey team the "Mighty Ducks" in order to take advantage of the recognition which flowed from the two movies (a third is planned) of the same name.

A third set of synergistic opportunities occurs through the creation of new businesses. One high-profile example is Dreamworks SKG, a company formed by three well-known Hollywood figures: record mogul David Geffen, former Disney executive Jeffrey Katzenberg and film director/producer Steven Spielberg. Dreamworks SKG constitutes a multifaceted entertainment factory whose projects include television production, movies, recordings and "Gameworks," a chain of super-arcades stocked with virtual reality games and other high-tech attractions.

Most of what I have discussed so far has been a matter of "brand extension," transferring the cachet of one well-known brand to a line of further products. Synergies in urban entertainment districts also have a "value-added" component. As used by economists, value-added suggests that the sum of the whole is worth more than the individual parts. A new car, for example, is something more than just tires, bumpers and seat covers. In its more popular usage, value-added means annexing new components so as to enhance the appeal of a venue or facility. It is possible to find examples of both in Fantasy City.

In spring 1997, the entertainment conglomerate, Viacom Inc., opened its first Viacom Entertainment Store on the "Magnificent Mile" along Michigan Avenue in Chicago. At the grand opening benefit party, Viacom boss, Summer Redstone, acknowledged that "Viacom is not a household name," but suggested that by combining six of the company's high-profile brands – MTV, VH1, Nickelodeon, Nick at Nite, Paramount Pictures and *Star Trek* – a valuable synergy would be achieved which would raise the profile of the company as a whole. "It will be a powerful licensing tool," Redstone declared, "to help drive sales [of Viacom merchandise] in other retail outlets. This store represents a major step in a companywide initiative to drive merchandising revenues" (M. McCormick, 1997).

Illustrative of the second meaning of value-added is the proposed building of a $20 million, 295,000-square foot factory outlet center in Jackson Township, New Jersey. Located less than a mile from the Six Flags Great Adventure Theme Park, the fifty-store center with well-known fashion brands such as Gap, Calvin Klein, Donna Karan and London Fog will be called the Six Flags Outlet Center. Further synergies will be cultivated through joint advertising and promotional efforts and by providing a free shuttle-bus between the factory outlet mall and the theme park. Juxtaposing the two facilities, announced Arnold Laubich, president of New Plan Realty Trust, the project developer, "provides enough alternatives to make it well worth the trip and a longer stay" ("Outlet center opens" 1997).

A longer stay, in fact, is the goal of most UED developments. Previously, suburban shopping malls served as social centers for a cross-section of groups in the community. On his two-year journey across America in the early 1980s, William Kowinski (1985) talked to teenagers who spent all of their leisure time at the mall, young mothers who browsed, shopped and schmoozed there, and even "mall rats," people who do nothing but hang out at malls. A decade later, this situation had changed. Many of the baby-boomer mothers had re-entered the workforce and had less leisure time. Hit by the corporate downsizing of the early 1990s, consumers embraced the concept of "value retail" – brand-name goods at prices lower than those offered by department and specialty stores (Siegel, 1996, p. 29). Tired of the hassle of fighting traffic on the freeways or muggers in the parking lot, millions of consumers looked to other alternatives – at-home catalogue shopping, on-line computer services, cable television shopping channels. Between 1982 and 1992, the average time spent on a mall visit dropped from ninety minutes to seventy-two minutes (Morgenson, 1993, p. 107). With the growing popularity of stand-alone big box stores such as Home Depot and Price Club, a new in-and-out style of shopping was adopted. This had the effect of jolting retailers and developers into coming up with new strategies aimed at drawing consumers back to downtown and suburban malls and, once inside, keeping them there for longer. Entertainment has been widely touted as one way of achieving this aim, inspiring consumers to remain in the mall or store as long as possible.

Furthermore, value-added entertainment features are seen as necessary to attract a new breed of consumer who is hooked on fun. New York retail designer, Simon Graj, has observed that these customers shop as if they were sightseeing: "They're looking for and having the same kind of experiences that they would if they were on vacation or on a tour. . . . So if a retailer wants to sell product, they have to entertain you" (Kaplan, 1997, p. 74). With this requirement to provide entertaining experiences, retailers as well as restauranteurs, arena and stadium managers and, increasingly, educators and cultural institutions turn to leisure providers such as the producers of simulation and giant-screen attractions. Notes veteran amusement park designer and producer Jack Rouse (no relation to James): "Theming is about adding value" (Zoltak, 1997, p. 18).

Converging Consumer Activity Systems

This aggressively themed, value-added component of Fantasy City manifests itself in particular in the pace and degree of mutual convergence and overlap of four consumer activity systems: shopping, dining, entertainment, and education and culture. This has given rise to three new hybrids which in the lexicon of the retail industry are known as shopertainment, eatertainment and edutainment.

Shopertainment

As far back as the 1890s, the great metropolitan department stores set out to attract downtown customers by providing free entertainment. For example, Siegel-Cooper, which opened at Sixth Avenue and 18th Street in New York in 1896, earned its reputation as "the big store" by offering an orchestra, art shows, tearooms and "spectacular extravaganzas" in its auditorium. One summer, the store mounted a six-week long, "Carnival of Nations," which climaxed in the August with an exotic show, *Phantasma, The Enchanted Bower*, utilizing light and color effects to high-light a cast which included a Turkish harem, a parade of Turkish dancing girls, a "genie of the lamp" and, in an early example of time–space compression, "Cleopatra of the Nile" (Leach, 1993, p. 138). Not to be outdone, Marshall Fields opened its twelve-storey department store in Chicago in 1902 complete with six-string orches-tras on various floors (Magyar, 1997). In a similar fashion, McWhirters, a turn-of-the-century dry goods store in Brisbane, Australia, offered a fourth-floor tea room where tired shoppers could enjoy a cool sea breeze and a charming view of the river and suburbs. The opening of McWhirters' new premises in August 1931, was promoted with a series of three-hour entertainments which included a dancing demonstration by Phyl and Ray, Australia's leading adagio dancers, and a live revue advertising a leading brand of corset (Reekie, 1992, pp. 173–4).

Another way in which retail and entertainment activities converged during this era was through the spectacular electrical signage advertising both local and national businesses. Some of these displays were almost shows in themselves. In the summer of 1924, the highlight of Times Square was a three-storey bottle of Cliquot Club Ginger Ale which pictured a giant sleigh driven by a smiling Eskimo boy wrapped in white furs. With successive snaps of a six-foot whip, the boy prodded three com-panions to pull the sleigh and to retrieve the ginger ale which then set the name of the product flashing in the sky (Leach, 1993, p. 341). Twelve years later, the City Bank Farmer's Trust Building, which contained a theater and a vast nightclub, the International Casino, was crowned by a huge electronic sign featuring a fish blowing bubbles advertising Wrigley's Spearmint gum (Gray, 1997).

After the Second World War, suburban malls displaced downtown shopping districts as popular consumer destinations. At first, these shopping centers marketed themselves on the basis of easy automobile access and free parking. By the mid-1950s, however, mall developers rediscovered the appeal of turn-of-the-century department stores, transforming indoor spaces into theatrical "sets" in which a form of retail drama could occur (Crawford, 1992, p. 22). The template for this new generation of enclosed malls was Southdale in Edina, Minnesota, a suburb of Minneapolis. Built by Victor Gruen, an Austrian urban architect who admired the covered pedestrian arcades in Europe, Southdale had as its focal point the "Garden Court of Perpetual Spring," an atrium filled with orchids, azaleas, magnolias and palms which bloomed even in the midst of the deep freeze of Minnesota winters. Enclosed malls like these increasingly took on a leisure role, playing host to movie theaters, restaurants, fashion shows, symphony concerts and high-school proms and other such public activities. Over time, however, these entertainment elements became routine; "the formula," complained Cesar Pelli, a renowned architect who was once a Gruen design partner, "is trite and everyone has learned how to reduce it to a minimum" (Kowinski, 1985, p. 123).

In contrast, the West Edmonton Mall (WEM) in Alberta, Canada, could never be accused of minimalism, the largest shopping center in the world to date. Its developers, the Ghermezian brothers, explicitly and ostentatiously set out to bring the world of the theme park to the environment of the shopping center. Among other things, WEM contains a 15-acre amusement park, a 10-acre water park, a full-size ice-skating rink, the Fantasyland Hotel, a faux version of Bourbon Street in New Orleans, and a 2.5 acre artificial lagoon complete with a replica of Christopher Columbus' ship, the *Santa Maria*, several mini submarines and electronically operated rubber sharks. Built in the early 1980s, the West Edmonton Mall is a bizarre almagamation of shopping, entertainment and social space. As Shields (1989, p. 158) has observed, WEM "is a world where Spanish galleons sail up Main Street past Marks and Spencer to put in at 'New Orleans.'" West Edmonton Mall also radically changed the shopping center formula, boosting the footage dedicated to entertainment up to 40 percent, the largest proportion up to that time in a suburban mall. Seven years later, the Ghermezians succeeded in cloning WEM with their first American project, the Mall of America in Bloomington. The centerpiece of the Mall of America is "Camp Snoopy," an amusement park.

Retail and entertainment further dovetailed in the festival market places of the 1970s and 1980s. In contrast to mega-malls such as those in Edmonton and Bloomington, the two activity systems here were not just juxtapositioned but merged. The shopping and dining experiences constituted the entertainment in a visual environment which projected an aura of historic preservation. In case consumer interest flagged, stand-alone cultural and entertainment attractions such as science museums and aquariums were positioned in close proximity, frequently along the urban waterfront.

In the theme park cities of the 1990s, shopping, fantasy and fun have further bonded in a number of ways. As Margaret Crawford has observed, the two activities have become part of the same loop: shopping has become intensely entertaining and this in turn encourages more shopping. Furthermore, theme parks themselves have begun to function as "disguised market places" (1992, p. 16). This convergence is described as "shopertainment," a term also used to describe the cable television shopping channels which feature Ivana Trump, among others, selling an array of mail-order merchandise.

One form of shopertainment is the themed retail experience known as "experiential retailing." This is represented by Nike Town, a retail theater showcase in New York. Opened in November 1996, on the site of the former Les Galeries Lafayette,

Nike's flagship store is "a fantasy environment, one part nostalgia to two parts high-tech, and it exists to bedazzle the customer, to give its merchandise sex appeal and establish Nike as the essence not just of athletic wear but also of our culture and way of life" (Goldberger, 1997, p. 45). According to its creative director, John Hoke III, the store is designed like a ship in a bottle. The bottle in question is a simulated, old-style gymnasium made to look as if it was built in the 1930s or 1940s. This sense of age is created on the exterior through an arched limestone and sandstone façade with the numbers PS 6453 added, a reference to a time when boxers trained in the gym of the local public school. Inside, the old gym theme is continued with aged brick detail, wooden sports flooring, wireglass windows, gym clocks, wrestling mats and "authentic" bleachers reclaimed from a gym on Long Island.

The ship which is dropped into this old gym bottle is a high-tech cross between a store, a museum and a media experience. The latter is represented by a multi-media show which combines video projection, theatrical lighting and sound design, retractable screens, and a sophisticated motion-and-show control system with which to show Nike mini-films celebrating the spirit of sports. In addition, the lobby is decorated with a giant elliptical media wall on to which the multi-media show is projected at regular intervals. Scattered throughout the four levels are screen bays where one can view a rotating series of short films about sports and sporting events, and banks of video monitors placed directly beneath which give the latest scores and other information in ticker-tape style. The museum aspect is represented by scattered exhibitions, showcases displaying sports trophies and memorabilia and a Nike shoe museum with 400 pairs of shoes which have been gathered over the years. The retail element of the store is more muted: one can buy Nike products at Nike Town but the store exists primarily to promote brand recognition.

There are other Nike Town stores in Portland, Seattle, Chicago, Atlanta and Los Angeles but the New York location best epitomizes the retail theater of the future. The production lighting and sound systems are highly sophisticated. The principal lighting designer counts among her credits Disney's Broadway production of *Beauty and the Beast* and EFx in Las Vegas. The show control system is similar to that employed at the T23D attraction at Universal Studios Florida. The chief sound designer worked on the show *Quidam*, staged by Cirque du Soleil, the Quebec circus troupe who have permanent shows running at the Treasure Island hotel in Las Vegas and at Disney World in Florida. Clearly then the best of Fantasy City entertainment technologies and design are incorporated in the service of retail programming.

Combining the same themes of nostalgia and interactivity is the 300,000 square foot, two-level Viacom Entertainment store in Chicago. Scattered throughout the store are thirty interactive stations or "experiential hooks" at which customers can morph the Nickelodeon Welcome Totem into the cable network's logo, send the logo spinning, respond via computer to an MTV poll or be "transported" from the Starship Enterprise using green-screen technology. Juxtaposing these stations are a number of props and activities which celebrate the golden past of television and motion pictures: the entrance way to the Nick at Nite area is designed as a 1950s living room, and the "Paramount Flip Book" recreates brief physical performances by visitors in a style reminiscent of the early movies (Muret, 1997).

Less technologically elaborate but more brazenly commercial are the ubiquitous, yet successful, Disney and Warner Bros. stores. Of these, Disney is the largest with

530 retail outlets spread over eleven countries, but Warner Bros. is said to have a greater appeal to adults who regard Bugs Bunny and other Warner Bros. cartoon characters as having a funkier image than their Disney equivalents. The Disney and Warner Bros. outlets are closer to traditional retail stores than Nike Town and the Viacom Entertainment Store, with television monitors dotted throughout the clothing and souvenir displays continually showing cartoons, film clips and promotional material. In addition, these stores explicitly target on-the-spot sales to tourists who are looking to bring home a branded memory.

In the late 1990s, Disney has opened a new chapter in shopertainment with the debut of its 50,000-square foot World of Disney megastore in the Disney Village Market place in Orlando. In contrast to the smaller downtown and shopping mall stores, World of Disney is organized into a series of themed rooms (the Villain's Room, the Enchanted Dining Room) radiating from a central display area. It offers an astounding array of products from flavored "Polynesian" salad dressing to a set of silk Mickey Mouse pajamas. If successful, it is envisaged that the World of Disney will be rolled out to strategic markets across the globe (Tippit, 1996).

Eatertainment

A second synapse of consumer activity systems in the city is "eatertainment" in which the former boundaries between eating and play are collapsed and recast into something new. The act of eating, notes David Altheide (1997, p. 21), becomes "eventful in many senses of the word," even to the extent that the food itself may become secondary to the amusement experience. Dining and entertainment, of course, have always been closely linked, from the time of medieval banquets with jugglers and bards to modern-day supper clubs with big-name Hollywood entertainment. One of the most popular and participatory forms has been the neighborhood diner with a jukebox in every booth. Indeed, the presentation and consumption of food is itself often a setting for entertaining displays: these can range from the pyrotechnics of the server flambéing a boozy dessert at the diners' table to the Benihana of Tokyo (a Japanese restaurant chain) chef who presents a dazzling display of swordmanship in dicing chicken and beef on the counter in front of restaurant patrons. This synergy between the two activities has reached its zenith, however, in the fashion for themed restaurants.

Themed restaurants

A combination of amusement park, diner, souvenir stand and museum, themed restaurants are projected to be a $5 billion business by the year 2000 (Angelo 1996). Most of the first generation of themed restaurants gross upwards of $10 million per year in revenue with several, notably the Planet Hollywood units at Disney World and the Forum Shops, grossing a record $45 million and $35 million respectively.

Themed restaurants, however, are not a recent phenomenon. *Amusement Business* publisher Karen Oertley (1996), remembers going as a child to a restaurant called the Hamburger Express where your meal was delivered to you from the kitchen on the flat car of a tooting, puffing, model train. When I was in graduate school in the mid-1970s, the place for celebrating a special event in Columbus, Ohio was the Kahiki, a Polynesian-themed eatery with exotic fish, a waterfall and various generic artifacts that suggested the South Seas via Hollywood.

The Hard Rock Cafe   The present generation of themed restaurants can trace their origins back to 1971 when Peter Morton and Isaac Tigrett, two footloose 22-year-olds from wealthy American families, created the Hard Rock concept in London. By most accounts, the Hard Rock's success was as much serendipity as it was strategic planning. When rock legend Eric Clapton's guitar was mounted on a hook on the café's wall, fellow pop star Pete Townshend of The Who insisted that his guitar join Clapton's, penning a note which read "Mine's as good as his." This initiated one of the Hard Rock's most distinctive features, its rock memorabilia collection, now centrally supplied from a warehouse in Orlando and rotated between venues at regular intervals. During the first few years, Tigrett and Morton moved into merchandising offering shirts, hats, watches and coffee mugs displaying the Hard Rock logo, items which contributed significantly to the company's revenue (Covell, 1996, p. 228). These items were popular with tourists because it allowed them to return home with the evidence that, not only had they gone to Europe, but that they had gone somewhere fashionable. Indeed, in its twelve years, the Hard Rock Cafe was primarily an outpost for American rock and roll culture abroad, complete with hamburgers, ribs and apple pie. It was also a magnet for celebrities from the entertainment world: Steven Spielberg, for example, reputedly ate lunch there every day during the filming of *Raiders of the Lost Ark*.

In 1982, the Hard Rock brought its concept to the USA, opening an outlet in Los Angeles. Among its financial backers were a handful of celebrities including Spielberg. This was the genesis of the concept of celebrity investors which has since been perfected by rival restaurants Planet Hollywood and the Official All Star Cafe. A year later, however, the co-founders who had been feuding for several years finally fell out and went their separate ways. As part of the corporate divorce, the world was divided with Morton's territory including the US from Chicago westwards, Israel, Australia and Brazil, and Tigrett's receiving the rest. Tigrett, a noted eccentric and follower of the Indian guru, Sai Baba, subsequently sold his stake to restauranteur Robert Earl in 1988 for $100 million. After a stormy five years, Earl, who had gone on to open Planet Hollywood, sold his shares to minority partner, British entertainment conglomerate Rank Organisation, leaving Rank with fifteen fully owned Hard Rock Cafes and twenty-six franchised units while Morton's company owned thirteen restaurants and oversaw four franchised outlets. In 1996, the Hard Rock Cafe empire was united again when Rank acquired Morton's share for $410 million. As part of the deal, Morton retained the right to license the Hard Rock Cafe name for the casino business in his former territory, having successfully marketed the concept in Las Vegas with the first Hard Rock Hotel and Casino (Orwall, 1996a).

Planet Hollywood   Inspired by an idea originally put forward in 1989 by film producer Keith Barrish for a restaurant called the Hollywood Cafe, Robert Earl opened the first Planet Hollywood in New York in 1991, one block away from the

New York Hard Rock Cafe. Instead of rock and roll, Earl and Barrish, working with Anton Furst, the set designer on the first *Batman* movie, decorated their restaurants with costumes and props from Hollywood movies. Although celebrities such as Henry Winkler, Willie Nelson and John Denver had invested in Morton's Hard Rock Cafe in Los Angeles, their involvement had been largely passive and their appearances at the restaurant informal. Earl deliberately courted celebrities such as Bruce Willis, Demi Moore, Arnold Schwarzenegger and Sylvester Stallone, convincing them to become investors and make scheduled live appearances. By November 1995, Planet Hollywood had expanded into a chain of twenty-eight restaurants: twenty-one in the US and seven overseas. Collectively, the chain grossed $270.6 million in 1995 (Levine, 1995, p. 184). Today their sites include New York, the Mall of America, the Forum Shops and Walt Disney World. In July 1997, Planet Hollywood announced a joint venture with AMC Entertainment Inc., a major operator of megaplex theaters. Together, the two companies plan to develop eight to ten "Planet Movies by AMC" complexes by the end of the millennium, and a further five to ten a year after that. Within the complexes, customers will be able to watch movies, eat at restaurants with movie themes and shop in stores selling movie-related merchandise ("Planet Hollywood and AMC in venture" 1997).

More than any other commercial player in Fantasy City, with the exception may be of Disney, Planet Hollywood has managed to ingratiate itself into the celebrity-soaked, media-purveyed public life of America. When American gymnast, Kerri Strug, achieved her fifteen minutes of fame in Atlanta by maintaining her landing despite a ripped left ankle ligament, it was not long before her Olympic leotard ended up on display in Planet Hollywood, San Diego (Friend, 1996).

Rainforest Cafe   The final member of the triumvirate of themed restaurant chains is the Rainforest Cafe. The brainchild of former nightclub owner, Steven Schussler, the Rainforest Cafe recreated the tropics in the Mall of America in Bloomington, Minnesota, complete with live parrots, mechanized birds and monkeys, a 20-foot high fiberglass giraffe, and fake thunder and lightning which can be heard every seventeen minutes. If the biology of the rainforest was not entirely accurate, Schussler's business sense was. The company's stock climbed from $6 a share at its initial public offering (IPO) in April 1995 to $22 in October, and by 1 July 1996 it had risen 700 percent before splitting three for two (Angelo, 1996). Its market capitalization now stands at roughly $450 million, with each café costing around $7 million to open (Damsell, 1997). Flush with the proceeds of its IPO, the company moved forward to open further restaurants at the Woodfield Mall, south of Chicago, Disney World in Orlando, the Gunnie Mill Mall (Illinois), Tyson's Corner mega-mall in McLean, Virginia and in the Stratosphere Tower in Las Vegas, following a marketing strategy of locating in the first or second highest ranked tourist attraction in each state (O'Brien, 1996a). In April 1997, Rainforest Cafe, Inc. announced a newly forged partnership with the Elephant & Castle Group, a Canadian company which operates British-style pub restaurants. A further six Rainforest Cafes are slated to open across Canada by the end of 1998 (Damsell, 1997).

Other themed restaurants   With the success of Planet Hollywood, the Hardrock Cafe and the Rainforest Cafe, the floodgates are opening to a tidal wave of new themed eateries. With a host of superstar athletes as partners (Shaquille O'Neal, Andre Agassi, Wayne Gretsky, Joe Montana, Ken Griffey Jr., Monica Seles), Robert Earl has gone on to open a 650-seat sports-themed restaurant, the Official All Star Cafe in Times Square and is initiating the concept elsewhere. He has further plans to launch a Marvel Mania chain themed around the popular comic superheroes and villains, in partnership with financier Ronald Perelman, formerly Marvel's controlling shareholder. Under the guidance of veteran developer and restaurant designer Larry Levy, Steven Spielberg, Jeffrey Katzenberg and Mirage Resorts chairman Steve Wynn have created The Dive, a nautically-themed restaurant which gives the impression of being underwater in a submarine. At present, The Dive has venues in Los Angeles, Barcelona and adjacent to the Fashion Mall in Las Vegas. Disney has joined forces with illusionist David Copperfield to build a chain of magic-themed restaurants called Copperfield's Magic Underground; the first two sites are due to open at the Walt Disney World Resort in Orlando and at the corner of Broadway and 49th Street in New York. The five-level Manhattan venue is to include a 430-seat restaurant with levitating tables and disappearing diners, a 2,000-square-foot magic retail shop, and even a well-marked "secret entry" ("Presto!", 1997). Other putative chains are themed around racecars (NASCAR Cafe, Race Rock) and motorcycles (Harley Davidson Cafe); soul music (Motown Cafe), 1950s music (Dick Clark's American Bandstand Grill) and country and western music (Country Star, Wildhorse Saloon); fashion (Fashion Cafe) and entertainment (Billboard Live).

Perhaps the most unusual establishment is the Jekyll and Hyde Club in Manhattan. As its name suggests, the theme is horror – four floors of it. Acting on a suggestion by staff from Walt Disney Imagineering who were dining at his pub, The Slaughtered Lamb, D. R. Finley, together with project designer Dan Hoffman, spent several years building what they intended to be the first fully fledged theme park restaurant. The Jekyll and Hyde Club has in residence a talking gargoyle and sphinx, animatronic musicians, Femur and Patella, and a Frankenstein act with a monster who descends from the roof of the club to the first-floor grand salon on a slab amid billowing clouds of dry ice (Cashill, 1996).

In contrast to UEDs in general, themed eateries aim at a slightly younger clientele – 16–35-year-olds. These restaurants, notes Art Carlson, an executive with the Dick Clark's chain, reflect the MTV generation where restaurant patrons not only eat out to enjoy the food but also expect to be bombarded with free entertainment (O'Brien, 1996b). This expectation is further enhanced when the themed restaurant is an integrated component of the food service in a theme park or urban entertainment destination – for example, the new 13,000-square-foot ESPN World at Disney's Boardwalk which includes a restaurant, broadcast center, sports bar and interactive sports arcade.

Themed eateries also differ from some other UED components in that they are seen by their owners as being compatible with casino gaming. Peter Morton is explicitly aiming to use his Hard Rock Hotel and Casino operations to attract a younger segment of the gambling market (Orwall, 1996b). Two Planet Hollywood casino hotels bankrolled by ITT, the parent of Caesar's Palace, are on the drawing board. The Rainforest Cafe has not yet announced plans to open a casino, but its largest shareholder is Lyle Berman, chairman of Grand Casinos, Inc.

Meanwhile, there is considerable concern in the hospitality industry that the themed restaurant market will eventually become saturated. "By the year 2000," warns Steve Routhier, vice-president of marketing for the Hard Rock Cafe, "the highway will be littered with themed restaurants gone awry" (O'Brien, 1996a, p. 3). Already we are seeing some evidence of this with many of the second generation restaurants finding it difficult to recreate the sense of excitement and the iconic status of the Hard Rock and Planet Hollywood. The Fashion Cafe is said to be dying; The Dive has been slow to catch on and even The Jekyll and Hyde Club has not attracted the crowds at its Village location in Manhattan that it has in midtown (Zoltak, 1997, p. 26).

Edutainment

A third location for converging consumer activity systems is in "edutainment" – the joining together of educational and cultural activities with the commerce and technology of the entertainment world. The notion that "learning is fun" has achieved almost canon-like status, and can be seen in evidence from the animated performing letters and numbers on *Sesame Street* to the laser-rock star shows in urban planetariums. Nowhere has this edutainment trend been more prolific than in the area of museums.

In the first decades of the twentieth century, the great museums in American cities were transformed from institutions which were seen as inaccessible to ordinary people, to become part and parcel of urban industrial life. Spearheading this alliance between museums and business was a new cohort of curators – Morris D'Camp Crawford (American Museum of Natural History), Stewart Culin (Brooklyn Museum), John Cotton Dana (Newark Museum) – all of whom imitated Fifth Avenue display strategies in their exhibits and offered their museum facilities to industrial designers from all walks of business (Leach, 1993, pp. 164–73).

At the same time, museums also began to make an effort to become more entertaining as well as educational. Displays became more sophisticated as collections were interpreted around distinct historical and cultural themes. Among the devices used to enliven exhibitions were period rooms, natural habitats, dioramas and live demonstrations (Glaser with Zenetou, 1996, p. 18). Museums in Fantasy City have taken this a stage further. They employ "new media, new techniques of interactivity and new styles which have more in common with the funfair or theatre than with a traditional museum" (Macdonald, 1996, p. 2). This is not accidental. The overwhelming commercial success of Disney theme parks in the 1970s and 1980s was recognized by museum directors and curators, many of whom have chosen to look to a winning formula to enhance their own marketability. As the commercial coordinator of a British history museum has been quoted as saying, "we're a family fun day out, not a stuffy museum – you can't afford not to be these days" (Wolfram, 1997).

What can museums learn from theme parks? On one level this can be seen as simply a case of museums needing to catch-up by adopting whiz-bang theme park technologies such as advanced audio-animatronics. EPCOT, Neil Postman (1991) notes, is "so to speak, the world's largest animated diorama," which suggests that the Disney imagineers have simply scooped their museum colleagues by updating and expanding a technology which was originally the province of the latter.

There may, however, be another sociocultural dimension to consider. Margaret King, a cultural analyst who once served as Development Director of the Please Touch Museum in Philadelphia, views the relationship between theme parks and museums as essentially "a question about the dynamics of and between education, entertainment and acculturation" (1991, p. 7). Theme parks, King suggests, attract customers because they offer a form of stability in a world where change has accelerated at a rapid pace (p. 8). By contrast, museums have tended to actively embrace change, mounting shows that attempt to reach out to diverse sections of the community. Or, to put it more bluntly, theme parks present a nostalgic vision of Main Street USA for affluent WASP visitors while museums try to promote cultural understanding of minority populations whose stories have heretofore been given short shrift.

In such situations, public museums often find themselves in a bind. Tourists, by and large, prefer romanticized and fictional representations of history and geography, even if these are distortions which are rife with postmodern currents of time–space compression. Museum programmers, on the other hand, take their educational role seriously, striving to reflect accurately local communities in time and space. Julia Harrison (1997) highlights this dilemma in her case study of the Bishop Museum of Ethnology in Hawaii. Faced with market competition from the Polynesian Culture Center theme park, the largest single attraction in the Islands, the Bishop Museum has attempted to broaden its appeal to a wider audience while at the same challenging "trivialized glosses" held by many tourists of what constitutes the local community and experience (1997, p. 36). Harrison argues that tourists are more open to the presentation of a distinctive "localness" than is generally assumed, especially if this is packaged using a wide range of high-tech media. So far, however, the Hawaii of the Polynesian Cultural Center and the Aloha Center festival market place seems to be winning.

With many other museums, however, the line between education and entertainment has blurred to the extent that it is difficult to know which is paramount. As a tie-in to the release of the blockbuster film *Jurrasic Park* in 1993, the Museum of Natural History in New York mounted an exhibition called "The Science of Jurassic Park" featuring movie robots and models. The sequel, *The Lost World*, was matched by another exhibit at the Museum – "The Lost World: The Life and Death of Dinosaurs" – which included dinosaur replicas contributed by Steven Spielberg's production company and a videotaped tour featuring actor Jeff Goldblum, who played a scientist in the movie, as one of the narrators. At times, it seemed "more like a movie set than a museum hall" (Gill, 1997, p. C-2), although the Museum, somewhat disingenuously defended the mix as helping visitors "distinguish fiction from reality" (Newborne, 1997, p. 94).

Science museums and space centers have also been embracing edutainment for some time. Blazing the trail was the Exploratorium, housed in the Palace of Fine Arts building in the Marina district of San Francisco. Founded in 1969, the Exploratorium, followed soon after by the Ontario Science Centre in Toronto, was one of the first museums to adopt an interactive, "hands-on" approach to science education. Another leader has been NASA's Johnson Space Center in Houston, Texas, which offers the audience both a simulated space flight experience and a chance to go behind the scenes and discover how things work. On the East Coast of Florida, the Kennedy Space Center Visitor Center attracted 2.5 million visitors in 1996. The newest attraction at the Kennedy Center is the Apollo/Saturn V Center which covers an area the size of the National Air and Space Museum in Washington, DC. Designed by Bob Rogers' company, BRC Imagination Arts, the presentation uses a historical storyline and theatrical effects to instruct visitors about the Apollo program. As the simulated flight begins in the Firing Room Theater, "the lights change, a rumble can be heard, and the room shakes just as it did during the real launch" (O'Brien, 1997). Also of note is the Pacific Space Centre in Vancouver, which is opening a new theater using a seventy-seat simulator and software package developed by SimEx Inc., a Toronto company which developed the Tour of the Universe Attraction at the CN Tower in Toronto in 1984. The Centre plans to show SimEx's "Virtual Voyages," a series of science speculation films.

If any one thing can be said to represent an obstacle for the advancement of public museums toward becoming full-scale entertainment destinations, it is the economics of edutainment. To deliver a level of technological sophistication equal to that of the theme parks, museums would have to charge theme park admission prices. There are several problems with this, not least of which is their present dependence on school tours which cannot afford to bear the higher tariff. One well-known big city museum recently commissioned plans from a theme park designer for a stunning, futuristic, high-tech makeover but has had to put the project on hold because of this dilemma.

One possibility is for museums and science centers to become privately operated institutions. In a sense this has already happened with the success of facilities such as EPCOT and the Rock and Roll Hall of Fame. In what is perhaps the Rolls Royce of simulated experiences, a private company, Casey Aerospace Corporation is poised to build a $50 million space station center in Orlando. For a fee of $10,000, would-be astronauts receive space flight education, experience weightlessness in a specially equipped aircraft, watch an IMAX film which shows the visual impact of space flight, and, to remember the experience, take home a videotape of their adventure together with a personal astronaut-style flight suit ("Next step: the space station" 1997). At this price, only a very special niche market is targeted, but it does suggest that in Fantasy City there will be increasing competition between the private and public sectors for the attention and dollars of tourists and other visitors.

REFERENCES

Altheide, D. 1997: "Media participation in everyday life." *Leisure Sciences* 19 (1): 17–29.

Angelo, B. 1996: "Hungary for theme dining." *Time*, 22 July: 30–2.

Bryman, A. 1995: *Disney and his Worlds*. London and New York: Routledge.

Cashill, R. 1996: "Jekyll & Hyde: Theatre vets cook up drop-dead Manhattan dining." *TCI (Theatre Crafts International)*. 30 (2): 44–7.

Covell, J. 1996: "Hard Rock Café International." In T. Grant (ed.). *International Directory of Company Histories*. Volume 12. Detroit MI and London: St. James Press.

Crawford, M. 1992: "The world in a shopping mall." In M. Sorkin (ed.). *Variations on a Theme Park*. New York: Hill and Wang.

Damsell, K. 1997: "Eateries hope to serve steady diet of profit." *The Financial Post*, 22 August: 18.

Fabrikant, G. 1997: "Of all that he sells, he sells himself best." *New York Times*, 1 June: 3–1.

Featherstone, M. 1995: *Globalization, Postmodernism and Identity*. London: Sage Publications.

Friend, T. 1996: "Strug vaults straight into life of fame." *New York Times*, 6 September: B – 17; 19.

Gelsi, S. 1997: "Sony's showcase at sea." *Brandweek* 3 February: 20–1

Gill, A. 1997: "Pop goes the highbrow cultural institution." *Globe & Mail*, 13 June: C-1, 2.

Glaser, J. (with A. A. Zenetou). 1996: *Museums: A Place to Work*. London and New York: Routledge/ Smithsonian Institution.

Gleick, E. 1997: "Tower of psychobabble." *Time*, 16 June: 59–61.

Goldberger, P. 1997: "The store strikes back." *New York Times Magazine*, 6 April: 45–9.

Gottdiener, M. 1997: *The Theming of America: Dreams, Visions, and Commercial Space*. Boulder, CO: Westview Press.

Gray, C. 1997: "When a big waterfall was a sign of Times Square." *New York Times*, 30 March: 9–5.

Harrison, J. 1997: "Museums and touristic expectations." *Annals of Tourism Research* 24 (1): 23–40.

Kaplan, D. 1997: "Music biz sees inspiration in experimental retailing." *Billboard*, 17 May: 1; 74.

King, M. 1991: "Never Land or Tomorrowland?" *Museum* 169 (1): 6–8.

Koselka, R. 1995: "Mergermania in medialand." (An interview with Michael J. Wolf). *Forbes*, 23 October: 252–9.

Kowinski, W. 1985: *The Malling of America*. New York: William Morris and Company.

Leach, W. 1993: *Land of Desire: Merchants, Power and the Rise of a New American Culture*. New York: Pantheon Books.

Levine, J. 1995: "Hamburgers and tennis socks." *Forbes*, 20 November: 184–5.

McCormick, M. 1997: "Viacom's flagship store opens." *Billboard*, 7 June: 67–8.

MacDonald, S. 1996: "Theorizing museums: An introduction." In S. Macdonald and G. Fyfe (eds.). *Theorizing Museums*. Oxford, England and Cambridge, MA: Blackwell Publishers/ The Sociological Review.

Magyar, L. F. 1997: "Back to the future: A Century of Selling." (Boxed insert) in "The store strikes back." *New York Times Magazine*, 6 April: 45–9.

Morgenson, G. 1993: "The fall of the mall." *Forbes*, 24 May: 106–12.

Muret, D. 1997: "Interactive Viacom Entertainment Store merges six of its most popular brands." *Amusement Business*, 9 June: 5.

Nasaw, D. 1993: *Going Out: The Rise and Fall of Public Amusements*. New York: Harper Collins.

Newborne, E. 1997: "This exhibit is brought to you by…" *Business Week*, 10 November: 91, 94.

"Next Step: the space station." (1997) *The E Zone* 1 (5): 4.

O'Brien, T. 1996a: "Themed eateries thriving on crowds of others, but how long will it last." *Amusement Business*, 4 March; 2–3; 38.

O'Brien, T. 1996b: "Themed eateries hit big time." *Amusement Business*, 13 May: 15–16.

O'Brien, T. 1997: "Kennedy Space Center Visitor Center predicts 10% increase in attendance." *Amusement Business*, 31 March: 34.

Oertley, K. 1996: "I theme, you theme, we all theme." *Amusement Business*, 8–14 April: 2.

Orwall, B. 1996a: "Hard Rock Café empire to be reunited as Morton plans to sell his half to Rank." *Wall Street Journal*, 10 June: B-8.

Orwall, B. 1996b: "Rank Organization and Trump Hotels to develop Hard Rock Café at casinos." *Wall Street Journal*, 3 October: A-4

"Outlet Center Opens near 6 Flags Park." (1997) *New York Times*, 4 May: 9–1.

Palen, J. J. 1995: *The Suburbs*. New York: McGraw-Hill, Inc.

"Planet Hollywood and AMC in venture." (1997) *New York Times*, 25 July: C-5.

Postman, N. 1985: *Amusing Ourselves to Death*. New York: Viking.

Postman, N. 1991: "Love your machines." *Museum* 169 (1): 9.

"Presto! A David Copperfield magic restaurant." (1997) *The New York Times*, 13 July: 9–1.

Purcell, K. 1997: "Review of Gottdiener (1997)." *Community and Urban Sociology Section Newsletter* (American Sociological Association), 25 (3): 12.

Reekie, G. 1992: "Changes in the Adamless Eden: The spatial and sexual transformation of a Brisbane department store 1930–90." In R. Shields (ed.). *Lifestyle Shopping: The Subject of Consumption*. London and New York: Routledge.

Ritzer, G. 1993: *The McDonaldization of Society*. Thousand Oaks, CA: Pine Forge Press.

Rowe, P. G. 1991: *Making a Middle Landscape*. Cambridge MA: The MIT Press.

Shields, R. 1989: "Social spatialization and built environment: The West Edmonton Mall." *Environment and Planning D: Society and Space*. 7: 147–64.

Siegel, L. C. 1996: "The changing face of value retail." *Urban Land* 55 (5): 29–32; 58–9.

Tippit, S. 1996: "Mickey's Megastore." *The Financial Post*, 5 October: 12.

Veblen, T. 1925: *The Theory of the Leisure Class*. London: Allen & Unwin.

Wolfram, J. 1997: "CultureBoom." *The E Zone* 1 (5): 6.

Zoltak, J. 1997: "Sports, trade shows and education on forefront of theming trends." *Amusement Business*, 9 June: 17–18; 25–6.

15

Whose Culture? Whose City?*

Sharon Zukin

Cities are often criticized because they represent the basest instincts of human society. They are built versions of Leviathan and Mammon, mapping the power of the bureaucratic machine or the social pressures of money. We who live in cities like to think of "culture" as the antidote to this crass vision. The Acropolis of the urban art museum or concert hall, the trendy art gallery and café, restaurants that fuse ethnic traditions into culinary logos – cultural activities are supposed to lift us out of the mire of our everyday lives and into the sacred spaces of ritualized pleasures.[1]

Yet culture is also a powerful means of controlling cities. As a source of images and memories, it symbolizes "who belongs" in specific places. As a set of architectural themes, it plays a leading role in urban redevelopment strategies based on historic preservation or local "heritage." With the disappearance of local manufacturing industries and periodic crises in government and finance, culture is more and more the business of cities – the basis of their tourist attractions and their unique, competitive edge. The growth of cultural consumption (of art, food, fashion, music, tourism) and the industries that cater to it fuels the city's symbolic economy, its visible ability to produce both symbols and space.

In recent years, culture has also become a more explicit site of conflicts over social differences and urban fears. Large numbers of new immigrants and ethnic minorities have put pressure on public institutions, from schools to political parties, to deal with their individual demands. Such high culture institutions as art museums and symphony orchestras have been driven to expand and diversify their offerings to appeal to a broader public. These pressures, broadly speaking, are both ethnic and aesthetic. By creating policies and ideologies of "multiculturalism," they have forced public institutions to change.

* Zukin, Sharon (1995) "Whose Culture? Whose City?" from *The Culture of Cities*, Blackwell Publishers, Oxford, pp. 1–45.

On a different level, city boosters increasingly compete for tourist dollars and financial investments by bolstering the city's image as a center of cultural innovation, including restaurants, avant garde performances, and architectural design. These cultural strategies of redevelopment have fewer critics than multiculturalism. But they often pit the self-interest of real estate developers, politicians, and expansion-minded cultural institutions against grassroots pressures from local communities.

At the same time, strangers mingling in public space and fears of violent crime have inspired the growth of private police forces, gated and barred communities, and a movement to design public spaces for maximum surveillance. These, too, are a source of contemporary urban culture. If one way of dealing with the material inequalities of city life has been to aestheticize diversity, another way has been to aestheticize fear.

Controlling the various cultures of cities suggests the possibility of controlling all sorts of urban ills, from violence and hate crime to economic decline. That this is an illusion has been amply shown by battles over multiculturalism and its warring factions – ethnic politics and urban riots. Yet the cultural power to create an image, to frame a vision, of the city has become more important as publics have become more mobile and diverse, and traditional institutions – both social classes and political parties – have become less relevant mechanisms of expressing identity. Those who create images stamp a collective identity. Whether they are media corporations like the Disney Company, art museums, or politicians, they are developing new spaces for public cultures. Significant public spaces of the late 19th and early 20th century – such as Central Park, the Broadway theater district, and the top of the Empire State Building – have been joined by Disney World, Bryant Park, and the entertainment-based retail shops of Sony Plaza. By accepting these spaces without questioning their representations of urban life, we risk succumbing to a visually seductive, privatized public culture.

The Symbolic Economy

Anyone who walks through midtown Manhattan comes face-to-face with the symbolic economy (see Figure 15.1). A significant number of new public spaces owe their particular shape and form to the intertwining of cultural symbols and entrepreneurial capital.

- The AT&T Building, whose Chippendale roof was a much criticized icon of postmodern architecture, has been sold to the Japanese entertainment giant Sony; the formerly open public areas at street level have been enclosed as retail stores and transformed into Sony Plaza. Each store sells Sony products: video cameras in one shop, clothes and accessories related to performers under contract to Sony's music or film division in another. Sony's interactive science museum features the opportunity to get hands-on experience with Sony video equipment. Sony had to get the city government's approval both to enclose these stores and set them up for retail shopping, for the original agreement to build the office tower had depended on providing *public* space. Critics charged that retail

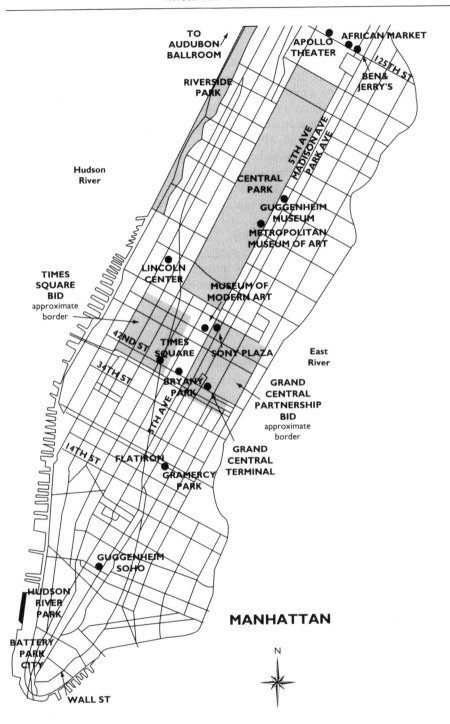

Figure 15.1 Manhattan

Note: A selective view of Manhattan's symbolic economy: Downtown financial district, parks, art museums, midtown business improvement districts and African market.

stores are not public space, and even the city planning commissioners admitted they were perplexed by the question (AIA Forum, "Sony Plaza: Public Space or Corporate Face," May 1994). "In return for the retail space," the chairman of the local community board said, "we would like to hold Sony to the original understanding to create a peaceful refuge, which certainly didn't include corporate banners and a television monitor." "We like it," the president of Sony Plaza replied. The banners "are seen as art and bring warmth and color to the space" (*New York Times*, January 30, 1994).

- Two blocks away, André Emmerich, a leading contemporary art dealer, rented an empty storefront in a former bank branch to show three huge abstract canvases by the painter Al Held. Entitled *Harry, If I Told You, Would You Know?*, the group of paintings was exhibited in raw space, amid falling plaster, peeling paint, exposed wires, and unfinished floors, and passersby viewed the exhibit from the street through large plate glass windows. The work of art was certainly for sale, yet it was displayed as if it were a free, public good; and it would never have been there had the storefront been rented by a more usual commercial tenant.

- On 42nd Street, across from my office, Bryant Park is considered one of the most successful public spaces to be created in New York City in recent years. After a period of decline, disuse, and daily occupation by vagrants and drug dealers, the park was taken over by a not-for-profit business association of local property owners and their major corporate tenants, called the Bryant Park Restoration Corporation. This group redesigned the park and organized daylong programs of cultural events; they renovated the kiosks and installed new food services; they hired a phalanx of private security guards. All this attracted nearby office workers, both women and men, who make the park a lively midday gathering place, as it had been prior to the mid 1970s – a public park under private control.

Building a city depends on how people combine the traditional economic factors of land, labor, and capital. But it also depends on how they manipulate symbolic languages of exclusion and entitlement. The look and feel of cities reflect decisions about what – and who – should be visible and what should not, on concepts of order and disorder, and on uses of aesthetic power. In this primal sense, the city has always had a symbolic economy. Modern cities also owe their existence to a second, more abstract symbolic economy devised by "place entrepreneurs" (Molotch 1976), officials and investors whose ability to deal with the symbols of growth yields "real" results in real estate development, new businesses, and jobs.

Related to this entrepreneurial activity is a third, traditional symbolic economy of city advocates and business elites who, through a combination of philanthropy, civic pride, and desire to establish their identity as a patrician class, build the majestic art museums, parks, and architectural complexes that represent a world-class city. What is new about the symbolic economy since the 1970s is its symbiosis of image and product, the scope and scale of selling images on a national and even a global level, and the role of the symbolic economy in speaking for, or representing, the city.

In the 1970s and 1980s, the symbolic economy rose to prominence against a background of industrial decline and financial speculation. The metamorphosis of American-made products into Mexican blue jeans, Japanese autos, and East Asian computers emptied the factories where those goods had been made. Companies that were the largest employers in their communities went out of business or were bought and restructured by takeover artists.

The entrepreneurial edge of the economy shifted toward deal making and selling investments and toward those creative products that could not easily be reproduced elsewhere. Product design – creating the look of a thing – was said to show economic genius. Hollywood film studios and media empires were bought and sold and bought again. In the 1990s, with the harnessing of new computer-based technologies to marketing campaigns, the "information superhighway" promised to join companies to consumers in a Manichean embrace of technology and entertainment. "The entertainment industry is now the driving force for new technology, as defense used to be," the CEO of a US software company said ("Entertainment Economy" 1994, p. 60).

The growth of the symbolic economy in finance, media, and entertainment may not change the way entrepreneurs do business. But it has already forced the growth of towns and cities, created a vast new workforce, and changed the way consumers and employees think. In the early 1990s, employment in "entertainment and recreation" in the United States grew slightly more than in health care and six times more than in the auto industry ("Entertainment Economy" 1994, p. 61). The facilities where these employees work – hotels, restaurants, expanses of new construction and undeveloped land – are more than just workplaces. They reshape geography and ecology; they are places of creation and transformation.

The Disney Company, for example, makes films and distributes them from Hollywood. It runs a television channel and sells commercial spinoffs, such as toys, books, and videos, from a national network of stores. Disney is also a real estate developer in Anaheim, Orlando, France, and Japan and the proposed developer of a theme park in Virginia and a hotel and theme park in Times Square. Moreover, as an employer, Disney has redefined work roles. Proposing a model for change in the emerging service economy, Disney has shifted from the white-collar worker described by C. Wright Mills in the 1950s to a new chameleon of "flexible" tasks. The planners at its corporate headquarters are "imagineers"; the costumed crowd-handlers at its theme parks are "cast members." Disney suggests that the symbolic economy is more than just the sum of the services it provides. The symbolic economy unifies material practices of finance, labor, art, performance, and design.

The prominence of culture industries also inspires a new language dealing with difference (Ewen, 1988). It offers a coded means of discrimination, an undertone to the dominant discourse of democratization. Styles that develop on the streets are cycled through mass media, especially fashion and "urban music" magazines and MTV, where, divorced from their social context, they become images of cool. On urban billboards advertising designer perfumes or jeans, they are recycled to the streets, where they become a provocation, breeding imitation and even violence. The beachheads of designer stores, from Armani to A/X, from Ralph Lauren to Polo, are fiercely parodied for the "props" of fashion-conscious teenagers in inner city ghettos. The cacophony of demands for justice is translated into a coherent demand for jeans. Claims for public space by culture industries inspire the counterpolitics of display in late 20th century urban riots.

The symbolic economy recycles real estate as it does designer clothes. Visual display matters in American and European cities today, because the identities of places are established by sites of delectation. The sensual display of fruit at an urban farmers' market or gourmet food store puts a neighborhood "on the map" of visual delights and reclaims it for gentrification. A sidewalk cafe takes back the street from casual workers and homeless people. In Bryant Park, enormous white tents and a canopied walkway set the scene for spring and fall showings of New York fashion designers. Twice a year, the park is filled by the fashion media, paparazzi, store buyers, and supermodels doing the business of culture and reclaiming Bryant Park as a vital, important place. We New Yorkers become willing participants in the drama of the fashion business. As cultural consumers, we are drawn into the interrelated production of symbols and space.

Mass suburbanization since the 1950s has made it unreasonable to expect that most middle-class men and women will want to live in cities. But developing small places within the city as sites of visual delectation creates urban oases where everyone *appears* to be middle class. In the fronts of the restaurants or stores, at least, consumers are strolling, looking, eating, drinking, sometimes speaking English and sometimes not. In the back regions, an ethnic division of labor guarantees that immigrant workers are preparing food and cleaning up. This is not just a game of representations: developing the city's symbolic economy involves recycling workers, sorting people in housing markets, luring investment, and negotiating political claims for public goods and ethnic promotion. Cities from New York to Los Angeles and Miami seem to thrive by developing small districts around specific themes. Whether it is Times Square or el Calle Ocho, a commercial or an "ethnic" district, the narrative web spun by the symbolic economy around a specific place relies on a vision of cultural consumption and a social and an ethnic division of labor.

As cities and societies place greater emphasis on visualization, the Disney Company and art museums play more prominent roles in defining public culture. I am speaking, first, of public culture as a process of negotiating images that are accepted by large numbers of people. In this sense, culture industries and cultural institutions have stepped into the vacuum left by government. At least since the 1970s' debacles of Watergate and the Vietnam War, through Irangate in the 1980s and the confessions of politicians in the 1990s, government has lacked the basic credibility to define the core values of a common culture. On the local level, most mayors and other elected officials have been too busy clearing budget deficits and dealing with constituents' complaints about crime and schools to project a common image. The "vision thing," as George Bush called it, has been supplied by religious leaders from Jerry Falwell to Jesse Jackson, and by those institutions whose visual resources permit or even require them to capitalize on culture.

I also see public culture as socially constructed on the micro-level. It is produced by the many social encounters that make up daily life in the streets, shops, and parks – the spaces in which we experience public life in cities. The right to be in these spaces, to use them in certain ways, to invest them with a sense of our selves and our communities – to claim them as ours and to be claimed in turn by them – make up a constantly changing public culture. People with economic and political power have the greatest opportunity to shape public culture by controlling the building of the city's public spaces in stone and concrete. Yet public space is inherently democratic. The question of who can occupy public space, and so define an image of the city, is open-ended.

Talking about the cultures of cities in purely visual terms does not do justice to the material practices of politics and economics that create a symbolic economy. But neither does a strictly political–economic approach suggest the subtle powers of visual and spatial strategies of social differentiation. As I suggested in *Landscapes of Power* (1991), the rise of the cities' symbolic economy is rooted in two long-term changes – the economic decline of cities compared to suburban and nonurban spaces and the expansion of abstract financial speculation – and in such short-term factors, dating from the 1970s and 1980s, as new mass immigration, the growth of cultural consumption, and the marketing of identity politics. This is an inclusive, structural, and materialist view. If I am right, we cannot speak about cities today without understanding:

- how cities use culture as an economic base,
- how capitalizing on culture spills over into the privatization and militarization of public space, and
- how the power of culture is related to the aesthetics of fear.

Ethnicity and private security services have shaped an urban public culture that simulates inclusion. The old civic virtues for mingling with strangers – civility, security, tact, and trust – have lost their meaning in the fear for physical safety and the dramatization of ethnic diversity. Every tabloid carries the news: public spaces are too dangerous for public culture. Elementary school pupils carry home-made arms, teenagers attack each other in crimes of sexual abuse. Even ethnically homogeneous subcultures lack solidarity. In most states, both crime victims and convicted criminals are disproportionately black and Latino and come from the same inner city ghettos (Ellis 1994). In the city around them, whatever its name, the symbolic geography of neighborhoods has been remade by selective abandonment and redevelopment. People who were perceived as part of "far away" worlds are present in the "here and now" (Shields, 1992). Spaces inherited from the modern city – department stores, schools and welfare offices, subways and buses – frame encounters that are both intimate and intrusive.

In everyday experience in the city, the "Other" might be the salesperson or waiter who speaks to you in a familiar tone, the supermarket cashier or bank teller who taps on computer keys with inch-long fingernails, the subway driver who roars into the station wearing a turban. At the same time, despite debates stretching from the Chicago School of the 1920s to the "underclass" school of the 1980s, many social practices that were once considered limited to "subcultures" now cross class and ethnic lines. Illegal drug use, out-of-wedlock births, and female-headed families are more common in all parts of the population. Whites watch and copy African-American rap artists ("gangstas," with a nod to previous generations of immigrants who made their mark on society). Lessons are taken from the struggle for existence, both social and sexual, of the older generation. Mass entertainment provides common icons and rituals. *Cocaculturalism*, as Henry Louis Gates, Jr. (1993, p. 117) calls the whole complex of commercial culture, is the most powerful form of public culture. If this is the only source of public culture, there is less distance between subcultures and between "ghetto" and "mainstream" identities. Then social distance is reestablished by developing new cultural differences, confirming the cultural power of fear.

In such a landscape, there are no safe places. The Los Angeles uprising of 1992 showed that, unlike in earlier riots, the powerless respect fewer geographical boundaries, except perhaps the neighborhoods where rich people live. Carjackings – the ultimate American violence – occur on the highway and in the parking lots of fast food restaurants. "If you can't feel safe at McDonald's," a driver in Connecticut says, "is there any place you can feel safe?" (*New York Times*, 27 February, 1993). Patrons of 24-hour automatic teller machines are robbed so often that the NYCE Network, with 10,000 machines in New York City, distributes a pamphlet of safety tips worthy of a military base: "As you approach an ATM, be aware of your surroundings.... When using an ATM at night, be sure it is located in a well lit area. And consider having someone accompany you." Someone, that is, other than the homeless man who stood by the door with an empty paper cup in his hand, until the New York City Council passed a law that forbade panhandlers to stand within 15 feet of an ATM. Or, as a Spanish-language subway advertisement cautions, "Mantengase alerta. Sus ojos, oidos y instinto son sus recursos naturales de seguridad en la ATM." In Chicago and Los Angeles, ATMs have been installed in police stations, so residents with bank accounts in the poorest neighborhoods will have a safe place to get cash.

For a brief moment in the late 1940s and early 1950s, working-class urban neighborhoods held the possibility of integrating white Americans and African-Americans in roughly the same social classes. This dream was laid to rest by movement to the suburbs, continued ethnic bias in employment, the decline of public services in expanding racial ghettos, criticism of integration movements for being associated with the Communist party, and fear of crime. Over the next 15 years, enough for a generation to grow up separate, the inner city developed its stereotyped image of "Otherness." The reality of minority groups' working-class life was demonized by a cultural view of the inner city "made up of four ideological domains: a physical environment of dilapidated houses, disused factories, and general dereliction; a romanticized notion of white working-class life with particular emphasis on the centrality of family life; a pathological image of black culture; and a stereotypical view of street culture" (Burgess, 1985).

By the 1980s, the development of a large black middle class with incomes more or less equal to white households' and the increase in immigrant groups raised a new possibility of developing ethnically and racially integrated cities. This time, however, there is a more explicit struggle over who will occupy the image of the city. Despite the real impoverishment of most urban populations, the larger issue is whether cities can again create an inclusive public culture. The forces of order have retreated into "small urban spaces," like privately managed public parks that can be refashioned to project an image of civility. Guardians of public institutions – teachers, cops – lack the time or inclination to *understand* the generalized ethnic Other. "We don't know how to reach Salvadoran refugees, Vietnamese boat people, African-Americans whose neighborhoods are full of crack," says a public school reformer in Los Angeles. "There is a widening gulf between those of us in charge and the successor generation. We can't relate to their reality" (*New York Times*, 16 February, 1993, p. A13).

Yet the groups that have inherited the city have a claim on its central symbolic spaces. Not only to the streets that serve as major parade routes, not only to the central parks, but also to the monumental spaces that confirm identity by offering visual testimony to a group's presence in history.

Many places that we think of as great public spaces have become so only over time. Some, like city halls, Grand Central Terminal, or the Metropolitan Museum of Art, were built as representations of centralized power. Others, like Times Square, are places of commercial rather than political culture (Taylor, 1992). Public spaces like the Mall in Washington, DC, may eventually become civic spaces, evoking a sense of citizenship and the memory of sacrifice or heroism that citizenship often requires. Or a public space can be rebuilt or reconfigured to repress the memory of citizenship. The Basilica of Sacré Coeur was built on Montmartre, site of the slaughter of Communards in 1871 (Harvey, 1985); traffic was rerouted around Columbus Circle, in New York, to end the left-wing rallies that gathered there in the 1920s and 1930s. Until 1914, we are told, "Times Square was the scene of many outdoor forums. When the square became too crowded these activities shifted northward; now in the open space below the [Columbus] monument impromptu discussions are held and groups listen to oratory on every conceivable subject from Thomas Paine and the *Age of Reason* to the advantages of a vegetable diet" (Federal Writers' Project 1939, 180). Now the discussion at Columbus Circle focuses on which developer is going to build a multistory speculative tower there and how little he will pay the city treasury for the right to build it.

Many social critics have begun to write about new public spaces formed by the "transactional space" of telecommunications and computer technology, but my interest in this book is in public spaces as places that are physically *there*, as geographical and symbolic centers, as points of assembly where strangers mingle. Many Americans, born and raised in the suburbs, accept shopping centers as the preeminent public spaces of our time. Yet, while shopping centers are undoubtedly gathering places, their private ownership has always raised questions about whether all the public has access to them and under what conditions. In the 1980s and 1990s, shopping centers became sites for hotels, post offices, and even schools, suggesting that public institutions can indeed function on private property. A recent decision by the New Jersey Supreme Court (*New York Times*, 21 December 1994), moreover, recognized that the great public spaces of modernity – "the parks, the squares, and the streets...have now been substantially displaced by [shopping] centers," and consequently, that the private owners of these shopping centers could no longer prevent people from exercising their Constitutional right of free speech. But it will take many years, and many changes in the culture of privatization, for shopping centers to develop into symbolic landscapes of public power. If suburbanization, computerization, and electronic media are to transform the social spaces of shopping malls and internets into public spaces, they require greater subjective legitimacy.

NOTE

1   Over the past few years, I have presented parts of this chapter at conferences or lectures at Oxford, Stanford, Columbia, Georgia State, Harvard, and Temple Universities and the

City University of New York Graduate Center. The discussion of Bryant Park always gets a buzz of recognition from the audience because the privatization of public space is such an important issue everywhere.

REFERENCES

AIA Forum. 1994. "Sony Plaza: Public Space or Corporate Face." May

Burgess, Jacquelin. 1985. "News from Nowhere: The Press, the Riots and the Myth of the Inner City." In Jacquelin Burgess and John R. Gold (eds.). *Geography, the Media and Popular Culture* London: Croom Helm, pp. 192–228.

Ellis, Edwin. 1994. "Return to Sender: Recidivism and Urban Geography." Lecture, Brooklyn College.

"Entertainment Economy." 1994. *Business Week*. March 14, p. 58–66.

Ewen, S. 1988. *All Consuming Images: The Politics of Style in Contemporary Culture*. New York: Basic Books.

Federal Writers' Project. 1939. *The Berkshire Hills*. New York: Funk and Wagnalls.

Gates, Henry Louis, Jr. 1993. "Culture of Complaint: The Fraying of America." *The New Yorker*, (19 April): 113–17.

Harvey, David. 1985. "Monument and Myth: The Building of the Basilica of the Sacred Heart." In *Consciousness and the Urban Experience: Studies in the History and Theory of Capitalist Urbanization*, Baltimore: Johns Hopkins University Press, pp. 221–49.

Molotch, H. 1976. "The City as a Growth Machine." *American Journal of Sociology* 82: 309–32.

New York Times. January 30, 1994.

Shields, R. 1992. "A Truant Proximity: Presence and Absence in the Space of Modernity." *Environment and Planning D: Society and Space* 10: 181–98.

Taylor, William R. 1992. "The Evolution of Public Space: The Commercial City as Showcase." In *In Pursuit of Gotham: Culture and Commerce in New York*, New York: Oxford University Press, pp. 35–50.

Zukin, S. 1991. *Landscapes of Power: From Detroit to Disney World*. Berkeley and Los Angeles: University of California Press.

16

See You in Disneyland*

Michael Sorkin

As he was led manacled away after his conviction, serial killer Richard Ramirez, Los Angeles's infamous "Night Stalker," turned to the courtroom audience and snarled "See you in Disneyland." America recognized the turn of phrase from the familiar TV ad that invariably follows the World Series or Super Bowl. After a montage of key plays – with "When You Wish upon a Star" swelling behind – the beaming hero of the game is caught striding off field and asked by the announcer, "What are you going to do now?"

The reply is invariable: "I'm going to Disney World."

Disney World, a theme park of theme parks, is America's stand-in for Elysium, the ultimate reward for quarterbacks and pitchers, the utopia of leisure. And it's not just America's: through those pearly gates in Orlando, Florida, lies the leading purely tourist destination on the planet, welcoming close to 100,000 people on good days, over 30 million a year, a throng that spends nearly a billion dollars each year. These staggering numbers include neither the original Disneyland in Anaheim, California, nor Tokyo Disneyland, nor Euro Disneyland, a building by the Marne. Thanks to Disney and like attractions, Orlando has become America's capital of transience, with more hotel rooms than Chicago, Los Angeles, or New York.

But the empire of Disney transcends these physical sites; its aura is all-pervasive. Decades of films have furnished a common iconography on generations. Now there's a television channel too. And years of shrewd and massive merchandising have sold billions of Disney things – videocassettes, comic books, pajamas, paper cups, postcards, and mouse-eared coin purses – which vaunt their participation in this exponentially expanding system of objects. The litter of Disneyland is underfoot in streets from New York to Shanghai. More people know Mickey than Jesus or Mao. Who doesn't live in Disney World?

* Sorkin, Michael (1992) "See You in Disneyland" from Michael Sorkin (ed.) *Variations on a Theme Park: The New American City and the End of Public Space*, Hill and Wang, New York, pp. 205–32.

The literal placemaking began with Disneyland. According to one hagiographer, the idea for the park came to Disney in 1938, on a trip to the Chicago Railroading Fair, where he was invited to don engineer's overalls and climb behind the throttle of a historic locomotive, fulfilling a childhood dream. Later, he built a miniature railroad around his own house, anticipating the rail-ringed parks to come. Another myth of the park's origins, much retold, recounts a visit by the Disney family to a conventional amusement park, and Disney's disgust at its failures of hygiene. These fantasies of transport and cleanliness culminated, one day in 1955, in Disneyland itself, the alpha point of hyperreality.

It was always to have been a utopia. Early publicity limns it:

> Disneyland will be based upon and dedicated to the ideals, the dreams, and the hard facts that have created America. And it will be uniquely equipped to dramatize these dreams and facts and send them forth as a source of courage and inspiration to all the world.
>
> Disneyland will be something of a fair, an exhibition, a playground, a community center, a museum of living facts, and a showplace of beauty and magic. It will be filled with the accomplishments, the joys, the hopes of the world we live in. And it will remind us and show us how to make those wonders part of our lives.

If this evocation is a tad fuzzy, Disneyland's immediate origins are specific. Television paid. Strapped for cash to finance spiraling construction costs, the previously TV-shy Disney cut a deal with ABC, then struggling far behind its two rivals. In return for the network's money, Disney offered his most precious commodity: the mouse. Disneyland and the Mickey Mouse Club were born as twins. The park was, as Thomas Hine has noted, "the first place ever conceived simultaneously with a TV series."

The coincidence is more than temporal. Television and Disneyland operate similarly, by means of extraction, reduction, and recombination, to create an entirely new, antigeographical space. On TV, the endlessly bizarre juxtapositions of the daily broadcast schedule continuously erode traditional strategies of coherence. The quintessential experience of television, that continuous program-hopping zap from the remote control, creates path after unique path through the infinity of televisual space. Likewise, Disneyland, with its channel-turning mingle of history and fantasy, reality and simulation, invents a way of encountering the physical world that increasingly characterizes daily life. The highly regulated, completely synthetic vision provides a simplified, sanitized experience that stands in for the more undisciplined complexities of the city.

There are more than ample precedents for such weird compendia: circuses, festivals, and fairs have long been with us. Disney is the cool P. T. Barnum – there's a simulation born every minute – and Disneyland the ultimate Big Top. Both circus and Disney entertainment are anti-carnivalesque, feasts of atomization, celebrations of the existing order of things in the guise of escape from it, Fordist fun. Disneyland, of course, also descends from the amusement park, especially that turn-of-the-century blossoming at Coney Island, inspiration to imitator parks from coast to coast. Like Disneyland, Coney Island offered itself as a kind of opposition, an Arden of leisure in symbiosis with the workaday city. Steeplechase Park, Luna Park, and Dreamland established the basic elements of this new machinery of pleasure. Their evocations of travel in time and space, lilliputianization, physics-defying rides, ecstatic relationship to new technology, efficient organizing architecture of spectacle and coercion, and aspirations to urbanism – all harbinger apotheosis at Disneyland.

The most direct ancestor, however, is the World's Fair. These spectacles evolved from the national manufacturing exhibitions that grew with the industrial revolution. Originating late in the eighteenth century, the form climaxed in the Great Exhibition of the Works of Industry of All Nations held in London in 1851 under the enormous glass roof of Joseph Paxton's Crystal Palace. William Thackeray described it in an ode written for the occasion as

> A Palace as for a fairy prince
> A rare pavilion, such as man
> Saw never since mankind began,
> And built and glazed.

This giddy positivism also shines through in the inaugural address of Prince Albert, a Mouseketeer *avant la lettre*:

Nobody who has paid any attention to the peculiar features of our present era will doubt for a moment that we are living at a period of most wonderful transition which tends rapidly to accomplish that great end, to which, indeed, all history points – the realization of the unity of mankind...The distances which separated the different nations and parts of the globe are rapidly vanishing before the achievements of modern invention, and we can traverse them with incredible ease; the languages of all nations are known, and their acquirement placed within the reach of everybody; thought is communicated with the rapidity, and even by the power, of lightning. On the other hand, the great principle of the division of labor, which may be called the moving power of civilization, is being extended to all branches of science, industry, and art...The products of all quarters of the globe are placed at our disposal, and we have only to choose which is the best and the cheapest for our purposes, and the powers of production are entrusted to the stimulus of competition and capital.[1]

The 1851 fair was the first great utopia of global capital. The Prince Consort's evocation of a world shrunk by technology and the division of labor is the ur-theme of the theme park, and Paxton's Crystal Palace made this visible by canny means. First, the wealth of nations was contained under one roof, housed in a single architectural space. And the construction itself embodied the progress of industry – assembled from a vast number of precisely prefabricated elements, the Crystal Palace was the great early expression of a manufactured building. Finally, the Palace depicted paradise. Not only was it laid out like a cathedral, with nave and transept, but it was also the largest greenhouse ever built, its interior filled with greenery as well as goods, a climate-controlled reconciliation of Arcadia and industry, a garden for machines.

Since efficiencies in the manufacture of glass had begun to make them possible late in the eighteenth century, such large structures had come to be both stand-ins for the ineffable and zoos for the menagerie of European colonialism. In the days of the dark satanic mills, winter gardens became hugely popular places of entertainment and assembly. Those tropical landscapes in Berlin or Brussels helped (along with the popular historical and geographical panoramas) to invent the idea of simulated travel, initiating the great touristic dialectic of appearance and reality. The decline in popularity of these environments toward the end of the century was the result of the spread of railways, which made actual exotic travel possible.

This dislocation is central. Whatever its other meanings, the theme park rhapsodizes on the relationship between transportation and geography. The winter garden evokes distance, the railroad proximity. The flicking destination board at JFK or Heathrow offers – in its graphic anonymity – a real trip to Tangier. The winter garden – the "hothouse" – is all artifice, about inaccessibility, about both its own simulations and the impossibility of being present at the scene evoked: it is not recollective, but a fantastic. At its core, the greenhouse – or Disneyland – offers a view of alien nature, edited, a better version, a kind of sublime. Indeed, the abiding theme of every park is nature's transformation from civilization's antithesis to its playground.

In time, these fairs became differentiated. Soon they embraced a variety of pavilions arranged thematically (manufacture, transport, science, etc.), then national and entertainment pavilions, eventually pavilions sponsored by corporations. From the first, these structures, while impermanent, competed in architectural extravagance. And, as the scope of the fairs grew, the ordering and connection of elements assumed paramount importance. Reaching the scale and density of small cities, the fairs also became models, adopted visionary urbanism as an aspect of their agendas, both offering themselves as models of urban organization and providing, within their pavilions, panoramic visions of even more advanced cities to come. The crucial role played by movement systems within the enlarging fairs was not simply a product of necessity but a paradigm for physical relations in the modern city. And the fairs quickly developed "urban problems," especially in relation to their peripheries. They were conceived as exemplars, and stultifying high-mindedness was a staple. As a result, the fairs often found themselves in symbiosis with disorderly carnivals of more "popular" entertainments just beyond their boundaries, with Little Egypt doing "exotic dancing" on the Midway or strippers plying their trade on the fringes of Flushing.

The years that saw the rise of the great universal exposition also witnessed a flowering of practical utopianism. Although much of the theory originated in Europe, America became the great blank canvas for utopian experiments. Not only were new cities being built at a vast clip, communitarian citizens – Fourierites, Owenites, Shakers, Quakers, Mormons, and other affinity groups – built a breathtaking array of intentional communities. While few of these enterprises can be said to have broken much new ground in terms of the physical life of the city, they did abet an atmosphere of renovation and reform that had direct consequences for urbanism. The contrast between this positivistic, optimist vision of the perfectible future and the increasingly degraded condition of the migrant-swollen industrial city precipitated a range of proposals that took increasingly physical form.

In fact, the 1982 Fair in Chicago – aptly called the White City, for the Fair was the urban analogue of the Great White Fleet that was to convey reform in other spheres – represents a summa of one influential impulse. The City Beautiful movement was the first great model for the new city to be born in America. Its prescriptions – baroque symmetries, monumental beaux-arts architecture, abundant parks and greenery – impressed themselves on scores of cities with frequently vivifying results. The City Beautiful's fascination with sumptuousness, visible order, and parks – with the monumental, "public" aspect of the city – anticipates the physical formula of the theme park, the abstraction of good public behavior from the total life of the city. The dazzling Chicago fair showed the potential for magnificence of such concentrated architectural firepower, and virtually every city in America has a civic quarter, however slight the remnant, created under its influence.

Concurrent with the City Beautiful, the pressure of mass settlement and expanding technology created other visions of regulation, less indebted to formal ideas culled from the past. These visions appeared both in imaginary architectural schemes and in a remarkable literary outpouring: novels about happy technologized utopias, like Bellamy's *Looking Backward*, with its strikingly prescient evocation of a world at leisure. These two expressions were focused on somewhat different territories. The visionary architectural proposals – many inspired by the development of the technology of tall buildings – were prompted by the prospect of skyscraper cities and especially by the intricate movement systems that would be required to sustain them. The novels, however, tended to be fantasies about the relations of production, scenes of happy regulation set in a technologically enabled culture of convenience.

These imaginings anticipated the urbanism promulgated by modernism itself, which shows two main strains. The first is the now maligned rationalist, geometric manner – Le Corbusier its main apostle – an enormity of regimentation plopped at regular intervals across a verdant landscape. Le Corbusier's vision has become the icon of alienation, dislodged from its original status as challenge to the insalubrious dreariness of the industrial city and reincarnated as faceless urban renewal and bland 1960s downtowns. It is this version of modernist urbanism that Disneyland's architectural apologists have in mind when they propose it as a restorative.

But modernism produced another version of the city, one more central to Disney's American imaginings. The movement for garden cities, expostulated by the Englishman Ebenezer Howard in his 1902 screed *Garden Cities for Tomorrow*, stands in approximately the same relationship to Le Corbusier's Cartesian fantasies as English landscape gardening did to French in the eighteenth century. The one was a romantic ode to "wild" nature, the other an essay in submission, nature bent to the paths of order. Both, though, were versions of the pastoral, embracing the idea that the renaturalization of the "denatured" city would strip it of its dread, that the reversion to the natural would have a salutary effect on human nature itself.

The garden city is the physical paradigm that presages Disney space, the park in the theme park. Its ideology embraces a number of formal specifics. To begin with, these were to be small cities constructed, ex novo, on the exurban perimeter of existing metropolises, to function as escape valve or release from the tension and overcrowding of the old city. A picturesque plan – the stuff of the early suburbs – was as indispensable as the strict regulation of traffic. Indeed, strategies of movement became the ultimate internal rationale and formal arbiter of the garden city. These included separation of pedestrians and vehicles and a scale of distances convenient for persons on foot. Formally, the result was generally a single center and a radial plan, united by loops of circulation.

Technology and the garden city conjoined in the two great world's fairs of the 1930s: the 1933 Century of Progress Exposition in Chicago and the 1939 World's Fair in New York City. The Chicago Fair was laid out along a meandering roadway meant to evoke "an evolving incipient roadtown," a garden city. Dispersed along this route – and strongly prefiguring the Disney solution – were a variety of pavilions celebrating scientific advance. Over it all soared the skyride: Chicago was the first fair to absolutely elevate the means of movement as its most visible symbol. The layout of the New York Fair evoked an earlier utopian order, the kind of geometric radiating plan characteristic of ideal communities from the Renaissance through the eighteenth century, inspiration to the garden city. However, New York also boasted two gigantic scale models of cities of the future, which between them embodied those two indispensable ideas of order – movement and the garden.

Both were the products of industrial designers, forerunners of Disney's imagineers. The first, "Democracity," the work of Henry Dreyfus, sat inside the famous Perisphere. Although its center was a jumbo skyscraper, the plan of the city – a constellation of sylvan towns on a green perimeter – was pure Ebenezer Howard. The second – and far more popular, perhaps because visitors rode past it in tiny cabs, Disney style – was Normal Bel Geddes's "City of 1960," designed for the General Motors Futurama. Here was the Corbusian version of modernity, a sea of skyscrapers set in green superblocks, ordered by a Cartesian grid. Of course, the rectilinear interstices swam with swift traffic, cars sailing unimpeded to the cardinal points, motion the fertilizing matrix in which the city grew.

The ideology of the garden city today has been dispersed into a wide variety of environments. Consider Opus, an office complex on the ring highway outside Minneapolis. Promotional brochures describe it as

> an imaginative, innovative development...a model for a whole new generation of office parks. Strategically located in southwest suburban Minneapolis, the beautifully landscaped 450-acre site is ribboned with pedestrian and bike paths, colored with flowers, shaded with trees... alive and inspiring. Nestled in acres of meadows, hills, and ponds, Opus is only minutes away from shopping centers, sports stadiums, the international airport, and the downtown business districts of Minneapolis and St. Paul. The site is linked to the interstate system by County Road 18 and Crosstown Highway 62.

A look at the plan for the development elucidates the hype: Opus is the garden city with pedestrians carefully separated from vehicular traffic and picturesque circulation routes organizing lots of different sizes. Yet one thing distinguishes Opus from the garden-variety garden city. Opus is an office development, the residential component an afterthough, a few parcels set aside for outside developers to build limited amounts of housing. Given the character of the work performed in each of the office parcels ("Opus gives new meaning to the word 'work'") and the location of most services and housing off the site, there's no real reason for the elaborate pedestrian links and the careful grade separations. They do, however, "urbanize" the site, giving it a stature in theory that it lacks in use. The pedestrian system signifies benign mobility, a map of motion without movement. The real links are the highway and airport connections and, more crucially, the invisible telecommunications system that is primarily responsible for enabling the dispersed developments that now figure as the major mode of American urbanism.

The perimeter road in Atlanta, Interstate 285, is often offered as a primal scene for the proliferation of this new exurbia. It developed fast. By 1980, central Atlanta had become a symbol of the Sunbelt reborn. The city had a new profile: a classic central place diagram with a clutch of shiny skyscrapers extruding value straight up at its center. By 1985, however, the pattern had just as suddenly shifted: 4.3 million square feet of office space had been added in the center of town, but 7.6 million had been built in the oxymoronic Perimeter Center at one interstate intersection and 10.6 million had gone up in Cumberland/Galleria at another. Perimeter office space is now predominant overall.

The circulation loop that organizes the building sites within Opus recapitulates the highway loop that arrays Opus and other fringe developments around cities like Minneapolis and Atlanta. The order is centrifugal, about perimeters rather than centers, a logic of dispersion. In such spatial hierarchies, circulation always dominates. First, its requirements are literally the largest. By one standard calculation, 1300 square feet of parking space are required for every 1000 square feet of office on the urban perimeter. The physiognomy of movement orders the most primary issues of architecture, deforming it to its requirements. Like the tail-wagged dog, the workspace at the end of the movement chain seems misplaced, out of sequence, a prisoner of the prodigious life-support system necessary to sustain it in its isolation. This incessant circulation mirrors the circuit of capital – that global chain letter, faithfully accumulating – which these offices on the endless perimeter serve to accelerate. If these new developments seem schematic, it is precisely because they represent, in their primary order, an abstraction: the mobility of the capital that enables them.

The organization and scale of Disney World and the Disneylands is precisely that of the garden city. Located on the urban perimeter, they are, as phenomena, comparable to the office parks at other intersections in the highway system, if sited now for convenience of access by leisure commuters. Internally, they are also ordered according to a strict model. Radiating from a strong center – occupied by the totemic castle of fantasy – the parks are arranged in thematic fiefs (Tomorrowland, Frontierland, etc.), which flow into one another. While the ground plane is given over to pedestrian circulation, the parks' perimeters and airspace are the terrain of elaborate transport systems: trains, monorails, and aerial gondolas.

Movement is ubiquitous and central. Disneyland and Disney World are, in the travel agent's parlance, "destinations." The implication is double, enfolding the acts of traveling and of arriving. The element of arrival is especially crucial, the idea that one is not passing through some intermediate station but has come to someplace where there is a definitive "there." In the larger discourse of travel, these places are vested with a kind of equivalence. The only relevant variable is motion. As the slogan for Busch Gardens, a rival theme park in Williamsburg, Virginia (hard by the first park, Colonial Williamsburg), proclaims – over the *Ode to Joy* – "If you want to see Europe, take a vacation in Virginia ... It's all the fun and color of old Europe ... but a lot closer!" (Not to mention, without pesky terrorists threatening to crimp your pleasures en route!)

Like world's fairs, both Busch Gardens and Disneyland offer intensifications of the present, the transformation of the world by an exponential increase in its commodities. World's fairs are microcosmic renditions of the "global marketplace," transnational shopping malls. At Disneyland, this monumentalized commodity fetishism is reduced to the pith of a haiku. While the nominal international "competition" at the orthodox fair centers on the "best" of national manufacture, the goods at Disneyland represent the degree zero of commodity signification. At Disney World, for example, the "national" pavilions groan with knick-knacks. These are not simply emblems of participation in the enterprise of the higher, global, shopping, they are stand-ins for the act of travel itself, ersatz souvenirs. A trip to Disneyland substitutes for a trip to Norway or Japan. "Norway" and "Japan" are contracted to their minimum negotiable signifiers, Vikings and Samurai, gravlax and sushi. It isn't that one hasn't traveled – movement feeds the system, after all. It's that all travel is equivalent.

Getting there, then, is not half the fun: it's all the fun. At Disneyland one is constantly poised in a condition of becoming, always someplace that is "like" someplace else. The simulation's referent is ever elsewhere; the "authenticity" of the substitution always depends on the knowledge, however faded, of some absent genuine. Disneyland is in perpetual shadow, propelling its visitors to an unvisitable past or future, or to some (inconvenient) geography. The whole system is validated, though, by the fact that one has literally traveled, that one has, after all, chosen to go to Disneyland in lieu of any of the actual geographies represented. One has gone nowhere in spite of the equivalent ease of going somewhere. One has preferred the simulation to the reality. For millions of visitors, Disneyland is just like the world, only better.

If culture is being Disneyfied (and there's no mistaking it!) the royal road there is precisely that: going for a ride. Whatever else they subsume, the Disney zones harbor an amusement park, a compendium of rides offering both kinesis narrativized (a trip, a fantasy voyage) and that mild empirical frisson of going one-on-one with Sir Isaac, testing the laws of everyday physics. The visitor travels in order to travel. Whether experienced at 37,000 feet, on the interstate, or padding between Mike Fink's Keel Boat Ride and Captain Eo in your new Nikes, the main experience – motion – is broadened, extended right back to your front door.

Each Disney park embodies a kind of thematic of transportation. Euro Disneyland, rising by the Marne, sits athwart a TGV line (the French bullet train – what a ride!), convenient to all Europe. Disney World exists in gravitational relationship to the airport at Orlando. Disneyland, superannuated Shangri-la of the American fifties, is an exit on the LA freeway. In each instance, the park sits as an intensely serviced node on a modern network of global reach. The urbanism of Disneyland is precisely the urbanism of universal equivalence. In this new city, the idea of distinct places is dispersed into a sea of universal placelessness as everyplace becomes destination and any destination can be anyplace. The world of traditional urban arrangements is colonized by the penetration of a new multinational corridor, leading always to a single human subject, the monadic consumer. The ultimate consequence is likely to be the increasing irrelevance of actual movement and the substitution of the even more completely artificial reality of electronic "virtual" space. (As the Frank Zappa lyric puts it, "How can you be two places at once when you're not anywhere at all?".) For the moment though, the system still spends its energies on sculpting more physical simulacra.

Consider the trip to the original Anaheim Disneyland. Conceived regionally, in the days before cheap air transport allowed its touristic reach to match its ideological grasp (who can forget poor Nikita Khrushchev's frustration at being denied a visit?), Disneyland was not simply designed for arrival by car, but was – like Los Angeles – begot by the car. One approaches Disneyland only after tooling across the vast Southern California sward of atomization, the bygone suburban utopia of universal accessibility that the automobile was supposed to guarantee.

Whatever else it represents, Disneyland is also a model of Los Angeles. Fantasyland, Frontierland, Tomorrowland – these are the historic themes of the city's own self-description, its main cultural tropes. The genius of the city, however, resides not simply in dispersal but in juxtaposition, the invention of the possibility of the Loirish Bungalow sitting chockablock with the Tudoroid. The view through the framing window of the passing car animates the townscape, cinematizing the city. This consumption of the city as spectacle, by means of mechanical movement through it, precapitulates the more global possibilities of both the multinational corridor created by air travel and the simultaneous electronic everywhere of television. Disneyland offers a space in which narrative depends on motion, and in which one is placed in a position of spectatorship of one's own spectatorship.

While the car may be LA's generator, it's also its "problem," motor of democracy and alienation both, repressor of pedestrianism and its happy random encounters. There's a school (popular along the learnedly kitsch axis of early architectural postmodernism) that exalts Disneyland as a solution to the dissipation of the public realm engendered by cars. This is achieved by relegating cars to a parking periphery, creating an auto-free zone at its center, and using efficient, technologized transport (that charismatic monorail) to mediate.

But this is only half the story. In fact, Disneyland less redeems LA than inverts it. The reason one circulates on foot in Disneyland is precisely to be able to ride. However, the central experience, by anyone's empirical calculation, is neither walking nor riding, but waiting in line. Most of a typical Disney day is thus spent in the very traffic jam one has putatively escaped, simply without benefit of car. Indeed, what's perfect, most ultimately viable, at Disneyland is riding. After hours of snaking through the sun with one's conscientiously well-behaved fellow citizens comes the kinetic payoff: brief, thrilling, and utterly controlled, a traffic engineer's wet dream.

There's a further inversion. Much of the riding at Disneyland – from Space Mountain to Mr. Toad's Wild Ride – takes place indoors. Driving a car in Los Angeles is at once an intensely private and very public activity: on the road, one is both isolated and fully visible. Disneyland surrealizes the ambiguity by making driving domestic, interior, even as it's regulated by being pared of control. Chez Mr. Toad, the line culminates in a quaint Olde English manse through which one is conveyed in . . . a quaint Olde English car. One drives in exactly the only place one expects to walk in the "real" city back home.

Getting to Disney World is a more intrinsically long-distance proposition, involving a long-distance automotive schlep or passage through the global air corridor (visitors are presently divided 50/50 between road and air). Let's say the journey begins at Kennedy Airport in New York. Kennedy is organized along exactly the same ring road principles as Disneyland itself. A big vehicular loop defines a perimeter along which are arrayed the terminals of the various airlines. These buildings – most of which were designed in the late fifties or early sixties – are conceived after the fashion of the national pavilions of the world's fairs of the period, modernist shrines whose signifying tasks are engaged via abstraction rather than representation: expressions of grandeur and consequence rather than any particular evocation of regional particulars. This exaltation of the node differs from the more current paradigm – visible at the airports of Chicago, Atlanta, Dallas/Fort Worth, or Orlando – with their emphasis on the seamlessness of the intermodal transfer. Indeed, at Kennedy, this primacy of the individual terminal is purchased at the cost of considerable inconvenience to travelers transferring between airlines, and a just-begun reconstruction of the airport aims to transform it with the introduction of a "people-mover" system, a linkage-ride like the Disney monorail.

The original arrangement, however, was suited to its Eisenhowerian age, an airport structured like a suburb, America's own version of the garden city. The suburbs, of course, were predicated on the preeminence of the family, its autonomy expressed by freestanding structures on clearly delineated plots. In a time of confidence, the visibility of the economic unit was paramount on the symbolic agenda: at Kennedy, as at Disney, the corporations are surrogates for the family, everybody's big brothers. And Kennedy is likewise afflicted with the same problems of transportation as the suburbs it emulated: difficult to get to, inefficient in its internal connections, dependent on a single mode – the car. At the center of the sea of parking within the Kennedy loop – in the symbolic position occupied by Disneyland's castle, Disney World's geodesic or the 1939 World's Fair Trylon and Perisphere – stand three concrete chapels, for Catholic, Protestant, and Jewish worship. Under the reconstruction plan, they are to be replaced by a more up-to-the-minute shrine: the central node of the new airport movement system. The obliteration of the three chapels, of course, also obviates the question of an absence they so directly beg. While this religious trinity may have been sufficient for the American imperium of the late fifties and early sixties, the accelerated globalism of today does not so easily slough off religions classed simply as Other. Certainly, those chapels had to go if only to avoid the question of the missing mosque. At "Kennedy" – America's leading memorial to the great initiatory act of modern terrorism – mingling Islam and air travel would clearly be too risky.

If airports have become the locale of choice for random terror, they're also arenas for other politics. The Tokyo airport, Narita, is a perennial protest site. Located many miles from the center of Tokyo in an agricultural area typified by small landholdings, Narita's plans to build a long new runway on expropriated farm land have repeatedly fallen afoul of the local left, and numerous, often violent, demonstrations have occurred. From an American vantage point, there's something at once quixotic and stirring in this rage on behalf of traditional life in a country that has become the emblem of breakneck modernization and globalized capital. But there's no mistaking the power of the runway, a spirit portal of virtually Egyptian intensity. Like an automatic teller machine, the runway is the point at which a vast, controlling, and invisible skein is made manifest. As each jumbo sets down, tarring its tread-trace in a puff of burnt rubber, the runway becomes rune-way, marker of that inescapable web.

Hartsdale airport in Atlanta is home base to Delta, the current "official" airline of Disney World. As with any fledgling nation-state, hocking its future for a pride of Boeings, an airline completes an indispensable circuit of status, a symbolic minimum apparatus of nationhood. Indeed, the world's most succinct and prospering nation, Singapore, embodies the shrunken vision to perfection. Almost no territory, an intense electronic and travel economy, a superb airline, and a bustling airport linked by modern rapid transit to a compact skyscrapered downtown, orderly to a fault, complete with hygienically retained ethnic and colonial quarters and regulated with scary draconian legality, it's a virtual Disney Nation, deftly substituting Uncle Harry for Uncle Walt. For Disney World, the relationship with Delta both opens another line of penetration into the Real World and affirms its status as perpetually offshore.

Unlike Kennedy, Hartsdale already has an automated "people-mover" transit system to link its terminal concourses. Vaunted as a panacea for urban congestion in the hardware-fixated sixties, the vision was of fleets of small, highly autonomous, "user-friendly" transit cars gliding silently on elevated tracks. People-movers were also seen as a replacement for the freeways – the previous solution – then coming to be viewed as hopelessly destructive to the urban body they were meant to heal. Although people-movers mainly proved too inefficient and expensive for city use, they were just the thing for the more specific and restricted requirements of airports, where exponential growth had stretched the distance from entry to gates to pituitary proportions.

The fantasy that undergirds the science of people-moving is regulation. It's a primal ordering: the Newtonian vision of the universe, bodies intricately meshing and revolving like ticking clockwork, divinity legible precisely in the Laws of Motion. For planners confronted by the irrationality of the city, the addition of computer-regulated, minutely responsive people-movers clearly meant bringing the global-motion net one step closer to the front door. In the space of capital, circulation is politics: its foregrounding at places like Disneyland is analogous to the barrierless vision of free trade that sparked the fairs of the nineteenth century. The driverless people-mover – its motions seemingly dictated by the invisible hand, mechanical creature of supply and demand – is symbol of this economic fantasy of perfect self-government.

On the Hartsdale people-mover, the recorded voice that signals the stops along the loop was originally female. Held to lack authority, it was changed, not to a male voice but to an electronic androgyne. This, then, is a welcome, the signal of an unspecifiable presentness of the system. Gliding to a stop, the car murmurs, "The next stop is terminal A. The color-coded maps and signs in this vehicle match the colors in the terminal." Indeed, the airport has become ("deregulation" notwithstanding) perhaps the most intensively regulated zone of common experience, a more visible version of the more discrete, concealed governings of the Disney Zones. The combined threats of narcotics and terror have given rise to unprecedented levels of policing and surveillance. Credit and passport checks, magnetic screening, irradiation of luggage, baleful agents vetting security "profiles," sniffer dogs: such are the quotidian experiences of air travel. Indeed, every year over a billion people pass through the airport security apparatus, terrified and terribly safe all at once.

The global corridor is the modern Panopticon, seething with surveillance. The genius of this system is, however, not just the drill but the invitation, the willingness of its subjects to participate. Take Williams Island, a typical upper-income enclaved community in Miami, advertised by spokesperson Sophia Loren as the "Florida Riviera." Williams offers at least a triple pitch. Its architectural centerpiece is indeed a complex of buildings meant to evoke Portofino or Saint Tropez, all tile roofs, waterside cafes, and bobbing boats. There's also an idealized movement system, consisting of footways and golf carts. In the context of the successive transformations of the garden city, the golf cart is an interesting modification. The cart is the ultimate reconciliation of machine and garden, a benign transport indigenous to leisure. And the golf course itself is a state of nature apt to the age: a vast acreage of greenery scrupulously regulated to support a network of tiny, shallow holes.

But security is the main feature. The first checkpoint at Williams Island is on the far side of a bridge from the mainland. Residents, once recognized, are admitted with a wave. Visitors undergo further scrutiny, and are directed along a succession of additional checkpoints. At buildings' edge, security becomes high-tech. Each resident of the complex has an electronic pass, like a credit card. To move through the sequence of security locks, he or she must insert the card in a slot. A central computer verifies the pass and opens the door. At the same time, a record of the cardholder's movement is printed out at the main guard post. Like the air traveler, the resident submits to an elaborate system of surveillance with the ultimate rationale of self-protection. Here, however, the surrender of privacy is a privilege. Moving through Williams Island recapitulates the larger experience of moving through the global corridor. The security checks, the certifying credit cards and passports, the disciplined, carefully segmented movements, the ersatz geography, the grafted cachet – this is Disneyville.

Arriving at Orlando airport offers the Disney-bound a hint of things to come. There's a brief people-mover ride from satellite to main terminal and a welter of advertising and Disney Reps in the main lobby. However, the cocooning shroud of automated movement stops at the main entrance. To get from the airport to Disney World, a car is required. Indeed, the only way to arrive at Disney World is by road. This obliges a key ritual of the corridor: the modulation of the means of movement. At the entrance to Disney, the process is inverted: one passes through a customs-like toll barrier, thence to relinquish one's car to hotel, campsite, or day-tripper's parking lots and enter the system. The toll booth is also the limit of a monetary zone: within Disney World, visitors can pay either with conventional instruments or with "Disney Dollars." These – exchangeable for US dollars one to one – confer absolutely no advantage, no discount, no speculative hedge. They do, however, concretize and differentiate the experience of exchange and boost the counterfeit aura of foreign-ness.

Visitors are welcomed by the mouse. Mickey – hairless, sexless, and harmless – is a summary: as Disney once put it, "Mickey is a *clean* mouse." Talk about a constructed subject – Mickey stands in the same relationship to human subjectivity as Disneyland does to urbanity. Rigorously and completely manipulated, the mouse's outward appearance is affective and cute. As a gloss on human speech, locomotion, and appearance, the mouse offers pratfalling, loopy variation. As an epistemology, Mickey sees things as we do. Mickey, like most cartoon characters, circulates in the cartoon state of nature, a place which collapses the best of Hobbes and Rousseau, a place where life's inevitable brutishness is always played for laughs, where impulses need not be censored because they are ultimately without consequences. The mechanical mouse, product of the animator's assembly line, also confirms a key switch: at Disney, nature is appearance, machine is reality.

Just as the image of the mouse on a million plastic souvenirs confers aura and legitimacy on them, so the vestiges of utopia in the Disney space certifies them as more than amusement parks. For Disneyzone – Disneyland, Disney World, and all the other Disney places – is also a state of nature, offering the fecund communism of abundance and leisure, a true technocratic postindustrial utopia. The industrial army, raised in the nineteenth century and rationalized in the twentieth, is, at Disneyzone, not dispersed but converted to a vast leisure army, sacrificing nothing in regimentation and discipline as it consumes its Taylorized fun. Disneyzone completes the circuit of world's fairism by converting the celebration of production into the production of celebration. The pivot on which this transformation turns is the essential alienation of the producer-turned-consumer, his or her dance to the routines of someone else's imagining.

The need for the efficient production of leisure activities has certainly not escaped the official strategizers of our collective future. In his 1976 *Between Two Ages*, Zbigniew Brzezinski warned his patrons of the exigencies to be faced in the coming "technotronic society." Describing the relationship between employers, labor, and the market in this new order, Brzezinski writes that "in the emerging new society questions relating to the obsolescence of skills security, vacations, leisure, and profit-sharing dominate the relationship, and the psychic well-being of millions of relatively secure but potentially aimless lower-middle-class blue-collar workers becomes a growing problem."[2]

The relation between work and leisure is part of the conceptual problematic that kept Disney's most ambitious, most conventionalized, utopian vision, the Experimental Prototype Community of Tomorrow (Epcot) from full fruition. Epcot was prompted by a number of impulses, one of them the literal realization of a full-scale version of the kind of well-regulated one-dimensional urbanism proposed in model form at the 1939 Fair. Perhaps more strongly motivating, however, was Disney's widely reported frustration at events in Anaheim. Like so many world's fairs, Disneyland was beleaguered by an undisciplined periphery: the huge success of the park prompted developers to buy up miles of surrounding countryside, which was promptly converted to a regulationless tangle of hotels and low commerce. For Disney the frustration was double. First, at the millions lost to others who were housing his visitors. (In the first ten years, Disneyland took in $273 million, the peripherals $555 million.) And second, the disorder of it all, the sullying of his vision by a sea of sleaze.

Redress, utopia's wellspring, was thus a major motivator for Disney's next go. With guile and stealth he accumulated 28,000 acres of land near Orlando, Florida, for Disney World and its subset Epcot. As intended, the scheme was to embrace both theme park (a clone of Anaheim) and a full-blown community, initially to house his own workers, eventually to include such additional industrial and residential development as he was able to attract. Spake Disney, "Epcot will always be in a state of becoming. It will never cease to be a living blueprint of the future, where people will live a life they can't find anywhere else in the world today." Disney was able to extract extraordinary, unprecedented concessions from the government of Florida, assuring him of virtually complete sovereignty (including rights of policing, taxation, and administration, and freedom from environmental controls) over his domain.

Unfortunately, death intervened before Disney was able to materialize his dream. Its realization was left in the hands of his successors, whose view of the matter was somewhat more jaundiced. Instead of a full-blown "community," Epcot was reduced to the status of simply another theme park. Indeed, it was to become the Disney empire's most literally world's-fairian incarnation. Organized according to the familiar schema – initiatory "main street," loop of attractions – it directly reproduced the components of its predecessor fairs. Materializing the covert agenda of previous Disney Main Streets (where the ITT pavilion lurks behind the malt-shoppe facade), its main street is flanked by the pavilions of major US corporations, each housing some version of a "ride" through a halcyon future. The GM pavilion with its ode to the car also offers up the Epcot theme song, the remorselessly repeated "It's a small world after all." The loop holds the pavilions of eight elected (and subsidizing) nations, an array projecting a sufficient (one from Asia, one from Latin America...) compendium of national diversity.

Even Epcot's symbol – a large geodesic sphere – is received. Its lineage proceeds backwards to the tacky Unisphere of the 1964 New York Fair (in which Disney participation was considerable – including an early Animatronic Abe Lincoln) and to Unisphere's own source, the mesmerizing Perisphere that accompanied the complementingly vertical Trylon to the 1939 Fair. In fact, the line extends – via the biospheres of the nineteenth century – back at least as far as the eighteenth-century French architect Boullée's proposal for a vast spherical cenotaph to Isaac Newton, its interior daubed with stars, a representation of the universe which Newton's mechanics had made so newly comprehensible. Epcot's ball is a degenerate – if still viable – totem of universality. In commercials, Mickey stands atop it, waving, an anti-colossus.

It somehow seems inevitable that this puny organ of Brzezinskian "psychic well-being" should stand in for the more literal variety that Disney's fuller first vision (actual homes, actual factories) represents. The two possibilities are clearly antithetical, the one destined to annihilate the other. After all, utopia is illusory, a representation. The careful structure of entertainment and social relations (nominal egalitarianism with segmenting opportunities: meals at up- and downscale restaurants; at night you sleep with your class at hostelries ranging from modest to luxe) at Disneyland relinquishes its power to draw if it fails as an alternative to daily life.

The Disney strategy, then, inscribes utopia on the terrain of the familiar and vice versa. The economy of its representations depends on a careful calculus of degrees of difference. Like any other consumer operation, it thrives on algorithms of both the desirable and the attainable. Thus, its images never really innovate, they intensify and reduce, winnowing complexity in the name of both quick access and easy digestibility. What's being promoted is not the exceptional but rather the paranormal. Just like the real thing, only better.

In an essay on montage, the Soviet film-maker Lev Kuleshov describes a scene shot in the early 1920s with the actors Khokhlova and Obolensky:

> Khokhlova is walking along Petrov Street in Moscow near the "Mostorg" store. Obolensky is walking along the embankment of the Moscow River – at a distance of about two miles away. They see each other, smile, and begin to walk toward one another. Their meeting is filmed at the Boulevard Prechistensk. This boulevard is in an entirely different section of the city. They clasp hands, with Gogol's monument as a background, and look – at the White House – for at this point, we cut in a segment from an American film, *The White House in Washington*. In the next shot they are once again on the Boulevard Prechistensk. Deciding to go farther, they leave and climb up the enormous staircase of the Cathedral of Christ the Savior. We film them, edit the film, and the result is that they are seen walking up the steps of the White House. For this we used no trick, no double exposure: the effect was achieved solely by the organization of the material through its cinematic treatment. This particular scene demonstrated the incredible potency of montage, which actually appeared so powerful that it was able to alter the very essence of the material.[3]

Kuleshov called this technique "creative geography." Like gene-splicing, the point is to create a new organism from the substance of the old. Indeed, in another famous experiment, Kuleshov used the technique to "fabricate" a new, recombinant woman, from fragments of several "other" women. The question here is whether the perpetrator is Prometheus or Frankenstein. To distinguish monstrosity from coherence, the practice of montage – and the practice of urbanism, its three-dimensional equivalent – requires a theory of juxtaposition. For the cinema, the theory is either about narrative or its interruption, about a sequence of images bound to time. Montage begs the question of the logic of this arrangement. The city is also joined in sequence. Both its construction and its politics devolve on principles of aggregation. The idealization of such principles creates utopia.

As a utopia, Disneyland's innovation lies not in its fantasy of regulation but in the elision of its place-making. Disneyland is the Holy See of creative geography, the place where the ephemeral reality of the cinema is concretized into the stuff of the city. It should come as no surprise that the most succinct manifestation to date of this crossover is the "Disney–MGM Studios" theme park, recently opened at Disney World. Here, the agenda of dislocated authenticity is carried back to its point of origin. The attraction (much indebted to its precursor, Universal Studios Tour, back in Los Angeles, now also in Orlando) is explicitly about movies, both the space of their realization (the "studio") and about the particular narrative spaces of particular movies.

Although the attraction is in Florida, at Disney World, and although its recreational agenda is precisely to purvey "creative geography," Disney–MGM is at pains to locate itself in a particularly referential space: Hollywood, the locus classicus of movie-making. Main Street's axial introduction is accomplished with an imaginative recasting of Hollywood Boulevard, heavy on the deco. Visitors enter through a gateway borrowed from the now-incinerated Pan-Pacific Auditorium, past a replica of the famous Crossroads of the World tower, a reincarnate Brown Derby, and a welter of familiar Los Angeles architecture, here scaled down and aggregated with an urbanity unknown at the unedited source.

At the head of this axis stands a re-created Grauman's Chinese. No longer exactly a movie palace, however, it's the queuing zone for the main event at the theme park, the Great Movie Ride, a forty-two-minute trip through scenes from well-known Disney and MGM movies, re-created by Animatronic robots. This is a fabulously compact rendition of the larger experience of Disneyfication, the suspension of the visitor in a serially realized apparatus of simulation. Like the global-corridor traveler, the visitor is propelled past a series of summary tableaux which stand in for some larger, sloughed-off, memory of reality. Of course, the Great Movie Ride goes the system one better, mechanically reproducing a mechanical reproduction.

One of the main effects of Disneyfication is the substitution of recreation for work, the production of leisure according to the routines of industry. Now, one of the products of postindustrialism is not simply the liberation of vast amounts of problematic leisure time, it's the reinvention of labor as spectacle, what Dean MacCannell has called "involuted differentiation." The positivist mythos having withered, culture turns in on itself, simply aestheticizing its internal operations, romanticizing especially those bygone. The tourist travels the world to see the wigged baker at the simulacrum of Colonial Williamsburg drawing hot-cross buns from an "authentic" brick oven or the Greek fisherman on the quay on Mykonos, mending his photogenic nets, or the Animatronic Gene Kelly "singing in the rain."

At the movie theme park this spectacle is multiplied. The "work" at Disney World is, of course, entertainment. The 26,000 employees of the place are all considered by management to be "cast-members." Transforming workers to actors presumably transforms their work into play. This plugs nicely into a familiar mode, an endless staple of the talk-show circuit: the performance of some overcompensated Hollywood sybarite talking about his or her "work" as if the activity were somehow comparable to the labors of the assembly line. It's the same grotesque operation found in the seasonal public negotiations (with frequent strikes) of overpaid sports figures which create a themed version of "old-fashioned" labor relations, rendering union–management relations ridiculous by exaggeration.

But the most important aim of this inversion is not to encourage delusional thinking by some harried cafeteria worker at Disney. It is rather to invent the empire of leisure that still differentiates Disneyworld from everyday life. Visitors to the Disney parks, polled about what they like best, cite first the cleanliness, next the friendliness of the employees. This is surely the redemption of the industrial metropolis: hygienic, staffed with unalienated workers apparently enjoying their contributions to the happy collectivity. The movie ride takes this theory of labor a logical step further. One imagines, to begin with, that the Gene Kelly automaton is working for considerably less than scale. The representation goes the "ideal" worker one better: entertaining itself – fun in the first place – has been fully automated.

Consider a further recursion. In all likelihood, as the tram rolls through the Animatronic Temple of Doom, a hundred video-cams whirringly record the "event" for later consumption at home. That tape is an astonishing artifact, unprecedented in human history. If postmodern culture can be said to be about the weaving of ever more elaborate fabrics of simulation, about successive displacements of "authentic" signifiers, then the Japanese family sitting in front of the Sony back in Nagasaki, watching their home videos of the Antimatronic re-creation of the creative geography of a Hollywood "original," all recorded at a simulacrum of Hollywood in central Florida, must be said to have achieved a truly weird apotheosis of raw referentiality. Interestingly, several years ago, the inventor Nolan Bushnell proposed a further efficiency in this circuit. His notion was to place little self-propelled robots, each with a video eye, in major tourist cities – Paris, Rome, London, perhaps even Disney World. These could then be driven around by folks in Phoenix or Dubuque, giving them the experience of prowling the Champs Elysées, Regent Street, or the Via Veneto, without actually leaving home. But this is just an incremental advance, economizing only on human mobility, still premised on an old notion of the superiority of old-style "reality."

Disney's ahead of this. The Disney–MGM studio tour offers a third order of re-creation, another involuted riff on the nature of place. Part of the complex is a functioning movie studio, affording visitors the authentic frisson of a brush with living stars, an actual "production." Strolling the backlot, tourists might pass down a set for a New York City street. Although this set is constructed in the same way and with the same creatively interpolative geography as nearby "Hollywood Boulevard," the spectator's relationship to it is different. Success here depends on the apprehension of this space not primarily as a zone of leisure (as on the Great Movie Ride or the stroll down the Boulevard) but as a workplace. It's another order of tourism, like watching the muffin-bakers and glass-blowers at Colonial Williamsburg, the addition of the pleasures of voyeurism to those of mere recreation.

If visitors are permitted the pleasure of circulating "backstage" at the movie studio, there's yet a further backstage that remains inaccessible. In true rational modernist fashion, the Disney parks are built on giant platforms. Underneath the attractions, a labyrinth of tunnels provides service and staff circulation for the public activities above. These areas are strictly off limits to visitors although they're often discussed in publicity as one of the keys to Disney's marvelous efficiency, and photographs – daffy shots of giant Mickey Mice padding down fluorescent-lit concrete corridors – are widely disseminated. This subterranean space inevitably conjures up other, more dystopian images, most notably the underworld in Lang's *Metropolis*, its workers trapped in carceral caverns dancing their robotic ballet like Martha Graham on Thorazine.

But – perhaps in part because a man in a mouse costume is a more genial image of dehumanization than a prole in chains – this "servant space" (in Louis Kahn's locution) has a generally happier reputation. It is, in fact, what makes Disneyland "clean." Not simply is this a venue for the efficient whisking away of the detritus of fun – the tons of Popsicle sticks and hot-dog wrappers generated daily – it divides labor into its clean, public face, and its less entertaining, less "magic" aspects. Like the tourist-popular sewers of Paris, this underworld is both alien and marvelous, "peopled" with strange denizens, inconspicuous yet indispensable, supporting the purer city of being above. It is the dream of each beleaguered city dweller: an apparatus for keeping every urban problem out of sight. In fact, though, it reverses the Langian schema. This disciplinary apparatus is not above but underground, a subterranean Panopticon, ready to spring up innumerable concealed passages to monitor and service the vast leisure army toiling at fun up above.

Such reveries of self-discipline are historic. Stuart Ewen cites a variety of sources celebrating the self-modified behavior of visitors to the White City of 1892. "Order reigned everywhere," wrote one, "no boisterousness, no unseemly merriment. It seemed as though the beauty of the place brought a gentleness, happiness, and self-respect to its visitors." Observed another, "No great multitude of people ever showed more love of order. The restraint and discipline were remarkable." And another, "Courtiers in Versailles and Fontainbleau could not have been more deferential and observant...the decorum of the place and occasion than these obscure and myriads of unknown laborers." Even Charlotte Brontë, visiting the Crystal Palace in 1851, opined that "the multitude...seems ruled and subdued by some invisible influence."[4]

Jeffrey Katzenberg, head of Disney's movie division, suggests that we "think of Disney World as a medium-sized city with a crime rate of zero." Although the claim is hyperbole (petty larceny mainly leads to expulsion from the kingdom, more serious infractions to the summoning of adjoining police forces), the perception is not: the environment is virtually self-policing. Disney World is clearly a version of a town ("Imagine a Disneyland as big as the city of San Francisco," goes a recent ad). And it's based on a particular urbanism, a crisp acceleration of trends everywhere visible but nowhere so acutely elaborated. The problems addressed by Disneyzone are quintessentially modern: crime, transportation, waste, the relationship of work and leisure, the transience of populations, the growing hegemony of the simulacrum.

But finally, Disneyzone isn't urban at all. Like the patent-medicine-plugging actor who advertises his bona fides as "I'm not a doctor but I play one on TV," Disney invokes an urbanism without producing a city. Rather, it produces a kind of aura-stripped hypercity, a city with billions of citizens (all who would consume) but no residents. Physicalized yet conceptual, it's the utopia of transience, a place where everyone is just passing through. This is its message for the city to be, a place everywhere and nowhere, assembled only through constant motion. Visitors to Disneyzone are reduced to the status of cartoon characters. (Indeed, one of the features of the studio tour is the opportunity for visitors to cinematically interpolate themselves into *Who Framed Roger Rabbit?*) This is a common failing in utopian subjectivity, the predication on a homogenized, underdimensioned citizenship. However, it's also true that there's probably no more acquiescent subject that the postindustrial tourist. And there's surely no question that a holidaymaker wants a version of life pared of its sting, that vacationing finds its fulfillment in escape. The Disney visitor seeks and delights in the relationship between what he or she finds and its obverse back home, terrain of crime, litter, and surliness.

In the Disney utopia, we all become involuntary flaneurs and flaneuses, global drifters, holding high our lamps as we look everywhere for an honest image. The search will get tougher and tougher for the fanned-out millions as the recombinant landscape crops up around the globe. One of the latest nodes appears about to be sprung at Surajkund, near New Delhi, where India's first theme park gleams in the eye of the local tourism department. "We have a whole integrated concept of a fun center," as the *New York Times* quotes S. K. Sharma, state secretary for tourism. "Like all big cities, Delhi is getting polluted. It is getting choked with people. People need amusement and clear air."[5]

Marcuse called utopia "the determinate sociohistorical negation of what exists."[6] Disneyzone – Toon Town in real stucco and metal – is a cartoon utopia, an urbanism for the electronic age. Like television, it is a machine for the continuous transformation of what exists (a panoply of images drawn from life) into what doesn't (an ever-increasing number of weird juxtapositions). It's a genetic utopia, where every product is some sort of mutant, maimed kids in Kabul brought to you on the nightly news by Metamucil, Dumbo in Japan in Florida. The only way to consume this narrative is to keep moving, keep changing channels, keep walking, get on another jet, pass through another airport, stay in another Ramada Inn. The only logic is the faint buzz of memories of something more or less similar... but so long ago, perhaps even yesterday.

NOTES

1 "Inaugural Address of the Prince Consort Albert, May 1, 1851," quoted in Wolfgang Freibe, *Buildings of the World Exhibitions* (Leipzig: Editions Leipzig, 1985), p. 13.
2 Zbigniew Brzezinski, *Between Two Ages: America's Role in the Technotronic Era* (New York: Viking, 1976), quoted in Collettivo Strategie, *Strategie* (Milan: Macchina Libri, 1981) included in Tony Solomonides and Les Levidow, eds., *Compulsive Technology: Computers as Culture* (London: Free Association, 1985), p. 130.
3 Lev Kuleshov, "Art of the Cinema," in Ronald Levaco, *Kuleshov on Film: Writings by Lev Kuleshov* (Berkeley: California University Press, 1974), p. 52.
4 Stewart Ewen. *All Consuming Images: The Politics of Style in Contemporary Culture* (New York: Basic Books, 1988), pp. 204–5.
5 *New York Times*, February 10, 1990.
6 Herbert Marcuse, "The End of Utopia," in *Five Lectures* (Boston: Beacon, 1970), p. 69.

17

The New Urbanism*

Douglas Kelbaugh

Pedestrian Pockets, TODs, and TNDs

If urban villages and zoning reform are good strategies for existing cities and suburbs, what strategies are needed for new suburban development? We desperately need new, compelling typologies for our suburbs – ones that take the low-density, homogenous net that has been thrown over the outskirts of our cities and gather it into finite knots that are bounded, contained, lively, and walkable communities. The old model of the single-family dwelling, large lawn, garage, swimming pool, curving cul-de-sac, and automobile commute to school, office park, shopping center, and recreation still lingers in the minds of many planners, developers, and design professionals. It also holds sway in the dreams of many home buyers.

One of the new models for suburban development to emerge in the 1980s was the Pedestrian Pocket. The idea was coined and developed by Peter Calthorpe, who came to the concept from an environmental ethic. A group of young architects who had been designing passive solar buildings came together with other environmentalists in the early 1980s for a design charrette on sustainable cities. Five years later this same group, plus a few others who had also been making contributions to passive solar architecture, coauthored *The Pedestrian Pocket Book* after the University of Washington charrette in 1988. Calthorpe and his colleagues have since applied its concepts to dozens of development projects around the country and in Australasia and lectured to numerous conferences here and abroad. This pioneering planning work is now coming to physical fruition in such projects as Laguna West in Sacramento, where the county has also adopted the principles as design guidelines for Transit-Oriented Development (TOD) in its unincorporated areas. Similar projects are on the drawing board or under construction in other states, such as Florida and Washington.

* Kelbaugh, Douglas S. (1997) "The New Urbanism" from *Common Place*, University of Washington Press, pp. 111–21. Reprinted by permission of the University of Washington Press.

What is a Pedestrian Pocket or TOD? It is a development model for a small, walkable community that mixes low-rise, medium-density housing for a variety of household types, with retail, civic, recreational, and employment centers along a main street – all within about a one-quarter-mile radius of a central transit stop for a bus or rail system. This tight node can be surrounded by a secondary area or belt of more conventional single-family homes, separated by a natural buffer but connected by pedestrian and vehicular links. Because it is not a stand-alone community, the pocket is connected by automobile, bike, and transit to other pockets and existing towns and cities, as well as to the shopping malls and office parks that it aims to replace. The Pedestrian Pocket is small – 30 to 150 acres – and, ideally, it is bounded by open space which keeps it from sprawling. Sufficient parking is provided for each dwelling unit to accommodate automobile ownership, but the number and length of trips is expected to be greatly reduced, perhaps by as much as 40 or 50 percent. Although the mix of land uses is similar from pocket to pocket, the master plan varies considerably to accept different physical constraints and citizen input, much like architectural types inflect into particular models or variations to recognize differences in local culture, climate, building materials, and practices. None of the Pedestrian Pocket precepts is new or extraordinary; taken singly they are embarrassingly obvious revivals of traditional patterns of settlement, but in concert they form a compelling new vision for urbanizing suburbia.

While Pedestrian Pockets and TODs were arising on the West Coast, the Traditional Neighborhood Design, or TND, had already taken root on the East Coast. Andres Duany and Elizabeth Plater-Zyberk were the pioneering authors of the concept and have continued to develop and apply it around the country and world. It is referred to as Neotraditionalism, a term that embraces architectural as well as town planning precepts. The two models have a great deal in common: small scale, mixed use, environmental sensitivity, internally consistent hierarchy of architectural, building, and street types, finite geometry with legible edges and a center, walkability, and alleys with accessory units and reliance on succinct graphic guidelines in lieu of traditional zoning codes. These are happy and significant convergences, especially given the fact that their respective authors come from different backgrounds and political ideologies. Pedestrian Pockets and TODs came from an energy and environmental design ethic. TNDs grew out of a more doctrinaire Euro-American urbanism. Pedestrian Pockets and TODs started with regionalism as a planning and environmental concept. TNDs originated more with traditional notions of city, town, type, and architecture, although they have a strong environmental record. Ideologically, one movement came from the left, one from the right.

While they share a great deal at the scale of the town or neighborhood, they diverge somewhat at other scales. TODs are predicated more on a regional transit and open space system, while TNDs are more rigorous about architectural typology, style, and detail. TNDs have architectural as well as urban design guidelines, regulating fence design and the color of architectural trim. Both are committed to establishing a hierarchy of known building types, but TNDs tend to be more literal in their architectural reinterpretation of historical precedent – at least at such places as the Kentlands in Maryland and Windsor in Florida. This dominance of Neotraditional architecture may lessen over time, as it has already at Seaside, Florida, the original TND and historic milestone in American town planning.

Despite their differences in origin and methodology, the East and West coast approaches are remarkably sympathetic and parallel in their results, spectacularly so given the myriad of design possibilities for a landscape as open as suburbia. They are both committed to environmental and social diversity, affordability, and sustainability, as well as transit and walkability. They both aim to restore a human-scaled, humane, and formally coherent sense of public and private place to American neighborhoods, towns, and cities before they dissolve further into endless, stereotypical sprawl and mindless imitations of themselves.

Congress for the New Urbanism

TODs and TNDs are so similar in intent and results that many architects and planners have embraced their principles with great fervor under the name of New Urbanism. In 1993, the first Congress for the New Urbanism (CNU) was convened in Alexandria, Virginia – called by founding members Duany, Plater-Zyberk, Calthorpe, Polyzoides, Moule, and Solomon. Since then three more congresses have been hosted, in increasing coalition with environmental and community organizations. The CNU's creed is indicative of the common polemic and concerns that have subsumed urban villages, Pedestrian Pockets, TODs, TNDs, Neotraditionalism and welded them into a single movement. Its values and goals are elaborated in the preamble to the Charter for the New Urbanism.

The Congress for the New Urbanism
views disinvestment in central cities, the spread of placeless sprawl, increasing separation by race and income, environmental deterioration, loss of agricultural lands and wilderness, and the erosion of society's built heritage as one interrelated community-building challenge.

We stand
for the restoration of existing urban centers and towns within coherent metropolitan regions, the reconfiguration of sprawling suburbs into communities of real neighborhoods and diverse districts, the conservation of natural environments, and the preservation of our built legacy.

We recognize
that physical solutions by themselves will not solve social and economic problems, but neither can economic vitality, community stability, and environmental health be sustained without a coherent and supportive physical framework.

We advocate
the restructuring of public policy and development practices to support the following principles: neighborhoods should be diverse in use and population; communities should be designed for the pedestrian and transit as well as the car; cities and towns should be shaped by physically defined and universally accessible public spaces and community institutions; urban places should be framed by architecture and landscape design that celebrate local history, climate, ecology, and building practice.

We represent
a broad-based citizenry, composed of public and private sector leaders, community activists, and multidisciplinary professionals. We are committed to reestablishing the

relationship between the art of building and the making of community, through citizen-based participatory planning and design.

We dedicate
ourselves to reclaiming our homes, blocks, streets, parks, neighborhoods, districts, towns, cities, regions, and environment.[1]

New Urbanism Criticized

As New Urbanists have stuck their chins further and further into the media stream, more and more critics have taken swipes at them. This is both natural and healthy in an open society, although it is unfortunate that much of the discourse is reduced to sound bites and short news pieces. Michael Dennis, urban designer and architecture professor at MIT, has commented that the New Urbanism is neither. Its principles and practices, he points out sympathetically and accurately, are old ones. And its primary focus, at least as reported in the press, has been suburban, not urban.

The first point is almost undeniable, but not quite. True, the New Urbanism revives many ideas about town and city planning that were mainstream before the Modern Movement. It is also true that New Urbanists believe a continued obsession with the "new" will not result in better neighborhoods, towns, cities, and regions and that there is nothing ethically or artistically wrong or weak about reviving and championing old, proven ideas. What *is* new about the New Urbanism is its totality. It attempts to promote a sort of unified design theory for an entire region – from the small scale (building block, street) through the intermediate scale (corridor, neighborhood, district) to the large scale (regional infrastructure and ecology). Although many of its ideas may seem obvious and old hat, the particular combination and orchestration of them are new. Also fresh is the New Urbanist insistence that physical placemaking must be carefully and thoroughly linked to public policy. New Urbanists have been more effective than their predecessors at reforming municipal, state, and federal policies.

The second point – that New Urbanism is not truly urban – is mistaken, although understandable given media coverage to date. The projects that have gotten the most attention are the Neotraditional towns like Seaside, Laguna West, Kentlands, and Harbor Town, most of which are located on greenfield sites in suburbia. The suburban agenda of the New Urbanists has been the most newsworthy because these new, imageable communities are built and occupied, flying in the face of conventional suburban development. But the New Urbanism is a regional strategy, with equally important ideas and proposals for downtown and inner city neighborhoods, as well as an interest in overall regional planning. (Of the seven design charrettes in Part II of this book, only one is in a classic suburban setting, and much of the CNU founders' work has been in urban areas.) Perhaps some of the confusion about the name could be cleared up by using "Neotraditional design," "Traditional Neighborhood Design," and "Pedestrian Pocket" to refer to suburban applications and "New Urbanism" as an umbrella term for the comprehensive regional strategy.

Another complaint has been about elitism within the movement. Specifically, the early Congresses for the New Urbanism were criticized for not being open to the public. This policy could be easily construed as a mark against a movement that is purportedly intended to build community. However, the conveners felt that restricting attendance to invitees was necessary to organize and focus the early events. In a sense, the early Congresses were meant to get ideas and principles on the table, clarified, ordered, and chartered before going public. Later conferences were opened up to anyone nominated by any previous attendee and ultimately to any paying registrant. This policy did step on many professional and academic toes and, in retrospect, may have resulted in more damage than operational advantage. CNU III in San Francisco in 1994 was a deliberate attempt to broaden the membership and build coalitions with other urban groups and environmental organizations. CNU IV in Charleston in 1996 invited known opponents of New Urbanism to debate openly its principles and practices. The Congresses, however, have never intended to be like the contemporary, open-ended conference or symposium, which typically asks more questions than it answers and often ends up in pluralist confusion. To design and build communities takes more than probing questions and an endless quest for all the answers. To act, we must settle on norms, standards, and specific designs, moving ahead even though all questions may not be fully resolved.

Perhaps the biggest challenge leveled at the New Urbanism is that it is another ideal vision conceived, ordained, and disseminated from above and not rooted in specific places or local cultures. This critique contends that architects and planners have always come up with beautiful, sanitized visions that will save the world and which, although provocative and even brilliant, are too idealized, ambitious, or disconnected from place or reality. To a large extent, that has been true of twentieth-century visions (Sant' Elia, Garnier, Le Corbusier, Wright, Krier). It does apply in some measure to the New Urbanism, which, it has been argued, is a "narrow representation or framework that denies the social, physical and economic diversity of the built North American landscape."[2] True, the proposed and built projects do try to apply an ideal diagram or plan. But any development that is faithful to the principles of the New Urbanism recognizes and celebrates what is unique about a place's history, cultures, climate, and architecture. Perhaps in the early going, TND and TOD site plans have been too formulaic – a design template from on high. But it takes this sort of single-minded effort and confidence, as well as a simple, clear diagram, to launch a new movement. In today's media circus, it takes more chest-beating, ego, and bombast than when Olmsted spawned the profession of landscape architecture or Ebenezer Howard founded the Garden City movement last century.

Related to this concern is the question of whether New Urbanist projects are too stand-alone, i.e., too separate and aloof from their existing physical and social context. This is a vexing issue, because their physical context is often too flawed or frayed to respect. A congested arterial strip with a monstrously wide roadway and a sea of asphalt parking lots ebbing and flowing with a tide of cars in front of low, cheap retail boxes is not a context worth honoring. In suburbia, there is generally not much good built fabric with which or off which a designer can work. In urbanized areas, especially those with substantial building stock, there is a stronger argument for both infill and reuse of existing buildings and infrastructure. In either case, dealing with the existing social fabric is very challenging. It is usually easier for designers and planners to work in an empty greenfield site than to knit and nudge new development into an existing neighborhood, where social, economic, and political groups and factions are in place and in many cases entrenched. If New Urbanism is to live up to its charter, it will have to take on successfully more of the messier and compromised work of infill and repair, whether in center city, urban neighborhoods, suburbia, new towns, or small towns.

Another criticism is that, despite all the hoopla, New Urbanist developments are not living up to their transportation promises and expectations. The argument has been made that there is a weakening link between land use and transportation in an increasingly automotive world and that pedestrian-oriented communities have only a marginal effect on household vehicle miles traveled (VMT). Pedestrian trips in TNDs and TODs, it is suggested, simply add to automobile trips rather than replace them.[3] While making walking and bicycling safer and more convenient may not be enough by itself to reduce auto dependence, it *is* an essential ingredient in an overall solution to auto dependency. Also necessary is reducing the subsidy, as well as the right-of-way, priority, and authority that automobiles enjoy in our society. And more and better public transit is needed with mixed-use development at every stop, so riders can walk or bike at either end of the trip. True, transit and walking will never displace private motorized vehicles, but the New Urbanism can ultimately reduce the number of trips from about ten per household to maybe six, as well as shorten the length of those trips (Figure 17.1). Also true, transit will never eliminate traffic congestion, because if and when highways become less crowded, transit riders will tend to drive more. But transit can put a lid on congestion. We must recognize that it will not be easy to change as deep a pattern as auto-dependence. It will take *all* of the programs, policies, and development strategies outlined in the CNU charter and in this and other books on the New Urbanism.

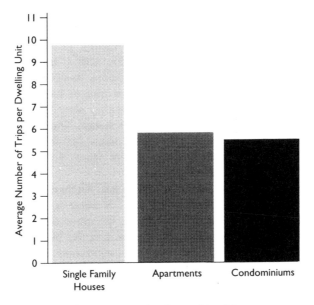

Figure 17.1 Weekday vehicle trip generation for residential areas

A final critique is that New Urbanist developments are not a marketing success and that people either are not ready for them or don't like them. It's clearly too early to measure marketability. As of early 1996, there were only several thousand housing units built in a handful of TNDs or TODs across the country. New urban villages in Seattle are still in the planning stages. Consumer surveys have produced mixed but generally favorable responses from home buyers and renters, as well as from prospective residents. Laguna West outside of Sacramento got off to a rocky financial start by falling into receivership during California's worst recession, but now the original developer has bought it back and sales have improved. Until the public has had a good chance to see the New Urbanism in fuller buildout and with more mature landscaping, it is too early to pronounce a verdict. And until the economic playing field is more nearly level, biases in pricing will also distort market responses. Also, superficial imitations of TNDs and TODs will inevitably muddy the waters and skew the results. (The same problem plagued the solar movement, with many impostors and exaggerated claims.)

Even if unbiased, the market is not always able to evaluate properly something as complicated as community. Humans do not always opt for what is in their best interests, especially long term interests that are hard to comprehend, such as sustainability. Sometimes human desires and needs are two different things. Other times, subsidies and penalties have accustomed people to habits they can no longer afford or have led them inadvertently into shortsighted behavior. Yes, the market-place must eventually accept New Urbanism if it is to succeed and endure. But only the test of elapsed time with market prices that reflect true costs will determine its true value and validity.

The New Urbanism has its flaws, to be sure. Some people want to cherry-pick the positive parts and reject the objectionable parts. Accept the walkability but reject the narrow lots; keep the overall coherence but dilute the overly symmetrical town plans; include the single-family dwelling but reduce social elitism; keep it urban but make it greener; build rapid transit but don't take away the car; etc. Unfortunately, communities come in packages. They cannot be ordered up à la carte. Community design consists of complex tradeoffs, with a limited number of win–win solutions. For the most part it is slow, arduous, iterative, pluralist, and contested, punctuated by creative breakthroughs from time to time. It is not exact work. Community design is an approximation, community development a compromise. But that is not to say that it is casual or provisional. Once adopted – however imperfect – comprehensive plans, neighborhood plans, and design guidelines need to be implemented with consistency and conviction. (Leon Krier suggests that violations should be treated as a criminal offense.)

Why build new suburbs at all, some urbanists ask. We have no choice, because all American suburbanites and their offspring are not going to return to the urban or rural communities from which they migrated. We most need the New Urbanist models for the periphery of our cities. Flawed as it is, the New Urbanism is clearly better than the other models being purveyed in conventional suburbs. TODs, TNDs, and urban villages are far superior in economic, social, environmental, and urban design terms to the prevailing models of suburban development. In many ways they *are* a win–win proposition. Sound economics, healthy ecology, social reform, and design integrity fit happily into the New Urbanist canon. Rarely do so many moral and economic entries fall on the positive side of the ledger.

The New Urbanism is taking hold in the Pacific Northwest. LUTRAQ in Portland and urban villages in Seattle have been heavily influenced by the New Urbanism. Peter Calthorpe's work has included projects with Weyerhaeuser Real Estate Company in DuPont and at Snoqualmie Ridge. Northwest Landing at DuPont is the first built new town in the Seattle Region to realize many of the principles of New Urbanism. Likewise, many of the University of Washington charrettes and studios have applied these same principles over the last decade to real sites in the Seattle region, in some cases, galvanizing projects that are now in the works.

NOTES

1   Charter, Congress for the New Urbanism IV, Charleston, SC, May 1996.
2   John Kaliski, "The New Urbanism: Vocational Excellence Versus Design Paradox," (draft), Lincoln Institute of Land Policy seminar on "The Influences of New Urbanism," Cambridge, MA, Dec. 1995.
3   Genevieve Giuliano, "The Weakening Land Use/Transportation Connection," *On the Ground*, Summer 1995, pp. 12–14.

18

Urban or Suburban?

A discussion held at the GSD in July 1996, with invited commentary*

Advocates of New Urbanism are helping achieve what once seemed impossible: making Americans question their devotion to conventional suburban development and their complacency about its attendant sprawl and lack of community. Powerful constituencies such as national home builder associations are paying attention to the movement, as are mayors, and even federal institutions such as the Department of Housing and Urban Development. The possibility that a cultural shift is underway only increases the need to distinguish "the hype from the hope." Insofar as the New Urbanists contribute to encouraging demand for alternatives to sprawl, they deserve our admiration. Insofar as their principles degenerate into ineffective panaceas and mere icons of community, or the fashion of neotraditional subdivisions produces yet more sprawl, then the New Urbanists warrant our ire. The following discussions address this most compelling recent phenomenon in American urban practice.

Alex Krieger, GSD Professor in Practice of Urban Design

* Burns, Carol, Robert Campbell, Andres Duany, Jarold Kayden and Alex Krieger (1997) "Urban or Suburban?" (Roundtable discussion), *Harvard Design Magazine* 1, Winter/Spring, pp. 47–61. Copyright © 1997 by the President and Fellows of Harvard College.
PARTICIPANTS: **Carol Burns**, associate professor of architecture, GSD; **Robert Campbell**, architecture critic, *The Boston Globe*; **Andres Duany**, principal, Duany, Plater-Zyberk & Company, Inc., Architects, Miami; **Jerold Kayden**, associate professor of urban planning, GSD; **Alex Krieger**, professor in practice of urban design, GSD; author, with Anne Mackin, of *A Design Primer for Cities and Towns* and editor, with William Lennertz, of *Towns and Town-Making Principles: Andres Duany and Elizabeth Plater-Zyberk*; **Nancy Levinson**, associate editor, *Harvard Design Magazine*; **William Saunders**, editor, *Harvard Design Magazine*
COMMENTARY BY: **Ellen Dunham-Jones**, assistant professor of architecture, MIT; member of the Congress for New Urbanism; **Gerald E. Frug**, Samuel R. Rosenthal Professor of Law, Harvard Law School; author of, most recently, "The Geography of Community," *Stanford Law Review*; **Alex Krieger** (also a participant); **William Morrish**, program director and professor of architecture, Design Center for American Urban Landscape, University of Minnesota, author of *Planning to Stay*; **John O. Norquist**, Mayor, Milwaukee, Wisconsin; **Edward Robbins**, lecturer in urban design, GSD; author of *Why Architects Draw*; **Gretchen Schneider**, MArch '97, GSD; **Daniel Solomon**, principal, Solomon Inc., San Francisco; author of *ReBuilding*; **Gwendolyn Wright**, professor of architecture, Columbia University; author of *The Politics of Design in French Colonial Urbanism*

Saunders: Andres, how has your thinking about town planning changed lately, given that several of your projects have been built and have thus allowed you to test your ideas against reality?

Duany: I've been confirming the original definition of "neotraditionalism," which isn't well known. It was a term conceptualized by Stanford Research in 1985; that firm was commissioned by the Disney Company to explore and predict the ethos of the baby boomers for the next three decades; in their presentation they defined "neotraditionalism" as a non-ideological selection of what's considered to be the best for home environments. The researchers illustrated their study: they showed a photograph of a Victorian mantelpiece with a Braun alarm clock sitting on it. The neotraditionalists, they argued, might choose an old-fashioned room, but they wouldn't buy a Victorian clock that has to be wound and might not be accurate. They would choose an up-to-the-minute German clock. Moreover, the neotraditionalists would have modern plumbing and kitchens in their old houses. Now, a traditionalist would restore a Victorian bathroom, claw-foot tub and all, while a modernist would think it improper to live in a Victorian house. The point is that neotraditionalism tries to incorporate, pragmatically, whatever works best.

Wright: This use of the word "pragmatically" diminishes the complexity of the concept. Thoughtful pragmatists don't simply act; they choose where to experiment and where to acquiesce, they speculate about the relative effects of any strategy, and they acknowledge and try to mitigate the inevitability that some people will be hurt by an action. If a plan of action seems self-evident, take heed: beware

of generalizing too broadly on the basis of one's own ideas (or those of a client), of treating these priorities as if they were obvious and natural. Andres Duany can't escape ideology, any more than the rest of us.

We have come to understand the value of eschewing ideology – of not falling in love with this or that, but of trying to find the best solution or model and implementing it through design. I've also come to regard developers not as barbarians to be educated, but as people who may know a thing or two. That's a fundamental change in our outlook.

Krieger: I'd like to venture a criticism of the New Urbanism. It's not uncommon that as a movement emerges and matures, it becomes rigid, even strident, too sure of its propositions. Now specifically, that might lead one to argue that Seaside, your first major development, was articulated in too narrow a range, and thus as a model is neither flexible nor productive.

Duany: I think you may be right. But its focus makes it an effective polemical statement.

Krieger: The buildings at Seaside are one-to-four stories high, counting roofs and attics, and they're primarily single-family houses. The size of the lots is more or less uniform. Now compare that, for example, to Harvard Street here in Cambridge. It's parallel to and one block north of Massachusetts Avenue, the commercial spine of Cambridge, and within a half mile or so it contains a great variety of residential types: houses just as highly designed as those at Seaside, as well as red-brick apartment buildings and a few concrete towers from the 1960s. I think it's a marvelous street, in large part because of this diversity – a diversity that accommodates both big single-family

Victorians and apartment buildings rented mostly to students. But here's the thing: if you were to try to write a formula, a code, for it, it would sound like a disaster.

Duany: Again, I agree with you. You've raised several interesting issues. Let me begin to respond by emphasizing the difference between our intentions and our just not knowing enough about the process of town making. For example, one thing we didn't know early on, when designing Seaside, was that a height limit, when applied to the top of pitched roofs, would result in buildings "pavilionizing," or breaking down in scale. So, one part of our practice has involved mastering the instrument of coding.

Another aspect has involved being in constant friction with the real world – there is no way that our ideas can become rigid when we're constantly being challenged by developers, clients, users, etc. We often collaborate with other planners and architects who are not necessarily sympathetic to our ideas. Our charrettes are tremendously educational to us. Lately we've been inviting people we want to learn from, to keep enriching the intellectual gene pool of New Urbanism. I'm very aware of how common it is for design offices that were once wonderful and creative to become tired, stodgy, deadhead. In fact, we've purchased land and plan to build an academy next door to our office. In the evenings our staff will teach. This will invigorate our work.

Now, although it's important to be flexible, open to new ideas, it's also important, when you confront the world, to maintain principles that are inviolate – one thing you can learn from Le Corbusier is that to influence and persuade, you must be polemical. You can't convince people by equivo-cating, by saying, "Well, on the one hand this, on the other that." You'll bore them, and they'll chew you up. As a polemicist, you have to clarify matters, as Corbu and Leon Krier did. And you have to attack. Whenever I'm invited to speak to the Urban Land Institute [ULI], I try to destabilize them with my certainty that they are wrong.

In important ways, the Congress for the New Urbanism [CNU] is modeled on CIAM. CIAM changed the world. Our ideology is different but our methodology is the same – congresses, charter, etc. And, like CIAM, we are selective – our membership is not open. You have to know what you're doing to be invited. We don't meet to teach, but to hone ideas. At the CNU we have fierce internal debates. The work of Calthorpe, Solomon, Moule, and Polyzoide might seem similar to outsiders, but we argue ferociously.

Levinson: What's the most trenchant critique that's come out of one of your internal debates recently?

Duany: Well, here's one: How do you define and draw the urban boundary? Is it drawn as a continuous circumventing line, as in Portland, or is it drawn according to the ideas of Benton MacKaye, where you protect what needs to be protected and let the city flow past? I would argue that the urban boundary drawn as an edge is essentially arbitrary; in this scenario the farmer within the boundary becomes a millionaire, and the farmer outside the limits stays a farmer. Such limits cannot hold, politically. But if you use Benton MacKaye's method – as you do here in the Boston region – you can protect in court that which is objectively defensible, such as a forest or a wetland; and the natural environment has some stability. But a lot of CNU members disagree with that approach.

Wright: Why is it only natural landscapes that merit such concerned intervention? Human ecologies must be protected, too. How can one identify and nurture, for instance, more and various modes of play and self-observation, of livelihood, or of responses to age?

Another debate within the CNU concerns style. Some felt we should state that neotraditionalism does *not* imply the use of vernacular styles. Actually, I think style is uncontrollable. In places like Toronto, for example, people select fairly modernist dwellings. In the US this is seldom the case. We pay attention to the public process. Then we use what we learn to write an urban code; a code is a neutral instrument that does not necessarily prescribe a popular style, but rather allows it.

Krieger: One of the interesting things about Harvard Street is that it's not coded.

Duany: Are you sure? I would think it's coded; almost everything is coded.

Krieger: If everything is coded, then nothing is coded. It's a question of definition.

Duany: By code I always mean the legal instrument, never the intellectual concept.

Kayden: It would be a disservice to claim that Duany Plater-Zyberk's codes resemble existing zoning codes, because one of your major contributions has been to undermine existing zoning. Your coding *is* different than the coding that exists in the Cambridge zoning ordinance and that determined much of Harvard Street.

Campbell: In this context it seems important to remember that the streets of Cambridge have developed over centuries and are the result of serial coding.

Duany: I wish I knew Harvard Street because I could probably give you six rules that would result in a similar street. You can code anything.

Campbell: Yes, but you've made two different statements. One is that you could code anything and the other that everything is coded.

Kayden: And you've made a much more substantive, normative statement about coding: you've converted the word "zoning" into a bad word, as opposed to a neutral one.

Duany: That was Krier's argument. To him zoning means the separation of uses.

Kayden: I agree that zoning is theoretically a neutral instrument; it's whatever we want it to be. You have, however, looked empirically at zoning, particularly in the suburbs, and you've said, "Shame on you, we need to change this." So "zoning" came to be seen as the culprit in the suburbs.

Duany: Right. But don't give us personally too much credit. The New Urbanism is a movement. Lizz [Plater-Zyberk] and I would argue that Krier clarified our understanding of zoning, and that, while I talk about it more than most, there are dozens of people doing this work.

Kayden: One of the great current debates in law, and zoning in particular, is the debate between present rules and the exercise of discretion on a case-by-case basis, perhaps guided by some rules. The Town and Country Planning Act, Great Britain's contribution to the world of planning, has operated to a large degree on the basis of discretion, whereas the German and then the American zoning system have tended to operate on the basis of present rules that can be read by everybody and are read especially by developers who, as a result of these rules, have the predictability and stability that they claim they want. Do you still see value in preset rules?

Duany: That's an ongoing debate. Will good architecture result from preset rules, or do such rules actually harm the work of creative architects such as Aldo Rossi, Richard Meier, etc.? For example, Seaside was built according to one of the most liberal architectural codes we've written, because [developer] Robert Davis has a sophisticated eye and knows how to use a discretionary code. Now, in other places, we've written much stricter codes because we didn't have the same confidence. We adjust the code to the situation.

Kayden: What if the developer is the public sector?

Duany: Well, you cannot fix the public sector permanently – the law can always be voted in and out of effect. We try to make codes for the public sector resistant to political change, by making them weaker, less prescriptive. We have lower expectations for public-sector architecture.

Burns: In what ways do you private and public codes differ? Is the street configuration changed, or the coding of individual buildings, or the quality of the architecture *per se*?

Duany: The code for Seaside is strong typologically and weak architectually; most people don't realize that. The architectural code is very informal, having to do with the use of real materials, minimum sizes for the rafters, and so on. Seaside looks the way it does largely because individual residents have commissioned certain styles. There are some modernist buildings at Seaside – but they're not very popular. In our experience, what happens when you free up the architectural code is that people tend to choose vernacular architecture. After Seaside,

we learned to code more precisely, both typologically and architecturally; but the prescriptions of a code are always adjustable. Some of our latest codes, for example, deal with frontage only; in these, we say very little about the buildings, other than the ways they perform relative to the street. By the way, we have found that there are only seven frontages in the world: seven ways that a building can engage the street.

One important way to ensure an appropriate measure of creativity is to allow civic buildings to remain wholly uncoded. We would not code a campus, a church, a city hall. The dialectic of urbanism is that private buildings are to be silent and behave coherently to create public spaces, whereas the civic buildings are to freely embody the aspirations of the society and of the artists who create them. Why should the work of architects like Richard Meier be coded? His architecture is suitable for civic buildings; but, if he wants to do a house, he has to behave, to get along with his neighbors.

Krieger: Of course, the irony here is that many would say that Meier's greatest buildings are private houses.

Kayden: One could also argue that there is a value to individualism in the design of houses, in expressing oneself through one's house.

Wright: We can't have it both ways. Our justified praise for the elegantly distinctive individualism of a Meier house is directly related to our usual critique of the excessive, often jarring gestures of individualism along many suburban streets. We can't expect people to defer willingly to our judgment about which architects (and which clients) should be allowed creative license and which should be content to fashion an anonymous background. As Duany rightly points out, even a great architect has to defer somewhat to the world beyond his or her own design. It's the relationship between the parts and the whole that needs oversight and maintenance, as much as visual cohesion *per se*.

A caveat, however, about controls. For the past century, at least, the most common regulations in American residential neighborhoods have involved restrictive convenants; and now there have developed more devious systems to exclude those people considered "undesirable" and to outlaw those activities deemed "deviant" (such as creating an independent home office or workshop, or renting out a room). As we all know, such paranoid desire for control has lately only intensified and extended. The New Urbanists must acknowledge the subtext of conformity and hostility that usually underlies any kind of code or guideline. Of course, this isn't to say that throwing away controls releases us from these problems.

Duany: Let me explain. In our projects we enable the owners to choose their own designer. Neotraditional design is not about selling a whole sector to a single developer but about dividing up the land so that someone can buy a small portion and control it.

It's interesting – builders have learned that people want their private houses to fit in. If only one house on the street has a porch, and the others don't, the house with the porch won't sell. The authentic personal expression in an American house currently takes place in the backyard. One problem with Seaside, in this regard, is that we made the backyards public, visually. One of the social experiments of Seaside was to create a network of paths that run by the backs of the houses; this was intended to encourage people to use their front porches. Well, this is exactly what happened, and the backyards are underused. But that's not fair, because as a result residents have no truly private outdoor places. Urbanism requires the creation of both community and privacy. In our later projects, such as Windsor, we were obsessive about private backyards; if you want to raise chickens out back, that's fine.

Kayden: Andres, do you see a distinction between government or the public sector adopting such rules and a private developer being converted to New Urbanism and adopting these rules in a private setting?

Duany: Typically, our initial work is for a private developer. We write a code for the new neighborhood or village. Often, we are subsequently asked to rewrite the existing code for the municipality.

Kayden: But it's one thing to change the law to respond to demands from customers represented by a developer and quite another for government to require in advance that people act in a certain way.

Duany: Government is always weaker than the private sector. When you buy into a private development, the code is referenced in the purchase agreement, and you contract to act in accordance. So private coding can be stronger.

Krieger: I'd like to return to something Andres said that seemed stunning – coding the private, not the public, sector. Historically, however, the public realm, including its civic monuments, has been the most tightly controlled, usually through an act of authority; and private development, including where people live, has been the least controlled.

Duany: I was imprecise: what I meant is that we control the general spatial and functional definition of the public realm but allow the specialized elements within it to be determined more freely. For example, we control the making of the street and the square, but not the expression of the civic buildings within the square or the light standards along the streets.

Krieger: Another of your statements struck me strongly as well, because it seemed so refreshing – I refer to your comment that the aesthetic debate is trivial. I would guess that a lot of people assume that aesthetics are central to New Urbanism.

Duany: It definitely is to some members; but we adjust the level of control in regard to the desired degree of harmony. The citizens usually decide the style. This is something that we usually offer potential residents by showing them images of different scenarios. I may show them slides, for example, of buildings that create a very harmonious whole, such as the Rue de Rivoli. Few Americans like that model. We show them other choices with strategic adjustments such as mandatory balcony lines, or specific percentages of solid to void, or vertically proportioned openings, or a set range of colors. Rules can create an urbanism, and we are concerned with that level of design rather than with the issue of whether the style is Victorian or neo-Modern. But when you give Americans choices, they usually respond with the same answer: vernacular. If you want to impose a modernist downtown, you really have to push them that way, because there's a strong preference for traditional architecture. It's seen as "normal" or "neutral."

Campbell: When you are criticized about Kentlands, you often argue that the criticisms are premature because the design will mature in the fullness of time. But nothing that you've said here so far has anything to do with the fullness of time. What you've been saying is, "Here it is, any student can do it, boom, let's go."

Duany: Well, first, much of the criticism about Kentlands concerns the town center – people say that it's not built. But I know that it is in the pipeline; the town center will be built, with a vengeance. But that's not the question you're asking.

Campbell: The question is: how are your towns going to change over the next half century?

Duany: I'll tell you how Kentlands was designed. We played a sort of game. There were five existing farm buildings, and each designer sequentially added buildings and spaces. In a sense, we were trying to compress history: to achieve in a short time what would happen over a longer period. Today this method is part of our process. The way we design is that Lizz or I do the parti, very crudely; we then hand it to the first designer, who has it for two hours before handing it over to the next designer, and so forth.

Burns: That's Surrealist methodology.

Wright: How fascinating that both New Urbanists and poststructuralists are trying to build contingency, plurality, and experimentation into the process of design! There may be the possibility of a larger architectural culture after all.

Duany: In the meantime, the other designers are running around, looking at the site, studying the architectural or urban history of the region, etc. We sequentially hand over the design not only to architects but also to landscape architects, engineers, and so on. You can see this in Kentlands. Kentlands has authentic variety, built-in disjunctions and inconsistencies. That's important. Our towns plans have a history, they're not finite designed places – mistakes are inscribed and, of course, they continue to accrue as the towns are built out.

Campbell: I'd like to put Kentlands in the framework of the larger issue of settlement patterns over time. Kentlands is often criticized as another stop on the highway, another suburb for commuters. At the same time, I suspect we're entering an era during which half the population will move to Montana and the other half will move downtown, because those are the two best places to live, and new communications technology lets you live anywhere. So what happens to the suburbs? Given this larger framework of settlement patterns, what happens to Kentlands?

Duany: Kentlands will be resilient. It was designed to comprise a balance of offices and shops as well as dwellings. The problem is that the office market was overbuilt at the time, and is still soft, so Kentlands won't have many offices. But, serendipitously, a new settlement that we are now designing on adjacent land, the former site of the National Geographic Society, will include offices. Also, Kentlands will contain many more live-work units than we originally envisioned. Places like Kentlands, with their small-scale platting and their variety of dwellings and flexible uses, can evolve organically. They will survive. The standard suburban monoculture is vulnerable to the forces that you refer to.

Saunders: Is it ever possible to *create* community? Can one make "instant" towns or cities with any organic integrity?

Duany: American towns are all instant. Look at the cities of the Midwest and West – all instant. American urbanism is designed quickly and built quickly.

Krieger: You're right about American towns. But one major difference is that

when Guthrie, Oklahoma – to give just one example – was designed in three days, it was the only town within a radius of about 100 miles. Therefore it became a real town. Today, your Kentlands is next to someone else's Windsor and down the road from yet someone else's Seaside. Thus they all need to be interactive; it's a very different situation to make a town today than it was a century ago. The townspeople of Guthrie had nowhere to shop but in the stores of Guthrie. The citizens of Kentlands can choose from any number of suburban DC malls. This is an important issue – it's not just about shopping *per se*, but about behavioral patterns. Can the way of life of Kentlands' residents really be defined as "urban"?

Duany: We asked that question of an anthropologist, Edward LiPuma, of the University of Miami, an expert on suburbia. We showed him what we were doing, explained our goals, and asked: will this work? He responded that it will work, but it will take a generation, which he defined as nineteen years.

In his view, there is an immature stage in new towns. It takes time, he said, to find the right mix, for the teenagers to find their hangouts, for the right shops to move in, for the jobs to appear so that people look for dwellings near their work, etc.

Wright: Whether it's Sigfried Giedion or Alexander Garvin, architects too easily use history and social science to legitimate their own preferences, rather than to challenge and expand their ideas. I'd like to evoke the historian and political scientist Charles Beard, who was deeply involved in urban planning in New York and Tokyo in the 1920s. His proposals always acknowledged contingency and provisionality. "Will it work?" has to be expanded, he contended, to ask "Whom will it work for? Who will be damaged? Who decides? Who doesn't have a voice? What haven't I thought about? What am I blocking out of my vision?"

Burns: I'd like to move from time to scale. One thing that any urbanism must do is to acknowledge several scales at once – the scale of the street, the neighborhood, the town, the city. These new greenfield suburban towns are no-brainers, in a sense; you could design many variations that would be successful by various criteria. To me, the potential interest of New Urbanism is how it confronts more difficult problems – for instance, inner-city sites. But I'd like you to address this issue of moving across scales, because it seems New Urbanism works very well up to the scale of the town, but not beyond that. So to take up the issue Alex raised – what kind of urbanism happens when you have Kentlands next to Windsor next to Seaside? Is that the image of the city that you want to be making as a *city*, not a town?

Solomon: Why do Seaside and Kentlands assert themselves in this conversation like toy punching bags that keep popping up again after you knock them down? TNDs, Kentlands, and Seaside are huge contributions, to be sure, but what do we have to do to broaden the discourse? What about other New Urbanist projects like those in Cleveland, Portland, San José? What about the repair of Boston, Seattle, San Francisco? What about the CNU initiatives with the federal Department of Housing and Urban Development? What about the Department of Transportation? Wake up, everybody. Something bigger is going on.

Duany: That's a very interesting question to which there's a very precise answer. The density of modern urban design is controlled by parking. That's important to understand. Density is parking, parking is density, parking is profits, parking is power: everything is controlled by parking. And when you start designing, you find that sixteen units per acre is the highest density that works with parking. Beyond that you have to use heroic measures to accommodate parking.

Solomon: Our San Francisco projects are 40 to 55 dwelling units/acre, with no heroic measures.

Burns: Such as underground or structured parking?

Duany: Yes. Now, this creates an interesting situation. At sixteen units per acre, everybody lives in townhouses, which results in a social monoculture. Townhouses are important, but so are other housing types. You need mansions, because the individuals who are likely to support the necessary civic buildings are wealthy and will want big houses. And once you start to include the standard 50, 70, 100, 120-foot lots to balance the society, density becomes eight units to the gross acre. Then there are the parks and the schools to fold in, lowering it still more. Beyond this you ratchet up in one leap to a metropolitan condition such as Boston, San Francisco, or Manhattan, where transit truly works and density is unlimited.

Solomon: San Francisco depends on cars, and most people drive.

Krieger: I would still argue, though, that the real issue is whether you – or any of us – can persuade Americans to accept denser housing patterns; because even sixteen units per acre will not support an effective system of mass transport.

Duany: According to Peter Calthorpe it will.

Krieger: Calthorpe's assertion remains to be proven. So how do you respond to those who say that you're perpetuating a low-density, car-dependent, *suburban* condition, albeit through design? Another way to put it is to ask whether the New Urbanism is not, in fact, the New Suburbanism. You refer to urban models in your speeches, but your projects do not reproduce the urbanity of, say, Boston or Providence. Are you not perpetuating suburbia, perhaps even making it more palatable, through better designs, for a new generation of homeowners?

Duany: You've asked a very complex question. What would happen if, let's say, Gaithersburg [the municipality in which Kentlands is located] were uniformly coded with a TND [Traditional Neighborhood Development] ordinance? There would then be a series of neighborhoods like Kentlands next to each other, and neighborhoods of that density make a town, not a city like Boston or Providence, but a good town like Alexandria, Virginia, or Annapolis, Maryland. In fact, Kentlands is much denser than many respectable American towns; it has many apartment buildings. Actually, what would result is a structure like that in Clarence Perry's 1929 diagram of the Neighborhood Unit. This differs from suburbia; this model attempts to locally balance and "micro-mesh" various uses, such as housing, workplaces, shops, schools, etc. Suburbia might be *statistically* identical to New Urbanist towns, but its form consists of discrete shopping centers, office parks, and housing subdivisions which, in fact, are segregated by income in an absolute way. A place like Kentlands, in contrast, mixes income groups radically. In a single block there's a variety of housing, from rental apartments to townhouses; in another area there are contiguous apartments, townhouses, and expensive single family houses. The ULI is astounded by this mixing of housing types. "How did you do it?" they asked. And I responded, "It wasn't an issue because the architectural vernacular of all the parts, being identical, acts as a kind of camouflage."

Wright: Does a mixture of architectural types and sizes guarantee the social diversity and interchanges we associate with urban life? Does this approach, in making a planned neighborhood more visually enticing, make it more expensive, and thus less affordable to a wide range of people, and hence less urban? That said, DPZ's commitment to variety is a step in the right direction. Like all of us, they need to find incentives and strategies to make the sociopolitical reality of urban diversity coalesce with the architectural representation of such diversity.

Here's a paradox: the architectural world thinks that all this is conservative; the development industry thinks it is radical to the danger point, courting the bankruptcy of the developer, and even endangering their entire industry. These are the two worlds and the two critiques that we are straddling. And – just for the record – the development world interests me much more than the architectural world.

Burns: You may be setting up polarities that do not in fact exist. Many of us here are also very interested in both worlds.

Duany: Point taken. But let me explain how we create these mixed-income communities, because it relates back to style. Empirically, we have found that there are two ways to convince developers to build – and people to live in – these intensely variegated new towns. One way is to code unit type – as we did at Seaside. At Seaside, the same unit types face each other across the street; there's an avenue of mansions, another of townhouses. People respond very strongly to their street frontage; what happens in the back can be another world as far as they're concerned. You can observe this phenomenon in aerial photographs everywhere. We use this method with the more conservative developers.

At Kentlands, we did something different: the platting of lots there is flexible, but the architectural language is coded. The great unifier is style. There might be a townhouse next to an apartment building, but the buildings are all brick, for instance, with vertically proportioned openings and shingled, pitched roofs. So mixing people is not an issue because the high-density housing looks like the low-density housing. This is a powerful tool. And what's more, it can integrate uses: offices, shops, and housing. If you control the look of buildings, everything is compatible. In this sense I think a common language is important. It can be a great instrument. If you don't code style – if you free up the architect to do an office building in glass and steel – then the whole thing, in a sense, explodes, and people can't stand being next to that which looks different.

Solomon: A very interesting idea far more easily realized along the East Coast, with its reasonably intact 300-year-old building traditions, than in the American West, where vernacular building traditions are far more deeply buried by debased modernism and developer kitsch.

Kayden: But there's distinction between what people say they want and what people really use.

Krieger: I agree; there's a difference between behavior and expression of desire. I happen to live within a short walk of a corner store; I'm very glad it's there, but if the proprietor depended upon the frequency with which I shop in his store, he wouldn't prosper. Most of the time I find it easier to shop at another store near where I'm working, or to buy in quantity at big supermarkets where the prices are lower.

Duany: Yes, but you may appreciate that store when you are old, and your children will probably use it often. I'd like to reemphasize the difficulty of analyzing new towns. We are looking at immature communities; they are not yet in balance and shouldn't be judged in the same way one would judge older places. Conversely, the problem with studying mature communities is that they're full of tourists who distort the statistics. There's such a scarcity of decent urbanism in this country that good cities are tourist attractions.

Burns: But I'd like to look again at this issue of market research. There's a study of worker productivity in which the workplace was first painted one color and productivity improved; then it was painted another color and productivity again improved. Then it was painted yet again, and productivity still increased. This continued for awhile, until researchers figured out that the key was not the color—

Duany: It was the change.

Burns: Yes; the workers were responding to the fact that their environment was being attended to.

Campbell: That raises the question of how one sustains a sense of attention to the environment.

Kayden: Or how one knows what in fact affects behavior.

Krieger: And, of course, behavior is not always predictable. We all understand the evils of high rise housing projects, and yet some of the most expensive real estate in the world is in high-rise buildings. So the human response to form is not constant.

Duany: Generally that's true; but it is predictable by other measures – age, class, region, ethnic group, etc. This is what sophisticated marketing studies determine.

Levinson: We could probably extend this idea to what you were talking about earlier, to the use of style as a unifier in New Urbanism. It occurs to me that many Americans who were raised in the "traditional" suburbs of the 1950s – in stylistically unified and conformist environments – reacted strongly against all that unity, which some saw as stultifying, and got the hell out. So I'm wondering whether all these studies that measure and predict human behavior are often too narrow in scope, too unaware of the range of human response to situations, of the fact, for instance, that what one generation embraces another generation rejects.

Duany: I see your point. But consider the context of postwar suburban development: typically one office or one developer designed an area of a great size. There's less variety than there would be if every building were designed by a different architect, which is what we propose as an ideal. There's infinitely more variety in the towns we design than in conventional suburbia. We divide the entire site into lots, and do not permit the same builder to build whole sectors, which, by the way, is a tremendous pain. You have to look at all this in the context of current practice, and, in that context, the variety of the New Urbanism is radical.

Krieger: What Nancy said reminded me of another critique of your work

that has lately emerged. In *Architecture*, Heidi Landecker wrote about her recent tour through half a dozen or so of the most progressive New Urbanist communities; she was struck by a sense of great homogeneity of appearance, scale, demographics, and observable activity at particular moments. She noted a general absence of public space and commercial activities. In short, she described these places as not all that radically different from older suburbs; and she suggests that they are producing, or maybe reinforcing, a new kind of conformity. She and others have surmised that these places foster a sense of security in a world that these days feels insecure, and they grant that this is comforting, although perhaps not appropriate or even desirable.

Campbell: It seems inevitable that any place created all at once will have a certain homogeneity.

Krieger: That wasn't Landecker's point, exactly. She was saying that the new towns in California looked, behaved, and felt like the ones in Massachusetts or Virginia and that they were populated by the same rather narrow spectrum of the population. Maybe she's a poor observer.

Duany: No, she's not necessarily a poor observer. There are many towns being built with picket fences and so forth that are not TNDs. You should see *Builder Magazine* this week. The cover story is all about supposedly New Urbanist towns, but not one is an authentic TND. They're all single-use communities. There's a lot of fake stuff out there, and a lot of writers can't tell the difference. This is now the great vulnerability of the movement.

Krieger: You've noted this often over the years, which raises the question: how do you avoid being co-opted?

Duany: Well, that's a problem.

Kayden: Andres, you said earlier that these towns are propositions. You quoted an anthropologist who suggested that they would require a generation nineteen years to mature. If we were sitting around this table nineteen years from now, and I asked you to cite three key improvements in human behavior that have made American society better and that result from New Urbanism, what would those three be?

Duany: First, I think the life of children will be richer. I think a generation of children will benefit from not growing up in cul-de-sacs, but in a network of streets providing access to parks, schools, stores, and the like. With a network of streets, kids can have the run of the entire neighborhood. Have you ever taken a kid who grew up in West Palm Beach County to Paris? Well, I took students to Paris a few years ago, and they found it scary. I had to say, "It's okay, you can go here, you can go out at night. Yes, I know it's dirty, but go ahead, it's all right." They were uneasy in Paris because they had grown up in an environment that was "perfect"; they had been vaccinated against urbanism. I don't believe that at this moment there's one piece of paper on a lawn anywhere in West Palm Beach County. It's maintained perfectly – and privately.

Wright: But aren't you making perfect places, or as close an approximation as possible? Isn't there a risk of hegemonic control, together with limited options outside that system? Is Kentlands a neotraditional Singapore?

Campbell: I had a similar experience when I brought a group of architecture students, most about thirty years old, from Tampa up to Boston. They stayed in Kenmore Square, and we walked from there to Newbury Street; and it became clear to me that they'd seen places like this in movies – they'd seen sidewalk cafés and people strolling the streets and looking in shop windows – but didn't realize that such places existed outside the media. They couldn't believe it.

Duany: It's amazing, isn't it? If it were not for Hollywood and even for Disney, many Americans simply wouldn't know about street life.

The second improvement that I believe the New Urbanism will help bring about is that it will be possible to age in place in these communities. They will be viable places in which to live when you lose your ability to drive, when you become fearful of driving at night or in the snow. Too often this makes people move into retirement communities. But New Urbanist towns are designed to make pedestrian mobility possible.

Levinson: The changes you've described would certainly be beneficial. But we're still a long way from the dirt and diversity of Paris.

Krieger: Robert, didn't you once describe Quincy Market as "a halfway house for disenfranchised suburbanites."

Campbell: "Recovering suburbanites" was the actual phrase—

Krieger: Andres, are Kentlands and other New Urbanist developments halfway houses for recovering suburbanites? Halfway there on the road toward a real recovery of urbanism, an urbanism that these places do not yet represent, because of the factors we've already mentioned?

Norquist: New Urbanism has appeal across the political spectrum, not just to environmentalists and neighborhood activists on the left. CNU has associations with conservative Paul Weyrich, who has written on the benefits of transit and TND to the construction of a moral society. The conservative American Enterprise Institute has published Andres Duany's thoughts.

Duany: That's a good question. The first thing to say is that not all of our projects are the same. Windsor is one thing, Kentlands another, and so on.

Campbell: For what it is, Windsor seems to me remarkably successful.

Duany: Windsor is about architecture – about *sobriety* in architecture; it's about sweating off the vulgarity that has taken over so much Florida architecture. It is in some ways a perfect place. Kentlands, on the other hand, is an extraordinarily imperfect place. Every time I visit I'm astonished at how like a real place it looks because of its imperfect character. Many of our projects are formally resolved to a high degree. For various reasons, though, Kentlands is almost a mess. But when I walk along its paths that don't always line up and that are made of asphalt, I say, "This is like Pittsburgh! This is great!" In fact, I would bet that in nineteen years, people won't realize that it was a planned community.

Campbell: Of course, that's the fate of many planned communities. What's the third answer to Jerold's question?

Kayden: Well, it obviously will have to do with advantages for the middle-aged – you've already covered children and the elderly.

Duany: Here's an example. My secretary lives in Kentlands, close to our office there. She's a divorcee who owns one car; she could not easily live in conventional suburbia because she has a daughter who also needs the car. So there's an instance of one person whose daily life has been positively affected by these places – and there will be many such cases. To be relieved of the *need* to own more than one car – that's a great thing. According to *USA Today*, it costs $6,400 a year to own a car. So if you figure that an extra $6,000 per year, at a 10 per cent mortgage rate, translates into $60,000 of housing purchase capability, this gives people the ability to improve their living situations enormously.

Levinson: So a couple living in a TND would need only one car?

Duany: It would be easier there than elsewhere. You can argue that their teenager won't need a car at all.

Kayden: I think that would have to be proved, and one would want to see the studies you cite.

Duany: Just wait nineteen years. There are fourteen years to go for Kentlands and I am confident there will be substantial statistical differences between Kentlands and more traditional developments.

Campbell: I think Andres has made a very valuable argument, without even discussing all the codes, roads, maintenance, and so on.

Burns: Income mixing is one of the more interesting aspects of New Urbanism. Income mixing in the suburbs has been rare, and it relates to an issue we have not yet raised. The New Urbanism, as it's matured, has managed to align a number of disparate groups – people who are interested in public housing, historic preservationists, environmentalists, interests that do not have much obviously in common. It's intriguing that each group sees New Urbanism as a way to address its own very specific issues. Different people have looked at these "traditional" environments and seen something in them that relates to their concerns. Among other things, this is an incredible testament to the power of the built environment to stimulate ways to think.

Duany: The CNU thinks of New Urbanism as a solution to *many* problems. In fact, we are soon going to ally the CNU South with a mature environmental organization, the Southern Environmental Law Center. We plan to bring together the groups and train them to represent each other's concerns.

Levinson: Will the CNU be trained by the environmentalists as well as vice versa?

Duany: Yes. We will theoretically be able to represent our agendas interchangeably, not as we do now, occasionally and tentatively, but completely and with full understanding. Can you imagine the power of such an alliance?

Burns: I would extend this idea of bringing together different worlds to the relationship between academia and practice: academics and practitioners are not in opposing worlds. Both realms can benefit from the other. I would even suggest that as New Urbanism develops, it could be less about salesmanship and could actually contribute to the sad state of architectural theory as it exists today, especially with respect to its own methodology. New Urbanism works in modes that are socially empirical, self-conscious in terms of discipline, and engaged in dialogue with others. These methodologies of bridging distinct realms could help foster a contribution to theory in architecture.

Duany: About salesmanship – I've been reading Daniel Boorstin's history of this country. He makes it clear that America was built on boosterism. The West could not have been colonized without outrageous boosterism. Boosterism supports our performance as a

movement – not just mine, which is perhaps an extreme version. We try to replicate the American style of getting things done quickly and effectively. I was reading Boorstin and thought, "This is how it was done back then. How it was always done. This is how Kansas City came to be."

I'd like to tell you about an analogy made by Christopher Alexander. Years ago he wanted to study the TND Ordinance; he said that if it did what we said it did, then it was a great thing. I replied that I didn't think it was as great as *A Pattern Language*. He then suggested that both the TND and *A Pattern Language* were like appliances needing power – and while his appliance might be better in an absolute way, our appliance is more practical because it plugs into the existing power grid.

We are constantly working on how this appliance can be plugged into the existing power grids. The appliance, the New Urbanism, is a timeless one, but it is necessary to design a variety of plugs.

Kayden: Andres, I want to ask you about an issue Carol raised, that of income mixing. Some people who've studied the field have looked at the numbers and claimed that there really isn't that much income mixing in New Urbanist communities. Could you describe, for example, what exactly is the percentage mixing of incomes based on constructed housing in Kentlands?

Duany: My secretary's townhouse sold for $160,000 next to a house that sold for $470,000 with an outbuilding that rents for $595 per month. There are also hundreds of rental apartments nearby. That's a very radical mix of incomes. In a nearby project, called Windcrest, there's actually subsidized housing right next to $280,000 houses.

Now the problem is this: I don't believe that you can construct a dwelling on a lot in the Washington area to sell for less than $150,000. That's the base price, which we can't control. Given that, one of the most honorable things about Kentlands, in my view, is that it is as mixed as possible. What more can you ask than to have rental apartments, townhouses, and mansions all next to each other?

Saunders: But you've also acknowledged that the class differences are diminishing as Kentlands has become known as a desirable place to live.

Duany: Yes. The rents are rising; house prices are rising. There are two possible ways to counteract this. One is to build enough great places so that the market doesn't overheat. The other solution – which is not serious – is to build places that do not connect with the popular taste culture. For example, Steven Holl's building at Seaside hasn't gone up in price at all; it is not viewed as desirable.

Burns: What an idea – maintaining long-term affordability through unpopular aesthetics!

Duany: Steven Holl, who is a friend, might see this is as an honorable contribution. He might argue that architecture must make its own culture.

Krieger: Andres, you tend to answer us primarily with assertions, and we all want to believe those assertions. But assertions are not proofs. It still remains to be observed and proved through statistics and experience whether all that you claim will actually come to be.

I'd like to raise again the issue of whether the New Urbanist pattern is, in certain ways, a good pattern – the issue of whether it will result in as much redundant peripheral development as "traditional" postwar suburban development has produced. There's a great risk of being co-opted, I think; and for every Kentlands, there are still dozens and dozens of underused, dilapidated, existing neighborhoods that could be revitalized – and that already have many of the urban attributes that you try to create at great effort and expense. Furthermore, this new peripheral development will further drain the vitality of struggling urban neighborhoods.

Norquist: I disagree. The urban form being revived in suburban New Urbanist design revalidates existing urban development. Each year that sprawl development is the only new development, the urban forms of older cities like Boston, St. Louis, and Milwaukee become a smaller proportion of total development.

For example, streets with sidewalks decline as a proportion of total streets. Apartments above shops have not only declined proportionally, but have become an historic relic, reproduced only as a novelty at Disney World and Disneyland.

Genuine traditional neighborhood development, built on the metro edge, awakens consumer taste for urban forms already existing in cities. As mayor of a 150-year-old city, I prefer suburban development that mirrors the design of my city to suburban development that is alien to what we have in Milwaukee. If New Urbanism catches on in suburbs, people might be more likely to choose the real thing in Milwaukee.

Kayden: What Alex is asking relates to the argument Andres raised earlier: the debate in the CNU about urban boundaries and whether there should be set boundaries or, as Benton MacKaye advocated, more fluid and flexible limits that allow precious resources to be protected. One could make the argument that New Urbanism could use its influence and power to create public policy that would intervene in the marketplace and force development to occur in cities, in the places where poor people actually live and which are genuinely diverse, places where the middle class is now reluctant to live. In this context the debate about boundaries becomes very significant; perhaps the Benton MacKaye approach would allow New Urbanism to exist in places like Kentlands, whereas the urban growth boundaries approach would to some extent stifle the Kentlands pattern.

Krieger: And to this argument we could add that New Urbanism has perhaps provided the middle classes with a politically correct incentive to abandon the city.

Duany: The first thing to say is that the New Urbanism has a dual purpose. Our skills and energy are being devoted equally to development in suburbia *and* in the inner city. Over one-third of our firm's projects are plans for existing fabric. To answer Jerold: yes, the urban growth boundary model would have the positive effect of stifling places like Kentlands. It would tend to compress development.

The problems of the urban growth boundary are, first, it needs the secondary structure of the neighborhood within its bounds if it is not to become just sprawl; second, it seems to me politically unsustainable. There has never been an urban growth boundary that has held, not even Portland's. And the reason for this is simple: such boundaries are arbitrary. What happens is that a city draws an arbitrary line – and there is inevitably an economic differential between inside and outside, and a democratic system cannot sustain the pressure of that differential. You cannot have many thousands of dollars per acre one place, and just beyond virtually no value. It is not organic.

Burns: It's not democracy that prevents this; it's the capital markets.

Duany: A good point; you're right.

Kayden: Actually though, such differences do exist in many places – they happen through zoning regulations. Zoning has made some land valuable; it's also prevented some people from making millions from their land.

Duany: But I would argue that such situations are not sustainable—

Krieger: Andres is right; no such boundary conditions have withstood long-term pressures from the market.

Kayden: Well, there's a debate about that, and I think the record is mixed. And, after all, New Urbanism itself is evidence that the conventional wisdom can be disproved. Five years ago people were saying your developments would never succeed.

Duany: But, you see, we are really not interested in expending a huge amount of political capital on something that isn't going to work. We don't want to create a place that's based on laws that would only hold for one political generation. I believe that the only way to develop places is to acknowledge that growth will occur and to give it a healthy pattern.

Kayden: So that's your pragmatic political judgment?

Duany: Yes, but it is not the position of the CNU, which is debating this issue.

Kayden: Were it not your pragmatic political judgment, would you think differently?

Duany: Lizz and I spend time studying plans that have failed. We have learned a lot; we've learned that there's too much failure in planning. And I'm not interested in participating in that tradition even though it includes the work of such distinguished thinkers as Lewis Mumford and John Nolen.

Krieger: Andres, tell us more about your work in the inner city.

Duany: First let me go back and say that I grant that by making suburbs with many of the attributes of towns, we are making it palatable for some people who abhor the idea of living in suburbia to live out on the periphery. People tell us all the time, "I'm so glad this new town is here, because I couldn't afford a house in Washington." Now there's little chance that our new development will threaten Georgetown or Alexandria. So don't worry: those who can afford Alexandria and Georgetown will still buy there.

Krieger: But Georgetown is not at a crisis point, as are some of the neighborhoods around Georgetown.

Duany: That's true. And I'm saying that you may be right about avoiding creating more places on the periphery. But we look at it like this: the overwhelming majority of what gets built in this country is on the periphery. Obviously, your perspective here in New England differs from that of much of the country. If you go out West, you can see clearly that the suburban train is hurtling forward at tremendous speed. So how do you respond to this train? Dan Solomon has suggested that you can either plant a flag on the runaway train, as Rem Koolhaas does, and say, "Hey, this train is inevitable so I will ride it in style"; or you can attempt to derail it. Much of what we do is an attempt to derail it, to say "No, this is not how the train should be moving. We understand it has to move, but we think the direction is wrong." One of the things I learned from Boorstin is that new growth is the American way. It is deep in our culture and our tradition.

Let me say one more thing about the consumption of land. I have learned about some statistics from the Lincoln Institute of Land Policy that suggest that if every American family were given an acre of land, only 2% of the continental United States would in this way be consumed. In other words, there is not a scarcity of land. This becomes obvious when you leave the Northeast. Outside the Northeast, land has little value; it is as widespread a commodity as there is.

Burns: That's an abstract argument, though, because 90% of the population lives within 100 miles of a coast. There is a lot of land in places where there are not many people to use it.

Duany: Let me tell you why New Urbanists are so often confident. There is little useful literature about this sort of development, so we work very much by observation. We're obsessive observers. So if we are certain that traffic behaves a certain way, it's not because we've read about it or theorized about it, but because we've observed it. I travel in planes a lot, and I always get a window and look down. I've seen how sparsely populated much of the country is; even the East Coast is very sparsely populated. I cannot be dissuaded from that knowledge acquired through observation.

Campbell: It's true that there's a trend today toward depopulation of the East. There's more undeveloped land in Connecticut now than there was 100 years ago.

Duany: In terms of the issues Alex has raised about the inner city, I might ask: isn't it important to deal with suburban development, since it makes up 90% of all development? Should we ignore it, because we don't approve of it? It seems to me that the crisis, at least statistically, is just as much in the suburbs as in the inner city. Many New Urbanists work on master plans for inner cities; the problem is, they're not as visible as our suburban work.

Burns: That is the problem. That's where the market is; the train that you're derailing, or building new rails for, is the train of capitalist development. And these days the train doesn't stop in the city. The problems of the city are not addressed by the mechanisms of the market. And there's another place that poses an important development challenge, which is the dying American small town. It's ironic: the small towns that are the model for New Urbanism are themselves struggling to survive.

Duany: WalMart is still killing them. Actually small towns are easy to work with, technically: as pure design problems they are a cinch. The impediment to working with them is political. The politics are usually very complicated; they use up all the time and budget.

Burns: That's part of the reason why greenfield sites are so attractive.

Duany: Last year, we did two plans for infill communities; our clients were idealistic developers, and every skill, every expense was applied – the best drawings, many meetings, the best cocktail parties to drum up support, etc. But guess what happened? These wonderful infill plans, for dense, mixed-use development, were voted down. Do you know how much money these young developers lost on these ventures? Do you think they're going to try again? Now, what are you going to do about that? Do you want us to keep working on wonderful plans that flop? So how do we balance the theoretical and the actual? Everybody says, "Work on the inner city." We try, but one-third of the work I personally did last year was infill projects, and none is being built.

Campbell: That raises an issue that we probably don't want to get into: the whole issue of the larger political framework. You've described suburban sprawl, or peripheral development, as if it were a response to real needs and desires. In fact, it is so heavily subsidized by the government that you could almost call it socialized planning. The public sector builds the highways and the infrastructure that make it possible. At the same time, the government does almost nothing to help the inner city. I would argue that that larger political framework is what killed your idealistic developers, and it's what is constantly driving the train you're trying to derail. The train is a subsidized, socialized vehicle.

Burns: That's such an important point. The market is subsidized.

Campbell: The political question is: can you change where the subsidies go?

Levinson: Do you see a way to use the growing influence of the Congress for New Urbanism to advocate for the kind of development you believe in?

Krieger: I think that is an important challenge for you; I think there is a risk that there will be a great divergence between your theory and ideas, on the one hand, and the behavior of communities in response to these ideas, on the other. Sadly, that's happened often. A history of American planning might blame Lewis Mumford or John Nolen or Clarence Perry and his famous diagram for certain unloved kinds of suburban development. So there may be some point at which you need to shift not your principles but the focus of your gamesmanship. You have redirected people's expectations and developers' behavior already. This suggests that you could dare to invent new patterns that might further redirect the development train, might steer it more to public or civic sites.

Duany: But about the question of refocusing our work: one difference between the suburbs and the inner city is that the suburban developers, in every way that counts, outperform the inner city and its developers. It's not a question simply of the suburbs being "subsidized." The first inner-city project we did was in a town called Stuart. We applied to it everything we had learned from suburban practice, and lo and behold, within two years it has become the hottest place. Every shop is filled; the city lowered the tax rate. What did we do? We applied suburban management techniques to the city. What's happened in America is not that the cities are worse than they ever were; it's that our expectations of municipal performance are much higher. Americans are spoiled. What we expect in terms of safety, of cleanliness, of government responsiveness, of sophistication in retail management, is now so drastically escalated that most cities do not meet our expectations. That is one of the insidious trends of history. If you study what cities were like in their heyday, you find that there was crime and dirt and inconvenience. But today, American middle-class standards are higher, having been raised by the superior management techniques of suburban developers.

Our inner-city work puts in place a variety of physical and managerial techniques. For example, one project now in our office involves taking a large unbuilt superblock of the 1970s prepared for national builders and subdividing it into smaller pieces for local individuals to work with. But we also talk to the sanitation department; we make them see that they've got to achieve near perfect performance. Just

as in the suburbs, not one piece of trash should remain on a sidewalk for more than five minutes. We've been talking with the police about the importance of creating localized no-crime areas. Now it's clear that these are not splashy projects – not the kind of stuff that gets into the magazines and certainly not what's taught in schools.

Campbell: Why is publicity so important?

Duany: Alex asked about how we can use our influence to change the agenda. This is largely done through the press. I'm saying that part of the agenda, the nonsuburban stuff, is too subtle for reporters.

Campbell: Well, magazine publicity is one thing. But if the word gets around among the people who deal with cities, isn't that all you need?

Duany: It's virtually anonymous, this urban work.

Campbell: Government publications don't cover things like that?

Duany: These projects are about tinkering. It's hard to make people understand what you've done. Some of the most important work really is about giving pep talks to the guy who runs the sanitation department.

Levinson: I'd like to raise again the issue of suburban infill. If it's true that people want to live in places like Kentlands, then doesn't this suggest there's a market that would be responsive to retrofitting existing suburbs – making them denser, building small commercial centers that people could walk to?

Duany: The retrofit of suburban housing is very difficult because of homeowners' associations and residents' outstanding mortgages, both of which tend to make suburbia resistant to significant change. Whenever you want to modify a housing subdivision – for example, to remove houses to build a community pool or a corner store – you find that the plan is frozen stiff by the mortgages and by the homeowners' association documents. They're instruments designed to retain real estate value through predictability. They are allergic to change.

Levinson: What about the retrofit and redesign of shopping centers?

Duany: It is quite possible to redesign such centers but only if they are successful enough so that the parking doesn't have to be surface parking. Decks can liberate areas for buildings to balance the retail. When we design a new center, we design the open parking lots and the infrastructure in such a way that it can later be urbanized as a town center.

Levinson: You've described your work with developers as a struggle to convince them of the worth of your ideas, but you've also described the developments as very successful. Why is there still such a struggle, then? Or is there?

Duany: I have a theory that suburbia was an accident, an inadvertent mistake of postwar policy. America was built for profit, one coast to the other. Developers built most of the beautiful places we now love, and so the profit motive is capable of creating wonderful towns, villages, cities – of creating New York, Boston, etc. What happened after the Second World War was that America made a mistake – the cheap loans were available only for housing. For the first time in history, developers performed the illogical and unprecedented act of building only housing. Now, when did it ever make sense to build only housing? Don't we need places to work and places to shop? When developers built Coral Gables they built a whole town; when they built Kansas City they built a whole

town. Developers have always built whole towns in America.

But because of this detail of government loan policy, we began to build Levittown. Then, a few years later, retailers figured out that their clients were in the suburbs and said, "Whoa, we'd better get out there." And they were permitted to build out there and they developed a typology that was also unprecedented, the shopping center. And still later, in the 1980s, when the chief executives realized that their workers were in the suburbs, they took the workplace out there and created the office park. So what's happening is that the ingredients to make towns are being built constantly, in the suburbs, but they are never assembled into towns. Now why is it difficult to unhinge that? The development industry has become specialized. Those who build townhouses don't build single-family houses and certainly don't know how to build retail; those who build retail don't know how to build offices. And, of course, the financial industry is now set up to accommodate this; they cannot absorb any product that is not standard. So across the board there are these enormous, impersonal forces. This is why we struggle.

Campbell: The next question is, what do we do about these forces?

Duany: Well, the only way to counter them is to build alternatives that are so spectacularly successful that they outperform the status quo. This is achieved three ways: faster permits, less cost, and faster sales. We concentrate on promoting success in these terms.

Krieger: Andres, how does the issue of style relate to this need to create places that succeed spectacularly? You've said often that style is extremely important, although you said earlier today that it doesn't particularly interest you.

Duany: As I said earlier, about Kentlands, it's important as a tool. It's not important as nostalgia. People say we're nostalgic for an Arts and Crafts, or a Victorian world. Style is a weapon. But if the style is unpopular, then nobody buys and the development goes bankrupt, and what is the use of that? Another paper project.

Campbell: In other words, your use of style is like your use of language, a way of concealing what you're doing.

Duany: Yes, exactly. Further, I would argue that by focusing on an unpopular style, modernist architects are marginalizing their discussion and marginalizing themselves. They are, in essence, separating themselves from where the power really is, which is the ability of architecture to transform society, to be of genuine social benefit.

Burns: I agree. And, along those lines, you noted the importance of mortgage lenders in determining development. I think it's tremendously important for architects to understand such things. For example, because banks prefer to give loans for two- or three-bedroom houses, bankers are, in essence, determining the program in housing. This is quite amazing, and not well understood. So I agree that style is not the most interesting subject in a critique of existing practices. This critique is exposing how we construct our environments, and not just New Urbanist environments.

Krieger: But here it seems important to note that emulation is not co-option. The New Urbanists want to be emulated; not co-opted. Unfortunately, in practice, the imitators are focusing on the styles, rather than on the principles, of New Urbanism. In this sense style is not such a trivial issue.

Duany: You're absolutely right.

Campbell: We're all interested in the language of architecture. It's a fascinating subject. It's just not relevant to what we're talking about.

Krieger: Oh, but it is. New Urbanism may be primarily about breaking conventions; but secondarily it has created or reinforced a convention of styles, which is resulting in an unfortunate homogenization of many environments.

Campbell: But that isn't bad in itself. There seem to me to be two different issues. The language of architecture, whether it's sentimental or inventive, involves one set of issues. The urbanistic innovations of New Urbanism involve a different set of issues.

Solomon: Sentiment versus invention does seem to be the dialectic that architectural discourse revolves around. Unfortunately, neither sentiment nor invention have any intrinsic value. Architectural journalism and criticism are mired in the opposition of two positions that don't mean much. Avant-garde revival versus revival revival – equally vacuous, equally irrelevant. Good building, good urban building, buildings good to inhabit can beg these questions. Tectonics, materiality, environmentalism, urbanity, utility – these are the real questions. We can have hair and comb it nicely without succumbing to the preoccupations that dominate discourse among hairdressers.

Campbell: You talked earlier about CIAM. CIAM lasted about a generation; then Team X came along. If the pattern repeats, we'll be due for another Team X in a few years. Where do you think they'll come from?

Duany: The CNU, I would argue, is the Team X to Team X, as we are completing the march toward the rediscovery of urbanism that they began.

Krieger: Well, I would be tremendously impressed if you came up with a latter-day Team X – a critique and redirection of CNU by one of its founders.

Duany: I'm very interested in that whole heroic period of CIAM and Team X, and in the ideas of social responsibility. I was at Princeton in the years just before Michael Graves and the formalists prevailed, and I still find that earlier era incredibly appealing. Of course, a lot of socially conscious stuff failed, but the reaction to this failure was erroneous. The conclusion was that architecture could not affect society, it could only affect itself; so we had postmodernism and two decades of self-referential design.

Campbell: Because architecture is so expensive and so slow, it lags about a generation behind other aspects of culture.

Duany: Well, we were certainly persuaded to forget about affecting society. We originally designed Seaside mainly in aesthetic terms. We wanted to make beautiful places. We subsequently observed that people behave differently in Seaside; they don't become better people, but aspects of their lives change. So now I feel very strongly that urbanism, if not architecture, can affect society. We sometimes think that the failure of places like Pruitt Igoe shows that architecture can't change the world. But I think the lesson of Pruitt Igoe is that architecture does affect us – in that particular case, for the worse.

Burns: Many people who have studied Pruitt Igoe argue that its failure had less to do with the buildings than with the management. But that relates exactly to the point you were making that urban management is not as good

as suburban management, and that access to resources is crucial.

Duany: Well, management matters, of course, but only to a point. I still say the design itself is critical.

Campbell: It's not one or the other, though, is it?

Duany: No. And don't misunderstand: we are not so unsophisticated as to actually believe that architecture is going to affect behavior in the moral sense. My point is that it can make some things possible. It can affect patterns of life, increase one's choices.

Campbell: Perhaps what people are reacting to when they accuse you of naiveté is the old idea that architecture can create utopia. Years ago I worked for Jose Luis Sert, who once told me that when he was a young man he believed that architecture was going to remake the world into a kind of utopia. There was a time when that hope was shared by many people. So whenever you say that architecture can affect how people live, some people will hear those utopian echoes. But I understand that that isn't what you mean.

Duany: By the way, in the ... debate on Seaside, Peter Eisenman critiqued the very idea of being utopian. He said that the last time the world had utopian visions, they led to the Holocaust.

But what disturbs me most is the accusation by many academics that we are "complicit" with power structures, that we pander to the people. Have you ever talked with poor people in the city about where they want to live? They want to live in a ranch house with small classical columns at the front. They don't want to live in anything experimental or "critical." Even Latinos want to live in Georgian houses. In my experience, the only people who want housing that differs from the conventional are the intellectuals. And this is often in theory only; it's rarely borne out in their own choice of dwelling.

One of the consequences of all this is that a generation of architecture students – not necessarily those at the GSD – are being encouraged to dissociate themselves from the world of construction and development. To deal with that world is to be "complicit" with developers. The result of this is that the design talent is encouraged to distance itself from very important problems – but these problems do not then disappear; they fall into the hands of the inept.

Campbell: I agree 100 percent.

Krieger: I'd like to defend academia somewhat. Debate and probing are the hallmarks of education. At the GSD we tried a more evangelical approach during the Gropius years; some of the results of this are precisely what is being challenged by the New Urbanists. I think what you are criticized for, sometimes, is your very great ability to conventionalize norms. In doing so, you might be influencing what people say they want and taking them further away from what they might actually want.

Duany: Well, that may be. Again, I suppose that is what the next generation can challenge us on. But the main thing is that they engage their talents in the real world.

19

Social Justice, Postmodernism, and the City*

David Harvey

The title of this chapter is a collage of two book titles of mine written nearly 20 years apart, *Social Justice and the City* and *The Condition of Postmodernity*. I here want to consider the relations between them, in part as a way to reflect on the intellectual and political journey many have travelled these last two decades in their attempts to grapple with urban issues, but also to examine how we now might think about urban problems and how by virtue of such thinking we can better position ourselves with respect to solutions. The question of *positionality* is, I shall argue, fundamental to all debates about how to create infra structures and urban environments for living and working in the twenty-first century.

Justice and the Postmodern Condition

I begin with a report by John Kifner in the *International Herald Tribune* (1 August 1989) concerning the hotly contested space of Tompkins Square Park in New York City – a space which has been repeatedly fought over, often violently, since the 'police riot' of August 1988. The neighbourhood mix around the park was the primary focus of Kifner's attention. Not only were there nearly 300 homeless people, but there were also:

> Skateboarders, basketball players, mothers with small children, radicals looking like 1960s retreads, spikey-haired punk rockers in torn black, skinheads in heavy working boots looking to beat up the radicals and punks, dreadlocked Rastafarians, heavy-metal bands, chess players, dog walkers – all occupy their spaces in the park, along with professionals carrying their dry-cleaned suits to the renovated 'gentrified' buildings that are changing the character of the neighbourhood.

* Harvey, David (1993) 'Social Justice, Postmodernism and the City' *International Journal of Urban and Regional Research* 16, 588–601. Reprinted by permission of Blackwell Publishers.

By night, Kifner notes, the contrasts in the park become even more bizarre:

> The Newcomers Motorcycle Club was having its annual block party at its clubhouse at
> 12th Street and Avenue B and the street was lined with chromed Harley Davidsons with
> raised 'ape-hanger' handlebars and beefy men and hefty women in black leather. A
> block north a rock concert had spilled out of a 'squat' – an abandoned city-owned
> building taken over by outlaw renovators, mostly young artists – and the street was
> filled with young people whose purple hair stood straight up in spikes. At the World
> Club just off Houston Street near Avenue C, black youths pulled up in the Jeep-type
> vehicles favored by cash-heavy teen-age crack moguls, high powered speakers blaring.
> At the corner of Avenue B and Third, considered one of the worst heroin blocks in New
> York, another concert was going on at an artists' space called The Garage, set in a
> former gas station walled off by plastic bottles and other found objects. The wall
> formed an enclosed garden looking up at burned-out, abandoned buildings: there was
> an eerie resemblance to Beirut. The crowd was white and fashionably dressed, and a
> police sergeant sent to check on the noise shook his head, bemused: 'It's all yuppies.'

This is, of course, the kind of scene that makes New York such a fascinating place,
that makes any great city into a stimulating and exciting maelstrom of cultural
conflict and change. It is the kind of scene that many a student of urban subcultures
would revel in, even seeing in it, as someone like Iain Chambers (1987) does, the
origins of that distinctive perspective we now call 'the postmodern':

> Postmodernism, whatever form its intellectualizing might take, has been fundamentally
> anticipated in the metropolitan cultures of the last twenty years: among the electronic
> signifiers of cinema, television and video, in recording studios and record players, in
> fashion and youth styles, in all those sounds, images and diverse histories that are daily
> mixed, recycled and 'scratched' together on that giant screen that is the contemporary
> city.

Armed with that insight, we could take the whole paraphernalia of postmodern
argumentation and technique and try to 'deconstruct' the seemingly disparate images
on that giant screen which is the city. We could dissect and celebrate the fragmentation, the co-presence of multiple discourses – of music, street and body language, dress
and technological accoutrements (such as the Harley Davidsons) – and, perhaps,
develop sophisticated empathies with the multiple and contradictory codings
with which highly differentiated social beings both present themselves to each other
and to the world and live out their daily lives. We could affirm or even celebrate
the bifurcations in cultural trajectory, the preservation of pre-existing and the creation of entirely new but distinctive 'othernesses' within an otherwise homogenizing
world.

On a good day, we could celebrate the scene within the park as a superb example
of urban tolerance for difference, an exemplar of what Iris Marion Young calls
'openness to unassimilated otherness.' In a just and civilized society, she argues, the
normative ideal of city life:

> instantiates social relations of difference without exclusion. Different groups dwell in
> the city alongside one another, of necessity interacting in city spaces. If city politics is to
> be democratic and not dominated by the point of view of one group, it must be a politics

that takes account of and provides voice for the different groups that dwell together in
the city without forming a community.   (Young, 1990, p. 227)

To the degree that the freedom of city life 'leads to group differentiation, to the
formation of affinity groups' (p. 238) of the sort which Kifner identifies in Tompkins
Square, so our conception of social justice 'requires not the melting away of differences, but institutions that promote reproduction of and respect for group differences without oppression' (p. 47). We must reject 'the concept of universality as
embodied in republican versions of Enlightenment reason' precisely because it
sought to 'suppress the popular and linguistic heterogeneity of the urban public'
(p. 108). 'In open and accessible public spaces and forums, one should expect to
encounter and hear from those who are different, whose social perspectives, experience and affiliations are different.' It then follows, Young argues, that a politics of
inclusion 'must promote the ideal of a heterogeneous public, in which persons stand
forth with their differences acknowledged and respected, though perhaps not completely understood, by others' (p. 119).

In similar vein, Roberto Unger, the philosophical guru of the critical legal studies
movement in the United States, might view the park as a manifestation of a new ideal
of community understood as a 'zone of heightened mutual vulnerability, within
which people gain a chance to resolve more fully the conflict between the enabling
conditions of self-assertion; between their need for attachment and for participation
in group life and their fear of subjugation and depersonalization with which such
engagement may threaten them' (Unger, 1987, p. 562). Tompkins Square seems a
place where the 'contrast between structure-preserving routine and structure-trans-
forming conflict' softens in such a way as to 'free sociability from its script and to
make us available to one another more as the originals we know ourselves to be and
less as the placeholders in a system of group contrasts.' The square might even be
interpreted as a site of that 'microlevel of cultural-revolutionary defiance and incon-
gruity' which periodically wells upwards into 'the macrolevel of institutional innovation' (p. 564). Unger is acutely aware, however, that the temptation to 'treat each
aspect of cultural revolution as a pretext for endless self-gratification and self-
concern' can lead to a failure to 'connect the revolutionary reform of institutional
arrangements with the cultural-revolutionary remaking of personal relations.'

So what should the urban policy maker do in the face of these strictures? The
best path is to pull out that well-thumbed copy of Jane Jacobs (1961) and insist that
we should both respect and provide for 'spontaneous self-diversification among
urban populations' in the formulation of our policies and plans. In so doing we
can avoid the critical wrath she directs at city designers, who 'seem neither to
recognize this force for self-diversification nor to be attracted by the esthetic problems of expressing it.' Such a strategy can help us to live up to expectations of the
sort which Young and Unger lay down. We should not, in short, aim to obliterate
differences within the park, homogenize it according to some conception of, say,
bourgeois taste or social order. We should engage, rather, with an aesthetics which
embraces or stimulates that 'spontaneous self-diversification' of which Jacobs
speaks. Yet there is an immediate question mark over that suggestion: in what
ways, for example, can homelessness be understood as spontaneous self-
diversification, and does this mean that we should respond to that problem with

designer-style cardboard boxes to make for more jolly and sightly shelters for the homeless? While Jane Jacobs has a point, and one which many urbanists have absorbed these last few years, there is, evidently, much more to the problem than her arguments encompass.

That difficulty is highlighted on a bad day in the park. So-called forces of law and order battle to evict the homeless, erect barriers between violently clashing factions. The park then becomes a locus of exploitation and oppression, an open wound from which bleed the five faces of oppression which Young defines as exploitation, marginalization, powerlessness, cultural imperialism and violence. The potentiality for 'openness to unassimilated otherness' breaks apart and, in much the same way that the cosmopolitan and eminently civilized Beirut of the 1950s suddenly collapsed into an urban maelstrom of warring factions and violent confrontation, so we find sociality collapsing into violence (Smith, 1989; 1992). This is not unique to New York City but is a condition of urban life in many of our large metropolitan areas – witness events in the *banlieues* of Paris and Lyons, in Brussels, in Liverpool, London and even Oxford in recent times.

In such circumstances Young's pursuit of a vision of justice that is assertive as to difference without reinforcing the forms of oppression gets torn to tatters and Unger's dreams of micro-revolutions in cultural practices which stimulate progressive rather than repressive institutional innovation became just that – dreams. The very best face that we can put upon the whole scene is to recognize that this is how class, ethnic, racial and gender struggle is, as Lefebvre (1991) would put it, being 'inscribed in space'. And what should the planner do? Here is how a subsequent article in the *New York Times* reflected on that dilemma:

> There are neighborhood associations clamoring for the city to close the park and others just as insistent that it remain a refuge for the city's downtrodden. The local Assemblyman, Steven Sanders, yesterday called for a curfew that would effectively evict more than a hundred homeless people camped out in the park. Councilwoman Miriam Friedlander instead recommended that Social Services, like healthcare and drug treatment, be brought directly to the people living in the tent city. 'We do not find the park is being used appropriately,' said Deputy Mayor Barbara J. Fife, 'but we recognize there are various interests.' There is, they go on to say, only one thing that is a consensus, first that there isn't a consensus over what should be done, except that any new plan is likely to provoke more disturbances, more violence.

On 8 June 1991, the question was resolved by evicting everyone from the park and closing it entirely 'for rehabilitation' under a permanent guard of at least 20 police officers. The New York authorities, situated on what Davis (1990, p. 224) calls 'the bad edge of postmodernity', militarize rather than liberate its public space. In so doing, power is deployed in support of a middle-class quest for 'personal insulation, in residential work, consumption and travel environments, from "unsavory" groups and individuals, even crowds in general'. Genuinely public space is extinguished, militarized or semi-privatized. The heterogeneity of open democracy, the mixing of classes, ethnicities, religions and divergent taste cultures within a common frame of public space is lost along with the capacity to celebrate unity and community in the midst of diversity. The ultimate irony, as Davis points out, is that 'as the walls have come down in Eastern Europe, they are being erected all over [our cities]'.

And what should the policy maker and planner do in the face of these conditions? Give up planning and join one of those burgeoning cultural studies programmes which revel in chaotic scenes of the Tompkins Square sort while simultaneously disengaging from any commitment to do something about them? Deploy all the critical powers of deconstruction and semiotics to seek new and engaging interpretations of graffiti which say 'Die, Yuppie Scum'? Should we join revolutionary and anarchist groups and fight for the rights of the poor and the culturally marginalized to express their rights and if necessary make a home for themselves in the park? Or should we throw away that dog-eared copy of Jane Jacobs and join with the forces of law and order and help impose some authoritarian solution on the problem?

Decisions of some sort have to be made and actions taken, as about any other facet of urban infrastructure. And while we might all agree that an urban park is a good thing in principle, what are we to make of the fact that the uses turn out to be so conflictual, and that even conceptions as to what the space is for and how it is to be managed diverge radically among competing factions? To hold all the divergent politics of need and desire together within some coherent frame may be a laudable aim, but in practice far too many of the interests are mutually exclusive to allow their mutual accommodation. Even the best shaped compromise (let alone the savagely imposed authoritarian solution) favours one or other factional interest. And that provokes the biggest question of all – what is the *conception* of 'the public' incorporated into the construction of public space?

To answer these questions requires some deeper understanding of the forces at work shaping conflict in the park. Kifner identified drugs and real estate – 'the two most powerful forces in [New York City] today'. Both of them are linked to organized crime and are major pillars of the political economy of contemporary capitalism. We cannot understand events within and around the park or strategize as to its future uses without contextualizing it against a background of the political–economic transformations now occurring in urban life. The problems of Tompkins Square Park have, in short, to be seen in terms of social processes which create homelessness, promote criminal activities of many sorts (from real estate swindles and the crack trade to street muggings), generate hierarchies of power between gentrifiers and the homeless, and facilitate the emergence of deep tensions along the major social fault-lines of class, gender, ethnicity, race and religion, lifestyle and place-bound preferences (Smith, 1992).

Social Justice and Modernity

I now leave this very contemporary situation and its associated conundrums and turn to an older story. It turned up when I unearthed from my files a yellowing manuscript, written sometime in the early 1970s, shortly after I finished *Social Justice and the City*. I there examined the case of a proposal to put a segment of the Interstate Highway System on an east–west trajectory right through the heart of Baltimore – a proposal first set out in the early 1940s and which has still not been fully resolved. I resurrect this case here in part to show that what we would now often depict as a quintessentially modernist problem was even at that time argued about in ways which contained the seeds, if not the essence, of much of what many now view as a distinctively postmodernist form of argumentation.

My interest in the case at that time, having looked at a lot of the discussion, attended hearings and read a lot of documentation, lay initially in the highly differentiated arguments, articulated by all kinds of different groups, concerning the rights and wrongs of the whole project. There were, I found, seven kinds of arguments being put forward:

1 An *efficiency* argument which concentrated on the relief of traffic congestion and facilitating the easier flow of goods and people throughout the region as well as within the city
2 An *economic growth* argument which looked to a projected increase (or prevention of loss) in investment and employment opportunities in the city consequent upon improvements in the transport system
3 An *aesthetic and historical heritage* argument which objected to the way sections of the proposed highway would either destroy or diminish urban environments deemed both attractive and of historical value
4 A *social and moral order* argument which held that prioritizing highway investment and subsidizing car owners rather than, for example, investing in housing and health care was quite wrong
5 An *environmentalist/ecological* argument which considered the impacts of the proposed highway on air quality, noise pollution and the destruction of certain valued environments (such as a river valley park)
6 A *distributive justice* argument which dwelt mainly on the benefits to business and predominantly white middle-class suburban commuters to the detriment of low-income and predominantly African-American inner-city residents
7 A *neighbourhood and communitarian* argument which considered the way in which close-knit but otherwise fragile and vulnerable communities might be destroyed, divided or disrupted by highway construction

The arguments were not mutually exclusive, of course, and several of them were merged by proponents of the highway into a common thread – for example, the efficiency of the transport system would stimulate growth and reduce pollution from congestion so as to advantage otherwise disadvantaged inner-city residents. It was also possible to break up each argument into quite distinct parts – the distributive impacts on women with children would be very different from those on male workers.

We would, in these heady postmodern times, be prone to describe these separate arguments as 'discourses', each with its own logic and imperatives. And we would not have to look too closely to see particular 'communities of interest' which articulated a particular discourse as if it was the only one that mattered. The particularistic arguments advanced by such groups proved effective in altering the alignment of the highway but did not stop the highway as a whole. The one group which tried to forge a coalition out of these disparate elements (the *Movement Against Destruction*, otherwise known as *MAD*) and to provide an umbrella for opposition to the highway as a whole turned out to be the least effective in mobilizing people and constituencies even though it was very articulate in its arguments.

The purpose of my own particular enquiry was to see how the arguments (or discourses) for and against the highway worked and if coalitions could be built in principle between seemingly disparate and often highly antagonistic interest groups via the construction of higher-order arguments (discourses) which could provide the basis for consensus. The multiplicity of views and forces has to be set against the fact that either the highway is built or it is not, although in Baltimore, with its wonderful way of doing things, we ended up with a portion of the highway that is called a boulevard (to make us understand that this six-lane two-mile segment of a monster cut through the heart of low-income and predominantly African-American West Baltimore is not what it really is) and another route on a completely different alignment, looping around the city core in such a way as to allay some of the worst political fears of influential communities.

Might there be, then, some higher-order discourse to which everyone could appeal in working out whether or not it made sense to build the highway? A dominant theme in the literature of the 1960s was that it was possible to identify some such higher-order arguments. The phrase that was most frequently used to describe it was *social rationality*. The idea of that did not seem implausible, because each of the seven seemingly distinctive arguments advanced a rational position of some sort and not infrequently appealed to some higher-order rationale to bolster its case. Those arguing on efficiency and growth grounds frequently invoked utilitarian arguments, notions of 'public good' and the greatest benefit to the greatest number, while recognizing (at their best) that individual sacrifices were inevitable and that it was right and proper to offer appropriate compensation for those who would be displaced. Ecologists or communitarians likewise appealed to higher-order arguments – the former to the values inherent in nature and the latter to some higher sense of communitarian values. For all of these reasons, consideration of higher-order arguments over social rationality did not seem unreasonable.

Dahl and Lindblom's *Politics, Economics and Welfare*, published in 1953, provides a classic statement along these lines. They argue that not only is socialism dead (a conclusion that many would certainly share these days) but also that capitalism is equally dead. What they signal by this is an intellectual tradition which arose out of the experience of the vast market and capitalistic failure of the Great Depression and the second world war and which concluded that some kind of middle ground had to be found between the extremism of a pure and unfettered market economy and the communist vision of an organized and highly centralized economy. They concentrated their theory on the question of rational social action and argued that this required 'processes for both rational *calculation* and effective *control*' (p. 21). Rational calculation and control, as far as they were concerned, depended upon the exercise of rational calculation through price-fixing markets, hierarchy (top-down decision making), polyarchy (democratic control of leadership) and bargaining (negotiation), and such means should be deployed to achieve the goals of 'freedom, rationality, democracy, subjective equality, security, progress, and appropriate inclusion' (p. 28). There is much that is interesting about Dahl and Lindblom's analysis and it is not too hard to imagine that after the recent highly problematic phase of market triumphalism, particularly in Britain and the United States, there will be some sort of search to resurrect the formulations they proposed. But in so doing it is also useful to remind ourselves of the intense criticism that was levelled during the 1960s and 1970s against their search for some universal prospectus on the socially rational society of the future.

Godelier, for example, in his book on *Rationality and Irrationality in Economics* (1972), savagely attacked the socialist thinking of Oscar Lange for its teleological view of rationality and its presumption that socialism should or could ever be the ultimate achievement of the rational life. Godelier did not attack this notion from the right but from a Marxist and historical materialist perspective. His point was that there are different definitions of rationality depending upon the form of social organization and that the rationality embedded in feudalism is different from that of capitalism, which should, presumably, be different again under socialism. Rationality defined from the standpoint of corporate capital is quite different from rationality defined from the standpoint of the working classes. Work of this type helped to fuel the growing radical critique of even the non-teleological and incrementalist thinking of the Dahl and Lindblom sort. This critique suggested that their definition of social rationality was connected to the perpetuation and rational management of a capitalist economic system rather than with the exploration of alternatives. To attack (or deconstruct, as we now would put it) their conception of social rationality was seen by the left at the time as a means to challenge the ideological hegemony of a dominant corporate capitalism. Feminists, those marginalized by racial characteristics, colonized peoples, ethnic and religious minorities echoed that refrain in their work, while adding their own conception of who was the enemy to be challenged and what were the dominant forms of rationality to be contested. The result was to show emphatically that there is no overwhelming and universally acceptable definition of social rationality to which we might appeal, but innumerable different rationalities depending upon social and material circumstances, group identities, and social objectives. Rationality is defined by the nature of the social group and its project rather than the project being dictated by social rationality. The deconstruction of universal claims of social rationality was one of the major achievements and continues to be one of the major legacies of the radical critique of the 1960s and 1970s.

Such a conclusion is, however, more than a little discomforting. It would suggest, to go back to the highway example, that there was no point whatsoever in searching for any higher-order arguments because such arguments simply could not have any purchase upon the political process of decision making. And it is indeed striking that the one group that tried to build such overall arguments, *MAD*, was the group that was least successful in actually mobilizing opposition. The fragmented discourses of those who sought to change the alignment of the highway had more effect than the more unified discourse precisely because the former were grounded in the specific and particular local circumstances in which individuals found themselves. Yet the fragmented discourses could never go beyond challenging the alignment of the highway. It did indeed need a more unified discourse, of the sort which *MAD* sought to articulate, to challenge the concept of the highway in general.

This poses a direct dilemma. If we accept that fragmented discourses are the only authentic discourses and that no unified discourse is possible, then there is no way to challenge the overall qualities of a social system. To mount that more general challenge we need some kind of unified or unifying set of arguments. For this reason, I chose, in this ageing and yellowing manuscript, to take a closer look at the particular question of social justice as a basic ideal that might have more universal appeal.

Social Justice

Social justice is but one of the seven criteria I worked with and I evidently hoped that careful investigation of it might rescue the argument from the abyss of formless relativism and infinitely variable discourses and interest grouping. But here, too, the enquiry proved frustrating. It revealed that there are as many competing theories of social justice as there are competing ideals of social rationality. Each ideal has its flaws and strengths. Egalitarian views, for example, immediately run into the problem that 'there is nothing more unequal than the equal treatment of unequals' (the modification of doctrines of equality of opportunity in the United States by requirements for affirmative action, for example, recognizes what a significant problem that is). By the time I had thoroughly reviewed positive law theories of justice, utilitarian views (the greatest good of the greatest number), social contract views historically attributed to Rousseau and powerfully revived by John Rawls (1971) in his *Theory of Justice* in the early 1970s, the various intuitionist, relative deprivation and other interpretations of justice, I found myself in a quandary as to precisely *which* theory of justice is the most just. The theories can, to some degree, be arranged in a hierarchy with respect to each other. The positive law view that justice is a matter of law can be challenged by a utilitarian view which allows us to discriminate between good and bad law on the basis of some greater good, while the social contract and natural rights views suggest that no amount of greater good for a greater number can justify the violation of certain inalienable rights. On the other hand, intuitionist and relative deprivation theories exist in an entirely different dimension.

Yet the basic problem remained. To argue for social justice meant the deployment of some initial criteria to define which theory of social justice was appropriate or more just than another. The infinite regress of higher-order criteria immediately looms, as does, in the other direction, the relative ease of total deconstruction of the notion of justice to the point where it means nothing whatsoever, except whatever people at some particular moment decide they want it to mean. Competing discourses about justice could not be disassociated from competing discourses about positionality in society.

There seemed two ways to go with that argument. The first was to look at how concepts of justice are embedded in language, and that led me to theories of meaning of the sort which Wittgenstein advanced:

> How many kinds of sentence are there? . . . There are countless kinds: countless different kinds of use to what we call 'symbols', 'words', 'sentences'. And this multiplicity is not something fixed, given once for all: but new types of language, new language games, as we may say, come into existence and others become obsolete and get forgotten . . . Here the term 'language-game' is meant to bring into prominence the fact that the speaking of language is part of an activity, or a form of life . . . How did we learn the meaning of this word ('good' for instance)? From what sort of examples? in what language games? Then it will be easier for us to see that the word must have a family of meanings.
>
> (Wittgenstein, 1967)

From this perspective, the concept of justice has to be understood in the way it is embedded in a particular language game. Each language game attaches to the particular social, experiential and perceptual world of the speaker. Justice has no universal meaning, but a whole 'family' of meanings. This finding is completely consistent, of course, with anthropological studies which show that justice among, say, the Nuer, means something completely different from the capitalistic conception of justice. We are back to the point of cultural, linguistic or discourse relativism.

The second path is to admit the relativism of discourses about justice, but to insist that discourses are expressions of social power. In this case, the idea of justice has to be set against the formation of certain hegemonic discourses which derive from the power exercised by any ruling class. This is an idea which goes back to Plato, who in the *Republic* has Thrasymachus argue that:

> Each ruling class makes laws that are in its own interest, a democracy democratic laws, a tyranny tyrannical ones and so on; and in making these laws they define as 'right' for their subjects what is in the interest of themselves, the rulers, and if anyone breaks their laws he is punished as a 'wrong-doer'. That is what I mean when I say that 'right' is the same in all states, namely the interest of the established ruling class ...   (Plato, 1965)

Consideration of these two paths brought me to accept a position which is most clearly articulated by Engels in the following terms:

> The stick used to measure what is right and what is not is the most abstract expression of right itself, namely justice ... The development of right for the jurists ... is nothing more than a striving to bring human conditions, so far as they are expressed in legal terms, ever closer to the ideal of justice, eternal justice. And always this justice is but the ideologized, glorified expression of the existing economic relations, now from their conservative and now from their revolutionary angle. The justice of the Greeks and Romans held slavery to be just; the justice of the bourgeois of 1789 demanded the abolition of feudalism on the ground it was unjust. The conception of eternal justice, therefore, varies not only with time and place, but also with the persons concerned ... While in everyday life ... expressions like right, wrong, justice, and sense of right are accepted without misunderstanding even with reference to social matters, they create ... the same hopeless confusion in any scientific investigation of economic relations as would be created, for instance, in modern chemistry if the terminology of the phlogiston theory were to be retained.   (Marx and Engels, 1951: 562–4)

It is a short step from this conception of Marx's critique of Proudhon, who, Marx (1967, pp. 88–9) claimed, took his ideal of justice 'from the juridical relations that correspond to the production of commodities' and in so doing was able to present commodity production as 'a form of production as everlasting as justice'. The parallel with Godelier's rebuttal of Lange's (and by extension Dahl and Lindblom's) views on rationality is exact. Taking capitalistic notions of social rationality or of justice, and treating them as universal values to be deployed under socialism, would merely mean the deeper instanciation of capitalist values by way of the socialist project.

The Transition from Modernist to Postmodernist Discourses

There are two general points I wish to draw out of the argument so far. First, the critique of social rationality and of conceptions such as social justice as policy tools was something that was originated and so ruthlessly pursued by the 'left' (including Marxists) in the 1960s that it began to generate radical doubt throughout civil society as to the veracity of all universal claims. From this it was a short, though as I shall shortly argue, unwarranted, step to conclude, as many postmodernists now do, that all forms of metatheory are either misplaced or illegitimate. Both steps in this process were further reinforced by the emergence of the so-called 'new' social movements – the peace and women's movements, the ecologists, the movements against colonization and racism – each of which came to articulate its own defin- itions of social justice and rationality. There then seemed to be, as Engels had argued, no philosophical, linguistic or logical way to resolve the resulting divergen- cies in conceptions of rationality and justice, and thereby find a way to reconcile competing claims or arbitrate between radically different discourses. The effect was to undermine the legitimacy of state policy, attack all conceptions of bureaucratic rationality and, at best, place social policy formulation in a quandary and, at worst, render it powerless except to articulate the ideological and value precepts of those in power. Some of those who participated in the revolutionary movements of the 1970s and 1980s considered that rendering transparent the power and class basis of supposedly universal claims was a necessary prelude to mass revolutionary action.

But there is a second and, I think, more subtle point to be made. If Engels is indeed right to insist that the conception of justice 'varies not only with time and place, but also with the persons concerned', then it seems important to look at the ways in which a particular society produces such variation in concepts. In so doing it seems important, following writers as diverse as Wittgenstein and Marx, to look at the material basis for the production of difference, in particular at the production of those radically different experiential worlds out of which divergent language games about social rationality and social justice could arise. This entails the application of historical–geographical materialist methods and principles to understand the pro- duction of those power differentials which, in turn, produce different conceptions of justice and embed them in a struggle over ideological hegemony between classes, races, ethnic and political groupings as well as across the gender divide. The philosophical, linguistic and logical critique of universal propositions such as justice and of social rationality can be upheld as perfectly correct without necessarily endangering the ontological or epistemological status of a metatheory which con- fronts the ideological and material functionings and bases of particular discourses. Only in this way can we begin to understand why it is that concepts such as justice which appear as 'hopelessly confused' when examined in abstraction can become such a powerful mobilizing force in everyday life, where, again to quote Engels, 'expressions like right, wrong, justice, and sense of right are accepted without misunderstanding even with reference to social matters'.

From this standpoint we can clearly see that concepts of justice and of rationality have not disappeared from our social and political world these last few years. But their definition and use has changed. The collapse of class compromise in the struggles of the late 1960s and the emergence of the socialist, communist and radical left movements, coinciding as it did with an acute crisis of overaccumulation of capital, posed a serious threat to the stability of the capitalist political–economic system. At the ideological level, the emergence of alternative definitions of both justice and rationality was part of that attack, and it was to this question that my earlier book, *Social Justice and the City*, was addressed (Harvey, 1973). But the recession/depression of 1973–5 signalled not only the savage devaluation of capital stock (through the first wave of deindustrialization visited upon the weaker sectors and regions of a world capitalist economy) but the beginning of an attack upon the power of organized labour via widespread unemployment, austerity programmes, restructuring and, eventually, in some instances (such as Britain) institutional reforms.

It was under such conditions that the left penchant for attacking what was interpreted as a capitalist power basis within the welfare state (with its dominant notions of social rationality and just redistributions) connected to an emerging right-wing agenda to defang the power of welfare state capitalism, to get away from any notion whatsoever of a social contract between capital and labour and to abandon political notions of social rationality in favour of market rationality. The important point about this transition, which was phased in over a number of years, though at a quite different pace from country to country (it is only now seriously occurring in Sweden, for example), was that the state was no longer obliged to define rationality and justice, since it was presumed that the market could best do it for us. The idea that just deserts are best arrived at through market behaviours, that a just distribution is whatever the market dictates and that a just organization of social life, of urban investments and of resource allocations (including those usually referred to as environmental) is best arrived at through the market is, of course, relatively old and well-tried. It implies conceptions of justice and rationality of a certain sort, rather than their total abandonment. Indeed, the idea that the market is the best way to achieve the most just and the most rational forms of social organization has become a powerful feature of the hegemonic discourses these last 20 years in both the United States and Britain. The collapse of centrally planned economies throughout much of the world has further boosted a market triumphalism which presumes that the rough justice administered through the market in the course of this transition is not only socially just but also deeply rational. The advantage of this solution, of course, is that there is no need for explicit theoretical, political and social argument over what is or is not socially rational just because it can be presumed that, provided the market functions properly, the outcome is nearly always just and rational. Universal claims about rationality and justice have in no way diminished. They are just as frequently asserted in justification of privatization and of market action as they ever were in support of welfare state capitalism.

The dilemmas inherent in reliance on the market are well known and no one holds to it without some qualification. Problems of market breakdown, of externality effects, the provision of public goods and infrastructures, the clear need for *some* co-ordination of disparate investment decisions, all of these require some level of government interventionism. Margaret Thatcher may thus have abolished Greater London government, but the business community wants some kind of replacement (though preferably non-elected), because without it city services are disintegrating and London is losing its competitive edge. But there are many voices that go beyond that minimal requirement since free-market capitalism has produced widespread unemployment, radical restructurings and devaluations of capital, slow growth, environmental degradation and a whole host of financial scandals and competitive difficulties, to say nothing of the widening disparities in income distributions in many countries and the social stresses that attach thereto. It is under such conditions that the never quite stilled voice of state regulation, welfare state capitalism, of state management of industrial development, of state planning of environmental quality, land use, transportation systems and physical and social infrastructures, of state incomes and taxation policies which achieve a modicum of redistribution either in kind (via housing, health care, educational services and the like) or through income transfers, is being reasserted. The political questions of social rationality and of social justice over and above that administered through the market are being taken off the back burner and moved to the forefront of the political agenda in many of the advanced capitalist countries. It was exactly in this mode, of course, that Dahl and Lindblom came in back in 1953.

It is here that we have to face up to what Unger (1987) calls the 'ideological embarrassment' of the history of politics these last hundred years: its tendency to move merely in repetitive cycles, swinging back and forth between *laissez-faire* and state interventionism without, it seems, finding any way to break out of this binary opposition to turn a spinning wheel of stasis into a spiral of human development. The breakdown of organized communism in eastern Europe and the Soviet Union here provides a major opportunity precisely because of the radical qualities of the break. Yet there are few signs of any similar penchant for ideological and insti-tutional renovation in the advanced capitalist countries, which at best seem to be steering towards another bout of bureaucratic management of capitalism embedded in a general politics of the Dahl and Lindblom sort and at worst to be continuing down the blind ideological track which says that the market always knows best. It is precisely at this political conjuncture that we should remind ourselves of what the radical critique of universal claims of justice and rationality has been all about, without falling into the postmodernist trap of denying the validity of *any* appeal to justice or to rationality as a war cry for political mobilization (even Lyotard, that father figure of postmodern philosophy, hopes for the reassertion of some 'pristine and non-consensual conception of justice' as a means to find a new kind of politics).

For my own part, I think Engels had it right. Justice and rationality take on different meanings across space and time and persons, yet the existence of everyday meanings to which people do attach importance and which to them appear unprob-lematic, gives the terms a political and mobilizing power than can never be neg-lected. Right and wrong are words that power revolutionary changes and no amount of negative deconstruction of such terms can deny that. So where, then, have the new social movements and the radical left in general got with their own conception, and how does it challenge both market and corporate welfare capitalism?

Young in her *Justice and the Politics of Difference* (1990) provides one of the best recent statements. She redefines the question of justice away from the purely redis-tributive mode of welfare state capitalism and focuses on what she calls the 'five faces' of oppression, and I think each of them is worth thinking about as we consider the struggle to create liveable cities and workable environments for the twenty-first century.

The first face of oppression conjoins the classic notion of exploitation in the workplace with the more recent focus on exploitation of labour in the living place (primarily, of course, that of women working in the domestic sphere). The classic forms of exploitation which Marx described are still omnipresent, though there have been many mutations such that, for example, control over the length of the working day may have been offset by increasing intensity of labour or exposure to more hazardous health conditions not only in blue-collar but also in white-collar occupations. The mitigation of the worst aspects of exploitation has been, to some degree, absorbed into the logic of welfare state capitalism in part through the sheer exercise of class power and trade union muscle. Yet there are still many terrains upon which chronic exploitation can be identified and which will only be addressed to the degree that active struggle raises issues. The conditions of the unemployed, the homeless, the lack of purchasing power for basic needs and services for substantial portions of the population (immigrants, women, children) absolutely have to be addressed. All of which leads to my first proposition: *that just planning and policy practices must confront directly the problem of creating forms of social and political organization and systems of production and consumption which minimize the exploitation of labour power both in the workplace and the living place.*

The second face of oppression arises out of what Young (1990) calls *'marginalization'*. 'Marginals', she writes, 'are people the system of labour cannot or will not use.' This is most typically the case with individuals marked by race, ethnicity, region, gender, immigration status, age, and the like. The consequence is that 'a whole category of people is expelled from useful participation in social life and thus potentially subjected to severe material deprivation and even extermination'. The characteristic response of welfare state capitalism has been either to place such marginal groups under tight surveillance or, at best, to induce a condition of dependency in which state support provides a justification to 'suspend all basic rights to privacy, respect, and individual choice'. The responses among the marginalized have sometimes been both violent and vociferous, in some instances turning their marginalization into a heroic stand against the state and against any form of inclusion into what has for long only ever offered them oppressive surveillance and demeaning subservience. Marginality is one of the crucial problems facing urban life in the twenty-first century and consideration of it leads to the second principle: *that just planning and policy practices must confront the phenomenon of marginalization in a non-paternalistic mode and find ways to organize and militate within the politics of marginalization in such a way as to liberate captive groups from this distinctive form of oppression.*

Powerlessness is, in certain ways, an even more widespread problem than marginality. We are here talking of the ability to express political power as well as to engage in the particular politics of self-expression which we encountered in Tompkins Square Park. The ability to be listened to with respect is strictly circumscribed within welfare state capitalism and failure on this score has played a key role in the collapse of state communism. Professional groups have advantages in this regard which place them in a different category to most others and the temptation always stands, for even the most politicized of us, to speak for others without listening to them. Political inclusion is, if anything, diminished by the decline of trade unionism, of political parties, and of traditional institutions, yet it is at the same time revived by the organization of new social movements. But the increasing scale of international dependency and interdependency makes it harder and harder to offset powerlessness in general. Like the struggle against the Baltimore expressway, the mobilization of political power among the oppressed in society is increasingly a local affair, unable to address the structural characteristics of either market or welfare state capitalism as a whole. This leads to my third proposition: *just planning and policy practices must empower rather than deprive the oppressed of access to political power and the ability to engage in self-expression.*

What Young (1990) calls '*cultural imperialism*' relates to the ways in which 'the dominant meanings of a society render the particular perspective of one's own group invisible at the same time as they stereotype one's group and mark it out as the Other'. Arguments of this sort have been most clearly articulated by feminists and black liberation theorists, but they are also implicit in liberation theology as well as in many domains of cultural theory. This is, in some respects, the most difficult form of oppression to identify clearly, yet there can surely be no doubt that there are many social groups in our societies who find or feel themselves 'defined from the outside, positioned, placed, by a network of dominant meanings they experience as arising from elsewhere, from those with whom they do not identify and who do not identify with them'. The alienation and social unrest to be found in many western European and North American cities (to say nothing of its re-emergence throughout much of eastern Europe) bears all the marks of a reaction to cultural imperialism, and here too, welfare state capitalism has in the past proved both unsympathetic and un-moved. From this comes a fourth proposition: *that just planning and policy practices must be particularly sensitive to issues of cultural imperialism and seek, by a variety of means, to eliminate the imperialist attitude both in the design of urban projects and modes of popular consultation.*

Fifth, there is the issue of *violence*. It is hard to consider urban futures and living environments into the twenty-first century without confronting the problem of burgeoning levels of physical violence. The fear of violence against persons and property, though often exaggerated, has a material grounding in the social condi-tions of market capitalism and calls for some kind of organized response. There is, furthermore, the intricate problem of the violence of organized crime and its inter-digitation with capitalist enterprise and state activities. The problem at the first level is, as Davis (1990) points out in his consideration of Los Angeles, that the most characteristic response is to search for defensible urban spaces, to militarize urban space and to create living environments which are more rather than less exclusion-ary. The difficulty with the second level is that the equivalent of the *mafiosi* in many cities (an emergent problem in the contemporary Soviet Union, for example) has become so powerful in urban governance that it is they, rather than elected officials and state bureaucrats, who hold the true reins of power. No society can function without certain forms of social control and we have to consider what that might be in the face of a Foucauldian insistence that all forms of social control are oppressive, no matter what the level of violence to which they are addressed. Here, too, there are innumerable dilemmas to be solved, but we surely know enough to advance a fifth proposition: *a just planning and policy practice must seek out non-exclusionary and non-militarized forms of social control to contain the increasing levels of both personal and institutionalized violence without destroying capacities for empower-ment and self-expression.*

Finally, I want to add a sixth principle to those which Young advances. This derives from the fact that all social projects are ecological projects and vice versa. While I resist the view that 'nature has rights' or that nature can be 'oppressed', the justice due to future generations and to other inhabitants of the globe requires intense scrutiny of all social projects for assessment of their ecological consequences. Human beings necessarily appropriate and transform the world around them in the course of making their own history, but they do not have to do so with such reckless abandon as to jeopardize the fate of peoples separated from us in either space or time. The final proposition is, then: *that just planning and policy practices will clearly recognize that the necessary ecological consequences of all social projects have impacts on future generations as well as upon distant peoples and take steps to ensure a reasonable mitigation of negative impacts.*

I do not argue that these six principles can or even should be unified, let alone turned into some convenient and formulaic composite strategy. Indeed, the six dimensions of justice here outlined are frequently in conflict with each other as far as their application to individual persons – the exploited male worker may be a cultural imperialist on matters of race and gender while the thoroughly oppressed person may be the bearer of social injustice as violence. On the other hand, I do not believe the principles can be applied in isolation from each other either. Simply to leave matters at the level of a 'non-consensual' conception of justice, as someone like Lyotard (1984) would do, is not to confront some central issues of the social processes which produce such a differentiated conception of justice in the first place. This then suggests that social policy and planning has to work at two levels. The different faces of oppression have to be confronted for what they are and as they are manifest in daily life, but in the longer term and at the same time the underlying sources of the different forms of oppression in the heart of the political economy of capitalism must also be confronted, not as the fount of all evil but in terms of capitalism's revolutionary dynamic which transforms, disrupts, deconstructs and reconstructs ways of living, working, relating to each other and to the environment. From such a standpoint the issue is never about whether or not there shall be change, but what sort of change we can anticipate, plan for, and proactively shape in the years to come.

I would hope that consideration of the varieties of justice as well as of this deeper problematic might set the tone for present deliberations. By appeal to them, we might see ways to break with the political, imaginative and institutional constraints which have for too long inhibited the advanced capitalist societies in their developmental path. The critique of universal notions of justice and rationality, no matter whether embedded in the market or in state welfare capitalism, still stands. But it is both valuable and potentially liberating to look at alternative conceptions of both justice and rationality as these have emerged within the new social movements these last two decades. And while it will in the end ever be true, as Marx and Plato observed, that 'between equal rights force decides', the authoritarian imposition of solutions to many of our urban ills these past few years and the inability to listen to alternative conceptions of both justice and rationality is very much a part of the problem. The conceptions I have outlined speak to many of the marginalized, the oppressed and the exploited in this time and place. For many of us, and for many of them, the formulations may well appear obvious, unproblematic and just plain common sense. And it is precisely because of such widely held conceptions that so much welfare-state paternalism and market rhetoric fails. It is, by the same token, precisely out of such conceptions that a genuinely liberatory and transformative politics can be made. 'Seize the time and the place', they would say around Tompkins Square Park, and this does indeed appear an appropriate time and place to do so. If some of the walls are coming down all over eastern Europe, then surely we can set about bringing them down in our own cities as well.

REFERENCES

Chambers I. (1987) Maps for the metropolis: A possible guide to the present. *Cultural Studies* 1, 1–22.

Dahl, R. and C. Lindblom (1953) *Politics, Economics and Welfare*. Harper, New York.

Davis, M. (1990) *City of Quartz: Excavating the Future in Los Angeles*. Verso, London.

Godelier, M. (1972) *Rationality and Irrationality in Economics*. New Left Books, London.

Harvey, D. (1973) *Social Justice and the City*. Edward Arnold, London.

Harvey, D. (1989) *The Condition of Postmodernity*. Blackwell, Oxford.

Jacobs, J. (1961) *The Death and Life of Great American Cities*. Vintage, New York.

Kifner, J. (1989) No miracles in the park: Homeless New Yorkers amid drug lords and slumlords. *International Herald Tribune*, 1 August 1989, p. 6.

Lefebvre, H. (1991) *The Production of Space*. Blackwell, Oxford.

Lyotard, J. (1984) *The Postmodern Condition*. Manchester University Press, Manchester.

Marx, K. (1967) *Capital*, vol. I. International Publishers, New York.

Marx, K. and F. Engels (1951) *Selected Works*, vol. I. Progress Publishers, Moscow.

Plato (1965) *The Republic*. Penguin Books, Harmondsworth, Middlesex.

Rawls, J. (1971) *A Theory of Justice*. Harvard University Press, Cambridge, MA.

Smith, N. (1989) Tompkins Square: Riots, rents and redskins. *Portable Lower East Side* 6, 1–36.

Smith, N. (1992) New city, new frontier: The Lower East Side as wild, wild west. In M. Sorkin (ed.). *Variations on a Theme Park: The New American City and the End of Public Space*, Noonday, New York.

Unger, R. (1987) *False Necessity: Anti-necessitarian Social Theory in the Service of Radical Democracy*. Cambridge University Press, Cambridge.

Wittgenstein, L. (1967) *Philosophical Investigations*. Blackwell, Oxford.

Young, I. M. (1990) *Justice and the Politics of Difference*. Princeton University Press, Princeton. NJ.

Index